MOON HANDBOOKS®

MEXICO CITY

© CHRIS HUMPHREY

Estado de México's bucolic countryside: Tenango de Arista

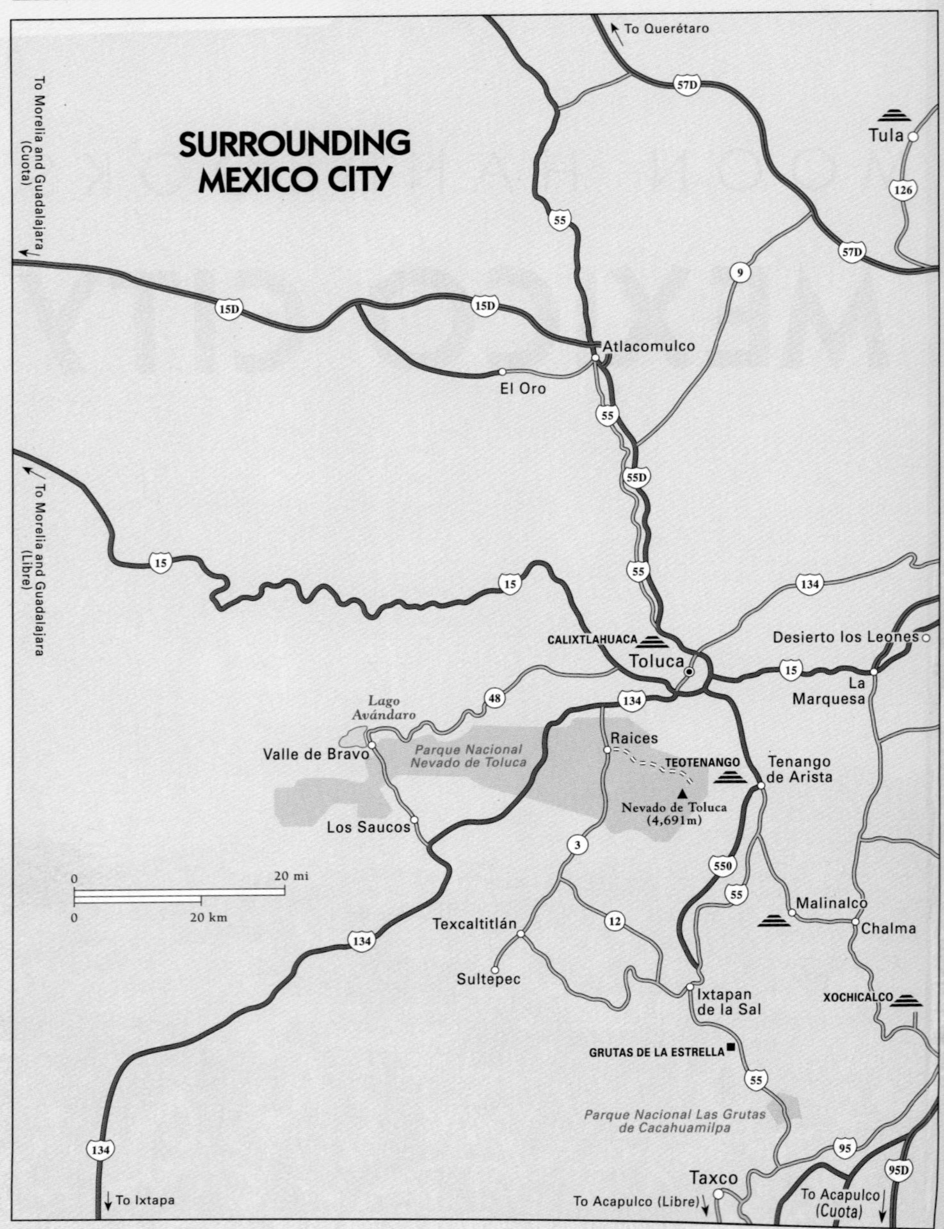
SURROUNDING MEXICO CITY
To Querétaro
57D
Tula
126
To Morelia and Guadalajara (Cuota)
55
57D
9
15D
15D
Atlacomulco
El Oro
55
55D
To Morelia and Guadalajara (Libre)
15
15
55
134
CALIXTLAHUACA
Desierto los Leones
Toluca
15
La Marquesa
48
134
Lago Avándaro
Raices
Valle de Bravo
Parque Nacional Nevado de Toluca
TEOTENANGO
Tenango de Arista
Nevado de Toluca (4,691m)
Los Saucos
3
550
0
20 mi
0
20 km
55
Malinalco
Chalma
Texcaltitlán
12
134
Sultepec
Ixtapan de la Sal
XOCHICALCO
GRUTAS DE LA ESTRELLA
55
Parque Nacional Las Grutas de Cacahuamilpa
134
95
95D
Taxco
To Ixtapa
To Acapulco (Libre)
To Acapulco (Cuota)

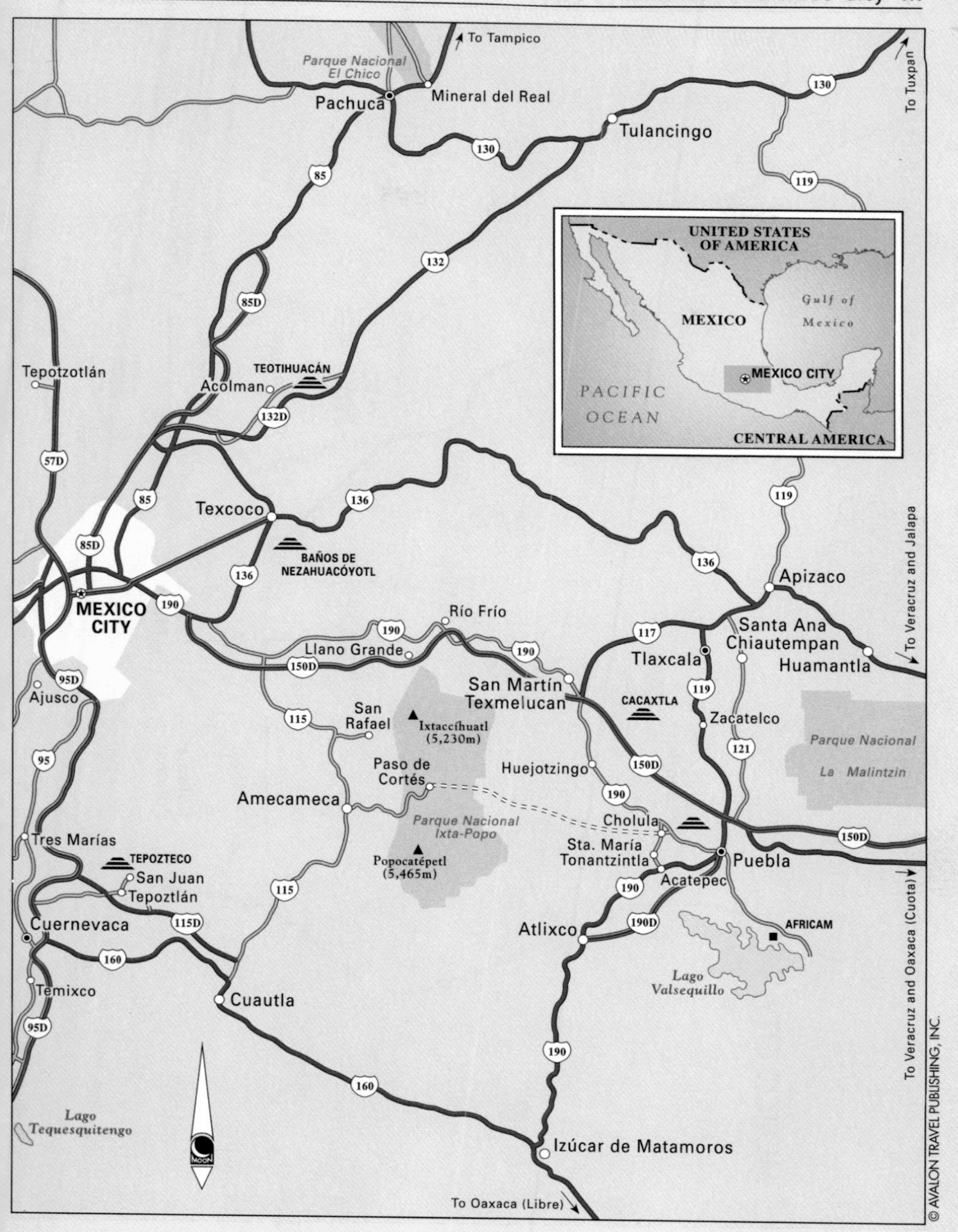

To Tampico
Parque Nacional El Chico
Pachuca
Mineral del Real
130
To Tuxpan
Tulancingo
85
119
UNITED STATES OF AMERICA
Gulf of Mexico
MEXICO
MEXICO CITY
PACIFIC OCEAN
CENTRAL AMERICA
132
85D
Tepotzotlán
TEOTIHUACÁN
Acolman
132D
57D
85
Texcoco
136
85D
BAÑOS DE NEZAHUACÓYOTL
136
Apizaco
MEXICO CITY
190
Río Frío
190
Santa Ana Chiautempan
117
To Veracruz and Jalapa
Llano Grande
190
Tlaxcala
Huamantla
150D
95D
Ajusco
San Martín Texmelucan
119
CACAXTLA
San Rafael
Ixtaccíhuatl (5,230m)
115
Zacatelco
95
121
Parque Nacional La Malintzin
Paso de Cortés
Huejotzingo
150D
Amecameca
190
Parque Nacional Ixta-Popo
Cholula
150D
Tres Marías
Sta. María Tonantzintla
Puebla
TEPOZTECO
Popocatépetl (5,465m)
San Juan Tepoztlán
190
Acatepec
115
To Veracruz and Oaxaca (Cuota)
Cuernevaca
115D
190D
Atlixco
AFRICAM
160
Temixco
Lago Valsequillo
Cuautla
95D
190
160
Lago Tequesquitengo
MOON
Izúcar de Matamoros
To Oaxaca (Libre)

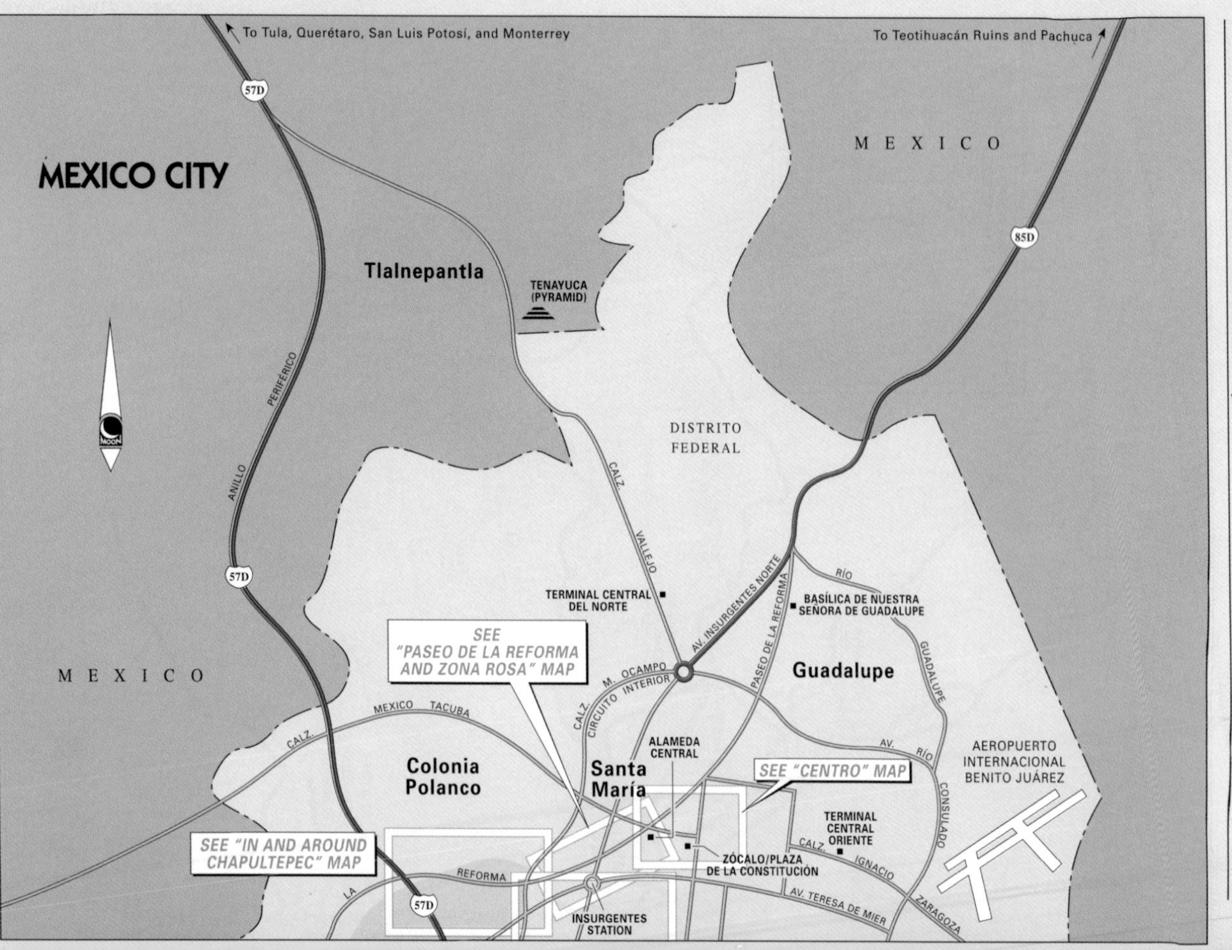

MEXICO CITY
To Tula, Querétaro, San Luis Potosí, and Monterrey
To Teotihuacán Ruins and Pachuca
MEXICO
MEXICO
DISTRITO FEDERAL
Tlalnepantla
TENAYUCA (PYRAMID)
57D
85D
57D
57D
ANILLO PERIFÉRICO
CALZ. VALLEJO
TERMINAL CENTRAL DEL NORTE
AV. INSURGENTES NORTE
PASEO DE LA REFORMA
RÍO GUADALUPE
BASÍLICA DE NUESTRA SEÑORA DE GUADALUPE
Guadalupe
SEE "PASEO DE LA REFORMA AND ZONA ROSA" MAP
CALZ. M. OCAMPO
CIRCUITO INTERIOR
CALZ. MEXICO TACUBA
Colonia Polanco
Santa María
ALAMEDA CENTRAL
SEE "CENTRO" MAP
AV. RÍO CONSULADO
AEROPUERTO INTERNACIONAL BENITO JUÁREZ
TERMINAL CENTRAL ORIENTE
CALZ. IGNACIO ZARAGOZA
ZÓCALO/PLAZA DE LA CONSTITUCIÓN
AV. TERESA DE MIER
SEE "IN AND AROUND CHAPULTEPEC" MAP
LA REFORMA
INSURGENTES STATION

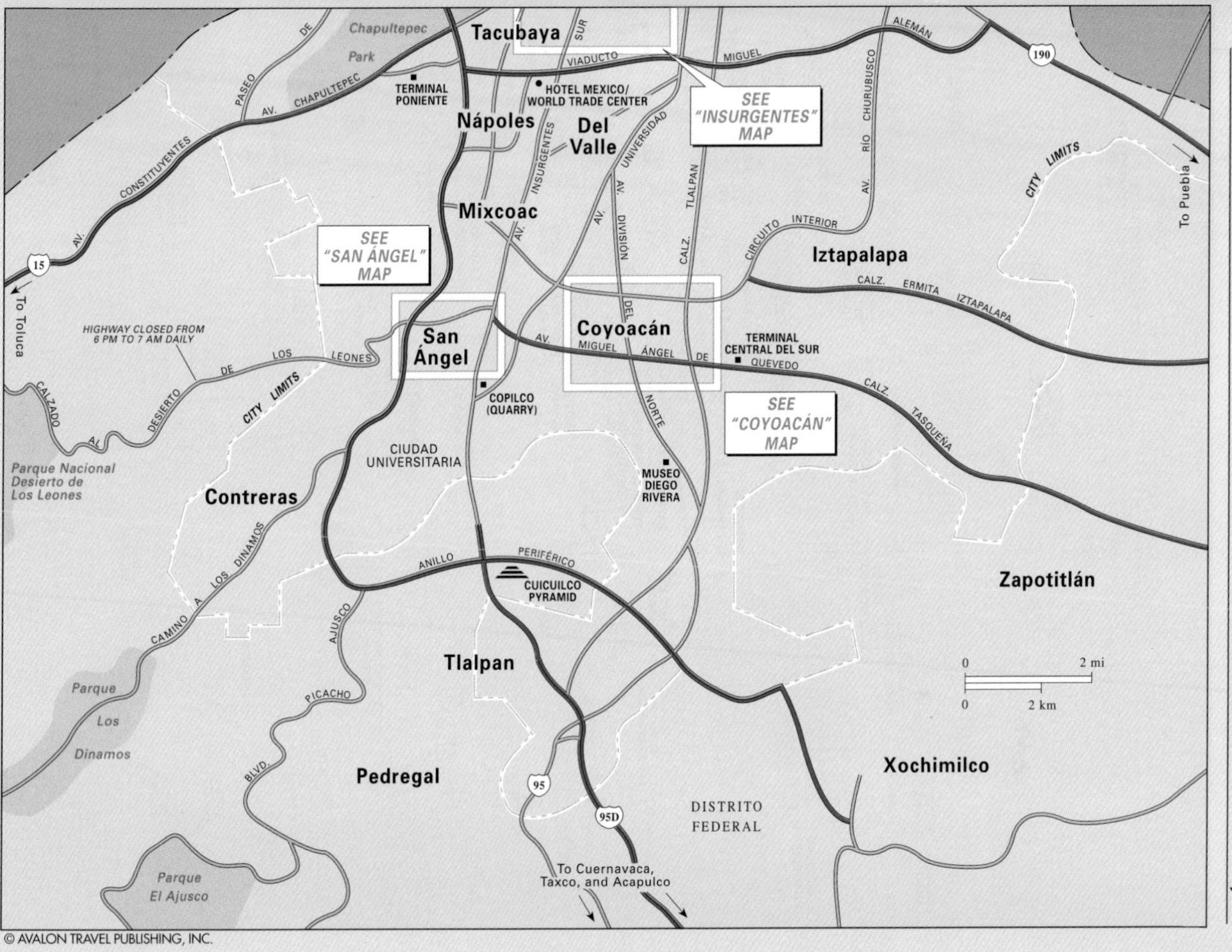
Chapultepec Park
Tacubaya
SUR
VIADUCTO
MIGUEL
ALEMÁN
190
PASEO DE
AV. CHAPULTEPEC
TERMINAL PONIENTE
HOTEL MEXICO/ WORLD TRADE CENTER
SEE "INSURGENTES" MAP
Nápoles
Del Valle
AV. INSURGENTES
AV. UNIVERSIDAD
AV. RÍO CHURUBUSCO
CITY LIMITS
To Puebla
AV. CONSTITUYENTES
Mixcoac
AV. DIVISIÓN DEL NORTE
CALZ. TLALPAN
CIRCUITO INTERIOR
Iztapalapa
15
To Toluca
SEE "SAN ÁNGEL" MAP
CALZ. ERMITA IZTAPALAPA
HIGHWAY CLOSED FROM 6 PM TO 7 AM DAILY
San Ángel
Coyoacán
AV. MIGUEL ÁNGEL DE QUEVEDO
TERMINAL CENTRAL DEL SUR
CALZADO AL DESIERTO DE LOS LEONES
CITY LIMITS
COPILCO (QUARRY)
SEE "COYOACÁN" MAP
CALZ. TASQUEÑA
CIUDAD UNIVERSITARIA
Parque Nacional Desierto de Los Leones
MUSEO DIEGO RIVERA
Contreras
ANILLO PERIFÉRICO
CUICUILCO PYRAMID
Zapotitlán
CAMINO A LOS DINAMOS
AJUSCO
Tlalpan
0
2 mi
0
2 km
Parque Los Dinamos
PICACHO
BLVD.
Pedregal
Xochimilco
95
95D
DISTRITO FEDERAL
Parque El Ajusco
To Cuernavaca, Taxco, and Acapulco

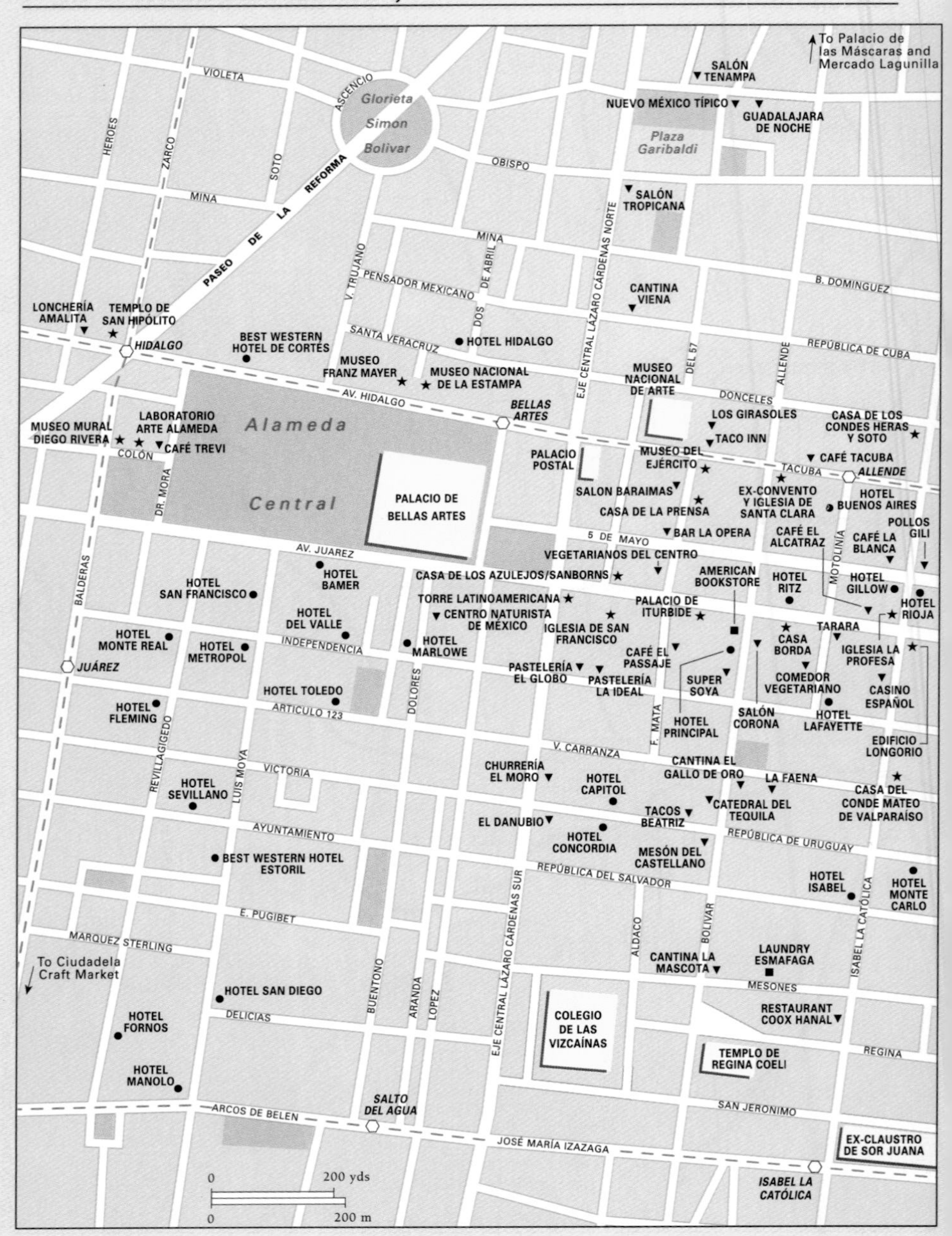

To Palacio de las Máscaras and Mercado Lagunilla
SALÓN TENAMPA
NUEVO MÉXICO TÍPICO
GUADALAJARA DE NOCHE
Plaza Garibaldi
Glorieta Simon Bolivar
VIOLETA
ASCENCIO
HEROES
ZARCO
SOTO
OBISPO
MINA
PASEO DE LA REFORMA
SALÓN TROPICANA
V. TRUJANO
DOS DE ABRIL
PENSADOR MEXICANO
EJE CENTRAL LÁZARO CÁRDENAS NORTE
CANTINA VIENA
B. DOMINGUEZ
LONCHERÍA AMALITA
TEMPLO DE SAN HIPÓLITO
HIDALGO
BEST WESTERN HOTEL DE CORTÉS
SANTA VERACRUZ
HOTEL HIDALGO
DEL 57
ALLENDE
REPÚBLICA DE CUBA
MUSEO FRANZ MAYER
MUSEO NACIONAL DE LA ESTAMPA
MUSEO NACIONAL DE ARTE
AV. HIDALGO
DONCELES
BELLAS ARTES
LOS GIRASOLES
CASA DE LOS CONDES HERAS Y SOTO
MUSEO MURAL DIEGO RIVERA
LABORATORIO ARTE ALAMEDA
CAFÉ TREVI
Alameda Central
COLÓN
TACO INN
PALACIO POSTAL
MUSEO DEL EJÉRCITO
CAFÉ TACUBA
TACUBA
ALLENDE
DR. MORA
PALACIO DE BELLAS ARTES
SALON BARAIMAS
EX-CONVENTO Y IGLESIA DE SANTA CLARA
HOTEL BUENOS AIRES
CASA DE LA PRENSA
POLLOS GILI
BAR LA OPERA
CAFÉ EL ALCATRAZ
CAFÉ LA BLANCA
5 DE MAYO
MOTOLINÍA
AV. JUAREZ
VEGETARIANOS DEL CENTRO
HOTEL BAMER
CASA DE LOS AZULEJOS/SANBORNS
AMERICAN BOOKSTORE
HOTEL RITZ
HOTEL GILLOW
HOTEL SAN FRANCISCO
TORRE LATINOAMERICANA
PALACIO DE ITURBIDE
HOTEL RIOJA
BALDERAS
HOTEL DEL VALLE
CENTRO NATURISTA DE MÉXICO
IGLESIA DE SAN FRANCISCO
TARARA
HOTEL MONTE REAL
HOTEL METROPOL
HOTEL MARLOWE
INDEPENDENCIA
CASA BORDA
IGLESIA LA PROFESA
CAFÉ EL PASSAJE
JUÁREZ
PASTELERÍA EL GLOBO
PASTELERÍA LA IDEAL
SUPER SOYA
COMEDOR VEGETARIANO
CASINO ESPAÑOL
HOTEL TOLEDO
HOTEL FLEMING
ARTICULO 123
DOLORES
F. MATA
HOTEL PRINCIPAL
SALÓN CORONA
HOTEL LAFAYETTE
REVILLAGIGEDO
EDIFICIO LONGORIO
V. CARRANZA
VICTORIA
LUIS MOYA
CHURRERÍA EL MORO
HOTEL CAPITOL
CANTINA EL GALLO DE ORO
LA FAENA
HOTEL SEVILLANO
CASA DEL CONDE MATEO DE VALPARAÍSO
CATEDRAL DEL TEQUILA
TACOS BEATRIZ
EL DANUBIO
AYUNTAMIENTO
HOTEL CONCORDIA
REPÚBLICA DE URUGUAY
MESÓN DEL CASTELLANO
BEST WESTERN HOTEL ESTORIL
REPÚBLICA DEL SALVADOR
HOTEL ISABEL
HOTEL MONTE CARLO
EJE CENTRAL LÁZARO CÁRDENAS SUR
E. PUGIBET
ALDACO
BOLIVAR
ISABEL LA CATÓLICA
MARQUEZ STERLING
To Ciudadela Craft Market
CANTINA LA MASCOTA
LAUNDRY ESMAFAGA
HOTEL SAN DIEGO
MESONES
BUENTONO
ARANDA
LOPEZ
HOTEL FORNOS
DELICIAS
COLEGIO DE LAS VIZCAÍNAS
RESTAURANT COOX HANAL
TEMPLO DE REGINA COELI
REGINA
HOTEL MANOLO
SALTO DEL AGUA
ARCOS DE BELEN
SAN JERONIMO
JOSÉ MARÍA IZAZAGA
EX-CLAUSTRO DE SOR JUANA
0
200 yds
0
200 m
ISABEL LA CATÓLICA

CENTRO
METRO
PEDESTRIANS ONLY
REPÚBLICA DE CHILE
REPÚBLICA DE HONDURAS
APARTADO
REPÚBLICA DE PERU
L. VALLE
REPÚBLICA DE BRASIL
REPÚBLICA DE ARGENTINA
REPÚBLICA DE BOLIVIA
J.J. HERRERA
PALACIO DE LA ESCUELA DE MEDICINA
TEMPLO DE SANTO DOMINGO
HOSTERÍA SANTO DOMINGO
REPÚBLICA DE COLOMBIA
RODRIGUEZ PUEBLA
LEONA VICARIO
Plaza de Santo Domingo
SECRETARÍA DE EDUCACIÓN PÚBLICA
REPÚBLICA DE VENEZUELA
MARGIL
CICERO CENTENARIO
PALMA
INTERNET LAFOEL
IGLESIA DE LA ENSEÑANZA
SN. ILDEFONSO
GENERAL M. ALEMÁN
ANTIGUO COLEGIO DE SAN ILDEFONSO
LAS ISABELES
COLEGIO DE CRISTO
HOTEL CATEDRAL
SAN ANTONIO
SUPER SOYA
BAR LEÓN
HOSTEL CATEDRAL
JUSTO SIERRA
TEMPLO MAYOR
MUSEO DEL TEMPLO MAYOR
PANADERÍA Y CAFETERÍA VASCONIA
LOS BISQUETS OBREGÓN
CASA DE LAS SIRENAS
MIXCALCO
NACIONAL MONTE DE PIEDAD
CATEDRAL
REPÚBLICA DE GUATEMALA
EX-SANTA TERESA
LIC. VERDAD
SAGRARIO
MUSEO DE LA SHCP
CASA DE LA IMPRENTA
MUSEO JOSÉ LUIS CUEVAS
EL CARDENAL
HOTEL ZAMORA/ CAFÉ POPULAR
HOLIDAY INN SELECT
HOSTAL MONEDA
IGLESIA DE LA SANTÍSIMA TRINIDAD
FCO. I. MADERO
MONEDA
BEST WESTERN HOTEL MAJESTIC
MUSEO DE LAS CULTURAS
ACADEMIA DE SAN CARLOS
RL REY DEL PAVO
Plaza de la Constitución
PALACIO NACIONAL
SOLEDAD
E. ZAPATA
GRAN HOTEL DE LA CIUDAD
ZÓCALO
16 DE SEPTIEMBRE
ZÓCALO
PALMA
SUPER SOYA
LORETO
SANTISIMA
ANILLO DE CIRCUVALACIÓN
RESTAURANT EL EHDEN
PERVERT/69
LIMÓN
EX-CONVENTO DE LA MERCED
ALHONDIGA
MANZANARES
MUSEO DE LA CIUDAD
ZAVALA
HOSPITAL DE JESÚS NARARENO
IGLESIA JESÚS NARARENO
CORREO MAYOR
LAS CRUCES
JESUS MARÍA
TALAVERA
GENERAL ANAYA
JOSÉ MARÍA PINO SUÁREZ
RESTAURANT AL ANDALÚZ
5 DE FEBRERO
20 DE NOVIEMBRE
MISIONEROS
RESTAURANT DON CHON
ROLDAN
SANTO TOMÁS
LA MERCED MARKET
SAN JERONIMO
PINO SUÁREZ
SAN PABLO
LA MERCED
To Sonora Market

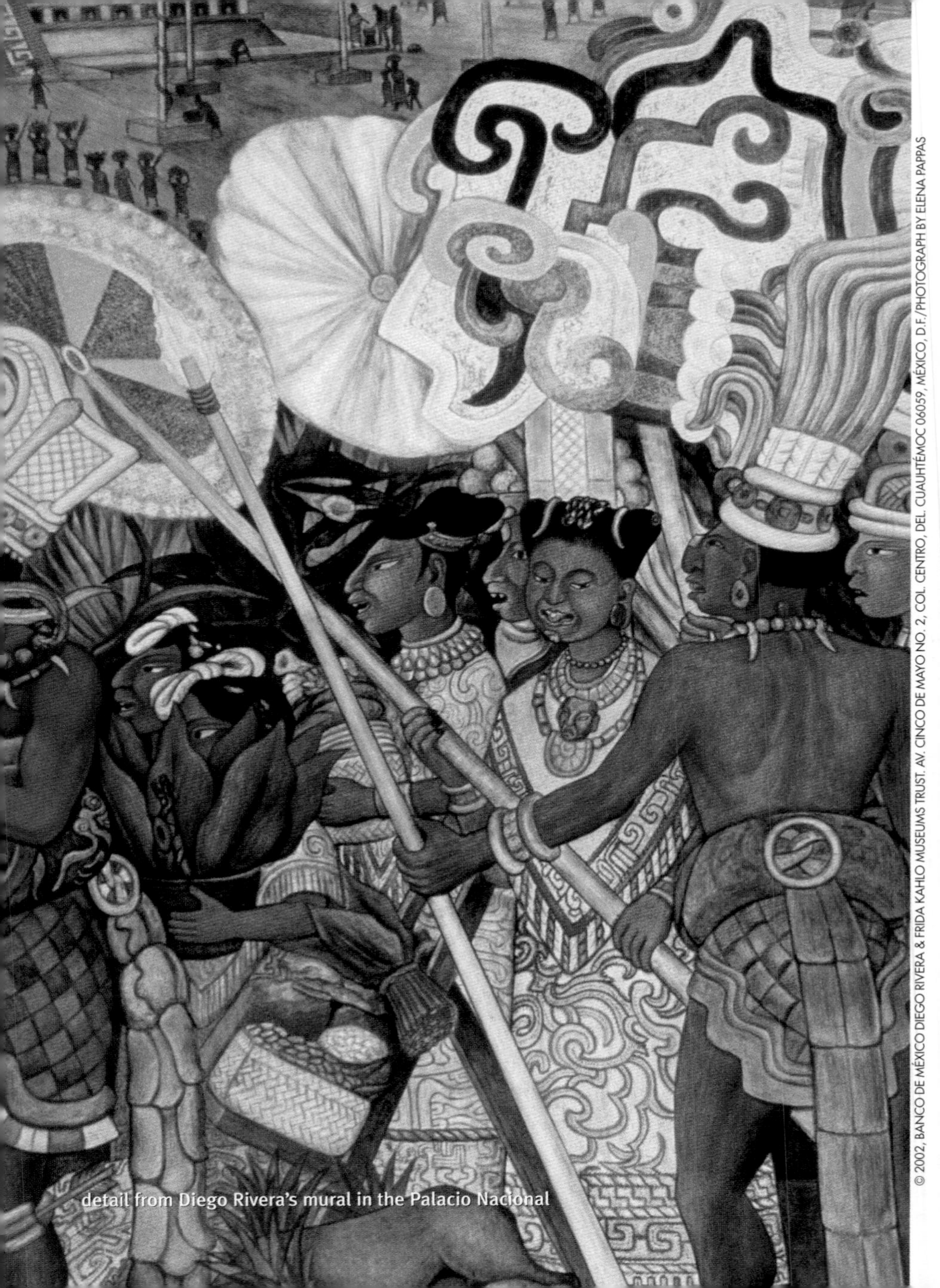

detail from Diego Rivera's mural in the Palacio Nacional

MOON HANDBOOKS®

MEXICO CITY

SECOND EDITION

CHRIS HUMPHREY & JOE CUMMINGS

SECOND EDITION REVISED AND UPDATED
BY CHRIS HUMPHREY

AVALON
TRAVEL

Moon Handbooks: Mexico City
Second Edition

Chris Humphrey and Joe Cummings

Published by
Avalon Travel Publishing
1400 65th Street, Suite 250
Emeryville, CA 94608, USA

Please send all comments, corrections, additions, amendments, and critiques to:

Moon Handbooks: Mexico City
Avalon Travel Publishing
1400 65th Street, Suite 250
Emeryville, CA 94608, USA
email: atpfeedback@avalonpub.com
www.moon.com

Printing History
1st edition—2000
2nd edition—January 2003
5 4 3 2 1

ISBN:1-56691-410-8
ISSN: 1541-9150

Editor: Rebecca K. Browning
Series Manager: Erin Van Rheenen
Copy Editor: Emily Lunceford
Proofreader/Indexer: Karen Gaynor Bleske
Graphics Coordinator: Susan Snyder
Production Coordinator: Darren Alessi
Cover Designer: Kari Gim
Interior Designers: Amber Pirker, Alvaro Villanueva, Kelly Pendragon
Map Editors: Olivia Solís, Naomi Adler Dancis
Cartographers: Mike Morgenfeld, Kat Kalamaras, Suzanne Service

Front cover photo: © Dave G. Houser/Houserstock 2001

Distributed by Publishers Group West

Printed in China through Colorcraft Ltd., Hong Kong

About the Authors

Chris Humphrey

© CARMEN OBERPARLEITER

Chris Humphrey began traveling at the tender age of five, when he ventured across town to a friend's grandmother's house. On a family vacation in Greece a few years later he wandered off through the streets of Athens, lost, but happily munching coconut macaroons until he found his hotel. When he took a year off from college to backpack through Africa and the Middle East, his parents saw the writing on the wall and gave up all efforts to worry about him.

Chris first went to Mexico in 1991 with a friend and a dilapidated Volvo, to meander the back roads for a month and a half. It was a dramatic trip, replete with spectacular scenery, fascinating people, and repeated mechanical failures. Thus was Chris introduced to the joys of Mexican roadside mechanics. Radiator sprung a leak? "Try cracking an egg in it, or better yet a handful of oatmeal..."

Chris continued to explore northern Mexico in his trusty, if recalcitrant, Swedish-made burro. On one such trip, while sipping coffee on the square of Alamos, Sonora, he ran across fellow Moon Handbooks author Joe Cummings, who gave him his start in travel writing. By 1994, Chris had moved to Mexico City to pursue his journalistic aspirations. On his second day of work for the English-language daily, *The News,* the peso crisis hit. Welcome to Mexico! Too bad you're getting paid in pesos.

Despite this inauspicious start, the intensity and excitement of living in one of the world's largest and most chaotic cities was addictive. For the next five years, Chris worked in Mexico City for a variety of publications covering Mexican business and politics. His first travel guide, *Moon Handbooks: Honduras,* was published in 1997.

Currently, Chris is finishing up a Master's degree in International Relations in Washington D.C. Wherever he lands next, good salsa music and somewhere to go rock climbing are absolute necessities.

About the Authors

Joe Cummings

Joe Cummings was born in New Orleans and raised in California, France, Texas, and Washington, D.C. He spent a good part of his childhood in San Antonio, Texas, where he ate his first taco in the 1960s during one of his family's frequent Mexican border town visits. After that he always preferred tacos to burgers, so his mom had to learn how to make them-well ahead of the Mexican food craze that would sweep across America in the 1970s.

Joe's love of Tex-Mex border culture drew him deeper into Mexico where he explored the Chihuahuan and Sonoran deserts and the famed Copper Canyon, to research and write *Moon Handbooks: Northern Mexico.* He took an epic road trip down Baja's Transpeninsular Highway in 1991 to write *Moon Handbooks: Baja.* Impressed by the juxtaposition of history, nature, and solitude that suited his restless spirit, he eventually built a Baja hideout five minutes from the Pacific Ocean.

In addition to authoring Moon Handbooks to Baja, Cabo, Mexico, Mexico City, and Northern Mexico, Joe has written numerous other guidebooks, phrasebooks, and atlases for countries around the world. As a freelance journalist, Joe has also contributed to dozens of periodicals, including *Ambassador, BBC Holidays, Car & Travel, Geographical, The Guardian, The Independent on Sunday, Los Angeles Times, Outside, San Francisco Examiner, South China Morning Post, Via,* and the *Wall Street Journal.* He has twice received the Lowell Thomas Travel Journalism Gold Award, and twice been a finalist in London's Thomas Cook Guidebook of the Year awards. In 2001, the government of Mexico awarded the Pluma de Plata (Silver Quill) to Joe for "outstanding foreign journalism" on Mexico. Joe divides his time between homes in Baja and Thailand.

Contents

SPECIAL TOPICS

Keeping Current

Between the time this book went to press and the time it got onto the shelves, hotels have opened and closed, restaurants have changed hands, and roads have been repaired (or fallen into disrepair). Also, prices have probably gone up; because of this, all prices herein should be regarded as approximations and are not guaranteed by the publisher or the author.

We want to keep this book as accurate and up-to-date as possible and would appreciate hearing about any errors or omissions you may encounter while using *Moon Handbooks: Mexico City.*

If you have any noteworthy experiences (good or bad) with establishments listed in this book, please pass them along to us. If something is out of place on a map, tell us; if the best restaurant in town is not included, we'd like to know. All contributions will be deeply appreciated and properly acknowledged. Address your letters to:

Chris Humphrey
Moon Handbooks: Mexico City
Avalon Travel Publishing
1400 65th Street, Suite 250
Emeryville, CA USA, 94608
email: atpfeedback@avalonpub.com

Maps

MAP SYMBOLS

Divided Highway
Primary Road
Secondary Road
Unpaved Road
Pedestrian Street
National Capital
State Capital
City/Town
Point of Interest
Accommodation
Restaurant/Bar
Other Location
Metro Station
Mountain
Archaeological Site

Foreword

From the first day of my first trip I was enchanted by Mexico. Yet I traveled through the provinces for five years before braving Mexico City. I was afraid of the capital, influenced by the prevalent propaganda dismissing it as a teeming, overpopulated mess, one of the most polluted locales in the world, full of horrific testimonies of insuperable poverty. Then, on one trip, I had an overnight layover and couldn't avoid it.

And in the half-hour taxi ride from the airport to my hotel, I fell in love. I was astonished by the twilit streets of the Centro Histórico, lined with massive stone buildings built by the Spanish conquerors in the 16th century. I was captivated by the contrast between the grandiosity of those edifices with their baroque ornamental details and the humility of the office workers wending their way home, the smiling shoeshine man at his bright-orange stand, the skinny matron in the blue skirt beseeching me to buy *tlacoyas* from a basket.

A crowd began to gather in the Zócalo, the city's enormous central square, in support of a teachers' strike. By nightfall it would be 200,000 strong. Yet a few hours later, everyone was gone, the plaza empty, as if the demonstration had been a hallucination.

That evening, I wandered along those streets dense with history. In a crowded cafeteria, all Formica and fluorescence, I ate tamales wrapped in banana leaves and stuffed with spicy shredded pork. I drank tequila in a dark bar, where a round man with a pencil mustache sang romantic songs, backed by three guitar players dexterously crowding notes into each phrase. I watched a lonely group of soldiers on drill in the, by that point, otherwise empty Zócalo.

I stumbled upon Plaza Garibaldi, the chaotic soul of the city. There, squadrons of musicians—mostly mariachis, with wide-brimmed sombreros and skin-tight, tin-studded black suits—trolled for customers willing to pay a few pesos for a melody. When they found temporary patrons, crowds gathered, and the most boisterous revelers sang along. It was a crowded Friday night, and the result was the most singular cacophony I'd ever heard.

In Garibaldi's most humble cantina—La Hermosa Hortensia, which dispenses *pulque,* a fermented cactus beverage that originated with the Aztecs—a staggeringly drunk man offered me his wife. She demonstrated her eagerness to consummate the proposition with a squeeze of my thigh and a smile, the seductiveness of which was undercut by the absence of several crucial teeth. I refused with as much courtesy as possible, after which he removed from his neck a string that held an emblem of Mexico's patron saint, the Virgin of Guadalupe. I felt safer accepting this gift.

The following morning, I entered the chapel that adjoins the Catedral Metropolitana and saw a weeping Indian, all in black, on her knees before a profusely bloody statue of Christ. Here was a glimpse of Mexico's past—the marriage between indigenous ritual and Catholic rite. It was more powerful than anything I'd seen in a European cathedral. Unfortunately, I had to leave Mexico City that day, after less than 24 hours. But I had been utterly seduced by the steady sensation of contrast, of surprise, even of tumult. The city so fascinated me that, less than three years later, I would be living there.

I have distinct images from my first months as a resident, walking everywhere armed with my *Guía Roji,* a 150-page street atlas. Dense throngs of people. Tall glasses of glistening juices—orange, grapefruit, or beet—dispensed at white-painted stands. The luscious aroma of frying tortillas and sizzling pork, mixed with that of charcoal-gray exhaust, farting in billows from a bus's back end. Oily, dark auto-repair shops. Boxy women in tight blue uniforms, grasping assault weapons, standing guard outside banks. Wheezy accordion music streaming past the swinging doors of a cantina. Signs on billboards, windows, and walls, in Spanish, English, and something in between: Bar Oxfort. Baby Creysi. Supergrupos Afroantillanos. Se Ponchan Llantas Gratis (this a caution to those who might park outside a private garage: Tires Flattened Free).

I'm recalling the thrill of discovery of one of the world's great cities. It is true that Mexico's capital has some serious, seemingly insurmountable problems—it is tragically polluted and impossibly crowded, the contrast between rich and poor is obscene, and the government has so far only begun to make progress in confronting a crime wave. Yet it is equally true, and unfortunately rarely acknowledged, that Mexico City is at the same time a world cultural mecca, an enchanting labyrinth of fascinating neighborhoods, and a bon vivant's garden of delights. Because of its enormity, it's not easy to get to know Mexico City; this guidebook will help to reveal its pleasures for you.

—by David Lida is the author of *Travel Advisory,* a collection of short stories set in contemporary Mexico.

Introduction

La Capital—also known as La Ciudad, México, el Distrito Federal, or simply "De Efe" for short—often astounds first-time visitors with its disarming combination of Old World charm, New World sophistication, and surprising friendliness. The city lures visitors with a long list of superlatives—it's the oldest and highest city in North America, possibly the largest in the world, and the only metropolis with two UNESCO World Heritage sites within its city limits.

Despite its legendary sprawl, it can be a remarkably attractive city, at least in certain areas—the historic downtown lined with colonial mansions and churches; broad, stately Paseo de la Reforma, buzzing with commerce; the art deco architecture, galleries, and cafés of the Roma and Condesa neighborhoods; and the upscale but cozy colonial areas of Coyoacán and San Ángel, home to many of the country's giants of art and literature. Museum-lovers could spend days, even weeks, touring all the different art, history, and technology museums. Amateur historians will admire the crumbling 17th-century palaces downtown, while partiers won't want to miss the epic, dawn-chasing nightlife for which the city is famous.

But it's the little discoveries that are addictive. A small café in continuous operation for seven decades, a used bookshop specializing in 19th-century engravings, street-corner vendors selling blue-corn *huaraches,* a colonial-era *plazuela* seemingly lost to all but local inhabitants—all conspire to pull you under the city's spell.

At the same time Mexico City sometimes seems as if it's hurtling from one disaster to the next. The city is reportedly sinking at a rate of several inches per year as wells suck the water table dry beneath the spongy lake bed upon which the city was laid out in the 16th century. During the dry season, a traffic-induced haze fills busy intersections—in a city where several hundred

Volcán Ajusco looming above the Periféro

MEXICO CITY METRO

EL ROSARIO
Tezozomoc
Azcapotzalco
Ferrería
Norte 45
Vallejo
Politécnico
INSTITUTO DEL PETRÓLEO
Indios Verdes
Lindavista
La Villa Basílica
MARTÍN CARRÉRA
Autobuses del Norte
Potrero
DEPORTIVO 18 DE MARZO
LA RAZA
Talismán
Misterios
Bondolito
Valle Gómez
Tlateloco
Aquiles Serdán
Camarones
Rernería
Panteones
Cuatro Caminos
TACUBA
Cuitláhuac
Popotla
Colegio Militar
Normal
San Cosme
Revolución
Buenavista
GUERRERO
GARIBALDI
Lagunilla
Tepito
MORELOS
CONSULADO
Eduardo Molina
Aragón
OCEANÍA
Bosque de Aragón
Tesoro
Valle de Aragón
Continentes
Campesire
Río de los Remedios
M. Muzquiz
Tecnológico
Olímpica
Plaza Aragón
Cd. Azteca
R. Rubio
Gran Canal
San Joaquín
HILDALGO
BELLAS ARTES
Allende
CANDELARIA
Zócalo
San Juan de Letrán
SAN LÁZARO
Terminal Aérea
Juárez
BALDERAS
Polanco
Cuauhtémoc
Insurgentes
SALTO DEL AGUA
Isabel La Católica
Merced
PINO SUAREZ
Balbuena
Aeropuerto
Gómez Farias
Zaragoza
Hangares
Auditorio
Sevilla
Chapultepec
Juanacatlán
Niños Heroes
Hospital General
Doctores
San Antonio Abad
Fray Servando
Velódromo
PANTITLAN
Constituyentes
Obrera
JAMAICA
Chilpancingo
Lazaro Cardenas
CHABACANO
Mixiuhca
Ciudad Deportiva
Puebla
Agrícola Oriental
TACUBAYA
Patriotismo
Observatorio
CENTRO MÉDICO
Viaducto
La Viga
SANTA ANITA
Canal de San Juan
Etiopia
Xola
Coyuya
San Pedro de los Pinos
Eugenia
Tepalcates
Villa de Cortés
Iztacalco
Guelatao
San Antonio
División del Norte
Apatlaco
Nativitas
Peñón Viejo
Mixcoac
Aculco
Zapata
Acatitla
Portales
Santa Marta
Escuadrón 201
Los Reyes
Barranca del Muerto
Coyoacán
Ermita
La Paz
Iztapalapa
C. de 1917
Atlalilco
Uampurisma
C. de la Estrella
Víveros
General Anaya
Miguel Angel Quevedo
Tasqueña
Copilco
Universidad

MOON

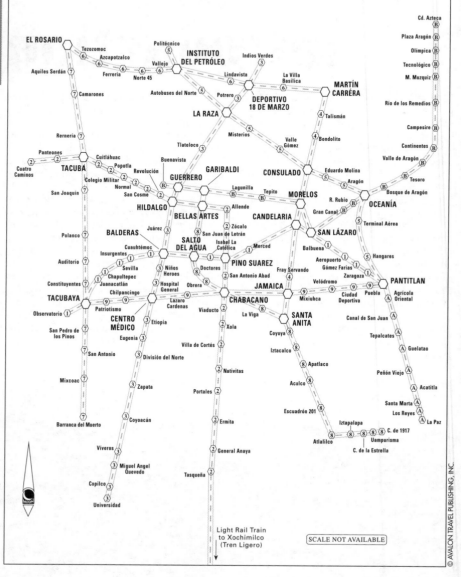

Light Rail Train to Xochimilco (Tren Ligero)

SCALE NOT AVAILABLE

new vehicles are registered every day. Nearly one-fifth of Mexico's population lives in the capital's metro area, and every bus from the provinces brings in yet more fortune-seekers, unfazed by the occasional 7.0 temblor.

Crazed? Definitely. But the amazing thing is how well the city works, how it reaches well beyond mere survival. You can zip across town by underground Metro or glide slowly around the Centro Histórico in a *bicitaxi* (pedicab). Dig into a steaming, chile-and-cheese tamal served by a sidewalk vendor for 35 cents while standing outside a US$200-a-night hotel. Catch a classic Mexican film at a local *cineclub,* then stroll through one of Latin America's most beautiful urban parks. Climb aboard a brightly painted *trajinera* (Mexican-style gondola) and disappear down the shaded waterways of Xochimilco. Aztec pyramids and Catholic cathedrals, punk rockers and *charro* serenaders, poverty-stricken slums and walled villas; they're all part of the phantasmagoric heart of *mexicanidad* or "Mexicanness" that is Mexico City. The longer you stay, the more intriguing it all seems to become.

Many casual visitors to Mexico arrive in the capital by plane and make an immediate beeline for the nearest exit, heading to the coastal resorts, colonial cities, or, basically, anywhere else. It's their loss. As huge and environmentally challenged as it is, Mexico City is a fascinating and vibrant cauldron of humanity, and anyone with a taste for cities can't afford to miss at least a visit of few days.

The Land

GEOLOGY

Mexico City takes up half the surface area of the roughly 3,100-square-km Valle de México, a unique land formation in the center of Mexico's volcanic central highlands. Technically not a valley—as it has no natural drainage—the basin is completely ringed by mountains. The worn down, low hills to the north rose 30 million years ago and were followed later by the steep-walled ridges on the east and west. A row of volcanoes to the south first erupted around two million years ago, thus sealing off the basin entirely. Several of Mexico's highest peaks—Popocatépetl (5,465 meters), Ixtaccíhuatl (5,230 meters), Ajusco (3,930 meters), Volcán Tláloc (3,690 meters), and Cerro Pelado (3,670 meters)—rim the valley to the south and southeast.

The valley floor, more than half of which was once covered by a series of broad, shallow lakes, varies between 2,100 and 2,400 meters in altitude and extends roughly 120 km north to south, depending on where you measure from (the northern boundary is a bit vague), and between 40 and 70 km from east to west. While mostly flat, the valley is punctuated by several anomalous mountains, mainly volcanic in origin, such as Cerro de la Estrella, Cerro de Chapultepec, and Cerro Tepeyac.

The Valle de México is very active seismically and experiences frequent earthquakes, most generated from the movement of geologic plates toward Mexico's Pacific coast. Because of the interaction between earthquake wave movement and the valley's weak subsoil, Mexico City sometimes feels the effects of a coastal quake more than places closer to the quake's actual epicenter. Such was the case in the 1985 earthquake, which left thousands dead in Mexico City despite the fact that its epicenter was more than 160 km (100 miles) away.

HYDROLOGY

One of the most vexing problems people settling in the Valle de México have had to deal with throughout its history is the complex water system. Before humans began making their modifications (originally under the Aztecs), five interconnected lakes in the valley fluctuated dramatically in size throughout the year depending on rainfall and evaporation rates. The highest of the lakes, Chalco, had the freshest

MEXICO CITY ENVIRONMENT

A 7.5 earthquake gently rocks the city. Phone calls will be interrupted and office workers will be ushered outside. But the traffic doesn't stop on the Eje Central and *chilangos* (Mexico City residents) take it as just another day in one of the world's largest cities. Talk about the environment here and residents will regale you with stories of contamination, natural disasters, and environmental neglect.

With its 16 million-plus population, Mexico City has a well-deserved reputation for being overcrowded and overpolluted. Long gone are the days when Carlos Fuentes could title his novel *Where the Air Is Clear.* And most people don't think of Mexico City as an environmental destination.

But keep an eye on this gargantuan metropolis—instead of being behind the curve, the Federal District may be leading the pack. The city is in fact quite green with its large number of landscaped city parks, including the 850-hectare (2,100-acre) Chapultepec Park and the cozy Alameda Park, immortalized in Diego Rivera's famous mural *Dream of a Sunday Afternoon in the Alameda.*

Air

Mexico City measures its Metropolitan Air Quality Index (Índice Metropolitana de Calidad de Aire, or Imeca) every hour every day. According to collected stats, air pollution is usually worse on the southern edge of town because the prevailing winds are from the north and the air is trapped by the Sierra Ajusco to the south. The winter months are the worst months for air pollution in the Valle de México, because of fewer and lighter air currents. Cooler air temperatures create thermal inversions, which keep car exhaust and industrial emissions hovering just above ground level, often causing respiratory, eye, and throat irritations.

The United Nations' World Health Organization classifies Imeca readings of more than 100 points as Unsatisfactory, readings of more than 200 points as Bad, and readings of 300 Dangerous. When the Imeca breaks 200 points, the city orders all outdoor activities for primary, secondary, and preschool canceled as the young are more susceptible to the ill effects of bad air.

A Phase One alert (called when the Imeca breaks 250 points) doubles the *Hoy No Circula* (No Driving Today) policy and 40 percent of privately owned vehicles and half of all government vehicles are kept off city streets the following day. Industries are also ordered to reduce their emissions. You can track the daily Imeca readings in *The News* or online at www.sima.com.mx/valle_de_mexico.

Are the policies working? Anecdotal and statistical evidence suggests that although Mexico City's air is still extremely poor, it is improving. During the first two months of 2002, 15 days were considered "satisfactory," with Imeca levels below 100; 42 were "unsatisfactory," with readings between 100 and 200; and two were "bad," with readings over 200. While this may hardly seem good, they are the best readings since readings have been kept for the months of January and February, which are traditionally extremely bad because of high-pressure systems and thermal inversions. The high point was hit on January 16, with a reading of 226, meaning no Phase One alerts were implemented. During this period, levels of nitrogen dioxide and carbon monoxide were considered satisfactory every day, while sulfur dioxide passed 100 on one day and PM10 (particulate matter) passed 100 on six days. The culprit was ozone, which passed 100 on 42 days and topped 200 twice. For recent reports (in Spanish) on air quality, look at the website for the Mexico City Secretaría de Medio Ambiente (Environment Secretariat) at www.sma.df.gob.mx.

The single biggest contributor to D.F.'s haze is the automobile, which accounts for an estimated 70 percent of detectable smog. The *Hoy No Círcula* program, which is supposed to ensure that every registered vehicle stays off the roads at least one day a week, seems to have exacerbated the problem. Instead of using public transport, the city's moneyed classes simply bought second or third vehicles, often cheaper used autos with higher emissions. Since the program was introduced, the number of private vehicles in circulation has soared an estimated 40 percent.

A better solution, according to world traffic experts, would be to institute a total ban on private vehicles in designated high-traffic, central business districts, where only public vehicles and mass-transit carriers would be permitted to operate. Such a program has been extremely successful in Singapore.

Water

The city has a seemingly unquenchable thirst for water. Most of the city's water supply is pumped from aquifers beneath the city. The removal of the groundwater has caused some of the buildings to sink more rapidly than usual. The water table has dropped by 32 meters (105 feet), and the city itself has sunk by seven meters since 1940. The city consumes 3.5 million cubic meters of water every day, twice the level of many industrialized countries. Why? Because up to a quarter of the city's water supply is lost through leaky pipes before it reaches household taps.

About 20–30 percent of the city's water is pumped uphill 1,000 meters (3,280 feet) from the Lerma and Cutzamala Rivers, 100 km (62 miles) to the west. The rest is pumped from underground aquifers. Sewage is disposed of out of town, much to the frustration of outlying communities. Built in 1900, the Gran Canal de Desagüe (Great Drainage Canal) project drove a pipeline through the northern hills to carry human waste and garbage outside the valley. At the beginning of the century, gravity was sufficient to pull the putrid black waters out of town. But as the city began to sink, 11 pumping stations were constructed. Today, another deep drainage system is under construction.

Is There Hope?

A reforestation program along the banks of the dwindling Lago de Texcoco has helped cut back on dust and recycle carbon dioxide, and it may also speed efforts to reclaim more rainwater in the lake basin.

Mexico City hosts a number of environmental groups dedicated to raising environmental awareness. The Centro de Ecología y Desarrollo (Cecodes) is one of the more persistent of the academic centers that review environmental issues. Cecodes (Chiapas 208, Dept. 7, tel. 5264-8758; email: cecodes@planeta.apc.org; website: www.planeta.com/ecotravel/mexico/ecologia/ecologia.html) produces numerous Spanish-language reports and studies on Mexico City environmental issues. Some reports have been collected in books available for purchase, and students and scholars can use its extensive library.

—by Ron Mader. Ron is author of the guidebook *Mexico: Adventures in Nature* (John Muir Publications, 1998) and host of the popular *Planeta.com* environmental travel website (www.planeta.com). For more information on environmental issues in Mexico City, see website: www.planeta.com/ecotravel/mexico/df/df.html.

water, while Texcoco, the largest and lowest-lying, was the saltiest.

This constant fluctuation in water levels vexed the Aztecs. Because all the best land on the lake shores had already been taken by the time they arrived, they settled on an island near the center of the lake. Thus when lake levels rose, their territory shrank on all sides. It was Nezahualcóyotl, the poet-king of neighboring Texcoco and an Aztec ally, who in the late 15th century oversaw the construction of a massive dike dividing Lake Texcoco into two halves, one salty and one fresh, as a means of controlling the annual floods. In addition, a network of canals was built for drainage control and transportation.

As part of his final assault on Tenochtitlán in 1521, Cortés ordered the breaching of the dike to flood the Aztec city. The water level was not high enough at that point to cause the damage he'd hoped for, but in the long run Cortés may have been more successful than he had planned. The Spaniards, not understanding the complexities of the ecosystem, left the dike in ruins when they rebuilt the city, and as a result saw their new colonial capital flooded repeatedly over the next few centuries. After repeated heavy rainy seasons, the entire city once remained underwater constantly for five years in the early 17th century, forcing many inhabitants to abandon their palaces and live temporarily on higher ground at the edge of the valley.

Thus a public works project was initiated that has seemingly continued unabated to this day, digging ever bigger tunnels and canals to completely drain the valley. Although successive colonial governments dug drainage canals, it was not until 1900, with the construction of the Gran Canal de Desagüe (Great Drainage Canal) under the administration of Porfirio Díaz, that the waters of Lago Texcoco were finally emptied almost entirely.

Currently the only major bodies of water in the valley are small tracts of Lago Xochimilco in the south, the lakes in Chapultepec, and the much reduced remnants of Lago Texcoco northeast of the city in the State of México. The dozen or so rivers that once flowed into the valley mainly from the western mountains, such as Río Mixcoac, Río de la Piedad, Río Tacubaya, and Río Churubusco, still exist but are canalized and sealed under major avenues, eventually draining into one of the five canals on the east side of the city, which in turn flow out of the valley to the northeast.

While only a few patches of lake still exist, flooding remains a yearly occurrence in many parts of the Mexico City metro area during the April–October rainy season. A huge new Drenaje Profundo (Deep Drainage) is on the drawing board and awaiting funding.

The results of all this drainage can be seen in the capital's uneven streets and settling architecture. Because much of the valley's ground water has been siphoned off, the sandy, unstable soil has sunk dramatically (about 7.5 meters in the last century), leaving many downtown buildings comically contorted as different parts sink at different rates. City air is also affected; the dried lake beds in the northeast part of the valley create swirling clouds of dust that are swept up into the atmosphere and moved to the southwest directly across the city by the prevailing winds, worsening the horrendous air pollution.

CLIMATE

Although Mexico City straddles the 19th parallel North, thus placing it squarely in the tropics, its 2,240-meter (7,350-foot) elevation can add a chill to the air, particularly during the December–January winter months, and at times during the summer rainy season due to the cloudy weather. Nights and early mornings can be chilly throughout the year. Generally the city has one of the mildest climates in Mexico, pleasant during the day and comfortable for sleeping at night.

The rains usually begin in April or May and continue sporadically until October. The rains often abate for two or three weeks in August, usually before the coming of the fall hurricane season. The violent high winds that lash Mexico's coasts during the frequent annual storms do not usually make it to Mexico City, but they can leave skies gray and rainy for days at a time, and sometimes flooding occurs.

Rain levels average 700–1,300 mm (27.5–51.2 inches) per year in the southwest mountains, and 400–600 mm (15.7–23.6 inches) per year in the more arid central and northern parts of the valley.

Temperature also varies depending on location, ranging from 12°C (50°F) on average in the western mountains to 16°C (60° F) in the center of town. The hottest months of the year are usually April and May, when temperatures sometimes hit 30°C (84°F) in the day, while the coldest are December and January, with daytime temperatures averaging 14°C (55°F). Humidity is low to moderate except during the rainy season.

Air Quality

Mexico City's Metropolitan Air Quality Index (Índice Metropolitana de Calidad de Aire, or Imeca) measures air quality hourly. Although folk wisdom says the air is worse in the winter months than the rest of the year, it really depends on wind patterns, which vary from year to year. (See the special topic Mexico City Environment for more information on Imeca.)

History

What follows is an effort to trace the general outlines of the history of urban development in the valley of Mexico. It does not pretend to comprehensively trace Mexico City's history, much less the history of the country as a whole, tasks which would require several volumes and many years of study. For suggestions on further reading, see the Recommended Reading section at the end of the book. Historical descriptions on different neighborhoods in the city are given in the Sights chapter.

PRE-HISPANIC HISTORY

First Arrivals

Mexico's earliest human inhabitants arrived slowly via the Bering Strait land bridge spanning the Asian and North American continents between 50,000 and 25,000 B.C. Descendants of Asia's late Paleolithic epoch, these nomadic hunter-gatherers dispersed throughout North America seeking food and benign natural conditions. No evidence of any sociocultural organization survives, although remains of hunted mammoth, mastodon, giant bison, and antelope near Puebla suggest humans arrived this far south by 24,000 B.C.

The First Inhabitants of the Valley

Groups of nomads are thought to have first found their way into the valley of Mexico sometime around 20,000 B.C. The advantages of an abundant water supply and the surrounding wall of the mountains—which served both as a natural defense and as a barrier for keeping game near at hand—must have made the valley an appealing place for these wandering bands to settle down and build small villages.

But this very appeal led to the extinction of the valley's large game between 9000 and 8000 B.C. Over the next several thousand years, the valley's population grew to rely on gathering fruits and grains, especially maize, until the third millennium B.C., when fully agricultural societies established themselves.

As in other parts of the world, this agricultural revolution created profound changes in social organization. Between 1500 and 650 B.C., villages around the edge of the valley's lakes grew in size, particularly in the northeast and in the south. The first full-fledged city to develop was Cuicuilco, centered around a pyramid site still seen at the junction of Insurgentes Sur and Periférico Sur. By 100 B.C. a second city was growing at Teotihuacán in the north, driven by springs which permitted irrigated agriculture.

The incipient rivalry between the two cities was dramatically cut short sometime in the second century A.D., when Volcán Xitle blew its top and covered Cuicuilco and much of the southeastern part of the valley with beds of lava. Following Cuicuilco's fiery demise, the population of Teotihuacán increased sharply, reaching a height of perhaps 200,000 in A.D. 750. Through a combination of excessive logging and over-in-

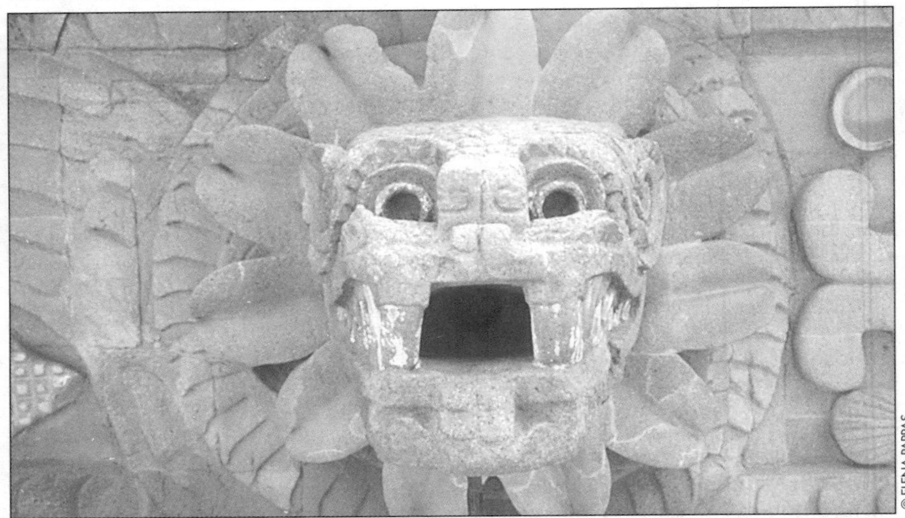

© ELENA PAPPAS

sculpture detail from the Templo de Quetzalcóatl, at Teotihuacán

tensive agriculture, the productivity of the once-fertile valley began to decline (even today the area has remained barren and arid), and the final blow was dealt by successive invasions by northern warrior tribes.

The Toltecs

Just before the end of the first millennium, the Toltecs—a culturally hybrid group dominated by Amerindians from northern Mexico—established a fortified capital at Tula in present-day Hidalgo, just north of Mexico City. Between A.D. 900 and 1200, Toltec centers developed as far north as Zacatecas and as far south as Guatemala; Toltec influence apparently extended to the post-Classic Maya architecture at Chichén Itzá as well.

The Toltec civilization never reached the heights achieved by Teotihuacán and slipped into decline after A.D. 1200. After suffering successive invasions by warrior tribes from the north, Tula was abandoned in the 13th century.

The Aztecs

In the wake of Tula's fall, control of the valley was divided between several competing communities, with population centers of 10,000–20,000 at Texcoco, Azcapoltzalco, Tacuba, Xochimilco, as well as dozens of smaller towns. Into this mix arrived yet another northern tribe, the Aztecs, in the mid-1200s. The fiercest warriors Mexico has ever known, the Aztecs claimed to come from an island in the north called Aztatlán or Aztlán (Place of Herons). According to Aztec chronicles, their war god Huitzilopochtli (Southern Hummingbird) led them to the valley after a century of wandering and gave the tribe a new name, Méxica.

Receiving a cold reception from the tribes already living around the lake, the Aztecs first settled on the insect-infested Cerro de Chapultepec in 1280 A.D. and tried to ingratiate themselves to the neighboring Tepanecs by serving as mercenaries. They quickly developed a reputation as fierce and bloodthirsty warriors. Around 1300 the Culhuacán, rivals of the Tepanecs, defeated the Aztecs in battle and took the survivors as slaves. After serving for 25 years as Culhuacán mercenaries, the Aztecs were eventually granted their freedom. In a telling sign of their vengefulness and brutality, they tricked the Culhuacán leader into giving them one of his daughters to marry their own ruler. At the Aztec "wedding" ceremony, the guest leader was greeted by the sight of the Aztec high priest wearing the flesh of his daughter.

Still weaker than the Culhuacán, the Aztecs fled to an uninhabited island named Tenochtitlán in the center of the lake, rather than risk a war they might lose. Legend has it that the sight of an eagle perched on a cactus, a snake in its beak, was the fulfillment of Aztec prophecy, which convinced the tribe to settle there for good. Historians cite the island's natural defenses and the existence of several small freshwater springs on the island as more prosaic reasons.

For a time the Aztecs returned as soldiers for their former Tepanec masters, but the fourth Aztec king, Itzcoatl, overthrew the Tepanecs in 1428 and, along with the leaders of nearby city-states Texcoco and Tlacopán, established the Triple Alliance to rule over the valley. Aztec hegemony in the alliance was implicit from the start and grew stronger over the next century.

Under Itzcoatl's mid-15th-century successors, all historical records belonging to other tribes were destroyed to cement the Aztec perspective of the Valley of Mexico, which revered the Toltecs as their spiritual ancestors and downplayed their nomadic past. Moctezuma I (1440–69) embarked on an expansionist program that brought the Huastec and Mixtec regions under Aztec control, and under Aztec monarch Ahuitzotl (1486–1502) all of central Mexico fell under Aztec sway, except for the fierce and copper-equipped Tarascan warriors of Michoacán and the doughty Tlaxcaltecas to the east, who would later prove key in the Spanish conquest.

Far from tempering their bloody ways as they grew in power, the empire Aztecs took their formerly modest practice of human sacrifice and occasional cannibalism to staggering heights. Historians continue to argue about the accuracy of the incredible number of victims Spanish chroniclers reported killed in single ceremonies (in the tens of thousands), but the Aztecs unquestionably sacrificed on a huge scale, reputedly believing it necessary to feed the sun with blood so it would rise each day.

Conquered by such a culture, vassal states obeyed the Aztecs from fear rather than loyalty. Tribute demanded by the Aztecs included gold, copper, gemstones, jade, amber, rubber, jaguar skins, tropical feathers, and chocolate. Apart from these material goods, other tribes were required to send victims for sacrifice. Even nominal Aztec enemies such as the Tlaxcaltecans and the Cholulans were forced into mock battles known as "flower wars," in which soldiers were rarely killed; instead they were taken as prisoners to have their hearts ripped out a few days later by Aztec priests.

The glittering city of Tenochtitlán was the heart of the great empire, an island command center measuring roughly three kilometers square and linked to the mainland only by four causeways that could be easily blocked from attack. Adjacent to Tenochtitlán, and eventually linked to it by continual land-fill projects, was the smaller island of Tlatelolco, the empire's principal market center.

Tenochtitlán was laid out in an orderly grid pattern and crisscrossed by a system of canals, which allowed for drainage during the flood season and also provided the principal means of transportation. The Spanish conquistadors (mostly young provincials with limited educations) who saw Tenochtitlán before they destroyed it were in utter awe of the pervasive cleanliness and order.

As the conquistador Bernal Díaz del Castillo put it in his book, *The Conquest of New Spain:*

> ***. . . we were struck with admiration and said that it all seemed like enchanted things from the book of Amadís, seeing the great towers and buildings which they had built in the water all made of plaster and stone, and some of our soldiers asked if what they saw was a dream, and how marvelous it was the things that I write about here, because it made one amazed. I don't know how to describe it, seeing things never heard of, never even dreamed of.***

In 1519, with a population of perhaps 250,000, Tenochtitlán was arguably the greatest city on earth.

SPANISH CONQUEST AND COLONIZATION OF MEXICO

The Spanish *Entrada*

In the wake of Columbus's momentous voyage in 1492, the Spaniards quickly took over several Caribbean islands, principally Hispaniola and Cuba. In 1518, Cuban Governor Diego Velázquez chose a 34-year-old Spaniard named Hernán Cortés from Medellín, a town in the poor province of Extremadura, Spain, to lead what was intended as a reconnaissance expedition to the Mexican coast.

Cortés, who at the time was working as a secretary for Velázquez, had other ideas in mind. The expedition of 530 soldiers landed in what is now the Gulf Coast state of Veracruz on April 20, 1519. After destroying his ships and convincing his men to risk all for glory, he made his way over the next several months to Tenochtitlán, gathering Aztec enemies as his allies along the way. According to many accounts, the superstitious Aztec Emperor Moctezuma II apparently became convinced that Cortés was the embodiment of the plumed serpent god Quetzalcóatl, who according to legend would return from the east. Because of this, or perhaps because of Cortés' clever diplomacy through Aztec messengers, Moctezuma eventually allowed the Spaniards into his city as protected guests when they finally arrived at Tenochtitlán in November of 1519. Through sheer force of personality and a series of psychological tactics, Cortés assumed a bizarre sort of mental control over Moctezuma, who was soon doing the bidding of the Spaniards and keeping them safe from an increasingly restive and angry Aztec elite.

While Cortés was away on an expedition to the coast, to fight off a group of rival conquistadors who had sailed from Cuba, the less subtle Pedro de Alvarado led a slaughter of Aztec nobility who were performing a ceremony that apparently he didn't like the looks of. Cortés hastened back, but the damage was done and the already unhappy populace rallied to expel the Spaniards from the city on July 1, 1520, known in Spanish history as the Noche Triste (Sad Night).

Cortés had hoped to hand over Tenochtitlán intact, as a sparkling jewel to the Spanish crown, but after several months of regrouping their forces, organizing allies around the valley, and building a flotilla of lake boats, the conquistadors mounted a brutal 90-day siege and then invaded the city. The Aztecs, already weakened by the diseases brought by the Spaniards and starving to death, fought to the bitter end under the iron leadership of a young warrior named Cuauhtémoc, who is today a national hero in Mexico.

To take the city, the conquistadors were forced to destroy it block by block, eliminating the high redoubts from which the Aztecs flung down rocks and spears, until eventually the remaining defenders, refusing to surrender, were killed in the main plaza of Tlatelolco. Cuauhtémoc was captured, tortured to reveal hidden stashes of gold (of which none remained—the Spaniards lost most of it during the Noche Triste), and was later executed by Cortés on a pretext.

Nueva España

Facing the rubble of Tenochtitlán, Cortés contemplated establishing the new colonial capital on the edge of the lake, but in the end chose to rebuild the old Aztec city, partly for defensive reasons, but also for the symbolic significance: in many ways, the Spaniards aimed to merely replace the Aztecs as the rulers of the already-existing empire system. So under the direction of Alonso García Bravo, a new city was laid out atop the old, utilizing much of the original Aztec street plan.

While the new conquerors often rationalized their right to rule Mexico on the grounds that they were converting the natives to Christianity, missionary zeal was hardly their only motive. Early Aztec gifts of gold and silver had tantalized the treasure-seeking Spaniards, and silver strikes in Taxco in 1522 presaged the fabulously rich mining industry that would form the basis of the colonial economy, and in fact that of all Europe as well.

All of the immense quantities of silver mined in New Spain passed through Mexico City—as the capital was soon called—on its way back to Spain. On top of this, the Mexico City merchants had an official monopoly on all trading in the colony. As a result of these convenient, royally granted advantages, the city grew immensely wealthy and came to be known throughout Europe as *la ciudad de los palacios* (the city of palaces).

With the decline of the silver industry, Mexico City stagnated in the late 17th and early 18th centuries, but the last decades of the 1700s saw a burst of reformist zeal under the new Bourbon kings, who appointed a series of activist viceroys, the colonial governors. Viceroy Conde de Revillagigedo ordered the creation of a master plan for the city's development, calling for all manner of urban improvements, including an overhaul of basic infrastructure such as sewage and street lighting, and building new, tree-lined avenues outside downtown, including La Viga and later Paseo de Bucareli.

MEXICO CITY AFTER INDEPENDENCE

Independence and Early Instability

Mexico's struggle for independence from Spain began on September 16, 1810, when Padre Miguel Hidalgo y Costilla gave his famous *grito de la independencia* (independence shout) from a church in Dolores, Guanajuato. Mexico City, which depended on the colonial trade monopoly for its living, remained a royalist holdout during the struggle, firmly opposed to independence. Hidalgo's anarchic rebellion, with racial and class overtones, was quickly put down, and independence was not consumated until royalist officer Agustín Iturbide switched sides and cut a deal with rebel Vicente Guerrero in 1821. Iturbide was appointed emperor of the new republic, but his reign lasted only two years before he was overthrown by another junta that established a federal republic called Los Estados Unidos de México—the United States of Mexico—in 1824. Under this republic, named for the Méxica (Aztec) tribe originally defeated by the Spanish, the 22 provinces of New Spain were divided into 19 states and four territories.

Over the next six years the Mexican republic endured two more coups; it wasn't until 1829 that all Spanish troops were expelled from Mexico. In 1833 Antonio López de Santa Anna, a megalomaniac, opium-addicted general in charge of enforcing the expulsion of Spanish troops, seized power and revoked the Constitution of 1824. Mexico in many ways was cursed by Santa Anna, who was a brilliant, charismatic general but utterly uninterested in the difficult tasks of administering a new nation. Santa Anna was in and out of power for the next decade, switching sides repeatedly between the feuding liberals and conservatives. The former favored reigning in the power of the church and proceeding with modernist reforms, while the latter felt that the only way for the country to survive was to maintain the social structure with a strong church and central government.

While Mexico was engrossed in this bitter infighting, its neighbor to the north was increasing its control on the Mexican territory of Texas and eyeing other territories covetously. In 1847, on a flimsy pretext, U.S. President James Polk ordered the invasion of Mexico, which ended with the U.S. occupation of Mexico City for 10 months. It was during this battle when six young military cadets, defending the Castillo de Chapultepec from the invading gringos, reputedly leapt to their deaths from the castle ramparts rather than surrender. For their Quixotic heroism, the six are remembered in Mexican history as the Niños Héroes, the Child Heroes. As a result of the unequal war, Mexico ceded almost half of its territory to the United States.

Juárez and Maximilian

Santa Anna returned to power after the war, but he was finally overthrown in 1855 by a Zapotec lawyer named Benito Juárez. The new president and his liberal allies promulgated a constitution in 1857 and passed laws restricting the financial powers of the church; all church property save for church buildings had to be sold or otherwise relinquished. These actions infuriated conservatives and, not surprisingly, the church, and led to the War of Reform, with self-appointed governments in Mexico City and Veracruz vying for national authority. A reactionary opposition group took control of Mexico City and fighting continued until 1861, when the liberals won and Juárez was elected president.

Once in power, Juárez promptly enacted the Reform Laws dispossessing the church of its property, a turn of events that would change the face of Mexico City. Much of the downtown area was at that time covered by large monasteries and convents, including San Agustín, San Francisco, Santo Domingo, La Merced, and others. After seizing the properties, city officials demolished parts of these religious compounds, running new streets through and walling off the old churches. While remnants of the old convents and monasteries still stand, none in the Centro Histórico are intact.

When guerrilla leader Pancho Villa took the capital (which he loathed) in 1915, he staged an elaborate ceremony to shame the city elite, forcing them to rename Plateros, the wealthiest street in the Centro, to Francisco I. Madero in honor of Villa's slain hero.

Between 1863 and 1867, Mexico was governed by Austrian Emperor Maximilian, installed by an invading French army. Maximilian's rule was brief and ended with his execution, but the modernist-minded emperor made a lasting mark on the city. Unhappy with the cold, gloomy palace on the Zócalo, Maximilian and his wife moved to and remodeled the Castillo de Chapultepec, now a popular tourist sight. To link the new palace with downtown, the Paseo de la Reforma (originally the Paseo de la Emperatriz), now the city's broadest boulevard, was laid out. He also overhauled the Zócalo itself, decorating it with trees, benches, and a Parisian-style kiosk.

MODERN MEXICO CITY

The *Porfiriato*

Juárez defeated the hapless Maximilian in 1867 and again took power, governing Mexico until his death in 1872, when political opponent Porfirio Díaz succeeded him. Díaz thoroughly dominated Mexico for the next 28 years, governing with a brutal and efficient authoritarianism, modernizing the country's education and transportation systems and opening the doors wide for foreign investors and speculators.

Although originally from rural Oaxaca, Díaz became so attached to Mexico City's pomp and ceremony that by the end of his regime he rarely left the city, a factor that took the formerly wily ruler out of touch with the country as a whole. He spent lavishly on city infrastructure, overhauled the police force, and did his best to convert the wealthy neighborhoods on the western side of the city into little pockets of Europe. The poor shanty towns east were ignored entirely, except when he unleashed the police on their inhabitants whenever they ventured into the "good" parts of town.

It was under Díaz that Mexico City began to systematically expand beyond the present-day Centro Histórico. The first neighborhoods established outside downtown were Guerrero and San Rafael, north and west of the Alameda, in the 1850s and 1860s. Under Díaz, this trend accelerated, first with the development of San Cosme and Santa María la Ribera farther west, and later Juárez and Cuauhtémoc on either side of the newly chic Paseo de la Reforma, and the Colonia Roma just to the south.

Interestingly, this division of the city between the wealthy west and poor east has continued to the present day. The likeliest explanation for the split, which began early in the colonial era, is that the elite were trying to keep as far away as possible from the floodwaters of Lago Texcoco, which lay on the east side of the city.

The Mexican Revolution

By the early 1900s, it was obvious that the gap between rich and poor was increasing, caused by the extreme pro-capitalist policies of the Díaz regime and the lack of a political voice for workers and peasants. Following the annulment of elections won by opposition candidate Francisco I. Madero in 1910, the Mexican Revolution unleashed itself upon the country, and 10 years of warring between different factions followed, until Sonoran General Álvaro Obregón established control in 1920.

As during the independence wars, Mexico City remained on the side of the conservatives throughout the conflict. The populace gave no sign of rising to defend Madero when General Victoriano Huerta staged a coup d'etat and had the liberal president executed in early 1913. In retaliation for this apathy, when guerrilla leader Pancho Villa took the capital (which he loathed) in 1915, he staged an elaborate ceremony to shame the city elite, forcing them to rename Plateros, the wealthiest street in the Centro, to Francisco I. Madero in honor of Villa's slain hero.

Mexico City under the PRI

Despite its antirevolutionary inclinations, there was never any doubt that the city would remain the heart of Mexico's political, social, and economic life. With the creation of a stable, single-party government under the Institutional Revolutionary Party (PRI), the capital embarked on a new path of explosive growth that has continued to the present day.

After the rule of General Álvaro Obregón (1920–24) and General Plutarco Elias Calles (1924–34), Lázaro Cárdenas was elected president in 1934. Cárdenas, a mestizo with Tarascan Indian heritage, was handpicked by Calles, who hoped to remain the power behind the throne, but he was quickly disabused of this notion. Cárdenas instituted the most sweeping social reforms of any national leader to date, effecting significant changes in education, labor, agriculture, and commerce. Because of his humble ways and his evident desire to improve the lot of the average Mexican, he is revered to this day throughout the country.

Cárdenas didn't devote a lot of attention to Mexico City in his reformist drive, but the reforms themselves would end up having a major impact on the capital. The new offices created to manage the myriad new programs would eventually lead to the Mexican "super state," a massive, bloated bureaucracy located entirely in Mexico City. "The dreams of the revolution, converted into a nightmare of centralization," as one historian put it.

Further catalysts to growth came from falling investment in the countryside, and policies encouraging all manner of new industry to spring up in Mexico City. Rather than trying to locate these factories outside of the city, successive governments actively encouraged them to stay, offering tax breaks and promising to build necessary infrastructure if industries would locate in northern suburbs such as Naucalpan, Azcapotzalco, Tlanepantla, and Ecatepec.

The lack of jobs in the countryside and the new industry in Mexico City kicked off waves of migration to the capital, which doubled the population in 20 years, from 906,000 in 1920 to 1,757,000 in 1940. To cope with its new residents, the city expanded in all directions. And as is immediately apparent when you fly over Mexico City, this expansion took place with very little planning or forethought. The government turned a blind eye to the impromptu settlements set up by rural immigrants, which would eventually become entire cities in their own right, and freely gave out permits to build new, upscale neighborhoods for the wealthy. First Colonia Condesa was the "in" place in the 1930s, and it was soon followed by Polanco and Lomas farther west in the 1940s.

The Post-World War II Boom

The dynamics of centralization and rural migration accelerated in step with Mexico's economic growth levels during and after World War II. The construction of the new national university complex in the south of the city in the early 1950s, and the expansion of Avenida Insurgentes to connect it to the city center, led to the buildup of the entire southwestern quadrant of the city in just a few short years. Wide open fields south of Roma were quickly converted into the Del Valle and Nápoles neighborhoods. In the early postwar years the formerly outlying villages of Mixoac, San Ángel, Tacuba, Tacubaya, and Coyoacán were formally incorporated into the city limits.

To the north, the industrial areas promoted by the government spurred the building of ever-greater numbers of houses, to the point where the remaining open land between them and the city itself soon disappeared entirely as the *mancha urbana* (urban stain) spread across the entire valley. When the middle-class suburb Ciudad Satelite was built with great optimism in the late 1950s, it was surrounded by open land, but in the intervening years the city gobbled it up completely, sprawling all the way to Tepozotlán, by the entrance of the tollway to Querétaro.

The poor, rural immigrants flooding into the city didn't have money to buy property or houses and simply erected shantytowns in the less desirable eastern side of the valley, once under the waters of Lago Texcoco. Over the years these *ciudades perdidas* (lost cities) have converted into increasingly permanent cities themselves, with infrastructure and local government. The classic *ciudad perdida* is Ciudad Nezahaulcóyotl (Ciudad Neza, for short), which saw its population increase from 65,000 in 1960 to 650,000 in 1970 to 1,233,868 in 1995, making it one of the largest cities in the country.

Immigration has fallen off somewhat in recent years, and city and federal governments make a lot of noise about controlling city growth, but the overall dynamic appears to have changed little. If anything, the changes under way due to NAFTA and the privatization of the communal farms will only drive more people out of rural Mexico, and if these migrants can't get to the United States, they'll come to Mexico City.

One example of the continuing relentless city growth can be seen in Chalco, in the southeastern corner of the valley. Still a farming community with miles of open fields, Chalco is now being "colonized" by immigrants from Ciudad Neza, and urban researchers say it's just a question of a few years before new roads will be built, power lines put in, and the new communities are regularized.

Government

Colonial Era

During the Spanish colonial era, Mexico City was governed as an *ayuntamiento,* the traditional Spanish form of town council. While subservient to the royal authorities, the *ayuntamiento* was a power to be reckoned with in colonial affairs.

The capital government became a *municipio* (roughly equivalent to a county in Anglo-American administrative systems) after independence from Spain and was declared the official seat of the federal government. City authorities managed to maintain a limited autonomy throughout the turbulent decades until the arrival of Porfirio Díaz, who centralized its authority (along with the rest of the country's) in his hands.

Under the PRI

In 1928, the revolutionary government of President Álvaro Obregón revoked the city's status as a *municipio,* creating the Distrito Federal, whose mayor was appointed directly by the president. The new entity encompassed what was previously the *municipio* of México and several outlying communities, converting them into 16 *delegaciones,* so named because their leaders were delegated by the federal government.

While these centralizing reforms were ostensibly intended to help modernize the city, in reality they created a bloated, incredibly inefficient, and numbingly corrupt bureaucracy. Taking care of any sort of *tramite* (official procedure) was an exercise in frustration, unless you were willing to pay the *mordida* (literally "the bite," a bribe) to speed up matters. Any kind of government contract became an opportunity for graft. The entire patronage system was managed by the long-ruling Institutional Revolutionary Party (PRI).

After seven decades as a badly managed appendage of the federal government, Mexico City's political reform began in 1989 with the birth of the Asemblía de Representantes del Distrito Federal (ARDF), housed in the old federal Congress in the Centro. After arduous negotiations, the city took its first step in modern democracy by voting for the first full elections of the assembly and mayor on July 6, 1997.

The PRD in Government

The election was a watershed. With 47 percent of the vote, Cuauhtémoc Cárdenas won by almost double the number of his closest competitor, the PRI's Alfredo del Mazo (25 percent).

© JOE CUMMINGS

Carlos Castillo Peraza of the center-right Partido Acción Nacional (PAN), early on thought to be the likely winner, finished with a distant 15 percent.

And on top of that, Cárdenas's leftist Partido de la Revolución Democrática (PRD) swept every single assembly district in direct vote. The PRI, PAN, and the smaller parties were able to capture seats only by proportional representation. With this overwhelming mandate, joyously expressed in the victory celebration in the Zócalo on election night, Cárdenas's possibilities seemed limitless.

But the euphoria evaporated quickly. Given only a shortened term of three years and facing a city with an array of complex problems, the Cárdenas administration was bound to fall short of public expectations. In addition, the federal government retained control of city finances, and during the 1999 federal budget debates in Congress, in a last-second jab at Cárdenas, the PAN and PRI factions denied a request to issue 10 billion pesos in debt, hamstringing the city budget.

Cárdenas, a former PRI member who had left the party to pursue democratic reforms, was also criticized for acting too cautiously and refusing to negotiate with the other parties. While the new government, filled with idealistic young reformers, clearly made some efforts to clean up bureaucracy in the *delegaciones* and fight corruption in the police, it did not manage to seize its golden opportunity as dramatically as it might have. Cárdenas's dour, uncommunicative style did not help the city government's poor public image.

The 2000 elections, as anyone who pays the slightest attention to Mexico knows, finally saw the PRI lose control of the presidency after seven decades in power to the PAN's Vicente Fox. Cárdenas ran a poor third place and appears to be a spent force in Mexican politics. But the PRD again easily won in Mexico City under Andrés Manuel López Obrador, irreverently known as "el pejelagarto," the "alligator mayor," because of his origins in the coastal state of Tabasco. A firey leftist politico who made his name fighting the PRI in Tabasco, López Obrador has had a mixed record running the city. As with Cárdenas, he is seen as setting himself up to run for president in 2006, and he has been very public in his criticisms of President Fox. Corruption and crime, the two issues most important to Mexico City residents, appear as bad as ever, but to be fair it will take years of hard work to make any changes in these areas. López Obrador's current grand scheme is to build a second story for the Viaducto city highway to help alleviate traffic.

Whatever the success of López Obrador, the PRD is firmly established as a major force in Mexico City politics, winning a majority of the 16 now-elected (formerly appointed) delegation heads. On a national level, the PRD remains riven with internal disputes and muddled on its platform, but in the city, it has found a niche. It seems appropriate: the PRD has a knack for street-level organization and is clearly focused on helping the poor, attributes that lend themselves well to city politics. The PAN, predictably, has better luck in the wealthier areas of the city, while the PRI seems to have lost its way in Mexico City, although this could change under the leadership of López Obrador's old Tabasco rival, new PRI president Roberto Madrazo.

Economy

As it has for centuries, Mexico City controls a far larger share of the country's economy than any other region. During the colonial era, the wealth came primarily from the monopolies held by Mexico City merchants on imports and exports between the colony and Europe. After independence from Spain, but especially under the rule of the PRI since the Revolution, a large part of the country's new industry was located in the city, which only accentuated the already-growing dominance of the capital.

Since the 1970s, Monterrey and Guadalajara have been developing industrial bases of their own, and in more recent years smaller cities such as Puebla, Querétaro, Aguascalientes, and Toluca have started industrializing as well. Mexico City completely controls the financial sector, as it is home to the stock exchange and all major banks and insurance companies, and plays a major role in the service economy. As it is the location of essentially all federal government offices, government jobs are also a major factor in the economy. In short, the Distrito Federal continues to dominate the national economy.

Employment and Wages

Because Mexico City is such a magnet to migrant workers from the countryside, it has a higher unemployment rate than the national average, despite the city's overall economic strength. The official unemployment figures—2.4 percent in September 1999—don't even come close to reflecting reality. With such a high proportion of the population participating in an informal, unregistered economy, accurate numbers are extremely difficult to come by.

Wages tend to be higher than the national average. The city is in the highest of the three minimum wage brackets, a daily minimum wage of around US$4.

No look at the Mexico City economy would be complete without mentioning the legendary armies of *ambulantes,* the informal street vendors seen all over the city, their wares spread out on the sidewalk. Guesses on the number of city *ambulantes* vary wildly, but they certainly number in the tens of thousands, and perhaps into the hundreds of thousands. As they have for generations, many new immigrants to the city begin their new urban lives hawking their modest wares from any street corner not already occupied by another seller.

For years the *ambulantes*—organized into disciplined groups that voted for the PRI and could be relied on to show up at pro-government rallies—were protected by the city police, despite the occasional crack down. But driven in part by a desire to clean up the downtown area, and also because of the severe increase in *ambulantes* in the wake of the 1994–95 crisis, city authorities have begun regular patrols to evict the vendors. Every once in a while riot police will chase vendors off the streets, sometimes resulting in violent clashes. You can always take the pulse of the conflict by walking along Corregidora east from the Zócalo—if the police are cracking down, the street will be deserted; otherwise it will be packed with hundreds of vendors.

DID YOU KNOW?

Mexico City's population, best estimate: 17.8 million
Number of registered cars and buses in the city: 2.6 million
Daily driving trips within the city: 29.2 million
Number of hotel rooms: 25,000
Hospitals: 344
Museums: 161
Art galleries: 106

People and Culture

Population Figures

Accurate population statistics for Mexico City are notoriously difficult to obtain. With an estimated 180,000 new arrivals flooding the metropolitan area each year, no one can claim to have a figure with a margin of error of less than three or four million. Between 1990 and 1995 alone, the metropolitan area added 1.5 million residents, or about 20,000 per month. The official Mexican government estimate for the population of México, D.F., the Federal District proper, is 8.6 million, and if you include the more densely populated *municipios* immediately adjacent to D.F. in the State of México, then the number rises to 17.8 million.

You'll hear a figure of 20 million bandied about with reference to the Federal District combined with the entire population of the State of México, which wraps around the top two-thirds of the district. By either reckoning this makes the metropolis not only Mexico's largest city, but one of the largest in the world. In terms of city limits proper, Buenos Aires is actually more populous than the D.F., but it doesn't come close in terms of metropolitan area.

According to the most recent statistics from the government's Institute of Statistics, Geography, and Information (Instituto de Edatísticas, Geografía e Información, or INEGI), the Federal District's population density averages about 5,600 people per square kilometer. Figures for the individual 32 states vary considerably, of course, ranging from very low rates in the states of Baja California Sur, Chihuahua, Sonora, Campeche, Durango, and Coahuila, each with fewer than 15 inhabitants per square kilometer, to the State of México, where there are 571 inhabitants per square kilometer. If we combine the densities of México state and the Distrito Federal—each of which account for about half the metro area's total population—then the density for the whole is 3,085 people per square kilometer. Compare with Mexico's overall average density of just 48 per square kilometer, and you'll get an idea just how intensely urbanized the city is, although it's less packed

***"Y es oro, cemento y playa* (And it's gold, cement and silver)"**

© RAUL ORTEGA

contemplative *capitalino*

than Hong Kong (6,364 per square kilometer) or Singapore (5,460).

INEGI claims that the total population of Mexico stands at 99 million, which means that the DF/México metro area harbors approximately 17 percent of the nation's inhabitants. Whether you count the percentage as low as 15 percent or as high as 20 percent (parlor estimates of 25 percent cannot be substantiated), this helps Mexico City meet the classic sociological definition of a primate city, i.e., one in which more than 10 percent of a nation's inhabitants live. Economic factors such as Mexico City's disproportionate share of national wealth (around 35 percent) and the fact that a preponderance of goods produced in the country as a whole end up in Mexico City complete the definition of urban primacy.

It's worth noting that Mexico City's growth has slowed considerably since the 1970s, when its population was expanding at an average rate of 4.5 percent per annum. Such vigorous growth came as a result of the dynamic social and economic environment that prevailed in the post-war era. Mexico's relative isolation in matters of international trade forced local manufacturers to concentrate on the internal market and, in particular, on the country's main center of consumption: Mexico City. This propelled the creation of an infrastructure whereby all the major routes of communication converged on the capital. The centralist attitude of the government also played an important role in this inward development.

Decentralization of the economy during the 1980s led to a slower growth of only 0.7 percent each year, well below both the national annual rate (2 percent), and the overall urban rate of growth (3.7 percent). The city now is Mexico's slowest growing metropolitan area.

Mestizaje

In Spanish colonial Mexico City, the most privileged class was the *gachupines,* pure-blooded Spaniards born in Spain, followed by *criollos,* pure-blooded Spaniards born in Mexico; mestizos, those of mixed Indian-Spanish blood born in Mexico; and *indios,* pure-blooded Indians. In many cases the Spanish lumped together *indios* and mestizos as *indígenas.* One of the ironies of the colonial caste system was that "pure-blooded" Spaniards were themselves

WHO'S BIGGER?

It is often claimed that Mexico's capital is "the largest city in the world," yet in our relatively exhaustive research into existing records, we could find no set of statistics that would back this claim. According to the International Data Base of the U.S. Bureau of the Census, part of the U.S. Department of Commerce (a government department with a keen interest in tracking foreign population statistics for trade purposes), a ranking of the world's largest urban "agglomerations" places Mexico City in the number two position, following Tokyo. According to this list, the Mexico City agglomeration numbered an estimated 27.8 million in the year 2000, while Tokyo was counted at 29.9 million, less than two million ahead of Mexico City. A second study, published by World Gazeteer, listed Tokyo in first place with 31 million, New York-Philadelphia (a rather generous lumping!) second with 29.9 million, and Mexico City third with a mere 20.9 million.

Another authoritative source, the United Nations Center for Human Settlements (HABITAT), published a report in 1996 with a very different ranking. According to this report, Mexico City contained an estimated 11.2 million in 1975—ranking it number four for that year—and was expected to reach 18.8 million by the year 2015. This latter projection would bring Mexico City down to a standing of 10th for that year. In first place for both HABITAT lists, again, was Tokyo (19.8 million in 1975; 28.7 million in 2015).

The apparent discrepancies among all these estimates can be explained by the fact that different organizations are tracking different statistical entities, from the 16 *delegaciones* of the Distrito Federal all the way to the entire Valle de México, which measures roughly 120 by 65 km, or more than 7,000 square km.

A middle-ground approach says that *la Ciudad de México*—or Zona Metropolitana de la Ciudad de México (ZMCM)—covers the Distrito Federal plus 21 *municipios* (a *municipio* is roughly equivalent to "county" in Anglophone countries) in the adjacent State of México. Using this definition, the Mexican Instituto Nacional de Estadística, Geografía e Informatica (INEGI) estimates the entire metro area at 17.8 million, a number that many independent observers consider the most realistic. According to INEGI's 2000 census, the population of the city proper is 8,591,309, which makes it the 11th most populous city in the world.

descended from a 700-year mixing of Moors and Iberians, the conquerors and the conquered—a pattern the Spaniards repeated in the New World.

The caste system still exists in a subtler and more simplified form throughout Mexico today. The national government recognizes *mestizaje* (mestizoism, or "mixing") as the root cultural characteristic of Mexico, yet distinguishes between two kinds of mestizos, the *indomestizos* of the South, "in whom indigenous characteristics predominate," and the *euromestizos* of the North, "in whom European traits prevail." Also recognized are smaller groups of *afromestizos* from the south Gulf coastal regions, particularly Veracruz, where toward the end of the colonial era the Spanish imported African slaves to fill labor shortages caused by the rapidly shrinking local population.

No statistical ethnic breakdown of the capital appears to be available to the public. However, according to the Mexican government, *mestizos* represent roughly 55 percent of the population of the whole nation. Caucasians are believed to represent another 14 percent; with 6 percent *indígenas,* that leaves 25 percent of the nation unaccounted for. An exact national ethnography obviously isn't one of the government's objectives. The Central Intelligence Agency claims a more exacting set of statistics: *mestizo* (Indian-Spanish) 60 percent; Amerindian or predominantly Amerindian 30 percent; Caucasian or predominantly Caucasian 9 percent; other 1 percent. Others break the population down with different numbers—it all depends on who gets slotted into which category, which in the end is a largely unscientific decision.

Representatives of virtually all 56 Amerindian groups recognized by the government can be found in Mexico City, along with many of the 90 officially cataloged native languages. Altogether around 100,000 inhabitants of the Mexico City metro area speak Amerindian languages, more than in any other city in the Americas.

Most numerous are the Náhua or Náhuatl-speaking people of Puebla, Veracruz, Hidalgo, Guerrero, Tlaxcala, Morelos, México, and San Luis Potosí. Most often described as progeny of the Aztecs, today's Nahuatl speakers are actually descendants of a number of disparate tribes whose individual languages were lost to the lingua franca of the Valley of Mexico.

Class Differences

The estimated distribution of wealth among *indomestizos, euromestizos,* and *afromestizos* remains roughly the same as it was when Mexico achieved independence from Spain. The *indígenas* occupy the statistical bottom, a colonial legacy still the standard throughout present-day North, Central, and South America.

While Indian values are publicly extolled, in practice almost anything labeled *indio* is considered low-caste. Political and economic power remains concentrated in the hands of an elite group of "pure" European descent, a social stratum sometimes referred to as the "Thousand Families."

RELIGION

Between the 16th and 19th centuries, Spanish missionaries indoctrinated the original inhabitants of the Valle de México in the ways of Roman Catholicism. That Catholicism is now the nation's majority religion is an amazing achievement considering it was laid over a vast variety of native belief systems in existence for thousands of years. About 90 percent of the population call themselves Catholics; Mexico is the second-largest Roman Catholic nation in the world after Brazil.

© CHRIS HUMPHREY

a carved wooden statue of Saint Christopher at Puebla's Museo Virreinal

Mexico's Protestant population consists mostly of Indians in the South missionized by North Americans in the 19th and 20th centuries. There are very few Protestants in Mexico City, which is considered the nation's most stalwart Catholic base after Guadalajara. Although many Spanish Jews arrived in the early days of European migration to Mexico, the Spanish Inquisition forced most to convert to Catholicism. Still, many more *capitalinos* identify themselves as "nonreligious" than in any other city in Mexico. The Mexican Constitution of 1917 guarantees freedom of religion; church and state are strictly separated.

Mexican Catholicism

Mexican Catholics tend to be devout practitioners of their faith. Mexican Catholicism, however, has its own variations that distinguish the religion from its European predecessors. Some differences are traceable to preexisting Indian spiritual traditions absorbed by the Catholic faith, and as such are localized according to tribe.

One variation common to all of Mexico is the Virgin of Guadalupe cult, which began in 1531 when a dark-skinned Virgin Mary appeared before Juan Diego, an Aztec nobleman formerly named Cuauhtaoctzin, in a series of three visions at Tepeyac, near Mexico City, previously a sacred Aztec site dedicated to the goddess Tonantzin. According to legend, in the third vision the Virgin commanded Diego to gather roses and present them to the local bishop, requesting that a church be built in her honor. When the devout Diego unfolded his rose-filled cloak, both he and the bishop beheld an image of the dark-skinned Virgin imprinted on the garment. This was deemed a miracle, and church construction commenced at once.

Today, many Mexican churches are named for Our Lady of Guadalupe, who has become so fused with Mexican identity that the slogan *¡Viva Guadalupe!* is commonly used at political rallies. The affectionate Mexican nickname for Guadalupe is La Morenita, "Little Dark One." She has become, as Mexican-American cultural commentator Richard Rodriguez puts it, the "official private flag of Mexico," and one way in which Catholicism has been absorbed by native cultures rather than vice versa. The official feast day for Guadalupe, December 12, is fervently celebrated in Mexico City and throughout the country. (For more information, see the entry on the Basílica de la Virgen de Guadalupe, in the Sights chapter.)

Mexican Saints

The legion of saints worshiped in Mexico runs the gamut of Catholic history. Three native saints warrant special mention. San Felipe de Jesús (1527–97), a Franciscan friar, became Mexico's first Catholic martyr when he was killed while performing missionary work in Nagasaki, Japan. His martyrdom was officially recognized by the church in 1627, and in 1629 Mexico named him the patron saint of the *virreinato* (the viceroyalty, i.e., the Spanish administration in Mexico). Santa Rosa de Lima (1586–1617), a Dominican nun, was canonized as a saint in 1671 and thus became the first *santa americana* (American female saint) within the Catholic tradition. After years of controversy, Juan Diego, the Aztec nobleman who saw the vision of the Virgen de Guadalupe, was declared a saint in 2002.

LANGUAGE

Mexico is the largest Spanish-speaking country in the world. The type of Spanish spoken in Mexico is usually referred to as Latin-American Spanish, in contrast to the Castilian Spanish spoken in Spain. Still, the Spanish here differs significantly from that of even other Spanish-speaking countries in the Western Hemisphere. Many Anglicisms have crept into the Mexican language. For example, the common Latin-American Spanish term for car is *coche,* but in Mexico you'll often hear *carro.*

While English is occasionally spoken by merchants, hotel staff, and travel agents in the Centro and in wealthier suburbs, first-time visitors are often surprised by how little English one hears in Mexico City compared to what might be encountered at popular beach resorts in Mexico. Outside areas of the city frequented by tourists, it's relatively rare to encounter anyone who speaks more than a few words of English.

Hence it's incumbent upon the visitor to learn at least enough Spanish to cope with everyday transactions. Knowing a little Spanish will not only mitigate communication problems, it will also bring you more respect among the local *capitalinos,* who quite naturally resent foreign visitors who expect Mexicans to abandon their mother tongue whenever a gringo approaches. Out of courtesy, you should at least attempt to communicate in Spanish whenever possible. See the Spanish Phrasebook at the end of the book for a list of useful words and phrases and a guide to Mexican-Spanish pronunciation. Also see the information on Spanish language courses in Mexico and recommended reference works.

CONDUCT AND CUSTOMS

Although Mexico City is extremely heterogeneous, collecting many regional differences in food, music, language, and life perspectives, a few generalizations can be made about how the "Mexican character" may appear to outsiders.

WHAT'S A *CHILANGO?*

Mexico City residents are often known by the epithet *chilango,* a word of mysterious provenance and dubious implication. Someone trying to get a definition of what the word literally means and where it came from is likely to get as many ideas as people he or she asks. Many suggest it's derived from the word *chile,* indicating the propensity of Mexico City denizen to eat spicy food. Others suggest it's a holdover from colonial times, from a Spanish word meaning to rape or conquer. Still others maintain that it comes from a Mayan word meaning intelligent or wise.

Whatever may be the original meaning of the word, if you travel around Mexico with a friend from the city, like as not you'll hear the word addressed at your companion in less than flattering tones. Much as Americans see New Yorkers as pushy, loud, fast-talking, and arrogant, Mexicans from the rest of the country do not hold capital city residents in the highest esteem, and unquestionably *chilango* has a negative connotation.

But much as black Americans have retaken the word "nigger" with a certain pride, so have some Mexico City residents, especially poorer ones, come to revel in their *chilango*-ness. One example is the popular song "Chilanga Banda," written by Juan Jaime López and made famous by the Mexico City group Café Tacuba, which glories in the fast-talking creative slang of the city. Some Mexico City folk, especially older ones, still find the word offensive, so if you want to be safe, use the neutral *capitalinos.*

First, however, consider this view of Americans through the eyes of María de los Angeles Jáuregui of Teocaltiche in southern Mexico:

> ***[In America] everything is scheduled by the clock. There is a specific time for everything. They spend all their days looking at their watches, and if they don't have a car, they can't do anything. If you don't know how to drive and there is no one to take you, you go nowhere. Here we keep our traditions even when people from here come back from the U.S. with new things. Here nobody plans their families. They have the children that God gives them.***

Time and Appointments

Of the many stereotypes of Mexican culture, the one about the Mexican sense of time being highly flexible is probably the most accurate. The reasons are too numerous and complex for the context of this book; read *The Labyrinth of Solitude* by Octavio Paz for a glimpse of an explanation. It's important to realize that the so-called *mañana* attitude is nothing more than a generalization; in many cases Mexican individuals are every bit as punctual as Americans, Canadians, or northern Europeans—especially when it comes to doing business with them.

If you make an appointment with a Mexican for dinner, a party, or other social engagement, you should figure the actual meeting time will occur an hour or two later than actually scheduled. As with business engagements, if the person involved has dealt frequently with Americans, Canadians, or northern Europeans, this might not always be the case. Also, Mexicans will typically accept an invitation rather than decline, even if they don't plan to attend the scheduled event. Within the Mexican social context, it is usually worse to refuse an invitation than not to show up. To avoid disappointment, prepare yourself for any of these scenarios.

When hiring any sort of guide, you can expect a modicum of punctuality—Mexicans in the tourist industry usually adapt themselves to the expectations of American and European tourists. Again, note the difference between business and social appointments.

Siesta

The stereotypical siesta, where everyone goes off to sleep for a couple of hours in the afternoon, is fast becoming a thing of the past throughout Mexico.

Nevertheless, a vestige of the siesta is preserved in the operating hours for offices and small businesses, which are typically closed 2–4 P.M. or 3–5 P.M. The first hour is reserved for *comida,* the midday meal, while the second hour is for relaxing or taking care of personal business. While to Americans and Canadians two hours may seem like a long lunch hour, the fact is that Mexican offices and businesses generally stay open much later than in the U.S. or Canada, until 7 or 8 P.M.

No matter what hours are posted for small businesses, the actual opening and closing times may vary with the whims of the proprietors. This is also true for tourist information offices. Banks usually follow their posted hours to the minute.

Terms of Address

Mexicans frequently use titles of respect when addressing one another. At a minimum, *"señor"* will do for men, *"señora"* for married women, and *"señorita"* for unmarried women or girls.

Professional titles can also be used for variety and to show additional respect. *Maestro* (master) or *maestra* (mistress) are common and can be used to address skilled workers (cobblers, auto mechanics, seamstresses, etc.) and any teacher except those at secondary schools and colleges or universities, who are *profesores* (men) or *profesoras* (women).

College graduates are *licenciado* (men) or *licenciada* (women), while doctors are *doctor* or *doctora.* Some other professional titles include *arquitecto* (architect), *abogado* (attorney), *ingeniero* (engineer), and *químico* (chemist).

Body Language

Mexicans tend to use their arms and hands more during verbal communication than do their American, Canadian, or northern European counterparts. Learning to read the more common gestures—but not necessarily imitate them—can greatly enhance your comprehension of everyday conversations, even when you don't understand every word being spoken.

One of the more confusing gestures for Americans and Canadians is the way Mexicans beckon to other people by holding the hand out, palm down, and waving in a downward motion. Holding the palm upward and crooking the fingers toward the body, the typical American or Canadian gesture for "come here," is a vaguely obscene gesture in Mexico.

Extending the thumb and forefinger from a closed hand and holding them about a half-inch apart means "a little bit" in the U.S. and Canada but in Mexico usually means "just a moment" or "wait a minute" (often accompanied by the utterance *"momentito"*).

The wagging of an upright forefinger means "no" or "don't do that." This is a good gesture to use when children hanging around at stoplights or gasoline pumps begin wiping your windshield and you don't want them to.

Mexicans commonly greet one another with handshakes, which are used between the sexes and among children and adults—in fact, with everybody. Mexican males who are friends will sometimes greet one another with a handshake, followed by an *abrazo* (embrace), and completed with another handshake, and urban women may kiss one another on the cheek. Foreigners should stick to the handshake until they establish more intimate relationships. Handshakes are also used upon parting and saying farewell.

Dress

Mexicans are relatively tolerant of the way visitors dress. Nonetheless, invisible lines exist, which, out of respect for Mexican custom, shouldn't be crossed. In Mexico City almost no one ever wears shorts; although this is mainly because of the cool year-round climate, it also demonstrates that *capitalinos* tend to be more formal in dress than Mexicans in many other cities, especially compared with coastal cities.

Upon entering a church or chapel in Mexico, men are expected to remove their hats. Many Mexican males will also remove their hats when passing in front of a church. More tradition-minded Mexican women will cover their heads when inside a church, but younger women usually don't and foreign females aren't expected to. Shorts, sleeveless shirts/blouses, sandals, or bare feet are considered improper dress for both men and women in churches, even for brief sightseeing visits.

Sights

SUGGESTED ITINERARIES

Statistics suggest that most visitors to Mexico City stay three days or fewer. We think it's worth at least a week, and two weeks would be just enough time to scratch the surface. Because not everyone will be able to schedule that much time, here are some recommendations for hitting the highlights during a shorter stay.

Reminder: Mexico City's 2,240-meter elevation makes it one of the highest country capitals in the world. If you're bothered by the altitude, go easy on strenuous activity for the first couple of days. Headaches, mild fatigue, and mild stomach upset may be symptoms of altitude sickness; doctors suggest staying away from alcoholic drinks and eating lightly for those first days.

Three Days

Start off in the heart of the city, at the **Zócalo,** and take in the **Catedral Metropolitana** and **Templo Mayor** (along with the Museo del Templo Mayor). If you like the look of the **Palacio Nacional,** also on the Zócalo, have a peek inside at Diego Rivera's famous murals. After touring the historical district, have lunch in one of the many nearby restaurants, then move west to the **Palacio de Bellas Artes** to admire the art nouveau/art deco architectural blend, the Tiffany glass curtain, and political murals. If you've got more energy to spare, finish up the day with a stroll across the

Palacio de Bellas Artes

©CHRIS HUMPHREY

On Av. Madero is the old Convento de San Francisco, one of the Centro's many colonial monasteries.

Alameda park to the eclectic applied-arts collection at the **Museo de Franz Mayer** or to the **Museo Mural Diego Rivera,** housing the mural, *Sueño de una tarde dominical en la Alameda Central* (Dream of a Sunday Afternoon in the Alameda Central). Or switch to market mode, visiting the handicrafts market at La Ciudadela and the antiques and furniture market at La Lagunilla in the Centro Histórico.

On your second day think about heading to Bosques de Chapultepec to see the world-famous **Museo Nacional de Antropología e Historia.** Even if you don't make it to all 23 exhibit halls (covering some 100,000 square feet), a visit should not be missed. Nearby you'll also find the former presidential residence, **Castillo de Chapultepec,** with commanding views over the city, and a couple of good art museums. Complete the day with a visit to one of the many fine restaurants or cafés in the leafy **Condesa** district nearby.

On day three you might consider heading south for a circuit through the upscale but charming colonial-era districts of **San Ángel** and **Coyoacán.** If you have time, take a ride on a *trajinera* (colorful Mexican-style gondolas) through the canals and floating gardens of **Xochimilco** farther south.

Four or Five Days

If you can add a day or two, think about getting outside the city to the majestic Mesoamerican pyramids at **Teotihuacán.** If you have an interest in religion, you can stop off at the **Basílica de Guadalupe,** home to Mexico's patron saint, the Virgin of Guadalupe, in the north of the city.

Also north of the city, but best visited on a separate half day, is the quaint colonial-era town of **Tepotzotlán,** home to one of the best ex-convent museums in Mexico (and a good place to try *pulque,* if you're curious about tequila's precursor). For your second half day, investigate the **Zona Rosa** and **Polanco** areas of Mexico City. While many guidebooks place these near the top of the list, the lack of historical, architectural, or traditional cultural interest leads us to consider them add-ons, not must-dos. An alternative afternoon might involve a look around the art galleries, cafés, and mansions of the **Roma** district, just south of the Zona Rosa.

If you're in Mexico City on a Sunday, you might be able to squeeze in a bullfight at the **Plaza de Toros** or catch a soccer match at the adjacent **Estadio Azul** or at **Estadio Azteca** in the south of the city.

A Week to 10 Days

After five days of sightseeing in or very near to Mexico City, you may be ready for a complete change of scenery. If so, consider going south to the colonial town-cum-suburb of **Cuernavaca** with a stop along the way at the village of **Tepoztlán** (not to be confused with the similar-sounding Tepotzotlán to the north of D.F.). Or head west to **Valle de Bravo,** a favorite weekend recreation getaway for Mexico City residents for its boating, mountain biking, and butterfly watching.

With more days at your disposal, the famed silver city of **Taxco** becomes a possibility, though we recommend at least one overnight there to fully appreciate the town's ambience. A more ambitious route would take in the triangle formed by **Tlaxcala, Cholula,** and **Puebla,** all three among the oldest and most important towns in Spain's colonial empire.

Centro Histórico

When the Aztecs first arrived in the Valle de México, they were forced to settle on a small island in the center of the great lake, as most of the more desirable land on the lake's shores was already populated by other tribes. This small island, known as Tenochtitlán, became the Aztec capital, and later the center of Spanish Mexico. As the centuries passed and the lakes and canals were gradually filled in and covered over, the Centro was physically joined to the rest of the city, but the rough outlines of the old island are still apparent, bordered on the west by Eje Central Lázaro Cárdenas, the north by Eje 1 Norte, the south by Avenida Izazaga or San Pablo, and the east by Avenida Circunvalación.

The downtown area, centered on the broad, wide-open Zócalo, is jam-packed with centuries-old palaces and churches—some crumbling to bits, others recently renovated—as well as museums, banks, and one of the city's main shopping districts. In any European city, an ancient central area would have long since been renovated, cleaned up, and gentrified, but despite the oft-stated plans of successive city governments, the Centro remains a chaotic place of crowded sidewalks, street vendors, political rallies, tourists both Mexican and foreign, peasants from the countryside, bustling office workers, and who knows who else. Not for nothing do locals jokingly call it the "Centro Histérico" (Hysterical Center).

In the summer of 2001, President Vicente Fox and Mexico City Mayor Andrés Manuel López Obrador jointly announced a plan to "rescue" the Centro. Top Mexican businessmen such

fountain inside Palacio Nacional

as Carlos Slim, historian Guillermo Tovar y Teresa, and even Cardenal Norberto Rivera signed on to support the plan. However, as one local newspaper laconically pointed out, a "new" plan to renovate the Centro seems to appear every decade or so. Time will tell whether this one is any different.

Although the sorry state of the many mistreated colonial buildings in the Centro can be a disheartening sight, somehow the very disrepair of it all adds to the downtown's charm, or at least its edge—this is no tourist theme park, but still the living heart of one of the world's largest cities. And just when you're being overwhelmed with the relentless urbanity of the Centro, you'll step off the street into the cool, blissfully calm courtyard of some colonial palace covered with marvelous stone carvings and wonder how this spot could be in the middle of such a city.

No matter how short your stay, at least a brief visit to the Centro is obligatory to admire the architecture and ambience of Mexico's ancient capital.

ORIENTATION

The Centro is quite a compact area, and its narrow streets and traffic make driving a major headache, so walking is unquestionably the best way to go. Should all the pavement-pounding wear you out, consider hopping onto one of the many bicycle taxis cruising around the Centro, which will charge you US$2–3 to peddle you from one destination to the next.

The sites in this section are divided into five walking tours, the first around the Zócalo and the other four through the neighborhoods in each direction from the Zócalo. Needless to say, readers will have their own ideas of what they would like to visit and should arrange their walks accordingly.

HIGHLIGHTS IN EL CENTRO

In case you don't have the time or inclination to see all the palaces, museums, churches, markets, and other sites described in this section, here are a few of the most important destinations, grouped by type, to help plan your selective tour. Conveniently, three of the arguably most important examples of Aztec, colonial religious, and colonial civil architecture—the Templo Mayor, Catedral, and Palacio Nacional, respectively—all face the Zócalo.

Can't Miss
- Zócalo
- Catedral Metropolitana
- Palacio Nacional
- Templo Mayor

Colonial Churches and Convents
- San Francisco (West)
- La Enseñanza (North)
- La Santísima (East)
- Regina Coeli (South)
- San Agustín (South)
- Universidad del Claustro de Sor Juana (South)

Museums and Murals
- Museo de Hacienda (East)
- Antiguo Colegio de San Ildefonso (North)
- Secretaría de Educación Pública (North)
- Museo Nacional de Arte (West)
- Museo de la Ciudad de México (South)

Palaces and Other Buildings
- Palacio de Iturbide (West)
- Casa de los Azulejos (West)
- Torre Latinoamericana (West)
- Casa de los Condes Heras y Soto (West)
- Casa de los Condes Mateo de Valparaíso (South)

Other Sites
- Mariachis at Plaza Garibaldi (North)
- Outdoor scribes at Plaza Santo Domingo (North)
- Weekend flea market at Lagunilla (see Shopping chapter)

ORIENTATION

As anyone who has flown into Mexico City on a relatively clear day can attest, the city is simply massive. It seems to stretch out forever in all directions. But the average traveler is interested in only certain parts of the Distrito Federal—mainly the center, the west, and the south. Mexico City is broken up into 350 *colonias* (neighborhoods), and, when you're trying to get somewhere, it's always a good idea to know what *colonia* your destination is in, whatever your means of transportation may be.

Just a few neighborhoods and main avenues form the core of what casual tourists are likely to see during a short stay in the city, and learning how to navigate through and between them is fairly quickly accomplished. Most visitors find the Metro subway system remarkably easy to use and convenient for getting around town. Buses are a bit more complicated, because of the infinite number of different routes around town, but some travelers prefer them because they offer a view of the city instead of the inside of concrete subway tubes. Taxis are everywhere and inexpensive, but the danger of mugging may deter some visitors from using them.

Finding specific addresses in the city can be tricky. The best tool is a good map, and the best portable map we've seen is Berndtson & Berndtson's *Mexico City,* which comes in a sturdy laminated folding sheet with a scale of 1:11,000 and is available in the U.S., Canada, and Europe for around US$7. In Mexico City, the most widely available Mexico City map is Guía Roji's *Ciudad de México Area Metropolitana,* a bright folding map with street indexes. It can be found in Sanborns or on many street corners and costs around US$8. A more detailed Guía Roji street atlas is also available, which is a veritable bible for anyone living in Mexico City. Casual tourists may find it a little excessive, though, and content themselves with the folding map.

Major Neighborhoods

The **Centro Histórico,** or historic center, has formed the core of Mexico City since the time of the Aztecs and is the most popular destination for tourists in Mexico City. The streets around the Zócalo (main plaza) and west to **La Alameda** park are lined with countless historical buildings and sites, including the Catedral, the Templo Mayor, the Palacio Nacional, various museums, centuries-old churches, and dozens of colonial palaces.

Running diagonally past the western end of the Alameda is the broad avenue **Paseo de la Reforma,** which angles southwest through the city's main financial district and alongside the **Zona Rosa** shopping and restaurant district to **Bosque de Chapultepec,** three km from the Alameda. Amid the grass meadows and tree groves of Chapultepec stand some of the city's finest art and history museums, including the world-class Museo Nacional de Antropología. North of Chapultepec, a short walk from the anthropology museum, lie the chic, modern hotels,

Watching Your Step

Most tourists will likely limit their explorations to the few blocks surrounding the Zócalo and the streets running west toward the Alameda park. Many historic buildings are in this district, and the streets are cleaner and less crowded than in other parts of the Centro. An area south and west of the Zócalo, between Avenida Madero and Avenida Izazaga, is a bit rundown and bustling with small businesses, but it hides a few minor treasures of colonial and 19th-century architecture, and it is generally safe for walking around.

But not too far beyond these areas is a ring of *barrios bravos* where it is not altogether wise to tread. North of the Zócalo past República de Venezuela, northwest between the Plaza Santo Domingo and Plaza Garibaldi and east past Lore-

restaurants, and high-end shops of **Polanco.** South of the Zona Rosa, on either side of Avenida Insurgentes, are the **Roma** and **Condesa** neighborhoods, populated with lots of trendy cafés, restaurants, art galleries, and parks.

Most of the neighborhoods north of downtown don't offer much to attract the casual visitor, apart from three significant religious shrines—the **Basílica de la Virgin de Guadalupe,** home to Mexico's Catholic patron, and the Toltec/Aztec temples at **Tenayuca** and **Santa Cecilia.** About eight and nine km south of the Centro, respectively, are two formerly outlying villages that have been incorporated into the endlessly growing city, **Coyoacán** and **San Ángel.** Both are peaceful enclaves of narrow cobblestone streets, markets, galleries, and bookstores within the hectic city.

In the southeast edge of the city, 24 km from downtown, is the neighborhood of **Xochimilco,** where visitors can travel along an ancient system of canals and floating farm-islands called *chinampas,* which once supplied the city's produce.

Major Streets

As might be expected, learning your way around a city of approximately 17 million can be confusing, but a familiarity with a couple of major avenues can help you stay oriented. **Avenida Insurgentes** is the longest boulevard in the city (also a major north/south route crossing Mexico City and the State of México). To the northeast, Insurgentes takes you to the exit to Pachuca and Teotihuacán; to the south, it continues past San Ángel to UNAM (the national university) to the exit to Cuernavaca and Acapulco.

Paseo de la Reforma is a broad avenue punctuated by large traffic circles *(glorietas),* most with a monument of some sort in the center. Originally, Reforma ran between the Alameda and Chapultepec, but now it extends west to the exit to Toluca and northeast to the Basílica de Guadalupe.

The city is circled by two ring highways—the inner **Circuito Interior** and the outer **Anillo Periférico.** The Circuito makes a complete loop, although it changes names variously to Río Churubusco, Río Mixcoac, Patriotismo, José Vasconcelos, and Revolución along the way. The Periférico, however, extends only three-quarters of the way, with a long northeast portion through a very rough part of the city, unfinished.

Cutting across these two loops is a grid of ***ejes,*** or axis roads running in one direction with traffic lights (somewhat) timed, either east-west or north-south. These are very useful for getting around the central part of the city. Other important roads include the east-west **Viaducto Miguel Alemán** and the south-to-center **Avenida Tlalpan,** both of which are major, two-way arteries with few stoplights.

to and Jesús María, the neighborhoods become dirtier and more crowded. It's not necessarily dangerous to venture out these directions, in the day at least, but go with your wits (and not your camera) about you. But meandering off into the blocks on the north side of Eje 1 Norte, east of Eje 1 Oriente Circunvalación, and south of Fray Servando Teresa de Mier is inviting trouble. The only reason to venture out this way would be to get a taste of the seamier side of street life in the Centro, as almost all of the main historical sites are close to the Zócalo.

Getting There and Getting Away

If you're not staying in a downtown hotel already, chances are you'll be somewhere near Paseo de la Reforma, Polanco, or another neighborhood to the west and south. The easiest and quickest way to get to the Centro is via Metro to one of the downtown stations: Zócalo, Allende, Bellas Artes, San Juan de Letrán, Salto de Agua, Isabel la Católica, Pino Suárez, or Garibaldi.

By car, you can reach the Centro Histórico either (from the west) along Paseo de la Reforma, then turning onto Avenida Juárez past the Alameda, and crossing into the Centro on Avenida Madero; or (from the south) by coming up Eje Central Lázaro Cárdenas and taking a right turn (east) on Avenida Madero. It's less expensive to park the car in one of the lots on the south side of the Alameda (for example, on Revillagigedo, Luis Moya, or Dolores Streets), as they only charge US$.75 per hour, whereas closer to the Zócalo the lots charge US$1.50 per hour. Two decent parking lots in the Centro which can be entered and left easily, even in traffic, can be found on Avenida Cinco de Mayo between Isabel la Católica and Bolívar just west of Café La Blanca, and on República del Salvador just east of Bolívar.

If you come downtown in a taxi, probably the easiest place to get off is at the corner of Juárez and the Eje Central, right in front of the Palacio de Bellas Artes. During the day, traffic can be heavy closer in toward the Zócalo, making it easier to get out and walk.

HISTORY

Until the mid-19th century, Mexico City essentially *was* the Centro Histórico. It was in this roughly 10-kilometer square area, surrounded by the shallow waters of Lago Texcoco, that the Aztecs first founded Tenochtitlán in the early 1300s, and in turn where the Spaniards erected their colonial capital after the conquest in 1521.

The Aztec city was divided into four *calpulli,* self-governing districts grouping several different clans, located in each quadrant of the city. At the intersection of the four districts was the broad central square, flanked by the Templo Mayor complex and the palaces of the Aztec nobility. Four causeways connected the island city to the mainland: Tacuba, to the west; Tenayuca, northwest; Tepeyac, to the north; and Iztapalapa, to the south.

Although its buildings were utterly destroyed during the Spanish siege, the basic street plan of the old city was nonetheless mostly preserved by Alonso García Bravo, who supervised the construction of the new colonial capital in 1521–22. The Aztec central square became the new Plaza Mayor, with the government palaces and the Catedral alongside. Many of the wealthier conquistadors built their mansions along Calle Tacuba to the west of the plaza, while the powerful missionary orders erected huge complexes all over the city. The poor, both *mestizo* (mixed-blood) and Amerindian, were left to their own devices to raise ramshackle warrens of shacks to the east and south of downtown, areas more prone to flooding during the annual rainy season.

By the time of independence from Spain, city authorities had relocated the markets from the Plaza Mayor to La Merced, a neighborhood surrounding the convent of the same name a few blocks southeast of the Plaza. La Merced would remain Mexico's largest marketplace until the Central de Abastos opened in 1992. Commerce also began invading the streets around Plaza Santo Domingo and near Tacuba, northwest of the Zócalo, driving the wealthiest residents to the new "in" street farther south, Plateros, now named Francisco I. Madero.

Armed by the Reform Laws of 1857, which dispossessed the once-mighty religious orders of their properties, city planners ordered the destruction of large chunks of the Centro's many convents and monasteries to lay down new streets such as Cinco de Mayo, Gante, Belisario Domínguez, and others, giving the Centro the street plan it has today.

When Mexico City finally started expanding beyond the boundaries of the original island, as Lago Texcoco began seriously shrinking in the mid-19th century, the city's elite were not slow to flee the increasingly crowded Centro to the new "suburbs." By the end of the Mexican Revolution, in 1920, most of the wealthiest families had long since relocated to the mansions along Paseo de la Reforma or the Roma. The largest merchants and textile producers in La Merced, many of whom were Syrians and Jews, had by the 1940s moved out to Roma, Condesa, and later Polanco.

The colonial mansions in the Centro were quickly taken over by the flood of new immigrants coming in from the countryside in the boom years after World War II. But rather than housing one family, as before, the erstwhile palaces now sheltered whole communities. The rent freeze in the 1940s sealed the fate of the Centro, as all the landlords got out as soon as possible and left their buildings to decay.

Successive city governments have promised great things with regard to renovating and rejuvenating the Centro, particularly after it was declared a World Heritage Site by UNESCO in 1987. Progress, however, has been very limited, and city officials are forthright in saying they simply have no money for major work. Much of the downtown area is still inhabited by low-income families, and the snobbish attitude most upper-class Mexicans have about the Centro makes gentrification (for better or worse) a distant possibility. In short, the Centro looks likely to continue as its majestically disheveled self for years to come.

IN AND AROUND THE ZÓCALO

Zócalo

Also called the Plaza de la Constitución, the Zócalo is the second-largest public plaza in the world after Red Square in Moscow. For most of the past two centuries it was lined with trees and grass (as are most plazas in Mexico). Now it's completely empty, save for the flagpole in the center. Although certainly a bit spartan, this massive open square in the very center of one of the most crowded environments on the globe makes a powerful spatial statement. Mexicans regularly fill the plaza for political rallies, protest demonstrations, or just to enjoy a sunny afternoon.

The Zócalo has formed the heart of Mexico City since the founding of the original Tenochtitlán in 1325. During the height of the Aztec empire, the space frequently served as a site for dances and celebrations, as well as the second most important market in the city. On the northeast corner towered the Templo Mayor, while the palaces of Aztec rulers lined the sides of the plaza. The causeways leading off the island of Tenochtitlán to the north, west, and south began at the plaza, now paved over by the avenues of República de Brasil, Tacuba, and 20 de Noviembre, respectively.

After the Spanish took over the Zócalo during the colonial years, the import merchants of El Parian market and secondhand traders of El Baratillo flea market filled the space. As in Aztec times, the square remained the city's main meeting place and a center of constant activity. By the end of the 18th century, the Zócalo was surrounded by the same buildings that flank it today:

THE EMPTY PEDESTAL

Shortly after independence from Spain in 1821, the square acquired its popular name, Zócalo, which is also often used for the main plazas in other Mexican towns. Historians agree the name derives from a pedestal (*zócalo* is an Arabic-derived Spanish word) which stood empty on the plaza for many years in the 19th century, but they disagree on what did or did not stand on the pedestal.

One camp maintains that the mercurial dictator Santa Anna ordered a monument to independence from Spain built in the 1830s, but that in the chaos of Santa Anna's erratic administration, only the pedestal was built.

Others say the pedestal was originally occupied by *El Caballito,* that peripatetic equestrian statue of Spanish King Carlos IV now standing in front of the Museo Nacional de Arte. The statue was originally erected in the plaza in 1803, but it was hastily removed shortly after the independence movement triumphed, leaving the pedestal behind. Perhaps Santa Anna didn't even get the pedestal built but merely wanted to use the one left behind from *El Caballito.*

Either way, the pedestal is long gone, but the name remains.

the Catedral Metropolitana on the north side, the Palacio Virreinal (now Palacio Nacional) on the east, the Palacio del Ayuntamiento (City Hall) on the south, and the merchants' arcades on the west. The only new building raised since that time is a second city hall building, the easterly of the two, built between 1941 and 1948. Just off the southeast corner of the Zócalo stood the smaller Plaza Volador, which housed a market of its own and also served as the city's bullfight ring. The Suprema Corte de Justicia (Supreme Court) building now occupies this spot.

The liberal-minded Emperor Maximilian banished the markets and tried to create his vision of a Parisian park in Mexico, replete with tree-lined walks, benches, and a wrought-iron kiosk in the center. With many modifications, the trees remained through the years of Porfirio Díaz, who took pains to cultivate European styles. To achieve its current vaguely social-realist monumental style, the Zócalo was cleared shortly after the 1910–20 revolution, perhaps in homage to the Soviet Red Square.

Now a towering flagpole in the center of the square is its only ornamentation. In strict military drill, a contingent of goose-stepping guards, in full battle gear, issue from the Palacio Nacional and then raise (in the morning) or lower (at sunset) a huge Mexican flag daily. The folding of the gigantic tricolor takes a half dozen soldiers a full 15 minutes to accomplish, accompanied by a fanfare of drums, bugles, and flugelhorns.

The city government has considered adding a row of trees along one side of the plaza, but that's yet to transpire. Even if it does, the Zócalo is unlikely ever to become just another one of the innumerable tree-lined plazas in Mexican cities, if only because Mexicans love taking advantage of this irresistible void in the center of one of the most populated cities on earth. Every day the plaza gathers a crowd of locals, tourists, street vendors, political activists, beggars, people looking for work, Aztec dancers, clowns, and much else besides.

The **Aztec dancers** perform most days, but always on weekends and also on certain celebration dates: August 13, the day Tenochtitlán fell to the Spaniards; September 21, the fall equinox; November 1 and 2, Días de los Muertos; December 21, the winter solstice;

EL GRITO

To see the Zócalo at its most vibrant, join the thousands of Mexicans who gather each year to watch the president stand on the balcony of the Palacio Nacional and shout *¡Viva México!* just before midnight each September 15, commemorating Padre Hidalgo's famous launch of the struggle for independence from Spain in 1810.

For the first decades after independence in 1821, Hidalgo was reviled by many (particularly Mexico's elite) as a rabble rouser, and his ill-fated rebellion was hardly the stuff of official myth. But in 1896 the legendary dictator Porfirio Díaz saw fit to rehabilitate Hidalgo by shouting the first official *Grito* in Mexican history. According to historians, Hidalgo's original shout was *"Vive la Virgen de Guadalupe y mueran los gachupines!"* ("Long live the Virgin of Guadalupe and death to the Spaniards!"), but Díaz thought it more diplomatic to shout, "Viva Mexico! Vivan los héroes de la Patria! Viva la Repúblic!"

It may seem odd that the *Grito* happens on September 15 at midnight, when Independence Day is September 16. As it turns out, Don Porfirio took a slight liberty with the dates, since his birthday was September 15.

The *Grito* has since become one of the main political ceremonies of the year. The scene in the square during and after the *Grito* is reminiscent of New Year's Eve in Times Square *a la mexicana.* If you go, be fully prepared to be plastered by the harmless shaving cream everyone is throwing around in jest.

© GREG BULL

The cathedral has been undergoing renovations for years.

March 21, the spring equinox; and June 21, the summer solstice.

For good, wide-angle views of the square, have a meal at the balcony restaurant of the Hotel Majestic, Gran Hotel de la Ciudad or Holiday Inn on the west side. The Hotel Majestic won't let you stay just for drinks, unless you're very persuasive and it's not crowded, but the Holiday Inn and Gran Hotel are more relaxed.

The *portales,* or archways, on the southwest side of the plaza often shelter temporary displays of paintings or photography.

The government has installed a tourist information booth on the Zócalo, on the west side of the Catedral (left side as you face it), where you can find maps and other information.

Catedral Metropolitana

In some ways the Zócalo, impressive though it may be, is but a stage for the magnificent Catedral. The government and private palaces pressed up against one another on the other three sides of the plaza seem merely the audience, as it were, to the Catedral's immense architectural performance.

The largest colonial cathedral in the Americas, the current Catedral stands on the site of a more humble chapel built by the Spanish conquistadors in 1524, immediately following the conquest of Tenochtitlán. Intended to symbolically replace the Aztec Templo Mayor, the first church was erected with the rubble of the temple and other buildings destroyed during the Spanish assault.

The rather modest size of Mexico's first cathedral prompted the colonists to develop plans for a structure more suitable to their idea of the city's greatness. Work on the foundations alone took 42 years, and the church would end up taking fully two and a half centuries to complete, from 1573 to 1813.

Because the Catedral took so long to build, different architects and changing architectural fashions left their mark in the building's interior and exterior ornamentation, which include elements of Gothic, baroque, Churrigueresque, and neoclassical styles. Despite the apparently eclectic mix, the church's styles come together with remarkable harmony. The north side of the Catedral, facing the plaza, is a perfect example: the exuberant baroque facades of the main church and the adjacent Sagrario seem tempered and balanced by the more austere neoclassical flanking towers and central clock tower, built in the late 18th and early 19th centuries.

Exterior: Built in the shape of a Latin cross, the cathedral's floor plan measures 109 meters long and 54 meters wide. The rear-facing northern facade was the first to be completed, followed by the eastern and western side facades, all done in Renaissance style, with just a few suggestions of baroque flair. The baroque front facade, finished in 1689, has one principal entrance and two side entrances, each flanked with columns and topped with a sculpted marble relief on the second level. In niches between the columns adjacent to the central portal are statues of Saints Pedro and Pablo, while Andrés and Jaime above frame a relief depicting the Asunción de la Virgen.

The side towers, measuring 67 meters, were designed by Mexican architect José Damián Ortiz de Castro and completed in 1790, while the central clock tower and dome were finished by Valenciana architect Manuel Tolsá in 1813.

Interior: The cathedral's cavernous interior contains a total of five naves, 14 side chapels, a central choir, and a sacristy, to name only the principal features, and a quantity of artistic detail that is almost impossible to fully absorb.

Upon entering the cathedral, visitors first come upon the golden Altar de Perdón (the Altar of Forgiveness) in the central nave, carved by Andalusian Jerónimo de Balbás. The altar, along

BENEATH THE CATHEDRAL

Recent archaeological and geological studies indicate that the Catedral is built over the site of a small spring, which may be why Aztecs chose the location as the center of their city when they first moved to the small island of Tenochtitlán. Thus, in what could be construed as unintended Aztec revenge on the Spanish for building the cathedral with stones from their destroyed temple, the Catedral stands on particularly weak, fissured ground.

Over the centuries the massive weight of the cathedral has forced the ground beneath to compress. The Catedral's slight tilt, easily visible if you look at the monument from the opposite side of the Zócalo, indicates how this geologic handicap has placed stress on its structure. Because of the irregularity of the soil, the compression has occurred unevenly, causing some parts of the building to sink more than others.

In a vain effort to halt the subsidence, a steel grid was placed underneath the cathedral's floor in 1940, and when that didn't help, new pilings were sunk to supposedly firmer subsoil 40 meters below the church. That didn't stop the sinking either, and by 1988 government authorities had wrapped the cathedral's columns in metal bands and erected braces and scaffolding to ensure the building didn't collapse outright.

At the same time, architectural engineers began an excavation project beneath the foundation, drilling 32 holes 25 meters deep, and carefully digging to the side in selected spots. The theory was to cause "high points" in the subsoil to collapse, and thus allow the cathedral to settle evenly. This was the same technique used at the famously leaning tower at Pisa, in Italy.

By late 1999, engineers estimated that different points of the cathedral floor were sinking at a maximum differential of 4–6 mm per year, rather than a previously measured 1.8 centimeters. The floor of the building is now about as close to "true" as it was in the 1930s. And as the fissures in the subsoil close, the sinking rate will continue to slow, meaning the cathedral's structure is likely to undergo less stress than in previous years.

As a result of the project, much of the scaffolding that has for years impeded the full admiration of one of the greatest example of Catholic architecture in the world has been removed, although metal supporting bands remain around the columns.

with the choir behind it, was damaged in a 1967 fire but has since been restored. The sculpted black Christ at the center of the altar has taken the place of a painting of the Virgen María, destroyed in the fire. The baroque choir, designed by Juan de Rojas, is made of cedar, while the metal latticework is a mix of gold, silver, and copper, cast in China.

The central altar at the front of the Catedral, the Altar de los Reyes (Altar of the Kings) houses a 25-meter high golden *retablo* decorated in such ornate baroque complexity that it's difficult for the eye even to begin to notice individual sculptures. The carvings, showing a veritable army of saints, cherubim, and other religious figures, were executed by Jerónimo de Balbas, while Francisco Martínez was responsible for covering the work in the gold leaf. Note the odd, squared-off *estípite* columns, one of the first uses of Churrigueresque elements in Mexico. The two paintings, both by Mexican painter Juan Rodríguez Juárez (1675–1728), depict the Three Wise Men paying homage to the baby Jesús (below) and the Asunción de la Virgen (above).

The 14 side chapels all date from the 17th century. The Capilla de los Ángeles is particularly impressive artistically, with its high baroque altarpiece and painting of San Miguel. The Capilla de San Felipe de Jesús is dedicated to Mexico's first saint, a missionary martyred in Japan, and contains a vase with the remains of Mexican Emperor Agustín de Iturbide (1783–1824), the country's often-denigrated leader in defeating the Spaniards in the war of independence.

Sagrario

Adjacent to the main church is the Sagrario, built between 1749 and 1768 by Spaniard Lorenzo Rodríguez. The white sculpted front of the Sagrario, considered by many to be the definitive Churrigueresque facade in Mexico (though other art historians place the Churrigueresque facade of the cathedral in Zacatecas at the top), is offset by flanking walls made with blocks of deep red *tezontle,* a volcanic stone. Closed for 10 years for repairs, the Sagrario reopened its doors in 2001, and now holds regular Masses. The bare, rather unimaginative altars (the originals were destroyed long ago by fire) don't compare to the magnificent exterior. A replica of the Virgen de Guadalupe painting is worth taking a look at, especially if you don't have the time or inclination to make the trip up to see the original at the Basílica de Guadalupe in the north of the city.

Templo Mayor de Tenochtitlán

At the time Cortés first laid eyes on the Templo Mayor (Teocalli to the Aztecs) in 1519, the holiest shrine in Tenochtitlán had been rebuilt at least six times and consisted of a walled complex of 78 buildings built on different levels, crowned with two tall pyramids. One was intended to symbolize the sacred hill of Coatepec, birthplace of the capricious and violent god Huitzilopochtli, while the other represented the hill of Tonacatepetl and was dedicated to the rain god Tlaloc. Each pyramid, in turn, was crowned with a small temple containing statues of the two gods. The Spanish conquistadors, on first entering the temples, were overwhelmed with righteous disgust at the gloomy atmosphere and the wild-looking priests, with long hair matted thick with blood, and insisted to the captive emperor Moctezuma II that they be destroyed.

To the Aztecs, the ritual sacrifices in the temple complex represented a key event in their mythology, namely when the new god Huitzilopochtli

SIGHTS

The Catedral (background) was built in part with stones originally taken from the Aztec Templo Mayor (foreground).

slew his sister Coyolxuahqui, the moon goddess, on Coatepec, and cast her body down to the foot of the hill. Some anthropologists have suggested this myth represented a changeover in Aztec politics from a society dominated by women to one ruled by men.

The rubble of the temple, which was razed during the battle for Tenochtitlán, served as building material for the cathedral and other buildings when the Spaniards rebuilt the city, and the remains of the temple were buried over and mostly forgotten. In 1911, 1933, and 1948 minor archaeological work uncovered remnants of the temple and some sculptures. Then in 1978 workers excavating for the Metro uncovered by chance an eight-ton round rock slab covered with carvings of the moon goddess Coyolxuahqui. The carving is now on display in the temple museum.

This magnificent work of art, found behind the Catedral near the corner of the streets República de Argentina and República de Guatemala, prompted authorities to begin a major archaeological project. After demolishing four city blocks over several years of excavations, archaeologists had uncovered a wealth of artifacts from the Aztec era.

A path leads visitors around the reconstructed foundations of the temple to view sculptures and faded murals. The **Museo de Templo Mayor** alongside the temple displays a model of the Aztec city and some 7,000 artifacts found at the site, including life-sized statues of eagle warriors standing menacingly over the skulls of their victims. The entrance to the museum, an oddly spartan building designed by Pedro Ramírez Vázquez of Museo de Antropología fame, is at Calle Seminario 8, on the east side of the Catedral. Open Tues.–Sun. 9 A.M.–5 P.M.; US$4 admission, US$3.50 extra for a video camera, free Sunday.

Palacio Nacional

Originally one of Hernán Cortés's many residences, this palace of red *tezontle* blocks stands on the site of Aztec emperor Moctezuma II's castle on the east side of the Zócalo. Martín Cortés, son of the conquistador, sold the palace to the crown in 1562, after which it became the Palacio Virreinal (Viceregal Palace), the main seat of colonial authority in Nueva España. Pro-church, anti-viceroy rioters destroyed the first building in 1624, and the current palace was built in 1628. Emperor Maximilian modified it significantly during his brief reign (1864–67), giving it much of its current European flavor. President Plutarco Elias Calles ordered the addition of a third floor and further modifications to the facade in 1926.

Padre Miguel Hidalgo rang the bell now hanging above the main entrance as he uttered his *grito* (shout) for Mexican independence from Spain in 1810, in the Guanajuato town of Dolores. President Porfirio Díaz moved the bell to the palace in 1896 and started the tradition of ringing the bell every year on September 15, just before midnight.

Between 1929 and 1935 Diego Rivera painted one of his best-known murals on the walls above the palace's central staircase. Divided into three parts, the mural is Rivera's vision of Mexican history, arranged chronologically right to left. The right-hand panel shows Aztec life before the conquest, while the central wall traces Mexico's history from the brutal conquest and colonial era, through independence from Spain, to the bloody revolution in 1910–20. The left-hand mural depicted Rivera's socialist view of Mexico's capitalist milieu and the inevitable workers' revolution yet to come.

On the walls of the second-floor corridor, Rivera painted a further eight mural panels between 1941 and 1952 to illustrate idealized aspects of Mexico's pre-Cortesian life, and a ninth depicts the arrival of Cortés.

Though the Palacio is the official residence of the Mexican president, recent presidents have opted to spend most of their time in a second residence known as Los Pinos, in the Bosque de Chapultepec.

The Palacio Nacional is open to the public daily 9 A.M.–5 P.M., and admission is free. Tourists must bring photo identification of some kind to leave with the guards at the entrance.

Nacional Monte de Piedad

This government-run pawnshop on the west side of the Zócalo, whose name means Mountain of

Mercy, has for more than two centuries offered low-interest loans to the needy. In times of economic crisis—not an uncommon situation during the last 20 years in Mexico—people line the surrounding blocks waiting to put their jewelry, musical instruments, and other personal possessions in hock for a loan.

Monte de Piedad sits over the site of another of Cortés's palaces, which in turn was built on the remains of Moctezuma I's residence. Cortés's huge original palace, which covered several city blocks, was divided up and sold in 1615, and the current structure was built in 1775 by Pedro Romero de Terreros, owner of the fabulously wealthy Regla silver mines near Pachuca. After independence from Spain, the government took over the building. At 7 Calle Monte de Piedad, tel. 5518-2206. Open Mon.–Fri. 8:30 A.M.–6 P.M., Sat. 8:30 A.M.–1 P.M.

WEST OF THE ZÓCALO

The corridor of streets between the Zócalo and the Alameda was, during most of the city's post-Aztec history, the Centro Histórico's most posh district. Although the city's wealthy have long since departed this neighborhood, it remains a more upscale area than other parts of the city center, and it is a favorite place for visitors to tour on foot.

While some older buildings have deteriorated or been replaced by poorly made modern structures or parking lots, much of the architecture remains remarkably intact. Because of its storied history and constant development, the buildings in this neighborhood—the colonial churches of La Profesa and San Francisco, the baroque Palacio de Iturbide and Casa de los Azulejos, the neoclassical Palacio de Minería, and the all-over-the-board Palacio Postal—represent a cross-section of the city's architectural styles. The Museo Nacional de Arte is worth a visit, both to admire the fine building and to tour the museum's collection of Mexican art, and several cafés and bars offer places to rest after tromping around. Unlike many other parts of the Centro, these streets are generally safe after dark, and are no problem at all during the day.

Iglesia de la Profesa (San Felipe Neri)

Two blocks west of the Zócalo on Avenida Madero, at the corner of Isabel la Católica, stands a hulking 18th-century church popularly known as La Profesa. Built in 1720 by the Jesuits, the church was turned over to the order of San Felipe in 1767 when the Jesuits were expelled from New Spain. It has since been officially named San Felipe Neri, but everyone still refers to it as La Profesa (The Professed, a euphemism for nun).

The early baroque facade is somewhat subdued compared to the flights of fancy decorating later churches, but it is attractive nonetheless. The interior is unusually compact, almost square in layout, with a neoclassical altarpiece by Manuel Tolsá. Several of the colonial religious paintings on the walls and in the adjacent art gallery, particularly those by famed painter Cristóbal de Villalpando, are worth a look.

Edificio Longoria

Diagonally opposite La Profesa on Avenida Madero, Edificio Longoria dates to 1890 and provides evidence of the passion for ornamentation that had become the architectural rage of the time. Have a look at the row of little heads peering down at you from the lintel dividing the second and third floors, and at the odd seashell-like ovals lining the top floor. La Esmeralda jewelry store, famed for its high-society clientele, once operated here. The bottom floor is now occupied by a MixUp music store, while the upper floors contain a nightclub.

Casa Borda

Continuing up Avenida Madero toward Eje Central you'll encounter Casa Borda, an 18th-century palace built by Taxco silver magnate José de Borda. In post-independence Mexico it served variously as public baths and one of Mexico City's first movie theaters before being bought by Banca Serfín in 1988. A small, free museum containing a display of Amerindian clothing is open Tuesday–Sunday 10 A.M.–6 P.M. Visitors cannot see the interior of the building, but the carved exterior is impressive enough.

Palacio de Iturbide

A block past Casa Borda on Avenida Madero

stands another former colonial palace, built in 1780 by a Mexico City *alcalde* (mayor), Conde de San Mateo Valparaíso. Fine stone carvings cover the outside of the *tezontle*-block building. Short-lived Mexican Emperor Iturbide occupied the palace in 1822, hence its current name. After serving as a hotel for many years, the mansion was purchased by Banamex and restored in 1965. It now houses bank offices as well as a free art museum. The revolving exhibits consist mainly of Mexican paintings, sometimes quite interesting, but it's worth looking in regardless to admire the four-story interior courtyard. Open daily 10 A.M.–7 P.M.

Iglesia y Ex-Convento de San Francisco

Near the western end of Madero, butting up against the back of the Torre Latinoamericana, are the sad, boxed-in remains of what was one of the greatest convents in Mexico City, San Francisco. Built on the site of Moctezuma II's famed zoo, the Convento de San Francisco and its associated chapels once covered the entire area now enclosed by Bolívar, Madero, Eje Central, and Venustiano Carranza.

After the passing of reform legislation against the Catholic Church in 1857, the Convento de San Francisco, along with other convents in Mexico City, saw their property seized and much of it destroyed to make way for the construction of new roads.

The main Iglesia de San Francisco is actually the third church built on this location, as earlier ones sank in the soft subsoil and had to be torn down. As visitors will notice from the steps leading *down* to the church, the third doesn't appear to be faring much better than the first two.

The church's main facade, dating from 1710, is walled in and thus cannot be seen. Visitors enter by walking through the smaller Capilla de Balvanera, which offers an impressive late baroque facade and a gilded altarpiece dedicated to the Virgin. The main church, with a neoclassical, gilded altar piece and several religious paintings, may be reached through a side door in the Capilla de Balvanera.

Though you wouldn't guess from its uninteresting exterior, the Methodist church at Calle Gante 5 is actually the remains of the San Francisco cloister. The church officials are usually quite friendly and allow visitors to take a look at the old cloister. And on Venustiano Carranza, the Panadería Ideal bakery was built using some of the old walls of the convent. City restoration officials have plans to reconnect some parts of the convent that are now sealed off and open them to the public. Although little progress has been made, a small square has been cleared between the Capilla de Balvanera and the back of the Torre Latinoamerica.

Casa de los Azulejos

Across Madero from the entrance to Iglesia de San Francisco is an exceptionally lovely tile-covered colonial mansion known as Casa de los Azulejos (House of Tiles). Originally built in the 16th century, it wasn't until the mid-18th century that the owners covered the exterior with blue Talavera tile from the State of Puebla. As legend has it, the son of one of the owners added the tiles to live down an insult from his father, who told him he would "never build a house of tiles," meaning that he would never amount to anything. Between 1891 and 1914 the house was home to the Jockey Club, the city's most exclusive social club at the time. During the Revolution, the Zapatista army occupied the building, and in 1919 Walter and Frank Sanborn opened a soda fountain, the first of what is now a national chain known simply as Sanborns. The atmospheric patio cafeteria inside is a popular place for Mexicans and foreigners alike to have a meal in luxurious surroundings. Take a walk upstairs to view José Clemente Orozco's 1925 staircase mural *Omniciencia* and to see the porcelain art on the upper floor surrounding the patio.

Torre Latinoamericana

To really get a feel for the immensity of Mexico City, air quality permitting, take an elevator ride to the top of the tallest building in the downtown area. Although not particularly attractive architecturally, the 182-meter-tall blue and gray tower, built between 1948 and 1956 at the corner of Eje Central and Avenida Madero, is specially designed to handle the earthquake-prone and flexible subsoil. Avoid weekends, when the small area at the top is packed and you'd be lucky to get an open spot to peer through the fence at the city below. Apart from the views across the valley, the tower affords a unique bird's-eye view of the layout of the downtown area. The roof platform is open daily 9:30 A.M.–10:30 P.M.; admission costs US$3.50 adults, US$2.50 kids 11 and under. Should you have a particular inclination for seeing fish at high altitude, check out the aquarium on the 38th floor, US$2.50 adults, US$2 kids 11 and under.

Palacio Postal

Normally a post office wouldn't make it as a tourist destination, but the old Mexico City "postal palace" is an unusual case. At the corner of Eje Central and Tacuba, the building is a Gothic/arabesque palace, with neoclassical, baroque, and art deco elements thrown in for good measure. In a word, eclectic. Designed in 1908 by Italian architect Adamo Boari, who also designed the Palacio de Bellas Artes across the street, the post office is made of a very light, almost translucent stone called *chiluca*. The exterior is covered with all sorts of fine detail, such as the wicked little iron dragon light fixtures and a wealth of stone carving around

EL CABALLITO

El Caballito (The Little Horse), as the equestrian statue of Spanish King Carlos IV in Roman garb is popularly known, is probably artist Manuel Tolsá's best-known work. Famed world traveler Alexander von Humboldt compared this beautiful bronze equestrian statue to Donatella's Erasmo Gattamelota masterpiece in Padua, Italy. Despite its five-meter-high, 21-ton mass, *El Caballito* has traveled around the city with some frequency since Tolsá cast the statue in 1803. Originally the figure stood in the center of the Zócalo, but public scorn for the mother country in the wake of independence from Spain almost led to *El Caballito*'s destruction. To safeguard the statue, city authorities hauled it off its pedestal and parked it in the courtyard of the national university, where the Suprema Corte de Justicia building now stands. There it remained until 1852, when it was moved again across the city to the mouth of Paseo de Bucareli, west of the Alameda.

An anonymous 19th-century poet used the occasion to lampoon General Santa Anna, who had just four years previously lost half of Mexico's national territory to the United States, and whose bust *El Caballito* passed on the way to its new home on Paseo Bucareli:

Goodbye bust of Santa Anna,
pointing to the north,
I'm going without a passport
and you stay here arrogant.
Perhaps the day after tomorrow
employment will become scarce
and you'll follow my path.
After all you've suffered
you'll go to jail
and I'll go to the Paseo.

As the city grew and the statue began to look a bit lost amidst all the traffic, the city moved it yet again to its current location in the middle of Plaza Manuel Tolsá in 1979. The huge, bright yellow sculpture now at the beginning of Bucareli is, presumably, meant to be an abstract vision of the original, although it's not easy to see the resemblance.

the windows and at the edge of the roof. The spacious interior is laden with different kinds of marble and much fine metalwork. Open Mon.–Fri. 8 A.M.–9 P.M., Sat. 8 A.M.–6 P.M.

Plaza Manuel Tolsá

Around the corner from the post office, one block east on Tacuba back toward the Zócalo, is a small square flanked by two imposing neoclassical buildings and crowned with a bronze equestrian statue of Spanish King Carlos IV. The statue and one of the buildings are the works of Manuel Tolsá, an architect and artist from Valencia, Spain, who came to Mexico City in 1791 to direct the Academia de San Carlos.

Tolsá was a disciple of a severe though elegant neoclassicism, and he strongly rejected the more ornate baroque styles favored in Mexico City up to that time. Dozens of his works, including buildings, paintings, and his oddly cold neoclassical altar pieces (such as those in the La Profesa and Santo Domingo Churches?), can be seen throughout the city. The frenetically productive Tolsá also found time to finish the Mexico City and Aguascalientes Cathedrals, supervise drainage and running water projects, and lay out Mexico City's first civil cemetery.

Mexican artist José Faustino Contreras badly burned his feet with molten bronze as he cast the Aztec emperor Cuauhtémoc, a gruesome coincidence considering that the Spanish had burned the feet of Cuauhtémoc in an effort to force him to reveal the whereabouts of hidden gold.

The **Museo Nacional de Arte** occupies the former Palacio de Comunicaciones building on the north side of Calle Tacuba. The reserved, gray palace was finished in 1910 under the supervision of Italian architect Silvio Contri and was converted into a museum in 1982. The building's cool, beautiful interior houses an overview of Mexican art dating from the early colonial period to the mid-20th century. Among the notable artists featured are colonial painters Miguel Cabrera, Cristóbal Villalpando, and Luis Juárez; 19th-century painters Juan Cordero, José María Velasco, and Ramón Sagredo; and the 20th century's Diego Rivera, Frida Kahlo, Rufino Tamayo, and others. Guide service is free and sometimes available in English. Major renovations were under way at last report, with only a temporary exhibit open to the public, but the permanent collection is set to reopen soon. At Calle Tacuba 8, tel. 5130-3400, open Tues.–Sun. 10 A.M.–5:30 P.M.; admission US$3, free on Sunday.

Across the street is Manuel Tolsá's three-story **Palacio de Minería,** built between 1797 and 1813 to house offices governing the colony's most important industry. The building now serves as the engineering school of UNAM, the national university. On one side is a small museum dedicated to Tolsá's life and work, open Tues.–Sun. 10 A.M.–7 P.M.; entrance US$1.50. In the main entrance to the building is a collection of meteorites from around Mexico. Guided tours of the entire building in English or Spanish, for a minimum of 10 people, can be arranged by calling 5623-2962.

Museo del Ejército

Across the narrow Calle Filomeno Mata from the Palacio de Minería is a museum dedicated to the soldiers of Mexico, housed in what was originally a Bethlehemite hospital and chapel. The museum contains armor worn by Spanish conquistadors and Aztec soldiers, plenty of old pistols and rifles, and other assorted military paraphernalia from across the centuries. There's no entrance fee, so it's worth taking a quick look inside if only to admire the interior of the old church. The museum also boasts a café and gift shop, attended by extremely efficient young soldiers. Open Tues.–Sat. 10 A.M.–6 P.M., Sun. 10 A.M.–4 P.M.

In a small garden outside the museum you'll see three large bronze sculptures of Nezahualcóyotl, Iztcoatl, and Totoquihuatzin, the creators of the Mesoamerican Triple Alliance, which ruled the Valle de México before the arrival of the Spaniards. In the entryway of the museum stands a fourth bronze of the heroic warrior and last

Aztec emperor, Cuauhtémoc. The sculptures were fashioned by Mexican artist José Faustino Contreras for Mexico's pavilion at the Paris Universal Exposition in 1898. Contreras badly burned his feet with molten bronze as he cast the Cuauhtémoc piece, a gruesome coincidence considering that the Spanish had burned the feet of the last Aztec emperor in an effort to force him to reveal the whereabouts of hidden gold.

Toward the Zócalo

Walking east along Calle Tacuba, on the right you'll pass the **Ex-Convento y Iglesia de Santa Clara,** which now houses the Biblioteca del Congreso, or Library of Congress (open to the public). Farther east, after Avenida Bolívar, Calle Motolinía heads south off Tacuba. Depending on how much the city government has been cracking down on *ambulantes,* or street vendors, a lively market usually fills the block of Motolinía between Tacuba and Cinco de Mayo.

Before reaching the Zócalo, take a one-block detour north on República de Chile to the corner of Donceles to admire one of the finest colonial palaces in the city, the **Casa de los Condes de Heras y Soto.** With exceptionally well-carved reliefs decorating the exterior, the building houses the offices of the Fideicomiso del Centro Histórico, an organization dedicated to restoring the downtown area. Visitors may enter and admire the courtyard Monday–Friday 9 A.M.–6 P.M. Around the corner, the block of Donceles between República de Chile and Palma is a secondhand book emporium of sorts, with around 10 shops on both sides of the street.

NORTH OF THE ZÓCALO

The blocks directly behind the Catedral contain several colonial buildings of note, including the churches of Santo Domingo and the ultrabaroque masterpiece La Enseñanza. The Antiguo Colegio de San Ildefonso, now a museum and cultural center, is worth visiting both to admire what is considered a classic example of colonial architecture and to see the first place where Mexico's renowned muralists began their art revolution in 1922. And the walls of the Secretaría de Educación Pública, housed in a former convent, are covered with more than 100 mural panels by Diego Rivera, making it a must-see for Rivera aficionados.

Those with an interest in the market life in Mexico City might walk farther north to check out Mercado Lagunilla and environs, and if you're feeling particularly brave, head across Eje 1 Norte into the Tepito "thieves' market."

If you've got a hankering for mariachi, Mexico's national music form, take a walk northwest to Plaza Garibaldi to see the many bands hanging out on the square.

While it's no problem walking this area during the day, it's best not to head over this way after dark. You might get away with it around Plaza Santo Domingo, but if you wandered into the streets around Garibaldi or Lagunilla at night you might as well hold out your wallet and save

© CHRIS HUMPHREY

dancers from the Yucatán at the Antiguo Colegio de San Ildefonso

the omnipresent *rateros* ("ratters," or thieves, in Mexican slang) the trouble of asking.

Antiguo Colegio de San Ildefonso

Running along the north side of the Templo Mayor is the imposing red-brick facade, divided by three baroque portals, of the Antiguo Colegio de San Ildefonso, first begun by Jesuit friars in 1588. Originally it was only a small school, but the Jesuits steadily expanded the building and the number of students until 1767, when the Spanish crown expelled the Jesuit order from New Spain and seized their properties. Shortly thereafter it served as a law school and medical school, before undergoing a mid-19th-century conversion into the Preparatoria Nacional, an institute that groomed students for the Universidad Nacional.

In 1922, shortly after the end of the Mexican revolution, idealistic Education Minister José Vasconcelos hired a number of young, then-unknown Mexican artists to paint the walls of the Antiguo Colegio with murals depicting their vision of the revolutionary nation, thus beginning the mural movement that would become so important to 20th-century Mexican art. Diego Rivera, José Clemente Orozco, Davíd Alfaro Siqueiros, Fermín Revueltas, Ramón Alva de la Canal, Fernando Leal, and Jean Charlot all painted different sections of the old school. While the painters worked, the school had to be barred and protected by the police on several occasions to protect the artists and murals from citizens who disagreed with the artists' sensibilities and leftist ideals.

At the entrance to the Patio Principal (Main Patio), you'll see the first mural painted, Alva de la Canal's *El desembarque de los españoles y la cruz plantada en tierras nuevas,* depicting the beginning of *mestizaje* (the cultural and genetic "mixing" of the Spanish and Indian peoples) and the birth of modern Mexico. Directly in front is *Alegoría de la Virgen de Guadalupe* by Revueltas. The Orozco murals on the walls of the main patio are famed for their intensity, particularly *Cortés y la Malinche,* showing the conquistador and his lover/interpreter holding hands naked.

In the Anfiteatro Bolívar, an addition built in 1911 at the front of the school and intended to copy the rest of the building's baroque style, Diego Rivera painted his first mural, *La creación.* He had just returned from living in Europe, and the artistic influence of the Old Continent can easily be spotted in the cubist elements and hints of Italian fresco style seen in the mural. Rivera's early interest in Asian symbolism is also apparent in the way an angel in the mural holds his hands in the classic Zen meditation pose. (A preliminary sketch for this detail in the private Gelman Collection is labeled "Wisdom," indicating that the hand gesture was no coincidence.)

In 1992 the Antiguo Colegio was converted into a museum and cultural center, and it often hosts exhibits and events of cultural interest. On weekends, music and dance groups from around Mexico frequently hold concerts in one of the two large courtyards. A small café on the second floor of the main patio is a fine spot to take a rest and drink in the atmosphere along with refreshments.

The Antiguo Colegio is at Justo Sierra 16, tel. 5789-2505 or 5702-6378. Open Sun.–Fri. 10 A.M.–6 P.M., Sat. 10 A.M.–9 P.M.; admission US$4, free on Tuesday.

Secretaría de Educación Pública

The Education Secretariat is housed in two separate but attached buildings: a former customs house at Brasil 31, facing the Plaza Santo Domingo, and the Ex-Convento de la Encarnación, with its entrance at Argentina 28. Built in 1729 (against the wishes of the nuns next door, who thought it would block their light), the customs house contains a Davíd Alfaro Siqueiros mural titled *Patricios and Patricidas* (Patricians and Patricide) in its main stairwell. The mural, begun in 1945 and completed in 1971, was continually interrupted by the artist's political work and temporary imprisonment.

While the Siqueiros mural is impressive, it's hard to compete with the ex-convent next door, where 124 Diego Rivera mural panels cover wall space that extends three stories high and two city blocks long. Rivera's work was commissioned by Education Secretary José Vasconcelos, who had been given the convent to serve as the secretariat's offices.

Rivera gave the nicknames Patio de Trabajo (Work Patio) and Patio de Fiesta (Party Patio) for the two courtyards, and filled each with images related to the two themes between 1923 and 1928. The first floor of the Patio de Trabajo depicts various industries, as well as religious themes, while the second floor is dedicated to science and intellectual pursuits. Whether because of the topics or some other consideration, the second floor murals consist of *grisallas,* or gray tones. On the stairwell to the third level is a self-portrait of Rivera.

The bottom level of the second courtyard, true to its nickname, depicts popular festival activities in Mexico, including scenes from Day of the Dead, the Danza del Venado (Deer Dance), and (demonstrating Rivera's socialist beliefs) Labor Day. The murals on the north side of the courtyard were painted by Rivera students Jean Charlot and Amado de la Cueva. Walls on the second floor carry the coats of arms of different Mexican states, painted by Charlot and de la Cueva, while the third floor features some superb Rivera murals dedicated to *corridos,* or traditional story-telling ballads. Particularly noteworthy are *En El Arsenal* (In the Arsenal), which shows Frida Kahlo handing out weapons, and *La Balada de Emiliano Zapata* (The Ballad of Emiliano Zapata).

The ex-convent is a quiet, restful place to enjoy the murals, or to take a seat and rest from sightseeing. The chapel of the convent, though reputedly lovely, is closed to visitors. The SEP is open Mon.–Fri. 9 A.M.–5 P.M.; admission is free.

Templo y Plaza de Santo Domingo

This ancient plaza, three blocks north of the Zócalo, is the site of the first monastery in Mexico and was the second-most important square in the city during the colonial period. Today the center of the plaza contains a statue of independence heroine La Corregidora Josefa Ortiz de Domínguez. A crowd of street sellers usually surrounds the statue, their wares displayed on blankets. Along the southwest side are the Portales de los Evangelistas, where low-budget scribes with mechanical printing presses have been ghost-writing love letters and legal documents since the late 19th century.

The first church was erected on the square in 1530, then a second in 1556. The existing Templo de Santo Domingo, on the plaza's north side, was built between 1717 and 1736. The baroque facade has statues of San Francisco and San Agustín on either side of the main door, a marble relief of Santo Domingo de Guzmán above, and another relief of the Virgin Mary on the top.

Inside is a neoclassical altarpiece sculpted by Manuel Tolsá early in the 19th century to take the place of an earlier baroque piece. The two side *retablos* are done in the ultrabaroque Churrigueresque style and date from the early 18th century.

Palacio de la Escuela de Medicina

Built between 1732 and 1736 by Pedro de Arrieta, the same architect who designed Iglesia La Profesa and worked on the Catedral, this palace first housed the dreaded Inquisition Tribunal before becoming a medical school in 1854. Although not dramatic on first glance, Arrieta's corner entrance was considered highly unusual in its time, as were the odd "hanging" arches in the interior courtyard. Visitors can pay US$2 to see the medicine museum or just take a quick free look inside to admire the courtyard. Open daily 9 A.M.–5 P.M.

Iglesia de la Enseñanza

On your way back to the Zócalo from Plaza Santo Domingo, take a detour left on Donceles to number 104, a church with an unusually narrow facade that now exhibits a severe backward tilt because of ground subsidence. Built in the 1770s as the Templo de Nuestra Señora del Pilar (but referred to as La Enseñanza, "The Teaching," because it was founded by the Marianists, a teaching order), the former church has an impressive late baroque facade, but the real reason to visit the church is for the nine ultrabaroque, gilt *retablos* (altarpieces) crammed into the small interior space. Infrequently visited, La Enseñanza is one of the Centro's hidden treasures and merits a few minutes' visit to marvel at the dazzling display inside. The church is packed on the feast day of its patron saint, Pilar, on October 12.

Colegio de Cristo

Right across the street from La Enseñanza is a former college dating from 1612, though the current building is from the 1770s. Now it serves as the Museo de Caricatura, a small homage to the political cartoonists who have enlivened Mexican newspapers and magazines over the years. At Donceles 99, open daily 10 A.M.–6 P.M.; entrance fee US$1.

Galería SCHP

If you're a starving artist, and you owe Mexico's government some back taxes, you may have a work in this little gallery housed in a colonial building right behind the Catedral on Avenida República de Guatemala 8, near the corner of República de Brasil. Here artists whose tax payments are delinquent may erase their tax debt by donating works of art. Those interested in seeing an eclectic collection of Mexican modern art might want to take a quick glance inside to see what they've got up. Open daily 10 A.M.–6 P.M.; free admission.

Plaza Garibaldi

Once a neighborhood square, this little plaza on Eje Central became a nightlife hotspot in the 1920s with the establishment of the Salón Tenampa and its mariachi band led by Cirilo Marmolejo. Because of the success of the bar and the group, the plaza became a magnet for mariachi musicians. Now you can see mariachi bands strolling around Garibaldi looking for clients at all hours of the afternoon or night. On weekend nights, competing groups line Eje Central between the Alameda and Garibaldi, relentlessly chasing down cars that slow down, trying to pick up gigs for private parties (US$220 per hour—the groups will arrange their own transport to and from the gig).

Groups will be glad to strike up a tune for you right there on the square for a rather steep US$11 per song, perhaps less if you bargain well. Or you can venture into one of the many nearby bars and put back a couple of tequilas to get properly into the spirit of things.

With its recent facelift (to install a parking lot and subway station underneath the square), Garibaldi is not too daunting during the afternoon for the average tourist. It's not uncommon to see a group of foreigners having a couple of beers in one of the taco restaurants on the northeast corner of the plaza, enjoying the activity around them. But if you really want to see Garibaldi in full swing, and you are in the mood for a night of partying *a la mexicana,* show up sometime after 10 P.M. (preferably later) on a weekend night with a group of friends and make your rounds of the bars. Although most bars at Garibaldi see their share of tourists and are generally okay, a couple of dives are to be avoided, so look before you leap. Under no circumstances should you walk on the back streets around Garibaldi after dark as you will promptly get robbed. Ask the bar to call you a *sitio* (taxi). If you need to walk back to downtown after dark, walk down Eje Central to Tacuba before turning east toward the Zócalo. (For more information on Garibaldi nightlife, see the Arts and Entertainment chapter.)

SOUTH OF THE ZÓCALO

Although not as frequented as other parts of the Centro, the blocks between the Zócalo and Avenida Izazaga hide several unique colonial buildings well worth taking a couple of hours to tour. Along Avenida Pino Suárez, which once was the old Aztec causeway leading south off the island capital, you'll find the Iglesia de Jesús Nazareno, on the spot where Cortés and Moctezuma first met when the conquistadors arrived in Mexico City and the site of Cortés's tomb. Across the street stands the Museo de la Ciudad, housed in an imposing colonial mansion. Farther south is the Ex-Convento de San Jerónimo, the colonial convent where Mexican poet Sor Juana wrote much of her famed verse, and nearby is the Templo de Regina Coeli, rivaled only by La Enseñanza for the quality of its interior baroque artwork.

Walking south from Avenida Madero, you'll notice the streets start to get a bit shabbier and commercial after Calle Mesones. While walking south of here during the day is no problem, it's best not to venture south of Mesones after dark.

Museo de la Ciudad de México

Three blocks south of the Zócalo on Avenida Pino Suárez, at the corner of Avenida República del Salvador, sits a colonial-era mansion that now serves as a small city museum. Historians surmise that one of the conquistadors built a house on the site shortly after the conquest, as the building's cornerstone is an impressive serpent head probably taken from the Templo Mayor after its destruction by the Spanish.

The Conde de Calimaya ordered the construction of the current high baroque mansion in 1781. The richly carved main portal leads to a quiet patio with a fountain on one side, overseen by a stone sculpture of a mermaid strumming a guitar. On the second floor you can see the restored office of one of the 19th-century occupants, as well as a small chapel to the Virgen de Guadalupe with three colonial-era religious paintings.

The museum's permanent exhibit displays some paintings and sketches of the city, but of more interest are the building itself, the rooms upstairs, and the frequently revolving displays of artwork (sometimes surprisingly alternative). Musical and cultural events are often hosted on weekends. At Av. Pino Suárez 30, tel. 5542-0487. Open daily 10 A.M.–6 P.M.; free admission.

Iglesia y Hospital de Jesús Nazareno

The unadorned red brick Iglesia de Jesús Nazareno, diagonally across Avenida Pino Suárez from the Museo de la Ciudad, is the final resting place of that much-maligned conquistador, Hernán Cortés. Perhaps reflecting the less than glorious image modern Mexicans have of Cortés, his tomb is marked only by a small plaque at the front of the bare church, to the left of the altar. Legend has it that at the same corner where the church now stands, Aztec Emperor Moctezuma II first met Cortés as the conquistadors rode into Tenochtitlán for the first time. A plaque on the rear of the church, facing Avenida Pino Suárez, commemorates the event. The ceiling of the *coro* (choir seating area) bears a José Clemente Orozco mural, *El apocalipsis.* The chapel is open Monday–Saturday 7 A.M.–8 P.M., Sunday 7 A.M.–1 P.M. and 5–8 P.M.

Half a block south on Avenida Pino Suárez from the church is the Hospital de Jesús, one of the oldest buildings still standing in Mexico City, now hidden by a modern facade. Take a walk through the unremarkable entrance into a tranquil two-story colonial courtyard, filled with plants and a fountain in the center. Past the central staircase, where there is a bust of Cortés, you'll come to a second courtyard. Cortés ordered its construction in 1524 to tend to soldiers wounded fighting the Aztecs. Amazingly, the building (much modified since Cortés's time) still functions as a hospital, but tourists are free to walk in and around the courtyards—there's very little activity in the hallways. Judging from the lack of patients, you're probably better off going to one of the better hospitals in Polanco or elsewhere if you had a medical problem, but in an emergency the *urgencias* at the Hospital de Jesús (Pino Suárez 35, tel. 5542-6501 or 5542-6507) is open all night, and convenient to Centro stays.

Ex-Convento de San Jerónimo

It was in this convent, during the late 17th century, where Mexican nun and poet Sor Juana Inés de la Cruz wrote much of her remarkable, passionate verse, and it is under the chapel inside the old convent where she is buried. The remains of the convent have now been converted into a small, private university with a humanist focus called the Universidad del Claustro de Sor Juana. Visitors can tour the school grounds, chapel, and museum at no charge. The entrance is on Avenida Izazaga, four blocks south and three blocks west of the Museo de la Ciudad.

The convent was founded in 1585 through the efforts of Isabel de Barrios, daughter of conquistador Andrés de Barrios, and her second husband, Diego de Guzmán. The couple's four daughters and one cousin eventually became nuns in the convent. The chapel, dedicated in 1626, has a somewhat severe Renaissance facade on the north side.

By the middle of the 19th century, when it

was closed by the Reform Laws, the convent had at least 200 permanent residents. After the nuns' expulsion, different parts of the convent were used variously as army barracks, a hospital, a stable, a hotel, dozens of private homes, and even a legendary1940s night spot called La Smyrna. Prompted by the complaints of people appalled that the burial site of a woman who is practically Mexico's national poet was being thus abused, government authorities intervened and expropriated the property in 1975, and shortly thereafter the university opened.

Visitors should bring some sort of photo identification to leave at the front gate entrance at Avenida Izazaga 92. After signing in and receiving a little badge, visitors can walk around the old chapel, which is now used for school theater productions and has been mostly stripped of its ornamentation, leaving it eerily bare. In the entrance is a large monument saying that the nuns of the convent, including Sor Juana, are buried under the church.

For more information (in Spanish) on upcoming exhibits and events at the school, call 5709-4066 or 5709-4126.

Near the chapel inside the university compound is the **Museo de la Indumentaria Mexicana,** which has rotating displays on traditional Amerindian and mestizo clothing from a large private collection belonging to photographer/folklorist Luis Marquéz Ramay. Exhibits of Mexican and international artists are frequently on display at different places in the university. It's worth taking a quick look into the large, two-story cloister where many nuns lived. The building postdates the time of Sor Juana, however: the poet is thought to have lived in a private home near the convent, which was common practice in her time. The museum is open Monday–Friday 10 A.M.–6 P.M.; admission is free.

Around on the north side of the convent, opposite the school entrance, one can walk through a pedestrian street to see the principal facade of the chapel. A statue of Sor Juana sits in the middle of a small square in front, which now serves as a soccer field for local boys. The pedestrian street here is seedy, so don't be surprised to see a drunk or two leaning on a bench.

Museo Nacional de la Charrería

The remains of a 16th-century Benedictine convent at Izazaga and Isabel la Católica is now home to the offices of the Asociación Nacional de la Charrería, a national organization dedicated to Mexico's passion for horsemanship and the *charreada,* often incorrectly referred to as "Mexican rodeo." A humble little museum housed inside the building contains a few displays of the famed outfits worn by *charros* from Mexico, Spain, Argentina, and Venezuela along with a collection of swords, saddles, and guns. A .44 caliber pistol once owned by Pancho Villa is the only labeled display. Historical inscriptions, however, are written in Spanish, English, and even French.

The museum is open Monday–Friday 10 A.M.–7 P.M. Admission is free. Call 5512-2523 for further information.

Templo de Regina Coeli

A hidden treasure of religious art in the Centro Histórico, this 17th-century church doesn't look overly spectacular on the outside, although the sculptures and reliefs are attractive enough. But inside, the church houses five separate carved, gilded *retablos,* masterpieces of late baroque colonial art. The principal altar, dedicated to the Regina Coeli and dating to 1671, has an oil painting of the Virgin in the center, and a statue of San José with the baby Jesus above. The *estípite* columns, characteristic of the Churrigueresque style of the church, are dazzlingly complex and fluid. The four side altars are dedicated to the Virgen de la Fuente, Virgen de Guadalupe, Virgen de la Soledad, and San Francisco de Asís.

The Convento de Regina Coeli began construction in 1573, and the church was completed in 1636. As with so many convents, the Regina Coeli was partitioned after the 19th century Reform Laws, and the eastern part became the Hospital Concepción Beistegui, which is now a run-down senior citizens' home. The church is at the corner of Bolívar and Regina.

Colegio de las Vizcainas

A block west of Regina Coeli sits a massive neglected relic of the colonial era, a three-story colonial building covering an entire city block.

© CHRIS HUMPHREY

The undulation lines of the Colegio de las Vizcainas are caused by subsidence.

This is the Colegio de las Vizcainas, a private university that is still, barely, in operation. Because it was always a lay (nonreligious) institution, the college was allowed to stay open after the Reform Laws, which shut down all religious schools.

It's not possible to enter the Colegio, unless you can sweet-talk the recalcitrant guards, but the beautiful front wall of the school on the north side is worth a look if you find yourself nearby. The heavy weight of the building coupled with the weak subsoil have led to a pronounced wobble in the building's foundation, easily visible from the neat rows of bricks now bent into curved lines. The school now occupies only part of the huge building, while private offices use the rest. The city government is hoping to revitalize this area, focusing particularly on the south side of the building, where there is a small park, but at the time of writing the streets around the Colegio were still fairly gritty.

Templo de San Agustín

Two blocks north of the Regina Coeli church and one block east, at the corner of Isabel la Católica and República de Uruguay, look for the Templo de San Agustín, along with what remains of the Augustinian convent. The huge church, built in 1692 on the site of an earlier, destroyed chapel, has an imposing front entrance topped with a sculpted relief of San Agustín sheltering several monks, flanked by double rows of Solomonic-style twisted columns. After the Reform, Mexico's government converted the church into the Biblioteca Nacional (National Library). The library has long since moved on, and the church itself is in a woeful state, evidenced by its dramatic east-to-west tilt. Only a small chapel on the south side, at República de El Salvador 76, is open to the public.

Casa del Conde Mateo del Valparaíso

A block north of the Templo de San Agustín on Isabel la Católica, at the corner of Venustiano Carranza, rises a two-story private palace with a third-story corner tower, built between 1769 and 1772 under the direction of architect Francisco Guerrero Torres. Sculpted reliefs decorate the tower and the area above the main entrance. Originally owned by the same count who erected the Palacio de Iturbide on Avenida Madero, this palace is now owned by Banamex and forms part of the bank's central offices.

Visitors can go into part of the old building through a Banamex branch in the adjacent building (itself an amusing modernist retake on the colonial palace, done in *tezontle*-flecked concrete), but to go all the way inside would require charming the guards and bringing along a photo identification to leave with them.

EAST OF THE ZÓCALO

In the few blocks behind the Palacio Nacional and Templo Mayor are several important and not frequently visited museums housed in buildings dating from the colonial area. Most of the sites are inexpensive or free and can easily be visited in an hour or two.

It's not recommended that tourists wander

too far off—more than about four blocks from the Zócalo—in an easterly direction, toward Avenida Circunvalación or Avenida San Pablo. Although much honest business goes on in these neighborhoods, which form part of La Merced market district, prostitutes patrol the main avenues while more suspicious-looking types walk the back streets. This is definitely not a place to go around toting a camera or looking confused. But all the sites listed below, with the exception of the Ex-Convento de la Merced and the Merced and Sonora markets, are close to the Zócalo and quite safe to walk to.

Museo de la Secretaría de Hacienda y Crédito Público

Facing the Palacio Nacional from the Zócalo, take the street heading east from the left (north) side of the Palace, known as Calle Moneda because the mint was for years located there. On the left side of the street, at Moneda 4, you'll find the former Palacio del Arzobispado (Archbishop's Palace), now a museum run by the Finance Secretariat. Built in the 1530s, it remained the seat of ecclesiastical authority in Mexico until 1867, when it was seized by the Juárez government along with most other church property.

With the remains of an Aztec palace in the basement, the building is one of the most historic in the city and worth a visit in its own right, but it also houses a sizeable collection of Mexican art given by artists or collectors to the government in lieu of tax payments. These include works by such greats as Diego Rivera and Rufino Tamayo, as well as contemporary artists such as Benjamín Domínguez and Vicente Rojo. Some rooms also contain modest displays of colonial art and artifacts. Free concerts and theater productions are held every Sunday between noon and 2 P.M.—get there before noon as it often fills up and the doors are closed until the show finishes. Open Tues.–Sun. 10 A.M.–5 P.M.; admission US$1; free on Sunday. Call 5228-1241 for further information.

Casa de la Imprenta

In this modest house at the corner of Calle Moneda and Calle Licenciado Primo de Verdad, early colonists cranked up the first printing machine in the Americas in 1536. Apart from a model of the press, the house contains a small exhibit of Aztec artifacts and occasional temporary exhibits. Open Mon.–Sat. 10 A.M.–5 P.M.; free admission; tel. 5522-1535.

Centro de Arte Alternativo Ex-Santa Teresa

In the shell of an old Carmelite chapel and convent, where famed 17th-century poet Sor Juana Inés de la Cruz briefly lived (after leaving the San Jerónimo convent), one of the few art spaces in Mexico City dedicated to young, alternative artists flourishes under the auspices of the Instituto Nacional de Bellas Artes. At Licenciado Primo de Verdad 6, just off Moneda. Open daily 10 A.M.–6 P.M.; free admission.

Museo de las Culturas

At Moneda 13, just past the north wall of the Palacio Nacional, stands a colonial-era building where the silver riches of Mexico's mines were once counted before being sent on to the Spanish crown's treasury each year by ship. The building, modified repeatedly over the centuries, served as Mexico's mint from the late 1500s until 1865, when Emperor Maximilian I converted it into a natural history museum. Since 1966 it has served as a museum for the cultures of the world. Mexican artist Rufino Tamayo painted the mural in the entrance way. While the permanent exhibit is nothing to write home about, occasional temporary shows can be of interest. As admission to the museum is free, you could spend just a few minutes walking around the rambling old building even if the exhibits aren't of interest. The museum has a good, government-run bookstore with plenty of historical and cultural books, postcards, posters, and other assorted trinkets. Open daily 9:30 A.M.–5:45 P.M.; free admission; tel. 5542-0187.

Museo José Luis Cuevas

Continuing east on Moneda past Correo Mayor to the corner of Academia, turn left and look for a bright red metal sculpture marking the entrance to this museum, established by one of Mexico's preeminent modern artists, José Luis Cuevas. Housed in the remodeled 16th-century

© CHRIS HUMPHREY

La giganta, at the Museo José Luis Cuevas

Convento de Santa Inés, the museum mounts new exhibits every month or two drawn from the artist's private collection, which he donated to create the museum. The collection contains works by Mexican artists Francisco Toledo, Vicente Rojo, and Arnold Belkin, among others, as well as foreign artists such as Pablo Picasso, Leonora Carrington, and Roberto Matta.

Erotica, found in a room draped in ominous black curtains on the first floor, contains a small display of rather tame erotic sketches by Cuevas. Several impressive Cuevas sculptures are placed throughout the museum. Particularly striking is the eight-meter-high bronze sculpture of a female figure that Cuevas designed especially for the center patio, titled *La giganta* (The Giantess). Open Tues.–Sun. 10 A.M.–5 P.M.; US$1 admission; free for students with ID; free on Sunday for the general public; tel. 5522-0156 or 5542-6198.

Academia San Carlos

Once the principal art school in Spanish America, the Academia de San Carlos began life early in the colonial era as a hospital, but it was occupied by the academy in 1790. To help train sculpture students, master artists made plaster copies of some of the great works of European art, such as *Venus de Milo* and *David,* and these casts line the school's two-story courtyard today. Visitors are free to look inside the school (now run by UNAM, the national university) during working hours (Mon.–Fri. 9 A.M.–2 P.M. and 5 P.M.–8 P.M.), although a fee is charged to take pictures. The school frequently mounts art exhibits by young Mexican artists. At Academia and Moneda; tel. 5522-3102.

Iglesia de la Santísima Trinidad

Popularly known simply as La Santísima, this is another little baroque masterpiece tucked away in the back streets of the Centro, at the corner of the pedestrian streets Emiliano Zapata and La Santísima. Built between 1755 and 1783, La Santísima is one of the most important Churrigueresque churches in the city, along with the Sagrario. The main facade, decorated with busts of the 12 apostles and a symbol of La Santísima Trinidad (the Holy Trinity), is stunning, and the deep relief carvings on the side entrance are also exceptional. The original altarpiece is long gone, so don't worry too much if the church happens to be closed up when you go by.

Ex-Convento de la Merced

Lost amid run-down streets a 15-minute walk southeast of the Zócalo is this convent, a gem of colonial architecture—although one in a sorry state of disrepair. The convent is now closed to the public, but if the guard is in a good mood, and you speak some Spanish, you might be able to convince him to let you in for a look at this masterpiece of colonial religious architecture.

The convent is considered by some to have the most beautifully sculpted cloister in all of the Americas. Unfortunately, much of the convent aside from the cloister was destroyed after the Reform Laws of 1857 allowed the government to expropriate church property, and the remains have further decayed. The government that came to power immediately after the Mexican Revolution threatened to demolish the cloister in 1920, but Mexican artist Dr. Atl (a pseudonym, meaning "water" in Náhuatl, for Mexican painter Gerardo Murillo) staged a hunger strike in the cloister in 1920 and successfully staved off its demise.

Thank you, Dr. Atl. The two stories of sculpted columns and arches around the patio of the cloister will cause rapture in those with an affinity for the best of Latin colonial religious architecture. The lower level was finished in 1656, in a somewhat reserved baroque that includes sculptures of various saints and biblical allusions decorating the stonework above the arches. Thirteen striking *portales,* with scalloped arches in the Arab-influenced Mudejar style, line each side of the top floor and represent Jesus and the 12 Apostles.

Unfortunately, the government's interest in La Merced appears not to have increased much since 1920. Probably because it is in a rough neighborhood unlikely to draw many tourists, the cloister is closed to the public and appears to be slowly decaying. The walls and sculptures all show signs of water and earthquake damage in urgent need of repair.

It's best to walk over this way on Sundays only, when the streets are mostly deserted. If you come during the rest of the week, when the area is packed with people and cars, it would be best to come in the company of *capitalinos* who know the area. If you're driving, proceed along Avenida República de El Salvador past Avenida Pino Suárez, continue four or five blocks farther east, then turn left (north) on Talavera or Roldán, and turn left again immediately on República de Uruguay. The convent will be on your right.

Mercado de la Merced and Mercado de Sonora

One of the largest retail and wholesale markets in Mexico, La Merced covers an entire block between the streets of Santa Escuela, General Anaya, Rosario, and Cerrada del Rosario in Col. Merced Balbuena, near the Ex-Convento de la Merced and just outside of Metro Merced. For most of the nearly two centuries since independence from Spain, La Merced was the city's principal market-

© CHRIS HUMPHREY

leaning towers: the listing Iglesia de Santa Veracruz on the Alameda

place and the centerpiece of a bustling commercial neighborhood. In 1983 the city inaugurated the Central de Abastos farther south, and it soon superceded La Merced in the wholesale business. But La Merced is still going strong, and many *capitalinos* still consider it the quintessential Mexico City market.

Across Avenida Fray Servando Teresa de Mier from La Merced is Mercado Sonora, the so-called "witches' market" of tourist brochures. Mexicans flock here to buy herbal remedies, love potions, talismans, and other assorted psychospiritual balms. The market also does a booming trade in endangered plants and animals, for which it is routinely raided by the police.

Beware of walking the back streets around the two markets, as the neighborhood is rough. Both are open daily 6 A.M.–6 P.M.

AROUND THE ALAMEDA CENTRAL

West of Eje Central Lázaro Cárdenas, the older colonial architecture of the Centro Histórico is interspersed with many modern structures and the city blocks begin to lengthen. Attractions in this area include one of the city's oldest and largest parks, the architectural gem Palacio de Bellas Artes, a small museum housing Diego Rivera's famed mural set in the Alameda, La Ciudadela handicraft market, and assorted smaller plazas and historic churches.

Palacio de Bellas Artes

Looming over the eastern end of the Alameda Central, at the corner of Avenida Juárez and Eje Central, is the huge, domed Palace of Fine Arts. Construction began in 1904, during the presidency of Porfirio Díaz, under the supervision of Italian architect Adamo Boari. Boari planned for the building to be a masterpiece of art nouveau architecture but, frustrated by interruptions wrought by the decade-long Mexican Revolution, he left Mexico in 1916 having completed only the grand facades.

One of Boari's Mexican apprentices, Federico Mariscal, took over the design in 1932 and finished off the interior of the building as well as the impressive cupolas in art deco. The exterior decoration mixes classical Greco-Roman statuary with Aztec motifs such as serpent heads and representations of Aztec warriors, most of it sculpted by Italian artists. For the main auditorium inside, Mexican painter Gerardo Murillo, also known as Dr. Atl, designed a huge stained-glass stage curtain *(cortina de cristal)* depicting the Ixtacíhuatl and Popocatépetl volcanoes. Tiffany Studios of New York assembled more than a million pieces of glass to realize the design. The building was completed in 1934.

From west to east, the building consists of: the entrance vestibule and reception rooms; the large mezzanine and stairwells, beneath the Palacio's three cupolas, plus art galleries; the theater and associated service rooms; and backstage areas and scenery workshops. Only the first two sections are open to the public on a daily basis (except Monday, when Bellas Artes is closed). The theater is reserved for performances—except on Sunday morning, when the public may visit—and the backstage areas and workshops are usually off limits to all but performers and staff.

The massive marble building is so heavy that it has already settled more than four and a half meters into the old lakebed. The exterior ornamentation of the Palacio has suffered from air pollution and neglect, particularly the copper-laminated cupolas, which are considered the best examples of art deco in Mexico.

Aside from admiring the interior architecture, you can visit the second and third floors of the mezzanine to view massive social-political works by Mexico's most famous muralists. Davíd Alfaro Siqueiros's 1944–45 *Nueva democracia* (New Democracy), on the north wall of the third level, is probably the most striking and clearly designed. Siqueiros's wife served as the model for the bare-breasted, helmeted woman breaking out of chains in the mural. For this painting, which is the central panel of a larger triptych, Siqueiros used pyroxilin, a commercial enamel used for airplanes and automobiles. Four other Siqueiros panels can also be seen on this floor. Diego Rivera's 1934 *El hombre contralor del Universo* (Man, Controller of the Universe) occupies another wall. On the

RIVERA AND ROCKEFELLER

When in 1933 Nelson Rockefeller decided he wanted a mural for the new RCA Building at Rockefeller Center, New York, he commissioned Diego Rivera (after receiving refusals from Picasso and Matisse) to carry out the work. Thumbing his nose at the Western world's primary proponent of free enterprise, Rivera chose to depict the modern worker at a symbolic junction of science, industry, capitalism, and socialism in a work provisionally titled *Man at the Crossroads Looking with Hope and High Vision to the Choosing of a New and Better Future.*

Among several influential world personalities portrayed in the fresco—including Edsel Ford, Jean Harlow, and Charlie Chaplin—Rivera included a figure of Russian communist leader Vladimir Lenin. When Rivera steadfastly refused Rockefeller's request to remove Lenin's portrait, Rockefeller had the entire fresco chiseled off the wall.

In 1934, Rivera reproduced the mural on an interior wall of the third level of the Palacio de Bellas Artes, where it can be seen today under the title *Man, Controller of the Universe.* In the second version he included not only Lenin, but Marx, Engels, and Trotsky. Taking revenge one step further, Rivera added a portrait of John D. Rockefeller Jr. standing in a nightclub and surrounded by sleek women. Just above Rockefeller's head stretches a microscopic view of a swirl of bacteria said to represent venereal diseases.

south wall, José Clemente Orozco's 1934–35 *La katharsis* depicts a confrontation of the mechanistic world with humanity in a swirl of guns, machines, and tortured human faces. Less interesting murals by Rufino Tamayo and Juan O'Gorman cover the remaining walls.

On the second floor of the mezzanine you'll see more murals by less-famous Mexican artists Roberto Montenegro, Jorge González Camarena, and Manuel Rodríguez Lozano. Camarena's 1963 *Humanidad librándose* (Humanity Liberating Itself) is especially worth noting. Like Siqueiros, Camarena's approach to color and line was bold and bright, almost psychedelic, but he had a much greater range of technique, which he could turn from abstraction to realism or super-realism. Also on this floor are a couple of galleries used for well-curated temporary exhibits.

The fourth floor of Bellas Artes, the **Museo de Arquitectura** (Museum of Architecture) exhibits floor plans, photos, and other archived memorabilia related to Mexico City's historic buildings, including many older structures that have disappeared from Roma, Juárez, San Rafael, Tacubaya, and other *barrios.*

The massive lobby, mezzanine, and galleries are open to the public Tuesday–Sunday 10 A.M.–6 P.M.; admission to the mezzanine and galleries is US$2.75, free on Sunday. On Sunday mornings visitors are also permitted to enter the theater to see the lighted Tiffany glass curtain. Off the north side of the lobby is a very pleasant and slightly upscale café. Ticket windows downstairs offer advance sales for the Orquestra Sinfónica Nacional (National Symphonic Orchestra) and for the famous Ballet Folklórico (see the Arts and Entertainment chapter for details). Other concerts and events are scheduled regularly. For further information, call 5512-2593, ext. 193.

Right next to the northwest corner of the Palacio is the Metro Bellas Artes subway station. The French government recently paid for a renovation of the Metro entrance, giving it the full art nouveau treatment like the famed Metro station entrances of Paris. Several *peseros* pass along Avenida Hidalgo to the immediate north.

Alameda Central

When the Spanish conquered Tenochtitlán, the area now occupied by the Alameda Central was an Aztec *tianguis* (open-air market). Spanish viceroy Don Luis de Velasco, as part of a plan to develop what was then the western edge of the city, ordered the construction of the first Alameda—named for the *álamos* or poplar trees originally planted throughout—between 1592 and 1595. More than 400 years later it is one of the most traditional and well-proportioned city parks in all of Mexico, and so beloved by Mexicans that parks of all sizes throughout the country take the name "Alameda" in homage.

The original park covered only about half the current area, from the Palacio de Bellas Artes to the park's Hemiciclo de Juárez. The newer western half took the place of an unadorned public square built during the Spanish Inquisition and known as El Quemadero (the Burning Place), as this was where "infidels" were tortured and burned at the stake with much public ceremony. The inquisitors wore special conical hats and yellow shirts emblazoned with devils, flames, alligators, and snakes, painted by the top religious artists of the era. By the 1760s, the Inquisition was all but over in Mexico, and in 1770 viceroy Marqués de Croix ordered the expansion of the park over El Quemadero.

The de Croix expansion was further amplified in 1791 by the Conde de Revillagigedo, who erected a wood fence around the perimeter in an attempt to reserve the park for the exclusive use of the aristocracy. A French designer installed five classical fountains inspired by Greco-Roman mythology, and more statuary, both classical and modern, was added in the 19th century. Gas lamps were erected in 1868, to be replaced by electric lighting in 1892, by which time the park had become a popular spot for all classes of Mexicans. Most of what you can see in the park today, from the starburst pathways set around fountains to the band kiosk, dates to the 19th and early 20th centuries.

The Alameda remains a favorite place for local romantics during the week and is *the* place to go on Sunday afternoon for a stroll with the family. Aside from being a pleasant place to walk and observe Mexican park life at its finest, the park features a couple of monuments worth visiting in and of themselves. Standing at the south side of the park, facing Avenida Juárez, is the **Hemiciclo de Benito Juárez,** a semicircle of eight marble Doric columns joined at the top. Inaugurated by dictator Porfirio Díaz in September 1910, the monument was intended to commemorate 100 years of independence from Spain but wasn't completed till 1919. Four columns stand on each side of a central obelisk topped with a statue of Juárez holding a copy of the Mexican constitution. The mythical Greek goddess Glory places a laurel crown on his head as Victory stands by with brandished sword.

Although any day of the week is a good time for a stroll through the leafy Alameda, the park is at its most festive on Sunday, when many food and trinket vendors set up along the pathways. An excellent children's puppet theater sometimes performs along the north side of the park toward the Hotel de Cortés around the middle of the day on Sunday, and occasionally a live symphonic ensemble mounts the kiosk to perform.

During the Christmas season the park is dotted with Santa Claus displays and other Christmas scenery, most of it oriented toward children; between Christmas and January 6, Día de los Reyes, the themes switch to the Three Kings.

Churches of the Plaza de la Santa Veracruz

This small plaza on the north side of Avenida Hidalgo, opposite the Alameda Central, is surrounded by four small architectural and artistic gems. At the south end of the plaza, which lies a couple of meters below the level of Avenida Hidalgo because of soil subsidence, stands dark **Iglesia de la Santa Veracruz.** Reportedly, the original church that once stood here was built by order of chief conquistador Hernán Cortés in 1521 to celebrate the arrival of his ships at Veracruz in 1519, making it the oldest church in Mexico City. The oldest sections of the present structure date to 1730, while the southern facade was redone in 1759 and 1764 in the baroque style. Neoclassical architect Manuel Tolsá—who abhorred baroque architecture—is entombed inside.

At the opposite end of the plaza, **Iglesia de San Juan de Dios** was completed in 1729 and features a unique concave facade. Inside is a figure of one of the most sought-after saints in the city, San Antonio de Padua. Local myth says San Antonio will help supplicants obtain a fiancée; to win the saint's favor, you must offer only coins obtained from strangers.

Both churches are open to visitors daily 10:30 A.M.–1:30 P.M. and 4:30–6:30 P.M.

Museo Nacional de la Estampa

Housed in a reconstructed 16th-century two-story mansion near the northeast corner of the Plaza de la Santa Veracruz, the Engraving Museum, tel. 5521-2244, is filled with a large collection of printmaking paraphernalia, from the clay seals and agave leaves of precolonial times to modern metal plates. There are also many displays of the prints themselves. Among the most interesting are those that were used to illustrate books and periodicals before the popularization of photography. The latter include works by Manuel Manilla (1830–90) and José Guadalupe Posadas (1852–1913), both of whom were famous satirical newspaper illustrators in the late 19th century.

The etchings of Aguascalientes native Posadas often feature variations of the *calavera* or skeleton figure associated with Mexico's Day of the Dead celebration. His most famous *calavera* engraving, *Catrina,* depicts a skeleton wearing an expensive lady's hat ("Catrina" was reportedly a popular name among aristocratic women in the 19th century) and is on display here, as is his noted Don Quijote skeleton. Great muralists Rivera and Orozco, who hung around his studio as novice artists, revered Posadas as the first truly Mexican artist in the country's history. Open Tues.–Sun. 10 A.M.–6 P.M.; admission US$2.

Museo Franz Mayer

In the northwest corner of the Plaza de la Santa Veracruz, a 16th-century former hospital contains the carefully and artfully displayed applied arts collection of German financier-philanthropist Franz Mayer. The fine selection, which extends to two floors, includes 16th- through 19th-century Mexican ceramics, antique *rebozos* (Mexican shawls), religious articles, furniture, textiles, silver and gold pieces, clocks, and even full *cocinas poblanas* (tiled Puebla-style kitchens)—a real treat for fans of Mexican culinary history. The museum contains a few canvases by European Renaissance artists as well, plus temporary exhibitions of often excellent quality. Call 5518-2266 for details.

A courtyard café toward the back of the museum is a quiet spot for reflection and refreshment. Both museum and café are open Tuesday–Sunday 10 A.M.–5 P.M. Museum admission on most days is US$2.50, but it's half price on Sunday and free on Tuesday.

Hotel Cortés (Ex-Hospicio de San Nicolás Tolentino de los Ermitaños de San Agustín)

Built in 1730 as an Augustinian hospice dedicated to providing shelter and food for the poor, this dark building with a baroque facade of *tezontle* block became a hostel for traveling tradesmen in 1860 and was completely refurbished and reopened as a hotel in 1943. Mexican and foreign visitors alike stop off for late breakfast or lunch in the cool stone courtyard of the hotel, which stands at the west end of Avenida Hidalgo near Paseo de la Reforma (see Accommodations for more information).

Museo Mural Diego Rivera

Opposite the southwest corner of Alameda Central, facing a smaller garden plaza, a small, modern museum houses the famous Diego Rivera mural called *Sueño de una tarde dominical en la Alameda Central* (Dream of a Sunday Afternoon in the Alameda Central). Rivera created this huge work for the lobby of the Hotel Del Prado in 1947–48. Mexico City's 1985 earthquake damaged the hotel beyond repair, but the mural survived and was moved to this museum built especially to exhibit the work in 1986. Also on display are various photos showing the work in progress as well as the effects of the quake on the Hotel Del Prado.

Dominating the museum's back wall, the 15- by 4-meter (49- by 13-foot) mural's park scene portrays many famous Mexican personalities, including Hernán Cortés, Porfirio Díaz, Francisco I. Madero, Gen. Antonio López de Santa Anna (handing the "keys" to Mexico to American Gen. Winfield Scott), Emperor Maximilian and wife Carlota, and many more. In the center of the cartoonlike mural, José Guadalupe Posadas, Mexico's most well-known engraver, walks arm in arm with La Calavera Catrina (see Museo Nacional de la Estampa), who is decked out in a feathered hat and serpent-headed boa. To the right of the *calavera* stands Frida Kahlo, holding in her left hand the Taoist yin-yang symbol. A self-portrait of Diego Rivera as a young boy stands in front of Kahlo. Open Tues.–Sun. 10 A.M.–6 P.M.; admission US$1.50; free on Sunday.

To commemorate the many people who died during the 1985 quake, the Mexico City government established the rectangular **Jardín de la Solidaridad** (Solidarity Garden) in front of the museum. The plaza lies on the former site of the Hotel Regis, which was destroyed during the cataclysm. Chess aficionados will be pleased to hear this is the favored spot for players to come spend hours playing the game of kings.

Laboratorio Arte Alameda

Right next to the mural, in what was formerly a museum for colonial art, is a new art space for young artists run by the Instituto Nacional de Bellas Artes. Temporary exhibits of experimental modern art are on display Tuesday–Sunday 9 A.M.–5 P.M.; US$1 admission; free on Sunday. At Dr. Mora 7; tel. 5510-2793. The colonial paintings have been moved to the Museo Nacional de Arte.

© CHRIS HUMPHREY

one of the many restored colonial mansions still found in the Centro: Casa de Cultura of the state of Tamaulipas, near the Ciudadela market

Proyecto Alameda (Alameda Project)

This work in progress encompasses more than a dozen city blocks south of the Alameda Central between Avenida Juárez and Calle Dondé/Calle Pugibet. It's all part of an urban restoration project that has the dual purpose of filling in blocks destroyed by the 1985 quake and renovating historic properties in the neighborhood for both residents and tourists.

Private funding focuses on a three-block area along Avenida Juárez between Balderas and Luis Moya, where the former Hotel De Prado was irreparably damaged by the quake and had to be razed. At last report, a brand-new Sheraton Hotel was half completed along Avenida Juárez, that when finished is expected to be the second-tallest building in the city. It's hoped that the hotel will trigger further private investments in the neighborhood.

Farther south, the project is busy renovating the small *barrio chino* (Chinatown) along Calle Dolores. Plans call for a large Chinese-designed gateway to be erected over the street.

Templo de San Hipólito

At the corner of Calle de Zarco and Avenida Hidalgo, slightly west of Paseo de la Reforma, this church was founded a year after the so-called Noche Triste or "Sad Night" (June 30, 1520), when Cortés's Spanish troops came under heavy Aztec attack and were forced to flee the city. Reputedly Cortés vowed to build a church at this spot, the beginning of the Aztec causeway leaving the island, when he returned. A small plaque in a corner of the church courtyard commemorates the infamous event. Cortés returned in 1521, took the city after a three-month siege, razed it, and captured the Aztec emperor Cuauhtémoc. The church was completely redone in 1577, when America's first mental hospital—Hospital de San Hipólito—was attached.

Worth a brief look is the church's dark *tezontle* and stone three-stage early baroque facade, topped by slender bell towers uniquely twisted so that their corners face toward the front.

Plaza de San Fernando

Two and a half blocks west of the Templo de San Hipólito, on the north side of Puente de Alvarado, sits the small, narrow landscaped Plaza de San Fernando. In the center of the plaza, surrounded by trees and benches, an inscribed obelisk is mounted by a statue of Mexican independence hero Vicente Guerrero (1782–1831). Guerrero led a provisional guerrilla government based in Michoacán 1817–21 and then served briefly as Mexican president April–December 1829.

The **Iglesia de San Fernando** can be seen just beyond the north end of the plaza. Franciscans from Querétaro established the San Fernando church and convent in 1734 to serve as a headquarters for the missionary effort. A century later the convent was badly damaged by an earthquake and the city razed the ruin in 1862. Around that same time the convent's surrounding orchards and pasturelands were divided and sold off to create Colonia Guerrero, named, of course, for Vicente. Once an elegant neighborhood, Guerrero is nowadays rather seedy, but if you stick to the plaza, church, and *panteón,* you shouldn't have any problems.

The church's facade of plastered stone and *tezontle* is standard baroque. The main attraction is the **Panteón Histórico de San Fernando,** an old cemetery extending from San Fernando's east side. Most of the grave markers—some grand tombs, others mere headstones—date to the 19th century. Revered Mexican President Benito Juárez is interred in a marble tomb surrounded with Greek columns. Atop the tomb is a marble sculpture of Juárez himself, dressed in Greco-Roman robes and dying in his mother's arms. Buried alongside the great hero are his wife and children. Many of the other gravesites and tombs contain military heroes from the 19th and early 20th centuries, including Vicente Guerrero, Ignacio Comonfort, Melchor Ocampo, Tomás Mejía, and Miguel Miramón.

The cemetery is open daily 8 A.M.–3 P.M.

La Ciudadela

Built as a tobacco factory in the 18th century, this thick-walled quadrangle served as a military barracks during the Mexican Revolution and is today home to the **Biblioteca de México** (Library of Mexico).

In the same building, the **Centro de la Imagen,** tel. 5709-6095, contains studios, classrooms, a bookshop, and exhibition space dedicated to the promotion and archiving of Mexican photography. The center issues a quarterly journal, *Luna Córnea,* which may be purchased in Imagen's bookshop. The exhibition hall is open Tuesday–Sunday 11 A.M.–5 P.M., while the Centro de la Imagen office is open Monday–Friday 10 A.M.–3 P.M. and 5–7 P.M.

The complex can be found six blocks south of the Alameda Central, on the west side of Avenida Balderas opposite Metro Balderas. The area surrounding La Ciudadela is sometimes referred to as "Plaza de la Ciudadela," although the plaza just north of the complex is also called "Plaza José María Morelos."

On the same side of Balderas, two blocks north at Calle Ayuntamiento, the **Centrol Artesenal La Ciudadela,** also called Mercado de Artesanías de la Ciudadela, is one of the better places to buy Mexican handicrafts in the center of the city. (See Shopping for additional comments.)

Parque Carlos Pacheco

Just across Avenida Balderas from Ciudadela, along Calle Ernesto Pugibet, is a small, quiet square surrounded by colonial buildings, many of which have been restored in recent years. Although none of the buildings could be considered a "sight" per se, visitors may enjoy spending a few peaceful moments in the park enjoying the colonial atmosphere after shopping at the Ciudadela market. At Pugibet 73 is the Casa de Cultura of the State of Tamaulipas, housed in a restored 18th-century palace moved to the current location from its original site at Venustiano Carranza 23; it's open to the public Monday–Friday 9 A.M.–5 P.M. at no charge.

Plaza de San Juan

This recently renovated small plaza, north of the Torre TelMex tower and west of the Eje

Central, was the center of a relatively major market area during the late colonial and early post-colonial eras. In an effort to revitalize the rather run-down neighborhood surrounding Plaza de San Juan, the city government lent money for the restoration of not only the plaza, but adjacent historic buildings and a handicrafts market, **Mercado de Artesanías San Juan,** which sits on the east side of the plaza. The district around the plaza consists mostly of shops selling housing accessories. (See Shopping for comments on the *artesanías* and on other shopping possibilities in the area.)

Facing the north end of the plaza is the **Basílica de San José de Nuestra Señora del Sagrado,** a small twin-towered church originally built in 1772, and rebuilt after earthquakes in 1857 and 1985.

Opposite the northwest corner of the plaza stands an imposing Republican-era building erected by the **Compañia Cigarrera Mexicana** back when Mexico City was a major tobacco entrepôt. Nowadays the building is subdivided into office space.

The San Juan de Letrán Metro station is only two blocks northeast of the Plaza de San Juan, on the corner of República de Uruguay and Eje Central Lázaro Cárdenas.

TLATELOLCO/PLAZA DE LAS TRES CULTURAS

Just northwest of the Centro Histórico, this plaza is so named (Plaza of the Three Cultures) because around it are the ruins of an ancient Aztec temple, the renovated 16th-century Iglesia de Santiago Tlatelolco, and a huge 1960s-era apartment complex—thus presenting three cultures in one wide-angle view. Walkways wind through the temple ruins, which contain the walls of 18 structures.

On the southeast side of the ruins stand the colonial church and adjacent Ex-Convento de San Buenaventura. The old monastery was founded in 1535 as one of the principal schools where children of Aztec nobility were educated in the ways of Catholicism and the Western world. The existing structure, now part of the Foreign Relations Secretariat, was built in the 1660s, while the unadorned church was built shortly thereafter.

The plaza can be reached by walking about a kilometer or so either from the Garibaldi or Tlatelolco Metro stations (the latter is a bit closer), or by driving or taking a taxi north on the Eje Central and getting off at the corner of Ricardo Flores Magón. From here the plaza is a short walk through the building complex to the northeast.

History

The plaza sits over the site of Tlatelolco, once a small island appended to Tenochtitlán and the market center of the Aztec empire. A group of Aztec dissidents, unhappy with the growing empire's power structure, established themselves here in the late 14th century. The island was allowed a degree of autonomy until 1473, when its leaders were executed and the island was annexed by Tenochtitlán.

When Cortés first arrived, Tlatelolco was a massive market complex trading in goods from as far away as Guatemala. Hundreds of products were bought, sold, or bartered (usually the latter) by thousands of people each day. Merchandise was grouped by category in specific areas, and government appointees oversaw the transactions. According to the memoirs of Cortés himself, the market traded more fabrics each day than did the great markets of Granada at that time. At the center of the market stood the main temple, with twin pyramids dedicated to Tlaloc and Huitzilopochtli as in Tenochtitlán. The ruins seen today are the remains of this temple.

Over the centuries, Tlatelolco has been the location of an unusual number of bloody tragedies. It was here that the fanatical defense of the Aztecs under Cuauhtémoc came to its gory finale, with thousands of Aztecs run through with Spanish steel. Again in the colonial period, during grain riots in 1692, an unknown number of poor protesters were killed on the square.

But when Mexicans hear the word Tlatelolco today, the first thing they think of was the massacre that took place on the plaza the night of October 2, 1968. In the preceding weeks, a series of student protests had swept Mexico

City. While the protests posed no immediate threat to the government, they took place shortly before the 1968 Olympics, and President Gustavo Díaz Ordaz did not want students causing any embarrassing problems. As the protests continued, the police responded with increasing violence.

Because of the perceived overreaction, the protests grew stronger, and on September 18 the Army occupied UNAM, the national university. Students continued to hold smaller demonstrations in different parts of the city and ended up at Tlatelolco the night of October 2. Exactly how the violence started remains a matter of great dispute. The government insists that protesters had guns and started the shootout, while many others hold that gun-toting government agents planted among the protesters provoked the army into opening fire.

However it started, it ended with several hundred protesters dead, and hundreds more wounded and under arrest. The student protests were indeed halted, and the Olympics took place without a hitch, but in the end it was a Pyrrhic victory, for the Tlatelolco massacre was in many ways the birth of the opposition to the long-ruling Institutional Revolutionary Party (PRI). By all accounts it was this brutal overreaction on the part of the government that, for many Mexicans, unmasked the dictatorship. The full truth about what happened that night will likely never be known, but it remains a touchstone event for modern Mexico.

As if the massacre weren't enough, the government-built Tlatelolco housing complex around the plaza was severely damaged during the 1985 earthquake. The Nuevo León building, in which residents had been complaining for months about evidence of shoddy construction, collapsed in a heap, killing an estimated thousand people who lived in it. Other buildings suffered heavy damage, and to this day the residents are engaged in a long-standing legal battle with the government over the state of the complex. Considering the Nuevo León collapse, and looking at the dramatic tilt and large cracks visible in many of the buildings, it's no surprise they want the government to pay for repairs.

Paseo de la Reforma and Zona Rosa

Designed by Emperor Maximilian to resemble Paris's famous Champs Elysées, the Paseo de la Reforma (often shortened to "Reforma") is Mexico City's grandest avenue, a broad boulevard that's home to the Bolsa Mexicana de Valores (Mexican Stock Exchange) as well as numerous banks, stock brokerage firms, and office buildings. Foreign visitors will likely find themselves on Paseo de la Reforma at some point during their visit, either on their way to Chapultepec or the Zona Rosa, or to avail themselves of the avenue's many banks, exchange houses, airline offices, hotels, and nearby embassies. South of Reforma lies the Zona Rosa shopping and restaurant district, much frequented by tourists, and on the avenue's north side is the imposing Monumento a la Revolución and two interesting and not oft-visited museums, El Chopo and San Carlos. A bit farther north are San Rafael and Santa María de la Ribera, two formerly wealthy neighborhoods now on the downside, but still replete with historical buildings.

HISTORY

For the 20-odd years after Maximilian first laid it out, Reforma remained a narrow street running through open fields, while Avenida Bucareli was the principal avenue outside the downtown area and the address of choice for the city's upper crust.

But under the francophilic dictator Porfirio Díaz, Reforma assumed the Parisian grandeur Maximilian had intended. Díaz ordered the laying out of a broad central avenue flanked by side lanes (*laterales*), and the city's elite flocked to build their new palaces (only a few of which remain standing) along what was to quickly become the most fashionable district in town.

Díaz decorated three of the avenue's five

© JIM BUDD

the Mexican Stock Exchange on the Paseo de la Reforma

glorietas (traffic circles) with sculptures of (from east to west) Spanish King Carlos IV, explorer Cristóbal Colón (known to Anglos as Christopher Columbus), and Aztec Emperor Cuauhtémoc. A fourth *glorieta* was crowned with the Monumento de la Independencia. Díaz also lined the boulevard with 70-odd busts of lesser figures of the late 19th-century-elite, most of which are still standing.

Historian Michael Johns, author of the well-written and engrossing *The City of Mexico in the Age of Díaz,* commented on the Porfiriato development of Reforma:

> ***They [the monuments] narrated a history of Mexico that aimed to reconcile the ideas and events of a real past with the ideals and needs of an inexperienced ruling class that was trying to guide a new nation. That story all but ignored Mexico's past as a colony while praising the European world that Spain had introduced it to.***

The *colonias,* or neighborhoods, that grew up along either side of Reforma, first Col. Juárez to the south and then Col. Cuauhtémoc to the north, were filled with mansions owned by Mexico's richest citizens, often built in bizarre, eclectic combinations of different European styles.

In the 1950s the cafés and bars in a triangular section of Col. Juárez bordered by the avenues Insurgentes, Reforma, and Florencia became the gathering spot of choice for the city's cultural elite, including famed writers Carlos Fuentes, Carlos Monsivaís, and composer Agustín Lara, to name only three of the most prominent. The district was soon the hip spot to be seen at night, and Mexican newspaper columnists soon christened it "la Zona Rosa" (the Pink Zone, perhaps in reference to the pinkish glow given off by the red neon lights) because of its legendary nightlife.

PASEO DE LA REFORMA

The central section of Reforma, between the Alameda and Chapultepec, features an eight-lane middle avenue and two-lane parallel side streets, punctuated with five *glorietas* (traffic circles), each with a monument in the center.

Although Reforma has expanded over the years to the northeast as far as La Villa de Guadalupe, and westward to the Toluca highway exit, the sights described below are along the original, century-old boulevard. Distances along the spacious walkways on Reforma are farther than they might appear, so it's best to try to arrive fairly close to your destination before walking.

Several Metro stations can be found near Reforma: Metro Hidalgo is close to the eastern end and the Monumento de Colón; Metro Insurgentes is next to the Zona Rosa; and Metro Chapultepec is at the avenue's western end, near Chapultepec park. For destinations close to the Monumento a la Revolución, get off at Metro Revolución, which is on Avenida Puente de Alvarado, a few blocks north of the monument.

Pesero buses run the entire central stretch of Paseo de la Reforma, beginning at the Hidalgo

Metro station and going west past the Chapultepec museums to the Auditorio Nacional. These are perhaps the most convenient way of moving up and down Reforma.

Should you have a car, plenty of metered parking places can be found both in the Zona Rosa and on side streets off the north side of Reforma. The *transitos* (traffic police, dressed in brown) take great pleasure in slapping metal "boots" on the wheels of cars who haven't fed the parking meters, so beware. Traffic tends to flow pretty well along Reforma day and night (unless you hit a protest march), but it can get tied up in the middle of the Zona Rosa, especially on Friday and Saturday nights.

Paseo de la Reforma Monuments

The **King Carlos IV statue** that originally marked the start of Reforma has since moved downtown, and in its place stands a bright yellow, modernist interpretation of the horse-riding king—so highly stylized as to be unrecognizable. The lettering on the sculpture, "Torre El Caballito," refers to the adjacent office building, suggesting the piece can't stand on its own merits.

Cast in 1877 by French sculptor Charles Cordier, the **Monumento de Colón** still stands despite the best efforts of political protesters who in an annual ritual sling ropes around the statue and try to pull it down. Once the protesters managed to snap off one of the Great Mariner's thumbs, but the city promptly reattached it.

At the intersection of the city's two most important avenues, Insurgentes and Reforma, stands a statue of the Aztec warrior-emperor **Cuauhtémoc** (Attacking Eagle), who fought in a desperate last stand against the Spaniards before the

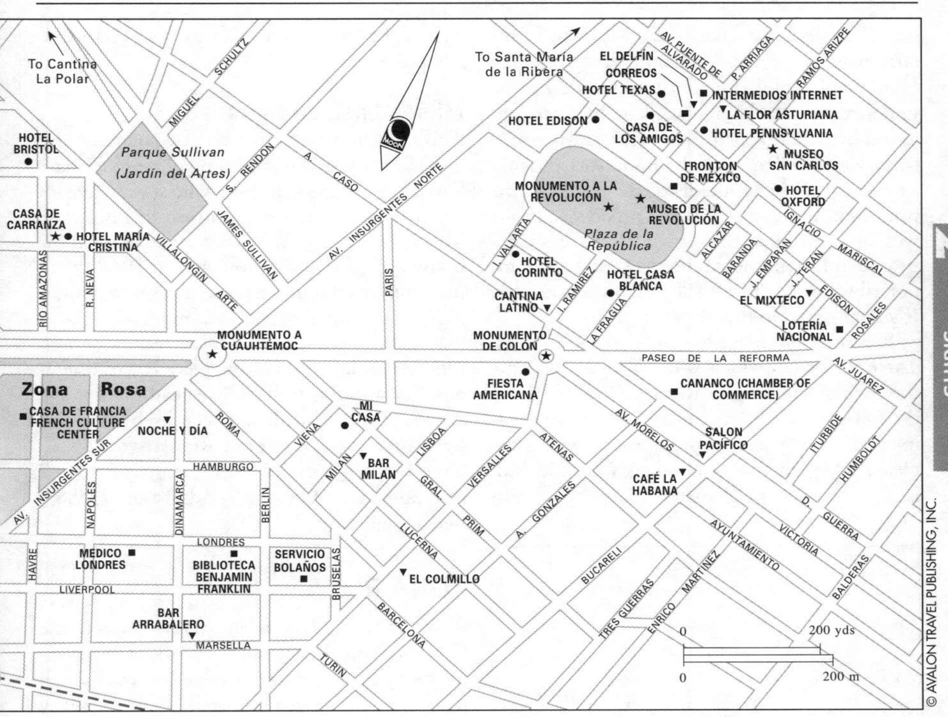

fall of Tenochtitlán. It is the work of Mexican sculptors Francisco Jiménez and Ramón Agea.

The *glorieta* beyond Cuauhtémoc has a single, tall palm tree in the center, while the next one southwest contains Mexico's **Monumento de la Independencia.** This 32-meter-high column, topped with the winged *Ángel de la Independencia,* was formally inaugurated by Porfirio Díaz on September 16, 1910, shortly before his overthrow and the start of the Revolution. The gold-sheathed angel, one of the city's landmark symbols, is the site of frequent political rallies and spontaneous street celebrations whenever the beloved *tricolor* (as Mexico's national soccer team is known) pulls off a victory. It's best to avoid such victory parties—the crowd is normally nonaggressive, if boisterous, but occasionally people have been beaten up or robbed amidst the celebration.

After dodging the traffic to cross Reforma, you can walk up the steps of the monument's base, pass through a door into the foot of the column, and walk around a small passageway wherein the remains of 12 heroes from the Independence struggle are stored in three niches: Miguel Hidalgo, José María Morelos, Ignacio Allende, Nicolás Bravo, Mariano Matamoros, Juan Aldama, Mariano Jiménez, Leona Vicario, Vicente Guerrero (whose remains are also supposed to be interred in a tomb at the Panteón Histórico de San Fernando), Francisco Javier Mina, Guadalupe Victoria, and Andrés Quintana Roo. All in all it's a bit spooky, particularly the faceless skull of Hidalgo in the second niche. Open daily 9 A.M.–6 P.M.; free admission.

At the westernmost *glorieta* stands a circular fountain and a statue of the Greek goddess **Diana Cazadora** (Diana the Huntress), aiming a bow.

Raised in 1942, the naked and voluptuous Diana stirred such a scandal that the sculptor, Juan Francisco Olabuíbel, was forced to add bronze undergarments to her loins. Olabuíbel later confessed he had attached the covering using only three weak solders, and the underwear was removed in 1967. Reputedly at the behest of the prudish wife of one of Mexico's presidents, Diana was again deemed too provocative for such a prominent monument, and the statue was temporarily relocated to a small park off Insurgentes. It was returned to the *glorieta* in 1992.

Reforma will soon boast another monument, **Torre Reforma,** which will reportedly become the highest building in Mexico City. Work on the tower, which began in late 1998, is proceeding at a leisurely pace and was not yet half completed at last report. The building, when finished, is expected to soar 225 meters above the western end of the avenue across from the entrance to Chapultepec.

© JIM BUDD

the once controversial statue of the Greek goddess Diana

Museo Casa de Carranza

This French-inspired mansion two blocks north of Reforma was the last home of revolutionary leader Venustiano Carranza, who stayed here for six months before his execution in Puebla on May 7, 1920. Carranza's widow was granted the house after the Revolution, and in 1942 she in turn converted it into a museum commemorating her husband. Art, period furniture, and memorabilia from Carranza's life fill the various rooms. One particularly interesting piece is an ambiguous Carranza portrait by Mexican painter Dr. Atl (Gerardo Murillo). The museum, at Río Lerma 35 at the corner of Río Amazonas, tel. 5546-6494, is open Tuesday–Saturday 9 A.M.–7 P.M., Sunday 11 A.M.–3 P.M. Admission is US$3, free on Sunday.

ZONA ROSA

A trendy area of bohemian bars and cafés in the '50s, the Zona Rosa is still one of the city's principal shopping and entertainment districts, though it's not as chic as it was in its earlier heydays. Many tourists will look around at the chain stores, fast-food restaurants, beggars, and young men offering to take them to nightclubs with "pretty ladies" and wonder why they came in the first place.

That said, the Zona Rosa is still a pleasant place to grab a cup of java in a European-style café or visit the one of the smart boutiques in the neighborhood. The Zona Rosa hotels are of good quality and are conveniently located for touring the city. You'll find shops and restaurants, nightclubs, major hotels, airlines, and banks in the area. There's an antiques market on Calle Londres, and many of the shopkeepers in the area speak English; some accept U.S. dollars. Calles Copenhagen and Génova are pedestrian-only streets full of shops and sidewalk cafés. (For more information, see Shopping.)

The Zona Rosa isn't all shopping and restaurants, however, and in fact today the area holds more than its share of "men's clubs," a euphemism for clubs that feature erotic dancing.

ALVARADO'S LEAP

Avenida Puente de Alvarado, site of the Metro Revolución station and the Museo San Carlos, extends over a former section of the old causeway running west from the former Aztec capital of Tenochtitlán, across what was then a lake, to the village of Tacuba (now part of the city). The avenue received its name, meaning "Alvarado's Bridge" (or "Alvarado's Leap," depending on the translation) from a possibly apocryphal story about the legendary conquistador Pedro de Alvarado, one of Cortés's most loyal and ferocious lieutenants. The story goes that on the night of the Noche Triste, when the Aztecs had rallied to expel the conquistadors from Tenochtitlán and the Spaniards fled along the causeway, Alvarado came to a gap in the causeway. Fending off the Aztec warriors trying to capture him, and with his horse lying dead underneath him, Alvarado reputedly ran up the causeway and, putting his lance into the mud, pole-vaulted over to safety on the far side.

While most of the galleries in the Zona Rosa are more oriented to collectibles and antiques, one modern art gallery is **Mexicanos Galería de Arte,** at Dinamarca 44-A, specializing in painters from the Oaxaca school such as Francisco Toledo, Rodolfo Morales, Jorge Barrios, and Alejandro Santiago.

AROUND THE MONUMENTO A LA REVOLUCIÓN

The lower-middle-class neighborhood around the Monumento a la Revolución, between Avenida Puente de Alvarado and Paseo de la Reforma, is slightly run-down but contains several budget hotels and two points of tourist interest: the Monumento a la Revolución and Museo San Carlos.

Monumento a la Revolución

This massive marble and basalt monument to Mexico's bloody 1910–20 revolution was begun by Porfirio Díaz to house his puppet Congress. Designed by the inevitable European architect, who clearly aimed for an art deco structure, the building ran into massive cost overruns and when the revolution began it was left an empty hulk for more than 20 years. When the government was on the verge of destroying the unfinished structure, Mexican architect Carlos Obregón Santacilia proposed to convert the shell into a monument to the revolution.

With the additions of several unsmiling, heroic-proletariat statues on the corners, evidently influenced by the socialist realism of Russia and the Eastern Bloc, work was completed in 1938. Crypts within the "feet" of the monument hold the remains of revolutionary heroes Venustiano Carranza, Francisco I. Madero, Francisco "Pancho" Villa, Plutarco Elias Calles, and Lázaro Cárdenas. It's a little ironic that the five men should end up buried in the same place, as they all despised and plotted against one another.

On weekends 10 A.M.–5:30 P.M. visitors may pass through the crypt of Plutarco Elias Calles and ride an elevator to the *mirador,* or viewpoint, in the monument's dome. And below the grand ramp running up to the eastern side of the monument lies the **Museo de la Revolución,** a small collection of photos and memorabilia related to the revolution. The museum is open Tuesday–Saturday 9 A.M.–5 P.M., Sunday 9 A.M.–3 P.M. Admission costs US$.75, except on Sunday when it's free.

On the northeast side of the plaza, the art deco **Frontón Nacional** contains a wooden court where jai alai—the world's fastest ball game—was played until a 1995 workers' strike closed it down.

Museo San Carlos

On the corner of Puente de Alvarado and Ramos Arizpe, amidst a row of otherwise drab buildings, stands an anomalous neoclassical palace that was once the home of the Marqués de Buenavista. Although the original plans have apparently been lost, it's thought to have been the work of that omnipresent Valencian architect and artist, Manuel Tolsá. The rooms of the former mansion, around the unusual oval-shaped courtyard, now house a remarkable collection of European artworks, including paintings by Rubens and Anton van Dyck, a series of sketches by Goya known as "Los Caprichos" (The Whims), and sculpture by Rodin and Manuel Vilar. Works by foreign masters who taught at the San Carlos school, such as Eugenio Landesio and Pelegrín Clavé, are also included.

King Carlos IV donated much of the art to the Academia de San Carlos when the art school opened in the late 18th century. Originally housed in the academy building in the Centro, these sculptures and paintings served as models for students learning their chosen medium.

The collection was opened to public viewing during the last years of the Spanish colony, thus establishing the first public art museum in the Americas. When the quantity of visitors began to overwhelm the art school in the Centro, many of the finest works were moved to the current museum. At Av. Puente de Alvarado 50, tel. 5566-8522. Open Wed.–Mon. 10 A.M.–6 P.M.; US$2.30 entrance, US$.75 extra for cameras, US$4 extra for video.

the Eiffelesque Museo El Chopo

© CHRIS HUMPHREY

SANTA MARÍA DE LA RIBERA AND SAN RAFAEL

West of Avenida Insurgentes and on either side of Avenida San Cosme (the extension of Avenida Tacuba) are these two *colonias* dating from the mid-19th century. Built for the wealthy residents of Mexico City eager to flee the growing squalidness of the downtown area, the streets of Santa María and San Rafael (both named for the ranches on which they were built) are lined with dozens of old mansions, some in sorry states of disrepair, others beautifully restored. Both neighborhoods are resolutely lower middle-class these days, although some predict they will soon be on the upswing again, particularly San Rafael. If you've got an extra afternoon for wandering, it's worth taking a stroll through this area to enjoy a corner of Mexico City little visited by foreigners. The Alameda of Santa María is a particularly fine spot, evocative of life in the city from years past.

Museo El Chopo

Built in Germany and moved to Mexico in pieces, this Eiffelesque structure of girders and glass first served as the Japanese pavilion at an industrial exposition in 1910, and then was moved to its current site to become a natural history museum. UNAM, the national university, took over the building in 1973 and uses it for revolving shows of modern art, mostly by young Mexican artists. Occasional theater shows are also staged in the cavernous interior, which has the ambience of a train station but boasts wonderful light from all the colored stained glass. A small café at the museum serves coffee and snacks. At the rear of the museum is the **Cinematógrafo del Chopo,** run by UNAM and showing art movies daily. For information check in the newspaper, call, or look it up on the Web at www.chopo.unam.mx. At Calle Dr. Enrique González 10, a block from the intersection of Insurgentes and San Cosme (look for the iron towers), tel. 5546-5484. San Cosme is the closest Metro stop. Open Tues.–Sun. 10 A.M.–2 P.M. and 3–7 P.M.; admission US$.70, free on Sunday.

Just around the museum on Avenida San Cosme is a fine colonial-era palace, **Casa de los Mascarones.** Now a branch of UNAM, the palace was built in the mid-19th century by José Vivero Hurtado de Mendoza, who also owned the Casa de los Azulejos downtown. Although there's not much to see apart from the building itself, if you happen to be in the area and have an interest in colonial buildings you could take a peek inside.

La Alameda de Santa María

The center of Santa María is the lovely Alameda, a leafy, tranquil park with an unusual brightly colored arabesque-style kiosk in the middle, built in 1904. On weekends the park is replete with local families out for an afternoon stroll, boys playing soccer, or young couples seeking out a quiet nook. On the west side of the Alameda is UNAM's **Museo de Geología,** housed in a beautiful old mansion. The displays of meteorites, fossils, and some impressive mammoth skeletons, as well as the opportunity to wander around the old building, are well worth the US$1 admission charge. Check out the imposing art nouveau wrought-iron staircase in the entryway. Guided tours of the museum can be arranged by calling ahead and are even available in English if the museum director (who speaks English) is around. Open Tues.–Sun. 10 A.M.–5 P.M.; tel. 5547-3900.

If you're craving a snack while in Santa María, stop into **La Querencia,** an inexpensive and popular little restaurant on the northeast corner of the Alameda, at the intersection of Atl and Carpio, open daily 8 A.M.–10 P.M.

Árbol de la Noche Triste

On the night of the Noche Triste, June 30, 1520, the Aztecs revolted and expelled the Spanish conquistadors from Tenochtitlán, driving them out of the city in the middle of the night along the Tacuba causeway, killing many and sending the rest fleeing for their lives. The story goes that when the remaining band of conquistadors finally managed to get to the far end of the causeway, on dry land again, Cortés leaned up against a tree and cried. And then, a testament to the will of this ferociously determined soldier, he pulled himself together and asked his company only one thing: did the carpenter survive? It turns out he had. And so Cortés immediately began his next move, the building of a fleet of brigantines that the Spaniards used to launch an amphibious assault on the city, eventually taking it.

If you can believe it, the tree that Cortés cried against still exists. It's along Avenida Mexico-Tacuba (which is the extension of Avenida Puente de Alvarado/San Cosme), between Metro stations Cuitlahuac and Popotla. The burnt-out, destroyed tree trunk, with a small bust of Cortés nestled inside and surrounded by a metal fence, is not much of a sight to see itself. But anyone with a fascination with Mexican history will feel a shiver at the legendary spot. If you go by Metro, get off at the Popotla station, but better yet hop a *microbus* or take a taxi along Avenida Mexico-Tacuba, and imagine yourself on the ancient Aztec causeway. Along the route you'll see a few old churches, the imposing Colegio Militar, and several old mansions from the years when this was the spot for wealthy residents to have their country homes.

San Rafael

South of Avenida Mexico-Tacuba is Colonia San Rafael, another once-upscale neighborhood that has slid into decline. In recent years younger, bohemian Mexicans, along with a smattering of expatriates, have begun moving into San Rafael, which could signal an impending re-gentrification of the neighborhood. To get a taste for the old *casonas* for which San Rafael was famous, take a walk down Calle Sadi Carnot, Avenida Mexico-Tacuba, and Monumento a la Madre, near the intersection of Insurgentes and Paseo de la Reforma. Numbers 33 and 35 are fine old mansions, and at 57 is the

Universidad de Del Valle, tel. 5628-6375, partly housed in a restored palace.

Farther south, at Francisco Pimentel 3, is **Ace Gallery,** tel. 5546-9001, an international art gallery with revolving exhibits of visual (and occasionally performance) art in a restored *casona.*

In and Around Chapultepec

Five kilometers west of the Zócalo along Paseo de la Reforma, Bosque de Chapultepec is filled with some of the city's finest museums, green grass and trees, small lakes, and plenty of families out for a stroll, especially on Sunday. At the eastern edge of the park, crowning a 60-meter bluff, is the 18th-century Castillo de Chapultepec, a city landmark.

Generations of *capitalinos* have used Bosque de Chapultepec's 1,655 acres of trees and meadows to escape the travails of the city. On weekends the grass is covered with families out for a picnic, lovers seeking secluded spots, and all manner of random folks out for a breath of fresh air. During the week the park is usually much more *tranquilo.* The main section of the park is closed on Monday.

Just north of Chapultepec is the wealthy neighborhood of Polanco, filled with upscale hotels, restaurants, and boutiques. To the south is Tacubaya, a run-down neighborhood with a couple of interesting museums housed in mansions from the area's more genteel past.

HISTORY

The hill and forests of Chapultepec ("Grasshopper Hill" in Náhuatl) have occupied a special place in Mexican history since the beginning of the Aztec era. On arriving in the Valle de México in the early 1200s from their original homeland in northern Mexico, the small band of Aztecs, unwelcomed by the valley's other inhabitants, found a temporary home on Chapultepec, and it was there that they held their first "New Fire" ceremony in the valley. Shortly thereafter, the Aztecs suffered their first great defeat on Chapultepec at the hands of the neighboring Tepanecs, who forced the tribe to serve as slave-mercenaries.

Once the Aztecs had emerged from servitude to dominate the valley, Chapultepec became the hunting grounds and summer retreat of successive Aztec rulers. Aztec ally Nezahualcóyotl, the famed poet-king of Texcoco, had his own palace on the hill. In 1465, with the inauguration of the first aqueduct, it also became the principal water supply for the island city of Tenochtitlán. Aztec leaders ordered their likenesses carved into the side of the hill, the fragments of which still exist today, although they are not visible to the public. The caves on the side of the rocky bluff were thought to be the sacred resting place of the last ruler of the Toltecs, whom the Aztecs believed to be their predecessors.

During the Spanish invasion of Mexico, a group of Spanish soldiers attacked an Aztec garrison at Chapultepec in 1521 and subsequently destroyed the aqueduct and cut Tenochtitlán's water supply in preparation for the subsequent siege of the city. The aqueduct was quickly repaired after the conquest, and in 1537 King Carlos V of Spain declared the forests around Chapultepec a protected area for "the good of the population," making it Mexico's first designated nature preserve.

Not that the colonial public was allowed to frolic in the woods, of course: it remained the favored retreat for the Spanish viceroys and governing elite. It was finally turned into a public park by President Lázaro Cárdenas in the 1930s.

Toward the end of the 19th century, the Chapultepec springs that supplied the city with *agua gorda* (literally "fat water," meaning rich in minerals) for more than 400 years finally dried up because of the drainage of the valley's lakes and the sinking level of groundwater. The only remaining traces of Chapultepec's once-great water system are the Baños de Moctezuma, now a concrete pool surrounded by a fence, and the grievously mistreated colonial fountain outside the Chapultepec Metro station, where the aqueduct began. Most of the aqueduct itself was destroyed around the beginning of the 20th century, but 22 of its original 904 arches still stand, looking a bit forlorn, along Avenida Chapultepec, near the Sevilla Metro station.

ORIENTATION

Chapultepec park extends from the eastern entrance on Paseo de la Reforma several miles to the west and is bordered on the south by Avenida Constituyentes and on the north (for much of the way at least) by Paseo de la Reforma. The park is divided into three sections: the first closest to downtown and containing most of the museums and sites of interest for tourists, and the second and third west of the Periférico, with an amusement park, children's museum, two restaurants, and plenty of spots for picnics or a jog.

Two tourist information booths can help visitors with basic questions in English and Spanish. One is at the corner of Reforma and Gandhi, near the Museo Rufino Tamayo, and the second is just inside the park from Reforma by the lakes. Both are open Tues.–Sun. 9 A.M.–6 P.M.

Getting There and Away

The first section of Chapultepec is accessible easily enough from the Chapultepec or Auditorio Metro stations. The Chapultepec station works better for El Castillo and the two art museums, while Auditorio is closer to the zoo. The Museo Nacional de Antropología lies more or less midway between the two stations. If you prefer to take a bus, hop one of the *peseros* marked Auditorio near the Hidalgo Metro station, at the western end of the Alameda. These run as far as the Auditorio Nacional. The public is not allowed to drive in the first section, though you may see the occasional park vehicle.

To get to the second section, catch a *pesero* marked La Feria, Papalote from the Chapultepec Metro station. *Peseros* to the third section also leave from Chapultepec Metro and are marked Panteón Dolores. Several roads cut through the second and third sections, making all the sites there accessible by car.

PRIMERA SECCIÓN (FIRST SECTION)

Closest to downtown and with most of Chapultepec's favorite sights, the Primera Sección is where most tourists are likely to end up. Here you'll find Cerro Chapultepec itself, crowned by the castle, as well as the zoo and three museums: Museo Nacional de Antropología, Museo de Arte Moderno, and Museo Rufino Tamayo. The grounds around Cerro Chapultepec, particularly to the south toward Avenida Constituyentes, have long shady paths perfect for strolling, cycling, or rollerblading. A small train leaves from near the castle for regular 20-minute narrated (in Spanish) tours around the park for US$1. Rent a bicycle to cruise the park near the Paseo de la Reforma entrance for US$3.50 per hour.

On the **Lago Mayor** (Bigger Lake) and **Lago Menor** (Smaller Lake) swans and ducks mingle with canoes and rowboats. Rent a rowboat for a paddle around the lake for US$1 per hour. The ballet *Swan Lake,* complete with live swans, is presented on an small island in Lago Mayor on weekends in February and March. In the verdant **Jardín de la Tercera Edad** (literally, Garden of the Third Age), the city's senior citizens practice aerobics, yoga, tai chi, and other fitness activities.

On the southwestern edge of the first section, surrounded by extensive grounds, stands the presidential mansion **Los Pinos.** Don't try hopping fences over that way unless you want to cause an international incident.

The first section of Bosque de Chapultepec is open Tuesday–Sunday 5 A.M.–4:30 P.M. Bicycles and rollerblades are allowed, but pets and alcoholic drinks are not.

Museo Nacional de Antropología e Historia

The largest museum in Latin America, and one of the great anthropological museums of the world, the Museo de Antropología is a must-see for most foreign visitors to Mexico City. The museum recounts the crossing of the first hunter-gatherers from Asia onto the North American continent and has magnificent archaeological

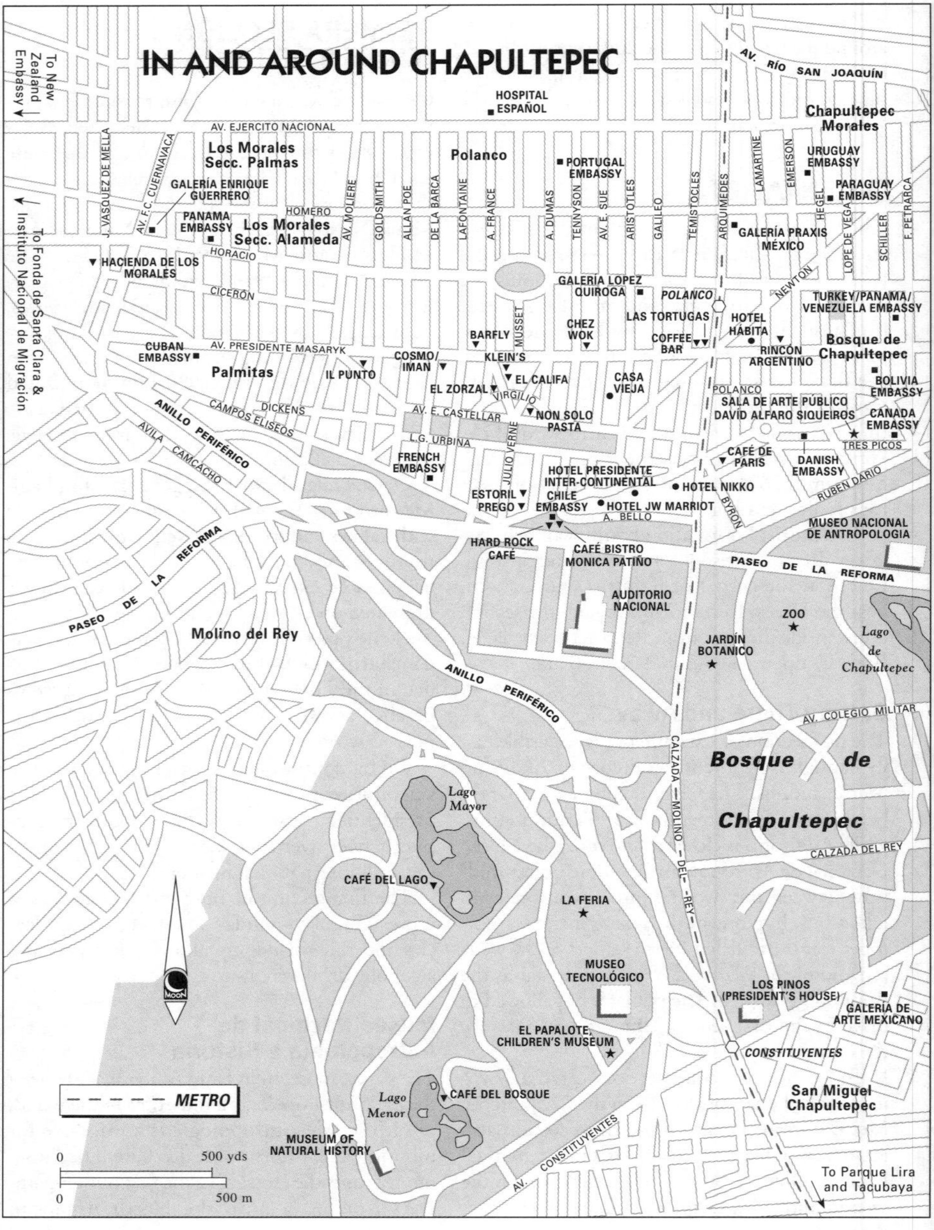
IN AND AROUND CHAPULTEPEC
To New Zealand Embassy
To Fonda de Santa Clara & Instituto Nacional de Migración
AV. RÍO SAN JOAQUÍN
HOSPITAL ESPAÑOL
Chapultepec Morales
AV. EJERCITO NACIONAL
Los Morales Secc. Palmas
Polanco
PORTUGAL EMBASSY
URUGUAY EMBASSY
PARAGUAY EMBASSY
J. VASQUEZ DE MELLA
AV. F.C. CUERNAVACA
GALERÍA ENRIQUE GUERRERO
PANAMA EMBASSY
Los Morales Secc. Alameda
HOMERO
HORACIO
AV. MOLIERE
GOLDSMITH
ALLAN POE
DE LA BARCA
LAFONTAINE
A. FRANCE
A. DUMAS
TENNYSON
AV. E. SUE
ARISTOTLES
GALILEO
TEMISTOCLES
ARQUIMEDES
LAMARTINE
EMERSON
HEGEL
LOPE DE VEGA
SCHILLER
F. PETRARCA
GALERÍA PRAXIS MÉXICO
HACIENDA DE LOS MORALES
CICERÓN
GALERÍA LOPEZ QUIROGA
POLANCO
NEWTON
TURKEY/PANAMA/ VENEZUELA EMBASSY
MUSSET
LAS TORTUGAS
HOTEL HÁBITA
CHEZ WOK
BARFLY
COFFEE BAR
RINCÓN ARGENTINO
Bosque de Chapultepec
CUBAN EMBASSY
AV. PRESIDENTE MASARYK
COSMO/ IMAN
KLEIN'S
IL PUNTO
Palmitas
EL CALIFA
CASA VIEJA
BOLIVIA EMBASSY
EL ZORZAL
VIRGILIO
POLANCO
SALA DE ARTE PÚBLICO DAVÍD ALFARO SIQUEIROS
CANADA EMBASSY
DICKENS
CAMPOS ELISEOS
AV. E. CASTELLAR
NON SOLO PASTA
TRES PICOS
ANILLO PERIFÉRICO
AVILA CAMCACHO
L.G. URBINA
FRENCH EMBASSY
JULIO VERNE
CAFÉ DE PARIS
DANISH EMBASSY
RUBEN DARIO
HOTEL PRESIDENTE INTER-CONTINENTAL
HOTEL NIKKO
ESTORIL
PREGO
CHILE EMBASSY
HOTEL JW MARRIOT
BYRON
A. BELLO
MUSEO NACIONAL DE ANTROPOLOGIA
HARD ROCK CAFÉ
CAFÉ BISTRO MONICA PATIÑO
PASEO DE LA REFORMA
AUDITORIO NACIONAL
ZOO
Lago de Chapultepec
JARDÍN BOTANICO
Molino del Rey
ANILLO PERIFÉRICO
AV. COLEGIO MILITAR
CALZADA MOLINO DEL REY
Bosque de Chapultepec
Lago Mayor
CALZADA DEL REY
CAFÉ DEL LAGO
LA FERIA
MOON
MUSEO TECNOLÓGICO
LOS PINOS (PRESIDENT'S HOUSE)
GALERÍA DE ARTE MEXICANO
EL PAPALOTE, CHILDREN'S MUSEUM
CONSTITUYENTES
METRO
Lago Menor
CAFÉ DEL BOSQUE
San Miguel Chapultepec
MUSEUM OF NATURAL HISTORY
AV. CONSTITUYENTES
0
500 yds
0
500 m
To Parque Lira and Tacubaya

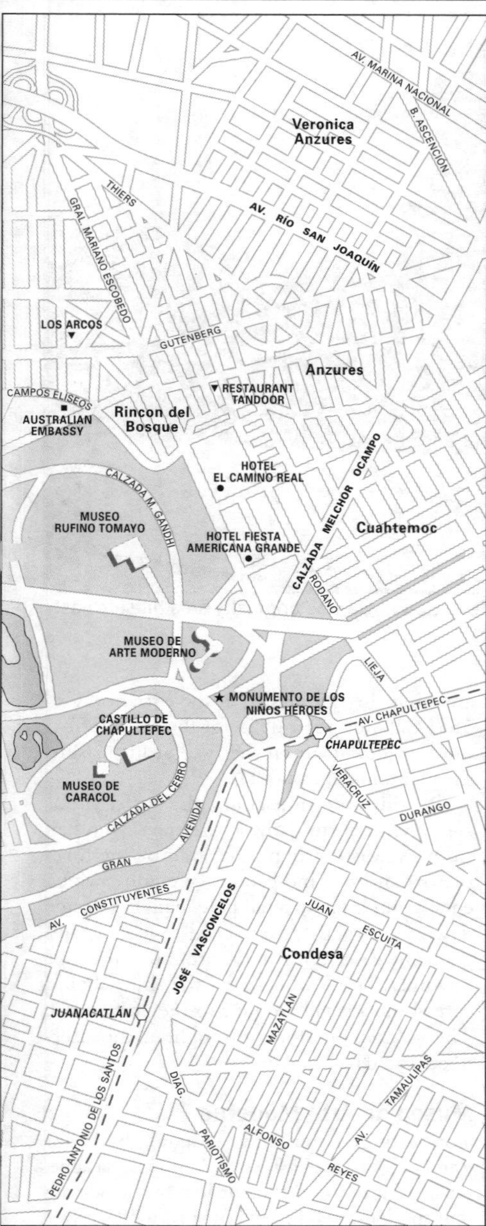

exhibits from early Mesoamerican societies as well as ethnological displays on Mexico's current Amerindian groups.

Apart from its archaeological and anthropological treasures, Pedro Ramírez Vásquez's building itself is an impressive work of art, with its understated exterior and dramatic central patio. In the middle of the patio, a sheer curtain of water flows from a huge overhang supported by a single concrete column. The column is covered with sculpted reliefs depicting events in Mexican history. Out front is a massive sculpture of Tlaloc, the Aztec god of rain, which came from a mountainside east of Mexico City.

The museum is laid out in two floors, with 23 exhibition rooms. Each room on the first floor is dedicated to the archaeology of particular geographic areas or cultures throughout Mexican history. Casual visitors may want to skip the first two rooms, dedicated to the profession of anthropology and Mesoamerica in general, and move directly to the "Origins" room. Here begins the chronological tracing of different civilizations that grew up in Mexico over the centuries, including Teotihuacanos, Toltecs, Olmecs, Zapotecs, and others, right up to the Aztecs. Many of the finest pieces of pre-Hispanic art anywhere in the world are found in the rooms on this floor. Upstairs, rooms focus on the anthropology and ethnography of different indigenous groups in Mexico today, including the Huichol, Cora, Purépecha, Otomí, Nahua, and different groups from the Sierra de Puebla, Oaxaca, and Gulf of Mexico region. The exhibits are exhaustively labeled in both Spanish and English, providing a veritable university course of anthropology for those who take the time to read them all.

A full day is required to get an adequate tour of the museum, and many people with a serious interest in Mexican history spend two. But don't be daunted: if you have just a casual interest in the subject, two or three hours of popping in and out of different halls will give you an excellent taste. Take in the museum's 20-minute orientation film before setting out to tour the five km of walkways, patios, and exhibit halls. If you need to catch your breath, have a snack at the

© ELENA PAPPAS

The Tlaloc rain god statue in front of the Museo de Antropología was originally on a hillside east of Mexico City near Texcoco.

lower-level café or check out the well-stocked bookstore (both English and Spanish titles are available). Rent headsets with taped information (in English or Spanish) for US$6—a good value to save your eyes from getting tired reading labels all day.

During 1999, the museum's rooms were in the process of overhaul, both to make display changes and to include new archaeological data in the exhibits' explanatory information. The work was to be completed by mid-2000, but has since dragged on. At last report several of the rooms were still closed, but let's hope they will reopen soon.

The museum is on Paseo de la Reforma, just west of the Museo Rufino Tamayo. Open Tues.–Sat. 9 A.M.–7 P.M., Sun. 10 A.M.–6 P.M. Entry to the museum costs US$4 per person, free on Sunday (when it's always packed), or US$10 for admission with a camera. **Note:** No flash photography is allowed. If you don't want to pay the fee, you can check your cameras and anything else not needed at the entrance. Call 5553-6285 or 5553-6554 for further information, or look it up on the Web at http://sunsite.unam.mx/antropol/.

Outside the museum, the vertiginous *voladores* perform daily. These men, who hail from the eastern State of Veracruz, perform their traditional indigenous ceremony, which entails climbing up a tall pole, hanging upside down with their feet attached to a rope, and gradually descending to the ground as the rope unwinds. Those who watch the show should contribute a small amount to the performers. The *voladores* perform throughout the afternoon Tuesday–Sunday.

Museo de Arte Moderno

This dark glass building, designed by Pedro Ramírez Vásquez of Museo de Antropología fame, looks a bit drab on the outside, but inside are four spacious, well-lit exhibition halls off a broad central stairway. Three rooms are dedicated to rotating exhibits of sometimes excellent quality (a fine show of Cartier-Bresson photography is one recent example), while the fourth displays selections from the museum's permanent collection, including Mexican greats Diego Rivera, José Clemente Orozco, Rufino Tamayo, Dr. Atl, and many others. One of the galleries contains Frida Kahlo's largest work, *Las Dos Fridas* (1939), in which twin portraits of the artist are joined by arteries looping from the exposed hearts of each figure. Also notable are some 1920s paintings by Ángel Zárraga.

The museum is between Paseo de la Reforma and the Monumento de los Niños Héroes (entrance on Reforma). Open Tues.–Sun. 10 A.M.–6 P.M.; admission US$2, free on Sunday. Call 5553-6233 for further information.

Museo de Arte Contemporáneo Internacional Rufino Tamayo

A Zapotec Indian born in Oaxaca in 1899, Rufino Tamayo is one of the great Mexican painters of the 20th century. Heavily influenced by his indigenous roots, Tamayo gained fame in the 1950s (when he was living in New York) for his dramatic use of colors, particularly the earth tones from his native state. In 1981, he and his wife, Olga, donated this museum along with a fabulous collection of modern art, consisting partly of his works, plus works of Salvador Dalí, Max Ernst, Gunther Gerzso, Alberto Giacometti, Willem de Kooning, René Magritte, Joan Miró, Andy Warhol, and many others. Tamayo died in 1991 at the age of 91.

A modernistic red sculpture sits in front of the odd, bunkerlike modernist building of concrete and white marble, hidden away amid a stand of trees. World-class traveling exhibits change frequently in the 10 halls around a central patio. Check the local newspapers or the tourist office for a current list of exhibits, or look up the museum on the Web at www.museotamayo.org. The museum installed a cyberlounge in 2001, dedicated to art on the Internet. The museum is east of the Museo Nacional de Antropología at Paseo de la Reforma and Gandhi. Open Tues.–Sun. 10 A.M.–6 P.M.; admission US$2, free on Sunday. Call 5286-5889 for further information.

El Castillo de Chapultepec

Standing at attention atop Cerro Chapultepec, the original Castillo was built by Viceroy Bernardo de Gálvez in 1785. While Chapultepec was historically the "weekend" home of Aztecs and viceroys, the previous villas had been on the southern side of the hill, near Chapultepec's spring, while a temple (either Aztec or Catholic) crowned the hilltop. Evidently Viceroy de Gálvez had defensive considerations in mind when he decided to build atop the hill. As it would happen El Castillo—at that time housing the nation's military college—would be the last, and ultimately unsuccessful, bastion of defense against the U.S. Army during its 1847 invasion of Mexico City.

The castle took its current shape during the brief rule of Emperor Maximilian (1863–67). Feeling uncomfortable in the tradition-laden Palacio Nacional downtown, Maximilian declared El Castillo to be his official residence, and he and his wife, Carlota, set about remodeling it to their liking during 1865 and 1866 in a vain effort to re-create a little corner of Europe that might shut out the problems of Maximilian's disastrous government. Mexicans heaped criticism on their short-lived emperor for spending so much money on the grand salons, flowered terraces, and rooftop garden.

After Maximilian and Carlota were overthrown by Benito Juárez, the castle was converted to the Mexican presidential residence. In 1876 Porfirio Díaz moved in, and under the dictator the castle's interior reached new heights of sumptuousness. President Lázaro Cárdenas, disliking the elaborate palace, moved to the more modest residence of Los Pinos in 1939, and the castle became a national history museum.

Perhaps because of its multiple historical roles, El Castillo looks as though it can't decide if it's a Gothic fortress or a Mediterranean palace. The two-story gray stone building is divided into two distinct sections. The Alcázar, formerly the living quarters of Maximilian and Díaz, is a series of rooms and terraces laid out around a central courtyard. The different rooms are filled with 19th-century furniture, artwork, and musical instruments. The patios, once open to the air,

© CHRIS HUMPHREY

El Castillo de Chapultepec

have been covered with glass to protect the antiques and art inside. The Alcázar was closed for a year in 1999–2000 for restoration and to allow archaeologists access to the grounds below the building to learn more about the past of this key location in Mexican history.

The more stolid, heavy-looking main wing of the castle houses a museum chronicling the nation's turbulent history between conquest and the Revolution. An extensive collection of artifacts, documents, and paintings of modern Mexican history is displayed in 20 rooms on both floors. Among the noteworthy art objects are murals by Juan O'Gorman (of Mexican history), Davíd Alfaro Siqueiros (of Revolutionary leaders), and José Clemente Orozco (of Benito Juárez).

Outside the castle, a side terrace garden makes a quiet place to sit, rest, and admire the views (air quality permitting). Just down the stairs from the terrace is a small, dingy snack shop (good for soft drinks at least).

The castle and Alcázar are open Tuesday–Sunday 10 A.M.–5 P.M.; admission US$4.

Museo Caracol

This museum, also known by the overlengthy name Museo Galería de la Lucha del Pueblo Mexicano por su Libertad (Gallery Museum of the Struggle of the Mexican People for Freedom), is housed in a snail-shaped building (hence the name, which means "snail") just below the entrance to the castle. The museum's exhibits consist mostly of historical dioramas of unremarkable quality, highlighted by a carved eagle looming over a replica of Mexico's 1917 Constitution. At last report the museum was closed for an overhaul, with several changes planned for the exhibits. One hopes the new displays are a step up from the old ones. Open Tues.–Sat. 9 A.M.–4:30 P.M., Sun. 10 A.M.–3:30 P.M.; admission US$1, free on Sunday. The entrance can be tricky to find—take the path down from the main entrance of the castle, and keep an eye out on your left. For further information, call 5553-6285.

Monumento de los Niños Héroes

Right below the castle at the foot of Cerro Chapultepec, this six-towered monument commemorates a heroic though ultimately doomed defense of the castle against invading U.S. troops during the Mexican-American War on the part of a thousand Mexican soldiers and a few dozen military cadets. On September 13, 1847, when it was clear the Americans would take the castle, six military cadets—Juan de la Barrera, Juan Escutia, Fernando Montes de Oca, Vicente Suárez, Francisco Marquéz, and Agustín Melgar—reputedly wrapped themselves in Mexican flags and jumped to their deaths from the castle ramparts rather than surrender. Their deaths are honored by six tall columns, each topped with a black eagle. On September 13, the Mexican president holds a solemn national ceremony honoring the cadets.

Behind the main monument, right up against the edge of the hill, is a smaller monument, a semicircle with paintings of each of the six cadets. Right behind the fence here, archaeologists have made some fascinating discoveries in recent years, including Aztec carvings in the rock and burials dating from the era of Teotihuacán, around the time of Christ. At the moment the area is closed to the public, but it may be opened in the future.

Zoológico de Chapultepec

The Chapultepec Zoo houses about 1,600 animals of 270 species, the most famous of which are a family of pandas. As zoos go it's relatively humane, giving most animals plenty of room to roam. If you're tired of walking take the minitrain from the station in the center of the zoo. Admission to the zoo is free, but there is a small charge for the train ride. Open Tues.–Sun. 9 A.M.–4:15 P.M. Next to the zoo is the park's botanical gardens.

Also next door is the **Casa del Lago,** a cultural center run by UNAM often showing art exhibits or holding cultural events. For more information, call at 5211-6093, or visit on the Web at www.casadellago.unam.mx.

Baños de Moctezuma

Around on the south side of Cerro Chapultepec, following the paved road from behind the Niños Héroes monument, lie the dilapidated remains of the Baños de Moctezuma. Legend has it Moctezuma once threw treasure into the well on the south side of hill to placate Tlaloc, the Aztec rain god, when the city was flooded. As a result, treasure hunters from across the centuries have dug all around the area, so far in vain. Even though the baths aren't much to see nowadays, it's worth wandering over that way to enjoy walking in a quieter part of the park.

Just above the *baños* one can see channels cut into the rock where the old springs welled up, supplying Mexico City with much of its drinking water. Up until the mid-1900s water still rose here, but it's now long gone.

SEGUNDA SECCIÓN (SECOND SECTION)

On the west side of the Periférico highway lies Chapultepec's second section. The main attractions here include a children's museum, an amusement park, and two upscale restaurants: Café del Lago and Café del Bosque (see Food and Drink). Mexico City residents seeking a place to exercise near the city frequent the meadows and stands of trees to jog and kick a soccer ball on weekends. Just up an old flight of steps in front of the roller coaster are several large, circular old water storage tanks that have been filled in with dirt and now serve as impromptu soccer fields.

La Feria de Chapultepec

This amusement park is found in the western section of the park, on the far side of the Periférico from El Castillo. It's easy to spot—just look for the towering *montaña rusa,* (Russian mountain, as roller coasters are known here). Admission costs US$7 and includes a pass for all rides. Open daily 10 A.M.–9 P.M.

Museo del Niño (Children's Museum)

Popularly known as El Papalote, the bright blue, oddly shaped building just south of the amusement park at the edge of the Periférico hosts an excellent interactive children's museum. On the premises are 380 "touch, play, and learn" exhibits on science, the human body, communications, and other subjects. The museum has limited capacity, meaning you may have to wait (usually not long) before being allowed into the museum. Admission costs US$3 adults, US$2.50 children, kids under two enter free. Tickets can be bought in advance through TicketMaster, tel. 5325-9000. Open Mon.–Fri. 9 A.M.–1 P.M. and 2–6 P.M., weekends 10 A.M.–2 P.M. and 3–7 P.M. For more information, call 5237-1881 or log onto the website: www.papalote.org.mx.

Museo Tecnológico

Unless you have a particular fascination with the Mexican government's heroic progress generating power for the country, there's not much to see in this electricity museum between the Papalote and the amusement park. Open daily 9 A.M.–5 P.M.; free.

TERCERA SECCIÓN (THIRD SECTION)

Past the Panteón Dolores is the newest section of Chapultepec, added only in the 1970s as the city expanded to the west. The third section is a jumble of ravines, meadows, patches of forest, and a few caves, not really developed for visitors beyond a few picnic tables set up by the roadside. Aside from the grounds of the horse club (see below), it's unfortunately not the safest place to go walking or jogging—better to stick to the first and second sections.

Water Parks

Right off Avenida Constituyentes, just west of the Panteón Dolores, is a playground with water rides and a wave pool (no surfboards) called **El Rollo.** It's open 10 A.M.–6 P.M. weekends and holidays only; admission is a steep US$7 for adults, US$3 for kids 1.2 meters and under.

Next door, **Atlantis** presents an animal show for kids, with jumping dolphins, theatrical parrots, and other amusements. Open weekends only 11 A.M.–6 P.M.; tel. 5277-7583.

Centro Hípico de la Ciudad de México

Deep in the middle of the third section, reached only by car, is a municipal horseback riding school and boarding stables for private horse-owners. Classes run US$110 per month for two lessons per week. No horse rental is available. For more information about classes, call 5540-4085.

A loop of paved road through a stretch of forest on the center's grounds is a popular spot for early-morning joggers, who appreciate the leafy surroundings and the center's guards, who keep away potential thieves. The grounds are open daily 6 A.M.–6 P.M. It costs US$1.50 to park your car on the grounds, or you can park outside for free.

Lienzo de Charro

Charreadas—the Mexican equivalent of the rodeo, but with considerably more finesse and pageantry—are held in the *charro* ring from time to time throughout the year. For current scheduling, contact the Asociación Nacional de la Charrería, tel. 5512-2523.

POLANCO

Opposite the Paseo de la Reforma from the first section of Chapultepec is Polanco, a Rodeo Drive–style area replete with modern high-rises, hotels, elegant shops, art galleries, embassies, and fine restaurants. Originally land belonging to a colonial silkworm farm known as Hacienda de los Morales, Polanco was subdivided and developed in the late 1930s and early 1940s and was for years the most exclusive neighborhood in Mexico City. While it is still the highest-end shopping district, many of the super-rich have moved farther west to Tecamachalco or Lomas.

Polanco may not have many tourist sites as such, but if you're after upscale lodgings, top-quality dining, and all the shopping you can handle, this is the place. Just be sure not to forget your wallet. Polanco is also home to many foreign embassies, so you may find yourself coming this way if you plan to travel elsewhere in Latin America from Mexico City. A perennial favorite among foreign visitors to Mexico City is **Hacienda de los Morales,** a superb restaurant specializing in traditional Mexican cuisine housed in a 16th-century hacienda. Find it near the Periférico at Calle Vázquez de Mella 525, tel. 5281-4703 or 5281-4554 (see Food and Drink for more details).

Fans of the Mexican muralist movement may

want to stop in **Museo Sala de Arte Público Davíd Alfaro Siqueiros,** Tres Picos 29, tel. 5203-5888. Here, in a private house donated by the artist shortly before his death in 1974, you'll find a permanent exhibit of his art, as well as temporary exhibits of other contemporary art. Open Tues.–Sun. 10 A.M.–6 P.M.; admission US$1.50.

Polanco is the home to some of Mexico City's finest art galleries, with both Mexican and international modern art. Three of the most established galleries are: **Galería Enrique Guerrero,** Horacio 1549A, tel. 5280-2941, focusing on more established artists; **Galería Lopez Quiroga,** Aristótles 169, tel. 5280-6218, specializing in contemporary Latin American and Mexican artists; and **Galería Praxis México,** Arquimedes 175, tel. 5254-8813, with more experimental Mexican and international art.

TACUBAYA

Now an unlovely neighborhood of elevated highways and rather dirty back streets, the sorely mistreated Colonia Tacubaya is one of the oldest settlement areas in the Valle de México. Although it's certainly not atop the list for tourists with a limited time in the city, those who have a more leisurely schedule or live in Mexico City might enjoy a day walking around the Tacubaya for a taste of an unusual corner of the city.

Tacubaya is situated at the edge of the long-gone lake, right where several small rivers come out of the hills; its name derives from an Aztec word meaning "where one drinks water." The area was controlled by the Tepanecas when the Aztecs arrived in the valley, but the intruders soon saw fit to conquer this strategic location. After the arrival of the Spanish, Tacubaya became one of the favored places for the colonial elite to live, because of its fresh air, clean water, and myriad orchards. For a brief time in the 17th century it was the colony's capital, when the downtown area was flooded for a period of five years. Tacubaya was also the birthplace of Mexican industry, with the construction of mills along the Becerra, Tacubaya, and de la Piedad Rivers. Only one mill, the Santo Domingo, still exists today, but it contains private homes and is not open for visitors.

Parque Lira and Casa de la Bola

A little corner of leafy tranquility amid the avenues of Tacubaya is this medium-sized park, easily reached from Metro Tacubaya, or via taxi along Avenida Parque Lira or Avenida Observatorio. Giving a magnificent taste of what life was like in Tacubaya during its era of colonial glory is the Casa de la Bola, an unusual and little-known museum in an old mansion in a corner of the park. Step off the noisy avenues through the doors of the Casa de la Bola and the blissfully calm courtyard and garden will make the city seem a distant dream.

Built in the early 1600s, this lovely mansion was first the home of Mexico's grand inquisitor, after which it changed hands frequently over the years before its last owner, Antonio Haghenbeck y de la Lama, donated it to the government in the 1940s. Haghenbeck maintained the two-story house much as it had looked during the colonial era, supplementing the decor with his own unusually rich tastes, judging from all the fine furniture, tapestries, and artwork inside.

The house opens for guided tours on Sunday only, 11 A.M.–5 P.M., or on other days by appointment only. Admission costs US$2.50. Casa de la Bola, tel. 5515-8825, stands at Av. Parque Lira 136, at the corner of Av. Observatorio.

At the northern end of Parque Lira is the **Delegación Miguel Hidalgo building,** the administrative offices for this part of the city. Evidently a former colonial hacienda, the sprawling red brick complex has the **Capilla de Nuestra Señora de Guadalupe** on site.

Across Avenida Parque Lira, a several-block walk through the San Miguel Chapultepec neighborhood, is the first still-operating art gallery in Mexico City, **Galería de Arte Mexicano,** Gobernador Rafael Rebollar 43, tel. 5273-1261, email: artgam@prodigy.net.mx.

Museo Nacional de la Cartografía

Seemingly trapped amid a sea of concrete and traffic, right at the intersection of the Periférico and Avenida Observatorio, is this former Franciscan convent dedicated to San Diego, built in 1590, with a chapel on one side erected a century later. The red domed building with a simple facade and a small park shaded with palm trees out front has seen a turbulent history. It was taken over by the Dominicans in the late 17th century, then closed in 1827 by the government because the convent authorities had supported the Spaniards against the Mexican independence movement. During the U.S. invasion in 1847, the church was the site of a prisoner exchange between the Mexicans and the invaders. It was briefly reopened as a church in the late 1800s but was taken over by the government in 1918.

Nowadays the building houses an interesting museum of maps and is run by the Mexican military. Inside are copies of old codices and many fascinating maps of Mexico City and the country as a whole, as well as old mapmaking gear such as compasses, cameras, projectors, and GPS instruments, all housed amid the bare walls of the old church. For an idea of how Mexico City has grown, check out the satellite photo showing how the city has changed over 110 years. Open Mon.–Sat. 10 A.M.–6 P.M., Sun. 10 A.M.–4 P.M.; free admission.

Insurgentes Sur

Along both sides of Avenida Insurgentes Sur, between the Zona Rosa and San Ángel, lies a series of residential neighborhoods, including Roma, Condesa, Del Valle, Nápoles, and Mixcoac. While only the Roma merits a visit in its own right for a casual tourist, the Condesa boasts probably the trendiest restaurant district in the city at the moment.

ROMA

A tree-lined residential neighborhood between Avenida Cuauhtémoc and Insurgentes, south of Avenida Chapultepec, the Roma was the most upscale area of the city when it was built in the early 1900s, and in recent years it has once again become fashionable. Many of the old mansions, left to decay over the decades, have been renovated by wealthy residents with a taste for the neighborhood's genteel ambience, while others now house cafés and art galleries.

While the Roma does not have many tourist sights apart from the Casa Lamm cultural center, visitors may enjoy a couple of hours strolling the quiet, leafy streets lined with *porfiriato*-era mansions. Most casual tourists will want to walk around the Roma for an hour or two, visit the Casa Lamm, and have a cup of coffee or a meal somewhere before returning to their home or hotel. If you're interested in contemporary Mexican and Latin American art, you may wish to spend a few more hours touring the half-dozen galleries in the neighborhood.

Orientation

The Roma has Metro stations at each of its four corners, clockwise from the northwest: Metro Insurgentes, Metro Cuauhtémoc, Metro Centro Médico, and Metro Chilpancingo. For the Roma Norte, where most visitors will likely be going, Metro Insurgentes is the closest.

By bus from the Centro, take a *pesero* to Insurgentes, and change on another bus going south on Insurgentes. Get off just past the large traffic circle, about one km south of Reforma. The Roma is on the left (east) side of Insurgentes.

If you're in the Zona Rosa, it's just a 10-minute walk over to the Roma.

History

The building of the Roma was, in a sense, the last gasp of the Mexico City elite from the era of Porfirio Díaz, a final burst of upper-middle class optimism before the deluge of the Revolution. The neatly planned streets and boulevards, complete with electricity, running water, and dozens of mansions shamelessly imitating European styles (sometimes several styles at once), all pointed to the vain efforts of Mexico City's upper crust to cre-

THE LONG AND NOT SO WINDING ROAD

An appropriately hyperbolic avenue for this city of excess, Insurgentes stretches a full 45 km in length, from just short of Ecatepec in the northeast, at the exit to Pachuca, across the entire valley to Tlalpan and the highway to Cuernavaca in the south. By one counting (a local one, admittedly), it's the longest avenue in the world.

Lengthy Insurgentes came into being in the 1950s, shortly after the construction of the new university complex south of San Ángel, as the city government linked up dozens of smaller, unconnected roads to form the avenue.

Traffic on Insurgentes is proverbial. One of the jokes going around says the city government should hang strings of garlic on lampposts up and down Insurgentes to improve circulation. At the intersection with Avenida Mixcoac, one of the dozens of tangled traffic interchanges that turn into battle zones along Insurgentes during the afternoon, 15,000 cars pass per minute during peak hours.

While in the U.S. or Europe such a traffic artery would be given over exclusively to vehicles, millions of pedestrians swarm on and around Insurgentes day and night. It's practically an elongated city in its own right, a sort of urban epiphany, literally a cross-section of Mexico City life. The avenue passes through 60 of the city's 300-odd *colonias* and five of its 16 *delegaciones.* As of 1999, Insurgentes claimed 217 restaurants, 172 bars, 97 banks, 30 department stores, 12 gas stations, seven Metro stations (soon to be eight), four federal secretariat offices, the headquarters of the Institutional Revolutionary Party (PRI), and UNAM (the national university), to name only a few of the most prominent *avenida*-dwellers.

ate their own little pseudo-Paris, from which the unpleasant realities of Porfiriato Mexico could be conveniently shut out, at least for a time.

The Roma was planned and developed by a group of foreigners operating together as the Compañía de Terrenos de la Calzada de Chapultepec. The principal partners were Edward Walter Orrin, British owner of a Mexican traveling circus, and U.S. engineer Casius Clay Lamm and his sons. Porfirio Díaz Jr. also participated, which no doubt eased government approval. With the city growing rapidly westward, especially around the newly chic Paseo de la Reforma, the wealthy were clamoring to move out of the crumbling downtown and into better neighborhoods.

The land on which the Roma now stands is thought to have originally been "grown" from *chinampas,* the floating islands made of twigs, earth, and compost that were built on the lake for agricultural purposes, and which eventually became solid chunks of land. After the conquest, it became part of the estate granted by the Spanish crown to Hernán Cortés in 1529—thus forming one of Mexico's first *ejidos*—and by the early 20th century it was owned by descendents of the Conde de Miravalle.

In 1903 the Díaz administration gave permission to Orrin, Lamm, and crew to divide up the land into lots and committed itself to provide public services to the new development. Construction began immediately, and the Roma quickly became the chosen place to live for the second-level elite, as it were: wealthy families eager to move out of the decaying Centro but who could not afford to build on Paseo de la Reforma.

In the 1930s, the neighboring Condesa district became fashionable, and by the 1940s and 1950s, the Roma was slipping into decay. Many of the "better" families moved on to newer developments farther west in Polanco or Lomas, while poorer families migrating to Mexico City began to take over the old mansions and turn them into apartment buildings.

Nonetheless Roma remained trendy, but for the genteel poverty favored by many Mexican artists and intelligentsia. Because so many writ-

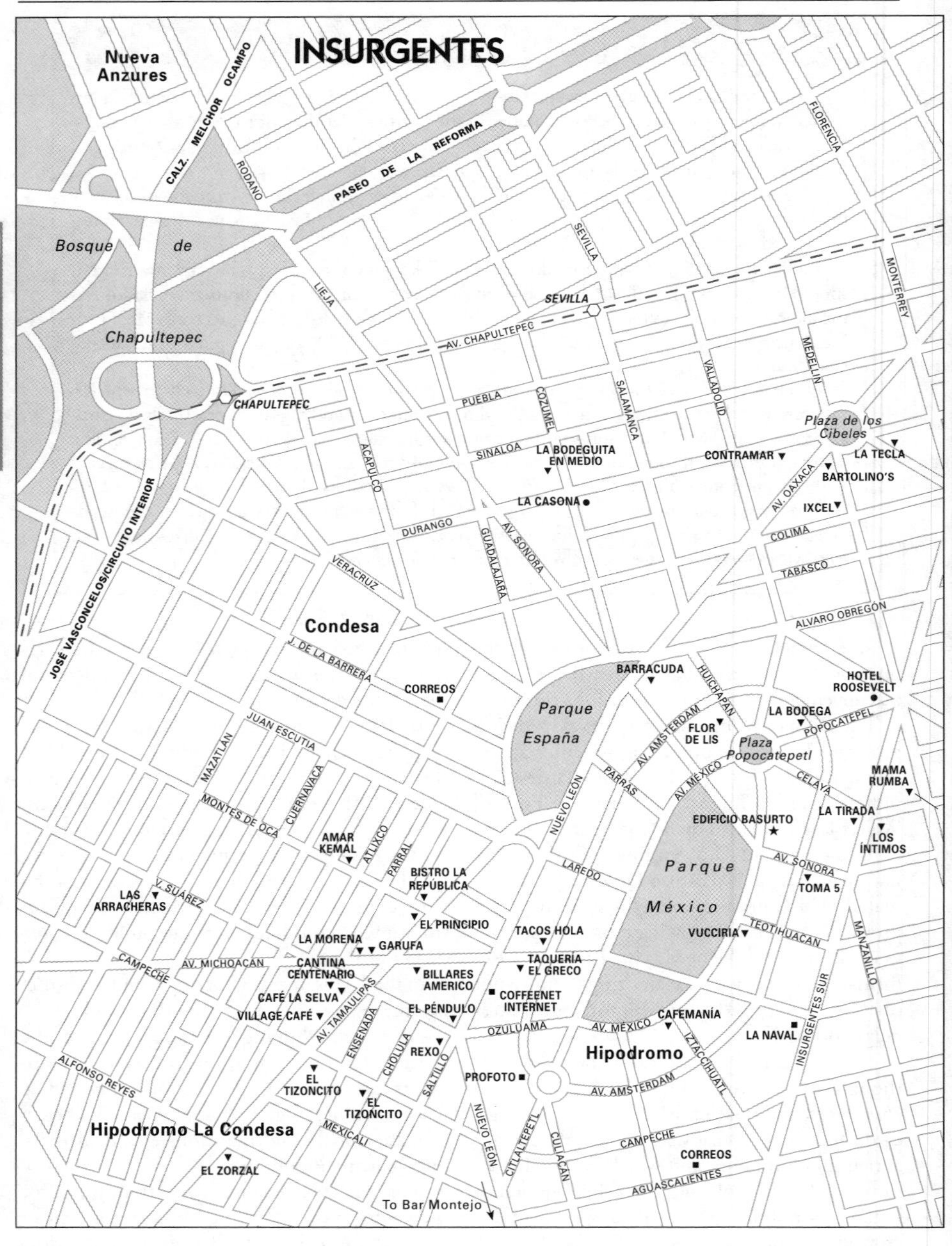

INSURGENTES
Nueva Anzures
CALZ. MELCHOR OCAMPO
PASEO DE LA REFORMA
RODANO
FLORENCIA
Bosque de Chapultepec
SEVILLA
LIEJA
MONTERREY
AV. CHAPULTEPEC
CHAPULTEPEC
MEDELLIN
VALLADOLID
SALAMANCA
COZUMEL
PUEBLA
Plaza de los Cibeles
SINALOA
LA BODEGUITA EN MEDIO
CONTRAMAR
LA TECLA
BARTOLINO'S
ACAPULCO
LA CASONA
AV. OAXACA
IXCEL
DURANGO
GUADALAJARA
AV. SONORA
COLIMA
TABASCO
VERACRUZ
ALVARO OBREGÓN
JOSÉ VASCONCELOS/CIRCUITO INTERIOR
Condesa
J. DE LA BARRERA
BARRACUDA
HUICHAPAN
HOTEL ROOSEVELT
CORREOS
Parque España
AV. AMSTERDAM
FLOR DE LIS
LA BODEGA
POPOCATEPETL
Plaza Popocatepetl
JUAN ESCUTIA
MAZATLAN
PARRAS
AV. MEXICO
CELAYA
MAMA RUMBA
NUEVO LEON
MONTES DE OCA
CUERNAVACA
EDIFICIO BASURTO
LA TIRADA
LOS ÍNTIMOS
AMAR KEMAL
ATLIXCO
PARRAL
LAREDO
Parque México
AV. SONORA
BISTRO LA REPÚBLICA
TOMA 5
LAS ARRACHERAS
V. SUAREZ
EL PRINCIPIO
TACOS HOLA
VUCCIRIA
TEOTIHUACAN
MANZANILLO
LA MORENA
GARUFA
CAMPECHE
AV. MICHOACÁN
CANTINA CENTENARIO
TAQUERÍA EL GRECO
BILLARES AMERICO
CAFÉ LA SELVA
AV. TAMAULIPAS
COFFEENET INTERNET
VILLAGE CAFÉ
EL PÉNDULO
ENSENADA
CAFEMANÍA
OZULUAMA
AV. MÉXICO
LA NAVAL
INSURGENTES SUR
REXO
CHOLULA
Hipodromo
ALFONSO REYES
EL TIZONCITO
PROFOTO
IZTACCIHUATL
SALTILLO
AV. AMSTERDAM
EL TIZONCITO
Hipodromo La Condesa
MEXICALI
NUEVO LEÓN
CITLALTEPETL
CULIACÁN
CAMPECHE
CORREOS
EL ZORZAL
AGUASCALIENTES
To Bar Montejo

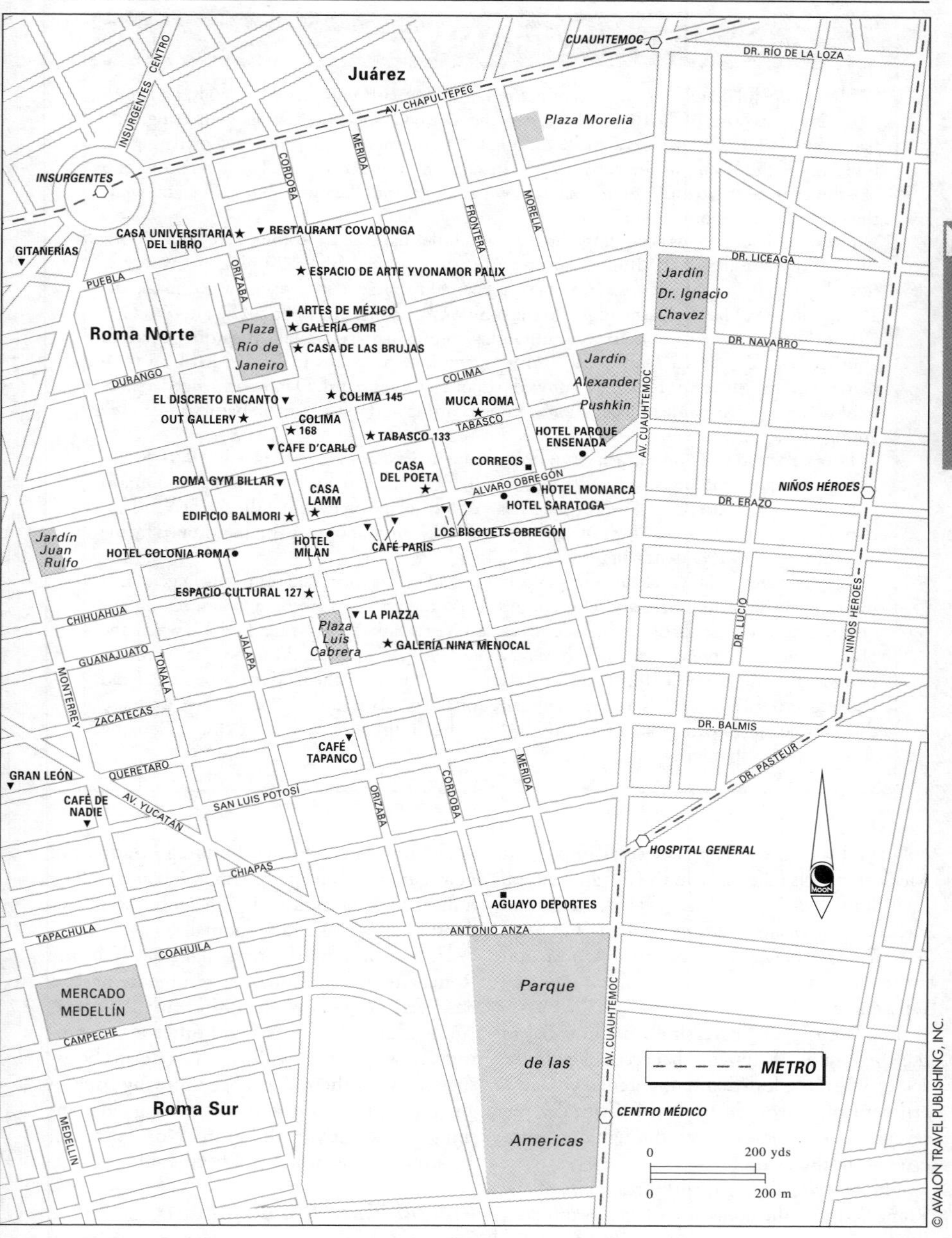
Juárez
CUAUHTEMOC
DR. RÍO DE LA LOZA
AV. CHAPULTEPEC
Plaza Morelia
INSURGENTES CENTRO
INSURGENTES
CORDOBA
MERIDA
FRONTERA
MORELIA
CASA UNIVERSITARIA DEL LIBRO
RESTAURANT COVADONGA
GITANERÍAS
ESPACIO DE ARTE YVONAMOR PALIX
PUEBLA
ORIZABA
ARTES DE MÉXICO
GALERÍA OMR
CASA DE LAS BRUJAS
Roma Norte
Plaza Río de Janeiro
DR. LICEAGA
Jardín Dr. Ignacio Chavez
DR. NAVARRO
Jardín Alexander Pushkin
AV. CUAUHTEMOC
DURANGO
COLIMA
EL DISCRETO ENCANTO
COLIMA 145
MUCA ROMA
OUT GALLERY
COLIMA 168
TABASCO
TABASCO 133
CAFE D'CARLO
HOTEL PARQUE ENSENADA
CORREOS
CASA DEL POETA
ROMA GYM BILLAR
CASA LAMM
ALVARO OBREGÓN
HOTEL MONARCA
HOTEL SARATOGA
NIÑOS HÉROES
DR. ERAZO
EDIFICIO BALMORI
HOTEL MILAN
CAFÉ PARIS
LOS BISQUETS OBREGÓN
Jardín Juan Rulfo
HOTEL COLONIA ROMA
ESPACIO CULTURAL 127
LA PIAZZA
CHIHUAHUA
Plaza Luis Cabrera
GALERÍA NINA MENOCAL
GUANAJUATO
TONALA
JALAPA
DR. LUCIO
NIÑOS HEROES
MONTERREY
ZACATECAS
DR. BALMIS
CAFÉ TAPANCO
DR. PASTEUR
GRAN LEÓN
QUERETARO
CAFÉ DE NADIE
AV. YUCATÁN
SAN LUIS POTOSÍ
ORIZABA
CORDOBA
MERIDA
HOSPITAL GENERAL
CHIAPAS
MOON
AGUAYO DEPORTES
ANTONIO ANZA
TAPACHULA
COAHUILA
MERCADO MEDELLÍN
CAMPECHE
Parque de las Americas
AV. CUAUHTEMOC
METRO
Roma Sur
CENTRO MÉDICO
MEDELLIN
0
200 yds
0
200 m
SIGHTS

LA ROMITA

The "shameful daughter of the Colonia Roma," as one early chronicler labeled it, La Romita is a tiny corner of the Roma Norte, near the Metro Chapultepec station, with a singularly bad reputation. La Romita was actually the original native village in the area, long predating the building of the Roma in the early 1900s. In fact, the original Roma developers fought a lengthy battle to try to incorporate what is now La Romita into their neighborhood plans, while the locals resisted tooth and nail.

From this inauspicious beginning, the plaza and little chapel of La Romita were off limits for the wealthy families of the Roma, who feared getting robbed by La Romita's many *rateros* (literally "ratters," i.e., thieves). La Romita even boasted two legendary female thieves during the 1930s and '40s, Plácida Hernández and the ominously named "La Loba" (The She-Wolf).

But the most famed crooks to come out of La Romita managed to take their dirty deeds to another level altogether. During the 1940s a gang known as Los Halcones, led by a thug named Arturo "El Negro" Durazo, controlled part of La Romita's turf. Durazo befriended a more bookish type by the name of José "Pepito" López Portillo and made sure no harm came to the young man.

López Portillo went on to a career in politics and arrived at the presidency in 1976–82. In Mexico one does not forget past favors lightly, so López Portillo made his old protector Durazo police chief of Mexico City. Thus began a reign of official terror, bringing the routine corruption of the city police to new lows of venality, until El Negro was ousted and imprisoned by the administration of President Miguel de la Madrid.

Los Halcones and their ilk are long gone, but in La Romita their aura somehow lingers. Trying to find the little square and church, just a few meters from Avenida Cuauhtémoc but only reached by a couple of narrow side streets, is no easy task. When you ask a local where the plaza is, the first reply is invariably to warn you about getting robbed. But on one recent afternoon, the only people in the shady little plaza were a young mother and her baby, and an old man eager to tell a foreign visitor stories of La Romita's legendary past. Of course, there were also three suspicious-looking young men huddled together in the alley next to the church, looking at the visitor with interest. . .

ers have lived in the Roma, several important Mexican novels take place in the neighborhood, including: *Batallas en el desierto* by José Emilio Pacheco, *Agua quemada* by Carlos Fuentes, *Manifestación de silencios* by Arturo Azuela, and more recently *El vampiro de la colonia Roma* by Luis Zapata.

The Roma grew increasingly commercial in the 1960s and '70s, a trend that accelerated in the 1980s when the less-than-enlightened city government of Mayor Carlos Hank González ran several *ejes,* or major avenues, through the southern part of the district.

The few remaining wealthy residents of the Roma fled after the devastating 1985 earthquake. Because it was built on soft, unstable subsoil, the quake rocked the Roma, toppling hundreds of new, shoddily built apartments and houses, killing hundreds if not thousands of neighborhood residents and leaving 15,000 homeless.

In part because the rents fell sharply in the Roma after the earthquake, a resurgence of sorts has been under way since the early 1990s. A younger crowd of artists and other urban hipsters, as well as the wealthy who want to be associated with them, have been moving back in and renovating many of the crumbling old mansions, particularly in the Roma Norte between Álvaro Obregón and Avenida Chapultepec.

Around Plaza Río de Janeiro

For a stroll around the Roma, the best place to start

is the old heart of the neighborhood, Plaza Río de Janeiro (originally called Plaza Roma), just a few blocks southeast of the Insurgentes Metro station.

Although a couple of remarkably ugly towers now scar the park's skyline, one can still enjoy the graceful mansions around the stately park, with its fountain and a replica of Michelangelo's *David* statue in the center. One building worth a look is **La Casa de las Brujas** (Witches' House), as the Edificio Río de Janeiro is popularly known. It's not hard to spot the striking red brick castle, built in 1908, on the east side of the park. Note the "face" formed by the windows right on the top floor of the corner tower, and the art deco entranceway, which was added in the 1930s.

A block north of the park, at Orizaba 24 at the corner of Puebla, is the **Casa Universitária del Libro,** the offices of a small publishing house run by the Universidad Nacional Autónoma de México (UNAM). During working hours, visitors may sign in and tour a small museum in the renovated mansion, which affords an opportunity to view the lovely wood interior and exceptional stained glass windows of the central atrium. Open Mon.–Fri. 10 A.M.–3 P.M. and 5 P.M.–8 P.M.

The blocks between Plaza Río de Janeiro and Álvaro Obregón are dotted with mansions built in the early 1900s, decorated in a variety of eclectic styles. A few noteworthy examples:

Tabasco 133, at the corner of Córdoba: a 1917 mansion with fine iron grillwork and stone carvings over the windows.

Colima 145 at Córdoba: a squat facade with subtle art nouveau stone details.

Colima 168: a Venetian-style palace with pink trim.

Álvaro Obregón and Orizaba: the reserved, elegant Edificio Balmori, overshadowed by a monstrous concrete tower right next door.

Three blocks south of Álvaro Obregón on Orizaba is another lovely small park called Plaza Luis Cabrera, the setting for part of José Emilio Pacheco's classic short story, *La batallas en el desierto.*

Casa Lamm

If you have time only for a brief visit to the Roma, at least make sure to take a look around Casa Lamm, a cultural center with an art gallery, a wonderful bookstore, and restaurant, all situated in a beautifully restored 1911 mansion at Álvaro Obregón 99, at the corner of Orizaba. Whether you're interested in seeing the art exhibits or not, the mansion is worth visiting to get an idea of how people lived in the heyday of the Roma.

It was built by Lewis Lamm, son of one of Roma's founders, but the architect never got around to living there and instead rented it for years to a religious orphanage. In 1939 the house was sold for US$100,000 to a private family who lived in it until 1990, saving the building from the depredations faced by other Roma mansions.

In 1993 Casa Lamm was renovated and opened as a private cultural institute that holds frequent exhibits and events and teaches a couple of dozen university-level courses each year on art, literature, music, politics, and society. Courses cost US$200–800 per four-month semester. A program of guided visits to 10 different art galleries in the city over the course of a semester costs US$250. For more information on courses, contact the school at tel. 5514-4899, email: lammacademico@mail.internet.com.mx.

Since it was opened, the Casa Lamm has mounted regular exhibits of all variety of art, but in 1999 the institute received stewardship of a large collection of art amassed by Mexican media giant Televisa. This collection had formerly been housed in the now-closed Centro de Arte Contemporáneo in Polanco. The collection contains hundreds of works by many famed Mexican and international artists, including Sergio Hernández, María Izquierdo, Francisco Toledo, Jasper Johns, Gerhard Richter, Manuel Álvarez Bravo, Tina Modotti, and Guillermo Kahlo (photographer and father of Frida).

Casa Lamm has built a new wing in the courtyard to house a rotating display of the Televisa collection. The visiting exhibits will continue as well, both in the atrium upstairs in the main house and in the annex. There is no charge to visit the exhibits; open daily 9 A.M.–6 P.M.

On the ground floor of the main house is **Librería Pegaso,** perhaps the most user-friendly bookstore in Mexico City, with free coffee and

JEWS IN MEXICO CITY

While a number of Spanish and Portuguese Jews came to Mexico after the conquest, fleeing the Holy Inquisition on the Iberian Peninsula, religious persecution followed them to the New World. Although the Inquisition was applied with less force and frequency in the colonies than in Spain, many Jewish immigrants were forced to practice their faith in secret or to convert to Christianity. Over a 265-year period—from the first Inquisition trial in Cuautla, Morelos, in 1614 to the last in Guanajuato in 1779—it was virtually impossible for a Jewish community to flourish openly. What little Jewish activity existed during this time was minutely described in the inquisitorial archives, the result of confessions elicited through torture.

By 1820, at the end of the colonial period, the Jewish presence in Mexico City was insignificant, and it was not until the government of Porfirio Díaz (1877–1911) that Jews began arriving in larger numbers, principally from western Europe, Russia, Syria, Turkey, and Greece. These early immigrants—mostly men—generally identified more with their nationality than with their religious faith or cultural origins. Some married Catholic Mexican women, others returned to Europe after a time in Mexico, and a few stayed and organized the beginnings of a Jewish community. Their principal meeting place was a Masonic temple in the Centro Histórico. The young Jewish men who decided to leave the Old World and *hacer la América* generally ventured off on their own, and once established in Mexico, sent for their families.

In the 1920s another wave of Jewish immigrants came from Eastern Europe. Together with the earlier Jewish immigrants from Asia Minor, those present in early 20th-century Mexico City formed the basis of the current Jewish community, which numbers roughly 45,000. Most live in Mexico City, with smaller communities in Guadalajara, Monterrey, and Tijuana.

The immigrants first settled certain sections of the Centro, particularly the streets of Loreto, Justo Sierra, Las Cruces, and, most of all (ironically enough) Jesús María. In these streets, a few blocks from the Zócalo, an entire form of Jewish life was re-created, with bakeries, kosher

comfy couches in the middle of the store to relax on. The store has an extensive selection of titles, many in English, and the art book collection is particularly good. All-day browsing is tolerated. Open daily 10 A.M.–8 P.M.; tel. 5208-0171 or 5208-0174.

The Casa Lamm also has a fine European-style restaurant, Flors del Mal (closed at last report for renovations), and an outdoor café.

Muca Roma

Museo Universitario de Ciencas y Artes Roma (Muca Roma), east of Plaza Río de Janeiro at Tabasco 73, is a UNAM-run art space in a early 1900s brick house. Eight rooms exhibit works of different Mexican and international artists, often very good. Open Mon.–Sat. 10 A.M.–6 P.M.; tel. 5511-0925; free entrance.

Casa del Poeta/ Museo Ramón López Velarde

One of Mexico's most famed poets, Ramón López Velarde, lived the last three years of his life (1918–21) in this *porfiriato*-era apartment building, and it has since been converted into a cultural center and small museum. Born in Jeréz de la Frontera, Zacatecas, in 1888, López Velarde wrote impassioned verse, often to a lover to whom he gave the pseudonym Fuensanta. He also penned *Suave Patria,* a hymn to Mexico considered something of a national poem.

Unless you're a López Velarde fan, the museum won't do much for you, but **Café La Hormiga,** upstairs, is a nice spot to relax and have a drink or coffee. The café hosts frequent poetry readings in the evenings, usually on Saturday. At Álvaro

butcher shops, stores, and workshops. The Jews lived in *vecindades,* multifamily complexes, with a central patio as the space for social life. The community built synagogues, organizations, and social and recreational centers.

Much as immigrants from other parts of Mexico are surviving today, the Jewish immigrants generally began life in the city as *vendedores ambulantes,* or street vendors, in the Centro. After putting together some savings, they then moved up to a stall in one of the local markets, and from there worked up to opening their own storefronts. Some eventually went into industry, particularly textile production.

The first Jewish organization in Mexico was the Alianza Monte Sinai (Mount Sinai Alliance), formed in 1912. While all Jews participated at first, eventually those from Syria, the Sephardic Jews from Turkey and Greece, and the Ashkenazi from Eastern Europe separated and created their own organizations. The Alianza Monte Sinai today remains the main representative of Jews originating from Damascus, Syria.

By the end of the 1920s many of the Syrian Jews had moved out of the Centro to the Roma district, while the Ashkenazi stayed on in the Centro until the 1950s and 1960s before moving to the Hipódromo Condesa. The Sephardic community moved at about the same time to the Roma and Del Valle.

Over the years many Jewish families moved on to Polanco, and more recently farther west to Tecamachalco, Bosques de las Lomas, La Herradura, El Oliva, and elsewhere. Currently, the Jewish community supports 24 synagogues, 15 schools, 10 *kolelim* (religious schools), youth organizations, and an organization for Mexican Jews regardless of origin (Comite Central Israeliti de Mexico, tel. 5540-7376, email: tribuna@ort.org.mx).

A great number of Jews have left their mark on Mexican literature, fine arts, cinema, history, architecture, television, and journalism. Mónica Unikel-Fasja of Jewish Tours, tel. 5202-2621, email: monikel@jewishtours.com.mx, website: www.jewishtours.com.mx, takes visitors on guided trips to Jewish historical sites in the Centro Histórico.

Obregón 73; tel. 5533-5456; open Mon.–Fri. 11 A.M.–10 P.M., Sat. 6–12 P.M.

Art Galleries

Since the Roma began its resurgence during the late 1980s and 1990s, it has become Mexico City's premier location for contemporary art galleries. Most galleries hold regular opening parties; call for info on upcoming exhibitions, or check out the very useful website www.arte-mexico.com.

Nina Menocal is owned by Cuban expatriates and carries contemporary Latin American art, with an emphasis on young Cuban artists. At Zacatecas 93; tel. 5564-7209 or 5564-7443; email: ninart@mail.internet.com.mx; open Mon.–Fri. 9 A.M.–7 P.M., Sat. 10 A.M.–3 P.M.

Out Gallery features younger, more experimental artists from Mexico and the U.S., displaying mainly painting and prints. At Colima 179; tel. 5525-4500; open Mon.–Fri. 11 A.M.–7 P.M., Sat. 11 A.M.–3 P.M.

Espacio Cultural Unodosiete is a small gallery with contemporary art. At Orizaba 127; tel. 5264-3039; open Mon.–Fri. 9 A.M.–3 P.M. and 4–7 P.M., Sat. 10 A.M.–2 P.M.

Galería OMR carries both Mexican and international contemporary art (mainly paintings and sculpture) in a converted mansion, with frequent group shows and monthly or bimonthly openings. At Plaza Río de Janeiro 54; tel. 5511-1179 or 5207-1080; open Mon.–Fri. 10 A.M.–3 P.M. and 4–7 P.M., Sat. 10 A.M.–2 P.M.

Espacio de Arte Yvonamor Palix, with another branch in Paris, has intermittent shows, mainly installations and photography exhibits, but some painting as well. At Córdoba 37–7;

tel. 5514-5384; open by appointment only, weekdays between 10 A.M. and 4 P.M.

CONDESA, NÁPOLES, AND DEL VALLE

After the Roma began filling up with mansions in the 1920s, the next neighborhood to develop was the Condesa, to the south and west of the Roma. Originally part of a hacienda owned by the Condesa de Miravalle (hence the name), the land had nothing on it but open pastures and a defunct horseracing track when a street plan was drawn up in 1924.

Rather than destroy the old racetrack, Mexican developers José Basurto and José de la Lama incorporated the shape into their street plan, giving us the oval Avenida Amsterdam, with Parque México in the middle. Many of the wealthier Catholic and Jewish families still living in the Centro began moving into Condesa in the 1930s and '40s. The time period is reflected in the local architecture, with art deco stylings on some of the older buildings.

The Condesa was not badly damaged in the 1985 earthquake, but many of the older Condesa families fled along with those from the Roma to newer suburbs farther west outside of the downtown area. And as with the Roma, the sudden drop in rents and increase in apartment openings led to a recolonization of sorts, this time with actors, gays, artists, journalists, and other bohemian types, who appreciate the local parks, attractive apartment buildings, and many restaurants.

Until the 1940s, south of what was then Río de la Piedad (and is now the Viaducto highway) there was nothing but open fields with a few scattered country houses until you reached San Ángel. But with the construction of Avenida Insurgentes, the Nápoles and Del Valle middle-class neighborhoods were developed. Farther south is Mixcoac, a former village which has long since been overtaken by the city, though it still has a couple of quiet squares and colonial buildings. Apart from visiting the Polyforum Siqueiros or passing along Insurgentes to get to San Ángel, casual tourists won't find much reason to come down this way.

Orientation

The Condesa is bordered on the east by Insurgentes Sur, on the south by Eje 3 Sur Baja California, on the west by Avenida Patriotismo (a section of the Circuito Interior), and on the north by the Roma Norte. The neighborhood itself is divided in two, the eastern half around Parque México called Hipódromo Condesa (because of the former horsetrack), and the section west of Nuevo León known as the Condesa. Many people now think of both parts simply as the Condesa.

The closest Metro station for the Hipódromo Condesa is Metro Chilpancingo, while the nearest to the restaurant district in the Condesa is Metro Patriotismo. If you drive to the Condesa, Parque México is a good place to park your car, as spots are usually available. The streets around the restaurant zone are more congested.

Metro Chilpancingo is the southernmost Metro station along Insurgentes, so to get anywhere between the Condesa and San Ángel along Insurgentes, hop any one of the thousands of *peseros* marked "San Ángel" (going south) and "Reforma/La Raza" (going north).

You won't find any Metro stops convenient to the Del Valle or Nápoles neighborhoods, but hop any *pesero* heading south along Insurgentes and get off wherever convenient. Metro Mixcoac is a short walk from the Mixcoac neighborhood.

Colonia Condesa

Despite the growing popularity of the Condesa among young Mexicans and foreigners as a place to live and hang out, there's not a whole lot for most visitors to do apart from eating out at one of the (generally pricey) restaurants. But if you feel like seeing something besides colonial churches and museums, you might consider walking around **Parque México** and surrounding streets for a couple of hours, or relaxing on a bench with a book or postcard in the park.

The large, oval-shaped park, built on the site of a horsetrack, is filled with remarkably lush, almost tropical vegetation, and it is a wonderful oasis of clean air in the midst of the city. If you're a runner, you might consider joining the many locals who get their daily exercise jogging, rollerblading, or just walking their dogs around the park.

While the hype of the Condesa as the most pristine art deco neighborhood outside of Miami's South Beach is overblown, there are several elegant deco/functionalist apartment houses facing Parque México. Near the north end of the park, right next to the Suburbia department store at the corner of Sonora, is **Edificio Basurto,** named in honor of its architect, and also one of the developers of the Condesa, José Basurto. For a brief time after its construction in the 1920s, this was the tallest building in Mexico City. It's hard to appreciate the architecture from the outside, but the circular atrium and apartments have clean, crisp lines.

Parque México is divided by two streets, Michoacán (in the middle) and Sonora (at the north end). Follow Michoacán four blocks to the west, across Nuevo León and Tamaulipas, and you'll find yourself in the middle of the Condesa restaurant and café zone. Following Sonora west from Parque México will take you across Nuevo León to **Parque España,** a second, smaller park, not as nice as Parque México because it's stranded next to a major avenue.

Poliforo Cultural Siqueiros

On Insurgentes Sur south of the Viaducto, in the shadow of the monstrous 50-story World Trade Center de México, is this eye-catching, geometric building covered with huge mural paintings inside and outside by Mexican artist Davíd Alfaro Siqueiros.

The Polyforum was the brain-child of ex-revolutionary and later businessman Manuel Suárez y Suárez, who originally conceived of the building for a location in Cuernavaca. But seeing the unique structure and the murals begun by Siqueiros, President Gustavo Díaz Ordaz convinced Suárez to relocate it to its present site.

The 12-sided building was designed to resemble a diamond sitting on four pillars. Inside are eight facet, and three horizontal levels. The first is the entrance, with a small, free museum about the Polyforum, while in the center, but set down a level, is a 500-seat circular theater often used for drama productions. Call the Polyforum for upcoming shows.

Upstairs is the main forum hall, frequently used for major events, particularly by the leftist Democratic Revolution Party (PRD), which perhaps feels an affinity for the socialist beliefs expressed in the monumental, three-dimensional mural created by Siqueiros inside the hall, titled *La marcha de la Humanidad* (The March of Humanity). At 11:30 A.M., 12:45 P.M., and 5 P.M. on weekends only, visitors can attend a sound-and-light show (US$3.50), narrated by Siqueiros, describing his vision in the mural.

At Insurgentes Sur 701; tel. 5536-4520; open daily 9 A.M.–7 P.M. Entrance to see the mural without the show is US$1.25, while the museum by the entrance hall is free.

Nápoles and Del Valle

South of the World Trade Center along Insurgentes are the Nápoles (west of Insurgentes) and Del Valle (east of Insurgentes) neighborhoods, residential areas developed in the 1950s. At the north end are two major stadiums, the **Estadio Azul** soccer stadium, and right next door the **Plaza de Toros México,** the largest bullfighting ring in the Americas. Farther south, between Eje 6 Sur and Eje 7 Sur, is **Parque Hundido** (Sunken Park), a large leafy park along Insurgentes, set below street level. The gravel and dirt paths of the park, lined with about 50 reproductions of pre-Hispanic sculptures, are a good place for a jog—as with Parque México in the Condesa, the trees seem to help keep out the fumes from traffic on nearby Insurgentes.

Across Insurgentes from Parque Hundido is the smaller **Parque San Lorenzo,** another tree-filled park. This one boasts a couple of basketball courts and a 16th-century chapel dedicated to San Lorenzo Martír, with a bare facade and a worn brick bell tower.

Mixcoac

Another one of the many "lost" neighborhoods populating unlikely corners of Mexico City, Mixcoac is a small oasis of cobblestoned streets and colonial buildings hidden between the noisy avenues of Insurgentes and Patriotismo. The only sight, per se, in the neighborhood is the **Instituto de Mora,** a library specializing in the history of Mexico, Latin America, and the

United States. Housed in what was briefly the home of ex-President Valentín Gómez Farías, the library is a wonderful place for anyone interested in history, and who can read Spanish. There's a peaceful garden to sit and read in, and a small cafeteria to buy coffee or snacks. At Plaza Valentín Gómez Farías 12; tel. 5598-3777; www.institutomora.edu.mx; open Mon.–Fri. 8 A.M.–7 P.M., Sat. 8 A.M.–3:30 P.M. In front of the building is a quiet, tree-filled square, and across the street is the colonial-era **Iglesia de San Juan.**

Several blocks south from the Instituto Mora, across Avenida Felix Cuevas, is what was the old center of Mixcoac, a remarkably quiet pedestrian area with three interconnecting plazas. Three buildings of note here are the **Casa de Cultura Juan Rulfo,** housed in what was the old Palacio Municipal; the 17th-century **Parroquia de Santo Domingo de Guzmán** church and adjacent convent complex; and the **Universidad Panamericana,** housed in what was an 18th-century textile factory and hacienda. In the archways of a building right opposite the university is **Café Los Arcos,** a sidewalk coffee shop invariably filled with students that makes a great spot for a soft drink or coffee.

By public transportation, the easiest way to get to Mixcoac is to go by Metro to the Mixcoac station, and walk from there.

Southern Mexico City

COYOACÁN

Eight km south of the Centro, Coyoacán is an affluent and influential *delegación* with some fine museums, plazas surrounded by outdoor cafés, and the historical fingerprint of Cortés side by side with the bohemian color provided by the area's many resident artists, writers, and musicians. Once a walled colonial village separated from Mexico City proper by farmland and lakes, it remains one of the most traditional neighborhoods in the Distrito Federal. After the Centro Histórico, this might be the most tour-worthy part of in the city—even if it didn't contain the highly popular Museo Frida Kahlo. Visitors who think that nearby San Ángel is too pricey or "precious" often find Coyoacán more to their taste.

The leafy plazas and narrow cobbled streets of Coyoacán, once part of huge haciendas and convents, are marvelous places for visitors to stroll and appreciate the neighborhood's relaxed ambience. Take a break from walking at one of the plaza cafés under brightly colored awnings, while organ grinders play beneath towering Indian laurel trees.

Coyoacán life is centered around its twin main plazas, Jardín del Centenario and Jardín Hidalgo. On weekends the plazas fill with all manner of street vendors, musicians, and passersby—so many that it can be difficult to find room to walk. Most attractions lie within walking distance of this central location. For tourist information, go through the main doorway of the Casa Municipal, on the north side of Jardín del Centenario, and immediately on your right you'll find the Centro de Información y Servicios Turísticos de Coyoacán, tel. 5658-0221. It's open daily 8 A.M.–8 P.M. At the northwest corner of the plaza is a Banamex where you can change money if needed.

To get to Coyoacán from the city center, take the Línea 3 Metro to the Miguel Ángel de Quevedo station and hop a *pesero* heading east on Avenida M. A. de Quevedo, telling the driver that you want to get off at Calle Tres Cruces. Walk north along Tres Cruces, which becomes Calle Centenario and reaches the west side of Jardín Centenario after five blocks. Two other Línea 3 Metro possibilities are the Coyoacán and Viveros stations, each about a 20-minute walk from the plazas. Another way to combine bus and Metro would be to catch a Línea 2 Metro to the Tasqueña station, southeast of Coyoacán, and from there hop a *pesero* directly to Plaza Centenario, Coyoacán. This takes a little longer but avoids having to walk into Coyoacán.

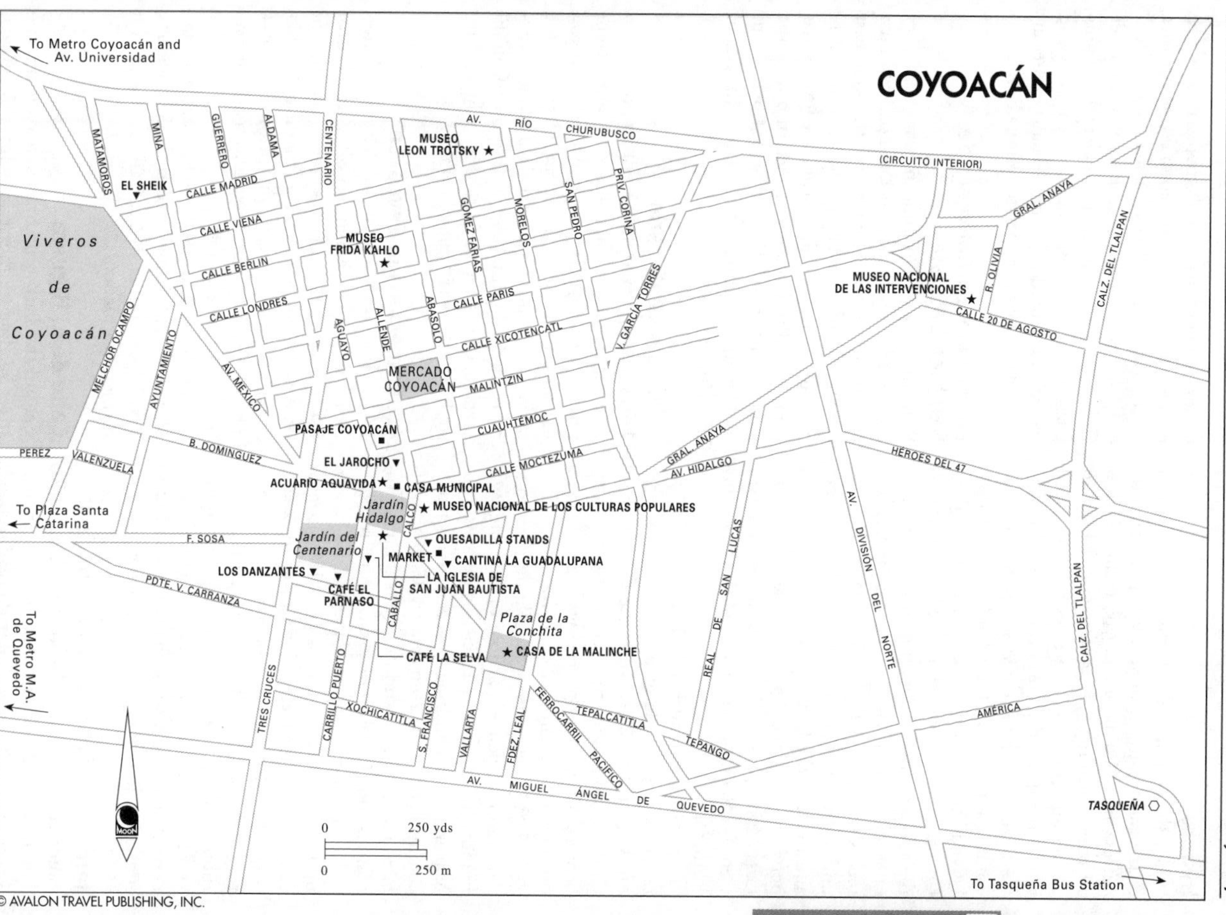
COYOACÁN
CALZ. DEL TLALPAN
TASQUEÑA
To Tasqueña Bus Station
GRAL. ANAYA
R. OLIVIA
CALLE 20 DE AGOSTO
(CIRCUITO INTERIOR)
MUSEO NACIONAL DE LAS INTERVENCIONES
HÉROES DEL 47
AMÉRICA
AV. DIVISIÓN DEL NORTE
REAL DE SAN LUCAS
TEPANGO
AV. HIDALGO
V. GARCÍA TORRES
QUEVEDO
DE
TEPALCATITLA
FERROCARRIL PACÍFICO
ANGEL
MIGUEL
AV.
AV. RÍO CHURUBUSCO
PRIV. CORINA
SAN PEDRO
MORELOS
GÓMEZ FARÍAS
ABASOLO
ALLENDE
AGUAYO
CENTENARIO
ALDAMA
GUERRERO
MINA
MATAMOROS
CALLE PARIS
CALLE XICOTENCATL
MALINTZIN
CUAUHTÉMOC
CALLE MOCTEZUMA
MUSEO LEON TROTSKY
MUSEO FRIDA KAHLO
MERCADO COYOACÁN
PASAJE COYOACÁN
EL JAROCHO
ACUARIO AQUAVIDA
CASA MUNICIPAL
MUSEO NACIONAL DE LOS CULTURAS POPULARES
Jardín Hidalgo
Jardín del Centenario
CALLO
QUESADILLA STANDS
CANTINA LA GUADALUPANA
MARKET
LA IGLESIA DE SAN JUAN BAUTISTA
CAFÉ EL PARNASO
LOS DANZANTES
CABALLO
CAFÉ LA SELVA
Plaza de la Conchita
CASA DE LA MALINCHE
FDEZ. LEAL
VALLARTA
S. FRANCISCO
XOCHICATITLA
CARRILLO PUERTO
TRES CRUCES
250 yds
250 m
0
CALLE MADRID
CALLE VIENA
CALLE BERLIN
CALLE LONDRES
AV. MEXICO
B. DOMINGUEZ
F. SOSA
PDTE. V. CARRANZA
AYUNTAMIENTO
MELCHOR OCAMPO
VALENZUELA
PEREZ
EL SHEIK
Viveros de Coyoacán
To Metro Coyoacán and Av. Universidad
To Plaza Santa Catarina
To Metro M.A. de Quevedo
MOON
© AVALON TRAVEL PUBLISHING, INC.

History

When the conquistadors arrived in Coyoacán in the early 16th century, it was populated by Aztecs who called the area Coyohuacan, a Náhuatl name meaning "place of coyotes." Hernán Cortés and his troops were very well received in Coyoacán by the area's earlier inhabitants, the Tepanecas, who resented the oppressive Aztec domination of their homelands. At that time Lago de Texcoco extended all the way south to Coyoacán, and Cortés chose the lakeside port as the spot for his headquarters during the conquest of Tenochtitlán, the Aztec capital. As the reconstruction of the conquered capital was under way, Cortés installed himself in Coyoacán and made it the first capital of Nueva España between 1521 and 1523. Coyoacán's current Casa Municipal sits at the north end of Jardín del Centenario on the site of one of Cortés's many former residences.

After Mexican independence from Spain, one of the most notable local historic events occurred on August 20, 1847, when the Convento de Churubusco became the scene of a fierce battle between Mexican troops and invading U.S. forces during the Mexican-American War.

In 1923, the famous Escuela de Pintura al Aire Libre (Open Air School of Painting) was founded in the former Hacienda de San Pedro Mártir, thus establishing Coyoacán as an artists' colony. Later in the 20th century, Coyoacán offered refuge to two world-renowned exiles, Romania's King Carol and Russia's Leon Trotsky.

Coyoacán became part of the Distrito Federal upon the ratification of Mexico's 1857 constitution. Today, the Delegación Coyoacán extends over 60 square km and is bisected by three waterways, including the channeled Río Churubusco, the partially channeled Río Chiquito, and the Canal Nacional. Around 640,000 residents live in Coyoacán, making it the fourth most populous of D.F.'s 16 *delegaciónes.*

Jardín Hidalgo and Casa Municipal

Bordered east, west, and north by Calles Carillo Puerto, Caballocalco, and B. Domínguez, Coyoacán's lovely *zócalo* is a traditional rectangle centered around a 19th-century kiosk. The kiosk features a stained-glass cupola topped by a bronze Republican eagle. Along the north side of the plaza lies the Casa Municipal, which houses local and federal government offices on the site of a former Cortés residence. An attached chapel contains Diego Rosales frescos narrating local history, while the Sala de Cabildos (Council Hall) features an elaborate mural by the painter Aurora Reyes.

Parroquía y Ex-Convento de San Juan Bautista

Built in 1589 by Dominican friars (and later transferred to the Franciscans), this parish church and former convent looms over the southeast corner of Jardín Hidalgo. The plastered early baroque facade is original, while the interior has been beautifully reconstructed. In one of the church's three naves, the Capilla de Rosario contains an ornate baroque *retablo* from the end of the 17th century.

Jardín del Centenario

This smaller plaza to the west of Jardín Hidalgo is centered around a fountain and bronze sculptures of two coyotes, a reference to the literal meaning of the name Coyoacán. The south side of the verdant plaza is lined with cafés and restaurants, including the very well-known Café El Parnaso, considered the perfect place for a philosophical chat over a cup of coffee.

Acuario Acuavida Coyoacán

Facing the north side of the Plaza del Centenario, this public aquarium offers exhibits of fishes, reptiles, live corals, aquatic plants, and other water-bound life, including the only freshwater manta ray in captivity in the Americas. The jungle courtyard is popular with kids, and refreshments are available.

Open Tues.–Fri. 10 A.M.–8 P.M., Sat. and Sun. 10 A.M.–10 P.M. Admission costs US$2 for adults, US$1 for children 3–11. Call 5659-2060 for further information.

Calle de la Higuera

Behind the Parroquía San Juan Bautista, this street heading southeast away from the plaza is lined with beautifully renovated colonial homes, including **Casa Colorada,** site of the first Spanish military encampment in the Valle de México.

A little farther southeast, Calle de la Higuera passes the **Plaza y Capilla de la Conchita.** A chapel constructed here in 1521 by order of Cortés was thought to have been the first Christian building in the city. Although officially known as Capilla de la Purísima Concepción, the chapel and surrounding garden are more commonly known by the affectionate nickname "La Conchita" (the little shell). The chapel is thought to be next to a spot where springs once provided water for Tenochititlán, now Mexico City proper.

A controversial piece of Hernán Cortés's past can be found just off Plaza de la Conchita at the **Casa de la Malinche,** the former house of the conqueror's Indian lover/interpreter. A complex woman, originally enslaved by rival tribes before being taken by Cortés, Malintzin (her Indian name) played a crucial role in the conquest of the Aztec empire, offering Cortés subtle advice along with her interpretations. She is reviled by many modern Mexicans for helping Cortés, to the point that the term *malinchista* refers to any Mexican (but particularly women) who idealizes foreigners and puts down Mexico.

Casa de los Camilos, on the right at the corner of the next block, was built in the 17th century as the residence and hospice of the Camillians, a religious order founded by San Camilo de Lelis (1550–1614), patron saint of hospitals and the sick. The stone-block structure's small but unique door of black stone is worth a look.

On the opposite side of the street, the **Jardín Frida Kahlo** is dedicated to the famous Coyoacán painter. A statue of Kahlo contemplates the garden that carries her name. A fountain completes the picture.

Running north along the west side of Jardín Frida Kahlo, tree-shaded **Calle de Fernández Leal** boasts a string of attractive country mansions and houses built around the beginning of the 20th century and typical of residential Coyoacán.

Museo Frida Kahlo

One of the most popular sights in Coyoacán, the Museo Frida Kahlo is a startlingly blue early 20th-century house in which the world-famous artist was born to a German father and Mexican mother in 1907. In recent years acclaimed by critics and collectors worldwide, Kahlo painted for years in the shadow of her famed muralist husband, Diego Rivera. She suffered a crippling injury in her early years, and her art suggests a stoic life full of pain and self-absorption. She lived with Rivera off and on for 25 years, until her death in 1954. Perhaps because the work she created seems to have transcended her difficult circumstances, Kahlo has become an emblem for contemporary female artists.

A selection of Kahlo's personal art collection is on display, including excellent pre-Hispanic artifacts and Mexican folk art (including jewelry and clothes, most of it inspired by Amerindian designs, which Kahlo herself wore) as well as works by well-known artists José María Velasco, Paul Klee, and, of course, her husband Rivera. Particularly interesting are Kahlo's self-portraits, which combine her own self-examination along with a fascination with Communist ideology and Amerindian folkways. For a larger exhibit of Kahlo's own paintings, head to the Museo Dolores Olmedo in Xochimilco. Kahlo was said to have had a love affair with Leon Trotsky, whose own museum is nearby. The garden here is a quiet spot to sit and write a letter or drink in the atmosphere. A small gift shop and café are on the premises. At Calle Londres 247; tel. 5554-5999; open Tues.–Sun. 10 A.M.–6 P.M.; admission US$3. Cameras aren't allowed inside the museum.

Museo León Trotsky

Leon Trotsky's house looks like a fortress—which is the function it served (albeit unsuccessfully) for this exiled Russian Bolshevik. Having lost to Josef Stalin in a struggle for rulership over the Soviet Union, Trotsky left the USSR in 1929 under the threat of execution. At the invitation of Diego Rivera and Frida Kahlo, he came to Mexico in 1937 to seek asylum and, after having an affair with Kahlo, moved to this building, just around the corner from Kahlo's home.

Trotsky, living in justifiable paranoia of Stalin, seldom left his house in an effort to protect himself from assassination attempts. But to no avail—in 1940, a Spanish Stalinist named Ramón Mercader convinced Trotsky to allow him in the house and promptly stabbed him with an ice pick as Trotsky looked the other way. The room in which he was killed has been left untouched; every paper and book remains in the same position. Among other artifacts on display are photographs of Trotsky, his wife, Natalia, and Rivera and Kahlo. Some visitors find the veneration expressed by the museum tour guides toward some of Trotsky's daily objects ("This was the spoon he stirred his coffee with!") a bit over the top.

The house is also headquarters for the **Instituto del Derecho de Asilo y las Libertades Públicas** (Institute for the Right of Asylum and Public Liberties), founded in 1990, and for the **Biblioteca Rafael Galván,** housing a collection of books focused on social themes. The IDALP organizes occasional expositions, conferences, and art activities. On Calle Viena 45, although the main museum entrance is around the corner at Río Churubusco 410; tel. 5658-8732; open Tues.–Sun. 10 A.M.–5 P.M.; admission US$2.50.

Museo Nacional de Culturas Populares

Established in 1982, this museum on Avenida Hidalgo, just a half block northeast of Plaza Hidalgo, is dedicated to Mexico's diverse artistic and cultural expressions. Visitors will encounter displays of both traditional and modern handicrafts, along with live demonstrations. Special courses and fairs with gastronomic or handicraft themes are also frequently hosted here. A cafeteria offers refreshment, while shops purvey a variety of books, magazines, and posters. Open Tues.–Thurs. 10 A.M.–6 P.M., Fri.–Sun. 10 A.M.–8 P.M.; donation requested.

Museo Nacional de las Intervenciones

If you walk farther northeast along Avenida Hidalgo from the east side of Plaza Hidalgo, and fork left at Calle General Anaya, after just under two km from the plaza you'll arrive at the 17th-century **Ex-Convento de Churubusco,** now home to one of Mexico's key historical museums. Housed in the former monastery where Mexican General Pedro Anaya surrendered his sword to U.S. forces in 1847, the museum's 13 rooms chronicle invasions of Mexico on the part of Spain in 1829, France in 1838, and the U.S. in 1846–47, 1914, and 1916. Administered by INAH, the museum also hosts temporary historical exhibitions, cultural extension courses, round-table discussions, conferences, and other educational/cultural activities.

In addition to weaponry, flags, paintings, lithographs, maps, photos, and documents, the casual visitor can admire large-scale dioramas depicting various battles against French and U.S. forces. The museum is of particular interest to history buffs, and all sides are treated fairly and without animosity in the displays. A plaque commemorates a group of Irish-American soldiers from Texas known as the St. Patrick's Battalion, who switched sides during the 1847 invasion, in large part because of to their religious affinity with the Mexicans. Those who survived the battle for Mexico City were executed by the Americans. On Calle 20 de Agosto at Gral. Anaya, right behind Metro Gral. Anaya; tel. 5604-0699; open Tues.–Sun. 9 A.M.–6 P.M.; admission US$3.50.

Viveros de Coyoacán

Once the private nurseries *(viveros)* and orchards of Miguel Ángel de Quevedo, since nationalization under President Venustiano Carranza this wide expanse of green has become a cool park where you might want to take a rest. Open to the public daily 6 A.M.–7 P.M.

Museo Anahuacalli/Diego Rivera

Mexican muralist Diego Rivera designed and built this Mesoamerican pyramid–inspired museum of volcanic stone to contain his prodigious collection of pre-Hispanic treasures. The museum displays 60,000 artifacts from the Zapotec, Toltec, Teotihuacán, Veracruz, Mixtec, and Aztec cultures. Upstairs a studio holds many personal belongings and sketches of Rivera, offering a window on this legendary artist's personal life. On

Calle de Museo 150; tel. 5617-4210; open Tues.–Sun. 10 A.M.–2 P.M. and 3–6 P.M.; admission US$1.50.

Parque Santa Catarina

A few blocks west of Parque Centenario along Calle Francisco Sosa is a beautiful small square, fronted by the brightly painted **Capilla de Santa Catarina** as well as several restored colonial-era houses. On one side is the **Casa de Cultura de Coyoacán,** Francisco Sosa 202, tel. 5658-7826, which often holds cultural events and art exhibits. It's worth taking a peek in to admire the rambling old hacienda or take a rest in the lush gardens in back. Heading back toward the center of Coyoacán you'll find the **Istituto Italiano di Cultura,** Francisco Sosa 77, tel. 5554-0044, with art exhibits and other events.

SAN ÁNGEL

During the colonial era, the village of San Ángel attracted wealthy Spaniards who found the pleasant climate and rural ambience perfect for their estates and summer homes. Nine km from the Centro, today it's a posh and attractive suburb that the spreading city has grown to meet. You'll still find cobblestone streets with marvelous old colonial-era homes and haciendas now inhabited by successful artists, writers, and actors. The Saturday art market is a favorite spot for tourists and Mexicans alike to go gift shopping.

A small tourist office in the **Centro Cultural de San Ángel,** Av. Revolución and Calle Madero, tel. 5277-6955, can answer questions about touring the *colonia.* You can also join a free **walking tour** around San Ángel here each Saturday at noon, 2 P.M., and 4 P.M.

Ex-Convento e Iglesia del Carmen

At this Carmelite ex-monastery built between 1615 and 1626, you'll find a diverse collection of colonial art by such *maestros* as Cristóbal de Villalpando, Juan Correa, and Juan Becerra, along with colonial furniture displays. Even more amazing is the basement crypt containing mummified remains of priests, nuns, and nobility, discovered during a building project.

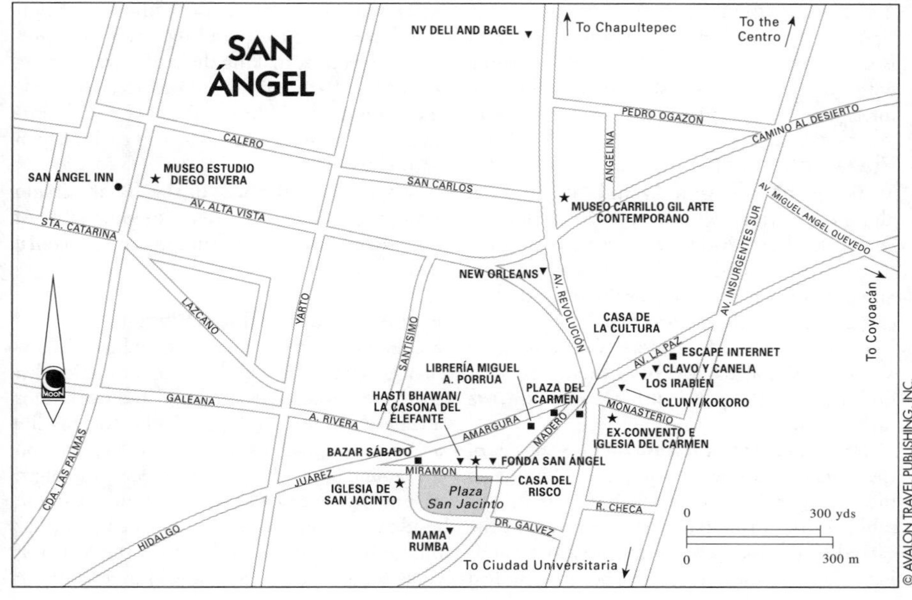

SIGHTS

The adjacent church, built in the usual Latin cross floor plan, contains colonial-era *retablos* of some interest. The museum, on Av. Revolución right near the intersection of Av. La Paz, is open Tues.–Sun. 10 A.M.–4:45 P.M.; admission US$2, free on Sunday.

Casa del Risco

Also known as the Casa del Mirador, this late 17th-century house on the north side of Plaza San Jacinto encloses a museum, a library, and two courtyards. The displays at the Museo Colonial Casa del Risco illustrate the fascination with European lifestyles felt by wealthy Mexicans in the colonial era. Upstairs in the Salón Barroco is a display of Mexican baroque art from the 17th century, mostly religious art and furniture. Two rooms feature portraits of European kings and nobility, and another room displays some collected art from the 19th and early 20th centuries. There's one large room downstairs where temporary exhibits of contemporary Mexican artists are mounted. Also in the building is the colonial library **Centro Cultural y Biblioteca Isidro Fabela.** Both are open Tues.–Sun. 10 A.M.–5 P.M.; free admission.

A large wall fountain in the eastern courtyard is decorated with whole Talavera plates (along with a few Spanish, English, and Japanese ones) interspersed with hand-painted tiles and seashells.

Plaza San Jacinto

Walk up the hill from Avenida Revolución along Calle Madero to this fine colonial plaza surrounded by period architecture. Although just a couple of blocks from a sea of traffic and asphalt, sitting in one of the relaxed plaza cafés, one can still imagine San Ángel as a village isolated from Mexico City. On Saturday, 9 A.M.–6 P.M., local artists offer their works for sale, turning the plaza into a *jardín del arte* (art garden).

The **Iglesia de San Jacinto** on the west side of the plaza was at one time part of a Dominican monastery built between 1564 and 1614. Notable are the principal *retablo* inside and the carved stone *cruz atrial* or atrium cross standing in front of the church. The beautiful walled gardens in front of the church are a favorite venue for weekend wedding parties.

Opposite the southeast side of the plaza, amid a row of shops and cafés, **Baños Colonial** is an old bath/steam establishment where you can shower for US$.75, take a public Turkish bath for US$3.50 (or US$5 for a private steam). It's open Mon.–Fri. 6 A.M. to 8 P.M., Sat. 6 A.M.–8.30 P.M., Sun. 6 A.M.–5:30 P.M. An attached soda fountain sells soft drinks and fresh juices.

A plaque on the square commemorates the execution of Irish-American U.S. soldiers (by order of Gen. Zachary Taylor) who switched sides during the 1847 U.S. invasion to fight for Mexico.

Bazar Sábado

On Saturday one of the finest craft and art markets in Mexico sets up in a 17th-century stone edifice along the northwest side of the Plaza San Jacinto. Talented artisans sell handcrafted items such as jewelry, pottery, leather, and clothing in the two-story plaza. Some of the more successful artists selling the highest quality crafts maintain regular shops here. Spurred by the success of the market, artists without a stall inside have taken to spreading out their wares across the plaza, making the entire area one big art market. Bargaining is not well-received inside the main market, but haggle all you wish outside. Snacks are available at the patio. Open Saturday only 10 A.M.–7 P.M..

Walk west and north of the Bazar Sábado along the cobblestone streets to view some of the neighborhood's most sumptuous ex-colonial mansions.

Museo Estudio Diego Rivera

Designed by architectural prodigy Juan O'Gorman in 1928, this tightly spaced, functionalist structure was where Rivera lived and worked for a time with his wife Frida Kahlo. Rivera's life and work (reproductions only) are depicted on the ground floor, while the upper floor is arranged as it might have looked when Rivera was still in residence, complete with unfinished paintings on easels. On Av. Diego Rivera at the corner of Altavista (next to the San Ángel Inn restaurant);

tel. 5550-1189; open Tues.–Sun. 10 A.M.–6 P.M.; US$2 admission.

Museo de Arte Carrillo Gil

This slick building at Avenida Revolución 1608 houses one of Mexico's finest modern art museums. Along with an excellent collection of works by Mexican greats such as Rivera, Siqueiros, Tamayo, and Toledo, along with more experimental current Mexican and international artists. Open Tues.–Sun. 10 A.M.–6 P.M.; tel. 5550-6289; admission US$1.50.

You can walk to the museum from the Plaza del Carmen.

Transport

San Ángel is easily accessible from downtown via Metro or bus. The closest Metro station to San Ángel is M.A. Quevedo. From this station, take a *pesero* marked "San Ángel." Tell the driver you want to go to Plaza San Jacinto. Just about any of the many buses heading down Insurgentes from Reforma will drop you off a short walk from San Ángel. Just ask the driver to let you know when to get off. Some of these buses continue south along Insurgentes to UNAM, Pedregal, and Cuicuilco.

If you come down to San Ángel on a bus along Insurgentes, take a look at **Polyforum Siqueiros** (Poliforo Cultural Siqueiros) on Avenida Insurgentes Sur at Filadelfia, adjacent to the World Trade Center de México—the largest building in Mexico.

UNAM/CIUDAD UNIVERSITARIA

Founded in 1551 by special charter from the king of Spain, this is the oldest university in the Western Hemisphere. The original campus was in Mexico City's historic center, but in the early 1950s it was moved to its present site southwest of the city center. So vast is the present campus of the **Universidad Nacional Autónoma de México** (UNAM)—covering 7.3 million square meters, much of it green areas—that it is referred to as the Ciudad Universitaria, or "University City."

With an enrollment of nearly half a million students and a teaching staff of 25,000, this is the single largest campus in the Americas. UNAM has a reputation for teaching left-leaning theories and as a center for political activism. The famed 1968 student riots, which ended in the bloodbath at Tlaltelolco, began among students from UNAM. In 1999, a group of students went on strike and closed the university for nine months. The strike was initially triggered by a government plan to raise the miniscule tuition, but it quickly broadened to a more general antigovernment and antiglobalization protest. Although the strike was eventually broken up when the government sent in the police (a major taboo at the fiercely independent UNAM) in the wee hours of the morning, groups of strikers were still occupying a couple of buildings at last report.

The modern buildings—many covered with elaborate murals—were built between 1950 and 1955 by Carlos Lazo. The campus is divided into two sections, with the northern part containing most of the faculty buildings. Sprawling over a huge area of lava fields, the university is laid out in groups of faculties *(facultades)* centered around the **Rectoría** administration building, whose south wall is covered with a three-dimensional Davíd Alfaro Siqueiros mural. Next to the Rectoría is the library, with an impressive Juan O'Gorman mosaic on Mexico's past and future. Just south of the Rectoría is the **Museo Universitario de Ciencias y Artes CU,** with free revolving exhibits. Open Mon.–Fri. 10 A.M.–7 P.M., weekends 10 A.M.–6 P.M. tel. 5622-0206. Right next to the museum are two bookstores, **El Sótano** and **Librería UNAM.**

Across Insurgentes from the Rectoría complex, the **Estadio Olímpico**—a broad, open stadium designed to mimic one of the many volcanic cones in the area—has a Rivera mosaic over the main entrance. Home to the UNAM Pumas soccer club, the stadium has a reputation for the rowdiest fans in the city. If you go to a game and can understand a bit of Spanish, you'll enjoy hearing the crowd chanting creative (and often profane) songs and mercilessly razzing the opposing team and fans.

For information about the university, stop in to

the **Dirección General de Orientación,** an office on the south side of the large lawn just below the library, open Mon.–Fri. 9 A.M.–5 P.M.

The southern part of the campus is centered on the **Centro Cultural Universitario,** a collection of arts buildings and theaters. Here is the **Sala Nezahualcóyotl,** considered to have the finest acoustics in the country. In the middle of the complex is a café where you can grab some refreshments, and the **Librería Julio Torri** bookstore. Just south of the Centro Cultural is the **Unidad Bibliográfica,** which houses part of the national library and the **Hemeroteca Nacional,** far and away the most comprehensive collection of newspapers and magazines in the country. Both are open Mon.–Fri. 9 A.M.–8 P.M., tel. 5622-6814. Next to the library is the **Espacio Escultórico,** a collection of huge, colorful, and bizarre metal sculptures rising out of a field of lava. The maze of trails through the shrubs around the sculptures is a favorite spot for students to go find a quiet nook to read, play music, or even do a bit of bouldering.

Getting to Ciudad Universitaria

The most direct way to reach University City is by bus traveling on Insurgentes Sur (Insurgentes passes the campus, on the east side of the road, and the stadium, on the west). The bus stops close to both sides, so it's an easy walk to the central part of the campus. Because of the amount of space the university takes up, walking around is feasible only in the north, main section. The closest Metro stop to the central area of campus is Copilco, but it's still a couple of kilometers walk from there.

Cuicuilco

Although only a few round ruins remain to be seen, the structures at Cuicuilco once housed a settlement of 20,000. The city was built in approximately 600 B.C. and the ceremonial center was active 600–200 B.C. The main "pyramid" (actually a rare round circular platform) measures 118 meters in diameter and 18 meters tall and was topped with a ceremonial altar. Volcán Xitle, which looms to the south, buried the base of the pyramid, along with the rest of the ceremonial center, with lava. Much of the lava has been removed, making it possible to see the construction of the pyramid. Excavations continue around the base of the pyramid.

Take a look at the small museum nearby for in-

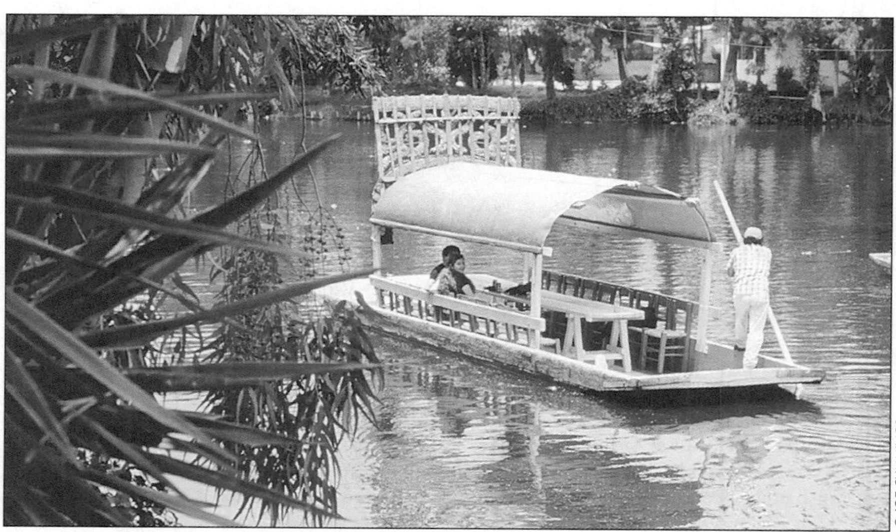

A *trajinera* glides down a canal at Xochimilco.

formation about the people and a few artifacts found at the site, along with descriptive paintings. Note the image of the fierce fire and volcano god. Cuicuilco site and the museum are open Mon.–Sat. 9 A.M.–5 P.M.; admission to the museum is US$2.50. Guided visits (in Spanish) are available Mon.–Fri. 9 A.M.–1 P.M.; call 5606-9758 for more information. It's easy to get here from the Ciudad Universitaria—take a bus marked "Cuicuilco" traveling south on Insurgentes. The site is south of the intersection of Insurgentes and Periférico Sur. In 1997, a Mexican company proposed construction of a mall complex right next to the ruins, an idea that raised an uproar and has yet to be definitively resolved.

XOCHIMILCO

According to the Códice Ramírez, Xochimilco (Place Where Flowers Grow) was originally founded on an island in Lago de Xochimilco in A.D. 919 by a Náhuatl-speaking tribe that called themselves Xochimilcas. Independent of the Aztecs, they fought many wars with neighboring tribes before the Spanish conquest. Today, the central *colonia* of Xochimilco serves as a living museum for pre-Hispanic Mexico City, conserving the ancient canals and *chinampas* (floating gardens) of a long-lost lifestyle. Hiring a boat to cruise the canals and have a floating party is a favorite weekend pastime for Mexico City residents.

Canals and *Chinampas*

Long before the Spanish arrived, the Xochimilcas had developed an imaginative solution to the difficulties of farming in the Valle de México. As the low-lying lake water could not easily be directed to the higher land on the islands and shoreline of Lago de Xochimilco, the Aztecs brought the soil to the lake and, assembling reeds, tree limbs, and soil, built the floating islands (the word *chinampa* means "terrain fenced by interwoven sticks") on which they planted their crops. The bottom soil proved to be extremely fertile, yielding two or three harvests a year, and as more *chinampas* were created, the lake was broken into a series of canals. Early European visitors often referred to Xochimilco as "the Venice of Mexico."

The Spaniards spared Xochimilco after the conquest because the area produced much of the city's food. Vegetables and flowers continue to grow on the *chinampas* today, and floriculture is the region's principle source of income. **Mercado Xóchitl,** in the center of town, **Mercado de Plantas Madreselva,** in the south of town, and **Mercado de Flores, Plantas y Hortilizas** next to the Parque Ecológico (see below), are the main plant markets. Native flora can be seen along the banks of the canals, including bulrushes, pepper trees, camphor, *jarilla, toloache,* and Mexican poppy.

Of the estimated 40,000 *chinampas* found in Xochimilco at the beginning of the 18th century, only 15,000 were left when the 20th century began. Canoe vendors began serving snacks to weekend visitors around 1920, followed quickly by the first restaurants on the embarcaderos (boat landings). Around this same time, traditional *trajineras,* poled barges used for transporting local cargo along the canals, were transformed into tour boats with the addition of seats, tables, tarp roofs, and flower-festooned facades (nowadays heavily painted, wired-together bunches of bulrushes). In 1987 UNESCO named Xochimilco a World Heritage Site to publicize its cultural importance.

Canal Touring

The Xochimilco canals are a popular spot for locals and visitors alike to rent colorful *trajineras turísticas,* drinking and picnicking onboard for an afternoon while the boatmen propel the craft down the canals with a long pole, somewhat reminiscent of the gondolas and gondoliers of Venice. Four sizes of *trajineras* are available, from the *toldo amarillo* (yellow tarp) with a capacity of four people for US$5.50 per hour up to the *toldo verde* (green tarp) holding up to 18 people for US$15 per hour. Although prices are posted and are the same for each boat, it is sometimes possible to negotiate cheaper rates, especially during the week. Each of these boats has a name, usually a woman's name such as Lupita or Julieta, so if you have a favorite it's easy to find the same boat and boatman on subsequent visits.

The main landings for *trajineras,* Embarcadero Caltonga and Embarcadero Nativitas, can be found near the center of town and the Parroquía de San Bernardino. An hour's rental is the minimum, but it's better to spend two or three hours to get farther out into the canals, see more, and have a more relaxing time. Be sure to confirm the price *before* you board. Also, give the boat a look; some are nicer than others.

A cheaper alternative would be to share a *lancha colectiva* (collective boat), which holds up to 60 people for US$.90 per person. These much larger boats run only on Sunday and holidays and leave only from Embarcadero Salitre and Embarcadero Caltongo. Food service is available on all the boats for around US$1.75–2.75 per dish. Of course it wouldn't be Mexican without the availability of live music, and, like the price of boat hire, the rates are regulated and publicly posted: a mariachi number costs US$3.50 (a bargain compared to Plaza Garibaldi), a *norteña* song is US$2.75, marimba US$1.70, and *salterio* (Mexican zither) or *acordeón* US$2.

Lots of souvenir stalls, as well as vendors on foot, sell blankets and trinkets at each of the piers. During the week, it's almost empty, so visit then if you want a peaceful ride. On the other hand if you want to see how the Mexicans most enjoy Xochimilco, the weekend would be the time to go.

Xochimilco is 24 km southeast of the Zócalo. Take Metro Línea 2 as far as Tasqueña, then board the Tren Ligero (Light Train or streetcar) to the Embarcadero streetcar station. From there follow the signs to the piers, which are about six short blocks to the northeast. Or take a "Xochimilco" bus or *pesero* from the Metro Tasqueña station all the way to the end of the line, which will put you in almost the same spot as the Tren Ligero. If you're driving, avoid Sunday, when traffic in Xochimilco can be very heavy.

Museo Dolores Olmedo Patiño

A lifelong friend and supporter of Diego Rivera (not to mention an occasional model for his paintings), Dolores Olmedo has donated a large part of her own house as a museum dedicated to Rivera and his wife, Frida Kahlo. The building itself, the lovingly restored 16th-century Hacienda La Noria, is worth a visit in and of itself, even if it weren't for the collection of more than 600 pre-Hispanic artifacts and pieces of native art, and works by Rivera (127 pieces) as well as Frida Kahlo. Although the Kahlo collection numbers only 25 pieces, this is the largest single private collection of the painter's work. Not all pieces are displayed at any given time, however.

The 6,000-square-meter Hacienda La Noria also displays colonial objects and furniture. The surrounding grounds, which together with the main building encompass 37,000 square meters, are beautifully landscaped with native trees and plants. You may also see Mexican turkeys and a few unique Xoloitzcuintle dogs, a rare pre-Hispanic canine species that is small, dark, and hairless.

The museum is about two km west of the main embarcaderos at Av. México 5843, Col. La Noria, tel. 5555-1016. Open Tues.–Sun. 10 A.M.–6 P.M.; admission US$1.50.

To reach the museum by public transport, take the Metro to the Tasqueña station, and then board the Tren Ligero from the metro station to La Noria streetcar terminal. From here, walk west along Avenida Guadalupe Ramírez till you come to a large three-way intersection, a distance of around 100 meters, and then make a sharp left (southeast) onto Antiguo Camino Xochimilco. After another 300 meters or so, you'll come to the museum on your left, at the intersection with Avenida México.

Parroquia de San Bernardino de Siena

In the center of town, not far from the main embarcaderos, rises this enormous parish church founded by Franciscans in 1535 but only inaugurated in 1590. The strong, stable architectural style has been described as "military monastic" with plain buttressed walls and ornate *portadas* (doorways). Exterior decoration mixes Greco-Roman, Gothic, and native motifs, while the interior of the attached convent shows Moorish influences. Inside, the principal *retablo* and 12 side *retablos* are authentic, late 16th-century jewels of art.

The Parroquia stands at Calles Violeta and Pino, about 100 meters northeast of the Mercado Xóchitl.

Mercado Xóchitl

This traditional municipal market, founded in 1957, stocks everything from fresh produce to clay, leather, and cane *artesanías.* It's southwest of the Parroquía, in a block bounded by Calles Madero, 16 de Septiembre, Guerrero, and Morelos. Open daily 5:30 A.M.–6 P.M.

Parque Ecológico de Xochimilco (PEX)

This relatively new educational/recreational park got its start in 1989 as part of the Ecological Rescue Plan for Xochimilco, an ambitious strategy to include water reclamation, agricultural reactivation, and historical and archaeological studies, all based on the traditional *chinampero* systems.

PEX covers about 300 hectares distributed into three areas, including the 13-hectare Mercado de Flores, Plantas y Hortilizas, reportedly the largest horticultural market in Latin America and the third largest in the world. A second part, the 67-hectare Deportivo Ecológico Cuemanco, is dedicated to water sports, leaving the 189-hectare Parque Ecológico de Xochimilco, or PEX.

About a quarter of the PEX consists of lakes, *ciénegas* (underground springs), and canals. Wide gravel and asphalt walking paths wind through the park, making this a great place to get some exercise and relatively fresh air. One path leads through the flower-lined Paseo de las Flores. A *chinampería* demonstrates how *chinampa* cultivation works. In addition to viewing natural and cultivated flora, visitors have a good chance of spotting herons, cormorants, egrets, ducks, and other waterfowl.

If you don't want to walk, a truck-pulled "train" takes visitors around the park frequently throughout the day. *Trajineras* are available on weekends. You can also rent mountain bikes and paddleboats any day of the week. Guards patrol the park, and it seems to be a very safe place to get out for some exercise without having to go all the way to Ajusco or Desierto de los Leones.

A museum near the front of the park offers historical, cultural, and natural history exhibits. There are also several children's playgrounds on the premises.

PEX is open Tues.–Sun. 9 A.M.–6 P.M. in the summer, 10 A.M.–7 P.M. in the winter. Admission is US$1.65 for adults, US$.60 over 60, or US$.25 under 12.

Northern Mexico City

BASÍLICA DE NUESTRA SEÑORA DE GUADALUPE

The church of Mexico's patron saint sees about 15 million visitors a year, and it's by far the most popular shrine in the country. It was here that Juan Diego, an Aztec nobleman named Cuauhtaoctzin before converting to Christianity, reported seeing his vision of the Virgen María on December 9, 1531, on the top of Cerro Tepeyac, a hill not far north of downtown Mexico City.

There has been a succession of chapels and *basílicas* on the hill, the most recent a very modern one. Whatever your religious proclivities, there's no denying that the latest Basílica has all the mystical aura of an airport terminal. For a slightly surreal, or at least postmodern, religious experience, take a conveyor-belt ride behind the altar to see the image of the Virgen. A religious art museum at the rear of the older 18th-century Basílica contains oil paintings and sculptures of the colonial period, including works by such famed masters as Cabrera, Villalpando, Correa, and Echave.

The original chapel at Tepeyac, built on the hilltop in the late 17th century over the site of the old temple to the Aztec mother goddess Tonanztin, can be reached by walking up through the hillside gardens.

In the days running up to December 12, were you to travel the highways around Mexico City, you would see a steady stream of pilgrims trudging or bicycling along the highways on their way to the Basílica. The night of the 12th is a crowded spectacle almost beyond imagining, a unique focus of Mexico's spiritual and national character. Unless you wish to pay your respects to the Virgin, or have a particular fascination with checking out the crowd, it's best to avoid the Basílica during most of the month of December.

Technically, the range of hills north of Tepeyac, known as the Sierra de Guadalupe, are protected as a national park. Unfortunately the hills are almost totally denuded of trees and would make for fairly desolate hiking. Because some of the neighborhoods surrounding and creeping up the sides of the hills are poor and rough, it's not recommended to venture into the range.

The easiest way to reach the Basílica is to take the Metro to the Basílica station and walk the short distance to the church. The gardens and pathways leading up the side of the hill are a relaxing place for a walk.

History

As the legend goes, Mexico City Bishop Juan de Zumárraga refused to believe Juan Diego's story that he had seen the Virgen on December 9 and demanded further evidence of his vision. On December 12 Juan had a second vision of the Virgen, surrounded by roses. This image was miraculously imprinted upon Juan Diego's cloak, and when he brought this to Zumárraga, the bishop was convinced of the miracle. After years of controversy, including a bizarre allegation by former Basílica Abbot Guillermo Shulenburg (of all people) that Juan Diego never existed, Pope John Paul II declared Juan Diego a Catholic saint in 2002.

Historians like to point out that Cerro Tepeyac was coincidentally, or perhaps not, the site of a temple dedicated to a major Aztec female deity, Tonantzin. Unsurprisingly, most Amerindian inhabitants of Mexico referred to the Virgen as Tonantzin well into the 17th century. It's also curious to note that the first Virgen de Guadalupe shrine was founded in a remote corner of the Spanish province of Extremadura, the home of many *conquistadores,* including Hernán Cortés. The Extremadura Virgen is also dark and appeared in the 1300s, during the

MORE MYSTERIES OF THE VIRGEN DE GUADALUPE

While modern historians might be quick to point to the historical situation at the time of the Guadalupe apparition to explain the "miracle," certain aspects of the original supposed spontaneous printing of the Virgen are less easy to explain away.

The color image appears to be painted onto a 2.2- by 1-meter piece of *ayate*—a paper-like cloth made from leaves of the agave using pre-Hispanic technology. While *ayate* was used by the Aztecs for their codices, it is a very difficult material on which to paint a detailed image such as this one. This anomaly alone is in fact one of the elements that convinced many of the validity of the miracle. Furthermore, after 116 years of leaving the cloth in the open, exposed to the elements and the hands of thousands of pilgrims, followed by another 352 years in a glass case, the image has retained most of its unusually brilliant colors. A reproduction done on *ayate* in the 17th century lasted only 30 years. And despite years of scientific investigation, the origin of the blue and skin-colored pigments remains a mystery.

The image is decorated with 47 stars, which for many years were thought to be located at random throughout the painting. But in recent years astronomers have charted the stars, and astoundingly they have confirmed that they represent the exact constellations seen over Mexico on the night of the winter solstice in 1531.

Computer studies of the Virgen's eyes in the painting have suggested that several minute figures lie hidden within, figures who some have interpreted as Juan Diego, Bishop Zumárraga, and others.

height of the conflict when the Spaniards were reconquering southern Spain from the darker-skinned Muslim Moors.

Whatever you make of the unusual coincidences surrounding the apparition, the New World Virgen de Guadalupe was an immediate success with Mexico's Amerindians and dramatically helped the Spanish missionaries with their work of conversion. Over the years *la Virgen morena* (the dark/Moorish Virgin, one of Guadalupe's epithets) has grown into the most revered religious figure in Mexico and is considered the protector of all Mexicans, the one who provides hope when all hope is lost. The number of miracles attributed to the icon of the Virgen runs into the many thousands, and her festival day of December 12 is the country's most important religious holiday.

The first church was a simple chapel built on the hilltop, where Juan Diego lived the rest of his days. The current hilltop chapel was built at the end of the 17th century, which is also when construction began on the first Basílica at the foot of the hill. Completed in 1709, by the 1970s the Basílica was sinking into the soft subsoil and could no longer accommodate the steady stream of pilgrims. So the modern Basílica, designed by Pedro Ramírez Vásquez of Museo Nacional de Antropología fame, was constructed in 1976 and is now the main place of worship at the site.

TENAYUCA AND SANTA CECELIA ACATITLÁN

Pirámide de Tenayuca

On the northern edge of Mexico City, technically in the State of Mexico suburb, Tlalnepantla, stands a pre-Aztec pyramid known as Tenayuca. Two parallel stairways climb the large, wide base and lead to temples on top. Occupied since at least the 11th century, six structures were raised here, each built over the other at 52-year intervals. Studies of the ruins indicate that the site was once occupied by Teotihuacáns at one point in time. The nicely landscaped grounds and attached small museum are open Tues.–Sun. 10 A.M.–4:45 P.M.; admission is US$2, free on Sunday and holidays.

To get to Tenayuca, go to the Metro La Raza station, then switch to a *pesero* marked "Pirámide."

Pirámide Santa Cecelia Acatitlán

A little farther north of Tenayuca in a *colonia* known as Santa Cecelia is the more interesting, but less visited, pyramid of Acatitlán. In the Náhuatl language Acatitlán means "place between the reeds," no doubt in reference to a time when the environs of Mexico City were much wetter. This archaeological site dates to the late post-classic period (A.D. 1200–1521) and is thought to have been a ceremonial center where Tláloc and Huitzilopochtli, the Mesoamerican gods of rain and war/sun respectively, were worshiped. The adjacent Parroquia de Santa Cecelia bears a large number of stones taken from the pyramid's base; with the arrival of the Spanish, Amerindian temples were usually ransacked, and the materials used for building Spanish churches and colonial houses.

The temple that tops the small, steeply sloped pyramid is one of the only intact pyramid temples in Mexico and is considered the most authentically restored. The first archaeological exploration of this site was carried out in 1923, and in 1961, archaeologist Eduardo Pareyón restored the pyramid's foundation. The work of this Mexican researcher has special merit because he reconstructed the upper temple that crowns the foundation after carrying out extensive research on the codices and archaeological materials (such as clay scale models) available. You can climb the steep steps to the top and walk inside the temple to see how these rooms were constructed, with wooden roofs, panels with embedded nails, an entrance with a wooden lintel, a bench, and a mezzanine or loft inside. On the outside, the temple is flanked by ceremonial arms. The entrance displays a carved sacrificial stone.

INAH-sponsored plaques on the grounds chronicle the history and architecture of Acatitlán in Spanish, English, and Náhuatl. Near the entrance to the grounds, the **Museo de la**

Escultura contains sculpture from the late post-classic period, (A.D. 1300–1521). Many of the carved stone figures on display represent flora and fauna, which no doubt had a direct relation to the Mesoamericans' daily lives. Anthropomorphic art in the museum tends toward the gruesome; a large stone receptacle, for example, is decorated in relief with various elements and symbols of human sacrifice—hearts, and severed arms, hands, and ears, which no doubt went into the stone bowl as offerings to Aztec gods. The museum building itself is a former Porfiriato home made of simple stone block and brick. A few rooms have been set aside to exhibit rustic antique furniture of the era, representing how the more common people of the era lived.

Admission and entry hours are the same as at Tenayuca. To get there from Tenayuca, either hop a taxi or get on a bus heading north along the Tenayuca-Santa Cecilia road, and ask the driver where to get off.

Parks near Mexico City

After a lengthy dose of Mexico City, visitors and expatriates will likely feel the need for a counterbalancing dose of fresh air and nature. The mountains ringing the southwest corner of the valley are home to four adjacent forest parks conducive to picnicking, hiking, and mountain biking. The parks enclose pine and oak forests from about 2,500 meters to the top of the hills marking the edge of the Valle de México. Parts of these forests are in fairly poor condition, because of air pollution and logging, while others are surprisingly healthy.

Mexico City is full of hidden parks and colonial churches, such as this one: Capilla San Lorenzo Martir in Colonia Del Valle.

The dirt roads and trails crossing the parks can be very rocky, so mountain bikes with shocks are a good choice if you plan to cycle off-road. Robberies have been reported in the more remote stretches of the parks, so if you venture away from the main areas and trails, it's best not to go alone. If you're thinking of a foray into the hills, ask other people in the parking lot or on the trail whether your planned route is safe. If you see other walkers, joggers, bird-watchers, or the like, you'll probably be fine.

DESIERTO DE LOS LEONES

Decreed Mexico's first national park in 1917, Desierto de los Leones is neither a desert nor populated with lions, but a pine and oak forest covering almost 1,529 hectares of mountainside, centered around the remains of an early 18th-century monastery. Picnickers frequent the groves and gardens around the semiruined Carmelite monastery, while hikers and mountain bikers roam the dirt roads and trails in the hills above. City authorities, in conjunction with the army, have in the last couple of years taken to patrolling the woods of Desierto de los Leones, particularly on weekends,

GREEN HOLDOUTS

Amazingly enough, 37 percent of Mexico City's territory (the city proper, not the entire valley) still consists of open land, mostly in the southern parts of the capital. Pine and oak forests cover 18 percent of the city, while cultivated lands make up 13 percent, and 6 percent serves as pasture land, meadows, or city parks.

The remaining forests in Mexico City are almost entirely concentrated in the Milpa Alta, Tlalpan, and Magdalena Contreras delegations on the steep mountains and narrow gorges in the south and southwestern parts of the valley. These forests are crucial for the continued health of the valley, as the trees help generate oxygen and their roots collect desperately needed ground water to replenish the dwindling aquifers.

Unfortunately, the forests have not fared well and face eventual extinction from clandestine logging and the continual encroachment of *paracaidistas* (parachutists), squatters who take up residence on the hilly outskirts of the city as if dropped from above.

But the effects of Mexico City's air pollution on the forests have been worse still. The winds in the valley blow from northeast to southwest, thereby sweeping much of the airborne pollution right into these forests. After decades of accumulating heavy metals and other toxins, the immune defenses of the forests have weakened, opening them up to repeated infestations by burrowing insects and other pests.

Between hunting and pesticide spraying, the pests' only natural predator, the woodpecker, has been driven to virtual extinction. The other technique used to prevent the pests from spreading has been to fell swaths of infested trees. Some observers claim such actions are a veiled attempt to justify logging for profit.

One stubborn local environmentalist, Dr. Luis Manuel Guerra, has taken on the lonely task of trying to reintroduce woodpeckers to the forests—we can only take our hats off to such dedication and wish there were more people like him around.

making it the safest and most recommendable park near Mexico City for hiking and biking. Regardless, ask one of the *vigilantes* (guards) at the monastery what the current situation is in the surrounding woods. Severe forest fires in 1998 ripped through parts of the Desierto, and burnt-out patches can still be seen in the upper reaches of the forest. The woods around the convent, however, were not touched by the fires.

The road into the park, **Camino al Desierto,** runs between the Toluca highway and San Ángel. Unless you're in the south of the city, the best way in for those driving motor vehicles is via the Toluca highway. A bus runs from the Metro Barranca del Muerto station up to the monastery on Saturday and Sunday only 6 A.M.–5 P.M. Bikers without a car would have to hire a taxi from the city, which would cost US$10–15 at least. Two gates at either end of the park collect a US$1 entrance fee from drivers 7 A.M.–6 P.M.

The Monastery

Desiertos were Carmelite monasteries first built in Spain in forests, meant to isolate the monks from the travails of urban life. The name is thought to be an allusion to Christ's 40 days in the desert. Started in 1606, Desierto de los Leones was the first such monastery built in the Americas. An earthquake destroyed the original building in 1711, and the current monastery was erected in 1722. The Carmelites moved away in 1801 to their present location in Mt. Niscongo above Tenancingo, in the State of Mexico.

Although there were likely some mountain lions in the area when the monastery was in operation, the second half of the monastery's name is thought to derive from the León family, who acted as the order's representative in affairs with the Spanish crown for many years.

Today the old monastery is a museum. Parts are a bit decrepit, but the main building is in good condition and features a lovely chapel. One large room has been converted into a restaurant, open for breakfast and lunch. On Sundays a crowd is usually milling around the hallways, but the gardens behind are always quiet, restful corners. Dotting the woods around the monastery are eight of the original 10 hermitages. The monastery building is open Tues.–Sun. 10 A.M. to 7 P.M.; there is a nominal admission fee of US$.20.

Hiking or Biking in the Forest

Although most visitors limit themselves to walking around the monastery grounds and the woods nearby, those seeking more energy expenditure should look for the turnoff to **Cruz Blanca,** .8 km (.5 mile) up the road from the monastery in the direction of San Ángel, on the right-hand side. A bumpy dirt road turns off the paved road (there's a small shack at the junction) uphill into the forest. Continue straight past the first junction (left to a forest workers' camp), then turn left (uphill) at the next junction a short distance farther to Cruz Blanca, a parking lot and ranger station in the forest. This is as far as unauthorized motor vehicles can go, and in fact it's probably better to park at the monastery and ride or walk up the dirt road, roughly 1.5 km (one mile) to the ranger station.

From Cruz Blanca, a dirt road used only by hikers and the occasional park vehicle winds parallel to a river valley, until a point where the road meets the river and forks, one branch crossing the river and the other continuing steeply up the mountain.

On the other side of the river, the trail climbs uphill briefly, then meets an old dirt road that has been closed off, winding along the side of the hills, without gaining or losing altitude for perhaps five km (three miles), finally coming out at Valle de los Conejos, near La Marquesa. This is a great place for bike riding or a long run in the woods. About halfway out along the road is an army camp, which means it's quite safe out this way.

At the far end of the road, toward Valle de los Conejos, a few robberies have been reported in recent years, so it's best to turn around near the army camp. If the situation improves, check out a great downhill mountain bike track leaving from the end of the dirt road out to the highway at Valle de los Conejos. Other single-tracks descend from this road too and eventually come out on the Mexico City-Toluca highway not far from La Marquesa.

Back at the river junction, the main dirt road heads steadily uphill, still on the left (east) side of the river valley, to the top of the mountain ridge forming the southwest corner of the Valle de México. It's a steep slog, taking an hour or two to the top depending on your lungs and legs, but the descent on bike is fast and fun. You can hike to the top of a nearby hilltop and catch the views (and your breath).

From where the dirt road comes to the top of the pass, other dirt tracks head off farther to the west and south, some looping back down toward the monastery and others leading to Los Dinamos and Ajusco. Although these are fun roads for riding if you like to explore, they pass through more isolated stretches of forest and are thus a bit more risky for the odd *bandito.* Most riders stick to returning to Cruz Blanca the way they came up (which is a great downhill on a bike, anyway) to avoid unpleasantness.

LA MARQUESA AND VICINITY

Just as the Mexico City-Toluca highway crosses the pass leaving the valley and starts its descent into the State of Mexico, the road passes through Parque Nacional La Marquesa, in a high valley surrounded by pine forest. Here visitors can find plenty of space to stretch out a blanket, kick around a soccer ball, bike off-road, buy fresh trout, and generally laze around and enjoy the clean, fresh air and greenery.

The forests above La Marquesa, particularly the trails around Valle de los Conejos, are filled with great single-track mountain bike trails, but unfortunately a few robberies have been reported here in recent years. Rock climbers, however, will be glad to hear of a rock pitch called Peñasco de los Perros, in the northwest part of La Marquesa, which is quite safe all week long.

If you feel the stomach rumbling when at

La Marquesa, be sure to enjoy local specialties such as *barbacoa* (pit-baked sheep meat), *sopa de hongo* (mushroom soup), *quesadillas de flor de calabaza,* (squash flower and cheese in a corn tortilla), as well as fresh rabbit and trout, served at the innumerable roadside restaurants around La Marquesa.

To get to La Marquesa without a car, visitors can catch a *pesero* bus at either Tacubaya or Juanacatlán Metro stations up to the park for US$2, taking 45–75 minutes, depending on traffic. The last bus returns to Mexico City at around 8 P.M. As well, you can go to the Observatorio bus station and catch an intercity bus to Tenancingo or Chalma, and get off at La Marquesa.

Valle de los Conejos

A grassy area behind a small group of roadside restaurants about three km (1.8 miles) south of La Marquesa, on the two-lane highway leading to Malinalco, Valle de los Conejos is a good spot to bring a mountain bike for exploring the forests above. The single-track rides leading uphill from the upper edge of Valle de los Conejos are great fun, so it's worth calling a Mexico City bike shop to ask whether the trails are safe; robberies have been reported.

Apart from biking, the meadows of the valley make a fine, out-of-the-way spot to relax on a sunny afternoon. If you don't have wheels, the easiest way out is to take a *pesero* from Metro Juanacatlán, or go to Observatorio bus station and take a bus marked "Chalma" or "Tenancingo," telling the driver you'd like to get off at Valle de los Conejos.

About five km southwest of Valle de los Conejos is Valle del Potrero, another grassy meadow in the forest. A dirt road winds up the mountains from here, eventually crossing over to Los Dinamos, Ajusco, or Desierto de los Leones. Because of its isolation, this may not be the safest road, but the full day trip across the mountains makes a heck of a mountain bike ride.

Climbing Peñasco de los Perros

A small rocky outcrop past the village of Salazar, at the northwest edge of the Marquesa valley, Los Perros is a great place for beginning and intermediate climbers to set up some basic topropes of not undue difficulty.

To get there, continue up the highway toward Toluca, past La Marquesa 2.4 km (1.5 miles) farther to a turnoff on the right, leading another .8 km (.5 mile) to Salazar. From the village, ask for the road to Los Perros. Take this dirt track heading north into a valley and, after arriving at a fork (1.6 km/one mile from the beginning of the track), take the right-hand turn, and you'll be facing Los Perros, a couple of hundred meters away across a field. You'll have to take a cab or walk if you don't have a car, as buses don't come out this way.

Leaving the car in a dirt lot to the left of the road, right at the base of the outcrop (there appear to be no problems with theft here), walk up a steep trail into the pine forest to the base of the 25–35 meter pitch. A scramble up a narrow trail leads to the top of the rock, where you'll find several anchors, as well as a few boulders to rope off of if you don't trust the anchors. Bring plenty of anchor rope, as you may have to hang the anchor to get the climbing rope all the way down to the ground. Facing the rock from the bottom, the crack to the left is the easiest climb (perhaps a 5.7), while the few farther to the right have more difficult entries and are more like 5.8–5.10. The most difficult route is the farthest to the right.

On weekends you may well have to wait your turn. Los Perros is very popular because it's easy to reach and suitable for novice climbers.

Without a car, visitors can get to Los Perros by taking a *pesero* from Metro Juanacatlán marked "Salazar" to the town, and from there either walking or taking a taxi out to the rock.

AJUSCO

The volcanic peak of El Ajusco (3,930 meters) looms large over the southern end of the valley of Mexico, visible to anyone looking down Insurgentes to the south on a semiclear day. Easily reached from downtown, the fields around the base of Ajusco are popular for weekend picknickers, who make good use of the soccer fields, horseback riding, dirt-bike tracks, and many small, rustic restaurants.

To get to Ajusco by car, get on Periférico Sur and look for the turnoff to Reino Aventura amusement park (lots of signs). The road, also called Camino al Ajusco, winds steadily uphill, past the amusement park on the left, through several kilometers of gradually less urban neighborhoods into fields and forest at the base of Volcán Ajusco. Here you'll find dozens of small stands selling tacos, quesadillas, *barbacoa,* and other munchies in the grassy meadows along the roadside. As the road approaches Ajusco it forks and ends up making a complete circle around the mountain in about 20 km (12.5 miles), a popular route for road cyclists on weekends. To get to Ajusco by bus, the easiest way is to go to Metro Tasqueña and from there take the light rail *(train ligero)* to the Estadio Azteca stop. Here look for a *pesero* marked "Ruta 39," which goes up to Ajusco for US$.50. The last one back down to the city leaves Ajusco around 9 P.M. Alternatively, you can catch a *pesero* at Metro CU, and transfer to the Route 39 bus.

At the high point in the circular road around Ajusco, opposite the place where a side paved road branches off out of the valley toward Toluca (also a popular bike ride), is a trail leading to the top of the peak in 1–2 hours' steep climb. It's best to go on this trail only on weekends during the day, when other people are around, to avoid any worries of robbery.

While the forested hills around Ajusco are great for hiking and mountain biking, it's generally not safe to go wandering too far from the road, as robberies are reported with regularity. However, a local *ejido* (communal farm), **San Nicolás Totolapan,** has cordoned off about 2,300 hectares of hillside crossed with dozens of kilometers of dirt roads and trails, ranging in altitude from 2,700 meters at the entrance (Km 11.5 on the Ajusco highway) up to 3,740 meters at its highest point, Montaña Nezehuiloya. The *ejido* patrols the forest, making it totally safe for hiking and biking. Some trails are for bikes only, others for walkers only, and some are for both. Guided trips in the forest can also be arranged; call the *ejido* office at 5630-8935 for more information, or look it up on the Web at www.parquesannicolas.com.mx. Bikes are usually available for rent on weekends at the park, but get there early if you want to get one as they go fast. The park charges US$1 for walkers, US$2 for bikers, and is open Mon.–Fri. 8 A.M.–4 P.M., weekends 7 A.M.–4:30 P.M. Because of the success of this park, it is often held up as a model for other ecotourism projects in Mexico involving local communities.

LOS DINAMOS

A spectacular gorge in the southwest corner of the Valle de México, Los Dinamos comprises 2,293 hectares of communally protected forest and offers some of the best rock climbing in the Mexico City region. The name refers to four generators *(dinamos),* only two of which are in operation, along the narrow Río Magdalena valley.

While the meadows and forest along the valley make a fine spot to pass a sunny afternoon biking on the single-track trails, the forest is best enjoyed on weekends when mounted police from the Magdalena Contreras *delegación* patrol the area. The area around the Segundo (Second) Dinamo, in particular, has been cleaned up and turned into an ecological park that's quite safe on weekends. But it's best not to wander too far from the beaten path, particularly in the forest above the Cuarto (Fourth) Dinamo.

The trails on either side of the river valley between the Segundo and Cuarto Dinamos are popular for mountain bikers and frequently used for local off-road bike races.

Rock-Climbing

Rock climbers will be happy to hear that much of the rock face on the western side of the Los Dinamos gorge is covered with dozens of climbing routes, making it one of the best climbing sites in central Mexico. Local climbers say the routes range mostly from a 5.9 to 5.12B, with lots of cracks and overhangs. The cliff directly opposite the Segundo Dinamo parking lot is dotted with climbers every weekend. The routes here are mostly bolted, and no top-roping routes appear to be available.

More bolted routes are found downriver by

the Primer Dinamo, while the climbs up at the Cuarto Dinamo are mostly bolt-free for the trad climbers out there.

For whatever reason (probably the steep hike to the base of the cliffs) climbers have not reported problems with theft, even before the police started patrolling the park.

Getting There

To reach Los Dinamos by car, take the Periférico Sur to the Magdalena Contreras exit, just west of the Ajusco exit. Follow the signs to "Contreras" and "Los Dinamos" through Santa Teresa and Magdalena Contreras to the edge of the forest, three km (two miles) from the Periférico. A paved road continues up the left side of the valley, reaching the Segundo Dinamo in three km (1.8 miles) and the Cuarto Dinamo, four km (2.5 miles) farther.

Those without a private vehicle can hop on the Metro to the Miguel Ángel de Quevedo or the Copilco stations, and from there look for the microbuses to Contreras. Get off at the end of the line, a small square faced on one side by food and handicraft shops and on the other by the 18th-century Santa María Magdalena Contreras chapel, with a fine guilded *retablo.* From this square, special buses continue farther up the road, on weekends only, stopping half a mile short of the Cuarto Dinamo. During the week, visitors have to walk or hire a taxi from the Contreras bus stop.

Accommodations

Places to stay in Mexico City run the gamut from spartan hostels to no-nonsense business hotels to plush inns in historic surroundings. In the expensive to premium categories, you can pretty well request and receive any service you desire. In the shoestring and budget classes, make sure you know what you're getting before moving in. If it's important to you to have a window, look before accepting a room. Check for security, too—is there a safe deposit box or some similar place to leave your valuables while touring? Though the weather in Mexico is usually mild, it can get cold at night in the winter; check for heat or ask for plenty of blankets. In the summer, it can get warm on occasion, so consider looking for air-conditioning or a fan.

Where to Stay?

Despite the great variety of accommodations the city offers, hotel locations remain concentrated in only a few areas, mainly in the Reforma-Zona Rosa-Centro Histórico area and along busy boulevards radiating from the center. Colonia Condesa, one of the more happening neighborhoods in the city these days, is ripe for someone to come in and build a few hotels or bed-and-breakfasts in any price category. There is nowhere to stay in this area other than the noisy Hotel Roosevelt on Insurgentes Sur, although there are a couple of places in the nearby Roma neighborhood. Coyoacán and San Ángel could also use some convenient accommodations—we searched high and low and there appears to be nothing available within 10 blocks of either area.

Most travelers on a tight budget opt to stay in the less expensive and centrally located hotels downtown and near the Monumento a la Revolución. Downtown and near the Zona Rosa are a good supply of midrange and higher-priced hotels, and the real luxury spots are found mostly in the Zona Rosa and Chapultepec/Polanco.

© CHRIS HUMPHREY

Estado de México's bucolic countryside: Tenango de Arista

Rates

Accommodations values, surprisingly, are among the best of any city in Mexico, probably because competition is keen. Except toward the high end, room rates tend to be moderate if not downright cheap to begin with, but you may still be able to save money by planning your stay for certain times of the year or days of the week.

Even in the priciest hotels you can often get some kind of a discount, especially at certain times of the year, if you arrive late at night, or if the hotel isn't filled. A few more possibilities: **American Automobile Association** (AAA) members generally can get 20 percent off. If you carry a **business card,** ask for a business discount. If you make **reservations** from the airport hotel desks, they frequently offer packages for a little less than the going rates. Or just ask for a discount after they quote a price. Obviously, it won't always work, but occasionally discounts come to those who ask. More upscale hotels often have better rates available on their web pages.

For business hotels along the Paseo de la Reforma, rates may be lower on weekends than during the week. At hotels in the Centro Histórico or at tourist-oriented hotels anywhere in the city, there's no difference between weekend and weekday stays.

Whatever the walk-in rate, you can sometimes bargain the price down except during peak periods such as Christmas or Easter. When checking in be sure to inquire whether the room rate includes breakfast—occasionally it does. Asking for a room without breakfast *(sin desayuno)* is an easy way to bring the rate down, or simply ask if there's anything more inexpensive available *("¿Hay algo más barato?")*. You can usually count on finding cheaper breakfasts outside the hotel.

In this book we use the following scale to categorize the pricing of accommodations:

Shoestring: less than US$15
Budget: US$15–30
Inexpensive: US$30–50
Moderate: US$50–75
Expensive: US$75–110
Premium: US$110 and up

The hotel sections below are organized by district, then by price category.

Taxes and Surcharges

Unless otherwise noted, the prices listed in this guide do not include 15 percent IVA and 2 percent city lodging tax. Some of the more expensive hotels also tack on a 10 percent service charge. Be sure to ask, before checking in, whether tax and service are included in quoted rates.

CENTRO HISTÓRICO

You'll find plenty of hotels in the Centro to suit almost any price range, particularly in the area from the Zócalo west to Eje Central. Budget travelers in particular will find a number of good deals to choose from, all conveniently located. Those looking for a bit more pampering have a few decent options, but if you're looking for a top-quality luxury hotel, head to the Zona Rosa or Polanco.

Shoestring

Two new hostels have opened in downtown, which are great options for budget travelers. Both are well-managed and receive rave reviews from the backpacker crowd. The first is **Hostal Moneda,** Moneda 8, tel. 5522-5821 or 5522-5803, www.hostalmoneda.com.mx, a member of Hostelling International (HI, formerly International Youth Hostel Federation). The hostel features 90 beds distributed in three-bed and four-bed communal rooms as well as private double and triple rooms. Downstairs is a kitchen, washing area, and Internet station, and on the roof is a small terrace café with great views. The location, just half a block east of the Zócalo, couldn't be better for exploring the Centro. The owner works with an adventure travel company that offers hiking, biking, and rafting trips in central Mexico. Rates: US$10–13 per bed, depending on number of beds per room; HI members receive a discount. Breakfast included.

On the other side of the Zócalo, right behind the Catedral, is **Hostel Catedral,** República de Guatemala 4, tel. 5518-1726, www.hostelcatedral.com. Slightly more upscale than the Hostal Moneda, the Catedral has 204 beds in dorm-style rooms with wooden floors, lockers, and new furniture. A few rooms have views out front toward the Catedral. Coin washing machines and small kitchen are available for guests. Downstairs is a pool hall, Internet café, travel agency, and patio restaurant. Rates: $10 for dorm beds with HI or International Student ID cards, $12 without, buffet breakfast included; $24 d for one of five private rooms; $34 d for a nicer private room with a small terrace.

Of the downtown hotels, **Hotel Zamora,** Cinco de Mayo 50, tel. 5512-1832, is a longtime favorite among the backpacker crowd, with 36 rooms in four stories around a small interior patio. The tiled building is kept clean but can be noisy. Rates: US$8 s, US$12 d with shared bath; US$10 s, US$14 d with private bath.

Near the Zamora, **Hotel Rioja,** Cinco de Mayo 45, tel. 5521-8333, seems to be in a near-permanent state of remodeling, but it has adequate, inexpensive rooms, each with private bath. Rates: US$9.50 s, US$11 d, US$16 for two beds for 1–4 people.

Hotel Buenos Aires, Motolinía 21, tel. 5518-2104, occupies an ancient two-story colonial building just off Cinco de Mayo. The rooms are surprisingly decent, considering how tattered the outside of the building looks. All rooms have TVs and high ceilings. Rates: US$9 s, US$12 d, less with shared bath.

On a pedestrian street three blocks west of the Zócalo, **Hotel Lafayette,** Motolinía 40, tel. 5521-9640, is a rather unattractive modern structure on the corner of 16 de Septiembre, but its TV-equipped rooms are a fair value and popular with many low-budget Mexican tourists. The interior rooms are a bit claustrophobic, but the exterior ones are well lit, and the pedestrian-only street is quiet after dark. Laundry services are available. Rates: US$12 s, US$14 d.

Budget

Four blocks southwest of the Zócalo, in a rambling old five-story building across from the Templo de San Agustín, the **Hotel Isabel,** Isabel la Católica 63, tel. 5518-1213, fax 5521-1233, is popular with young foreign travelers. The 74 rooms have high ceilings, private or shared bath, TV, and phone. Exterior rooms are less stuffy than interior rooms, but also noisier. A restaurant and bar are on the premises, and the staff speaks English. Rates: US$15 s, US$18 d, or less with shared bath.

Around the corner from the Isabel, on the other side of the Templo San Agustín, **Hotel Monte Carlo,** República de Uruguay 89, tel. 5521-2559, offers 60 rooms housed in what used to be part of the Augustinian convent. With the recent interior makeover (pink paint-job and all), it's hard to notice the colonial flavor, but the rooms do have high ceilings. Famed authors D. H. Lawrence and Somerset Maugham both stayed here in the early 20th century. Parking available. Rates: US$16 s, US$18 d, less with shared bath.

Four blocks west of the Zócalo in an older, four-story building, **Hotel Principal,** Bolívar 29, tel. 5521-1333, features basic, clean rooms with TV and phone. It's a known favorite among backpackers. Rates: US$17 s, US$19 d with one bed, US$24 d with two beds, lower rates if you don't mind sharing the hallway bathroom.

Inexpensive

Behind the Catedral Metropolitana, and half a block from Templo Mayor, **Hotel Catedral,** Donceles 95, tel. 5518-5232, fax 5512-4344, email: hcatedra@mpsnet.com.mx, is a clean, modern, and very comfortable place with a friendly and helpful staff. Another major plus: all local calls are free, and you can make data as well as voice calls, unlike at many Mexico City hotels that cost much more. The hotel features a good restaurant and bar, as well as a travel agency, all on the ground floor. One drawback is the traffic on Donceles in front of the hotel, which can be quite thick during rush hour; keep this in mind if you're planning to catch a taxi to the airport or bus station. Rates: US$32 s, US$40 d, junior suites US$49.

Hotel Capitol, Uruguay 12 between Eje Central and Bolívar, tel. 5518-1750, fax 5521-1149, has a distinctly sanitized, chain-motel feel despite being housed in a colonial-era building with an inner courtyard. The decor is less than elegant, but the rooms are functional. Rates: US$33 s/d, US$39 d with two beds.

Hotel Gillow, Isabel la Católica 17, tel. 5510-

0791, has 103 clean if somewhat characterless rooms, each with private bath and TV. The hotel is conveniently located just off the Zócalo and the restaurant is good. Rates: US$34 s, US$39 d with one bed, US$46 d with two beds.

Similar, though less expensive, is the nearby **Hotel Canadá,** Cinco de Mayo 47, tel. 5518-2106, fax 5512-9310. Rates: US$29 s, US$32 d one bed, US$35 d two beds.

Moderate

Hotel Ritz, Madero 30, tel. 5518-1340, fax 5518-3466, www.hotelritzdf.com.mx, has 130 rooms decorated with '60s lounge-style furniture (not chic, but comfortable) and carpets that have seen better days. The attached Vips restaurant offers room service, and the seven-floor hotel has a rooftop terrace. Rates: US$57 s/d, US$80 suite; breakfast included.

Expensive

The **Gran Hotel de la Ciudad,** Av. 16 de Septiembre 82, tel. 5510-4040, fax 5512-6772, www.granhotel.com.mx, was built on the west side of the Zócalo in 1899 as a trading house. The dazzling art-deco interior includes a large Tiffany stained-glass dome and wrought-iron elevators. Unfortunately most of the rooms are quite bare and don't live up to the promise of the building's style. Some have been remodeled and are reasonably attractive—have a look first to make sure you get one of those. Rates: US$92 d, US$160 suite, rooms facing the Zócalo cost more.

Adjacent to the Gran Hotel on the same block, but with its entrance on Avenida Madero, is the **Best Western Hotel Majestic,** Av. F. Madero 73, tel. 5521-8600, fax 5518-3466, U.S./Canada tel. 800/528-1234, www.majestic.com.mx. The rooms are small and nothing to write home about, but the location on the Zócalo is hard to beat. The patio restaurant is a fine spot for a meal overlooking the square, whether or not you're staying at the hotel. Rates: US$105 s/d, suites US$160, rooms facing the Zócalo cost more.

A new entrant in the upscale market in the Centro is the **Holiday Inn Select,** also on the west side of the Zócalo with its entrance on Cinco de Mayo, tel. 5521-2121, toll free in Mexico 800/990-9999, www.holidayinnzocalo.com.mx. In operation only since 1998, this hotel has 110 rooms that are a bit cramped but well stocked

ACCOMMODATIONS

lobby, Hotel Majestic

with new furniture and accoutrements, and the service is very good. Like the adjacent Hotel Majestic, the Holiday Inn has a rooftop patio restaurant, a good spot for a bird's-eye view of the square. Rates: US$95 s/d, up to US$165 for the master suite.

ALAMEDA CENTRAL

Shoestring

Hotel Conde, Pescaditos 15, tel. 5521-1084, offers good value—clean, bright, efficient rooms with tile baths. The hotel's lounge includes an upright piano, TV, and several sofas for relaxing. Parking is available. Rates: US$14 s or d, US$17 t.

Across the street from a lively square rests **Hotel del Valle,** Independencia 35, tel. 5521-8067. The rooms are a little musty and dark, but the hotel restaurant is always teeming with locals and travelers. A remarkably tacky bar adjoins the eatery. Rates: US$12 s, US$14 d, US$17 t.

If treacherous stairs, dubious stains, and no toilet seats don't bother you, **Hotel Sevillano,** Ayuntamiento 78, tel. 5512-6715, is about as cheap as it gets in Mexico City. The hotel allows no visitors, but condoms, toiletries, and snacks are available at the front desk. Rates: US$9 s, US$12 d, US$14 t, US$15 q.

Budget

A block north of the Alameda, **Hotel Hidalgo,** Santa Veracruz 37, tel. 5521-8771, has 100 clean, modest rooms with large bathrooms. The hotel is in a funkier neighborhood than most budget offerings but the service is excellent. Rates: US$22 s, US$27 d, US$30 t, US$34 q.

Hotel Manolo, Luis Moya 111, tel. 5521-3739, has dark but clean rooms with a large enclosed garage as well as a cavernlike contemporary lobby with a TV. Rates: US$18 s or d.

The 87-room **Hotel San Diego,** Luis Moya 98, tel. 5510-3523, is yet another affable and affordable option on Luis Moya. The street boasts a number of these medium-sized cheapies. This one offers room service and a central garden. Rates: US$15 s, US$16 d, US$25 t.

Hotel Fornos, Revillagigedo 92, tel. 5521-9594, fax 5510-4732, has a large, gated parking lot entrance on Luis Moya. The hotel has a busy bar and restaurant and offers rooms with hot tubs for a premium. Rates: US$17 s, US$20 d.

Inexpensive

Hotel Fleming, Revillagigedo 35, tel. 5510-4530, fax 5512-0284, features 80 rooms, 20 junior suites with hot tubs, ample parking, and a decent coffee shop. Very clean, and a good bargain. Rates: US$31 s, US$37 d, US$40 t.

With a modern facade and a welcoming sculpture-and-cactus garden, the **Hotel Marlowe,** Independencia 17, tel. 5521-9540, fax 5518-6862, offers 120 newer rooms including some with terraces. Rates: US$35 s, US$41 d, US$45 t.

The clean, friendly **Hotel Monte Real,** Revillagigedo 23, tel. 5518-1149, fax 5512-6419, is an efficiently run, crisply decorated venue with a restaurant/bar and a 24-hour café stuffed with Mexican handicrafts. There's an interior courtyard, though it's not accessible to guests, and the 135 rooms have satellite TVs but are a bit cramped. Parking is available. Rates: US$43 s or d.

Near the Palacio Bellas Artes, **Hotel Ambassador,** Humboldt 38, tel. 5518-0110, fax 5510-9645, is a similar 151-room establishment with the added advantage of being very near Fonda Santa Anita, one of the Centro's most authentic Mexican eateries. Rates: US$37 s, US$42 d.

Moderate

A refreshing combination of modern convenience and Mexican decor, the **Hotel San Francisco,** Luis Moya 11, tel. 5521-8960, fax 5510-8831, www.sanfrancisco.com.mx, is half a block from the Alameda's southern esplanade. The hotel's lobby boasts bright, modern Mexican murals and rustic seating. The rooms, including suites with large balconies (some with Alameda views), are spacious and tasteful. Rates: US$50 s or d, US$52 t.

Another good value is the modern **Hotel Metropol,** Luis Moya 39, tel. 5510-8660, fax 5512-1273, two blocks south of the Alameda. The 160 clean rooms have telephones and new color TVs, and hotel service is generally very good. The hotel has a restaurant/bar and travel agency as well as room service. Rates: US$51 s, US$59 d.

Hotel Bamer, Av. Juárez 52, tel. 5521-9060, fax 5510-1793, has been a traveler's old-reliable for years. The hotel faces the Alameda and is within walking distance of many attractions. Rooms and suites are spacious and have comfy beds; some also have sweeping views of the Alameda. A small *tabaquería* (tobacco shop) sells essentials, a lobby bar dispenses libation, and a brightly lit cafeteria is open daily 7 A.M.–11 P.M. Rates: US$48 s, US$53 d.

Expensive

The **Best Western Hotel de Cortés,** Av. Hidalgo 85, tel. 5518-2184, fax 5512-1863, U.S./Canada tel. 800/528-1234, www.bestwestern.com/reservations/mx, opposite the northwest corner of the Alameda, has lots of historical ambience. Originally built in 1730 as the Hospice of Saint Nicolás Tolentino of the Saint Augustine Hermits, it was originally dedicated to providing housing and food for the poor. Closed for several years following Mexican Independence, the building reopened in 1860 as a hostel for traveling tradesmen on local market days. The owners inaugurated the Hotel de Cortés in 1943, and today it offers 27 rooms and suites along with a small restaurant/bar and a beautiful courtyard dining area. Corner suites feature separate sitting areas; a few nonsmoking rooms are available. Although the rooms are nothing spectacular, the beautiful two-story terra cotta–colored courtyard, with its fountain, lush foliage, and caged songbirds, is a lovely place to have a relaxed meal. *Trovadores* often perform in the afternoon. The 2 P.M. check-out time is another plus. Rates: US$108 s or d, US$154 suite, plus tax.

The 246-room **Hotel Fontan,** Colón 27, tel. 5518-5460, fax 5521-9240, is a big multistory glass-front hotel next to the Hidalgo Metro station. A travel agency and restaurant are attached. Rates: US$89 s, US$102 d.

PASEO DE LA REFORMA AND ZONA ROSA

Because of its central location, the availability of services, and the relatively easy access to transportation, the Reforma/Zona Rosa area makes a good base from which to tour Mexico City. The hotels in the Zona Rosa and on Reforma fall toward the higher end of the scale, while attractive midrange accommodations can be found just off Reforma, both near the Monumento de Colón and behind the U.S. embassy. Budget travelers will find plenty of low-priced hotels of varying quality in the few blocks between the Monumento a la Revolución and Avenida Puente de Alvarado.

Shoestring

Near the Monumento a la Revolución, **Casa de los Amigos,** Ignacio Mariscal 132, tel. 5705-0521, fax 5705-0771, www.avantel.net/~friends, is run by Quakers and often serves as a base for people doing social work in Mexico and Central America. Don't worry, they don't proselytize, but you are asked not to bring alcohol into the hostel. Reception closes at 10 P.M., so arrive before that on your first night. Guests may also use the kitchen, which can help save pesos. There is a minimum stay of four days and a maximum of 15 days per month. Rates: US$9 for dorm bed, US$11 s or US$20 d for small private rooms. One studio double with a small kitchen rents for US$33.

Nearby but of a very different social milieu is **Hotel Oxford,** Ignacio Mariscal 67, tel. 5566-0500, which serves as a part-time brothel, but it remains popular with backpackers because it offers reasonably clean, inexpensive rooms. It has decent little bar inside for late-night drinks. Rates: US$11 s, US$13 d.

Just up the street from the Oxford is **Hotel Pennsylvania,** Ignacio Mariscal 101, tel. 5703-1384, also a bit worn but functional for those on a budget. Rates: US$13 s, US$16 d.

Budget

One block from the Monumento a la Revolución, **Hotel Edison,** Calle Thomas A. Edison 106, tel. 5566-0933, is a modest, inexpensive hotel. Each of the carpeted rooms has a writing desk, TV, telephone, and chairs with well-worn cushions. Check your mattress as some are severely mushy. Parking available. Rates: US$19 s, US$22 d.

Almost opposite Casa de los Amigos is the modern **Hotel Texas,** Ignacio Mariscal 129, tel. 5705-5782, with an attached parking lot. Rates: US$19 s, US$22 d, US$26 d with two beds.

Inexpensive

A couple of blocks north of Reforma, the 150-room **María Christina,** Río Lerma 31, tel. 5566-9688, fax 5566-9194, is a decent hotel in a four-story colonial-style building featuring interior gardens frequented by midrange travelers. The large suites are a good value, and each is furnished with a wet bar. The attached coffee shop is popular with guests and nonguests alike. A good selections of magazines can be found in the hotel bookshop. Rates: US$39 s, US$44 d, US$54–61 suites.

Casa González, Río Sena 69 at Río Lerma, tel. 5514-3302, fax 5511-0702, is a small inn consisting of a cluster of colonial and post-colonial houses close to the U.S. and British embassies. The owner and his family still live in one wing, and staying here is a little like staying in an old, rambling home. The separate buildings, each painted a cheerful white with blue trim and containing several rooms, are situated around a landscaped courtyard. Several of the 22 rooms have their own little patios, which make lovely spots to sit outside, relax, and listen to the birds sing. It's best to call ahead for reservations. Off-street parking isn't available at the hotel, but there's a public pay lot next door. Rates: US$24 for very small singles, US$27 for larger singles or US$33 d, or up to US$55 for one of the better rooms.

Hotel Corinto, Calle Vallarta 24, tel. 5566-6555, fax 5546-6888, is a 10-story, 155-room building one block south of the Monumento a la Revolución. The modern rooms are a bit on the small side but comfortable and a good value, with a tiled bath, TV, and phone. Parking is available, and the hotel also has a small pool. Rates: US$34 s, US$36 d.

Moderate

The 148-room **Hotel Bristol,** Plaza Necaxa 17, tel. 5208-1717, fax 5533-6060, is behind the U.S. embassy, three blocks from Paseo de la Reforma, and near the Zona Rosa. Recently remodeled, the rooms are very clean and modern with air-conditioning and large TVs. Amenities include a restaurant, bar, free parking, and an efficient staff. Rates: US$47 s, US$54 d for interior rooms; US$51 s, US$58 d for exterior rooms; US$56–65 for junior suites; and up to US$100 for penthouse suites. Tax included.

About halfway between the Zona Rosa and the Alameda is **Mi Casa,** General Prim 101, tel. 5566-6711, an inexpensive apartment-hotel with 27 modern rooms equipped with full kitchens. Rates: US$47 s, US$54 d, suites up to US$65.

Expensive

The 12-story **Casa Blanca,** La Fragua 7, tel. 5705-1300, fax 5705-4197, U.S./Canada tel. 800/972-2162, www.hotel-casablanca.com.mx, is a thoroughly modern hotel with 270 pastel rooms, each with wall-to-wall carpeting, subdued fluorescent lighting, marble-tiled baths, comfortable chairs and tables, piped-in music, and air-conditioning. A rooftop pool and bar overlook the city. Rates: US$84 s, US$105 d.

Premium

In front of the Monumento de Colón, the venerable **Fiesta Americana,** Paseo de la Reforma 80, tel. 5705-1515, fax 5705-1313, www.fiestaamericana.com, does well with the middle-class business crowd. Rooms are large and comfortable and the restaurant has a good reputation for quality Mexican food. On the downside, telephone lines in guest rooms do not have data transmission capability. Rates: US$125 s/d.

A higher-end choice for international businesspeople is the **Hotel Four Seasons,** Paseo de la Reforma 500, tel. 5230-1818, fax 5230-1808, toll-free in Mexico 800/906-7500, www.fourseasons.com/mexico. In an eight-story neocolonial building at the western end of Reforma, the rooms are unusually homey, filled with plants and comfortable furniture, and the courtyard café is a lovely spot for breakfast. The hotel restaurant is frequented by politicos and businessfolk negotiating deals. Rates: US$320 s/d, US$340 suite.

Galería Plaza, Hamburgo 195, tel. 5230-1717, fax 5207-5867, www.brisas.com.mx, is a luxury favorite in the middle of the Zona Rosa, with 439 elegantly decorated rooms, each with a marble bathroom and all the amenities. The hotel's Île de France restaurant is frequently recommended. Rates: US$180 s/d, suites US$260–290.

Another Zona Rosa base popular with business travelers is **Hotel Krystal Rosa,** Liverpool 155, tel. 5228-9928, fax 5511-3490, U.S./Canada tel. 800/231-9860, www.krystalzonarosa.com.mx. Guests will find a good selection in the restaurants and lively nightlife in the various lounges. Rates: US$185 s/d.

The concrete and steel **Hotel Marco Polo,** Amberes 27, tel. 5207-1893, fax 5533-3727, U.S. tel. 800/448-8355, www.marcopolo.com.mx, sits near the heart of the Zona Rosa on a quiet side street just off Reforma. The 60 carpeted rooms have a somewhat postmodern feel, and the staff do their best to pamper guests. A restaurant and piano bar can be found on the hotel's ground floor. Rates: US$137 s, US$153 d; cheaper rates frequently available on the web page.

A pink granite-and-glass structure on the western section of Reforma, with hints of art deco lines, **Hotel Marquis Reforma,** Paseo de la Reforma 465, tel. 5229-1200, fax 5229-1212, U.S. tel. 800/235-2387, Canada tel. 877/818-5011, www.marquisreformahl.com.mx, contains 208 rooms and 84 suites with soft-toned modern styling and vaguely antique-looking furniture. All rooms have data ports and faxes, and cellular telephone rental is available. Female guests can choose to room on a floor reserved for women only. On the premises are the stylish international restaurant La Jolla, a bar, and a gym with sauna and hot tub. Rates: US$265 s/d, US$320 regular suite.

CHAPULTEPEC/POLANCO

The area around Chapultepec and Polanco has some of the finest and most expensive hotels in the city, favored by many businesspeople and wealthier tourists. Low-budget travelers won't find anything in their price range here.

Camino Real Mexico City fills the corners of its unique whitewashed, cubist building with a flamboyant selection of modern art, including a Rufino Tamayo mural in the lobby and masterworks elsewhere by Alexander Calder, Pedro Coronel, Davíd Alfaro Siqueiros, and Gunther Gerzo.

Premium

A short distance from the edge of Chapultepec, the Ricardo Legorreta-designed **Camino Real Mexico City,** Av. Mariano Escobedo 700, tel. 5263-8888, U.S./Canada tel. 800/722-6466, www.caminoreal.com/mexicocity, fills the corners of its unique whitewashed, cubist building with a flamboyant selection of modern art, including a Rufino Tamayo mural in the lobby and masterworks elsewhere by Alexander Calder, Pedro Coronel, Davíd Alfaro Siqueiros, and Gunther Gerzo. Wandering around the palatial corridors of the five-story main building, lined with banquet halls and bars, one could be forgiven for forgetting that it's a hotel. The 713 airy rooms, decorated in solid colors, are practically hidden in the corners of the hotel, which also boasts three swimming pools, four rooftop tennis courts (illuminated for night play), and an excellent health club available to nonguests for US$10 per visit. The hotel has several restaurants and bars to choose from, including a branch of Fouquet's de Paris, one of the best French restaurants in Mexico. Rates: US$210–230 s/d, US$310 executive floor.

Just off Paseo de la Reforma, opposite the first section of Chapultepec, three more of Mexico City's best hotels dominate the skyline. The 38-story tower of **Hotel Nikko México,** Campos Eliseos 204, tel. 5280-1111, fax 5280-9191, www.nikkohotels.com, is visible from much of the city on a clear day. The Nikko boasts a complete business center, health club with pool and tennis courts, a golf driving range, several restaurants and bars, and a wealth of other amenities. The 745 rooms are rather standard looking, considering the price. Rates: US$210 s/d, US$245 executive room, US$600 suite

Right next door to the Nikko, the **Presidente**

Inter-Continental Mexico City, Campos Eliseos 218, tel. 5327-7700, fax 5327-7730, U.S./Canada tel. 800/327-0200, www.interconti.com, was built in 1977, making it the oldest of the park hotels. A multistory pyramid lobby topped with an immense skylight never fails to impress. The 660 rooms, though not exceptional, are well equipped, and executive suites equipped with Internet connections and fax machines are available. The hotel has a "gourmet center" with seven restaurants featuring different world cuisines, and the Balmoral tea room serves an excellent English-style high tea and snacks. Rates: US$240 s/d, US$325 executive (lower rates are often available).

A half a block from the Nikko and Presidente, at Campos Eliseos and Andrés Bello, the **JW Marriott,** Andrés Bello 29, tel. 5999-0000, fax 5999-0001, U.S./Canada tel. 888/813-2776, www.marriott.com, is considered by many to have the best rooms of the "big three." The Marriott has 300 rooms and 20 suites and has a reputation for top-notch service. Rates: US$265 standard, US$295 executive (rates as low as US$190 standard are often available).

A relative newcomer to the area is the **Fiesta Americana Grande,** Mariano Escobedo 756, tel. 5281-1500, toll free in Mexico 800/504-5000, U.S. tel. 800/343-7821, http://fiestaamericana.com. A complement to the venerable Fiesta Americana on Paseo de la Reforma, this sleek new tower houses 203 rooms and 14 suites, with a full spa and business center and three executive floors. Rates: US$190 s/d, or up to $310 for the standard suite.

A change from the high-powered high-rise hotels, though even more pricey, is **Casa Vieja,** Eugenio Sue 45, tel. 5282-0067, fax 5281-3780, www.casavieja.com, a converted late 19th–century mansion ideally located in the center of Polanco along a quiet side street. The 10 rooms all have a kitchen, stereo, fax machine, desk, and satellite TV and are decorated in Mexican style with bright solid colors, tiles, woven rugs, and wooden furniture. Rates: US$350 d for a one-bedroom suite, US$550 for a one-bedroom suite with living room, US$850 two-bedroom suite with living room (corporate rates and other discounts frequently available).

Also a change of pace, but of a very different variety, is **Hotel Hábita,** Av. Masaryk 201, tel. 5282-3100, www.hotelhabita.com. A member of Small Luxury Hotels and Design Hotels, Hábita is done up in a ultramodern style with lots of glass and sleek styling. Each of the 36 carpeted rooms is elegently simple, with futons and a small terrace. Suites are only slightly larger than the regular rooms. Each room has direct Internet data ports, and the hotel has a business/conference center. On the roof is a glassed-in exercise room and open-air pool, as well as a popular hipster lounge bar called El Área. The restaurant downstairs is very tasty and is also frequented by nonguests. Rates: US$195 s, US$225 d, US$275 suite.

ROMA/CONDESA

As Condesa and Roma are a bit off the tourist track, not a lot of hotel options are to be found in these neighborhoods. But the section of Álvaro Obregón between Insurgentes and Cuauhtémoc, Roma's main drag, has a few decent lower-priced hotels to choose from. Closer toward the Zona Rosa and Reforma is La Casona, the area's only upscale hotel.

Budget

The bright pink **Hotel Colonia Roma,** Jalapa 100 at Álvaro Obregón, tel. 5584-1396, offers 50 small, carpeted rooms with TV and telephone. Rates: US$16 s/d.

Three blocks east is **Hotel Monarca,** Álvaro Obregón 32, tel. 5584-0461, an unattractive five-story building which nonetheless has inexpensive and decent rooms. Popular among middle-class Mexicans. Rates: US$17 s/d.

Although the vaguely elegant lobby promises more than the rooms deliver, **Hotel Saratoga,** Álvaro Obregón 38, tel. 5147-8233, is reasonably well kept and not a bad deal. Rates: US$17 s, US$21 d; or US$26 s, US$30 d for a larger room.

Inexpensive

Hotel Milan, Álvaro Obregón 94, tel. 5584-0222, fax 5584-0696, has a remarkably ugly facade, but the rooms are modern and very livable.

The hotel has a restaurant/bar and parking. Rates: US$38 s, US$42 d.

The only hotel in Condesa, right on Insurgentes but with easy access to Parque México, is **Hotel Roosevelt,** Insurgentes Sur 287, tel. 5208-6813. The hotel, with 75 modern rooms, each with cable TV and telephone, has a sanitized, motel-like feel. A reasonably priced coffee shop and parking garage are on the ground floor. Rates: US$33 s/d, US$38 king-sized bed.

Moderate

An excellent midrange hotel in the Roma Norte is **Hotel Parque Ensenada,** Álvaro Obregón 13, tel. 5208-0052, with 140 comfortable, carpeted modern rooms, each equipped with bedside fan, small fridge, TV, and phone. Hotel staff are efficient and friendly. Rates: US$53 s, US$57 d.

Premium

In a residential area of the Roma neighborhood, near the Zona Rosa, **La Casona,** Durango 280, tel. 5286-3001, fax 5211-0871, www.hotellacasona.com.mx, is housed in a refurbished late-19th-century mansion. The small but luxurious hotel contains a very good café-restaurant, a gym, services for business travelers, and 30 rooms filled with wooden writing desks, and lacy curtains. A great alternative to the upscale tower hotels along Reforma. Rates: US$181 s/d with breakfast included.

COYOACÁN/SAN ÁNGEL

Although as yet there is nothing available in central Coyoacán or San Ángel, a cluster of three hotels can be found on Calzada de Tlapan near the Metro Tasqueña station, the southern terminus for Metro Línea 2. Also near this area is the Terminal Central del Sur bus station. It's a relatively short taxi or *pesero* ride to Coyoacán and San Ángel to the west.

Inexpensive

Hotel Cibeles, Calz. de Tlalpan 1507, tel. 5672-2244, offers basic rooms equipped with cable TV and air-conditioning in a modern building. The hotel has a restaurant with room service and a bar. Rates: US$41 s/d one bed, US$53 d with two beds.

Comfortable **Hotel Montreal,** Calz. de Tlalpan 2073, tel. 5689-0011, has 91 rooms with all the normal amenities. Rates: US$31 s/d one bed, US$46 d with two beds.

The best choice of the three is the modern, 128-room **Hotel Finisterre,** Calz. de Tlalpan 2043, tel. 5689-9544, fax 5689-9720. Rates: US$27 s, US$38 d, US$44 d with whirlpool bath.

NEAR THE AIRPORT

Inexpensive

The closest decent low-priced hotel near the airport is **Hotel Aeropuerto,** Boulevard Aeropuerto 380, tel. 5785-5888 or 5785-5851, just across the Circuito Interior from the airport. To get there on foot, walk all the way past the domestic terminal, follow the street around to the left past the Metro station entrance, and cross the Circuito Interior via the nearby pedestrian bridge. The hotel, with 52 basic rooms with TVs and telephones, is right on the far side of the bridge. Rates: US$35 s/d one bed, US$44 d two beds.

Expensive

Next door to Hotel Aeropuerto is **Hotel Jr Plaza,** Boulevard Aeropuerto 390, tel. 5785-5200 or 5785-6500, a major step up in price and quality. Rates: US$82 s or d.

Premium

Connected to the domestic terminal (near Sala B) via a pedestrian bridge is the **Airport Marriott Hotel,** Puerto México 80, tel. 5133-0033, fax 5133-0030, www.marriotthotels.com, a 583-room monster of a hotel with a very pleasant, leafy lobby. Guests (and the general public, for US$10) have access to a full health club and indoor pool. The hotel has three restaurants, a bar, a 24-hour café, and a 24-hour business center. Even if you don't spend the night in the hotel, the coffee shop is a much nicer place to spend layover time than comparable facilities at the airport. Rates: US$165 s/d.

The newer **Airport Hilton,** tel./fax 5133-0505, www.hilton.com, is actually built on top of the international terminal—take the elevator up to the fourth floor, and you will be in the lobby. The 129 rooms all have a separate phone line for computers. Rates: US$160 s/d.

NEAR BUS TERMINALS

Terminal Central del Norte

Budget: Hotel Brasilia, Av. de Los Cien Metros, tel. 5587-8577, is just two blocks from the Terminal Norte, easily walkable if you don't have too much luggage. The hotel is no great shakes, but it's more than adequate for an overnight stay if you come in late or need to leave early and don't have time to get into town for a nicer place. The hotel has a decent restaurant attached. Rates: US$27 s/d.

Terminal Central del Sur

See the Coyoacán/San Ángel entries in this chapter.

Food and Drink

Mexican cuisine isn't a single, monolithic cooking style. By blending New World and Old World influences, Mexicans have developed a range of specialties that form recognizable local cuisines. Mexico City brings together regional specialties from all over the nation, from coastal seafood to Altiplano beef to Oaxacan mole.

Many of the ingredients and cooking techniques seen in Mexico City kitchens today were observed by the Spanish when they first arrived in the capital's Aztec-dominated antecedent, Tenochtitlán, in the 1520s. At that time the local Amerindians were farming chiles, corn, beans, tomatoes, cacao, sweet potatoes, squash, onions, and other vegetables and legumes that they combined with trout, lobster, crab, oyster, frog, armadillo, dog, turkey, and deer to produce a cuisine that may not have differed a great deal from traditional Mexican cuisine as we know it today. The *comal* (flat griddle) and *cazuela* (fired clay bowl) were in use, and corn was ground and mixed with water to make *masa,* a cornmeal dough with which tortillas and tamales were made. Spain's main contributions to the diet were beef, pork, cheese, and wheat flour.

WHERE TO EAT

In this city that draws migrants from every corner of the country, you'll find every sort of dining venue, from humble sidewalk taco stands to five-star hotel restaurants.

Cheap and Fast

At the ***taquería,*** tacos are assembled before your eyes—more or less the Mexican equivalent to the old-fashioned American hamburger stand. *Taquerías* are most often located in areas where there's

© ELENA PAPPAS

Fresh fruit is everywhere in Mexico City, like at this stand in Coyoacán.

a lot of foot traffic. The good ones will be packed with taco eaters in the early evening.

Another economical choice is any ***lonchería,*** a small, café-style place that usually serves *almuerzo* (late breakfast/early lunch) and *comida* (the main, midday meal). *Lonchería* hours are typically 11 A.M.–5 P.M. Mexico City markets will often have a row of *loncherías* where basic meals and *antojitos* (snacks or one-plate dishes) are quite inexpensive. Many *loncherías* offer *comida corrida,* a daily fixed-price meal that includes a beverage, an entrée or two, plus side dishes, and possibly dessert.

A ***comedor*** is usually a more basic version of a *lonchería.* **Cafés** are similar to *loncherías;* they may open earlier and serve *desayuno* (breakfast) in addition to other meals. A ***cafetería,*** a larger coffee shop with a full menu, is often attached to a large department store or hotel. Table service is the norm; Mexican *cafeterías* rarely serve food in what Americans call "cafeteria-style."

Don't miss one of the most convivial places for an evening meal in Mexico City—the cantina. Unlike in many other towns in Mexico, the cantinas of Mexico City often welcome both women and men.

More basic yet are ***fondas,*** tentlike stalls usually found in outdoor market areas. Traditionally a *fonda* specializes in one or two dishes only, although nowadays some serve whole meals. A particularly successful *fonda* may even open a regular restaurant while retaining the word *"fonda"* in its name.

Restaurantes and Cantinas

More formal meals are available at *restaurantes,* which tend to serve *plato fuertes* (main dishes) rather than *antojitos* (though plenty of restaurant menus offer both). Male waiter service and the use of tablecloths often distinguish *restaurantes* from simpler venues.

One of the most convivial places for an evening meal in Mexico City is the cantina. Unlike in many other towns in Mexico, the cantinas of Mexico City often welcome both women and men. Food at cantinas can be very good and relatively inexpensive. Some cantinas offer free *botanas* (snacks) for a couple of

Fonda Las Margaritas

© ELENA PAPPAS

Mexico City's *panaderías* offer dozens of sweet treats to please the palate.

hours in the afternoon and (sometimes) early evening.

Bakeries

Mexico City's many *panaderías* or bakeries produce especially tasty *bolillos* (Mexican rolls), *pasteles* (cakes), and *pan dulce* (cookies and sweet pastries). To select bakery items from the shelves of a *panadería,* simply imitate the other customers—pick up a pair of tongs and a tray from the counter near the cash register and help yourself, cafeteria-style.

Ordering and Paying

You really don't need that much Spanish to get by in a Mexican restaurant. Stating what you want, plus *"por favor"* ("please"), will usually do the trick (e.g., *"dos cervezas, por favor,"* "two beers, please"). Don't forget to say *"gracias"* ("thank you"). The menu is called *el menú* or *la carta.* As a last resort, you can always point to what you want on the menu.

La cuenta is the bill. A tip *(propina)* of 10–15 percent is expected at any restaurant with table service; look to see if it's already been added to the bill before placing it on the table. In small *comedores, fondas,* or *taquerías,* tips are not expected.

WHAT TO EAT

Breakfasts

Mexicans traditionally have two kinds of breakfasts, an early one called *desayuno,* eaten shortly after rising, and a second called *almuerzo* that's usually taken about 11 A.M.

The most common Mexican *desayuno* is simply *pan dulce* (sweet pastry) and/or *bolillos* (torpedo-shaped, European-style rolls) with coffee and/or milk. Cereal is also sometimes eaten for *desayuno,* e.g., *avena* (oatmeal), *crema de trigo* (cream of wheat), or *hojuelas de maíz* (corn flakes).

The heavier eggs-and-frijoles dishes known widely as "Mexican breakfasts" in the U.S. and Canada are usually taken as *almuerzo,* the late breakfast, which is most typically reserved for weekends and holidays. Eggs come in a variety of ways, including *huevos revueltos* (scrambled eggs), *huevos duros* (hard-boiled eggs), *huevos tibios* (coddled eggs, but not "soft-boiled" as sometimes translated), *huevos escafaldos* (soft-boiled eggs), *huevos estrellados* or *huevos fritos* (eggs fried sunny side up), *huevos a la mexicana* (also *huevos mexicanos,* eggs scrambled with chopped tomato, onion, and chile), *huevos rancheros* (fried eggs served on a tortilla), and *huevos divorciados* (two *huevos estrellados* separated by beans, each egg usually topped with a different salsa).

Eggs also come *con chorizo* (eggs scrambled with ground sausage), *con machaca* (with dried, shredded meat), *con tocino* (with bacon), or *con jamón* (with ham). All egg dishes usually come with frijoles and tortillas. The biggest *almuerzo* package on the menu is typically called *almuerzo albañil* ("brickmason's *almuerzo*") or *huevos albañil* ("brickmason's eggs"); this means eggs with one or more varieties of meat on the side.

One of the cheapest and tastiest *almuerzos* is *chilaquiles,* tortilla chips in a chile gravy with

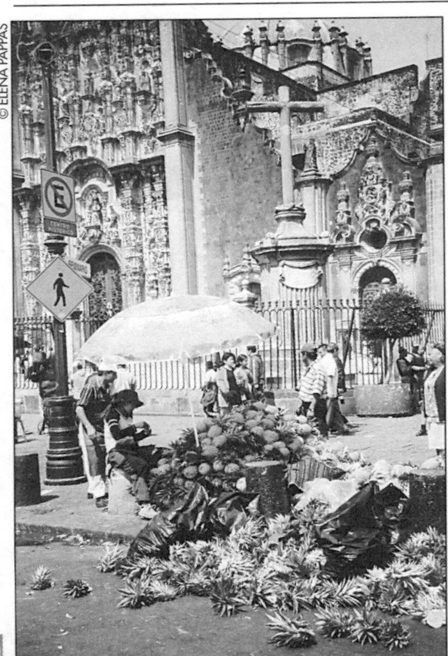
© ELENA PAPPAS

can't get enough pineapple: fruit sellers in front of the Sagrario

crumbled cheese on top. Eggs and/or chicken can be added to *chilaquiles* as options. In Mexico City a very similar dish called *migas* ("crumbs") usually includes eggs. Another economic choice is *molletes,* a split *bolillo* spread with mashed beans and melted cheese, served with salsa on the side. *Molletes* are usually only US$1–2 an order; they're often served with juice and coffee as a "university breakfast" *(desayuno universitario)* for US$2.50 or less. A quick breakfast frequently sold on the street by roving sellers is a *tamal* (steamed corn meal stuffed with a bit of meat or cheese) and a cup of *atole,* a hot, corn-based drink.

In Mexico City, the *desayuno/almuerzo* distinction has been fading fast, no doubt because of the exigencies of modern urban life. Nowadays, most *capitalinos* simply have one morning meal, called *desayuno,* the contents of which depend more often than not on one's budget. Middle-class and wealthier people have large meals with eggs, while poorer folk content themselves with a bit of bread and a coffee.

Comida

Capitalinos typically eat the main meal of the day, *comida,* sometime between 2 and 5 P.M. The *comida* is where Mexicans pack on most of the day's calories. Whether eaten at home or in a cantina, *lonchería,* restaurant, or bar, this meal will usually consist of several different dishes, including rice, soup, and a *plato fuerte* (main dish).

Many restaurants offer a *comida corrida* or *comida del día,* a special fixed-price, multicourse menu costing anywhere from US$2.50 to US$5. The typical *comida corrida* includes soup, a plate of flavored rice (served as an appetizer), a main dish, one or two side dishes, dessert, and a nonalcoholic beverage (often an *agua fresca*).

Cena

The large afternoon *comida* will sustain most Mexicans till at least 8 P.M. or so, when it's time for *cena,* traditionally a light evening meal usually consisting of *pan dulce* (Mexican pastries) with herb tea or coffee. While the light evening meal is still eaten by many Mexicans, an increasing number have a heartier dinner, especially in Mexico City. A favorite with kids (and the young at heart) is the *merienda,* a light snack of crackers or a sweet usually eaten around 6 P.M., between the *comida* and the *cena.*

Tortillas

A Mexican meal is not a meal without tortillas, the round, flat, pancake-like disks that are eaten with nearly any nondessert dish, including salads, meats, seafood, beans, and vegetables. Food experts have cataloged 166 kinds of tortillas in Mexico. Very large, thin wheat tortillas are known as *tortillas de agua,* or *sobaqueras* for example, while *coyotas* are small, thick, wheat tortillas. *Huaraches* are large oval-shaped flatbreads that look somewhat like flattened footballs; these are topped with chopped fried meats, onions, tomatoes, and spices and served as a complete *antojito.* A string of street vendors along the east end of Avenida Hidalgo, just north of the Palacio de Bellas Artes, sell delicious blue-corn *huaraches.*

Both corn and wheat tortillas are consumed in great quantity, although *capitalinos* clearly have an overall preference for corn tortillas. Some Mexicans claim meat and poultry dishes taste best with flour tortillas while vegetable dishes go best with corn. Restaurants sometimes offer a choice of the two; if you order tortillas without specifying, you may get *"¿De harina o de maíz?"* as a response.

Common variations on the standard corn tortilla include the *gordita,* a small, thick tortilla filled with spiced meat and vegetables, and the *sope,* a small, tart-shaped corn flatbread that is topped with a similar mixture plus crumbled cheese.

Incidentally, a tortilla has two sides, an inside and an outside, that dictate which direction the tortilla is best folded when wrapping it around food. The side with the thinner layer—sometimes called the *pancita,* or belly—should face the inside when folding the tortilla. If you notice the outside of your tortilla cracking, with pieces peeling off onto the table, you've probably folded it with the *pancita* outside instead of inside.

Antojitos

This word literally means "little whims," thus implying snacks to many people. However, the word also refers to any food that can be ordered, served, and eaten quickly—in other words, Mexican fast food. Typical *antojitos* include tamales, enchiladas, burritos, *flautas,* chiles rellenos, *chalupas, picadillos,* quesadillas, *tortas,* and tacos.

Visitors who identify these terms with dishes at Mexican restaurants in their home countries are sometimes confused by the different shapes and forms they may take in Mexico. Tacos can be rolled as well as folded, and enchiladas can be folded or stacked as well as rolled; shape is irrelevant. An enchilada (literally "chilied") is any *antojito* made with a tortilla dipped or cooked in a chile sauce; an *entomada* (or *entomatada*) is the equivalent made with tomatoes, while the *enfrijolada* is the same made with a thin bean sauce.

A taco is any type of plain tortilla surrounding other ingredients. In some eateries you can order tacos either *suave,* heated, soft tortillas stuffed with meat and vegetable fillings; or *dorado* ("golden"), thin corn tortillas stuffed tightly with meat, then deep-fried whole and served with lettuce and grated cheese. You'll be sure to get a smile at a *taquería* if you order your taco *"con fotocopia y jardín."* Literally this means "with photocopy and garden," which is to say, with two tortillas and all the veggie fixings, like cilantro and onions.

Platos Fuertes

The main dish or *el plato fuerte* of any meal can be a grander version of an *antojito,* a regional specialty (*mole poblano,* for example), or something the *cocineros* (cooks) dream up themselves. Typical entrées are centered around meats, seafood, or poultry.

Meats

Common meats include *carne de res* (beef), *puerco* (pork), and *cabrito* (kid goat). *Jamón* (ham), *chorizo* (sausage), and *tocino* (bacon) are usually reserved for *desayuno.*

Steak may appear on menus as *bistec, bistek,* or *biftec.* Poultry dishes include *pollo* (chicken), *pavo* (turkey), and, less frequently, *pato* (duck) and *codorniz* (quail).

Carnitas

This dish from the State of Michoacán belongs in a category all its own and is usually sold only at butcher shops or at restaurants specializing in it. The usual method for producing *carnitas* is to slowly braise an entire pig in huge pot, along with a variety of flavorings that are a closely guarded secret among *carnitas* purveyors. The results are chopped into thin slices and eaten with stacks of tortillas, pickled vegetables and chiles, guacamole, and various salsas.

Carnitas are always sold by weight, even in *carnitas* restaurants. You can order by the *kilo* (one kg, about 2.2 pounds), *medio* (half kg), *cuarto* (one-fourth kg), or sometimes in 100-gram increments *(cien gramos).* Figure on a quarter kg (about a half pound) per hungry person and you shouldn't have much left over.

COMMON *ANTOJITOS*

birria—lamb or goat stew in a sauce spiced with chiles, cinnamon, cloves, cumin, and oregano

burrito—a flour tortilla rolled around meat, beans, or seafood fillings; rather rare in Mexico City

chalupa—a crisp, whole tortilla topped with beans, meat, etc. (also known as a tostada); or a thicker, canoe-shaped cornmeal tortilla filled with same

chile relleno—a mild poblano chile stuffed with cheese, deep-fried in egg batter, and covered with a sauce of tomatoes, onions, and chiles

chimichanga—tortilla, usually flour, with beans, ham, and cheese

enchilada—a corn tortilla dipped in chile sauce, then folded or rolled around a filling of meat, chicken, seafood, or cheese and baked in an oven

enfrijolada—same as enchilada except dipped in a sauce of thinned refried beans instead of chile sauce

entomatada—same as enchilada except dipped in a tomato sauce instead of chile sauce

flauta—a small corn tortilla roll, usually stuffed with beef or chicken and fried

gordita—a small, thick, corn tortilla stuffed with a spicy meat mixture; a common street vendor offering

huarache—literally, "sandal"; a large, flat, thick, oval-shaped tortilla topped with fried meat and chiles; a common street vendor offering

menudo—a thick soup made with cows' feet and stomachs (and less commonly, intestines), and garnished with *chiles de árbol,* oregano, and fresh chopped onion; reputedly a sure hangover cure

pancita—the Mexico City equivalent of *menudo*

pozole—hominy stew made with pork or chicken and garnished with radishes, oregano, onions, chile powder, salt, and lime

picadillo—a spicy salad of chopped or ground meat with chiles and onions (also known as *salpicón*)

quesadilla—a flour tortilla folded over sliced cheese and grilled; some cooks can add *chiles rajas* (pepper strips), *flor de calabaza* (squash flower), *champiñones* (mushrooms), or *huitlacoche* (a truffle-like fungus that grows on fresh corn) on request

sincronizada—deep fried corn tortilla with beans, ham, and cheese, topped with guacamole

sope—a small, thick, round corn cake with dimpled edges, topped with a spicy meat mixture and crumbled cheese

taco—a corn tortilla folded or rolled around anything and eaten with the hands; *tacos al pastor,*

Fajitas

The name means "little belts" or "little skirts" and refers to a beef cut known in English as "skirt steak," often considered an unusable cut by butchers outside Mexico. In Mexico, *ranchero* cooks usually slice skirt steaks into strips, grill them quickly over very hot coals, and serve them with fresh flour tortillas, *salsa fresca* (called *pico de gallo* in some places), grilled onions, guacamole, and beans.

In Mexico City, fajitas may be called *arracheras.* Some restaurants make a distinction between skirt steaks cooked in strips and those cooked whole, calling the former fajitas and the latter *arracheras.* Neither dish is as popular in Mexico City as in northern Mexico or the United States.

Seafood

Although Mexico City is a minimum four-hour drive from the nearest seacoast, plenty of seafood finds its way to the capital from the Gulf of Mexico, Sea of Cortez, Caribbean Sea, and Pacific Ocean. *Pescado* (cooked fish) entrées on the menu are often seasonal or dependent on the "catch of the day." Often just the word *"pescado,"* along with the method of cooking (e.g., *pescado al mojo de ajo*), will appear. If you need to know exactly what kind of fish, just ask *"¿Cuál tipo de pescado hay?",* although in some cases the only response you'll get is something generic such as *pescado blanco* (white fish).

Shellfish *(mariscos)* is quite popular in the capital as elsewhere in Mexico: *ostiones* (oysters), *almejas* (clams), *callos* (scallops), *jaibas* (small

made with thin slivers of spit-cooked pork marinated in reddish *adobo* sauce, are the most popular Mexico City variation

tamal—plural tamales; cornmeal *(masa)* dough wrapped in a corn husk and steamed; sometimes stuffed with cheese, chile strips, corn, olives, pork, or turkey; popularly seen on street corners

torta—a Mexican-style sandwich made with *pan telera,* a large, flat roll

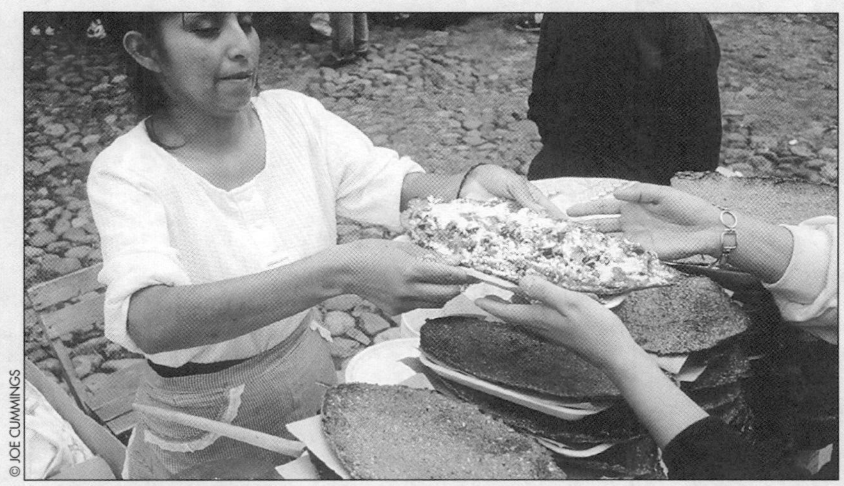

huarache **vendor, Tepozotlán**

crab), *cangrejo* (large crab), *camarones* (shrimp), *langostina* (crayfish, also called *cucarachas*), *langosta* (lobster), and *abulón* (abalone). All can be ordered as *cocteles* (cocktails, steamed or boiled and served with lime and salsa), *en sus conchas* (in the shell), ceviche (raw fish or shellfish marinated in lime juice, onions, and chiles until "cooked" by the acidic juices), or many other ways.

Beans

The beans most preferred in Mexico are pinto beans, usually dried beans *(frijól)* that are boiled until soft, then mashed and fried with lard or vegetable oil (usually the former) to make *frijoles.* Often this preparation is called *frijoles refritos* or "refried beans" although they're not really refried except when reheated. Sometimes the beans are served whole, in their own broth, as *frijoles de olla* (boiled beans, literally "pot beans") or with bits of roast pork as *frijoles charros* (ranch-style beans). *Frijoles* can be served with any meal of the day, including breakfast. In the south, *frijoles negros* (black beans) are as common as pintos and in southern Mexican restaurants in the capital you'll often be served black beans.

Cheese

Mexicans produce a great variety of cheeses. Among the most commonly used are *queso cotijo* (also called *queso añejo*), *queso chihuahua* (called *queso menonita* in the State of Chihuahua), *queso manchego, queso oaxaqueño,* and *queso asadero.*

Queso menonita or *queso chihuahua* ("Mennonite" or Chihuahuan cheese) is a mild, white

COOKING METHODS

Entrées, whether meat, poultry, or seafood, are most commonly prepared in one of the following styles:

adobo, adobada—marinated or stewed in a sauce of vinegar, chiles, and spices, often reddened by the addition of annatto seed extract
a la parrilla—broiled or grilled
albóndigas—meatballs
al carbón—charcoal-grilled
a la veracruzana—seafood, often *huachinango* (red snapper), cooked with tomatoes, onions, chiles, and olives
al mojo de ajo—in a garlic sauce
al pastor—slowly roasted on a vertical spit
al vapor—steamed
asado/asada—grilled
barbacoa—pit-roasted
con arroz—with rice
encebollado—cooked with onions
enpapelada—baked in parchment
empanizada—breaded
frito—fried
guisado—in a spicy stew

cheddar produced in wheels by Mennonite colonists in Chihuahua and Durango. Spanish import (though also made in Mexico) *queso manchego* is similar but usually softer. *Queso asadero* (griller cheese) is a braided cheese somewhat similar to Armenian string cheese, made by combining sour milk with fresh milk. *Chihuahua* is a common ingredient in dishes stuffed with cheese, such as enchiladas or chiles rellenos, that won't receive high, direct heat. *Asadero* melts well at high temperatures, without burning or separating, and as such is well suited to *chile con queso* (hot, blended chile-cheese dip), *queso fundido* (hot melted cheese topped with *chorizo* or mushrooms), and other dishes in which the cheese is directly exposed to high heat. *Queso oaxaqueño,* also called *quesillo,* is a lump-style cheese similar to *asadero* but a little softer—close to mozzarella. It's popular in *tortas* or Mexican-style sandwiches.

Cotijo or *añejo* is a crumbly aged cheese that resists melting and is commonly used as a topping for enchiladas and beans; the flavor and texture is somewhat like a cross between feta and Parmesan.

Occasionally you'll also come across *panela,* an extra-rich cheese made from heavy cream, usually sliced and served as a side dish all its own.

Vegetables

Although vegetables are sometimes served as side dishes with *comidas corridas,* with restaurant entrées, or in salads *(ensaladas),* they're seldom listed separately on the menu. Among the more exotic vegetables you may be served in Mexico City are the light and delicate *flor de calabaza* (squash flower) and the trufflelike delicacy *huitlacoche* (sometimes spelled *cuitlacoche,* a blue-black fungus that grows on fresh corn). Both are delicious.

Soup

The general menu term for soup is *sopa,* although a thick soup with lots of ingredients is usually a *caldo* or *caldillo.* Frequently a *crema,* or cream of vegetable soup, is one of the soup options with a *comida corrida. Menudo,* a soup made with hominy *(nixtamal),* cow's feet, and stomach (or, less commonly, intestine) in a savory, reddish-brown broth served with chopped onions, chiles, and crumbled oregano, is seen throughout Mexico and is highly prized as a hangover remedy. Mexico City has its own version of *menudo,* and it's called *pancita* (little stomach). *Pozole*—eaten since Aztec times, when it was known as *pozolli*—is a thick stew made with a much lighter-colored broth and filled with corn and some kind of meat.

Other tasty soups include *sopa de tortillas, sopa azteca,* and *sopa tlapeña,* all featuring varying combinations of artfully seasoned chicken broth garnished with *totopos* (tortilla wedges) and sliced avocado.

Bread and *Pan Dulce*

Bread *(pan)* arrived in Mexico not with the Spanish but during the brief era of French rule in the late 19th century. It is more commonly served in Mexico City than just about anywhere else in the country. Traditional Mexican dishes that would always come with a plate of tortillas elsewhere in Mexico may arrive with a basket of rolls or bread instead (if you prefer tortillas, just ask).

The most common bread you'll encounter is the *bolillo* (little ball), a small torpedo-shaped roll, usually rather hard on the outside. *Pan telera* ("scissor bread," so named for the two clefts on top) resemble *bolillos* but are larger and flatter; they're mainly used for making *tortas,* the ubiquitous Mexican sandwich. *Pan de barra,* American-style sliced bread, is also occasionally available but never measures up to crusty *bolillos* or *teleras.*

Sweetened breads or pastries are known as *pan dulce* (sweet bread). Common types of *pan dulce* include *buñuelos* (crisp, round, flat pastries fried and coated with cinnamon sugar), *campechanas* (flaky, sugar-glazed puff pastries), *canastas* (thick, round, fruit-filled cookies), *capirotada* (bread pudding), *cortadillos* (cake squares topped with jelly and finely shredded coconut), *cuernitos* (small crescent rolls rolled in cinnamon sugar), *galletas* (cookies), *palmitas* (flat, fan-shaped, crispy pastries), *pan de huevos* (spongy yeast bread with patterned sugar toppings), and *polvorones* (small shortbread cookies).

pancita

CHILANGO COOKING

Although most Mexican dishes commonly served in Mexico City had their culinary origins outside the capital, a few have been claimed as the city's own. One common dish in this category includes *barbacoa,* lamb that has been wrapped in *maguey* leaves and slowly pit-barbecued. Some restaurants serve *barbacoa* with a *salsa borracha,* a sauce made with chiles and *pulque.*

Another *capitalino* dish is *budín azteca,* in which tortillas, chicken, puréed tomatillos, roasted chiles, cheese, and various seasonings are baked in a *cazuela* or earthenware bowl—basically a casserole version of *chilaquiles.* Economic necessity in the infamous market ghetto of Tepito gave birth to *migas,* literally "crumbs," made by frying broken pieces of dried tortilla with eggs, onions, chiles, and whatever else is available.

Caldo tlalpeño, originally from the village of Tlalpan, now a suburb of southern Mexico City, is a very popular soup made by stewing chicken in a broth flavored with *chipotles* (smoked jalapeños), and served with garnishes of cilantro and avocado. This smoky-flavored *caldo* has become a menu standard throughout Mexico.

Street vendors sell a wide variety of foods that originated in the Mexican countryside but which have taken on their own Mexico City style. *Tacos al pastor,* made with layers of meat marinated in orange-red *adobo* sauce and cooked on a vertical spit, have become so ubiquitous in the capital that *al pastor* is now considered a D.F. specialty. On many street corners in the Centro, you'll also see steel washtubs filled with steaming tamales that tend to be larger than those you might encounter in Mexican villages. Served with a hot cup of *atole*—a drink made with cornmeal and chocolate—a Mexico City tamal makes a filling breakfast for only around US$.70. Other common street foods, especially in the Centro, include *huaraches* and *sopes.*

Salsas and Condiments

Any restaurant, café, *cafetería, lonchería, taquería,* or *comedor* will offer a variety of salsas. Sometimes only certain salsas are served with certain dishes, while at other times one, two, or even three salsas are stationed on every table. Often each place has its own unique salsa recipes—canned or bottled salsas are rarely used. The one ingredient common to all salsas is chile peppers, varying in heat from mild to incendiary.

There are as many types of salsas as there are Mexican dishes—red, green, yellow, brown, hot, mild, salty, sweet, thick, thin, blended, and chunky. It would take a separate book to describe them all. The most typical is the *salsa casera* (house salsa), a simple, fresh concoction of chopped chiles, onions, and tomatoes mixed with salt, lime juice, and cilantro. This is what you usually get with the free basket of *totopos* (tortilla chips) served at the beginning of many Mexican restaurant meals. Another common offering is *salsa verde* (green salsa), made with a base of tomatillos, a small, tart, green tomatolike vegetable. Some salsas are quite *picante* or spicy hot, so it's always a good idea to test a bit before pouring the stuff over everything on your plate.

Sliced, pickled chiles and carrots are sometimes served on the side as a condiment, especially with tacos and tortas, and are called *rajas.* In Mexico City's few Sonoran restaurants you may see a bowl of *chiltepines* (sometimes spelled *chilpetines* or *chiles pequines*), small, round, fiery red peppers. The kick of the *chiltepín* is exceeded only by that of the *chile habanero,* the world's hottest pepper and a regular table condiment at restaurants featuring dishes from the State of Yucatán.

Salt *(sal)* is usually on the table, although it's rarely needed since Mexican dishes tend to be prepared with plenty of salt. Black pepper is *pimiento negro,* and if it's not on the table it's normally available for the asking. Butter is *mantequilla,* sometimes served with bread.

In *taquerías,* guacamole (mashed avocado

blended with onions, chiles, salt, and other optional ingredients) is frequently served as a condiment. In restaurants it may be served as a salad or with tortilla chips. "Guacamole" sometimes refers to a very spicy paste of tomatillos and green chiles that may resemble avocado guacamole—always taste before heaping it on your plate.

Mole

From the states of Puebla and Oaxaca comes a genre of thick brown sauces called moles (MO-lays), usually served over chicken or turkey. The sauce is typically made from a lengthy list of ingredients that may include unsweetened chocolate, sesame seeds, and chiles. A similar but green-hued sauce made with pumpkin seeds is called *pipián.* Both are ancient dishes dating to Mexico's pre-Hispanic cultures. There are at least seven different kinds of mole.

Desserts and Sweets

The most popular of Mexican desserts, or *postres,* is a delicious egg custard called *flan.* It's listed on virtually every tourist restaurant menu, along with *helado* (ice cream). Other sweet alternatives include pastries found in *panaderías* (bakeries) and the frosty offerings at *paleterías.* Strictly speaking, a *paletería* serves only *paletas,* fruit-flavored ice on sticks (like American popsicles but with a much wider range of flavors), but many also serve *nieve,* literally "snow," flavored grated ice served in bowls or cones like ice cream.

Another street vendor sweet is *churros,* a sweet fried pastry that's something like a doughnut stick sprinkled with sugar and cinnamon. If this sounds even slightly appealing, be sure to visit the Churrería El Moro, on Eje Central between Uruguay and V. Carranza, where you'll find the city's best *churros* 24 hours a day.

One of the great joys of traveling or living in Mexico is to wander to a nearby street corner* licuado *stand and order a mix with whatever fruits strike your fancy for under US$1.

Vegetarians

It's difficult but not impossible to practice a vegetarian regime in Mexico City. Lacto-vegetarians can eat quesadillas, but ask for corn tortillas, which do not contain lard (most flour tortillas do) or *enchiladas de queso* (cheese enchiladas). With some luck, you'll stumble across restaurants that can prepare a variety of interesting cheese dishes, including *queso fundido con champiñones* (melted cheese with mushrooms, eaten with tortillas) and quesadillas made with *flor de calabeza* or squash flower. Some places make beans without lard *(sin manteca)* but you'll have to ask to find out. Many Mexico City restaurants offer pizza, usually offered in vegetarian versions (often called *pizza margherita*). You'll also find vegetarian/health food stores (usually called *tiendas naturistas*) with small dining sections as well as bulk foods.

Ovo-lacto-vegetarians can add egg dishes and flan to their menus. Vegans for the most part will do best to prepare their own food. Look for shops with signs reading *semillas* (seeds) to pin down a good selection of nuts and dried beans. Of course you'll find plenty of fresh fruits and vegetables in markets and grocery stores.

NONALCOHOLIC BEVERAGES

Water

The water and ice served in restaurants in Mexico is always purified—it's not necessary to order *agua mineral* (mineral water) unless you need the minerals. Likewise, the water used as an ingredient in "handmade" drinks, e.g., *licuados* or *aguas frescas,* comes from purified sources.

Soft Drinks

Licuados are similar to American smoothies—fruit blended with water, ice, honey or sugar, and sometimes milk or raw eggs to produce something like a fruit shake. One of the great joys of traveling or living in Mexico is to wander to a nearby street corner *licuado* stand and order a mix with whatever fruits strike your fancy for under US$1. In Mexico, *tuna* (not the fish but the prickly-pear cactus fruit) *licuados* are particularly delicious. Other tasty and nutritious additives include oats *(avena)* and wheat germ *(germen de trigo).* Most places that make *licuados* also offer fruit juices such as orange juice *(jugo de naranja)* or carrot juice *(jugo de zanahoria).*

Aguas frescas are the colorful beverages sold from huge glass jars in markets and occasionally on the streets. They're made by boiling the pulp of various fruits, grains, or seeds with water, then straining it and adding large chunks of ice. *Arroz* (rice), *horchata* (melon-seed), and *jamaica* (hibiscus flower) are three of the tastiest *aguas. Licuados* and *aguas frescas* are often sold from colorful storefronts invariably named La Flor de Michoacán or La Michoacana.

American soft drinks *(refrescos)* such as 7UP, Coke, and Pepsi are quite common. Local varieties, made in a variety of flavors, include Boing and Jarritos, as well as an apple-flavored soft drink called Manzanita. Less common, but very good, is Peñafiel, a flavored mineral water drink.

Hot Drinks

Coffee is served in a variety of ways. The best—when you can find it—is traditional Mexican-style coffee, made by filtering near-boiling water through fine-ground coffee in a slender cloth sack. Instant coffee *(nescafé)* is often served at small restaurants and cafés; a jar of instant coffee may be sitting on the table for you to add to hot water or milk. When there's a choice, a request for *café de olla* (boiled coffee) should bring you real brewed coffee. In some restaurants and cafés, *café de olla* means brewed coffee flavored with cinnamon, clove, or other spices. Several cafés in Mexico City offer superlative strong coffee; one classic spot is Café La Habana (see below under Paseo de la Reforma for details). The Roma, Condesa, and Coyoacán neighborhoods are also known for their many cafés.

Café con leche is the Mexican version of café au lait, i.e., coffee and hot milk mixed in near-equal proportions. *Café con crema* (coffee with cream) is not as available; when it is, it usually means nondairy powdered creamer.

Centuries ago, Mesoamericans mixed honey and spices with a bitter extract of the cacao bean to produce *atolli,* a warm chocolate drink popular among the upper classes. Today hot chocolate *(chocolate)* is still commonly found on Mexican menus. It's usually served very sweet and may contain cinnamon, ground almonds, and other flavorings. A modern version of *atole* is frequently served with *tamales* for an inexpensive breakfast, though these days it's often made without chocolate.

Black tea *(té negro)* is not popular among *mexicanos* although you may see it on tourist menus. Ask for *té helado* if you want iced tea. At home many Mexicans drink *té de manzanilla* (chamomile tea) or *té de yerba buena* (mint tea) in the evenings. Both *manzanilla* and *limón* ("lime," actually dried lemongrass) teas are often available in restaurants if you ask, and these make nice herbal substitutes if you're avoiding caffeine.

ALCOHOLIC BEVERAGES

The legal drinking age in Mexico is 18 years, and it's illegal to carry an open container of alcoholic beverages in a vehicle. Booze of every kind is widely available in bars, restaurants, grocery stores, and *licorerías* or liquor stores. *Borracho* means both "drunk" (as an adjective) and "drunkard."

Cerveza

Mexican beers are appreciated around the world as smooth, light- to medium-weight brews. In spite of their popularity, you can't really compare the beers sold in Mexico with their export equivalents outside Mexico; Mexican breweries produce a separate brew for American consumption, for example, that's lighter in taste and lighter on the alcohol content. It's always better in Mexico, where beer-brewing is big business.

The nation's largest brewer, Femsa, supplies about half the domestic market with Tecate, Carta Blanca, Superior, and Dos Equis. Grupo Modelo, which brews Victoria, Corona, Modelo, Negra Modelo, and others, is the world's 10th-largest brewer and now partially owned by Anheuser-Busch.

In Mexico City the most popular and available brand is probably Victoria, whose smooth, thirst-quenching flavor is very close to Corona. A great variety of other labels is of course available, including such major Mexican brands such as Dos Equis (XX), Corona, Superior, Carta Blanca, Bohemia, Negra Modelo, and Modelo. In *yucateca* restaurants and cantinas you may be able to order León Negro and Montejo, both darker beers brewed in the Yucatán. Some restaurants also serve Pacífico, a tasty brew from northwestern Mexico.

It's really a matter of personal taste which of these brands will most satisfy a visiting beer-drinker, though beer connoisseurs most often cite Bohemia as the country's best brew. *Mexicanos* usually ask for "lager" (la-GAIR) to order Dos Equis. Corona has become one of the most popular beers in urban Mexico, thanks to an aggressive ad campaign emphasizing its success in America (where it is now the largest-selling import, beating the previous favorite, Heineken). It's available in the familiar longneck bottle or in smaller Coronitas, which often come stuffed in ice buckets.

While the microbrew craze that swept the United States has not really made it south of the border, Mexico now does have one quality craft brew, Casta, made in Monterrey and distributed in Mexico City. The beer comes in four varieties, each with a label designed by different Mexican artists. Although very good, it sells at a fair markup from other Mexican beers and is found mainly in supermarkets and some upscale restaurants, not in your average corner store.

Wine

Virtually all Mexican wines hail from northern Mexico—particularly the states of Coahuila, Aguascalientes, Baja California, and Zacatecas—and some Mexico City restaurants serve a broad selection of domestically produced varietals, including cabernet sauvignon, chardonnay, chenin blanc, pinot noir, barbera, and zinfandel. These and other grapes are also blended to produce cheaper *vino tinto* (red wine) and *vino blanco* (white wine). When ordering wine in Spanish at a bar, you may want to specify *vino de uva* (grape wine), as *vino* alone can be used to refer to distilled liquors as well as wine. *Vino blanco,* in fact, can be interpreted as cheap tequila. Labels to look for include Baja California's Monte Xanic and Viñas de Camou. If you can find it, Monte Xanic's 1995 Cabernet y Merlot is considered one of the finest wines ever produced in Mexico. Camou makes an excellent *coupage* of cabernet franc, cabernet sauvignon, and merlot, which, although labeled *vino tinto,* is not an inexpensive table wine.

One of the best places to buy wine by the bottle in central Mexico City is **La Naval,** Av. Insurgentes Sur 373 at Michoacán, tel. 5584-3500, in the Condesa district. La Naval is open Mon.–Sat. 8 A.M.–9 P.M. Another good store, with several branches around the city, is **La Europea.** One branch near downtown is at Ayuntamiento 21, a couple of blocks west of the Eje Central and south of the Alameda, near Mercado San Juan, tel. 5512-6005.

Liquor

Tequila is the *capitalino* liquor of choice; the second most popular is *ron* (rum), followed closely by brandy, both produced in Mexico for export as well as domestic consumption. Among brandies, Presidente is the biggest seller, but Don Pedro Reserva Especial is better quality. A favorite rum drink is the *cuba libre* (free Cuba), called *cuba* for short—a mix of rum, Coke, and lime juice over ice. An alternative made with Mexican brandy is called *cuba de uva* (grape Cuba). Other hard liquors—gin, vodka, scotch—may be available only at hotel bars and tourist restaurants. Drinks that contain imported liquor typically cost about twice as much as those with domestic liquor (*nacional* on most bar menus). However, because of recent agave shortages, the price of tequila is fast catching up to imported liquors.

CENTRO HISTÓRICO

Downtown Mexico City is positively crammed with restaurants of all types, with plenty of choices for travelers in all price ranges. The emphasis among almost all of the Centro eateries is Mexican cuisine in all its myriad variations, varying from some great hole-in-the-wall taco joints to veritable pageants of traditional Mexican dishes served in renovated colonial mansions. Among the few in-

THE LIQUID HEART OF MEXICO

Mexico's national drink has been in production, in prototypical form, since at least the time of the Aztecs. The Aztecs in fact called themselves Mexicas in direct reference to the special spiritual role mescal—tequila's forerunner—played in their culture via Mextli, the god of agave (the desert plant from which mescal and tequila are derived). These names, as interpreted by the Spanish, eventually yielded "Mexico."

The first true distillers of mescal—as opposed to pre-Hispanic forms of fermented maguey juice such as *pulque*—are thought to have been Filipinos who accompanied the Spanish to Mexico aboard the famous Manila galleons. Although modern historians once assumed the distilling technique for tequila came from Europe, tequila stills—now as in the past—copy Southeast Asian rather than European methods of distilling, eschewing the familiar coiled piping for a simple distillation dome over the boilers.

The Spaniards levied a tax on tequila as early as 1608, and in 1795, King Carlos IV granted the first legal concession to produce tequila to Don José María Guadalupe Cuervo. The liquor's name was taken from the Ticuila Indians of Jalisco, who mastered the technique of baking the heart of the *Agave tequiliana weber,* or **blue agave,** and extracting its juice, a process employed by tequila distilleries today. Native to Jalisco, this succulent is the only agave that produces true tequila as certified by the Mexican government. All liquors labeled "tequila" must contain at least 51 percent blue agave distillates. Sugarcane juice or extracts from other agaves usually makes up the rest. Contrary to the myth that all true tequila must come from Tequila, Jalisco, Mexican law enumerates specific districts in five different Mexican states where tequila may be legally produced.

Despite the fact that tequila sales are booming today, much of the tequila-making process is still carried out *a mano* (by hand). In the traditional method, the mature heart of the tequila agave, which looks like a huge pineapple and weighs 50–150 pounds, is roasted in pits for 24 hours, then shredded and ground by mule- or horse-powered mills. After the juice is extracted from the pulp and fermented in ceramic pots, it's distilled in copper stills to produce the basic tequila, which is always clear and colorless, with an alcohol content of around 40 percent.

True "gold" tequilas are produced by aging the tequila in imported oak barrels to achieve a slightly mellowed flavor. The *reposado* or "rested" type is oak-aged for at least two months, while *añejo* or "aged" tequila must stay in barrels at least a year. Inferior "gold" tequilas may be nothing more than the silver stuff mixed with caramel coloring—always look for *reposado* or *añejo* on the label if you want the true gold.

José Cuervo, Sauza, and Herradura are well-established, inexpensive to medium-priced tequila labels with international notoriety. Of these three, Herradura is said to employ the most traditional methods; tequila connoisseurs prefer it over the other two. Other, smaller, much more expensive "boutique" tequila-makers use 100 percent blue agave, rather than mixing in sugarcane distillates.

Many tasters claim a label called Reserva del Patrón (sold simply as "Patrón" north of the Mexican border) is the finest and smoothest tequila tipple of them all. Other fine *tequilas reposadas* include Las Trancas, Ecuario Gonzales, La Perseverancia,

FOOD AND DRINK

Tesoro de Don Felipe, and our personal favorite for flavor and price, Herradura. To emphasize the limited production nature of these private reserve distillations, these brands are usually sold in numbered bottles with fancy labels. Less expensive but also good are the Jimador, Centenario, Cazadores, and Orendain labels. As with wine, it's all a matter of personal preference; try a few *probaditos* ("little tastes" or shots) for yourself to determine which brand best tickles your palate. One key characteristic is whether the tequila is 100 percent agave or not—the lesser brands are often only 51 percent agave, mixed with distillates from other kinds of cacti. The fancier tequilas may be served in brandy snifters instead of the traditional tall, narrow shot glass *(caballito).*

Mescal and the Worm

The distillate of other agave plants—also known as magueys or century plants—is called mescal (sometimes spelled "mezcal"), not to be confused with the non-distilled mescal—*pulque*—prepared in pre-Hispanic Mexico. The same roasting and distilling process is used for today's mescal as for tequila. Actually, tequila is a mescal, but no drinker calls it that, just as no one in a U.S. bar orders "whiskey" rather than specify scotch or bourbon. Although many states in Mexico produce mescal, the best is often said to come from the State of Oaxaca.

The caterpillar-like grub or *gusano de maguey* (maguey worm) at the bottom of a bottle of mescal lives on the maguey plant itself. They're safe to eat—just about anything pickled in mescal would be—but not particularly appetizing. By the time you hit the bottom of the bottle, who cares? Maguey worms are often fried and eaten with fresh corn tortillas and salsa—a delicious appetizer.

Tequila Drinks

The usual way to drink tequila is straight up, followed by a water or beer chaser. Licking a few grains of salt before taking a shot and sucking a lime wedge afterward makes it go down smoother. The salt raises a protective coating of saliva on the tongue while the lime juice scours the tongue of salt and tequila residues.

Tequila con sangrita, in which a shot of tequila is chased with a shot of *sangrita* (not to be confused with *sangría,* the wine-and-fruit punch), is a slightly more elegant method of consumption. Sangrita is a bright red mix of tomato juice, lime juice, grenadine, red chile powder, and salt.

An old tequila standby is the much-abused margarita, a tart Tex-Mex cocktail made with tequila, lime juice, and Cointreau (usually "Controy" or triple-sec in Mexico) served in a salt-rimmed glass. A true margarita is shaken and served on the rocks (crushed or blended ice tends to kill the flavor), but just about every other gringo seems to drink "frozen" margaritas, in which the ice is mixed in a blender with the other ingredients. If you detect a noticeable difference between the taste of margaritas north or south of the border, it may be because bartenders in the U.S. and Canada tend to use bigger and less flavorful Persian limes *(Citrus latifolia)* while in Mexico they use the smaller, sweeter Key or Mexican lime *(Citrus aurantifolia swingle).*

More popular than margaritas among Mexican drinkers is a sort of Mexican highball, mixing tequila with Seven-Up, Squirt (a Mexican soft drink), or some other grapefruit-tasting soda.

Tequila is a pallid flame that passes through walls and soars over tile roofs to allay despair.

—Álvaro Mútis, *Tequila: Panegyric and Emblem.*

ternational restaurants are the usual fast-food joints, two Arab restaurants, and the Casino Español.

Tacos, Sandwiches, Snacks

On the east end of Plaza Manuel Tolsá, near the Museo Nacional de Arte, **Taco Inn,** Calle Tacuba 10 (next door to Los Girasoles), is an upscale taco restaurant with hygienically prepared tacos and other *antojitos* at slightly higher than normal prices (for tacos). The steaming *café de olla,* served in ceramic mugs, is excellent. Open daily 8 A.M.–11 P.M.

A more traditional taco spot, infrequently visited by tourists but mobbed by locals, is **Tacos Beatriz,** at Uruguay 30. This little hole-in-the-wall might seem less than appealing at first, but the cheerful ladies running it keep everything clean, and the tacos are delicious and cheap. Open daily 10 A.M.–4:45 P.M.

Las Isabeles, Calle Palma Norte 308, tel. 5521-7805, near the corner of Tacuba, is a good choice for breakfast or lunch, with *licuados, jugos, tortas,* tacos, and other light fare. Beer is also served here, along with *comida corrida.* This popular spot is clean, inexpensive, and has a bit more ambience than your usual taco/torta place. Open Mon.–Sat. until 5 P.M.

Lonchería Vasconia is attached to the bakery of the same name, at the corner of Tacuba and Palma (all one big space, with separate signs on the building out front). It serves *tacos al pastor* and roast chicken; a good place for a quick, inexpensive bite to eat. Open Mon.–Sat. 7:30 A.M.–9 P.M., Sun. 7:30 A.M.–8 P.M.

CULINARY HIGHLIGHTS OF MEXICO CITY

For many visitors, one of the great pleasures of coming to Mexico is the opportunity to enjoy the country's mouthwateringly delicious cuisine. Sometimes, depending on the chile content, it's more like eye-wateringly delicious! As the nation's capital, Mexico City has restaurants offering all types of cuisine from across the country and the world. Below are a few of our personal favorites, some expensive and some not at all. Look in the chapter for details on each.

Classic Mexican

Hacienda de los Morales, Polanco
Hostería Santo Domingo, Centro
Café Tacuba, Centro
El Cardenal, Centro
La Tecla, Roma
San Ángel Inn, San Ángel

Tacos, Quesadillas, and Other Antojitos

Tizoncito, Condesa and Coyoacán
Las Lupitas, Coyoacán
Tacos Beatriz, Centro

Cantinas

La Única de Guerrero, Alameda
La Mascota, Centro
La Polar, Reforma
La Guadalupana, Coyoacán

Seafood

El Danubio, Centro
Contramar, Roma
Mercado Medellín, Roma
Los Arcos, Polanco

International

Argentine: El Zorzal, Polanco and Condesa
Chinese: Chez Wok, Polanco; and Blossom, Del Valle
French: Bistrot Salut les Copains, Zona Rosa; Champs Elysees, Zona Rosa; and Cluny, San Ángel.
Indian/Pakistani: Tandoor, Polanco
Italian: Il Punto, Polanco
Japanese: Diakoku, Reforma; and Nagaoka, Nápoles
Middle Eastern: Al Andaluz, Centro; and Amar Kemal, Condesa
Spanish: Covadonga, Roma

Right behind Iglesia La Profesa on Avenida Madero, **Café El Alcatraz** offers a few tables set on a terrace below street level where you can rest from your tour with a snack or soda. Open Mon.–Sat. 1–6 P.M.

Mexican—Less Expensive

Café El Popular has two branches downtown, both on Cinco de Mayo, one at number 50 near the Zócalo and the other at number 10, next to Bar La Ópera. El Popular is an example of the gradually disappearing *bisquet* café or *café chino*—operated by Chinese families and once popular in the 1940s and 1950s in Mexico City. The menu is unspectacular but reliable. The branch of El Popular nearer the Zócalo is smaller and has more character, though you may have to wait briefly by the cash register for an open table. It's also open 24 hours a day, while the other branch is open daily 8 A.M.–1 A.M.

Another popular *bisquet* restaurant is **Los Bisquets Obregón,** at Tacuba 85 near Palma, a branch of the famous diner in the Roma neighborhood. On weekends there's often a line for tables, a testament to the reliable, reasonably priced meals. Open daily 7:30 A.M.–10 P.M.

At the 1930-vintage **Café La Blanca,** Av. Cinco de Mayo 40, the simple tables and Formica counter, topped with plastic placemats, are always filled with men poring over newspapers while sipping strong coffee. The reliable though unexceptional menu focuses on Mexican specialties. Breakfasts are a good deal here. Lithographs on the walls depict Mexico City of yesteryear. Open daily 7 A.M.–11 P.M.

If you'd like to try *comida yucateca* (food from the Yucatán region), head over to **Coox Hanal** now at a new location at Isabel la Católica 83, tel. 5709-3613, a breakfast and lunch joint always swarming with locals gobbling down the restaurant's inexpensive specialties such as *sopa de lima, cochinita pibil, panuchos* or *papadzules.* Open Mon.–Sat. 9 A.M.–5 P.M., and invariably packed around 3 P.M.

Turkey-lovers should stop by **El Rey del Pavo,** at Palma 32 between Av. Madero and Av. 16 de Septiembre. Here you can get a full meal for US$2–3, or tasty turkey *tortas* topped with guacamole for US$1.20 each in a clean cafeteria-style restaurant. Open Mon.–Sat. 11 A.M.–6:30 P.M.

Also specializing in fowl is **Pollos Gili,** at the corner of Cinco de Mayo and Isabel la Católica. Gili offers delicious and inexpensive roast chickens and chicken tacos. Open Mon.–Sat. noon–9 P.M., Sun. noon–8 P.M.

For a *torta* or shrimp cocktail, and a mug of cold beer to wash it down, drop into **Salón Corona,** Bolívar 24, tel. 5512-9007, a family restaurant/cantina in business since 1928. Large *tarros* (mugs) of draft Corona—light, dark, or mixed together *(campechana)*—cost US$1.20. The *caldo de camarón* (shrimp stew) comes in a glass and is excellent. This a very popular spot on Sunday afternoons, when many other downtown spots are closed, and anytime there's a soccer game on TV. Open daily 8 A.M.–11:30 P.M.

If you'd like to eat in an old-style cantina, check out **El Gallo de Oro,** at Carranza 35 at the corner of Bolivar, open Mon.–Fri. noon–10 P.M., Sat. noon–7 P.M. Another very good cantina is the well-lit, friendly **La Mascota,** Mesones 20, open daily noon–11 P.M. Both places offer *botanas,* snacks offered free with drinks during the late afternoon, or multicourse fixed meals.

While most **Sanborns** feel somewhat like a Mexican-style Denny's, the historic original restaurant on Madero is an exception. Set in the two-story courtyard of the Casa de los Azulejos, Av. Madero 4, tel. 5512-9820, a 16th-century palace covered in blue tiles, the spacious restaurant is always packed with businessmen, politicians, tourists, and others. The Mexican menu is unexceptional but hygienic and reasonably priced. Open Mon.–Sat. 7 A.M.–midnight, Sun. 7 A.M.–11 P.M.

Mexican—More Expensive

Hostería Santo Domingo, Calle Belisario Dominguez 72, tel. 5510-1434, has been serving classic Mexican dishes since 1860. The *chiles en nogada* are superb, considered by some to be the best in the city, and the *mole poblano* is also legendary. A full meal costs around US$7–10. Musicians frequently serenade diners. On weekends expect a long wait for a table, particularly during the middle of the afternoon. Open Mon.–Sat. 9 A.M.–10 P.M., Sun. 9 A.M.–9 P.M.

Set in a converted 17th-century colonial mansion, **Café Tacuba,** Calle Tacuba 28, tel. 5521-2048, is a wonderful place to enjoy a well-prepared, traditional Mexican meal amid historic ambience. The restaurant is very popular with both Mexicans and visitors and has been in operation since 1912. One excellent choice, *cuatro cositas* (four little things), comes with a large, moist, and tasty tamal filled with cheese and fresh *epazote,* an *enchilada Tacuba* (chicken rolled up in a corn tortilla bathed in a house sauce), rice, beans, and guacamole. Be prepared to wait for your meal: while the food is excellent, the service can be terrible. Open daily 8 A.M.–11 P.M.

If you'd like to take in a little history with a meal or cold *cerveza,* stop in at **Bar La Ópera,** Av. 5 de Mayo 10, tel. 5512-8959, where Pancho Villa left bullet holes in the ceiling while riding around inside on his horse during the Revolution. This dark, baroque cavern of a place was built with plenty of wood and huge, mirrored booths big enough to hold large parties of revelers (or conceal couples deep in the recesses). The menu is large, the food is good, and entrées average US$8–10. Open Mon.–Sat. 1–11:30 P.M., Sun. 1–5:30 P.M.

La Casa de las Sirenas, behind the Catedral at Av. República de Guatemala 32, tel. 5704-3345 or 5704-3225, makes an excellent choice for a relaxing midday meal while sightseeing. The restaurant serves well-prepared Mexican classics such as *mole poblano, chiles en nogada,* and *pozole,* all pricey but good. It's on the second and third floors of a colonial-era mansion; the second floor patio is favored by Mexico City politicians. Open Mon.–Sat. 8 A.M.–11 P.M., Sun. 8 A.M.–6 P.M.

Another top-notch Mexican restaurant, but with very reasonable prices, is **El Cardenal,** Palma 23, tel. 5521-8815, serving dishes such as sea bass in barbecue sauce or veal cutlet in the quietly elegant dining room. Open daily 9 A.M.–8 P.M.

Los Girasoles, tel. 5510-0630, on the pedestrian-only Calle Xicotencatl, on the east end of Plaza Manuel Tolsá off Calle Tacuba, is a formal restaurant frequented by senators and their staff from the federal Senate next door. The menu offers some interesting *nueva cocina* specialties, such as *tacos de pato* (duck tacos) and trout cooked in mezcal sauce, at around US$8–12 per entrée. Open Mon.–Sat. 1:30 P.M.–midnight, Sun. 1:30 P.M.–6 P.M.

In a spacious, peaceful dining room in an old building on the northwest corner of the Zócalo, **Mexico Viejo,** Tacuba 87, tel. 5510-3748, is a popular spot with foreign and Mexican tourists visiting the downtown area. The extensive menu (available in English) offers specialties such as *crepas huitlacoche* and *chilaquiles con pollo.* It also has a reasonably priced *comida del día* (meal of the day). Breakfasts are good and not expensive. Open Mon.–Sat. 8 A.M.–9 P.M., Sun. 9 A.M.–6 P.M.

EL CAFÉ CHINO

One type of restaurant you aren't likely to find anywhere in Mexico except in the capital is the *café chino* (Chinese café), a tradition started by Chinese immigrants a century ago. Despite the name, the only dish resembling Chinese cuisine typically served at these small coffee shops is "chop suey" (a gooey stir-fry of vegetables with pieces of chicken or pork, served with rice), which is said to have originated among Chinese railroad workers in North America. Fried rice *(arroz frito)* is also occasionally available, but the real foci of the *café chino* are Mexican breakfasts, *antojitos,* and the *bisquet.* Like chop suey, the *bisquet*—doughy rolls or biscuits of various shapes and flavors—may be a Chinese immigrant adaptation of local ingredients, in this case Mexican *pan dulce.* To go with the latter, hot chocolate is usually served in three styles—*mexicano* (made with water), *frances* (with milk), and *español* (thicker, with milk and spices). Although the heyday of the *café chino* is sadly passing, and many have closed during the last couple of decades, one D.F. spot that appears to be more popular than ever is Bisquets Obregón, with branches in both the Roma and Centro districts.

For culinary adventure-seekers after a taste of exotic pre-Hispanic cuisine, including *gusanos de maguey* (cactus worms), *venado con huitlacoche* (deer meat with corn fungus), or other Aztec delicacies, try the famed **Fonda de Don Chon,** Calle Regina 160, southeast of the Zócalo. The surrounding neighborhood is rather run-down, so watch your step heading over this way, especially after dark. Open Mon.–Sat. noon–8 P.M.

Food with a View

Umbrella-shaded tables on the restaurant veranda on the top floor of the historic **Best Western Hotel Majestic,** Madero 73 at Monte de Piedad, tel. 5521-8600, look east out over the Zócalo, affording good views of the Catedral, Sagrario, Palacio Nacional, and the twice-daily flag ceremonies in the center of the plaza. Prices are moderate, considering the view, and the food is quite respectable if not the most exciting in the capital. Among the dishes we've enjoyed are *pollo almendrado* (chicken baked in a tasty almond sauce) and **crema de queso Sonora** (a rich Sonoran cheese soup). If you're just dropping by for dessert, try the *crepas de cajeta al tequila* (crepes in a goat-milk caramel and tequila sauce). Open daily 8 A.M.–11 P.M. The **Gran Hotel de la Ciudad** and the **Holiday Inn** also have rooftop restaurants overlooking the Zócalo.

Vegetarian

Decent vegetarian meals can be found at the dinerlike **Vegetarianos del Centro,** Calle Filomeno Mata 13 near Cinco de Mayo, tel. 5510-0113. A fixed vegetarian menu is served every day, or you can order dishes à la carte, including stuffed avocados, baked potatoes, and lots of egg dishes, all at low prices. Open Mon.–Sat. 8 A.M.–8 P.M., Sun. 9 A.M.–8 P.M.

Another veggie place worth trying is **Comedor Vegetariano,** at Motolinía 31, 2nd floor. Don't be deterred by the somewhat dingy entranceway—the restaurant itself is clean, and the food good and inexpensive. Open daily 1–6 P.M.

The **Super Soya** chain of health food store/lunch counters serves vegetarian *tortas, comida corridas,* and juices. There are three branches in the downtown area: 16 de Septiembre 79, open Mon.–Sat. 11 A.M.–9 P.M., Sun. 11 A.M.–8 P.M.; Brasil 11, open Mon.–Fri. 9 A.M.–8:30 P.M., weekends 10 A.M.–7 P.M.; and Bolívar 31-A, open Mon.–Sat. 9 A.M.–9 P.M., Sun. 9 A.M.–7 P.M.

Bakeries and Coffee Shops

For a late-night treat, head for the 1935-vintage **Churrería El Moro,** at Eje Central 42 between Uruguay and V. Carranza, tel. 5512-0896. Warning: *Churros,* deep-fried, sugary pastries meant to be dipped in hot chocolate before eating, can be very addictive. Open 24 hours.

Two bakeries next to one another on Avenida 16 de Septiembre near Eje Central, **Pastelería La Ideal** and **El Globo,** offer huge selections of pastries, both European and Mexican style. Both are open daily until 8 P.M.

Founded in 1927, the original **Panadería Ideal,** west of Eje Central on the north side of Calle República de Uruguay, may be the ultimate Mexican bakery. It's worth a visit just to see the marvelous cakes on display and the seemingly endless variety of *pan dulce.*

At the corner of Tacuba and Palma it's hard to miss **Panadería y Pastelería Vasconia,** a good bakery with a huge selection. Pick up a tray and tongs and serve yourself, then sit down and have some coffee at one of the tables inside.

Just off Avenida Madero, the upscale **Café El Passaje,** Calle Gante 6, serves espresso drinks and sweet treats Monday–Saturday 9 A.M.–9 P.M. The tables, some set up on the pedestrian-only street and some inside, are a fine place to sip a cup and read one of the international or Mexican papers sold at the café.

Café Emir, Uruguay 45, serves a good strong cup of java to drink at its collection of small tables. Open Mon.–Sat. 9 A.M.–6 P.M.

Seafood

Refined, quiet **El Danubio,** Calle Uruguay 3, just off Eje Central, tel. 5512-0912, is the place to go for top-quality seafood downtown at midrange prices. Some say it has the best seafood in the city. The weekday *comida corrida* (served 2–5 P.M. only) is a bargain at US$8, and entrées run US$8–12. Open daily 1–10 P.M.

SANBORNS ALL OVER

Multiple generations of Mexican families have grown up with Sanborns department stores—and their attached restaurants—during the nearly 100 years the company has been in existence. With well over a hundred branches throughout the Mexican republic, Sanborns has set the standard for Mexico-based retail chains and still enjoys a higher profile than any imported franchise.

It all began in 1903, when American brothers Walter and Frank Sanborn founded the Farmacia Americana in Mexico City to fill a perceived market for international pharmaceuticals in a nation where most Mexicans still relied on herbal remedies—many of which were, and still are, very effective, but many of which could also be classified as quackery.

Around 1919 the Sanborn brothers moved their growing business into the prestigious Casa de los Azulejos (House of Tiles) in the Centro Histórico and expanded services to include a pharmacy, gift shop, curios shop, and elegant tea salon—thus creating Mexico's first department store.

Today the typical department store operated by Sanborn Hermanos, S.A., integrates the services of a Mexican restaurant, bar, and large retail store with departments offering books, magazines, games, sweets, jewelry, fashion accessories for ladies, arts and crafts, audio and video equipment, baked goods, and, of course, a pharmacy. Newer on the scene has been the establishment of Sanborns Café outlets, which focus on food service only. Menu choices and prices at all Sanborns restaurants tend to be the same, a consistency that Sanborns regulars—Mexican businesspeople, upper middle class families, and tourists—have come to count on.

not your average cafeteria: Sanborns' Casa de los Azulejos

Spanish

A gathering place for Spaniards living in Mexico, the **Casino Español,** Isabel la Católica 31, tel. 5521-8894, is housed in a sumptuous early 20th-century building. Open only for lunch, the Casino's restaurant serves an excellent Spanish-style *comida del día* with five dishes for US$10, as well as a selection of specialties from the menu. The Casino is particularly popular on weekends. Open daily 1–6 P.M.

Middle Eastern

Three blocks southeast of the Zócalo is **El Ehden,** Venustiano Carranza 148, 2nd floor, tel. 5542-2320, a cafeteria-like restaurant run by a Lebanese woman and her Mexican husband. They serve a wide selection of Middle Eastern dishes, including stuffed grape leaves, hummus, falafel, *baba ganoush,* tabouli, and more, all at around US$3–5 per entrée. Open daily noon–6 P.M.

Considered to have some of the best Middle Eastern food in the city, but tucked into a not altogether pleasant neighborhood about seven blocks southeast of the Zócalo, is **Al Andaluz,** at Mesones 171, between Las Cruces and Jesús María, tel. 5522-2528. The restaurant, which caters principally to the Arab community who work in the neighborhood textile trade, is hidden in a cozy, renovated, two-story colonial house, an oasis from the surrounding streets. Specialties include *baba ganoush, shwarma,* hummus, and *kepa bola* (this last a mix of wheat, ground beef, and onion). Top off your meal with a cup of strong Arab coffee. Prices are very reasonable and the quality is excellent. Because of the location, Al Andaluz is not frequented by tourists. Open Mon.–Sat. 9 A.M.–6 P.M.

ALAMEDA CENTRAL

The area around the Alameda can't claim a great profusion of restaurants, although there are several worth seeking out if you're in the area.

Mexican

Just west of Templo de San Hipólito, on the ground floor of an old colonial building, modest and inexpensive **Lonchería Amalita,** Av. Hidalgo 105, has been grilling classic quesadillas for more than half a century. It's open Mon.–Sat. 10 A.M.–5 P.M.

South of the Alameda, **Fonda Santa Anita,** Humboldt 48, tel. 5518-4609, is a traditional Mexican restaurant offering tasty home-cooked standards at inexpensive to moderate prices. Open daily 1:30–6 P.M.

Inexpensive *comida corridas* can be found in the **Mercado San Juan,** off Calle Pugibet, open daily until 5 P.M.

Right next to the FONART handicraft shop, near the Metro Hidalgo station, is a 24-hour **Sanborns Café.** At the southeast corner of Calles López and Juárez, you'll find yet another branch of **Sanborns,** open daily for breakfast, lunch, and dinner.

For a more upscale meal, try the **Café del Palacio** inside the Palacio de Bellas Artes. Despite the good quality and elegant ambience, prices are quite reasonable. A *menú* including an appetizer, main course (such as grilled red snapper or steak), salad, and drinks costs US$16, while a main course by itself runs around US$10. If you just want a snack, try a pâté, quiche, or *cazuelitas de salpicón,* a dish of beans, shredded beef, onion, potato, lettuce, olive oil, and vinegar. This is also a fine spot to enjoy a strong espresso and dessert. Open daily 11 A.M.–7 P.M., or until 8:30 P.M. on Wednesday and Sunday (for the Ballet Folklórico).

Cantinas

Since 1933, **Cantina La Única de Guerrero,** Guerrero 258 at Marte, tel. 5526-6854, has preserved a legacy of culinary tradition that many other city cantinas aspire to. Popular with writers and intellectuals, "La Única" (also commonly known as "La U de G") dispenses good *caldo de camarón* (shrimp stew) and plenty of other cantina favorites (but no free *botanas*). Live *salterio* (Mexican zither) music is played from 3 P.M. onward, with an emphasis on sad *valses* (waltzes). To find it, go a block south of Avenida Ricardo Flores Magón on Guerrero, turn right (west) at Calle Martes, and look for the cantina at the southwest corner of the intersection. Open Mon.–Sat. 10 A.M.–10 P.M., Sun. (restaurant only) noon–8 P.M.

Cantina La Única de Guerrero

Salón Cantina La Victoria, Magnolia 3 at Eje Central Lázaro Cárdenas, tel. 5526-3667, specializes in regional dishes from many parts of Mexico. It offers a choice of seven daily platters. Two blocks south of the Metro Plaza Garibaldi on the west side of Eje Central. Open Mon.–Sat. noon–11 P.M., Sun. noon–8 P.M. Although La Única and La Victoria are anything but rough themselves, this isn't a great neighborhood for an after-dark stroll, so consider using taxi service at night when going to or from these cantinas.

Vegetarian

On the east side of Dolores, one-half block south of the Alameda between Avenida Juárez and Calle Independencia, basic, inexpensive **Centro Naturista de México** is a vegetarian restaurant and health food store featuring a daily vegetarian buffet.

Chinese

South of the Alameda, a small Chinatown runs along Calle Dolores north of Calle Artículo 123. An attempt is under way to create a pedestrian walkway here with decorations and street lamps, but so far this hasn't kept cars off the street. In this area you'll find **Restaurant Bar Nuevo Cantón, Restaurant Bar Chung King, Restaurant Bar Oriental, Restaurant Tong Fong, Restaurant Bar Shang Hai, Cuatro Mares,** and **Restaurant Hong King,** all serving reasonable Cantonese food. Shanghai and Tong Fong are two of the better ones. **Dinastia Lee** on Calle Dolores is more of a *café chino,* serving *bisquets,* chop suey, and Mexican breakfasts.

Italian

Friendly **Cafe Trevi,** Colón 1 at the western end of the Alameda, tel. 5512-3020, has been in operation since 1955, serving inexpensive pizza, pasta, breakfasts, and snacks. There's also a full bar; open daily 8 A.M.–11:30 P.M.

REFORMA/ZONA ROSA

Restaurants in the Zona Rosa and around Reforma are generally more upscale than in the Centro Histórico or Alameda Central, and prices are accordingly higher. Visitors can choose from several international cuisine styles as well as upscale Mexican fare. But those on a budget need not fear, lower-priced meals can be found in the surrounding neighborhoods, particularly at the markets and in little *comida corrida* eateries. McDonald's, KFC, and other fast-food chains have outlets in the Zona Rosa for those desperate for a taste of Americana.

Tortas and Tacos

Just off the pedestrian-only Calle Génova in the Zona Rosa, **Taco Inn,** Hamburgo 96, has rather pricey but very good tacos and is open daily 7 A.M.–4 A.M., making it convenient for breakfast as well as a late-night snack.

Mexican—Less Expensive

The lowest-priced meals around Reforma are, predictably, to be found in the markets. While the **Mercado Insurgentes** in the Zona Rosa, in the first block east of Florencia between Liverpool and Londres, is mainly dedicated to handicrafts, one corner of the market has a number of hygienic *comida corrida* stands where a meal will set you back around US$3. Open Mon.–Sat. 9 A.M.–7 P.M., Sun. 10 A.M.–3 P.M.

Directly behind the U.S. embassy on Río Lerma, **Mercado Cuauhtémoc** is a regular neighborhood market, though a touch pricier than most because of the relatively upscale clientele. The food stands inside serve tasty *comidas corridas* for US$2–4 and *antojitos* for US$1–3 and are open during the week until 6 P.M. and on weekends until 4 P.M.

At the corner of Avenida Cuauhtémoc and Morelos, at the eastern edge of the Reforma area, is the legendary coffeehouse and restaurant **La Habana,** Morelos 62, tel. 5535-2620, frequented by generations of journalists who work in the surrounding blocks. This is a wonderful spot to enjoy a strong cup of coffee and a good breakfast at leisure. Many regulars swear by the *huevos con machaca* (eggs with dried, shredded beef in a spicy sauce), but there are plenty of other options. The Formica and plastic decor comes straight from the 1950s, along with the old photos of Cuba on the walls. When government bribery of journalists was more common than it is nowadays, the men's room of La Habana was reputedly where most of the *chayotes* (a slang word for payoffs made for flattering stories) were passed along. Ground or whole-bean Veracruz coffee can be purchased to go here. Open Mon.–Sat. 8 A.M.–midnight.

On the west side of the Lotería Nacional building at the corner of Thomas A. Edison is **El Mixteco,** a classic little hole-in-the-wall spot specializing in cuisine from the Mixtec region of Oaxaca, including *tlayuda,* (a tortilla with salsa, onions, shredded beef, and special sauce), *tazajo* (a beef or shrimp dish), and exotica such as *chapulines* (grasshoppers). It offers a *comida corrida* with fresh-squeezed fruit drink for US$4.50. Open for lunch on weekdays only, closing before 5 P.M.

A more traditional *comida corrida* restaurant is **La Conexión,** on a quiet side street in the Zona Rosa at Belgrado 19, tel. 5208-7063. The food is a step up from the usual *corridas* (US$5), and service is good. It also serves breakfasts and dinners. Open Mon.–Fri. 9 A.M.–9 P.M., Sat. 9 A.M.–6 P.M.

El Faisan, also known as **Kobá-ich** (which means "pheasant" in Yucatán Maya), in the heart of the Zona Rosa at Londres 136, tel. 5208-5791, specializes in moderately priced *yucateca* dishes, including *panuchos, cochinita pibil,* and *papadzules,* among others. Open Mon.–Sat. 8 A.M.–10 P.M.

In the center of the Zona Rosa on Calle Londres 142 is **Bohemio's,** tel. 5514-0790, a somewhat upscale cantina that manages to stay entertaining and rowdy nonetheless with live Mexican music and many pitchers of light and dark Kloster beer swinging among the crowded tables. The food is traditional Mexican and of good quality. Try the *tampiqueña,* a piece of tender beef served with guacamole, a couple of enchiladas, and other fixings, for US$10. Open Mon.–Sat. 1 P.M.–1 A.M.

For very possibly the best *birria* in Mexico City, stop off at **La Polar,** Guillermo Prieto 129 at the corner of the Circuito Interior, in the San Rafael neighborhood, tel. 5546-5066. This classic, old-style cantina has several rooms, usually filled with crowds of Mexicans enjoying their legendary bowls of *birria,* a stew of shredded lamb in a spicy broth, served with tortillas, onion, salsa, and avocado. *Birria* is famed as a great hangover cure, to which the bleary-eyed crowds on Saturday and Sunday around noon can attest. La Polar also has beer on tap, and entertainment is provided by roving *norteña* and mariachi bands. Open daily 9 A.M.–midnight, or until 2 A.M. on Friday. It also serves *birria* to go from a take-out window.

Mexican—More Expensive

An all-time Zona Rosa favorite, **Fonda del Refugio,** Liverpool 166, tel. 5525-8128, serves traditional Mexican dishes such as *chiles en nogada, tacos de huitlacoche,* along with imaginative daily specials such as *albóndigas chipotle* (meatballs with chipotle chile sauce) in the quiet, relaxed ambience of an old two-story colonial house. The restaurant displays the folk art collection of the late Judit van Beuren, a writer who founded the restaurant in the 1950s. If you have a hard time with the Spanish menu, ask for the English version. Open Mon.–Sat. 1 P.M.–midnight, Sun. 1–10 P.M.

Behind the Hotel Melía Reforma at Antonio Caso 17, tel. 5564-0800, **Cantina Latino** is a large cantina-style place with large wooden booths. It's a popular spot for business lunches. The menu has a heavy emphasis on meats, including *arrachera* steaks, *cabrito* (kid goat), *chistorra,* and a selection of Spanish hams and sausages. It also has a full bar. Open Mon.–Fri. 11 A.M.–midnight, Sat. 11 A.M.–6 P.M.

Popular with tourists visiting the Zona Rosa is **Focalare,** at Hamburgo 87 between Niza and Copenhague, tel. 5207-8850, offering a wide selection of good-quality Mexican cuisine, including *cochinita pibil* and shrimp in tequila sauce. Mariachis play daily 9–11 P.M. Open daily 8 A.M.–11 P.M.

Vegetarian

Yug, Varsovia 3 at Paseo de la Reforma, tel. 5533-3296, goes beyond the standard health-store ambience of most D.F. veggie restaurants to serve vegetarian crepes, potato latkes, and a variety of fruit and vegetable juices. Open Mon.–Fri. 7 A.M.–10 P.M., Sat. 8 A.M.–8 P.M., Sun. 1–8 P.M.

North of Reforma, **Restaurante Vegetariano Las Fuentas,** Río Pánuco 127, at Río Tiber, tel. 5525-7095, offers good breakfasts and *comidas corridas* and is open daily 8 A.M.–6 P.M.

Seafood

Clean and inexpensive **Mariscos del Camaronero,** at Calle Ignacio Ramírez 21B, north of Paseo de la Reforma, serves delicious shrimp and fish tacos, ceviche, and seafood cocktails. Open Mon.–Sat. 10 A.M.–10 P.M.

A few blocks farther north, past the Monumento a la Revolución, is **Restaurante El Delfín,** at Arriaga 7, with similar, inexpensive fare. Open daily 10 A.M.–7 P.M..

Asian

If you're looking for Japanese cuisine in Mexico, try **Daikoku,** at Río Pánuco 170 at Río Nilo, tel. 5525-6520, a couple of blocks north of Reforma. Japanese living in Mexico City say they favor the sushi and sashimi in this restaurant over any other in the capital. Open daily 1–11 P.M.

Sushi Itto, Hamburgo 141, tel. 5525-2635, whips up (very quickly) sushi of the mass-produced variety, but it's reliable and hygienic, and the miso soup is tasty. Open daily 1–10:30 P.M.

In the middle of the Zona Rosa, **Luau's,** Niza 38, tel. 5525-7474, serves decent Cantonese food amid an amusingly kitsch decor. House specialties include *cha siu* (barbecued pork) and the ever-popular *chow mein cantonés.* The hearty multicourse set meals are a good value at US$7–9. Open Mon.–Sat. noon–11 P.M., Sun. noon–10 P.M.

French

A block and a half north of Reforma near the British embassy, **Les Moustaches,** Río Sena 88, tel. 5533-3390, is a very posh restaurant in a converted old *casona.* The service and authentic French food are top-notch, and it's not as expensive as one might expect considering the quality. Specialties include duck in a green olive sauce and chicory-leaf salad with goat cheese. Soft piano music adds to the ambience. Open Mon.–Sat. 1 P.M.–11:30 P.M.

Champs Elysees, Paseo de la Reforma 316 between Estocolmo and Amberes, tel. 5533-

3698, is frequently recommended for its exemplary foie gras and *confit de pato* (duck confit). Attached to the restaurant is a deli with fresh baguettes and a selection of French wines and other specialties. Open Mon.–Sat. 1–11 P.M.

At the Casa de Francia, a cultural organization run by the French Embassy, is the excellent **Bistrot Salut les Copains,** Havre 15, tel. 5511-3151. The quality of the food is very good, but the setting—with an outdoor patio—is more relaxed and informal than the above restaurants, and prices are lower. Is has a very good set meal during the day for US$10. It's also a fine spot to have a strong cup of coffee and enjoy a book. Open Mon.–Sat. 10 A.M.–6 P.M.

Greek

Run by an amiable U.S./Greek expat, **Zorba's,** Estrasbourgo 31 (near the corner of Amberes), tel. 5514-6122, offers a great selection of all your favorite Greek specialties at very reasonable prices. You'll often find a number of foreigners tipping back cold beers at the sidewalk tables. Open daily noon–10 P.M.

International

Difficult to classify, but well worth visiting if you're tired of tortas and *comida corridas* for lunch, is **Café Mangia,** Río Sena 85, a deli-style restaurant catering to the local office-and-embassy crowd with superb breakfasts such as croissants stuffed with egg, cheddar cheese, avocado, and bacon, or eggs scrambled with Gruyère cheese for US$2–5. Italian-style panini sandwiches are US$4–8. It also has a very good daily set meal, often some type of pasta, for US$5–7. Open Mon.–Fri. 8 A.M.–6 P.M.

Italian

La Gondola Restaurante in the Zona Rosa at Génova 21, tel. 5514-0743, has been serving Italian food for many years. If you'd like to dine alfresco, arrive before 8 P.M., or you probably won't get a table. The veal scallopini with lemon is tangy and tender and the fettuccine Alfredo is creamy and sweet. The restaurant offers a decent wine selection. Expect to pay about US$15 for salad and entrée. Open daily 1–11 P.M.

Spanish

A sidewalk restaurant in the Zona Rosa, **Mesón del Perro Andalúz,** Copenhague 28, tel. 5533-5306, has a reliable menu of Spanish dishes such as paella, tapas, and *tortilla española* at somewhat upscale prices. Open daily 1 P.M.–1 A.M.

Steaks

Angus, at Copenhague 31 between Hamburgo and Reforma, tel. 5208-2828, is a perennial favorite with the upper-class business crowd. Here you will certainly sate your craving for meat in short order—even the potatoes come with ham in them. The waitresses, dressed in skimpy Santa Fe–style cowgirl outfits, seem puzzled that one could want a plain potato. Expect to drop an easy US$20–40 per person for a full meal with drinks.

The chain restaurant **La Mansión** has a branch in the Zona Rosa at Hamburgo 77, tel. 5514-3425, serving hearty Argentine steaks, empanadas, and wine. Open Wed.–Sat. 1 P.M.–1 A.M., Sun.–Tues. 1–11 P.M.

Cafés and Tea Rooms

Near the corner of Florencia in the Zona Rosa is **Salón de Té Auseba,** Hamburgo 179, a great place to sit and relax in the comfortable '50s-style vinyl chairs and recharge with small sandwiches, pastries, and strong coffee. Open Mon.–Sat. 8 A.M.–10:30 P.M., Sun. 11 A.M.–10:30 P.M.

Nearby **Salón de Té Duca d'Este,** Hamburgo 164, is more "civilized," with strolling mandolin players and an endless display of cakes and pastries, along with very good coffee. A good spot to read the newspaper or people-watch over a leisurely coffee and snack. Open Sun.–Thurs. 8 A.M.–11 P.M., Fri. and Sat. 8 A.M.–midnight.

CHAPULTEPEC/POLANCO

As with hotels in this zone, Chapuletec/Polanco restaurants tend to be upscale and pricey, but they offer excellent quality. Polanco in particular features some of the best "ethnic" restaurants in the city. Reservations are recommended for many of these spots, particularly during the afternoon meal hours, and most credit cards are accepted.

Coffee, Breakfast, and Light Meals

Klein's Restaurant, tel. 5281-0862, in the strip of eateries along Presidente Mazaryk between Alejandro Dumas and Anatole France, is about the closest you'll come to a New York diner in Mexico. Klein's serves inexpensive sandwiches and meals. Open Mon.–Sat. 7 A.M.–1 A.M., Sun. 9 A.M.–1 A.M. It's usually packed for the 2–4 P.M. midday meal.

A good place to grab a quick, tasty breakfast is **Paris Croissant,** J. Verne 89, tel. 5281-0980, serving stuffed croissants, crepes, omelettes, and of course good coffee. Open Mon.–Fri. 8 A.M.–7 P.M., Sat. 9 A.M.–7 P.M.

Those after a quick *torta* or *comida corrida* in Polanco can head over to **Las Tortugas,** Presidente Mazaryk 249 (at Arquimedes), tel. 5280-1290, open daily 9 A.M.–11 P.M.; delivery available. Another decent spot is **Doña Torta,** right in the center of the Polanco shopping district at Virgilio 4, tel. 5281-6521.

El Califa, at Oscar Wilde 21A, a block off Mazaryk, is a long-time Polanco standby for tasty and sanitary tacos. Try the *taco gaonera,* with a cut of grilled, tender beef. Open daily until 4 A.M.

Grab an inexpensive Lebanese-style meal of stuffed grape leaves, falafel, or *tacos arabes* (tacos with meat cut from a rotating spit) at **Yamil,** Virgilio 9, tel. 8589-8142. Open 1–6 P.M. daily.

If you need a caffeine injection to revive you after touring the museums, stop in at **The Coffee Bar,** at the intersection of Temistocles and Presidente Mazaryk. The Coffee Bar has a large selection of international magazines and newspapers. Another branch can be found at Presidente Mazaryk and Moliere. Open Mon.–Fri. 8 A.M.–10 P.M., Sat. 9 A.M.–10 P.M., Sun. noon–10 P.M.

The **Balmoral Tea Room** at the Inter-Continental Presidente is also a pleasant, though more expensive, place to relax and recharge the batteries in the finest English style.

Mexican

Next to the Periférico, the superlative **Hacienda de los Morales,** Calle Vázquez de Mella 525, tel. 5281-4703 or 5281-4554, dates from the 1500s and was originally a silk-producing hacienda (hence the name, from *moral,* the mulberry tree groves in which the worms lived) in what was then a rural area west of Mexico City. The city has long since surrounded the hacienda, but this oasis of colonial calm is renowned for its Mexican cuisine, good service, and beautiful gardens. Well-prepared Mexican specialties include *chiles en nogada* (meat-stuffed chiles *poblanos* in a cream and nut sauce), shrimp in tequila sauce, and *cabrito norteño* (northern Mexican–style barbecued goat) for US$10–20 an entrée. The clientele tends to dress up to dine here, so don't come in shorts and a T-shirt. Open daily 1 P.M.–midnight.

Nearby **Fonda de Santa Clara,** Homero 1910, tel. 5557-6144, specializes in *cocina poblana* (cuisine from Puebla), including an extensive choice of moles (thick sauces made from chocolate), chiles, sesame, and myriad other spices. The *tinga poblana,* a flavorful dish made with shredded pork, is excellent. A musical trio performs during lunch and dinner. Open Mon.–Sat. 8 A.M.–11 P.M., Sun. 8 A.M.–6 P.M.

A converted mansion near the Paseo de la Reforma houses **Estoril,** Alejandro Dumas 24, tel. 5280-3414, a restaurant favored by wealthy Mexicans who enjoy the restaurant's cool ambience, attentive service, and top-quality Mexican specialties such as *nopales rellenos de huitlacoche* (cactus pads stuffed with corn fungus—a lot better than it sounds). This is a favorite power lunch spot, and entrées on the short menu will set you back US$10–17. Open Mon.–Sat. 1–11 P.M., reservations essential during the midday meal.

Seafood

A rival to downtown restaurant Danubio for having the best seafood in the city is **Los Arcos,** Torcuato Tasso 330, just off Mazaryk, tel. 5254-5624, the Mexico City branch of the famed Sinaloa restaurant. Fresh fish is flown in daily. Be ready to drop an easy US$20 per plate with drinks, but rest assured your stomach will thank you profusely. Everything is superb, but be sure to try the house specialty appetizer, *callo de hacha,* a scallop dish. Open Mon.–Wed. noon–10 P.M., Thurs.–Sat. noon–11 P.M., Sun. noon–8 P.M.

Chapultepec

Bosque de Chapultepec contains two restaurants, each overlooking a lake in the second section of the park. After walking through an entranceway that seems part of an elegant spaceship, you'll be seated in the spacious dining room of **Café del Lago,** tel. 5515-9586, which features one glass wall facing the lake. The restaurant is a favored haunt of Mexican politicians and other power brokers seeking a quiet place to hold their negotiations. The contemporary Mexican food (heavy emphasis on seafood) runs US$17–23 per entrée. The restaurant is open Mon.–Sat. 1:30–11:30 P.M., Sun. 1:30–5 P.M. Reservations recommended.

Café del Bosque, tel. 5516-4214, is a bit less upscale but still attracts a wealthy crowd, particularly for its weekend brunches (breakfast 8 A.M.–1 P.M., US$10; lunch 1:30–6 P.M., US$18). Open during the week 7:30 A.M.–midnight.

Sunday Brunch

Even if you're not staying in Polanco but feel like a splurge, the Sunday morning buffet at the **JW Grill** in the JW Marriott, Andrés Bello 29, tel. 5282-8888, is a great way to greet the day. Open 8–11 A.M.; US$13 for all you can eat.

Azulejos, in the Camino Real, Av. Mariano Escobedo 700, tel. 5263-8888, serves an afternoon brunch buffet on Sunday 1:30–5 P.M., with a huge array of cheeses, smoked fish, cold cuts, and half a dozen main dishes to choose from, for US$20.

In Chapultepec park, both **Café del Lago** and **Café del Bosque** serve Sunday brunch; the Café del Lago's buffet is more expensive but of higher quality.

Argentine

Rincón Argentino, Presidente Mazaryk 177, tel. 5254-8744, has some of the best Argentine food in the city, with succulent steaks, sausages, pastas, and wines. Started by an Argentine soccer star who played in Mexico for years, the cavernous, log-cabin style restaurant is always packed. Entrées run US$8–17. Open Mon.–Sat. 1–11 P.M., Sun. 1–10 P.M.

At the other end of Mazaryk, at the corner of Anatole France, is **El Zorzal,** tel. 5280-0111, a branch of the original restaurant in the Condesa. The *corte criollo,* a thick, juicy steak, is delicious, as are the empanadas. Open Mon.–Thurs. 1–11 P.M., Fri. and Sat. 1 P.M.–midnight, Sun. 1–7 P.M.

Asian

For those hot after authentic Chinese cuisine, never mind the bill, **Chez Wok,** Tennyson 117, tel. 5281-2921, is the place. On the second floor of a converted house at the corner of Presidente Mazaryk, you can savor a superb Peking duck, steak in orange sauce, and many other specialties from the extensive menu. Most meals are meant to be shared among two–six people. Dim sum is served on weekends only. Open Mon.–Sat. 1:30–4:45 P.M. and 7:30–11:45 P.M., Sun. 1:30–4:45 P.M.

Restaurant Tandoor, Copernico 156, at Leibniz, tel. 5203-0045, serves excellent Pakistani and Indian dishes at reasonable prices in a quiet house near the Hotel Camino Real. Mexicans apparently find the taste of Indian food rather odd, as the place usually contains only foreign customers. The chicken tandoor is the house specialty, and vegetarians will love the *palak paneer,* a tasty spinach and cheese dish. Service is excellent. Open Mon.–Sat. 1–11 P.M., Sun. 1–7 P.M.

International

An unusual mix of Asian and Latin cuisine is the specialty at the chic, upscale **Café Bistro Monica Patiño,** A. Bello 10, tel. 5280-2506 or 5281-0592. Enjoy dim sum, pizza, entrecôte with wasabi, or Thai sirloin with tamarind and mangos in a sleek, modern dining room decorated with Asian art. Open Mon.–Sat. 1:30 P.M.–midnight, Sun. 1:30–6 P.M.

Another upscale restaurant with an eclectic menu is **Iman,** Mazaryk 410 at Calderon de la Barca, tel. 5281-4412, offering international dishes such as foie gras and carpaccio, along with Mexican-inspired concoctions such as spaghetti with *arrachera* steak, shiitake mushrooms, and nopal cactus. Open Mon.–Sat. 1:30 P.M.–1 A.M.; reservations recommended. Next door to the swank Cosmo nightclub, Iman is a favorite spot for wealthy hipsters to start their night.

Italian

Mexico City is not known for its Italian restaurants, but **Il Punto,** at Emilio Castelar 213 B, tel. 5280-3623, is one of the best in town. Specialties include pizzas baked in a wood oven (US$17–20), *farfalle tequila* (pasta and shrimp with a tequila cream sauce, US$10), and *canelones Il Punto* (with tuna and a tomato cream sauce, US$10). Open daily 1 P.M.–midnight.

Another good option is **Prego,** A. Dumas 10, tel. 5281-0203, in a converted mansion just off Campos Eliseos. Prego offers an extensive menu of pastas, salads, cuts of beef, and wines. Open Mon.–Sat. 1 P.M.–midnight, Sun. 1–6 P.M.

A bit less stuffy, with more of a corner bistro feel, is **Non Solo Pasta,** Julio Verne 89, tel. 5280-9706, in the center of the Polanco commercial district. Run by a friendly French expat, this is a fine spot to enjoy a relaxing glass of wine with pasta for US$8–10. Open Mon.–Sat. 1 P.M.–1 A.M.

ROMA/CONDESA/ INSURGENTES SUR

Starting in the early 1990s, an increasing number of excellent restaurants have been opening in the Condesa neighborhood. The epicenter, as it were, is near the intersection of Vicente Suárez and Michoacán, where you'll find literally a dozen places to choose from, but many eateries have also opened on nearby streets such as Tamaulipas and around Parque México. Emphasis is definitely international— several taco joints and the like still occupy the neighborhood, but the real attraction is the more upscale places. It's gotten to the point where local residents are getting annoyed by all the traffic on weekends, with people coming from across the city to dine in what is now one of the hippest parts of town. Many restaurants have sidewalk dining, which makes a lovely way to spend a couple of hours tucking in a fine meal and a bottle or two of wine with some friends. The nearby Roma neighborhood also has some very good restaurants, although not as many and not as concentrated as the Condesa.

Tacos and Snacks

El Tizoncito offers two Condesa locations, a stool-and-bar, eat-and-run affair at the corner of Campeche and Tamaulipas, and a more formal sit-down restaurant two blocks east at Campeche and Cholula. Both serve delicious *tacos al pastor* (US$.50 each) and a variety of other *antojitos* along with beer and soft drinks. Prices are a bit higher than most *taquerías,* but the food is reliably hygienic. Open Sun.–Thurs. noon–3 A.M., Fri. and Sat. noon–4:30 A.M.

Another excellent Condesa taco stand is **Taquería El Greco,** at Michoacán 54 near the corner of Nuevo León. The inexpensive *pitatacos* are a popular Mexican culinary fusion experiment, as the regular crowds in the little restaurant will attest. Open Mon.–Sat. 2–10 P.M.

A block away, at Amsterdam 135 at the corner of Michoacán, diagonally opposite the Superama supermarket, is **Hola's** taco stand with delicious and inexpensive (US$.75 each) tacos of all varieties. It even serves a couple of vegetarian tacos, believe it or not, one with spinach and the other with squash and corn. There's a constant line for tacos in the afternoon calling out orders to the cheerful servers. Open Mon.–Sat. until 4 P.M.

Toma 5, at Sonora 201 one block from Insurgentes, has decent, filling meals and *antojitos* served amid photos of old Mexican and U.S. movies. The *zorba griego* salad (US$4), complete with goat cheese, spinach, lettuce, olives, walnuts, and even some pita bread on the side, is remarkably good for a place that serves mostly tacos. Open daily 8 A.M.–4 A.M., until 6 A.M. on weekends.

The block between Toma 5 and Insurgentes is lined with all sorts of taco-and-*torta* joints of varying styles and qualities (and all reputed to be owned by the same person) open until the wee hours of the night.

Mexican—Less Expensive

While Condesa has a market on the corner of Calles Tamaulipas and Michoacán, it's small and fairly pricey, which is no surprise considering the neighborhood. Far better is the **Mercado Medellín,** in Roma, bounded by Calles Medellín, Campeche, Monterrey, and Coahuila. A spacious, well-lit market with mountains of fresh produce, Medellín is also known for its excellent seafood, sold both in bulk and cooked in the many market restaurants. Shrimp cocktails are a tasty treat for a mere US$2.50. Open daily 8 A.M.–5 P.M.

Los Tamales, Álvaro Obregón 154, tel. 5574-2078, is an inexpensive and good-quality Mexican restaurant in the heart of Roma serving breakfast, lunch, and dinner, as well as its namesake tamales. Try the *oaxaqueño,* with mole and chicken; the *chiapaneco,* with mole, chicken, olives, almonds, plums, egg, and pepper; or the *yucatecos,* with Gouda cheese, strips of green *poblana* peppers, and *guajillo* chile sauce. Open Mon.–Sat. 8 A.M.–9 P.M., Sun. 9 A.M.–5 P.M.

Another restaurant specializing in *tamales* is **Flor de Lis,** Huichapán 17, tel. 5286-2229. In operation in Condesa since 1918, the simple cafeteria is a great place to enjoy a top-quality tamal stuffed with mushrooms or chicken and green chiles (US$2 each), or an assortment of other Mexican dishes at midrange prices. Open daily 8:30 A.M.–9 P.M.

If you're in the mood for some beef, but don't want to spend a whole lot of money, stop in at **Las Arracheras,** an unpretentious eatery in Condesa at Vicente Suarez 110 at the corner of Mazatlán. It serves reasonably priced, good-quality *arrachera* steaks, as well as very tasty *alambres,* a stir-fry of sorts with chopped steak, green peppers, onions, and a bit of bacon for flavor, eaten with tortillas. The green salsa here is hot and tasty. Open daily 1:30–8 P.M.

The cantina **Bar Montejo,** Benjamín Franklin 261 on the corner of Nuevo León, offers a full bar, inexpensive and good quality *comida yucateca* (Yucatán cuisine), and even a couple of tasty, full-bodied *yucateca* beers, Montejo and León. The service is exemplary. Open Mon.–Sat. 10 A.M.–midnight.

Mexican/International—More Expensive

One of the first of the trendy restaurants in Condesa, and still considered one of the best, is **Garufa,** Michoacán 93, tel. 5286-8293, with tables inside and on the sidewalk. Among the excellent pastas are cannelloni with spinach or corn and *fettucini hindú,* chicken breast in a tangy yogurt and ginger sauce over a bed of pasta. It has great steaks too. Open Sun.–Thurs. 1–11 P.M., Fri. and Sat. 1 P.M.–1 A.M.

Similar in quality and style to Garufa, but a bit more comfortable for sitting, is **El Principio,** in the Condesa at Tamaulipas 61 at the corner of Montes de Oca, diagonally across the street from its previous location, tel. 5286-0657. The *risotto con pato,* a rice and cheese dish with shredded duck (US$7), is sinfully rich. Open daily 1:30 P.M.–midnight.

Half a block away from El Princípio, but more relaxed in style, is **Bistro La República,** Montes de Oca 23, tel. 5553-1027, with healthy, creative salads and light meals at midrange prices. Popular with the local art crowd, this is a good spot to enjoy a relaxed glass of wine with a friend even if you don't want to eat. Open Mon.–Sat. noon–midnight, or sometimes later if customers are still around.

Café Los Asombros, in the bookstore El Péndulo at Av. Nuevo León 115 in Condesa, tel. 5286-9493, offers meals with a literary theme, such as beef *el pre-socrático* or *ensalada de pollo Neruda,* in a fittingly refined atmosphere. Breakfasts here are particularly good, and on weekend mornings it often has live classical music to aid your digestion. While the food is very good, service is often slow, so don't come in a hurry. Open Mon.–Fri. 8 A.M.–11 P.M., weekends 10 A.M.–11 P.M.

Restaurante-Bar La Tecla, Durango 186-A, tel. 5525-4920, is one of the better all-Mexican restaurants in Roma. Prices are reasonable, too; a *menú de degustación* (tasting menu) is available Monday–Thursday nights for just US$4.40. The daily set menu for both lunch and dinner is an excellent value. Main dishes include trout, steak with roquefort cheese and *huitlacoche,* or squash flower stuffed with goat cheese in a chipotle sauce.

In a converted old Roma mansion is **Ixcel,** Medellin 65, tel. 5280-4055, formerly a nightclub and now a very hip, popular upscale restaurant, still with something of a club feel to it. The Blue Room upstairs is particularly loungelike, if that's what you're looking for. The food is an eclectic mix of Mexican and international, including grilled shrimp with couscous, ravioli stuffed with spinach and goat cheese, duck meat tacos with plum sauce, and Vietnamese spring rolls. It's best to call ahead for a table, particularly on weekends. Open Mon. and Tues. 1:30 P.M.–midnight, Wed.–Sun. 1:30 P.M.–2 A.M.

An interesting updated version of a traditional Mexican restaurant/cantina, set amidst vaguely Gothic décor, is **El Candelero,** Insurgentes Sur 1333 in Colonia Mixcoac, tel. 5598-9008. Grab a table in the cozy bar or in the high-ceilinged, spacious central area and order from the menu of excellent quality Mexican specialties whilst enjoying the strains of the roaming mariachi or *trio* bands. A great spot for late night drinks *a la mexicana* as well. Open Mon.–Sat. 1:30 P.M.–2 A.M., Sun. 1:30–6 P.M.

Seafood

Contramar, Durango 200 in Roma, tel. 5514-9217 or 5514-3169, serves outstanding seafood in a bright, airy dining room bustling with waiters attending the 20-odd tables. Start off with the delicious *tacos de camarón* (US$5), stuffed with minced shrimp and more reminiscent of an Asian-style spring roll than a taco, then move on to the succulent *filete Contramar* (US$15), served on a wooden platter and lightly coated with sauce. Open daily 1–6 P.M. only.

Another good seafood restaurant is **La Morena,** in the center of the Condesa restaurant district at Atlixco 94, tel. 5211-0250. The *tostada ceviche a la peruana* is a great appetizer, as are the shrimp quesadillas. For a main course try the excellent, meaty *huachinango* (red snapper). Open Mon.–Wed. 1–11 P.M., Thurs.–Sun. 1 P.M.–midnight or later.

Bisquets

Roma remains a holdout for the classic Mexico City *café chino,* and the most famous of them all (and now a citywide chain), is **Bisquets Obregón,** at Álvaro Obregón and Mérida. Because of the popularity of the original 1950s-style restaurant, a new, McDonald's-style, multistory Bisquets is now open across the street. Both serve a large menu of inexpensive Mexican meals (breakfasts are a good deal), as well as the mandatory *bisquets* and chop suey. Open daily 7 A.M.–midnight.

A block west on Álvaro Obregón, at Córdoba, are the two branches of **Café Paris,** another longtime Roma favorite with bright purple booths and a similar menu to Bisquets Obregón. Open daily 7:30 A.M.–midnight.

Argentine

Specializing in hearty cuts of imported steak (the *corte criollo* and the *arrachera* are both topnotch), as well as sublime spinach-and-cheese empanadas, large salads, pastas, and wines, is **El Zorzal,** at Tamaulipas at the corner of Alfonso Reyes, tel. 5273-6023. A full meal runs US$20—well worth it for the superb quality. Open Sun.–Thurs. 1:30–11 P.M., Fri. and Sat. 1:30 P.M.–midnight.

Asian

Nagaoka, in a converted house on a quiet side street at Arkansas 38 in the Nápoles neighborhood, tel. 5543-9530, has some of the finest Japanese food in the city. After walking in past the stands of bamboo at the entrance, take a seat in the peaceful dining room and enjoy the excellent sushi, *teppanyaki,* and other dishes. Open Tues.–Sat. 1–10 P.M., Sun. 1–7 P.M.

Not as formal, **Tequila Sushi,** Arizona 77, tel. 5523-7936, is an inexpensive little restaurant with reasonably priced sushi, sashimi, *maki* roll, *misoshisu* soup, and other specialties. The set meals (US$4–7) are a good value. Open Mon.–Sat. 1–10 P.M., Sun. 1–6 P.M.

Blossom, in Colonia Del Valle at San Francisco 360, corner of Luz Saviñon, tel. 5523-8516, has some of the better Chinese food in Mexico City. The zippy *filete mongol* steak, with chile and spices, runs US$10, while the sumptuous *pescado blossom* (fried red snapper with shrimp and vegetables in a sweet and sour sauce) will set you back US$17. The restaurant has set lunch and dinner menus costing US$17. Open Mon.–Sat. 1–11 P.M., Sun. 1–6:30 P.M.

Italian

On Roma's tranquil Plaza Luis Cabrera, at the corner of Guanajuato and Orizaba, **La Piazza,** tel. 5264-5556, serves good, if not superlative, Italian cuisine in a wonderfully relaxed ambience. If the night is balmy (and it usually is), take a table out on the sidewalk. Prices are reasonable. Open Mon.–Sat. 1:30–11 P.M., Sun. 1:30–7 P.M.

On the ground floor of a 1930s apartment building on a shady corner of Parque México in Condesa, upscale **Vucciria,** Av. México 157, tel. 5264-0993, specializes in *tagliata al rosmarino,* strips of sirloin on a bed of spinach (US$9). Portions are not large considering the prices, but the quality is high. Open Sun.–Thurs. 2–11 P.M., Fri. and Sat. 2 P.M.–1 A.M.

Bartolino's, at Glorieta de las Cibeles 22 on the corner of Oaxaca, tel. 5535-5468, serves Mediterranean/Italian cuisine, including a very tasty *risotto de cetas* (mushroom risotto), escargot, and linguine with shrimp. Entrées run US$7–12. Open Mon.–Sat. 1:30–10:30 P.M., Sun. 1:30–6 P.M.

Haute cuisine in the most literal sense, **Bellini's** perches on the 45th floor of the World Trade Center de México, on Av. Insurgentes Sur at Filedelfia, in Col. Nápoles, tel. 5628-8304 or 5628-8305. Sweeping views over the city accompany respectable and surprisingly moderately priced Italian food. Apart from Italian favorites such as *fettucine tres quesos* (with provolone, manchego, and Roquefort cheeses), the restaurant also features an international array of dishes such as Latin American ceviche, English-style prime rib, and French foie gras; US$6–10 per entrée. The Sunday brunch (US$16; 9 A.M.–2 P.M.) is bountiful. Jacket and tie are required for men. Open Mon.–Sat. 1 P.M.–1 A.M., Sun. 9 A.M.–11 P.M.

Middle Eastern

Amar Kemal, Fernando Montes de Oca 43, near the corner of Atlixco, tel. 5211-2649, serves a variety of very healthy Arabic dishes, all prepared with organic ingredients. Falafel, *shwarma,* tabouli, kebabs, and other entrées all come with a salad; US$4–6 per dish. Open Mon.–Sat. 1:30–11:30 P.M., Sun. 1:30–8 P.M. Delivery available within Condesa.

Spanish

Restaurant Covadonga, in Roma Norte at Puebla 121, tel. 5533-2701, is a well-kept cantina/restaurant in a cavernous room with a bar at one end and a couple dozen tables populated mostly by men playing dominoes. Women will feel quite comfortable here, unlike some cantinas. Many artists and art scene followers converge at Covadonga after an exhibit opening in the neighborhood. Covadonga has an extensive menu filled with reasonably priced Spanish-style fish and meat dishes, appetizers such as *tortilla española,* soups, salads, and a midday set meal (US$7). The paella is excellent. Open Mon.–Fri. 1 P.M.–2 A.M.

Cafés and Sweets

Café D'Carlo, Orizaba 87, is a great little hole-in-the-wall Roma coffee shop with a few tables on the sidewalk, often filled with an interesting assortment of artist-hipster types, long-time Roma residents, and occasional foreigners sipping a strong espresso. Open Mon.–Fri. 8 A.M.–10 P.M., Sat. 8 A.M.–9 P.M.

Another Roma café, serving very tasty and inexpensive breakfasts and light meals along with the coffee, is **Café Tapanco,** Orizaba 161, tel. 5564-2274. Popular with local artists, this friendly café often has art displays on the wall. Open Mon.–Thurs. 8 A.M.–11 P.M., Fri. and Sat. 9 A.M.–11 P.M., Sun. 9 A.M.–10 P.M.

In Condesa **Café La Selva,** Vicente Suárez 38 D, tel. 5211-5170, is part of a socially conscious cafe chain serving only organically grown coffee from Chiapas collectives. It's now even opened a branch in Atlanta, Georgia. The java is excellent and wickedly strong. Open daily 9 A.M.–10:30 P.M.

For a more comfortable place to sit down, walk around the corner to the **Village Café,** Tamaulipas 99, tel. 5211-0346, a funky little coffee shop with Beatles memorabilia and stacks of old magazines. Seating is available in two quiet rooms or at outdoor tables. Open Mon.–Sat. 8:30 A.M.–11 P.M., Sun. 11 A.M.–11 P.M.

Another popular spot to while away the hours while sipping espresso and reading a newspaper or chatting with friends is **Cafemanía,** Parque México 123 at the corner of Ixtaccíhuatl, tel. 5264-0577. Apart from coffee drinks, it also serves light meals and pasteries. Open Mon.–Fri. 9 A.M.–10 P.M., weekends 10 A.M.–10 P.M., or sometimes later.

Café de Nadie, at San Luis Potosí 131, tel. 5264-3420, is something of a hipster institution in the Roma. Situated upstairs in a converted old *casona,* the café is frequently the site of poetry readings, one-act plays, and bohemian music (Jaime López plays frequently). Along with the good coffee, it serves interesting teas mixed with herbs and spices, such as the *sueño de nadie* or the *psyche.* Open Mon.–Sat. 3 P.M.–midnight; music Wed.–Sat. usually 9–11 P.M.

© JOE CUMMINGS

in the *seccíon comidas,* Mercado Coyoacán

COYOACÁN

This upper-class bohemian neighborhood in southern Mexico City offers some of the capital's finest and most traditional dining options.

Mexican—Less Expensive

A half block east of Jardín Hidalgo in Coyoacán, on the north side of Calle de la Higuera, a cluster of semi-indoor ***antojito* stands** serve quesadillas with your choice of cheese, cheese with pepper strips, cheese with beans, potato, *panza* (beef stomach), *seso* (beef cheeks), *huitlacoche,* mushrooms, *flor de calabaza* (squash flower), and chicken or beef *tinga,* along with *sopes* and tostadas with choice of toppings. It's all under one roof; plain cheese quesadillas start at US$.60 each. Also on hand are delicious *flautas* and *pozole.*

Nearly next door on Higuera, **Cantina la Guadalupana,** tel. 5554-6253, is one of the city's most traditional and most popular *cantinas familiares* (family cantinas). The full menu covers all the Mexican standards. Open Mon.–Sat. 10 A.M.–midnight.

At Calles Aguayo and Cuauhtémoc, opposite Pasaje Coyoacán, **El Tizoncito** offers a delicious variety of tacos and other *antojitos* along with beer and soft drinks. Prices are a bit higher than in most *taquerías,* but the food is very reliable. Open Sun.–Thurs. noon–2 A.M., Fri.–Sat. noon–4 A.M.

A neighborhood legend, attracting visitors from across the city to munch on the tasty Mexican specialities in a colorful tiled dining room, is **Las Lupitas,** on Francisco Sosa at the corner of Plaza Santa Catarina, about six blocks west of Jardín Centenario. Try the *enchiladas potosinas,* one of the specialties. Open Mon.–Fri. 9 A.M.–5 P.M. and 7–11 P.M., weekends 9 A.M.–11 P.M.

Inside the relatively plush Mercado Coyoacán you'll find a string of *marisquerías,* countertop purveyors of fresh seafood. Popular choices included *tostada de ceviche* (crisp corn tortillas topped with ceviche), *pulpo en su tinta* (octopus cooked in its own ink), and *sopa de mariscos* (seafood soup). Other *comedores* are sprinkled throughout the market, and most are very clean. Off to one side of the market there's also a *sección comidas,* where you'll find big *cazuelas* bubbling with *pancita,* Mexico City's answer to *menudo.* Mercado Coyoacán is three blocks north of Jardín Hidalgo off Calle Allende.

Mexican—More Expensive

At the south end of Jardín del Centenario, **Los Danzantes,** tel. 5658-6451, offers plaza-side tables as well as indoor seating on the ground floor of a two-story, colonial-style mansion. The Swiss-trained chef's lyrical way with food lives up to the name, which means "the dancers." The menu emphasizes Mexican fusion cuisine, offering such house specialties as *fettuccine con salsa de jitomate, ostiones ahumados, y chile pasilla* (fettucine topped with a sauce of smoked oysters, tomato, and chocolate-colored dried chiles) and *pechuga rellena de queso con salsa de cabuches* (chicken breast filled with cheese and covered with the fruit of the barrel cactus). The plush bar offers a wide selection of high-quality tequilas. Prices are high, but this is probably one of the best restaurants in the capital, so foodies should find it a worthwhile splurge. Open Sun.–Thurs. noon–11 P.M., Fri.–Sat. noon–1 A.M.

Facing the east side of Jardín Hidalgo in Coyoacán, **Restaurant Caballocalco,** Calle de la Higuera 2, tel. 5659-8059, serves moderately priced Mexican meals in a semiformal setting; open daily 8 A.M.–11 P.M.

Popular, tile-faced **Fonda El Morral,** Allende 2, a little north of Jardín Hidalgo in Coyoacán, specializes in regional dishes. Have a complete breakfast (US$4.50), *antojitos* (US$3–5), or entrées of fish, fowl, and beef (US$8–15), all served in a colorful and festive environment. Open Sun.–Fri. 8 A.M.–10 P.M., Fri.–Sat. till midnight.

International

Fabio's, in an upstairs dining room on the east side of Calle Caballocalco opposite the north end of Jardín Hidalgo in Coyoacán, serves an economical Mediterranean and Italian menu that includes pizzas, olive and eggplant appetizers, a Lebanese platter, and pastries. Open daily 8 A.M.–10 P.M.

El Sheik, at Madrid 129, a few blocks northwest of Jardín Hidalgo, tel. 5659-3311, is a popular Arab restaurant, with specialties such as hummus and tabouli (US$3.50) or a mixed plate of goodies for US$12. Open daily 8 A.M.–7 P.M.

Bakeries and Cafés

Around Coyoacán's twin plazas, both residents and visitors appear to sustain themselves on a steady diet of coffee and pastries. At the corner of Caballocalco and Avenida Hidalgo, opposite the east side of Coyoacán's Jardín Hidalgo, stands a branch of **Panadería El Globo,** one of Mexico City's best bakeries. Founded in 1884, El Globo now has several branches in the capital, and this is one of the fancier ones; most of the pastries come prewrapped, and there's a section dedicated to *pan rustico europeo* (rustic European breads). El Globo is open Mon.–Sat. 8 A.M.–7 P.M., Sun. 10 A.M.–5 P.M. On the opposite corner of Avenida Hidalgo, a bakery/deli called **América** offers more economical pastries, along with wines and various other comestibles.

If you're looking for intellectual stimulation, you might find it over a cappuccino at the **Cafe El Parnaso,** a cluster of wrought-iron tables just outside the ground floor of an old three-story colonial near the southeast corner of Jardín del Centenario, tel. 5554-2225. The attached bookstore offers tomes covering all subjects, mostly in Spanish, as well as music CDs. Try the empanadas, filled with your choice of tuna, spinach, ground beef, or other fillings, or share a *plato combinado* piled with empanadas, *tortilla española* (thick egg and potato omelette), cheeses, and *pan dulce.* Open Mon.–Fri. 9 A.M.–10 P.M., Sat.–Sun. 9 A.M.–11 P.M.

Facing the southwest corner of Jardín del Centenario, the casual outdoor tables at **Caffe Latte** appear to rival Café El Parnaso's in popularity. Then tucked away in a small courtyard at the southeast corner of adjacent Jardín Hidalgo, **Café La Selva** is packed with coffee drinkers savoring organic, politically correct Chiapas coffee all day long.

Politics aside, some claim that tiny **El Jarocho,** at Calle Cuauhtémoc 134 at the corner of Allende north of Jardín Hidalgo, serves the best Mexican coffee in Mexico City. There is no seat-

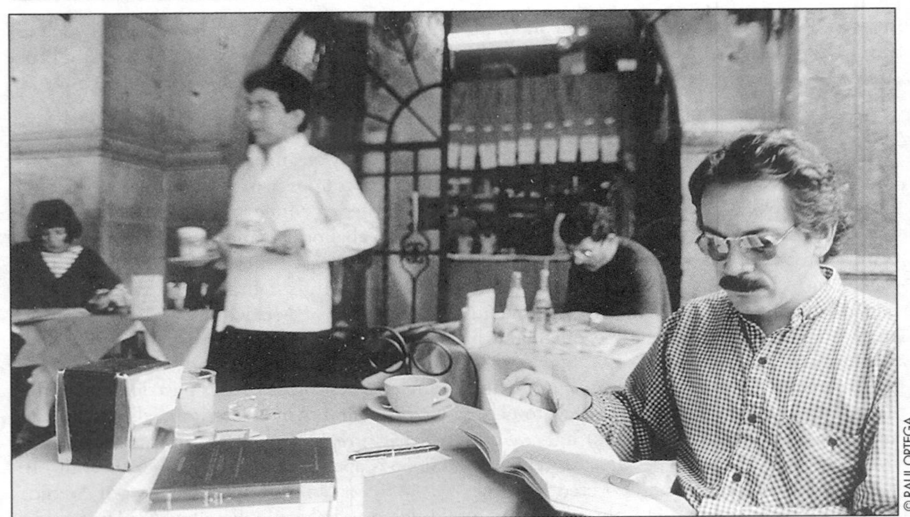
© RAUL ORTEGA

Café El Parnaso

ing inside the small shop, which has been serving fresh-roasted, fresh-brewed java since 1953, but if you're lucky you'll find space on a bench outside. You can buy whole-bean coffee by the kilo and half kilo here, and it also sells *tortas.*

To get away from the plaza scene a bit, check out **Cafetería Moheli** on the north side of Avenida Francisco Sosa west of Jardín del Centenario. Like El Parnaso, it's a popular place for those addicted to both books and caffeine.

SAN ÁNGEL

Restaurants in relatively upmarket San Ángel tend to be substantially pricier than those in Coyoacán.

Mexican

Ostionería la Curva de San Ángel, Altavista 1, at Av. Insurgentes, tel. 5661-4049, serves *chiles en nogada* stuffed with seafood as well as the usual set of shellfish *cocteles* and ceviche. Open Mon.–Sat. 10 A.M.–9 P.M.

Built in the 17th century as an opulent Carmelite monastery, and later home to Spanish viceroys—and, briefly, Emperor Maximilian and his wife Carlota—the **San Ángel Inn,** Diego Rivera 50, tel. 5616-0973 or 5616-1527, has seen a variety of guests over its three centuries, including Santa Anna and his troops, and, during the Revolution, Emiliano Zapata and Pancho Villa. Today, though still called San Ángel Inn, it's a restaurant only. It usually serves excellent food, though it's pricey and the dining room is often crowded. Try to come at a slow time—large groups on tour buses distract the chef. For a complete multicourse lunch and dinner, expect to pay US$20–28 and up. Open Mon.–Sat. 1 P.M.–1 A.M., Sun. 1–10 P.M.

Right on Plaza San Jacinto in a two-story colonial building is **Fonda San Ángel,** San Jacinto 3, tel. 5550-1641, with a lovely ambience but only so-so food. A good place to have a drink after a hot Saturday morning of shopping.

La Camelia, also on the plaza, tel. 5616-4668, serves excellent though pricey Mexican seafood dishes. Open Mon.–Wed. noon–9 P.M., Thurs.–Sun. 10 A.M.–11 P.M.

Clavo y Canela, Av. de la Paz 39, tel. 5550-4338, offers a daily Mexican buffet starting at 1 P.M. The prices are reasonable and the service is attentive.

International

If you've been dying for a bagel after eating all those tortillas, stop in at **NY Deli & Bagel,** Av. Revolución 1321, tel. 5651-0510, between San Ángel and the Metro Barranca del Muerto station. Breakfasts and lunches are hearty and excellent, although not cheap—many ingredients are imported. The expatriate owner offers several different homemade spreads to top your bagel. Food is also sold to go. Open daily 8 A.M.–midnight.

In the mood for Indian food? Next door to the Casa de Risco in an old colonial building is **Hasti Bhawan,** also known as **La Casa del Elefante,** where acceptable (though not exceptional) Indian cuisine is served either indoors or in a pleasant outdoor seating area. Open daily 11 A.M.–10 P.M.

Los Irabién, Av. de la Paz 45, tel. 5616-0014, focuses on Arab as well as *nueva mexicana* (new Mexican) cuisine at moderate prices. Open Wed.–Sat. 11 A.M.–11 P.M., Sun. 10 A.M.–9 P.M.

For a definite culinary adventure, check out **Kokoro,** Av. La Paz 57, local 37, tel. 5550-0185, offering a sometimes bizarre but scrumptious combination of Japanese and Mexican cuisine, for example, sushi with ripened banana and *chipotle* sauce. Food is not cheap, but the quality is very good. Open Mon.–Sat. 1 P.M.–midnight, Sun. 1–8 P.M.

In the heart of San Ángel, **Voilà Bistro,** Altavista 4 and 5D, tel. 5616-5286, serves classical Parisian bistro fare. Open Mon.–Wed. 1 P.M.–midnight, Thurs.–Sat. 1 P.M.–1 A.M., Sun. 1–10 P.M. Credit cards accepted.

Another restaurant with French cuisine is **Cluny,** Av. La Paz 57, tel. 5550-7350, with a selection of delectable crepes for US$7–10 each. You can choose between "salty" crepes with ingredients such as chicken, corn, cheese, *huitlacoche* (a type of fungus—trust us, it's good), or sweet ones with strawberries and cream or carmel and nuts. It also has very good salads. Open Mon.–Sat. 1 P.M.–midnight, Sun. 1–10 P.M.

Arts and Entertainment

I never lived in Greenwich Village in New York, so its bohemian life—in the old days when it was bohemian—was outside my orbit. Although once I lived for a year in Montmarte in Paris, I lived there as a worker, not as an artist. So the nearest I've ever come to **la vie de bohème** *was my winter in Mexico when my friends were almost all writers and artists. . .*

—**Langston Hughes,** *describing his life in Mexico City in 1933–34, from* **I Wonder as I Wander,** *originally published in 1956.*

In their relentless quest for diversion, *capitalinos* have turned their city into a world-class source of art and entertainment for virtually every taste. Whether you're into avant-garde theater, gallery art exhibitions, blockbuster cinema, symphonic music, mariachi music, salsa dancing, or just a great corner cantina, you'll find some part of the city dedicated to that particular form of expression.

Aztec dancers perform most days in the Zócalo, right next to the Catedral.

Fine Arts

Literature

Elaborate hieroglyphic books and a priest-dominated literary tradition existed in the New World before the arrival of the Spaniards. But many scholars consider the fantastic chronicles of newly arrived Spanish soldiers, explorers, and priests as the first flowering of a truly Mexican literature, early expressions of what would become enduring Mexican themes: being caught between Indian and European worlds, and the fall from (or destruction of) an Edenic paradise.

Two examples of this genre, widely available in English translation, make for compelling reading. Bernal Diaz del Castillo's *Conquest of New Spain* is the memoir of a foot soldier in Cortés's military campaign against the Aztec empire. With just 400 men, superior weaponry, horses, and the help of Indian tribes in thrall to the Aztecs, the Spaniards marched into Tenochtitlán, the heart of the empire, and triumphed against an army numbering in the tens of thousands.

A very different view can be found in Bartolomé de las Casas's *Brevísima relación de la destrucción de las Indias (Brief Account of the Devastation of the Indies),* which details the astounding brutality that the invaders visited upon the people of not just the West Indies but much of what was then called the New World. A priest who accompanied many expeditions, de las Casas raised the first voice of protest against Spanish destruction of native peoples and cultures.

The colonial era produced many authors who tried to imitate the prevailing styles in Europe. One colonial-era writer whose work has outlived that of most of her contemporaries is Sor Juana Inés de la Cruz, a remarkable nun, poet, and playwright. Her *Repuesta (The Reply),* a reply to a bishop who censured her and wrote of how women's role in the Catholic church should be severely limited, has become a feminist classic and is available in English translation, often accompanied by her poems, the best known of which is *Primer Sueño (First Dream).*

Modern Mexican writers—including Juan Rulfo, Octavio Paz, Carlos Fuentes, Mariano Azuela, Agustín Yáñez, Elena Poniatowska, and Rosario Castellanos—enjoy success outside of Mexico as well as in their native land. Rulfo's *Pedro Páramo,* published in 1955, is a hallucinatory novel well worth deciphering. Some consider it Latin America's first magical realist novel. Paz's *Labyrinth of Solitude* comprises classic essays that address the mysteries of Mexican identity. Poniatowska's *Massacre in Mexico* is an account of the 1968 killings of protesting Mexico City students by government troops. All are available in English translation. Another excellent observer of Mexican character and society is Carlos Monsiváis, whose *Rituales del Caos* is a collection of essays on life in Mexico City, available in Spanish only.

Two Colombian writers long resident in Mexico City, Gabriel García Marquéz and Álvaro Mútis, have also garnered international acclaim for their fiction, which is set in Latin American locales and imbued with a distinctly Latin perspective. The fact that these two literary stars have chosen to live and write in Mexico City says much about the capital's intellectual environment. Both have several works available in English translation.

Paco Ignacio Taibo II writes detective novels set in Mexico City, often from the bicultural view of a character or characters who move back and forth between Mexico and the United States. Taibo novels available in English translation include *De Paso, Four Hands, Just Passing Through, Some Clouds,* and *Leonardo's Bicycle.*

Of the many current Mexican writers, Guillermo Fadanelli is definitely worth a read, if your Spanish is up to it. His gritty, realistic, and funny novels and stories are set in contemporary Mexico City. Two of his better-known works are *¿Te veré en el desayuno?* and *La otra cara de Rock Hudson.* José Emilio Pacheco's novella *Las batallas en el desierto,* set in the Roma neighborhood of Mexico City, is a great read and easy to follow even if your Spanish is not excellent. Other current fiction writers include Sara Shefkovich, Mario González Suárez, Mario Bellatin, and Mauricio Montiel. Works by

DIEGO AND FRIDA

Mexico City in the 1920s stood on the threshold of a new era. Although the country had won its independence from Spain in 1821, it became obvious by the early 1900s that the economic gap between rich and poor—and the social gap between the Spanish descendant and Amerindian descendant—had only increased after the departure of the Spanish. Sparked by the populist escapades of colorful bandit-turned-revolutionary Francisco "Pancho" Villa and peasant-hero Emiliano Zapata, Mexico endured a decade of civil war before the newly established Partido Revolucionario Nacional (PNR, which later became the PRI) began steering the nation in a new, socialist-inspired direction in 1920.

The capital swarmed with optimism as the PNR vowed to make *mestizaje*—the blending of Amerindian and European patrimonies—the national zeitgeist. For Mexico, and especially for the intellectuals, artists, and academicians of Mexico City, the armed battles had ended but the cultural struggle was just beginning.

Under the 1920–24 presidency of Álvaro Obregón, the government decided that public works of art could play an important role in restoring a nationhood tattered by civil war. Commissioned to create a number of murals at the National Preparatory School at the University of Mexico in 1922, painter Diego Rivera took on the task of conceiving a new art medium that avoided a Eurocentric orientation and instead celebrated Mexican heritage from early Mesoamerica through the Revolution. Rivera was joined by a number of other similarly commissioned Mexican artists, who together formed the Syndicate of Technical Workers, Painters, and Sculptors. In a public tract issued by the Syndicate in 1922, fellow muralist Davíd Alfaro Siqueiros urged Mexican artists to "repudiate so-called easel painting and every kind of art favored by the ultra intellectual circles, because it is aristocratic, and praise monumental art in all its forms, because it is public property."

While the colonial art of Mexico and Latin America had from time to time incorporated Indian decorative motifs—sculpting squash foliage or pineapple patterns in stone to fill the space between religious figures on churches and cathedrals, for example—the overall design concepts, styles, and techniques employed were always Spanish. A painted *bodegón* or pantry scene might contain corn and cacao instead of oranges and grapes yet it remained the patented European still life, muted in color and devoid of human presence.

The soon-to-be-dubbed Mexican Modernist School abandoned the solemn and detached art of Europe and instead embraced bold New World imagery full of color and human activity. Looking for a medium beyond the confines of canvas and church porticoes, they settled on the vast, undecorated walls of Mexico's governmental edifices. Like the Aztecs and Maya of earlier eras, who painted on the walls of their temples and tombs, the Mexican muralists left their public buildings awash with color. And as did their Mesoamerican predecessors, they took native subjects as their inspiration. Instead of creating portraits of Spanish aristocrats, they glorified the everyday lives of the contemporary Amerindian population; in place of Franciscan friars fingering rosaries, they painted peasants tilling the soil.

Although many Mexican artists participated in the muralist movement, three names quickly came to the fore in Mexico City: Diego Rivera, Davíd Alfaro Siqueiros, and José Clemente Orozco. One of Rivera's earliest mural efforts emblazoned the courtyard of the Secretaría de Educación Pública with a series of dancing Tehuanas (natives of Tehuantepec in southern Mexico). This four-year project went on to incorporate many other contemporary Amerindian themes, and it eventually encompassed 124 frescoes that extended three stories high and two city blocks long. Such prodigious output, along with the predominance of native elements, had a profound effect on the Mexican art scene.

But as famous as the Mexico City murals made Rivera and his colleagues, a star-crossed romance with a teenaged National Preparatory School student named Frida Kahlo drew Rivera into a living tableau that for much of the world has symbolized the 20th-century Mexican art milieu seemingly for all eternity. Kahlo and Rivera married in 1929 and nearly overnight became a charismatic, celebrated couple on the art and society circuit around Mexico, the United States, and Europe. Their tumultuous relationship and Rivera's notorious infidelity only seemed to propel their mythic status. "I have suffered two accidents in my life," Kahlo is quoted as saying in the Malka Drucker biography, *Frida Kahlo: Torment and Triumph in Her Life and Art.* "One in which a streetcar ran over me [at age 18]. The other is Diego."

The aftermath of the streetcar accident, which included more than 30 surgical procedures and 28 plaster corsets designed to support her damaged spine, forms a recurring theme in Kahlo's famous self portraits. But more than the sometimes tortuously clinical details in these *autoretratos,* it's her iconic facial features—the batwing eyebrows, the stern, rose-like mouth, and secretive, sidelong glance fixed on the viewer—that one most remembers. A pronounced sexual ambiguity is also often present. In one portrait she suggests androgyny by merging her face with Diego's while another portrays Kahlo sporting shorn hair and a man's suit and tie. In a now-famous family photo from 1926 her hair is pulled back tightly and she again is dressed like a man.

In spite of her preference for personal rather than overtly political themes, Kahlo's work formed a central part of the Mexican Renaissance in its employment of native Mexican elements. Many of her paintings show an influence rooted in the tradition of Mexican religious folk culture, yet in a sense her work was post-modernist since she didn't completely turn away from traditional European presentation concepts. In *The Little Deer* (1946), Kahlo superimposed her head on the body of a stag (once again blending genders), whose body is pierced by numerous arrows. The painting recalls the martyrdom of St. Sebastian—a popular European theme in medieval religious art—while evoking the *danza del venado,* a mythic deer-hunting dance ritual common among Amerindian tribes throughout Mexico.

Although she didn't participate in public works of art like the muralists—in her physical condition she could hardly be expected to mount scaffolds—Kahlo in her own way became just as influential in her promotion of Mexican cultural nationalism. She decorated her home not with European and American art and accessories, but with Mexican handicrafts and folk art. Rivera and his colleagues typically dressed in the European fashions of the day, while Kahlo, though born of a German immigrant father, most often wore Amerindian dresses, shawls, and jewelry. Although she was born in 1907, she usually gave 1910—the year the Mexican Revolution began—as her birth date.

Kahlo died in 1954, and Rivera followed her three years later. Of all the Mexican artists who have worked in the 20th century, Diego and Frida are the most loved and remembered. In spite of the dynamic couple's original living-legend status, over the last decade Kahlo's international reputation has grown beyond that of her contemporaries as well as that of her husband Rivera. At a recent San Francisco Museum of Modern Art exhibition of the Gelman Collection—one of the largest private collections of paintings by the Mexican Modernists—museumgoers paid scant attention to paintings by Rivera, Siqueiros, and Orozco, but they stood four deep around the Kahlo paintings.

all of these authors can be found in many Mexico City bookstores. Two good ones are Gandhi, on the Alameda and in Coyoacán, and El Péndulo, in Condesa and Polanco. See the Shopping chapter for more details.

Architecture

Architectural styles in Mexico City vary from ancient Aztec pyramids to flamboyantly colored, cubistic high-rise office buildings. **Colonial architecture** in the capital extends from simple early-16th-century churches to the highly ornate late baroque or Churrigueresque styles that flourished in the 18th century.

The **baroque** period in Spanish church architecture was a response to the Protestant Reform and formed part of a Catholic religious movement known as the *contrareforma* during which many Catholics felt a strong need to elaborate on the mysteries of their faith. The baroque style permitted artists to experiment more freely with ornamentation, developing the twisted Solomonic column in the 17th century and the *estípite* (sections of columns and ornamentation layered vertically) in the 18th century.

As Mexican nationalism surged toward the end of the 18th century, government buildings adopted a more restrained, French-influenced **neoclassic style,** also known as Republican style. For colonial and neoclassic architecture the Centro Histórico is far and away the best district for touring, followed by Coyoacán and San Ángel.

For a taste of **art deco** architecture, take a couple of hours to tour around the Condesa neighborhood, particularly around Parque México, which began its boom in the 1930s. Across Avenida Insurgentes in the Roma are scores of century-old mansions built in homage to the Parisian styles to which the owners aspired.

Paseo de la Reforma, Polanco, and Chapultepec showcase styles of **modern architecture** created by such renowned 20th-century architects as Ricardo Legoretta, Luis Barragán, and Pedro Ramírez Vásquez.

Colonial Painting

You'll find the best overall collection of colonial-era painting—most of which was religious art meant for churches, cathedrals, and convents—in the Museo Nacional de Arte in the Centro Histórico. (See Centro Histórico in the Sights chapter for further details.) You'll also find much colonial painting in the older churches around the city, and in other museums.

© CHRIS HUMPHREY

Siqueiros's unusual three-dimensional mural at the national university

Mexican Modernism

Postrevolutionary nationalism in Mexico inspired grand works of art in painting and mosaics on the walls of public buildings throughout the nation. Often containing social and political criticism, Mexican murals have become one of the most imitated visual art forms in the Americas. Among the country's most famous muralists are José Clemente Orozco, Diego Rivera, Davíd Alfaro Siqueiros, Jean Charlot, Rufino Tamayo, and Juan O'Gorman. See the Sights chapter for listings of public places where such mural art may be viewed.

Diego Rivera (1886–1958) stands out as the most famous Mexican artist of the last century. No other renowned painter of the early 20th century except Picasso was considered as technically erudite as Rivera in terms of the range of his technique. According to MacKinley Helms, author of the 1941 *Modern Mexican Painters,* "[Rivera] painted in scores of styles before he developed his unmistakably personal formulas on Mexican walls." Among his Paris society friends were the artists Picasso, Braque, Gris, Modigliani, and Derain.

In the U.S., the status of Rivera's wife, German-Mexican artist Frida Kahlo (1907–54), has eclipsed that of Diego himself over the last decade. Most of Kahlo's work is held by private collectors; her tortured self-portraits fetch record auction prices, and art connoisseurs brave long lines whenever a Kahlo exhibit visits an American museum. The best place to view Kahlo's work is the Museo Dolores Olmedo Patiño in Xochimilco; the Museo Frida Kahlo in Coyoacán is more about the artist's life and her own art collection. The Museo de Arte Moderno holds on permanent exhibit Kahlo's most famous work in Mexico, *The Two Fridas.*

Contemporary Art

What, if any, legacy have the Mexican Modernists left to younger artists working in Mexico City today? At the Museo de Arte Moderno, museum director Teresa del Conde told us that "Diego Rivera stopped having followers in Mexico after the 1950s, perhaps because he had so much exposure. Siqueiros continues to be a minor influence, while Orozco's work has lasted among young and middle-aged artists working in Mexico today because of his opposition to commercialism." Del Conde also suggested that the nationalism of the Mexican Modernist School has been replaced by *neomexicanismo,* a slightly surreal, somewhat kitsch and postmodern slant on popular rather than historical Mexican culture.

Serving as a bridge between the highly symbolic and often political art of the early 20th century and the more representational art of younger artists are two older contemporary Mexico City painters, Gunther Gerzso and José Luis Cuevas. Gerzso abandoned symbolism for intensely abstract works that today are highly collectible. Cuevas rebelled against the idea that art had to serve a higher moral or political purpose and instead invested his talents in intensely personal explorations in concept, technique, and media, producing everything from labeled vials of his own semen to elaborate metal sculptures.

ART GALLERIES IN MEXICO CITY

Although not as well known as Guadalajara as a center for art galleries and festivals, Mexico City nonetheless has a vibrant art scene. The **Festival del Centro Histórico** held in three weeks in March includes a major art show. The Roma and Polanco neighborhoods, in particular, are where most art galleries are found. Check on the Web at www.arte-mexico.com for an excellent listing of galleries with upcoming openings. Below are some of the best-known galleries in the city, carrying both Mexican and international art. (See the Sights chapter for more details on each.)

Galería Enrique Guerrero, Horacio 1549A, tel. 5280-2941, Polanco

Galería Lopez Quiroga, Aristótles 169, tel. 5280-6218, Polanco

Galería Praxis México, Arquimedes 175, tel. 5254-8813, Polanco

Galería de Arte Mexicano, Gobernador Rafael Rebollar 43, tel. 5273-1261, San Miguel Chapultepec

Nina Menocal, Zacatecas 93, tel. 5564-7209 or 5564-7443, Roma

Out Gallery, Colima 179, tel. 5525-4500, Roma

Espacio Cultural Unodosiete, Orizaba 127, tel. 5264-3039, Roma

Galería OMR, Plaza Río de Janeiro 54, tel. 5511-1179 or 5207-1080, Roma

Ace Gallery, Francisco Pimentel 3, tel. 5546-9001, San Rafael

Currently extremely popular on the international art scene is the Oaxaca School of painters, a movement that was kicked off by Rufino Tamayo in the 1950s and continues to the present day with the whimsical, dreamlike works of Francisco Toledo.

Modern Art Museums

Museo Estudio Diego Rivera: This tightly spaced, functionalist, two-story studio was designed by architectural prodigy Juan O'Gorman, who was a friend of Rivera's. Reproductions of Rivera's work are displayed in a biographical section of the museum, along with a number of Rivera portraits donated by his subjects after his death (including one of doe-eyed actress Dolores del Río). Diego Rivera 2, San Ángel, tel. 5550-1518; open Tues.–Sun. 10 A.M.–6 P.M.; US$1 admission.

Museo de Arte Carrillo Gil: Created to house the private collection of the museum's namesake, this modern building contains significant works by Diego Rivera, Davíd Alfaro Siqueiros, José Clemente Orozco, and Gunther Gerzso. Av. Revolución 1608, San Ángel, tel. 5550-6260, www.macg.inba.gob.mx; open Tues.–Sun. 10 A.M.–6 P.M.; admission US$1.

Museo de Arte Contemporáneo Internacional Rufino Tamayo: Tamayo joined the ranks of noted Mexican muralists with images that bordered on the abstract. The museum dedicated to his art also houses work by Salvador Dalí, Max Ernst, Gunther Gerzso, Alberto Giacometti, Willem de Kooning, René Magritte, Joan Miró, Andy Warhol, and many other world-renowned names. Paseo de la Reforma and Gandhi, Chapultepec Park, tel. 5286-5889; open Tues.–Sun. 10 A.M.–6 P.M.; admission US$2, free on Sunday.

Museo de Arte Moderno: Mexico City's premier government-sponsored contemporary art space has two large rooms devoted to permanent collections of 20th-century Mexican art, particularly those of the Mexican Modernist School. Kahlo's *The Two Fridas* (1939) occupies an important display position. Paseo de la Reforma and Gandhi, Chapultepec Park, tel. 5553-6233; open Tues.–Sun. 10 A.M.–6 P.M.; admission US$2, free on Sunday.

Museo José Luis Cuevas: One of Mexico's preeminent modern artists, Cuevas donated works by himself and other Mexican artists such as Francisco Toledo, Vicente Rojo, and Arnold Belkin, among others, as well as foreign artists such as Pablo Picasso, Leonora Carrington, and Roberto Matta to this museum housed in a remodeled 16th-century convent. At Academia and Moneda, tel. 5522-0156, open Tues.–Sun. 10 A.M.–5 P.M.; US$1 admission; free for students with ID; free on Sunday for the general public.

Museo Dolores Olmedo Patiño: Olmedo, an intimate of Rivera's, has turned her home—a former convent—into a small museum exhibiting a number of works by Rivera, Kahlo, and others. She has the largest single collection of Kahlo's work. Av. México 5843, La Noria Xochimilco; tel. 5555-1016; open Tues.–Sun. 10 A.M.–6 P.M.; admission US$1.50.

Museo Frida Kahlo: Kahlo's traditional courtyard-style family residence became her home and studio, and after her death, a museum. Several of the rooms contain Kahlo paintings, including lots of nonself-portrait work, as well as works by French, German, and Mexican artists, including José María Velasco, Paul Klee, and José Clemente Orozco. Londres 247, Col. Del Carmen, Coyoacán, tel. 5554-5999; open Tues.–Sun. 10 A.M.–6 P.M.; admission US$1.50.

Museo Mural Diego Rivera: The government established this small museum to house Rivera's remarkable *Dream of a Sunday Afternoon in the Alameda,* which measures 15.6 by 4.3 meters and was created in 1947 for the Hotel Del Prado. Mexico City's 1985 earthquake damaged the hotel beyond repair, but the mural survived and was moved to this spot. Plaza Solidaridad, Centro Histórico, tel. 5512-0754; open Tues.–Sun. 10 A.M.–6 P.M.; admission US$1.50, free on Sunday.

To see more of the famed murals of Rivera, as well as other greats Siqueiros and Orozco, visit **Palacio Nacional, Secretaría de Educación Pública, Antiguo Colegio de San Ildefonso,** and **Palacio de Bellas Artes,** all in the Centro Histórico (see Sights for details). Farther afield, Rivera painted a unique mural inside a colonial chapel at the **Universidad de Chapingo,** in Texcoco (see Excursions chapter for more information).

Centro de Arte Alternativo Ex-Santa Teresa: In the shell of an old Carmelite chapel and convent, where famed 17th-century poet Sor Juana Inés de la Cruz briefly lived, one of the few art spaces in Mexico City dedicated to young, alternative art flourishes under the auspices of INBA. At Licenciado Primo de Verdad 6, just off Moneda. Open daily 10 A.M.–6 P.M.; free admission.

Laboratorio Arte Alameda: This new art space, also run by the INBA, has temporary exhibits of experimental modern art on display. Dr. Mora 7, tel. 5510-2793; open Tues.–Sun. 9 A.M.–5 P.M.; US$1 admission or free on Sunday.

Museo El Chopo: This Eiffelesque structure of girders and glass first served as the Japanese pavilion at an industrial exposition in 1910, and it is now a national university museum dedicated to modern art, mostly by young Mexican artists. At Calle Dr. Enrique González 10, a block from the intersection of Insurgentes and San Cosme (look for the iron towers), tel. 5546-5484. San Cosme is the closest Metro stop. Open Tues.–Sun. 10 A.M.–2 P.M. and 3–7 P.M.; admission $US.70, free on Sunday.

Nightlife

LIVE MUSIC

Mexico claims a rich musical heritage, from the traditional folk *chileñas* of the southwestern states to the Latino ska of Mexico City. Because of Mexico's position between the U.S. and the rest of Latin America, an unusually vibrant cross-fertilization results in an astonishing variety of musical styles that only an ethnomusicological survey could adequately convey.

Since 1998, when Mexico City was first governed by an opposition party, the city government has been much more amenable to holding open-air concerts in the Zócalo. Recent free concerts, with at times more than 100,000 in attendence, include Manu Chao, Café Tacuba, Tigres del Norte, and the Afro Cuban All Stars. Concerts are also occasionally held in Parque México in Colonia Condesa on weekend afternoons.

Because of a tragic fire in a nightclub a few years back, Dolores Padierna, the head of the Cuauhtémoc delegation (which includes downtown, Roma, Condesa, and several other *colonias*), has launched a campaign of closing bars and clubs left and right. One hopes her crusade manages to clean up many of the more grievious regulation violations without shutting down the city's vibrant nightlife. But by the looks of all the bright yellow closure stickers around the city, she appears to be erring on the side of the latter. Don't be unduly surprised if a place listed below is closed when you go by.

Legions of mariachis fill Garibaldi every day and night. A foreign visitor interested in experiencing a night of partying* a la mexicana *should go to Garibaldi forthwith, preferably on a Friday or Saturday evening from about 11 P.M.

Plaza Garibaldi

This little square along the east side of Eje Central Lázaro Cárdenas, a few blocks north of Bellas Artes, has been one of the main centers of traditional Mexican nightlife in the capital since the 1920s, when Cirilo Marmolejo and his mariachi band first took up residence at the Salón Tenampa. Marmolejo is long gone, but legions of fellow mariachis still fill Garibaldi every day and night. A foreign visitor interested in experiencing a night of partying *a la mexicana* should go to Garibaldi forthwith, preferably on a Friday or Saturday evening from about 11 P.M. onward. Just make sure you get a *sitio* cab or other type of safe ride home afterward, as the gangs of *rateros* (thieves) lingering in the back streets a couple of blocks

MARIACHI TRIVIA

- The word mariachi comes from the French word mariage; the music first became popular at weddings during the French occupation of Mexico (1862–67).
- Mexico's first nationally known mariachi ensemble was headed by Concho Andrade in the 1920s.
- A traditional troupe features 10 performers—four violinists, three guitarists (actually guitarrón, guitar, and vihuela), and three trumpet players.
- The male mariachi's tight-fitting, silver-studded costume is inspired by Mexican charro (horseman) suits.
- About 20 percent of all mariachi musicians are women, whose trademark coronela or china poblana outfits feature embroidered blouses and long, billowing, brightly colored skirts.

from Garibaldi are almost as famous as the mariachis themselves. The main square, however, is quite safe.

Salón Tenampa, on the north side of the square, is still going strong every day of the week until 3 A.M. (till 4 A.M. on Friday and Saturday). Two other favorites on the east side are **Guadalajara de Noche** and **Nuevo México Típico,** both open daily 8 P.M.–2 A.M., later on weekends. On the south side adjacent to Eje Central is **Tropicana,** open daily 9 P.M.–4 A.M.

The adventurous tourist may wish to try *pulque,* an unusual alcoholic drink favored by the Aztecs and made from fermented agave hearts. Although not the most traditional *pulquería* in the city, **Pulquería Hermosa Hortensia** on the north side of the square is a relatively safe place to try the drink; open Wed.–Mon. 5 P.M.–2 A.M.

While Garibaldi is in true form mainly at night, tourists may enjoy coming by on a sunny afternoon, having a beer and a couple of tacos at one of the little restaurants on the square's north side, watching the mariachis ply their trade. A group will gladly strike up an impassioned tune for you right then and there on the square, but it's not cheap—usually US$10 for a song, although sometimes you can convince them to play two for the price of one.

Folkloric Music and Dance

Música folklórica, ethnic folk music, has its roots at the local level in Mexico's rural areas, with differing *son* or song forms and instrumentation tied to particular regions of Mexico, such as the *sandunga* in Oaxaca, *jarabe* in Jalisco, *jarana* in Yucatán, *danzón* in Veracruz, or *huapango* in Tamaulipas and San Luis Potosí. Such song forms are for the most part restricted to regional festivals or, in Mexico City, at shows staged for the benefit of tourists.

The best of the latter, the **Ballet Folklórico de Amalia Hernández,** performs regularly at the Palacio de Bellas Artes. This troupe has accumulated 56 folk dances from around Mexico, which have been extracted from context and choreographed for Mexico City and foreign tastes into 30 separate "ballets." The costuming, settings, and music for these performances are superb, although the true Mexicophile may find the dance presentations themselves somewhat artificial, removed as they are from their native cultural habitats. Some of the choreography—such as the "Aztec" dances—are by nature highly speculative but also among the most dramatic. Performances at Bellas Artes are offered only two days a week, on Wednesday at 8:30 P.M. and on Sunday at 9:30 A.M. and 8:30 P.M. Tickets run US$20–40, depending on seating. Call 5512-

2593, ext. 193, for further information. Although the Amalia Hernández troupe is the most well known and is the permanent Bellas Artes troupe, other folkloric dance companies, such as the Compañia Nacional de Danza Folklórica, perform at Bellas Artes and elsewhere in the city.

A Mexican record label called Discos Corasón produces an excellent series of tapes and CDs focusing on folkloric music of Mexico and the Caribbean. Corasón's three-CD set *Antología del Son de México (An Anthology of Mexican Folk Music)* is a good place to start. It's distributed in the U.S. by Rounder, America's largest independent record label.

Música Antillana and *Salones de Baile*

From the lower Gulf of Mexico coast, Afro-Caribbean styles, from rumba to reggae, have made serious inroads in the Mexico City music and dance scene. Tropical *cumbia* from Colombia and salsa from New York and Puerto Rico have also become standards in the capital. All of these Afro-Caribbean forms are generally referred to as *música antillana* (music from the Antilles) or *música tropical.*

In the city center just behind the Catedral, **Bar León,** Brasil 5, tel. 5510-3093, is one of the most traditional *antillana* clubs in town, regularly attracting top-quality bands and a lively crowd. Open Thurs.–Sat. 9 P.M.–3 A.M.; cover costs US$5. If you go in a big group, check your bill carefully as it has been known to add on extra charges.

Salón Baraimas, Filomena Mata 7, between Tacuba and 5 de Mayo in the Centro Histórico, tel. 5510-4488, creates a similar mix of salsa and merengue music fueled by plenty of *mojitos* and daiquiris. Open Friday and Saturday only, cover US$8 men or US$4 women. Another good spot downtown is **Tarara,** at Madero 39 right above the McDonald's, tel. 5521-0102 or 5521-0123, often with live music in a slightly more refined environment than Baraimas. Open Friday and Saturday only; salsa classes on Saturday starting at 5 P.M.

In the Roma, **Mama Rumba,** Querétaro 230 at the corner of Monterrey, tel. 5564-6920, is a hugely popular Cuban bar with a live *son* (sort of a Cuban proto-salsa) band nightly, a lively crowd, and plenty of *mojitos* (a Cuban drink with rum and mint). Although the club has expanded in the last couple of years to cope with the crowds, Mama Rumba is still packed every weekend, and it can be difficult to get a table or find space on the packed dance floor. Open Tues.–Sat. for lunch 1–6 P.M., no cover; and at night 9 P.M.–5 A.M., US$6 cover. **Mama Rumba Sur,** by the same owners, is now open in San Ángel at Plaza San Jacinto 23, tel. 5550-8099. Open Wed.–Sat. 9 P.M.–3 A.M., US$5 cover.

More or less across the street from Mama Rumba in the Roma, and not quite as chic, is **Gran León,** Querétaro 225, tel. 5564-7110, originally established by the same people who ran the famed Bar León in the city center. Pepé Arévalo y sus Mulatos keep the crowd swinging their hips until the wee hours with salsa and merengue tunes. Tuesday is *danzón* night. Seating is available in the main hall downstairs by the dance floor or in the smaller balcony. Check out the egg-carton soundproofing on the walls and the fake palm trees. Open Tues.–Sat. 9 P.M.–3:30 A.M., US$5 cover.

A more old-fashioned version of the tropical dance club, the *salón de baile* (dance salon), which reached its peak between the 1930s and 1950s in Mexico City, has managed to hang on into the 21st century. The loyal clientele tend to be lower middle class Mexicans, but anyone who enjoys dancing is made to feel very welcome. Made famous by the Mexican film of the same name, the legendary **Salón México,** Pensador Mexicano 11, at San Juan de Dios near the Alameda, tel. 5518-0931, was remodeled and reopened in 1993. The spacious club hosts large bands playing salsa, merengue, and sometimes *danzón* and attracts a wide selection of Mexicans from different social classes and age groups. Open Thurs.–Sat. 9 P.M.–3:30 A.M., or on other nights for special events; cover usually runs around US$3–4. Another in this vicinity, and equally legendary, is the **Salón Los Angeles,** Lerdo 206 (between Ricardo Flores Magón and Estrella), tel. 5597-5181. **Salón Tropicana,** next to Plaza Garibaldi, is somewhat seedier and as the name suggests, the music tends toward *antillana.* In San Rafael is **Antillanos,** at Francisco Pimentel, tel. 5592-0439, with live salsa and merengue Thursday–Saturday after 9 P.M.; US$9 cover.

Keep in mind that the surrounding neighborhoods of Col. Guerrero and Col. San Rafael are not safe to walk around in at night, so be sure to take a cab there and have the staff call a cab when you're ready to leave.

The self-proclaimed "Palacio de Baile" of Mexico City is **Salón California,** in the Portales neighborhood well south of the Centro at Calz. Tlalpan 1189, tel. 5539-3631. This is an old-style, traditional dance hall where the clients take their dancing seriously, and don't do a lot of drinking. Open Fri.–Sun.; cover varies according to the bands. Although it's not near any tourist neighborhoods, the club is just off Line 2 (blue line) of the Metro, not far from the Portales station.

A more upscale Cuban-style club can be found in Polanco at **Barfly,** in Plaza Mazaryk, on Pres. Mazaryk between La Fontaine and A. France, with a live band playing from 10 P.M. onward Thursday–Saturday.

Just north of Polanco, at Lago Andómaco 17 near the corner of Moliere, is **Salón 21,** tel. 5255-1496 or 5255-5322. Formerly a regular dance hall, it is now only open for special events, but it often has really excellent music and a great dance floor. Worth calling to see what's on.

La Bodeguita en Medio, in the Roma at Cozumel 37, tel. 5553-0246, is styled after the famed Havana bar of the same name. There's no dancing here, but order a *mojito* and enjoy the small band that wanders from table to table. Open Mon.–Wed. 1–11 P.M., Thurs.–Sat. 1 P.M.–1 A.M., Sun. 1–5 P.M. Another place to enjoy a drink and listen to a small Cuban band is **La Bodega,** at the corner of Popocatépetl and Amsterdam in the Condesa, just off Parque México, tel. 5511-7390.

Rancheras, Corridos, and *Boleros*

The most popular song forms among the middle class and among the older generation in Mexico City are *rancheras* (similar to American country and western), *corridos* (Mexican ballads), and *boleros* (based on a traditional Andalusian form)—sometimes collectively known as *bohemio* (Bohemian). At any bar, cantina, or restaurant where *trovadores* (strolling musicians) play, you'll hear plenty of music of this sort. In most bars or cantinas, you can expect to pay about US$3 for a song played by a guitar trio at your table. If you're not sure which Mexican chestnut to name, ask for anything by Mexican composer Agustín Lara.

One of the more legendary performers of this sort of music, Paquita la del Barrio, has her own modest club in Col. Guerrero, **La Casa de Paquita la del Barrio,** Zarco 202, tel. 5583-

¡AY!

One of the quickest conduits to understanding and differentiating among musical genres is musical satire, at which Mexican vocalist Astrid Hadad excels. Her successful album *¡Ay!* includes *Me Golpeaste Tanto Anoche (You Beat Me So Last Night),* a send-up of the classic *ranchera* lamenting rural, working-class womanhood, as well as *Corazón Sangrante (Bleeding Heart),* sung in the staggering mariachi ballad style.

Even better than listening to Hadad's recorded work is seeing her perform live. Inspired by 1930s European cabaret and expressionism and by the *carpa,* a folk circus-opera popular in 1920s and '30s Mexico, she dons a succession of strongly visual costumes and makeup to match each number (e.g., a bodice festooned with a bleeding foam heart for *Corazón Sangrante*). Backed by a very accomplished group of musicians called Los Tarzanes, Hadad respectfully parodies the great vocalists of Mexico's past, including Lucha Reyes and Lola Beltrán. Although the lyrics and visual performances are much exaggerated, the musical arrangements themselves are always polished and potent.

8131, open Thurs.–Sat. nights, US$10 cover. Paquita continues the Lola Beltrán tradition of castigating men for their abuse of love through dramatic *boleros.* She occasionally performs at larger venues around the city such as the Teatro Metropolitán.

To get it all in one show, along with the even more melodramatic, sombrero-topped *charro* (horseman) style of *ranchera* delivery, check out La Tradicional Revista Musical del Blanquita (Blanquita Traditional Musical Revue) at **Teatro Blanquita,** opposite Plaza Garibaldi on Eje Central Lázaro Cárdenas. Shows usually mix musical numbers with comedic skits, not unlike the vaudeville shows of the early 20th century. There may be no better way to gain a quick insight into mainstream popular Mexican culture than to attend one of these shows, which are offered Thursday–Saturday 6.30 P.M. and 9 P.M., Sunday 5.30 P.M. and 8 P.M. Admission costs US$5.50–13, depending on theater seating; ignore ticket touts in front of the theater and buy your tickets directly from one of the ticket windows or else you'll end up paying 30–50 percent more than the face value of the tickets.

Astrid Hadad y los Tarzanes perform amusing, politically sharp, yet respectful takeoffs on Mexico's *rancheras* and *boleros* in the upstairs *teatro* at **La Bodega,** Popocatépetl and Amsterdam, tel. 5511-7390, in the Condesa on occasional weekends. Lately Hadad has taken to including a healthy dose of rumba in her repertoire as well. Hadad is worth seeing for her stage sets and costume changes alone, and her backing band is excellent. Check the weekly *Tiempo Libre* for scheduling.

Grupera

This is the latest name for a musical genre that basically has northern Mexican origins. The name itself refers to music performed by large ensembles blending the *ranchera*-and-polka *música norteña* of groups such Los Tigres del Norte with Sinaloan *perrada* or *tambora sinaloense.* The latter is a type of brass-and-drum band music originally brought by German immigrants but adopted and adapted in Sinaloa to become the "music of the people" when string music was still for the elite; during the 1910–20 Mexican Revolution it became a rallying soundtrack for the *constitucionalistas.*

The immense popularity can be explained not only by the cheerful horn and accordion instrumentation (brass carries the quality most cherished by the Mexican mainstream, *alegría* or joy), but because today's *grupera* lyrics reflect the daily lives and sentiments of Mexican peasants, sometimes with a political edge. *Norteña* lyrics often chronicle the tragedies and triumphs of *mota* (marijuana) smugglers and other *narcotraficantes* on the run from law enforcement. Some *grupera* songs have been banned by the Mexican government and can be heard only from bootleg tapes that circulate at cantinas or local fiestas.

Although touring *grupera* ensembles play at Mexico City theaters and auditoriums almost every weekend, one regular club venue where you can hear the music is the **Alamo Zona Rosa,** Hamburgo 96, in the Zona Rosa, tel. 5525-8352, with music daily after 9 P.M. Another is **Salón Pacífico,** Paseo Bucareli at Morelos, tel. 5592-2778, weekends only.

Rock en español/La Nueva Onda/Guacarock

Although lyrically descended from Latin American *nuevo canto* folk/rock music, *rock en español* takes its major musical inspiration from Anglo-American rock and Anglo-Jamaican ska. With Mexico City the premier center for the movement, this international genre has spread all over Latin America, particularly to Argentina and Brazil. *Rock en español,* also known as La Nueva Onda (The New Wave), began reaching critical popular mass in the mid-1980s; many observers speculate that the 1985 earthquake served as a major catalyst.

In the late 1980s, Botellita de Jeréz (Little Bottle of Sherry) and Maldita Vecindad (Cursed Neighborhood) began blending ska, punk, rock, jazz, and traditional Mexican elements as part of a movement within La Onda Nueva known by the descriptive *guacarock,* a reference to the mix of influences that are blended together like the ingredients in guacamole. Maldita Vecindad's first major hit was "Mojado" (Wetback), a tribute to transborder Mexican workers. Botellita has since disbanded, but Maldita Vecindad still flourishes at the center of the *guacarock* movement.

Also popular is rock fusion/art group Café Tacuba, a band that mixes alternative rock sounds with some Amerindian instrumentation and inspired live performances very much in the *guacarock* tradition. Santa Sabina adds a hint of Latin jazz improvisations to the mix, giving the band an art rock feel. All the major groups working in this medium come from D.F. or the State of México except for ¡Tijuana No!, possibly the most political of all the recent bands (the name signifies a plea not to flee Tijuana for the U.S.). One of its CDs, *Transgresores de la ley (Lawbreakers),* is more or less a tribute to the EZLN (Zapatista National Liberation Army) of Chiapas. Former band singer Julieta Venegas has now branched out on her own and with her two albums *Aquí* and *Bueninvento* is quickly establishing a name for herself as an immensely talented singer/songwriter. Two excellent Mexican rap/rock bands very popular in recent years are Control Machete and Molotov. Control Machete's "Sí Señor" is the theme song to a recent Levi's ad shown in the U.S., depicting a wobbly-legged young tough with a walkman ambling through the streets of some Mexican city.

Other Mexican rock groups still playing in Mexico include the venerable El Tri (kind of a Mexican Rolling Stones), CuCa, Maná (with a lead vocalist who sounds exactly like Sting), Los Jaguares, Caifanes, Plexo Solar, La Castañeda, La Barranca, El Sr. Gonzalez, La Lupita, Amantes de Lola, and Fobia. You may also come across bands who sing in Spanish but cleave more closely to Anglo styles, such as the glam/metal/goth Víctimas del Doctor Cerebro and Plastilina Mosh, or the punk/metal/rap sounds of Mauricio Garces.

None of these bands were the first in Mexico to play rock music; Los Apson and Los Locos del Ritmo created Spanish versions of Chuck Berry and Bill Haley in the 1950s, and 1960s indie garage rock produced sufficient output to fill two current CD compilations available in the U.S., *Mexican Rock and Roll Rumble* and *Psych-Out South of the Border.*

To get an idea of what young Mexicans are listening to, watch MTV Latino (formerly MTV Internacional), the Spanish version of America's MTV music channel available via cable or satellite throughout Mexico and in selected markets throughout the Americas, including the United States. The selections present a balance of English-language performances by groups from the U.S. or the U.K., Mexican performances in Spanish, and a good dose of Spanish-language videos from Spain and Latin America.

A number of venues in Mexico City are dedicated to modern rock music. **Bulldog,** Rubens 6 at the corner of Av. Revolución, San Juan Mixcoac, has live rock Friday and Saturday in a laid-back, unpretentious, atmosphere inside a converted arabesque mansion. Cover US$25 men, US$4 women.

Another popular spot to catch live rock bands is **Rockotitlán Sur,** Canal de Miramontes 2640, Coyoacán, tel. 5677-7374, a reincarnation of the old Rockotitlán on Insurgentes. Open Thur.–Sat.; US$9 cover men, women free.

A more underground club is **Alisa,** Cuauhtémoc 91 in the Roma, tel. 5767-1690, a bare room with a small stage, which can pack in a few hundred patrons on a good night. Many of the Mexican bands, mostly but not exclusively from Mexico City, play here regularly. Usually three acts play each night, Thursday–Saturday from 9 P.M. until sometime in the morning. Admission costs US$3–5. The telephone works only intermittently, so you're better to either come by or keep an eye out for the posters plastered all over the city advertising concerts.

El Péndulo in Condesa, at Nuevo León 115, tel. 5286-9493, frequently has small concerts of major bands in a coffeehouse atmosphere. Call for upcoming shows.

Mexico City's **Hard Rock Café,** Campos Eliseos 278 at Paseo de la Reforma, tel. 5327-7101, is always reliable. The club consists of a main restaurant/bar area and a separate small auditorium for live concerts. Tickets are also available through TicketMaster, tel. 5325-9000.

Reggae fans can catch live bands at **Casa Rasta,** Insurgentes Norte 149 in Col. San Rafael, tel. 5705-0086, open weekends only; US$20 cover men, US$4 women, free bar.

Larger *rockero* shows are held in the 3,000-seat **Teatro Metropolitana,** Independencia 90, tel. 5510-3448, or the even larger **Auditorio Nacional,** Paseo de la Reforma 50, tel. 5280-9250.

Probably the best place in Mexico City to shop for CDs and cassette tapes of *rock en español* (along with *antillana*) is the three-story **Tower Records** in the Zona Rosa. See the entry for Tower Records—and for **Mercado El Chopo,** a flea market for all kinds of Mexican and Latin rock CDs/cassettes—under Shopping.

Jazz/Coffeehouse

Other than the Latin jazz of hard-swinging Cuban bands in the city, it's difficult to find straight-ahead jazz ensembles in D.F. **New Orleans,** Av. Revolución 1655, tel. 5550-1908, in San Ángel, and **Pasta Jazz,** Alfonso Reyes at Saltillo, tel. 5271-9207, in Hipódromo Condesa, take a stab at it. The upstairs interior bar at **El Colmillo** (see Bars and Dance Clubs, below) takes jazz a little more seriously, but on Thursday evenings only, beginning around 9:30 P.M.

Los Íntimos, in the Roma at Querétaro 244, tel. 5264-2390, often has jazz acts, as well as Cuban music or rock bands, in a small club atmosphere. Open Tues.–Sun.; admission depends on the event (usually around US$10).

Café de Nadie, at San Luis Potosí 131, tel. 5264-3420, is something of a hipster institution in the Roma. Situated upstairs in a converted old *casona,* the café is frequently the site of poetry readings, one-act plays, and bohemian music (Jaime López plays frequently). Open Mon.–Sat. 3 P.M.–midnight; music Wed.–Sat. usually 9–11 P.M.

Upstairs at La Bodega restaurant is **Bataclán,** a performance space with a variety of different acts during the week, from jazz/blues to vocalists to comedians. Famed performance artist/musician Astrid Hadad plays regularly. At Popocatéptl and Amsterdam in the Condesa, tel. 5511-7390.

Flamenco

Although not Mexican per se (except for the flamenco-tinged sounds of mariachi bullfight fanfares), flamenco music has a small but strong following the capital. We found three clubs serving up hot flamenco: **Gitanerias,** Oaxaca 15, tel. 5514-2027, in the Roma (Tues.–Sun., first show at 9 P.M., second at midnight; cover US$11 men, US$5.50 women); **Mesón de la Guitarra,** Félix Cuevas 332, tel. 5559-2435, in Del Valle (Thurs.–Sat. starting at 7 P.M.; cover US$5); and **Mesón Triana,** Oaxaca 90, tel. 5525-3880, in the Roma (Tues.–Sat. 9:30 P.M.; cover US$7–9).

Tango

For live tango music, and some excellent dancers, check out **Bar Arrabalero** at the Hotel Viena, in Col. Juárez right near the Zona Rosa at the corner of Marsella and Dinamarca, tel. 5524-4864. Shows are on Friday at 9 P.M.

Classical Music

The **Auditorio Nacional,** Paseo de la Reforma 50, tel. 5280-9250, is a common venue for domestic and visiting international orchestras, major concerts by Mexico's top performers, or visiting international groups. The theater at the **Palacio de Bellas Artes,** tel. 5512-2593, in the Centro also hosts symphonic music from time to time, including weekly performances by the **Orquestra Sinfónica Nacional** (National Symphony Orchestra). Tickets for most events can be purchased through TicketMaster, tel. 5325-9000.

The national university, UNAM, hosts classical music in several venues. The **Orquestra Filarmónica de la UNAM** plays regularly at the Sala Nezahualcóyotl (tel. 5622-7125) and Sala Carlos Chávez (tel. 5622-7137) on the main campus. Other concerts are often held at the Casa del Lago in Chapultepec, tel. 5211-6093, and at Anfiteatro Simón Bolívar downtown at Justo Sierra 16, within the Antiguo Colegio de San Ildefonso, tel. 5702-4221. For more information look them up on the web at http://cartelera.musica.unam.mx.

BARS AND DANCE CLUBS

Cantinas and Bars

Mexico City's older, more traditional bars are mostly men-only hangouts, but a woman arriving in the company of males will feel comfortable

BAR LINGO

botanas—snacks
cantinero/cantinera—bartender
casco—"helmet," empty bottle
cerveza—beer
chela—slang for beer
chupar—slang verb for drinking
con hielo—with ice
copa—glass (for wine)
copita—"little cup," a drink
envase, botella—bottle
hasta atrás—drunk
hasta las chanclas—drunk
la cruda—"crude," hangover
sin hielo—without ice
tarro—mug (beer)
tragito—"little swallow," a drink
una fría—a cold one
vaso—glass (for most drinks)

in all the places listed below. Mexico City's many cantinas are wonderful places to toss back a few *tragitos* (swallows, i.e., drinks) with friends while listening to the music of strolling *trovadores.* Since most true cantinas serve food, you'll find several cantina listings in the Food chapter. At the other end of the social scale are plenty of sleek, chic bars, particularly in Polanco and Condesa, along with several laid-back, middle-of-the road watering holes in various neighborhoods.

Centro: Two very good cantinas downtown are **Bar La India,** Salvador 42, open Mon.–Sat. noon–1 A.M.; and **Cantina La Mascota,** Mesones 20, open daily noon–11 P.M. Both are clean, well-lit, and comfortable for foreigners and women.

A slightly seedy downtown bar with lots of ambience is **El Mesón del Castellano,** Bolívar 51, at República de Uruguay. Downstairs is a regular cantina, while upstairs is a dance hall with ladies hired to dance or sit and talk with male clients. The music upstairs is loud and invariably bad, but in a back room on the second floor you'll find a decent billiards room where you can shoot a few games of Mexican pool and drink inexpensive beer.

Also with lots of atmosphere, although of a different variety, is **La Faena,** V. Carranza 49, tel. 5510-4417. This high-ceilinged bar/restaurant pays homage to the *fiesta brava,* bullfighting. Stylish old bullfighting costumes fill the glass cases around the room. It often has tacky live music and occasionally alternative music events. Either way, it's an interestingly weird place to have a couple of drinks. Open Sun.–Thurs. noon–10 P.M., Fri. and Sat. noon–2 A.M.

A more traditional, upscale bar in the Centro is **La Ópera,** Av. 5 de Mayo 10, tel. 5512-8959, where Pancho Villa left bullet holes in the ceiling while riding around inside on his horse during the Revolution. This dark, baroque cavern of a place was built with plenty of wood and huge, mirrored booths big enough to hold large parties of revelers. The food is very good. Open Mon.–Sat. 1–11:30 P.M., Sun. 1–5:30 P.M.

In an extraordinarily baroque-styled house between República de Chile and Palma is **Cicero Centenario,** República de Cuba 79, tel. 5512-1510. The food is good, but the main attractions are the drinks and the bands of roaming musicians. As in La Ópera, the ambience is a bit more formal than in cantinas, so don't show up in shorts. This is a good place to go with a group of friends for a few hours of drinking, chatting, and listening to music in a lively atmosphere. Open Mon.–Sat. 1 P.M.–1 A.M., Sun. 1–8 P.M.

Paseo de la Reforma/Zona Rosa: In the center of the Zona Rosa on Calle Londres 142 is **Bohemio's,** tel. 5514-0790, a somewhat upscale cantina that manages to stay entertaining and rowdy nonetheless with live Mexican music and many pitchers of light and dark Kloster beer swinging among the crowded tables. The food is traditional Mexican and of good quality. Open Mon.–Sat. 1 P.M.–1 A.M.

La Flor Asturiana, at Puente de Alvarado 80 near the Monumento a la Revolución, 5535-4353, is a low-key neighborhood cantina with tasty *botanas* free with the drinks in the late afternoon. Live music Wednesday through Friday from 5 P.M. onward. It's a good quiet spot for early evening drinks and snacks, particularly if you're staying at one of the nearby hotels. Open Mon.–Sat. noon–11 P.M.

A bit more refined, but still relaxed, is **Cantina Latino,** at Antonio Caso 17 a block from Reforma, tel. 5564-0800. No free *botanas,* but it offers tasty meat dishes such as Spanish ham, sausage, *cabrito, chistorra,* or *arrachera.*

Almost more a club than a bar, considering its hipster clientele, **Bar Milan,** Milan 16, just east of Insurgentes near Reforma, tel. 5592-0031, is a dark little bar with strange, pizzalike sculptures on the wall and groovy music (but no dance floor). On first entering, you must buy a sort of monopoly money to pay for drinks at the bar—US$2.50–5, depending on what you get. Open daily 9 P.M.–2 A.M.

Looking something like an English ale house, with its wooden bar and hunting decorations, **El Chato,** at Londres 117, tel. 5533-2854, is a fine Zona Rosa spot to pull up a stool and share a drink and a few words with a friend. The bar is open Mon.–Sat. noon–midnight. In the back is a sort of karaoke-piano bar, open Mon.–Sat. 6 P.M.–midnight, where a pianist plays popular old-time Mexican tunes, and audience members take turns belting out the lyrics on a microphone.

Straight out of a David Lynch movie, **Noche y Día** is a most unusual late-night drinking spot just outside the Zona Rosa at Dinamarca 13, right across from McDonald's, tel. 5535-6074. An odd cross between a seedy dive bar and a vaguely baroque lounge with innumerable cigarette burns in the carpet, this ground-floor bar is populated principally by hard-core drinkers, but of a middle-class, nonthreatening variety. Drinks are a bit pricier than most, but since it's open 24 hours a day, it's a place to go at all hours after other bars close. Not for everyone.

Polanco: At the other end of the decor spectrum is **El Área,** in the Hotel Hábita, Av. Masaryk 201, tel. 5282-3100, a modernist bar looking like a transplant from Miami to the roof of a Polanco hotel. The jetset clientele lounges in relaxing sofas outside, admiring one another and the huge videos projected on a nearby building wall.

Insurgentes Sur: Right in the center of the Condesa restaurant district is **Cantina Centenario,** at Vicente Suarez 42. This cantina has been "gentrified" somewhat in recent years by the Condesa hipster set but still has its contingent of regular clients and a laid-back atmosphere. Open Mon.–Sat. noon–1 A.M.

Barracuda, Nuevo León 4A in the Condesa, is a very upscale, hip bar, styled as a lounge/diner, with overpriced food but plenty of atmosphere for having a few drinks. The clientele pulls up in droves on weekends in fancy cars, parked four-wide out into the street. It has live jazz most Wednesday nights, and sometimes on Thursday night and Sunday afternoon also. Open Tues.–Sat. 2 P.M.–2 A.M., Sun. 2 P.M.–midnight.

Another upscale spot favored by the well-dressed set in the Condesa is **Rexo,** a sleek glass and metal restaurant/bar at Saltillo 1, on the corner of Nuevo León, tel. 5553-1300. The martinis are strong and tasty.

Restaurant Covadonga, in Roma Norte at Puebla 121, tel. 5533-2701, is a well-kept cantina-restaurant in a cavernous room with a bar at one end and a couple dozen tables populated mostly by men playing dominoes. Many artists and art scene followers converge at Covadonga after an exhibit opening in the neighborhood to enjoy a few drinks and the very good Spanish-style food. Open Mon.–Fri. 1 P.M.–2 A.M.

The same owners as Cicero Centenario in the Centro also run the similar **El Candelero,** Insurgentes Sur 1333 in Colonia Mixcoac, tel. 5598-9008. Grab a table in the cozier bar or in the high-ceilinged, spacious central area and enjoy the strains of the roaming mariachi or *trio* bands. A great spot for late-night drinks as well as good, traditional Mexican food. Open Mon.–Sat. 1:30 P.M.–2 A.M., Sun. 1:30–6 P.M.

Coyoacán: It's hard to go wrong with the ever-popular **El Hijo del Cuervo,** at Jardín Centenario 17, tel. 5658-7824, open Mon.–Wed. 5–11 P.M., Thurs.–Sun. 1 P.M.–1 A.M.

Cantina la Guadalupana, just off Jardín Hidalgo on Higuera, tel. 5554-6253, is one of the city's most traditional and most popular *cantinas familiares* (family cantinas). The full menu covers all the Mexican standards. Open Mon.–Sat. 10 A.M.–midnight.

Tequilerías

Although tequila is served in virtually every bar or cantina in the city, a few places make a point of

PULQUE

Let some maguey cactus sap ferment and you have *pulque,* an ancient Mexican drink infused with more mystique than even tequila. Usually served in rustic establishments called *pulquerías,* the nutty-flavored, somewhat viscous liquid has an alcohol level comparable to beer and is said to be loaded with protein, vitamins, and minerals. *Pulquerías* are men-only establishments where outsiders are sometimes viewed with mild but real suspicion; it's best to enter with a regular. In Mexico City, you can easily find *pulque* at Pulquería La Hortensia in Plaza Garibaldi. In the nearby states of Tlaxcala, Hidalgo, and México, you will also find the occasional *ambulante* (street vendor) selling the beverage, often blended with fruit or nut extracts to produce a colorful display of bottles.

Before the arrival of the Spanish, Aztec priests drank *pulque*—Mexico's first alcoholic beverage—only during religious rituals. A temple dedicated to Tepoztecatl, the Mesoamerican god of *pulque,* still graces a hilltop near present-day Tepoztlán. Spanish colonization and later Mexican independence secularized and democratized the consumption of *pulque* and by 1883 Mexico City denizens were imbibing 100,000 tons of the inebriating liquid. Under Porfirio Díaz consumption in the capital tripled as huge haciendas in nearby Apam, Soltepec, Omestuco, Otumba, Apizaco, and Guadalupe dedicated themselves to cultivation of the agave plant and *pulque* production. By 1905 Mexico City boasted well over a thousand *pulquerías*—one for every 300 residents. The popularity of *pulque* waned considerably after World War II, when *capitalinos* became more accustomed to beer, brandy, and tequila.

The method for making the ancient drink has varied little over the last thousand years. When an agave or *maguey* is about to flower, a *tlachiquero* or harvester slices the top off the plant and scoops out the middle of the plant's heart (often referred to as the *piña* for its pineapple-like shape). The sweet sap of the plant will naturally accumulate in the resulting hollow. Several times daily the *tlachiquero* collects this *aguamiel* (literally "honey water") by inserting a long tube into the hollow and siphoning the juice into a shoulder-slung sack. One *maguey* will continue to produce *aguamiel* for two or three months before drying up. Left to stand, the sweet juice will ferment on its own into *pulque,* but the process is usually helped along by adding *madre* ("mother," previously fermented *pulque*), which will turn the entire batch into *pulque* in just one day. The results must be drunk within 24 hours, before the beverage goes bad.

providing a full range of Mexico's better tequilas. Because of the emphasis on quality, these can be pricey places to drink, but if you fancy yourself a tequila aficionado—or if you mean to become one—*tequilerías* are a must. In addition to the usual Jimador, Herradura, and Cazadores, you'll find such illustrious brands as Garañón, Los García, Don Jesús, El Tesoro de Don Felipe, Pura Sangre, Los Corrales, Dos Amigos, Tres Mujeres, Sombrero Negro, Don Leoncio, Cimarrón, Misión Imperial, Don Tacho, Las Iguanas, Bambarria, Los Tres Alegres Compadres, La Cava del Villano, Tenoch, Las Trancas, Reserva del Patrón, Zafarrancho, El Grito, Los Valientes, Chamuco Reposado, and many more.

Behind the Catedral Metropolitana in the Centro Histórico, **Salones Tequila de la Casa de las Sirenas,** República de Guatemala 32, tel. 5704-3273, occupies three rooms of a beautiful former *casona* built of volcanic stone. Last we checked the bar offered more than 120 labels of tequila. Service includes all the elements for tackling your assignment: salt, *chile piquín,* and limes. Open Mon.–Thurs. 1–11 P.M., Fri. and Sat. 1 P.M.–2 A.M., Sun. 1–6 P.M. Restaurant service available.

Another Centro Histórico establishment, **La Catedral del Tequila,** Bolívar 41, tel. 5512-9706, features a grandiose "altar" displaying hundreds of bottles of tequila in its three varieties—*blanco* (white), *reposado* ("rested," i.e., aged for one year), and *anejo* (aged more than a year), etc. The restaurant serves Mexican food. Open Mon.–Wed. 1–8 P.M., Thurs.–Sat. until 2 A.M.

Despite its name, **Salón España,** Luis González Obregón 25 at República de Argentina (Centro Histórico), tel. 5702-1719, is a cantina devoted to Mexico's national drink. In a section of the former *convento* of La Enseñanza (see Sights), you'll find more than 215 brands of tequila costing US$2–18 per glass. Don't be deterred by the less than impressive entryway; the interior is clean and orderly. Three or four different free *botanas* (appetizers) are served daily, along with a menu of traditional *antojitos* and a *comida corrida* costing only US$2.50. Open Mon.–Sat. 10 A.M.–11:30 P.M.

In the luxurious Hotel Camino Real, **María Bonita,** Mariano Escobedo 700, tel. 5203-2121, pours more than 120 kinds of tequila. If straight tequila isn't to your liking, the bartenders will mix up tequila cocktails, including a *margarita azul,* tequila sunrise, *cucaracha, iguana, chilango, México lindo,* or a *tecama. Bolero* trios wander the floor, and there are assorted free *botanas.* Open Mon.–Sat. 5 P.M.–1 A.M.

Pulquerías

Places that specialize in brewing and serving *pulque,* the fermented juice of the agave plant, could be found on virtually every street corner in the city before World War II. Nowadays they are few in number, though a few classics hold on. One of these, **Pulquería Las Duelistas,** Aranda 30 between Ayuntamiento and Puente de Peredo, next to Mercado San Juan in the Centro, has been serving *pulque* for more than 50 years. Especially good are the *curados* (*pulque* mixed with fruit or nut extracts). The *rockola* (jukebox) specializes in José Alfredo Jiménez, one of the great *ranchera* singers. Open Mon.–Sat. 9 A.M.–9 P.M.

Other *pulquerías* include **La Hortensia,** Amargura 4, Plaza Garibaldi (take along a friend or two, and don't walk to or from Garibaldi at night); **La Antigua Roma,** Allende and República de Perú in the Centro; and **La Reina Xóxitl,** 18 de Marzo 31, Xochimilco.

Microbreweries

The microbrew craze that has swept the U.S. (and has existed in Europe for centuries) has yet to make much of a dent in the Mexican market, but **Cervecería San Ángel,** Insurgentes Sur 1869, tel.

Pulquería Las Duelistas

5661-7729, is doing its best to create converts, offering eight different beers brewed in the huge vats inside. The beer is good, but the bar is certainly geared to a moneyed crowd: a large mug *(tarro)* costs US$5, while a glass is US$3. Plenty of hearty pub grub can be found on the menu, including Gruyère-and-Gouda sandwiches, chicken kebabs, cheeseburgers, and salads. Live bands play covers of international rock tunes Thursday–Saturday 9 P.M.–midnight. Open Mon.–Thurs. 1 P.M.–midnight, Fri. and Sat. 1 P.M.–3 A.M.

Another new place, also reputed to have very good beer (although we can't say from personal experience), is **Beer Factory Cuicuilco,** near Periférico Sur at Av. San Fernando 649, tel. 5606-0612. Open Mon.–Wed. until midnight, Thurs.–Sat. until 2 A.M., Sun. until 10 P.M.

Billiards

Roma Gym Billar, Orizaba 99 in Roma Norte, tel. 5207-8441, is a traditional Mexican pool hall, with local men drinking beer and shooting Mexican pool beneath fluorescent lights. The tables are in good condition, and chess and backgammon sets are available also. The game of choice here, as at most Mexican billiard parlors, is "pool," wherein balls 1–15 are lined up along the side of the table and are sunk in order. Several players, rather than just two, frequently shoot this game. Second in popularity is *ocho bola* or eight-ball, played much like it is in the United States. Also on hand are a couple of *carambola* tables, which feature three balls and no pockets; you use one ball to strike the other two, but only after it has touched three rails of the table. US$3 an hour per table. Open Mon.–Fri. 11 A.M.–11 P.M., Sat. 4–11 P.M., Sun. 4–10 P.M.

A block north of Calle Sonora in Roma-Condesa, **La Tirada,** Insurgentes Sur 317, tel. 5584-3642, is easily recognized by the painted sign of a voluptuous woman aiming a pool cue. Popular with young Mexicans, the bar/pool hall has 10 tables on two floors and good music. There are plenty of tables where you can hang out, drink a beer, and play a game of backgammon if you have to wait for a pool table to open up. US$3 an hour per table. Open Mon.–Thurs. 10 A.M.–11 P.M., Fri.–Sat. 10 A.M.–3 A.M., Sun. 4–11 P.M.

In the center of Condesa, **Billares Américo,** Michoacán 78, tel. 5553-5138, offers 12 pool tables in a converted warehouse, filled with young Condesa hipsters every night. Come in the afternoon or early evening to avoid a wait, or sit and watch the crowd until a table opens up, enjoying the great music. US$3.50 an hour per table. Open Mon.–Wed. 10 A.M.–midnight, Thurs.–Sat. 11 A.M.–1 P.M., Sun. noon–midnight.

In the Zona Rosa is **Brownsville Café Billar,** upstairs at Hamburgo 158, tel. 5511-9223, with a dozen tables but not a lot of atmosphere. Open Mon.–Sat. noon–11 P.M.

One place downtown to shoot some pool is **Ups & Downs,** Isabel la Catolica 83, tel. 5709-1539, open daily 10 A.M.–10 P.M..

Karaoke

If you're in the mood for it, you can visit three karaoke bars right next to one another on Florencia, between Liverpool and Londres, in the Zona Rosa: **Melodika, Canta Bar,** and **Bar 56,** at, respectively, numbers 52, 54, and 56. They are all about the same—filled with slightly inebriated people belting out their cherished favorites with great gusto to karaoke videos. Open daily 8 P.M.–4 A.M.

Tangas

Mexico City's many topless "table dance" bars (called *tangas* in D.F.) are perhaps best left for so-inclined individuals to discover on their own, but **El Closet,** in the Condesa at Saltillo 67, tel. 5286-5041, is so well established it's practically respectable to be seen there. You'll see lots of nicely dressed middle-aged men and barely dressed young ladies. Open Mon.–Sat. 8 P.M.–early morning. The Zona Rosa has *tanga* clubs on almost every other block.

Discos and Modern Dance Clubs

Because of both the current spate of club closures by city authorities, and the generally very fast turnover of clubs among the trend-concious crowd, listing good dance clubs is a dangerous idea. Those listed below seem to have withstood the test of time, and we hope they will be around for some time.

A long-running popular spot is the Centro Histórico club **Pervert Lounge,** Uruguay 70, tel. 5510-4454, with DJs spinning house, techno, and other club music to a young dance-happy crowd. Open Wed.–Sat. 11 P.M.–5 A.M. or so; cover US$6.

Run by a group of young Brits, **El Colmillo,** Versalles 52, tel. 5582-6164, in Col. Juárez near the Zona Rosa has been going strong since its inception in 1997. The club has two rooms, a straight-ahead house music disco and bar downstairs, and a more refined jazz/swing/groove bar (sometimes with live bands) upstairs. The downstairs section can be packed on weekends. Open Thurs.–Sun. 9 P.M.–4 A.M.; cover US$5 (free 9–11 P.M.).

Another exclusive Zona Rosa spot for after-hours, die-hard partiers is **Doberman,** Amberes 14A. Open only Fri.–Sun. 3–8 A.M. (that is, the mornings following Thurs.–Sat.); cover US$10 for men, free for women.

One good club in Polanco is **Cosmo,** at Mazaryk 410, tel. 5281-4412. This newer spot has some excellent DJs who bring the mood up slowly with groovier acid jazz, progressing subtly into more upbeat house music later in the evening. Open Wed.–Sat. until 2 A.M. or later.

The Roma's **Living Room,** Orizaba 146 in Roma, tel. 5584-7468, has been through several name changes in past years, and it is now a mainly gay club but worth visiting for straight people looking for the thumping electronic music. Open Friday and Saturday only; cover US$10.

More of an underground scene can be found in the weird little dive bar that has been colonized by young alternative hipsters called **La Perla,** República de Cuba 44. Normally it has techno/house music on Thursday and a mixed bag of random music and events on Friday and Saturday. Open until 4 A.M.

Gay and Lesbian Scene

For a supposedly macho country, Mexico has a surprisingly vibrant gay and lesbian subculture. It may not be as in the open as in Europe or the United States, but it's a lot more apparent than in much of Latin America. The capital's gay and lesbian scene is replete with hangouts of all different styles, from old-time gay cantinas to techno discos to transvestite dance revues. Pamphlets such as "La Otra Guia" or "Sergay" have listings of "in" clubs and can be picked up at several of the places written up below. Most of these clubs welcome women as well as men, although the females will be heavily outnumbered.

Unfortunately, the authorities have recently been closing down nightspots all over the city in a clean-up drive. Hangouts geared toward gays and lesbians are not the only targets, but they are easy ones. Some of the information here may soon be out of date. Best check the Internet: www.sergay.com.mx and www.gaymexico.net both have information in English.

In the Mexico City gay and lesbian scene you can observe a class/race/social divide that rich Mexicans rarely acknowledge. The expensive clubs attract the whiter, better-off clientele with independent lives, while the cheaper joints are jammed with poorer and darker-skinned men who are more likely to live with their families, perhaps in the closet.

The Zona Rosa, whose streets also become a cruising zone for men on weekend afternoons and evenings, contains a bunch of places. One longtime favorite is **El Taller/El Almacén,** Florencia 37, tel. 5533-4984 or 5207-0727, which is two clubs in one: upstairs is a mixed crowd, while downstairs is only men. It has popular tunes, videos, strippers and lots of men on the make. Tuesday and weekend nights are particularly strong. This is also a good place to find out about other "in" spots. Open daily; US$6 cover charge only on Thursday–Sunday.

Also in the Zona Rosa are several places along Calle Londres. **El Antro,** at no. 77, tel. 5511-1613 (disco/bar/piano bar, Thurs.–Sun.; US$5), has a mixed crowd, while **El Celo,** no. 104, tel. 5514-4766 (bar, Wed.–Sun.; US$6), and **El Cabare-tito Teatro,** no. 117-Bis, tel. 5207-2554 (bar/restaurant, every day; no cover), are meeting points for younger men. Seedier, little more than a sex club, is **La Estación,** on Hamburgo 234, tel. 5514-4707. Open daily, no cover, but you have to drink at least US$3 worth.

Down in the Colonia Roma, **Anyway,** Monterrey 47, tel. 5533-1691, is another veteran D.F.

gay club, with three different levels of dance floors and drag cabarets on weekend nights. Some nights one floor is reserved for women only; this is one of the few clubs in Mexico that caters to female clients.

For the hippest clubs try the **Box,** a vast ex-warehouse at Moliere 425, at the northwestern end of Colonia Polanco, tel. 5203-3356 or 5203-3365, www.boxmexico.com.mx. Only open on Friday and Saturday, Box is always packed mostly with young men but some women too, and it features Mexico's finest go-go dancers and occasional celebrity acts. The US$14 cover makes for a more affluent clientele than in the places downtown. Similar price and people are found at the more house-and-techno music **Living Room,** on Orizaba 137, Colonia Roma, which has an agreeable chill-out area upstairs. Upscale too, but less pretentious, is **La Victoria,** Coahuila 92, corner of Jalapa, Colonia Roma, tel. 5574-1762, a converted dance salon, on Wednesday (US$7) and Sunday (US$11) nights. It is always packed for its good 2 A.M. cabaret show on Sunday—don't these people have jobs?

Farther south and further down-market, **Tom's Leather Bar** at Insurgentes Sur 357, in Colonia Hipodromo Condesa, has precious little leather but does boast strippers, porn videos, a dark Gothic interior and a backroom, and eclectic music—the only gay bar where you might croon along with Ella Fitzgerald singing "Summertime." The US$8 cover includes one drink, and it opens daily except Monday. Farther south still, another supposedly leathery joint is **La Cantina del Vaquero,** at Alcegiras 26, Colonia Insurgentes Mixcoac, tel. 5598-2195. At the same address is **El Ansia,** tel. 5611-6118, an intriguing dive where, if you so choose, you may wear a numbered badge allowing potential beaux to leave notes for you in the corresponding message box.

Among the more working-class places is the **Cantina Viena,** a bar at República de Cuba 3, near the Eje Central, which looks just like any other Mexican cantina you might see, even down to the fact that men are the only clients. It's open daily, no cover. There are a few other gay bars nearby, some of them extremely seedy, but be wary in the dark streets. Farther south, at Izazaga 9 near the Eje Central, is **Buterflies,** a big club that holds the city's best drag revue by far, and it is always packed on Friday and Saturday nights. The US$6 cover includes a drink.

The notorious **14,** famed for its live heterosexual sex shows, has closed for good, and **15** ("Quince"), a pale imitation, has opened nearby on Ecuador 24, Colonia Centro, tel. 8589-9966; no live sex, but it attracts the same peculiar, sleazy, mixed heterosexual-homosexual crowd.

Many gays and lesbians live in the Colonia Condesa neighborhood, and a stroll through its streets or around the ellipse of Parque México is a pleasant way to spend a couple of hours. There are several gay-owned eateries in the Condesa restaurant hub centered around the streets of Tamaulipas, Vicente Suarez, and Michoacán. Places open and close so fast here that it's not worth mentioning any, but walk around and explore the options.

Finally, if after all this hedonism you are missing something spiritual in your life, you'll be welcome at Mexico City's only gay church, the **Instituto de la Comunidad Metropolitana,** Norte 77, no. 3218, in Azcapotzalco, to the north, tel. 5556-2172 or 5396-7768. It is an ecumenical chapel in the house of Father Jorge and Father Rodolfo, two priests who have been partners for more than 20 years. Mass is on Sunday at 10 A.M., 12.30 P.M., and 7 P.M. and lasts 1.5–2 hours. Take the Metro to Cuitlahuac station, and from there either take a taxi to the address, or walk 100 yards down the road to Avenida Cuitlahuac and take a *pesero* heading northeast until you reach a big roundabout—the Glorieta de los Camarones. Get off just before the roundabout, turn right, and it's the first street on your right.

THEATER

Mexico City is very rich in live theater, and if you understand Spanish you will undoubtedly find something entertaining, not to mention educational. The weekly *Tiempo Libre* is one of the best sources of info on theater, typically devoting a dozen pages to what's playing and where. The Consejo Nacional para la Cultura y las Artes

(Conaculta, the National Council for Culture and the Arts) funds many plays. Recent Conaculta-sponsored offerings at the **El Teatro en México,** Av. Revolución 1500, tel. 5562-8674, included *Los hermanos siameses, La muerte se va a Granada, Ubu rey, Salir al mundo,* and *Búfalo Herido.* Several other theaters in the city also host Conaculta-sponsored productions. On the Web you can find the latest information on such shows at www.conaculta.gob.mx.

A smaller, experimental theater also in Roma Sur is **Foco Luces de Bohemia,** Orizaba 193, tel. 5264-8380. Productions (usually US$5 admission) are held regularly, and less formal shows, with directors reading from works in progress, are frequent. Call for information about upcoming performances.

Other theaters with regular programming include: **Teatros Alameda,** Av. Cuauhtémoc 19 Altos at Chapultepec, tel. 5514-3300, ext. 221; **Teatro de las Artes,** Tlapan and Churubusco, Country Club (Metro Gral. Anaya), tel. 5420-4400; **Teatro Insurgentes,** Av. Insurgentes Sur 1587, tel. 5611-4253; **Teatro Isabela Corona,** Prol. Eje Central Lázaro Cárdenas 445, tel. 5782-1646; **Teatro Rafael Solana, Centro Cultural y Social Veracruzano,** Miguel Ángel Quevedo 687, Coyoacán, tel. 5554-1633.

CINEMA

Like other megalopolises such as New York, London, or Tokyo, Mexico City boasts a thriving cinema scene, with many world-class cinema facilities for viewing commercially distributed films—both international and Mexican—as well as institutes and clubs where films and filmmaking are dissected, critiqued, studied, and treated as a serious art form.

Film fans will find plenty of *cines* (cinemas) and *cineclubes* (film clubs) to choose from for an evening's entertainment, any night of the week. Many cinemas screen first-run American films, typically of the blockbuster genre (but a few art films sneak in as well), along with Mexican reels of all kinds. (See the special topic Cine Mexicano for a discussion of Mexican film.)

Foreign-language films—most of them American, with lesser numbers of French, German, and Italian films—are almost always projected in the original language, with Spanish subtitling. Ticket prices differ depending on the neighborhood and the movie house. Even branches of the same cinema chain will vary admission price according to the location. Movie theaters operated by Cinemex, one of the capital's better chains, can vary from US$2.40 general admission at one theater (Cinemex Real, on Av. Colón near Metro Hidalgo) to US$3.50 at another (Cinemex Galerias, at Ocampo and Bahía de Asención in the Centro). Compared to cinema-going in other world capitals, viewing first-run, international films in modern Mexico City facilities (usually with DDS or DSS audio) at these prices is already a bargain, but you can do even better if you attend showings before 6 P.M. (a slight discount most days of the week) or on specified days. In general the theaters in Polanco have the best projection and sound systems—and the highest prices. Note: Almost all Mexico City movie theaters offer half-price tickets on Wednesday.

Tiempo Libre carries extensive listings for current cinema showings in the capital, along with critical reviews in Spanish. The bigger daily newspapers also carry film listings; *Reforma* offers one of the more complete ones.

At least two local chains maintain their own websites, complete with addresses and phone numbers for all cinema outlets, ticket prices, and the titles of current film screenings: www.cinemex.com.mx and www.cinepolis.com.mx. Tickets for films showing at Cinemex theaters can be booked by phone at 5257-6969.

The following cinemas tend to show a preponderance of first-run American films, both independent and major studio productions, interspersed with occasional Mexican, Italian, and French films.

Cinemark Polanco, Miguel de Cervantes Saavedra 397, Polanco, tel. 5580-0506. **Cinemex Casa de Arte,** Anatole France 120, Polanco, tel. 5280-9156. **Cinemex Loreto,** Altamirano 46, Tizapán San Ángel, tel. 5550-0914. **Cinemex Palacio Chino,** Iturbide 21, Metro Hidalgo, Juárez, tel. 5512-0348. **Cinemex Plaza Insurgentes,** San Luis Potosí 214 at Insurgentes Sur,

CINE MEXICANO

Mexico's first cinema opened on Avenida Plateros (now Avenida Madero) in Mexico City on August 16, 1896, a few months after the Lumière brothers had premiered their famous cinematic projection system in Paris. *Capitalinos* took to the silver screen with great enthusiasm; statistics indicate that by 1902 Mexico City boasted more than 300 cinemas and 1,000 separate screenings per year.

Popular Mexican films run the gamut from drama to comedy to action pictures, with a high number of what might be called "cops and cowboys" films that focus on struggles between Mexican police agencies and *narcotraficantes.* As in the *narco-corridos* that celebrate the exploits of Robin Hood–like drug smugglers in song, such movies often extol smugglers' honor over police corruption. *Lucha libre* (professional Mexican wrestling, in which the opponents wear full head masks) films make up another curious subgenre of Mexican film. The longest-lasting of these is a series of B horror/detective films featuring el Santo, Mexico's most famous *luchador,* with such titles as *Santo contra los zombies (Santo against the Zombies), Santo contra las mujeres vampiro (Santo against the Vampire Women),* and *Santo: la leyenda del enmascarado de plata (Santo: The Legend of the Silver Masking).* Other Mexican productions have inserted masked wrestlers into all sorts of movie formulae.

In the 1940s and 1950s, Mexican films went through a high point known today as *la época de oro* (the golden age) for the quality of films produced. This was the era of great singer/actors such as Pedro Infante and Jorge Negrete, the dazzling actresses Maria Felix and Dolores del Río, and legendary comedian Cantínflas. Of the many top directors of the era, two of the best-known are Emilio "El Indio" Fernández and Alejandro Galindo, and cinematographer Gabriel Figueroa is considered one of the best ever in Mexico.

Mexico's cinematic tradition slipped in the '60s and '70s, with only a few classics shot during these years. An exception was the work of the father of cinematic surrealism, Luis Buñuel. Born in Spain in 1900, Buñuel moved to Mexico in the 1940s and directed some of his greatest cinematic works in his adopted homeland, including *Los olvidados* (1950), *Él* (1955), and *El ángel exterminador* (1962), before dying in Mexico City in 1983.

Another watershed art film made in Mexico, *El Topo* (1971), sees a nameless gunfighter travel from one bizarre village landscape to another in what could be a surreal version of a Kurosawa or Sergio Leone/Clint Eastwood epic. Chilean-born but Mexican resident Alejandro Jodorowsky directed the film, wrote the story, composed most of the music, and designed both sets and costumes. Both Buñuel and Jodorowsky were major influences on American director David Lynch.

Ariel de Oro (the Mexican equivalent of the Oscar) winner *Cronos,* directed in 1992 by Guadalajara native Guillermo del Toro, employs del Toro's trademark insect imagery and fondness for religious relics to create a story of a Mexican antique dealer who comes upon a strange scarablike mechanism that promises eternal life yet leads to the inevitable tragic end.

Roma, tel. 5264-2345. **Cinemex Real,** Colón 17, Centro, tel. 5512-9599. **Cinépolis Bucareli,** Bucareli 63, Metro Balderas, tel. 5535-9002. **El Plaza Condesa,** Juan Escutia 4, Condesa, tel. 5286-4973. **Lumiere Hipódromo Condesa,** Calle Progreso 1, between Av. Jalisco and Av. Revolución, Col. Tacubaya, tel. 5272-2649. **Lumiere Reforma,** Río Guadalquivir 104 and Paseo de la Reforma, tel. 5514-0000. **Lumiere Zona Rosa,** Londres 127 and Hamburgo 126, Zona Rosa, 5511-1309. **Multimax Continental,** Av. Coyoacán 116, at Xola, Del Valle, tel. 5687-5457.

Cineclubes

Several nonprofit venues screen smaller independent films and art films, typically for one

A more international hit was 1992's *Like Water for Chocolate (Como agua para chocolate).* Based on Laura Esquivel's recipe-studded novel of love, lust, and gustation, and adapted for the screen by her director husband Alfonso Arau, the film is considered one of the most successful transitions of Latin American literature's magic realism to the screen. *Chocolate* was filmed in Piedras Negras, Coahuila, near the U.S.-Mexico border. Two other films shot in *la frontera* that have become cult international hits include action thrillers *El Mariachi* (1992) and *Desperado* (1995), both directed by Mexican-American Richard Rodriguez on shoestring budgets.

In 1995 *El callejón de los Milagros (Alley of Miracles)* not only won Mexico's Ariel de Oro but became the most critically acclaimed film in Mexican history, earning 49 cinema awards around the globe. Loosely based on a novel by renowned Egyptian author Naguib Mahfouz and directed by Jorge Fons, the film paints a complex portrait of the interwoven lives of a cantina owner, a tarot card reader, a prostitute, and a small-time landlady in downtown Mexico City. Like several other Mexican art films, it was produced by the Universidad de Guadalajara with support from the Instituto Mexicano de Cinematografía (Mexican Institute of Cinematography, or Imcine) and Fondo de Fomento a la Calidad Cinematográfica (Fund in Support of Cinematic Quality).

In recent years Mexican cinema seems to be on the upswing again, with several excellent releases that have done well both in Mexico and abroad. In 1999, *La Ley de Herodes (Herod's Law),* directed by Luis Estrada, is an extremely entertaining political satire which for the first time in Mexican movies explicitly skewered the then-ruling PRI party, as well as the now-ruling PAN, the Catholic church, and much else besides. It chronicles the travails of a PRI flunky in a small village in the 1950s who is picked to be town mayor, and who proves quite adept at extorting, lying, cheating, and murdering his way to PRI glory.

But the real international breakthrough came with the brilliant *Amores Perros (dubiously translated in the English release as Love's A Bitch*), filmed in 2000 by Alejandro González Iñárritu. The harrowing, at times painfully realistic, movie follows the stories of three groups of Mexico City residents whose lives are brought together by a horrific car accident. By far the most moving of the stories is of a lower-class youth (played by rising film start Gael García Bernal) who falls in love with his brother's wife, and who begins to make money by bringing his pet Rottweiler Coffee to underground dog fights. The movie won more than 30 prizes around the world, and was nominated for an Oscar for best foreign film.

Filmed in 2001, and released in the U.S. in 2002, *Y Tu Mamá También,* directed by Alfonso Cuaron, looks set to garner plenty of foreign attention as well. The story, starring (again) García Bernal along with Diego Luna and Maribel Verdu, is a road movie of sorts with a heavy sexual emphasis, following the trip of two young friends who take an older Spanish woman with them to the beach. Although flawed, the movie is entertaining and marks a significant step in the pushing back of boundaries for sexual content in mainstream Mexican film.

or two nights only. One of the premier facilities is the government-supported **Cineteca Nacional,** Av. México Coyoacán 389, tel. 5422-1100, in the Centro Cultural Universitario on the UNAM campus in Ciudad Universitaria. Typical admission prices are US$3 general admission, US$1 for students with identification. The Cineteca Nacional was moved here after losing its original site at Viaducto Tlalpan and Avenida Río de Churubusco to fire. Its new home, originally constructed by the Sociedad de Autores y Compositores de México (Society of Mexican Authors and Composers) in 1978, contains five projection rooms, which means five different films are screened every night of the week. Also on the premises are a library and bookstore. For the latest schedule, see *Tiempo Libre* or the Friday arts section of *Reforma.* Classes in film history, such as "La historia de México, vista a través del cine" (The History of Mexico Viewed through Cinema) and "Cine y literatura" (Cinema and Literature) are offered on weekday nights and on Saturday.

Another nonprofit venue, especially for film festivals screening new cinema, is the **Cinematógrafo del Chopo,** Dr. Atl 37, Santa María La Ribera, tel. 5535-0447, where admission prices are the same as at the Cineteca Nacional. General admission is US$2, students US$1.

Other *cineclub* showings occur in a screening room at the **Museo de Arte Carrillo Gil** in San Ángel and at these three Centro Histórico locations: **Biblioteca de México,** La Ciudadela 4; **Biblioteca Nacional de Educación,** Leandro Valle 20; and **Salón Cinematográfico Fósforo,** San Ildefonso 43.

Holidays, Festivals, and Events

Like Mexicans around the country, *capitalinos* love a fiesta. Any occasion will suffice as an excuse to hold a celebration, from a birthday or promotion to a chile harvest. Add to all the civic possibilities the vast number of Mexican Catholic religious holidays, and there's potential for some kind of public fiesta at least every week of the year, if not all 365 days. Besides the national religious holidays, there are feast days for 115 Catholic saints per year, nine or 10 each month. Any pueblo or *colonia* named for a saint will usually hold a fiesta on the feast day of its namesake. Individuals named for saints, too, will often host parties on their *día de santo* (saint's day).

The primary requisites of a fiesta are plenty of food (especially tamales, considered a festive dish), beer and liquor, music, and dancing. More elaborate celebrations include parades, exhibitions, *charreadas* and, occasional fireworks.

© GREG BULL

reenacting the Pasíon at Taxco

Some of the more memorable yearly events and public holidays observed in Mexico City are highlighted below by month. Actual dates may vary from year to year, so be sure to check with the appropriate tourist office in advance.

Government offices and some businesses close on national holidays. These closings are not always mentioned in the text; you may want to call ahead to find out.

January

- **New Year's Day:** January 1 is an official holiday.
- **Día de los Santos Reyes:** January 6. See Las Posadas under December.

February

- **Constitution Day:** February 5 is an official holiday.
- **Flag Day:** February 24 is an official holiday.

March

- **Feria de la Flor Más Bella del Ejido:** Xochimilco celebrates its floriculture, its main claim to fame for at least 400 years. Among the events are a beauty contest; cooking demos; exhibitions of agriculture, cattle, and handicrafts; and a contest for the best-decorated *trajinera.* Dates vary from year to year.
- **Día de San José:** Celebrated in Iztapalapa, Santa Ana Tlacotenco (Milpa Alta), Tláhuac, Santiago Tepalcatlalpan (Xochimilco), and San Bernabé Ocotepec (Contreras) with music, processions, dances, fireworks and fairs; March 17.

- **Birthday of Benito Juárez:** March 21 is an official holiday.

March/April

- **Festival de Centro Histórico:** This three-week cultural celebration, held in Mexico City's historic district in the Centro, features concerts, theater performances, art exhibits, seminars, dance, gastronomical events, and activities for children. This festival usually coincides with an especially beautiful time of the year in Mexico City when the jacaranda trees are in full bloom. Dates vary from year to year.
- **Feria de Nieves:** Santiago Tulyehualco (Xochimilco). Exhibition and sale of ice creams and *nieves* (Mexican ices), from the usual favorites to more exotic flavors, including mole, tequila, and nopal. Dates vary from year to year.

April

- **Semana Santa:** Easter Week or "Holy Week" (usually in April, sometimes in late March) is second only to Christmas as the most important holiday period of the year. One of the most prominent Semana Santa customs is breaking *cascarones,* colored eggs stuffed with confetti, over the heads of friends and family. Besides attending Mass on Good Friday and Easter Sunday, many Mexicans take this opportunity to go on vacations. Mexican beach resorts can be overcrowded this week with a large influx of both Mexicans and North Americans.

  The Passion of Christ is reenacted at Iztapalapa, a *colonia* nine km southeast of the Zócalo. A young man portrays Christ and a young woman becomes Mary—both must be locally born virgins. On Good Friday around 150 people gather in Iztapalapa's central plaza to watch the Christ figure suffer mock beatings and a real crown of thorns. Then the young man must drag a 80-kg wooden cross for a distance of four km to the summit of Cerro de la Estrella, a hill sacred since the pre-Hispanic era. There he will be tied to the cross and ritually "crucified" before his attendants carry him back down the hill (and to a hospital to make sure he's still healthy).

May

- **International Worker's Day:** May 1 is an official holiday.
- **Cinco de Mayo:** Held on May 5, this festival commemorates the defeat of an attempted French invasion at Puebla de los Angeles on Mexico's Gulf of Mexico coast in 1862. Features music, dance, food, and other cultural events. In the capital, the biggest celebration is held at Iztapalapa.
- **Mother's Day** (Día de las Madres): Held on May 10.

June

- **Navy Day:** June 1 is an official holiday.

July

- **Dia de Santiago:** This fiesta for St. James is held in the Plaza de las Tres Culturas, where a great number of groups gather to perform their folkloric dances, wearing traditional costumes. Fireworks, art exhibits, and a handicrafts market are also on hand; July 25.

August

- **Commemoration of the Defense of Mexico and the Fall of Tenochtitlán:** At the Plaza de las Tres Culturas, the handsomely costumed *concheros* and many other groups entertain with dances to celebrate the temporary victory of the Aztecs over the Spaniards before the fall of Tenochtitlán. Aspects of the celebration are also held on elegant Paseo de la Reforma, in the Zócalo, and in front of the monument to Cuauhtémoc—the Aztec Emperor who led his armies in defense of the city; August 13.

September

- **Mexican Independence Day** (Fiesta Patria de la Independencia): Also called *diez y seis,* since it falls on September 16, this holiday celebrates the country's independence from Spain, as announced in 1810 by Father Hidalgo in the town of Dolores, Guanajuato. Festivities actually begin on the 15th and last two days, with fireworks, parades, *charreadas,* music, and folk dance performances.

Activities in Mexico City are centered on the Zócalo, where at 11 P.M. on the 15th, the president of Mexico—and the crowds congregated on the square below—call out Father Hidalgo's cry for independence—*El Grito.* There is a huge parade through the Centro Histórico on the 16th.

October

- **Día de la Raza:** Celebrated as Columbus Day north of the border, October 12 in Mexico commemorates the founding of the Mexican "race" *(raza)* as heralded by the arrival of Columbus in the New World.

November

- **Día de los Muertos:** The "Day of the Dead" is Mexico's third most important holiday, corresponding to Europe's All Saints' Day except that it's celebrated on the 1st and 2nd of November instead of only the 1st. Some of the festivities are held in cemeteries, where children clean the headstones and crucifixes of their deceased relatives *(los difuntos)* and play games unique to this fiesta. In some areas the faithful spend an entire day and night beside the family graves. Roadside shrines throughout Mexico are laid with fresh flowers and other tributes to the dead. Offerings of *pan de los muertos* (bread of the dead) and food and liquor are placed before family altars on behalf of deceased family members, along with papier-mâché or sugar skulls *(calaveras)* and skeletons. Short plays are occasionally performed in local theaters or large cemeteries, especially the melodrama *Don Juan Tenorio,* in which a murderer finds redemption through his victim's ghost. Colorful remembrances, with smaller crowds, are held in San Lucas Xochimanca (Iztapalapa), Santa Cecilia Tepetlapa (Xochimilco), and San Antonio Tecómitl (Milpa Alta). This holiday is also referred to as Fiesta de Todos los Santos (All Saints' Festival) and Festival de los Fieles Difuntos (Festival of the Deceased Faithful).
- **Día de la Revolución:** The anniversary of the 1910 Revolution, on November 20, is an official holiday.

December

- **Día de Nuestra Señora de Guadalupe:** The feast day of the Virgin of Guadalupe, Mexico's patron saint, is December 12; special Masses are held that day throughout Mexico. The nearest Sunday to the 12th also features special events such as mariachi Masses, food booths, and games. The celebrations at the Basílica de Nuestra Señora de Guadalupe in northern Mexico City are particularly well attended, and the *basílica* becomes an annual focus of pilgrimage, especially among Mexico's Amerindians. It's also called Fiesta Guadalupana.
- **Las Posadas:** Beginning on December 16, Mexicans hold nightly *posadas*—candlelight processions terminating at elaborate, community-built nativity scenes—in commemoration of the Holy Family's search for lodging. The processions continue for nine consecutive nights. Other activities include piñata parties where children break open hanging papier-mâché figures filled with small gifts and candy. Churches large and small hold continuous Christmas Masses beginning at midnight on the 25th (Día de la Navidad).

Las Posadas culminates on January 6, which is Día de los Santos Reyes—literally "Day of the King-Saints," referring to the story of the Three Wise Men. On this day Mexican children receive their Christmas gifts and family and friends gather to eat a wreath-shaped fruitcake called *rosca de reyes* (wreath of the kings) baked especially for this occasion. Hidden inside each *rosca* is a small clay figurine *(muñeco)* that represents the infant Jesus. While sharing the *rosca* on this day, the person whose slice contains the *muñeco* is obliged to host a *candelaria,* or Candlemas party, on February 2 for everyone present.

At the *candelaria*—which commemorates the day the newborn Jesus was first presented at the temple in Jerusalem—the host traditionally displays a larger Christ-infant figure and serves tamales and *atole,* a thick, hot grain drink flavored with fruit or chocolate.

Sports and Recreation

HIKING AND CLIMBING

If the pollution and stress of the city are getting you down, the nearby mountains of central Mexico offer plenty of opportunities to get some fresh air, exercise, and adventure within a couple of hours' drive or bus ride.

Two very good Spanish-language websites with lots of links and contact information for mountaineering in Mexico are the national university's www.montanismo.org.mx and the privately run www.xpmexico.com. The latter also has lots of information on other outdoor adventure sports, such as rock-climbing and mountain biking.

Hiking and Mountaineering

The mountain parks at the southwestern edge of the Valle de México—Ajusco, Los Dinamos, Desierto de los Leones, and La Marquesa—still (despite logging and pollution) support sizable patches of pine and oak forests, crisscrossed with dirt roads and trails.

Farther away from Mexico City are many patches of lovely forest that are safe for walkers. Among the many popular places to hike are: Parque Nacional El Chico, near Pachuca; the mountains above Tepoztlán in Morelos; and the spectacular forested countryside around Valle de Bravo, west of Toluca in the State of Mexico.

© ELENA PAPPAS

carved serpent head on the ancient stairways of the Templo Mayor, in the heart of Mexico City

Altitude addicts will be pleased to hear of several challenging peaks in the vicinity of Mexico City. **Popocatépetl** (5,465 meters) was once probably the most popular climb in the country, but recent volcanic rumblings have kept that mountain off-limits since 1994, and it will remain so for the foreseeable future. For the latest on Popo's rumbles, look on the Web at www.prueba.cenapred.unam.mx/mvolcan.html. However, the adjacent **Ixtaccíhuatl** (5,230 meters) is open for climbers. It presents a nontechnical but very exhausting 1–2 day climb across mostly rock with some patches of ice.

Between the cities of Puebla and Tlaxcala, east of Mexico City, is **La Malinche** (4,462 meters), an extinct volcano rising well above the treeline but low enough to be free of snow. Climbable in one full day without too much strain, this is a good acclimatizing hike for higher climbs or just for enjoying a less strenuous hike.

Farther east is the granddaddy of them all, **Pico de Orizaba** (5,611 meters), a major climb across a steep glacier not to be taken lightly. Climbers start the trip from the town of Tlachichuca, Puebla, on the western flank of the mountain. Pico de Orizaba falls outside the range of this book—for more information, call one of the shops or guide companies listed below. For information on any of the three peaks, buy a copy of *Mexico's Volcanoes: A Climbing Guide* by R.J. Secor, revised in 2001.

Guides

If you're looking for a guided trip up one of these peaks, there are several options. One U.S. company which has been running trips to Mexico for more than 20 years and has an excellent reputation is the **Colorado Mountain School,** based in Estes Park, Colorado, tel. 970/586-5758, www.cmschool.com. The company offers 10-day trips to Ixtaccíhuatl and Pico de Orizaba, all included, for US$1,700 per person.

The Oaxaca-based company **Tierra Dentro,** tel. 951/514-9284, www.tierradentro.com, offers four-day trips up Pico de Orizaba from Mexico City for US$260 per person. The national university UNAM has a mountaineering club that offers guided trips, as well as classes (in Spanish). Contact the club at www.montanismo.org.mx.

A group of experienced mountain and river guides living in Mexico City offer a variety of adventure travel trips around central Mexico under the name of **Eco Grupos,** tel. 5522-5821 or 5522-5803 (the number of Hostel Moneda, owned by Eco Grupo partner Juan Pablo Rico). Apart from the standard ascents of Pico de Orizaba, Ixtaccíhuatl, and La Malinche, the company runs guided rock-climbing trips (1–3 days, roughly US$40 per day) to Peña de Bernal in Querétaro, El Chico in Hidalgo, and to Los Dinamos near Mexico City.

Río y Montaña, Prado Norte 450, Col. Lomas de Chapultepec, tel. 5520-2041 or 5520-5018, email: rioymontana@compuserve.com.mx, also offers two-night trips up either Ixtaccíhuatl (US$250 per person) or Pico de Orizaba (US$325 per person).

Rock-climbing

Rock-climbing has not reached the fanatical level in Mexico that it has in the U.S., Europe, and elsewhere, but a determined community of climbers has established several areas with well-defined, often bolted climbs. Perhaps because they tend to stick together in one area rather than wandering off into the forests, rock climbers seem to have no problems at all with the *banditos* who occasionally hold up the unlucky biker or hiker.

Within the Mexico City limits, at **Los Dinamos** in the southwest part of the city, cliffs are dotted with dozens of 5.8–5.12 bolted routes. Near Parque Nacional La Marquesa, on the highway to Toluca, is **Peñasco de los Perros,** with only a handful of 5.7–5.11 routes, but unlike Los Dinamos, there are several places to set up a top-rope.

A bit farther afield, above the city of Pachuca two hours northeast of Mexico City, is **Parque Nacional El Chico,** one of the premier climbing areas in the country. A jumble of rocky outcrops and ridgelines, El Chico is a great place to camp for a few days and try your hand at a few of the dozens of mostly 5.8–5.9 routes (though more complicated multirope pitches are also available).

In a gritty neighborhood near the Instituto Politécnico Nacional in the north part of the city is a rock gym called **Escalódromo Carlos Carsolio,** Técnicos Mexicanos 18, Col. Santa María Ticomán, tel. 5752-7574, www.escalodromo.com. The easiest way to get there is get to Metro Indios Verdes, and from there take any *colectivo* marked "Ticomán." Get off at the Restaurant Galeón Español—the gym is directly behind the restaurant. Entrance is US$6 for unlimited use of 1,200 square meters of climbing walls. For the first visit equipment is provided free; after that either bring your own or rent shoes for US$2.50 and a harness for US$2. Four-hour introductory classes are available for US$27. Open Tues.–Fri 2–10 P.M., Sat. 9 A.M.–7 P.M., Sun. 9 A.M.–5 P.M.

Several of the lava chunks out in the Espacio Escultórico in Ciudad Universitaria, in southern Mexico City, are great for bouldering. Two of the gear shops listed below, Vertimania and El Séptimo Grado, can help find guides for rock-climbing trips. **Eco Grupos,** tel. 5522-5821 or 5522-5803 (the phone of Hostal Moneda), also organizes rock-climbing trips near Mexico City.

Gear and Rental Shops

Amid the couple of dozen sporting goods stores downtown on the long block of Venustiano Carranza between the Eje Central and Bolivar, most of which carry a huge selection of soccer cleats and uniforms, is **Deportes Rubéns,** Venustiano Carranza 17, tel. 5518-5636, which rents ice axes and crampons (no boots) for US$11 a set per weekend, plus a US$42 cash or voucher deposit. The store sells a decent selection of outdoor clothing, backpacking supplies, and climbing gear, both Mexican and imported. Open Mon.–Sat. 10 A.M.–7:30 P.M.

Tucked into a small shop in the Roma neighborhood is **Aguayo Deportes,** Coahuila 40, tel. 5574-9683, which rents ice axes and crampons. Despite its tiny size, the shop has plenty of imported and national rock-climbing and mountaineering gear. Open Mon.–Fri. 10 A.M.–7 P.M., Sat. 10 A.M.–3 P.M.

Probably the best-stocked rock- and ice-climbing shop around Mexico City is **Vertimania,** Frederico de la Chica 11B near the Plaza Satelite shopping center, tel. 5393-5287, in Ciudad Satelite northwest of the city. It rents better-quality crampons than the above stores for US$9 per weekend, and ice axes for US$7 per weekend. Open Mon.–Fri. 11 A.M.–8 P.M., Sat. 11 A.M.–6 P.M.

Also with good gear for sale (not for rent) is **El Séptimo Grado,** Fernando Montes de Oca 61 in the Condesa, tel. 5553-3777.

Another high-end gear shop is **Equipo de Aventura,** with locations in Plaza Satelite, tel. 5393-2794, and in Centro Comercial Santa Fe, near the highway exit to Toluca, tel. 5257-2028. Both are open daily 11:30 A.M.–8:30 P.M.

MOUNTAIN BIKING

Close to the city, probably the safest places for biking are the dirt roads and trails in Parque Nacional Desierto de los Leones and in the privately run **Ejido San Nicolás** at Ajusco (see Excursions from Mexico City for more details).

More extensive forests and trails for mountain biking are found around the flanks of Ixtaccíhuatl volcano, at Parque Nacional El Chico in Hidalgo, or in the countryside around Valle de Bravo, State of Mexico (see Excursions from Mexico City for details).

Guides

Advent-Ciclismo de Montaña, tel. 5681-4714, www.advent.com.mx, runs excellent bike trips to little-known areas near Mexico City and farther afield in Mexico. Bikers can join in on a set program of weekly rides or organize special group expeditions. Bike rental is available.

Río y Montaña, Prado Norte 450, Col. Lomas de Chapultepec, tel. 5520-2041, runs three-night trips to the northern Oaxaca mountains for US$310 per person, as well as day trips to San Miguel Regla, near Parque Nacional El Chico in Hidalgo.

For general information about mountain biking in Mexico, as well as lots of contacts and links, check out www.mtbmexico.com.

Bike Shops

If you're just looking for an inexpensive mountain bike to thrash around on either in the city or the hills, a couple dozen shops sell Benotto (the local brand) bikes for US$100–150 on Avenida San Pablo near the intersection of Avenida Circunvalación. Don't be surprised by all the prostitutes hanging out in between the bike shops—it's a seedy neighborhood but safe during the day.

Several shops in Mexico City specialize in higher-end imported and national mountain and road bikes. The shop staff also service bikes and sometimes they're a good source of advice about where to go biking. Among the better shops are: **BiciGato,** Eugenia 425, Col. Del Valle, tel. 5669-1896; **Rhoda,** Periférico Sur 2930, at the start of Calz. Desierto los Leones, tel. 5595-2387; and **Interbici,** Arquimedes 55, Col. Polanco, tel. 5280-9581.

OTHER SPORTS

Horseback Riding

The only place in the city itself to ride a horse is at the Centro Hípico de la Ciudad de México, in the Tercera Sección of Chapultepec, and then only if you have your own horse or want to sign up for several weeks of classes.

In the forest parks around Mexico City, such as Desierto de los Leones, La Marquesa, and Ajusco, local men are out on weekends at the main parking lots with fairly docile horses for rent, usually US$5–10 an hour. Near Valle de Bravo, in the State of Mexico about a 2.5-hour drive west of Mexico City, tourists can visit a monarch butterfly sanctuary in the pine forests on horseback from the village of Los Saucos, during the migration season, between November and March (January is the height of the season). For more details, look in the Excursions from Mexico City chapter.

Boating

Unless you want to go all the way down to the ocean, the closest place to do any sailing is Lake Avándaro, at Valle de Bravo. This three-by-seven-km lake, created by a dam built in the 1940s, is a favorite of yachties and, to a lesser degree (so far), windsurfers. (See Valle de Bravo for more information.)

Flying

Valle de Bravo is the most popular place in central Mexico for hang gliding and paragliding, with

tocando billares

steady thermals created out over the lake, and perfect launch and landing sites. (For details on courses and rentals in this region, see Valle de Bravo.)

Hot-air balloon rides are also available around Mexico City with at least two companies: **Globo Aventura,** tel. 5662-4023, www.globoaventura.com, out of Tenancingo in the Estado de Mexico; and **Sunrise Ballooning Club** in Yautepec, Morelos, tel. 5782-3414 (in Mexico City).

Rugby

Yes, if you can believe it, there's actually a rugby league in Mexico City, comprising perhaps half expatriates of various countries (France, England, Argentina, U.S.) and half Mexicans. They usually have two seasons, one in the fall and one in the spring, with a couple of 10-a-side tournaments as well. Quality of play is not top-notch, but it is good and has been improving dramatically in the past few years. Games are held at Dos Ríos, a group of sports fields just below the town of Huixquilucan, in the State of Mexico near the highway to Toluca. If you'd like to watch a game or join a team, look on the Web at www.mexrugby.com for more information.

Exercise

If you're looking for a good place in the city to go jogging or in-line skating, the roads and pathways of the **Primera Sección (First Section) of Chapultepec** are quiet and safe (open Tues.–Sat. 5 A.M.–4:30 P.M.). The Segunda (Second) and Tercera (Third) sections are more isolated and consequently not as safe. Smaller parks, including **Parque México** in the Condesa or **Parque Hundido** on Insurgentes Sur are other daytime options. If you can make your way up to **Parque Nacional Desierto de los Leones,** southwest of Mexico City, you'll find plenty of forest trails and dirt roads, and lots of other trail-runners on weekends.

Ciudad Deportiva is a huge sports complex with dozens of tennis and basketball courts and ball fields, open to the public. It's in central-eastern Mexico City near the highway exit to Puebla; the easiest way to get there is hop the Metro and get off at the Ciudad Deportiva station. Hoops players can usually get a decent pickup game of basketball there on weekends. The complex also has a great track, but it appears to be open for special events only.

The **Hotel Camino Real,** Av. Mariano Escobedo 700, tel. 5263-8888, has a very good fully equipped gymnasium open to nonguests for a US$11 fee.

SPECTATOR SPORTS

For general information on Mexican sports, nothing can top *El Afición,* a daily newspaper sold at any newsstand, devoted to all types of professional athletics, but principally to the sacred orb, *fútbol.*

Soccer

Soccer (or *fútbol,* as it's called here) is by far Mexico's favorite sport, and the sports fan may want to go catch a league game during the two-part, winter-summer seasons, one between August and January and the other between March and June. Tickets cost US$2–10, depending on the seat, and are best bought at the stadium ticket office the day before the game, or the same day. If the tickets sell out (although they usually don't), a vociferous crew of *revendedores* (scalpers) can be found selling tickets for a markup.

Mexico's largest stadium is the 120,000-seat **Estadio Azteca,** in the southern part of the city at Calzada de Tlalpan 3465, tel. 5617-8080, home of Las Águilas del América and Los Rayos de Necaxa (both owned by media giant Televisa). Call for times or check in the sports section of local papers for upcoming games. The massive iron sculpture presiding over the stadium entrance is called *Red Sun* and is one of American artist Alexander Calder's more famous pieces.

Also in the south is **Estadio Universitario,** on Insurgentes Sur just south of Eje 10 Sur at Ciudad Universitaria, home to the UNAM Pumas. While it's not always among the best teams in the league, going to see a Pumas game at Estadio Universitario is always good fun, as the *porras* (fan clubs) of the Pumas are well known for their elaborate and often hilarious chants and cheers.

The closest stadium to downtown Mexico City is **Estadio Azul,** just off Insurgentes Sur at Holbein,

Col. Ciudad de los Deportes, right next to the Plaza México bullfighting ring. This is home to the Cementeros de Cruz Azul, the second-most popular team in the city after América.

Other teams in Mexico City are the Potros de Atlante, which seems to be shuffled around to different stadiums but mostly plays at Estadio Azteca; and Toros Neza, with its stadium in the rough eastern suburb of Nezahualcóyotl. Toros Neza slid down to the Primera A division a couple of years back (despite hiring Brazilian Bebeto to help it) and is currently struggling to return to the top league.

Often the best matches to watch are the big rivalries, such as the *Superclásico* each season between the Chivas of Guadalajara and América, and the cross-town match between the city's two most popular teams, América and Cruz Azul. In recent years Necaxa, Cruz Azul, Atlas of Guadalajara, Los Diablos Rojos of Toluca, and América have consistently been among the best and most fun teams to watch.

Attending a match in Mexico is a remarkably relaxed affair, especially for those accustomed to European football matches. Fans from opposing teams often sit right next to each other and exchange mock angry commentary throughout the game. Actual fights among fans are very rare, though like most fans in the world they take great glee in flinging whatever they can onto the field, particularly rolls of toilet paper.

Among the several Internet sites related to Mexican soccer are: http://204.202.129.27/soccer/standings/mexico/index.html (general information); www.mexred.com.mx/Paginazteca/ (general information); www.futbolmundial.com.mx/ (general information); www.seleccionmexicana.com.mx (national team); Águilas del América: www.televisa.com.mx/america/index.asp; Chivas de Guadalajara: http://chivas.com.mx/; Cruz Azul: www.cruz-azul.com.mx/

Baseball

Although it can't quite compare to soccer, *béisbol* is extremely popular in Mexico, particularly in the northern part of the country but also in the center and south. Mexico has two leagues, the Liga del Pacífico, which plays in the northwestern part of the country, and the Liga Mexicana de Béisbol, which fields teams pretty much everywhere else. The Liga Mexicana has 16 teams, of which two are from Mexico City: the Tigres Capitalinos and the Diablos Rojos. Because of falling attendance, the Tigres now play in the nearby city of Puebla, which is a shame because their venerable old stadium in Mexico City was a great place to watch a game. The Diablos Rojos—perennial playoff contenders—play at the Foro Sol, tel. 5639-8722, which seats 26,000 spectators and is in Ciudad Deportiva, right at the junction of the Viaducto and the Circuito Interior in the eastern side of the city. Tickets run between US$1.50 and US$8, a bargain for an afternoon of kicking back, watching a game, and having a beer. The season is between March and July, with the playoffs in August. Sunday games are held at noon; on other days it's either 4 or 6:30 P.M. For more information, see the team website at www.diablos.com.mx, or the league website at www.lmb.com.mx.

Charreada

Decreed the national sport of Mexico in 1933 by presidential edict, the *charreada* (rodeo) is more popular in Mexico than bullfighting. *Charreadas* are staged in skillet-shaped *lienzos charros* (*charro* rings) by private *charro* associations to demonstrate equestrian and ranching skills, much like the U.S. counterpart inspired by the *charreada.* Though open to everyone, *charrería* (the *charro* art) is a rather expensive pastime requiring the maintenance of trained horses and elaborate clothing, somewhat analogous to polo in the Anglo world.

Scoring and Events: Unlike in American rodeo, *charros* and *charras* (gentleman and lady riders) compete for team, not individual, awards. Each team fields 6–8 people, who singly or in combination perform a series of nine *suertes* (maneuvers or events); upon completion of all *suertes,* the team with the most points wins. *Charreada* points are usually scored for style rather than speed. Live mariachi music adds drama and romance.

One of the more thrilling *suertes* is the *paso de la muerte,* in which a *charro* leaps from the back of a horse onto the back of an unbroken mare, with both horses at full gallop! In the *coleadero,* a *char-*

ro leans from his horse to throw a steer by catching its tail with his leg. For a *terna en el ruedo,* three mounted *charros* rope a wild bull, bringing it to the ground within 10 minutes or three casts of *la reata* (origin of the English word "lariat"); points are scored for complexity and style of rope work, not speed.

Also striking is the *escaramuza charra,* a women's event featuring rapid, precision-timed, and carefully choreographed and executed equestrian moves by a group of 6–10 riders. This extremely colorful and popular event owes its name to the Italian *scaramuccia,* a 16th-century cavalry maneuver.

In the bullriding event *(jinete de toro),* the rider must stay atop the bull until it stops bucking, then dismount with cinch in hand, landing on both feet simultaneously. The American rodeo counterpart to this event only requires a cowboy to stay mounted eight seconds.

Dress: A serious *charreada* regular maintains four *charro* suits: the *traje de faena,* or plain working outfit; the *traje de media gala,* a semiformal suit with embroidery; and two *trajes de gala,* the silver-buttoned *traje de etiqueta* or dress suit and the *traje de ceremonia,* an elegant tuxedo outfit for special ceremonies. Each *traje* consists of a broad-brimmed sombrero, tight-fitting trousers of cloth or leather, a short-waisted jacket, boots, and, when the *charro* is mounted, deerskin *chaparreras* ("chaps"). *Charras* generally dress in outfits of *coronela* or *china poblana* style, with full, embroidered blouses and long, billowing, brightly colored skirts with layers of lace and petticoats.

Information: The Asociación Nacional de la Charrería, Izazaga and Isabel la Católica, tel. 5512-2523, can tell you where to find *charreadas* in or near the capital, or check with the Mexico City tourist office.

Lucha Libre

The professional wrestling spectacle is alive and well in Mexico City, with several arenas scattered around town at which to watch the elaborate choreographed battles between such local masked heroes as Mr. Nieblas, Felino, El Rey Bucanero, and Tigre Blanco. The crowd is invariably raucous, supporting either the *rudos* ("brutes") or the *técnicos* ("technicians"), the two "styles" that characterize each fighter. Although many *luchadores* are clearly thick at the waist and pushing middle age, they do pull off some remarkably acrobatic maneuvers.

Arena México, at Dr. LaVista and Dr. Lucio in Colonia Doctores, a short walk east of the Cuauhtémoc Metro station, tel. 5588-0508, has *lucha* every Friday night 8:30–11 P.M., usually four or five fights, tickets US$5–7. On Saturday the arena hosts boxing matches 6:30–10 P.M., tickets US$6–10. Although the neighborhood around the arena is not the best (watch out after dark), inside it's suprisingly clean and nonthreatening. Also surprising, although beers are on sale, the crowd does not tend to get overly drunk here. Beware of taking a seat in the front rows, as fighters invariably come flying out of the ring, especially toward the end of matches.

In the Centro Histórico is **Arena Coliseo,** República de Perú 77, near República de Chile, tel. 5526-1687, with five *luchas* every Tuesday starting at 8:30 P.M. and Sunday starting at 5 P.M. Admission costs US$3–5.

Horse Racing

Mexico City's only horse-racing track is the **Hipódromo de las Américas,** at Av. Industria Militar just west of the Periférico, beyond Polanco in Colonia Lomas de Sotelo, tel. 5387-0600, www.hipodromo.com.mx. The 1.5-km oval course is a diverting place to spend an afternoon, tipping drinks in one of the various bars, watching the horses and riders parade around and race, and of course placing a few bets to keep the excitement up. The officials at the betting windows are usually all too happy to explain the general betting rules to a novice. Races are held Thursday 5:30–10 P.M. and Friday–Sunday 3–8 P.M. Entrance fee is US$2 general admission or US$5 for box/mezzanine seating. Minimum bet US$.10. By public transport, get off at either Chapultepec or Auditorio Metro stations, and look for buses marked "Hipódromo" driving west on Paseo de la Reforma.

Jai Alai

Known as "the fastest ballgame in the world," jai alai (pronounced "HAI-lai"), a Basque term meaning merry festival, descended from *pelota,* a 200-year-old Basque game that is also the forerunner of handball, squash, and racquetball. The Frontón Palacio Jai Alai de México, an art deco–style structure in the Centro, is the capital's main venue and the second largest *frontón* in the world. Unfortunately for would-be spectators of this unique sport, the workers of the stadium have been on strike since 1995, and it doesn't appear that games will be held again any time soon. To see if the Frontón has reopened, either walk by the building itself (just to one side of the Monumento a la Revolución) or contact the Mexico City tourist office.

LA CORRIDA

Alternately called *la corrida de toros* (the running of bulls), *la fiesta brava* (the brave festival), *la lidia de toros* (the fighting of bulls), or *sombra y sol* (shade and sun, in reference to the stadium seating), the bullfight can be perceived as a sport, an art, or a gory spectacle, depending on the social conditioning of the observer.

To the aficionado, the *lidia* is a ritual drama that rolls together courage, fate, pathos, and death in one symbolic event. But no matter how you may feel toward the bullfight, it is undeniably an integral part of Mexican history and culture.

History

Ritualistic encounters with bulls have been traced as far back as 3000 B.C. when, on the Greek island of Crete, the Minoans would perform ritual dives over the horns of attacking wild bulls. A closer antecedent developed around 2000 B.C. on the Iberian peninsula, where a breed of fierce, wild bulls roamed the plains. Iberian hunters—ancestors of the Spanish and Portuguese—figured out how to evade the dangerous bulls at close quarters while delivering a fatal blow with an axe or spear. When the Romans heard about this practice they began importing wild Spanish bulls and accomplished bullfighters for their Colosseum games—possibly the first public bullfights.

During the Middle Ages, bullfighting became a royal sport that was practiced on horseback by the Spanish and the occupying Moors, who both used lances to dispatch the wild bulls. As the toreros began dismounting and confronting the bulls on the ground, the game eventually evolved into the current *corrida,* as performed in Spain, Portugal, Mexico, and throughout much of Latin America.

Mexico City's first bullfight took place in the Plaza Mayor (as the Zócalo was then called) on August 21, 1529, to commemorate the eighth anniversary of the fall of Tenochtitlán. Between 1554 and 1810, bullfights were held in the adjacent Plaza Voladores (currently the Corte Suprema de Justicia). By the 18th century, they were also held on the south side of the Alameda, and in the 19th century at the now defunct Plaza de Toros San Diego (near the current site of the Monumento a la Revolución).

In the early years the only payment the torero received was the bull's carcass after the event. Nowadays bullfighters receive performance fees that vary according to their status within the profession.

El Toro

The bulls used in the ring, *toros de lidia* (fighting bulls), are descendants of wild Iberian bulls that for more than four centuries have been bred especially for their combative spirit. They're not trained in any way for the ring nor goaded into viciousness, but as a breed they are naturally quick to anger. The fighting bull's neck muscles are much larger than those of any other cattle breed in the world, making the animal capable of tossing a torero and his horse into the air with one upward sweep.

Bulls who show an acceptable degree of bravery by the age of two are let loose in huge pastures (averaging 10,000 acres per animal) in Zacatecas, San Luis Potosí, or Guanajuato to live as wild beasts until they reach four years, the age of combat. By the time *el toro* enters the ring, he stands around 127 cm (50 inches) high at the withers (higher at the shoulder, but they aren't measured there because the neck muscle expands to varying degrees when the bull is preparing to attack) and weighs 500 kg (1,100 pounds) or more.

The carcass of a bull killed in the ring does not go to waste, at least not from a meat-eater's perspective. Immediately after it's taken from the ring, it's butchered and dressed, and the meat is sold to the public.

The Torero

The bullfighter is rated by his agility, control, and, as surprising as it may seem to the uninitiated, his compassion. The torero who teases a bull or who is unable to kill it quickly when the moment of truth arrives is considered a cruel brute. In order to be judged a worthy competitor by the spectators, he must excel in three areas: *parar,* or standing still as the bull charges (as opposed to stepping away from the bull, even as little as an inch)—only the cape and the torero's upper body should move; *templar,* or timing and grace—the movements must be smooth, well timed, and of the right proportion; and *mandar,* or command, the degree to which he masters the entire *lidia* through his bravery, technique, and understanding of the bull, neither intimidating the animal nor being intimidated by it.

Standard equipment for the torero is the *capote de brega,* the larger cape used in the first two-thirds of the *lidia;* the *muleta,* a smaller cape used during the final third; the *estoque* or matador's sword; and the *traje de luces* or suit of lights, the colorful torero's costume originally designed by the Spanish artist Goya.

La Lidia

The regulated maneuvers or *suertes* followed in a bullfight date from 18th-century Spain. Anywhere from four to eight bulls may appear in a *corrida* (typically six), and one torero is on hand for every two bulls scheduled. The order of appearance for the toreros is based on seniority. Toreros who have proven their skills in several bullfighting seasons as *novilleros* (novice fighters) are called *matadores de toros* (bull killers). Ordinarily each torero will fight two bulls; if he is gored or otherwise put out of action, another torero will take his place even if it means facing more than his allotment of bulls.

Each *lidia* is divided into three *tercios* or thirds. In *el tercio de varas,* the bull enters the ring and the matador performs *capeos,* a cape maneuver that doesn't expose the matador's body to the bull's horns but is meant to test the bull or lead it to another spot in the ring. He then "lances," a cape maneuver that exposes the matador's body to the horns and brings the bull closer to him, while two horsemen receive the bull's charge with eight-foot *varas* or lances. The *varas* have short, pyramid-shaped points that are aimed at the bull's neck muscle but do not penetrate very deeply on contact.

The purpose of the encounter is both to punish the neck muscle so that the bull lowers its horns, and to give the bull the confidence of meeting something solid so that it won't be frustrated by the emptiness of the cape as the *lidia* proceeds. Usually only two *vara* blows are administered but more are permitted if necessary to produce the intended effect (the lowering of the head). The crowd protests, however, when more than two are administered, as it wants the matador to face a strong bull.

In *el tercio de banderillas,* the bull's shoulders receive the banderillas—26-inch wooden sticks decorated with colored paper frills, each tipped with a small, sharp, iron barb. They can be placed by the matador himself or more often by hired assistant toreros (called banderilleros when performing this function). The purpose of the banderilla placement is to "correct" the bull's posture; the added punishment also reportedly makes the bull more crafty in his charges. Placed in pairs, up to six banderillas may be applied to the bull, varying in number and position according to the needs of the individual animal.

At the end of the *tercio de banderillas,* signaled by a bugle fanfare, the matador takes up his *muleta* and sword and walks before the box of the *juez* or judge presiding over the *lidia.* He looks to the *juez* for permission to proceed with the killing of the bull and, after receiving a nod, offers his *brindis* or dedication. The *brindis* may be made to an individual spectator, to a section of the plaza, or to the entire audience. If the dedication is to an individual, he will present his *montera* (matador's hat) to that person (who will return it, with a present inside, to the matador after the *lidia*). Otherwise, he tosses his hat onto the sand after waving it at the crowd; he remains hatless for the final *tercio,* a gesture of respect for the bull during its last moments alive.

The final round of the lidia is called *el tercio de muerte,* the third of death. The main activity of this *tercio* is *la faena,* the work, involving cape and sword, during which a special set of passes leads to the killing of the bull. For the first two *tercios* there is no time limit; for the last, however, the matador has only 15 minutes within which to kill the bull, or else he is considered defeated and the bull is led from the ring (where it is killed immediately by the plaza butcher).

In a good *faena,* a matador will tempt fate over and over again, bringing the bull's horns close to his own heart. The time for the kill arrives when the bull has so tired from the *faena* that it stands still, forelegs squared as if ready to receive the sword. Then, with his cape the matador must draw the bull into a final charge while he himself moves forward, bringing the sword out from under the cape, sighting down the blade, and driving the blade over the horns and between the animal's shoulders. A perfect sword thrust severs the aorta, resulting in instant death. If the thrust is off, the matador must try again until the bull dies from one of the thrusts.

It is not necessary to kill the bull in one stroke (quite an extraordinary accomplishment); the matador's honor is preserved as long as he goes in over the horns, thus risking his own life, every time. If the bull falls to its knees but isn't dead, another torero on hand immediately comes forward and thrusts a dagger *(puntilla)* behind the base of the skull to sever the spinal cord and put the beast out of its misery. When the bull is dead, the *lidia* is over. If the matador has shown bravery and artistry, the crowd will let him know with its applause; an unusually dramatic performance will see lots of hats and flowers thrown into the ring.

Monumental Plaza de Toros México

Often referred to by its shorter name, Plaza México, Mexico City's bullfighting stadium is the largest and best-outfitted in the world. Begun in 1944 as part of a huge sports complex that was to include a bullring, soccer stadium, tennis courts, *frontón* (jai alai court), restaurants, the project was suspended after the *corrida* and soccer stadiums were finished. The plaza was inaugurated on February 5, 1946 with a *cartel* (program) that featured the legendary Luis "El Soldado" Castro, Manuel "Manolete" Rodríguez, and Luis Procuna. The stadium can hold an astounding 41,262 spectators.

Practicalities

Plaza México stands at Agusto Rodín 241, Col. Ciudad de los Deportes, just west of Insurgentes Sur. Winter (November–February) is the main bullfighting season, with full-fledged matadors pitted against the largest and most ferocious bulls. May to September is reserved for *novilladas,* in which *novilleros* (novice bullfighters) fight *novillos*—younger, smaller bulls.

It's usually a good idea to buy tickets for a *corrida* in advance if possible. Check with the tourist office to find out if they're available, since it's not unusual for an event to sell out (in which case you might still be able to buy a ticket—at higher prices—from a scalper or *revendedor*). Spectator sections are divided into the *sol* (sunny side) and *sombra* (shaded side), then subdivided according to how close the seats are to the bullring itself. The *sol* tickets aren't bad, since the *corrida* usually doesn't begin until around 4 P.M.; bring a hat, sunglasses, and sunscreen, plus plenty of pesos for beverages (tequila and beer are usually available, along with soft drinks).

Corridas or *novilladas* alternate irregularly between Saturday and Sunday, but always beginning at 4 P.M. Ticket offices are open to special pass holders Thursday and Friday only; the general public must buy their tickets Saturday–Sunday 9:30 A.M.–1 P.M. and 3:30–7 P.M. Ticket prices range US$1–10 in the *sol* section or US$2–20 on the *sombra* side.

Further Information

The News, Mexico City's main English-language newspaper, runs an entertaining bullfighting column each Thursday called "Blood on the Sand," written (in a most colorful prose) by Ricardo Morales Castillo. If you can read Spanish, *Matador,* a glossy monthly devoted to tauromania, is full of history, folklore, and current information on Mexican bullfighting.

For scheduling details, check local newspapers or call Plaza México directly at 5563-3961.

Shopping

WHAT TO BUY

Textiles and Clothing

Mexican Indians still produce pre-Hispanic-style textiles such as the *huipil* (sleeveless tunic) and *quechquemitl* (close-shouldered cape) in the states of Morelos, Guerrero, Oaxaca, and Chiapas, and on the Yucatán Peninsula. Another Yucateco specialty, the cool *guayabera* shirt worn by men in the tropics worldwide, is made in Mérida. The nearby weaving center of Tixkokob produces the country's finest hammocks.

Mexico's famous *rebozos* (shawls) come from San Luis Potosí, while the finest serapes and *jorongos* (ponchos) are made in Saltillo and Zacatecas, amid Mexico's largest wool-producing region.

Among the many types of embroidered, woven, and beaded shoulder bags produced throughout Mexico, those of the Huicholes in Jalisco, Nayarit, and Durango are the most popular. Also often sought are bright, psychedelic Huichol yarn paintings.

The states of Zacatecas, Durango, Nuevo León, and Tamaulipas produce the finest *charreada* costumery—sequined sombreros, embroidered *charro* jackets, and tight-fitting, *concho*-studded trousers.

Ceramics

Mexico boasts an astounding number of potters and pottery styles, natural legacies of ancient Amerindian ceramic traditions. Among the most highly valued by collectors are polychromatic Pueblo-style ceramics from Chihuahua's Casas Grandes area, green-

© CHRIS HUMPHREY

Puebla's ceramic art has centuries of tradition: this painted plate dates from the 18th century.

glazed pots from Michoacán, rainbow-hued vessels and black Zapotec jars from Oaxaca, and Puebla's famous tin-glazed Talavera plates and bowls. Potters immigrating from Talavera de la Reina in Spain settled in Puebla, where they fashioned *majolica*-inspired pottery that became known as Talavera. Although the best pieces still hail from Puebla, much Talavera today comes from potters' workshops in Dolores Hidalgo, in the State of Guanajuato. Usually the place of origin will be marked on the bottom of the piece, but after a while you may be able to tell the difference without checking the inscriptions.

Smaller ceramic pieces fashioned into brightly colored human and animal shapes—some functioning as candelabras or receptacles, others purely decorative—are everyday folk art throughout the country.

The enamel used to color-finish some Mexican ceramic products may contain lead. This doesn't usually pose a health problem for decorative pieces but if you plan to use Mexican pottery as cooking or eating utensils, you should buy articles *sin plomo* (without lead) to avoid accidental lead ingestion. Although cynics point out that Mexicans have been using leaded utensils for centuries without any perceived harm to themselves, it doesn't hurt to be on the cautious side. Nowadays many Mexican ceramicists create lead-free products whose characteristics surpass those of traditional enamelware and which are available at accessible prices. As recommended by FONART (Fomento de las Artesanías), such pieces may be marked EBT-SP, signifying *esmalte baja temperatura sin plomo* (low temperature enamelware without lead).

Jewelry

Well-crafted silver *(plata)* jewelry is plentiful and relatively inexpensive throughout Mexico. The finest work comes from Taxco, Guanajuato, and Zacatecas. Look for .925 stamped into silver products; this means they're 92.5 percent silver, the highest quality. You'll also come across *alpaca,* an alloy of copper, nickel, and zinc that looks like silver and costs a third to a half less than the real thing.

The best gold *(oro)* jewelry is said to come from Oaxaca, where Zapotec women regard gold adornments as the most important source of portable wealth. Most pieces are fashioned from 12-carat gold, though some may feature 24-carat plating.

Elaborate earrings, bracelets, and necklaces strung together from semiprecious or nonprecious materials such as turquoise, amber, beads, bone, and onyx have been popular throughout Mexico since the artist Frida Kahlo painted herself wearing pre-Hispanic jewelry. Though fashioned mostly in the central and southern states, this jewelry is sold all over the country.

Leatherwork and Saddlery

Mexico is home to many expert leatherworkers, a tradition inherited from Spain. Workers in the ranching areas of northern Mexico—particularly the states of Zacatecas, Coahuila, Nuevo León, and Tamaulipas—produce the best belts, *bolos* (leather string ties), boots, leather jackets, gloves, chaps, spurs, bridles, and saddles.

Basketry and Hats

A wide range of plant materials are used to fashion Mexican baskets, including palm strips, agave fibers, grass, pine needles, and henequen. High-quality baskets *(cesta, canasta)* are handwoven by the Seri, Yaqui, and Papago Indians of Sonora, the Tarahumara of Chihuahua, and the Mixtecs of Oaxaca. Seri baskets are woven so tightly they're capable of holding liquids; the Seri once used large baskets as rafts to cross the Río Colorado.

Rural Mexicans and Amerindians make and wear an incredible variety of hats, from the wavy-brimmed but stiff Texas-style headgear in Chihuahua to the flat-brimmed, round-crowned sunbusters of the Yucatán. A Mexican hat blocker can reshape just about any woven, natural-fiber hat to fit your head.

Wood

Wood-carving thrives as a folk art applied to everyday housewares as well as decorative objects. Orangewood combs from Oaxaca, guitars from Michoacán, and cedar *rebozo* boxes from San Luis Potosí are some of the more notable wood arts. Many different Mexican Indian cultures throughout Mexico fashion finely carved and lacquered wooden masks for use in tribal ceremonies; most of the masks seen in souvenir shops are knockoffs produced by carvers in Guerrero or Michoacán.

Other Crafts

Retablos, religious paintings on wood or tin, are commonly found near religious centers. Lacquered gourds and boxes from Guerrero, Michoacán, and Chiapas represent Mexico's finest lacquerwork.

Ironwork, another legacy of the Spanish, is a specialty of central Mexico, though wrought-iron furniture, gates, doors, and windows are common throughout the country.

Alebrijes are brightly painted, fantastically shaped animal-like sculptures carved of wood or fashioned from papier-mâché. The very first *alebrijes* were created in Mexico City by Pedro Linares, who created the figures after they appeared to him in a series of dreams, or nightmares, during a long illness. Seeing that the figures sold well among tourists and collectors, residents of Oaxaca later took up the craft and today the pieces are available throughout Mexico.

> ***The very first* alebrijes *were created in Mexico City by Pedro Linares, who created the figures after they appeared to him in a series of dreams, or nightmares, during a long illness.***

Glasswork is a popular purchase in Mexico for foreign tourists. Most handicraft shops carry a variety of colored or tinted glass sets.

To get an inkling of the full range of arts and crafts in Mexico, visit the Museo Nacional de Artes e Industrias Populares and Museo Nacional de Culturas Populares (see Sights).

WHERE TO SHOP

Antiques

Plaza del Ángel Antiques Center (Centro de Antigüedades), off Calle Hamburgo in the Zona Rosa, brings together more than 30 stores selling antique furniture, paintings, art objects, silver, and other articles, much of it high-end goods from the 19th century. Most shops can arrange shipping anywhere in the world. The plaza is open daily 10 A.M.–8 P.M., though some shops have more erratic hours. On Saturday and Sunday a flea market in antiques, typically featuring more than 100 exhibitors, convenes in the open hallways of the plaza, 10 A.M.–4 P.M.

Bookshops

In the Centro Histórico, the best overall bookshop for both English and Spanish language books is **Librería Gandhi,** Av. Juárez 4. Gandhi also sells audio CDs. Gandhi has another branch in Coyoacán at Av. M. A. de Quevedo 134; this one features an upstairs café. The **American Bookstore** recently moved to a smaller space at Bolívar 23, just south of Madero, and doesn't have the excellent selection of old, but you'll find a decent collection of English-language novels and history books.

The bookstore on the ground floor of the **Palacio de Bellas Artes** is chock-full of English-and Spanish-language books on art. Most of Mexico City's larger art museums contain similarly oriented bookshops.

Ciudad de México, in a large colonial-era building on the northeast corner of Eje Central Lázaro Cárdenas and Calle Carranza, is a good spot for Mexican textbooks in all academic disciplines.

Calle Donceles is lined with shops selling used books east of Calle Palma Norte, more or less behind the Catedral Metropolitana. **Librería Hermanos de Hoja** is good for art books; **El Mercader de Libros** has a large general-interest selection; and **El Laberinto** across the street is also good hunting grounds.

In San Ángel, **Librería Miguel Ángel Porrúa,** Amargura 4, near the Plaza del Carmen, is a bookstore that also happens to be a publisher of finely bound and printed books on Mexican history and art. Very little in English is available, but if you read Spanish and are interested in these fields, you'll find plenty to spend your money on. Miguel Ángel Porrúa operates other branches at the Antigua Escuela Nacional de Jurisprudencia, Facultad de Derecho, UNAM,

San Ildefonso 28, Centro Histórico; and at the Museo Nacional de Las Culturas, INAH, Moneda 13, Centro, tel. 5542-0901.

The Roma has one of the best bookstores in the city, **Librería Pegaso,** at the Casa Lamm in Roma, Orizaba 99, tel. 5208-0171. Nearby, along Avenida Álvaro Obregón, is a string of stores with both new and used books. Two right next to each other are **Através del Espejo,** A. Obregon 118-A, tel. 5264-0246, and **Librería Atico,** A. Obregón 118-B, tel. 5584-7627. In the Condesa is **El Péndulo,** Av. Nuevo León 115, tel. 5286-9493, with an excellent selection of Spanish-language books.

If you read Spanish and are interested in literature on Mexican history, archaeology, or culture, stop into the **Librería del Instituto Nacional de Antropología e Historia,** in the Roma at Córdoba 43, tel. 5514-0420, open Mon.–Fri. 9 A.M.–6 P.M., Sat. 9 A.M.–3 P.M.

Most branches of **Sanborns** carry a limited selection of Spanish and English-language books, newspapers, and magazines.

Tower Records, Niza 19A, tel. 5525-4829, in the Zona Rosa carries a good selection of books and magazines in English.

Cigar Shops

Cigar smokers will love Mexico City, which abounds in places to indulge one's taste for brown torpedoes. In the **Galerías Insurgentes,** a large mall just south of Eje 7 Sur Felix Cuevas at Insurgentes 1352, are two good cigar stores with well-stocked humidors. **Sir Walter Raleigh,** on the basement floor, has the largest selection of the two and is a bit pricier. On the top floor, **La Casa del Fumador** is similar. In the Roma, **Los Puros de la Roma,** Zacatecas 184, between Monterrey and Tonalá, tel. 5264-4076, specializes in Cuban cigars starting from US$5. Just up the street, at Zacatecas 172, is **Puros Churchill,** tel. 5584-0239, a small cigar factory using leaf from Veracruz, in eastern Mexico. Factory tours (in Spanish) can be arranged by calling in advance. It also has a small store in front.

In the Centro, **Little Havana Cigar Shop,** Av. San Jerónimo 630, tel. 5568-1891, is another Cuban specialist. **La Hoja del Tabaco,** Uruguay 12, tel. 5518-5200, also in the Centro, emphasizes Mexican brands but also carries *cubanos.*

Note that if you're planning on bringing Cuban cigars to the U.S., you'll be violating the American trade embargo against Cuba. If U.S. customs finds a couple of cigars during an inspection of your luggage, the usual practice is to confiscate them, nothing more, although you're legally liable for a very stiff fine. If you try to smuggle in a full box or more, you might be in for trouble.

Handicrafts

FONART's **Museo de Artes Populares,** Av. Juárez 89, tel. 5521-0171, near the Alameda, is a combination handicraft museum/store. The merchandise—silver, onyx, pottery, baskets, textiles, and more—is of excellent quality; prices are non-negotiable. Open Mon.–Sat. 10 A.M.–7 P.M. FONART has a slightly larger branch at Patriotismo 691, tel. 5563-4060, open Mon.–Sat. 9 A.M.–8 P.M., Sun. 10 A.M.–7 P.M. A private shop in the Centro, **Victor Artes Populares,** Madero 8, Suite 305, also offers a quality selection.

Palacio de las Máscaras (Galería Eugenio), Allende 84, tel. 5529-2849, opposite the furniture building of the Mercado Lagunilla, displays room after room of handmade Amerindian masks from Guerrero and other parts of Mexico—it claims to have more than 5,000 masks in all. Most of the masks are 30–50 years old and cost, on average, US$30. Open daily 10 A.M.–5 P.M.

The offices of the art magazine ***Artes de México,*** on the east side of the park at Plaza Río de Janeiro 52, tel. 5525-5905, has a small but good handicrafts shop. The store also carries back issues of the magazine, which features informative articles on different Mexican arts and handicrafts. Open Mon.–Fri. 9 A.M.–3 P.M. and 4–6 P.M.

(For more on handicrafts, see the Markets section in this chapter.)

Liquor and Wine

Mexico City offers an abundance of places selling *licores* and *vinos.* One of the best places to buy fine-quality alcohol by the bottle in central Mexico City is **La Naval,** Av. Insurgentes Sur 373 at

Michoacán, tel. 5584-3500, in the Condesa district. La Naval is open Mon.–Sat. 8 A.M.–9 P.M. Downtown is **La Europea,** at Ayuntamiento 21, tel. 5512-6005 (very good prices here), also with a store in Polanco at the corner of Arquimedes and Horacio. Also downtown is **Los Viñedos,** Ayuntamiento 14. Should you be looking for a bottle in the Zona Rosa, you could do worse than **Licores La Central,** Florencia 70 at the corner of Liverpool.

Music CDs and Tapes

Mixup, the best Mexican-owned chain retailing CDs and audio cassettes, has branches at Calle Genova 76 between Liverpool and Londres in the Zona Rosa; Isabel la Católica and Madero in the Centro Histórico; Galerías Insurgentes in Col. Felix Cuevas; and at Plaza Loreto in San Ángel. Typically open Mon.–Sat. 9 A.M.–midnight, Sun. 9 A.M.–10 P.M.

Even better is the Zona Rosa **Tower Records,** Niza 19A, tel. 5525-4829, with three floors packed with CDs from all genres of Mexican and international music. It looks like any other Tower Records except a three-story faux-Amerindian mural covers one wall; the book section stocks everything from Octavio Paz to Aztec histories. Open Sun.–Thurs. 10 A.M.–10 P.M., Fri. and Sat. 10 A.M.–midnight.

Librería Gandhi (see Bookshops) also stocks a good CD collection, especially for American jazz and Mexican folk.

Mercado El Chopo is the place to go for alternative Mexican rock. (See Markets later in this chapter.)

Musical Instruments

You can buy Mexican-made guitars and other stringed instruments at three shops on Calle Bolívar in the Centro, **ABC Musical Instrumentos,** Bolivar 62, tel. 5512-0159, **Hollywood Music Center,** Bolívar 46, tel. 5521-8028, and **Music Club Bolívar,** Bolívar 86, tel. 5709-6005.

Miscellanea

A string of **computer shops** along República de Uruguay, between Bolívar and Eje Central Lázaro Cárdenas in the Centro, sell just about any hardware or software available in Mexico. Calle Carranza, running east off Eje Central in the same general vicinity, holds several stores specializing in **sporting goods** and **camping equipment.** Overall, Ruben's is the best place for camping gear, Marti for sports gear.

Two booths selling traditional **Mexican calendars,** including reproductions of the late Jesús Helguera's colorful idealized scenes of early 20th-century Mexico and the ubiquitous Aztec warriors bending over swooning Aztec maidens, can be found on either side of Callejón de Filomena Mata.

Right behind the Catedral downtown are three stores next to one another specializing in **religious art,** where you can pick up that Virgin de Guadalupe poster you've always been looking for: El Vaticano and La Exposición, both at Guatemala 20, and La Catedral at Guatemala 26.

Two very well-stocked **paper** and **art supply** stores in the Centro are Lumen, República del Salvador 66, and Lozano, República del Salvador 48; both open Mon.–Sat. 9 A.M.–7 P.M.

MARKETS

Artesanías de Ciudadela

On Calle Balderas at Ayuntamiento, a few blocks south of the Alameda, Ciudadela is the best all-around place in the Centro Histórico if you're looking for a great variety of Mexican handicrafts. In addition to all the usual things, Ciudadela's complex of vendor booths is especially good for leather goods, ceramics, silver jewelry, blankets, and hammocks. Toward the southern end of the market, almost an annex to the main complex, is a luthier's shop with lots of handmade guitars. Bargaining is expected. Open daily 8 A.M.–6 P.M. Nearest Metro station: Balderas.

On Calle Balderas just south of the Ciudadela, heading toward Balderas Metro station, is a flea market on the street with all sorts of random goods for sale, including music, used clothing, handicrafts, and much else besides.

Mercado de Artesanías San Juan

Also known as Mercado de Artesanías Xochicalco or La Casa de las Flores, this renovated handicrafts market along the east side of the Plaza de San Juan (at Calles Ayuntamiento and Aranda; nearest Metro station: San Juan de Letrán) stands on the site of one of Mexico City's oldest colonial-era markets. It reopened in 1999 as a cooperative venture among Mexican artisans, but it's still feeling its way in terms of quality. Prices are good, especially if you bargain, but the selection is not quite as varied as at La Ciudadela. Open Mon.–Sat. 9 A.M.–7 P.M., Sun. 9 A.M.–4 P.M.

Nearby **Mercado de San Juan,** between Calles Pugibet and Luis Moya, offers a good selection of fruits, vegetables, meats, and Mexican delicatessen items. Open daily 6 A.M.–5 P.M.

Centro Artesanal Buena Vista

Several blocks north of Reforma on Avenida Insurgentes Norte, near the railroad station, this sprawling market at Aldama 187 is one of the best places for people who hate to shop but feel guilty returning home empty-handed. Here under one roof you'll find an incredibly large selection of everything made or sold in Mexico. The only drawback is that it's a bit out of the way. Open daily 9 A.M.–5 P.M. Nearest Metro station: Buenavista.

Mercado El Chopo

Just north of Centro Artesanal Buena Vista, the *rockero* street market of El Chopo convenes on Saturday only and has become *the* place for Mexican punks and rockers to hang out. It's in a warehouse district behind the Buena Vista train station on Insurgentes Norte; walk up Eje 1 Norte to Calle Aldama, turn left (north) and follow the crowd of rockers into the market area. More than 200 vendors sell all kinds of Mexican and Latin rock cassettes and CDs, with sections that specialize in thrash metal, hard-core punk, and rarities such as out-of-print Three Souls in My Mind (El Tri) records with psychedelic covers. Bootleg live cassettes are also available and even tolerated by many Mexican artists (Café Tacuba's Joselo Rangel says it was on the basis of the number of Tacuba bootlegs sold at El Chopo that they got their first record contract). Rock paraphernalia—T-shirts, jewelry, tattoo artistry, even hair-dyeing stands—are also on hand.

The market is open Saturday 10 A.M.–5 P.M. Nearest Metro station: Buenavista.

Mercado La Lagunilla

About 10 blocks northwest of the Zócalo, just south and north of the Eje 1 Norte, is a cluster of three market buildings known collectively as La Lagunilla, favored by lower middle class shoppers. Off the east side of Calle Allende, the building marked 1 stocks clothes, while building 2 focuses on inexpensive wooden furniture and lighting accessories. Building 3, north of Eje 1 Norte at República de Chile and Libertad, specializes in food products. All sorts of other merchandise trades hands in the shops and streets around the market buildings.

Be sure to check out **Palacio de las Máscaras** (also known as Galería Eugenio), opposite La Lagunilla building 2 at Calle Allende 84, tel. 5529-2849, an unassuming little storefront that

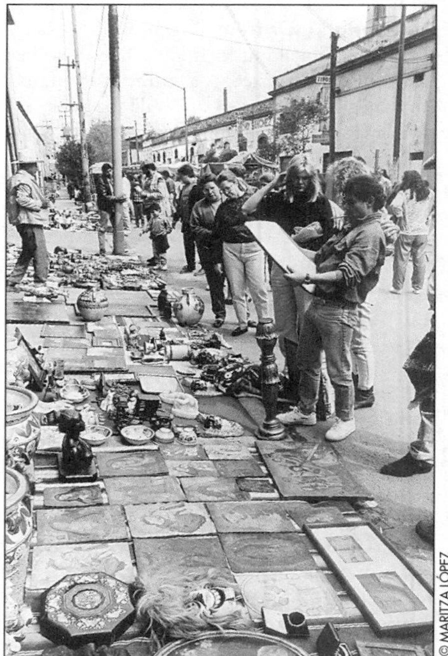

La Lagunilla flea market

hides literally thousands of Amerindian masks from around Mexico, mainly from the State of Guerrero. Whether you plan to buy or not, it's a fascinating place to walk around for a few minutes. Open daily 10 A.M.–5 P.M.

On Sunday, a flea market or *mercado de pulgas* also known as La Lagunilla sets up on the *lateral* (side lane) along the east side of Paseo de la Reforma just north of the Eje 1 Norte, and on a few side streets heading east into Tepito from Reforma. Although the prices are not as rock-bottom as they once were, it's a great place to wander around for an hour or two and check out the heaps of old books, toys, silverware, movie posters, antique and not-so-antique furniture, and all manner of other paraphernalia spread out on the streets and sidewalks. The side streets are quite safe—just don't walk all the way to their ends, where they meet infamous Tepito. Nearest Metro station: Garibaldi.

Mercado Tepito

On the north side of Eje 1 Norte lies this 500-year-old market neighborhood of legendary ill repute. During the colonial era, Mexico City's city gate and customs office were nearby, and the area became a focus for the smuggling of contraband into the city. By the beginning of the 20th century an extensive *zona de tolerancia* ("zone of tolerance" within which brothels are permitted to operate) of the lowest category had been established here. During the Revolution poor Mexicans from all over the country migrated to Tepito, especially from Guanajuato, and most of the prostitutes moved on to other (probably safer) areas of the city. Street markets proliferated, the population grew and Tepito developed its own culture complete with a unique dialect. The barrio's tough street life produced some of Mexico's best boxers throughout much of the 20th century.

Today street vendors selling everything from secondhand clothing to cheap electronics set up daily throughout the area except Tuesday. Although known as a "thieves' market," where one goes to look for the camera stolen the previous week, many of the goods sold in Tepito are not stolen, but rather are smuggled into the country (mostly from the U.S.) to avoid import taxes. In Mexican slang, such contraband is known as *fayuca,* and those who peddle it are *fayuqueros.* Drug trafficking is another Tepito specialty. Beware of heading into less-traveled back streets or you might just find yourself dispossessed at the point of a knife or gun. Nearest Metro station: Garibaldi.

Mexicans flock to Mercado Sonora—the so-called "witches' market"—to buy herbal remedies, love potions, talismans, and other assorted psychospiritual balms.

Mercado de la Merced and Mercado de Sonora

One of the largest retail and wholesale markets in Mexico, La Merced covers an entire block between the streets of Santa Escuela, General Anaya, Rosario, and Cerrada del Rosario in Col. Merced Balbuena, near the Ex-Convento de la Merced (see the Sights chapter). For most of the nearly two centuries since independence from Spain, La Merced has been the city's principal marketplace and the centerpiece of a bustling commercial neighborhood. In 1983 the city inaugurated the Central de Abastos farther south, and it soon superceded La Merced in the wholesale business. But La Merced is still going strong, and many *capitalinos* still consider it the quintessential Mexico City market.

Across Avenida Fray Servando Teresa de Mier from La Merced is Mercado Sonora, the so-called "witches' market" of tourist brochures. Mexicans flock here to buy herbal remedies, love potions, talismans, and other assorted psychospiritual balms. The market also does a booming trade in endangered plants and animals, for which it is routinely raided by the police.

Should you be interested in visiting either market, it's best to take the Metro to the Merced station rather than walk. The distance from the Zócalo may not be long, but the neighborhoods are dicey. Open daily 6 A.M.–6 P.M.

La Central de Abastos del Distrito Federal (CEDA)

Covering 328 hectares (approximately four square km), La Central de Abastos is said to be the "heart" that pumps the food into that great "body" that is Mexico City and surrounding Valle de México. An armada of up to 17,000 cargo trucks docks at this huge complex each day, handling an estimated 24,000 tons of fruits and vegetables that represent no less than 40 percent of Mexico's national harvest, along with 3,600 tons of dry groceries and other provisions.

CEDA (an acronym taken from Central de Abastos) was founded in 1992 to supply food wholesale and retail services that had outgrown Mercado de Merced in the north, and purportedly to create more cooperative and equitable leasing opportunities for vendor and *bodega* (warehouse) space. Although not a mainstream tourist attraction by any means, if you want to see the largest food market in the country, this is it. In the southeast part of the complex, a nine-hectare seafood section called La Nueva Viga displays virtually every kind of fish from all over the country, far more than any one Mexican port.

In addition to the food markets, the central corridors of the *bodegas* contain 18 banks representing 10 Mexican banking institutions, along with a number of small businesses—truck repair shops, tire shops, stationery stores, post and telegraph offices, travel agencies, pharmacies, bakeries, medical clinics, record stores, moneychangers, restaurants of all types, beauty shops, perfume stores, video stores, dry cleaners, clothing stores, tortilla factories—in short, everything essential to maintain this city within a city. Nearest Metro station: La Viga.

Excursions from Mexico City

Roads radiate from Mexico City in all directions, providing ample opportunities for day-trippers and weekenders to explore the region. This chapter covers the major cities and sights within about a 400-km (250-mile) radius from the nation's capital.

While most visitors will want to make trips on their own and explore, the Mexican government Instituto Nacional de Antropología e Historia (INAH) offers various trips every weekend to destinations around Mexico City. The trips, called Paseos Culturales de INAH, typically cost US$22–28 per day, with transportation, guide, and entrance fee to sites included. All the prescheduled trips are in Spanish, but special trips can be arranged with English-speaking guides for groups. For more information, contact the INAH office in the Museo Nacional de Antropología at tel. 5553-2365 or 5553-3822, or look it up on the Web at www.inah.gob.mx.

© CHRIS HUMPHREY

El Oro's Teatro Juárez

North of Mexico City

SAN JUAN TEOTIHUACÁN

Little is known about the people who built the ancient city of Teotihuacán, one of the largest, most impressive archaeological sites in the Americas. During the city's heydey it was Mesoamerica's most powerful social and political hub. The structures were built between 100 B.C. and A.D. 250, accommodating as many as 200,000 people and forming the largest and most sophisticated city in the Western Hemisphere and comparable with its contemporaries in the Roman Empire. During its height, the influence of the Teotihuacano empire was felt throughout Mesoamerica. Whatever civilization produced Teotihuacán lasted roughly until the 7th century A.D., but despite its obviously complex technology, left behind no writing system or any other hints as to who built the city. It is clear from the types of artifacts excavated within the pyramids and temples that the builders of Teotihuacán were a heavily militarized society, not unlike the later Aztec and Maya. More than 1,200 human skeletons have been discovered amid the ruins, all of them thought to have been sacrificial victims.

Archaeologists believe a four-chambered lava-tube cave in the Valle de Teotihuacán prompted the choice of location for the construction of the original monuments. Considered places where gods and ancestors emerged, as well as doors to a magical underworld, caves played an important role in Mesoamerican religion. Teotihuacán's Pyramid of the Sun was built directly over the cave in the 2nd century A.D.

The site flourished until about A.D. 750, when it was abandoned and set afire. Some researchers suggest the calamity may have been a war between Teotihuacán and Cacaxtla, a smaller contemporary city in nearby Tlaxcala. Over the centuries, pyramids, citadel, temples, palaces, plazas, and paved streets remained deserted and forgotten until the Aztecs arrived in A.D. 1200. Recognizing the site's formidable history, the Aztecs named the ruins Teotihuacán, or "place where gods are born." The Aztecs used Teotihuacán as a pilgrimage center; according to Aztec legend, the sun, moon, and universe itself were created here. Though awestruck by the city's size, the Aztecs probably knew less about the site than we know today.

The most visited archaeological site in Mexico, it is also among the world's most researched and excavated archaeological sites—"loved to death" according to some. Even though it is a national icon and a major center of tourism, government support has been ambivalent and commercial exploitation of Teotihuacán has been ongoing. UNESCO has designated the ruins a World Heritage Site, and the World Monuments Fund added them to its list of the world's 100 most

TEOTIHUACÁN'S NEWEST DISCOVERY

In 1999, a burial chamber containing what may be the remains of a retainer of an early Teotihuacán ruler was discovered in the Pyramid of the Moon by an excavation team led by American and Mexican archaeologists. Inside the chamber, which has been dated to A.D. 150, the team found the skeleton of an adult male who had been bound and sacrificed. Surrounding the skeleton were more than 400 burial offerings, including obsidian and greenstone figurines, ceremonial obsidian blades and spear points, pyrite mirrors, conch and other shells, along with the remains of eight hawks or falcons, two jaguars, a wolf, a puma, and various serpents, all of which may have been buried alive. The buried individual is thought to be a royal retainer, and archaeologists were hoping to find a royal tomb in the center of the pyramid when they complete their excavations in 2002. In 2000, the same researcher team came across the skulls of 17 sacrificial victims.

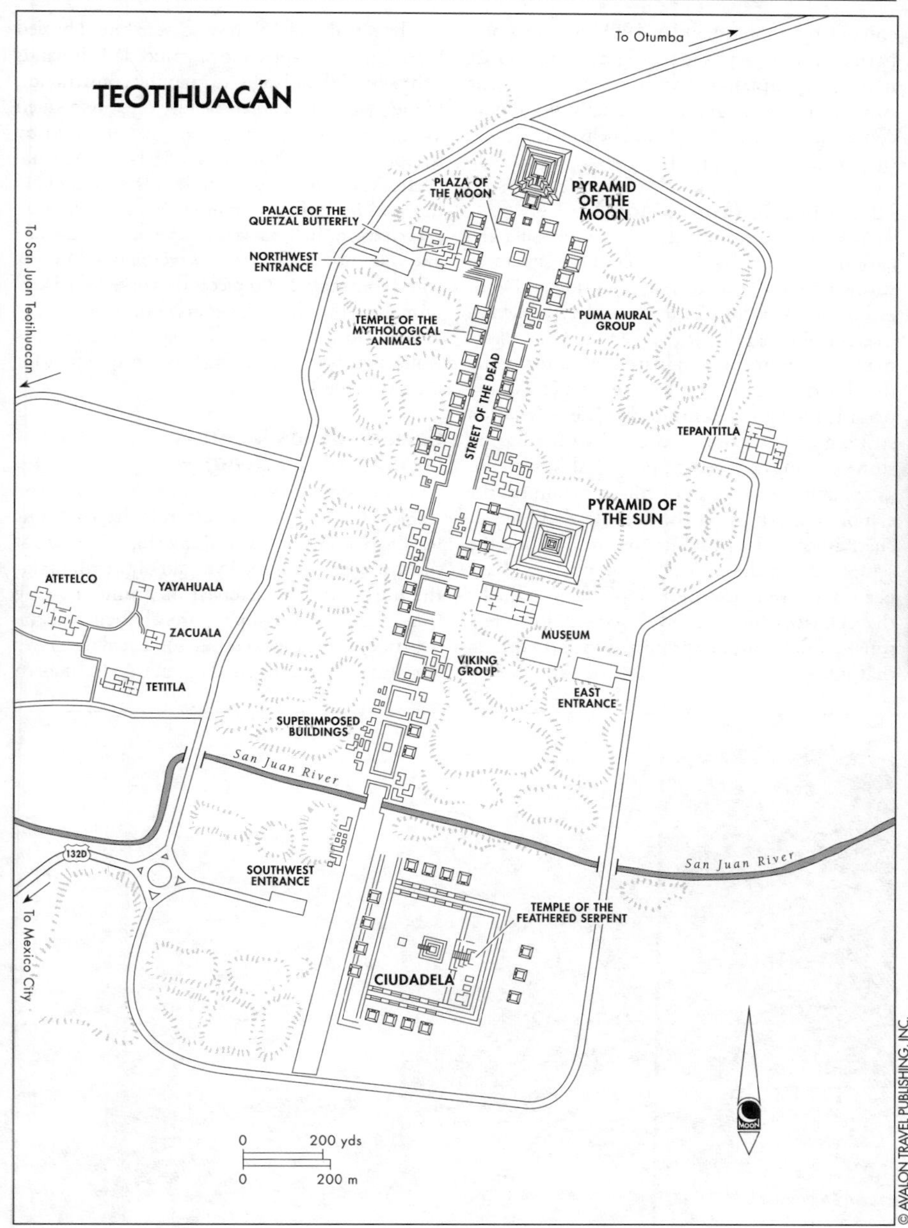
TEOTIHUACÁN
To Otumba
PLAZA OF THE MOON
PYRAMID OF THE MOON
PALACE OF THE QUETZAL BUTTERFLY
NORTHWEST ENTRANCE
TEMPLE OF THE MYTHOLOGICAL ANIMALS
PUMA MURAL GROUP
To San Juan Teotihuacan
STREET OF THE DEAD
TEPANTITLA
PYRAMID OF THE SUN
ATETELCO
YAYAHUALA
ZACUALA
TETITLA
MUSEUM
VIKING GROUP
EAST ENTRANCE
SUPERIMPOSED BUILDINGS
San Juan River
132D
SOUTHWEST ENTRANCE
San Juan River
TEMPLE OF THE FEATHERED SERPENT
To Mexico City
CIUDADELA
MOON
0
200 yds
0
200 m

endangered monuments in 1998, noting that a permanent conservation program and tourist management plan are badly needed. A recent American Express grant may establish a model conservation methodology and help leverage further government support.

La Ciudadela (The Citadel)

Across from the visitors' center is a fortresslike enclosure in the geographic center of the city, measuring about 400 meters on each side and with estimated room for 100,000 people. Archaeologists surmise that this area, called the Main Plaza, may have been the designated place for many ritual performances. At the southeast end of the plaza is the famed **Templo de Quetzalcóatl,** a striking construction decorated with amazing stone carvings of serpent heads. Although not as tall as either the Sun or Moon pyramids, the elaborate carvings on the Templo de Quetzalcóatl attest to its ritual importance. While the sculptures on three sides of the pyramid have been destroyed, a protective platform built by the *teotihuacanos* themselves (for unknown reasons) on the front has protected the artwork on that side.

The remains of 137 people were found buried here. They were apparently sacrificed, their hands tied behind their backs, during the construction of the pyramid. Scholars believe they were killed as part of a warfare cult that was regulated by the position of Venus in its 584-day celestial cycle. Many of these individuals wore collars made of imitation human jawbones with teeth carved from shell, as well as several real maxillae and mandibles. The corpses were placed in pits with more than 2,100 pieces of worked shell and numerous obsidian blades and points.

Next to the pyramid are two large palaces which may have been living quarters or offices for the city's rulers.

Calzada de los Muertos (Avenue of the Dead)

This causeway, now probably about half the length of when the city was in its heyday, runs north-to-south between the visitors' center (at the south end) and the Pyramid of the Moon (at the north end). It received its ominous name from the Aztecs, who apparently believed the structures lining the causeway contained the graves of giants who had died and become gods. Modern

Pirámide del Sol, Teotihuacán

archaeologists instead believe these buildings were ancient residential complexes.

Pirámide del Sol (Pyramid of the Sun)

This is one of the largest, most impressive pyramids in the world. As it now stands, the pyramid (actually five stepped platforms) measures 225 meters on each side and just under 70 meters in height. Two tunnels burrowed by modern researchers into the core of the pyramid, however, indicate that it was first 215 meters on each side and 63 meters high and later enlarged to its current height. The hike up is steep and, on the frequent dusty, hot days, exhausting. Take your time, but be prepared for some fantastic views on a clear day. The stark, unadorned lines of the pyramid add a certain austere grandeur to the imposing structure. A temple once stood atop the pyramid, but it has long since been destroyed.

In 1971, a long stairway was discovered that ended in a four-chamber lava cave 100 meters long under the pyramid. Archaeologists believe the cave was considered a sacred entryway to another world by the city's builders, who chose the location to build their largest pyramid because of it.

Pirámide de la Luna (Pyramid of the Moon)

At the north end of the Calzada de los Muertos is the Pyramid of the Moon, centered on the Plaza of the Moon, which along with the Main Plaza at the Ciudadela was one of the principal ritual areas in the city. Built later than the other principal monuments in the city, the Pyramid of the Moon is 46 meters high and not as steep a climb as the Pyramid of the Sun, but the views over the city and surrounding countryside are still great. When approaching the pyramid along the Avenida de los Muertos, note how the outline of the structure mirrors that of Cerro Gordo, the mountain behind it.

Visitors' Center

Back at the south end of the site, the visitors' center holds a museum, several craft shops, a bookstore, a restaurant, and restrooms. The second-floor restaurant is open Mon.–Fri. 9 A.M.–midnight, Sat. 11 A.M.–11 P.M., Sun. 10 A.M.–6 P.M.; it enjoys a captive audience so is a bit overpriced.

Tips and Information

Wear good walking shoes—the Avenue of the Dead alone stretches about four km. A hat, sunblock, and water are musts to carry with you. Remember, you are at an altitude of 2,300 meters; unless you're accustomed to this, take the steep stairs slowly. The site is open daily 8 A.M.–5 P.M. The best time of day for pictures and peace is 8 A.M., when the ticket-takers open the gate. The tour buses start arriving around 10 A.M. Weekends are the busiest, especially on Sunday when admission is free; the rest of the week admission is US$3. A parking fee is also charged.

Acolman

Along the free road to Teotihuacán from Mexico City, and easily visible from the toll road, is the 16th-century Augustinian church and monastary complex of Acolman, noted for its fine Plateresque facade and the churchyard cross in front, carved with a mix of Catholic and Amerindian motifs. Inside the cloister are a series of religious murals. The fortresslike monastary makes a great stop-off while visiting Teotihuacán, especially if you've got your own car. By public transport, you'd have to take the local (not direct) bus between San Juan Teotihuacán and Indios Verdes Metro stop in Mexico City.

Getting to Teotihuacán

The ruins lie about 50 km northeast of Mexico City. To get there by bus from Mexico City, look for the sign **Autobuses Sahagun** at the northwest end of the Terminal Central del Norte. Buses leave the terminal every 30 minutes 5 A.M.–6 P.M.; the trip to Teotihuacán takes about an hour. You want the bus marked "Los Pirámides," otherwise you may end up at the nearby city of San Juan Teotihuacán. Another option is to take Metro line 3 as far as Indios Verdes. As you leave the station, note the signs directing you to the Teotihuacán buses (at the last bus platform). Only local buses leave from Indios Verdes, however, making it a long slow trip with lots of stops. Better to go to the Terminal del Norte. To return to the city, catch your bus at the entrance gate of the museum. The last bus leaves the main entrance at 6 P.M.

If you're driving from Mexico City to Teotihuacán, you have a choice of toll-free México 132D or the toll road *(cuota),* México 85D. The toll road isn't much faster but does have lighter traffic.

TEXCOCO

A large, dusty town northeast of Mexico City, on what used to be the eastern shores of the nearly vanished Lake Texcoco, Texcoco is not much to see itself, but it has three interesting sites to visit nearby, little seen by foreigners: Molino de Flores, Universidad de Chapingo, and the Baños de Nezahualcóyotl.

Texcoco was founded originally around 1200 A.D. by the Toltecs and later became the seat of the Acolhua empire, which was one of the principal allies of Aztecs. The city reached its height under Acolmiztli Nezahualcóyotl (1402–1472), the famed king of Texcoco. Not only was he a brilliant poet (his verse remains powerful to modern readers), but he was also a budding monotheist and a superlative engineer. It was Nezahualcóyotl who designed the complex of dams controlling the interlocking lakes of the valley which were destroyed by Cortés during the conquest. Because of its importance, Franciscan monks established one of the first missions in Mexico nearby at Acolman, just off the highway to Teotihuacán.

© CHRIS HUMPHREY

the little-visited Baños de Nezahuacóyotl ruins, near Texcoco

The hills to the east of Texcoco, forming part of the valley of Mexico, remain a heavily indigenous area, populated by Nahua farming communities. In many of these villages, the residents still don't speak Spanish. Ruins from the pre-Hispanic era are found all over this little-explored region. San Miguel Coatlinchan, a village in the hills southeast of Texcoco, is the original site of the Tlaloc statue that now sits outside of the Museo Nacional de Antropología. Although the statue was taken decades ago, the villagers are still reputed to be extremely angry that their rain god was stolen by the government. A 16th-century church and convent in town is worth a visit. Another nearby village with many ruins around is San Luis Huexotla.

Nowadays Texcoco is a primarily agricultural town, and to celebrate that, the town holds the annual **Feria del Caballo** just before Easter (Semana Santa). This blowout bash features horse shows, bullfights, lots of good food, and lots of *ranchera* music.

There are plenty of restaurants in Texcoco should you want to grab a meal on your way through town. One right on the plaza is **Oasis del Naturismo,** a good place for breakfasts, light meals, or fruit drinks. Open daily 7 A.M.–9 P.M.

To get to Texcoco, take a Primera Plus bus leaving every five minutes from the Tapo eastern terminal in Mexico City. The 15-minute ride costs US$2. By car, take the Circuito Interior, and look for the exit to Texcoco (Via Rápida Texcoco) just north of the airport. The toll costs US$2 but is definitely worth it rather than struggling through the maze of back roads and slums on the free road.

EXCURSIONS

Universidad de Chapingo

Three kilometers south of Texcoco is this university, one of the premier agricultural schools in the country. The university, started in 1923, is not a particular attraction in itself, although the grassy grounds are nice enough. But in one of the main buildings is the **Capilla Riveriana,** a chapel painted by famed Mexican muralist Diego Rivera between 1924 and 1927. The socialist proclivities of Rivera are much in evidence here, with hammer and sickle symbols throughout the murals. Also prominent is an earth mother theme, possibly a nod to the school's agricultural focus. Check out the wooden doors at the entrance, carved by Abraham López according to a design by Rivera. Entrance to the building is US$4 for foreigners or US$1.50 for Mexicans; hours are Mon.–Fri. 10 A.M.–3 P.M., Sat. 10 A.M.–5 P.M. Guides offer a complete tour of the chapel and the adjacent building, a hacienda dating from 1690, for US$1.50. Check out the pre-Hispanic stone carving in the entrance to the hacienda. To get to the university from Texcoco, hop a *microbus* from downtown for US$.50, or take a taxi for US$2–3.

Parque Nacional Molino de Flores

The ruins of this 16th-century hacienda, three kilometers east of Texcoco in a small, tree-filled valley, is now a park frequented on weekends by local folks. The old hacienda was originally built in 1567 to produce cloth, and 20 years later it became a wheat mill. The mill passed through a variety of hands over the next centuries and continued functioning until the 1910–1920 Mexican revolution. It was expropriated by the government in 1937.

Some of the hacienda buildings have been restored, while others remain in ruins, but all are very beautiful and well worth a visit to get an idea of what life might have been like on a hacienda. Free guided tours are available, in Spanish only. The park is mobbed on weekends, so it's best to come during the week. Open Mon.–Fri. 9 A.M.–2 P.M., weekends 11 A.M.–5 P.M. Taxis from downtown Texcoco cost US$2.50, or you can hop a bus for US$.50.

Baños de Nezahualcóyotl

These ruins, surprisingly impressive considering how little-known they are, cover a hill just above the town of San Nicolás, about six km east of Texcoco. Whether they were built by Nezahualcóyotl himself or not is not certain, but one can be sure he made use of them. To get to the ruins, either take a bus from Texcoco to San Nicolás (US$1) or a taxi (US$3.50). By car, follow the road to Molino de Flores, and just before arriving at the park, look for a right turn continuing uphill. From this junction it's three km to San Nicolás.

There's no charge to visit Baños de Nezahualcóyotl, and it makes for a great alternative day trip from Mexico City instead of going to the same tourist destinations as everyone else.

Right at the entrance to San Nicolás, a dirt road to the right leads to a modern public swimming pool (where you can leave your car if you came in one). Just behind the parking lot, a dirt road leads uphill; it quickly becomes a footpath. Passing a carved cave, you will come to a rebuilt staircase leading to the first stone bath, facing west over the valley. Here you can continue uphill to more baths or take side paths winding around the hillside. Wherever you go, you'll find carved stones and baths all over the place. On the back (east) side are the reconstructed ruins of a major temple built into the hillside, as well as the remains of a causeway and aqueduct leading up into the mountains. More ruins are found continuing east. There's no charge to visit this site, and it makes for a great alternative day trip from Mexico City instead of going to the same tourist destinations as everyone else. On your way back down, you might consider taking a refreshing dip in the public pool for US$3 adults, US$2.50 kids under 12.

TEPOTZOTLÁN

Known for its magnificent Churrigueresque convent and church, Tepotzotlán also holds a cobbled-street colonial city center—mostly unspoiled either by modernization or chic restorations—and the country's largest and most complete colonial-history museum. Very popular with *capitalino* tourists, the small town makes a good day-trip destination from Mexico City, about an hour away (43 km) by bus from the Terminal del Norte. If you're driving up from the capital, take México 57D about 37 km north toward Querétaro. The well-marked turnoff to Tepotzotlán lies just before the tollbooth.

Templo de San Francisco Javier and Plaza Hidalgo

This single-towered Spanish church, and the attached convent, forms the nucleus of the town's tourist attractions. The simple early baroque side *portada* (entry) facing the main street corresponds to the first stage of the construction of the church, 1670–82, and is topped by a niche containing an image of San Ignacio de Loyola. The front entry facing the Plaza Hidalgo is classic late baroque or *churrigueresco* and was crafted between 1760 and 1762. This much larger facade consists of many *estípites* filled with saints—we lost count at 22. San Francisco Javier, of course, stands in the main niche, right above a rosette window.

Sunday is a very popular time to visit the plaza and church, not just for Mass but to visit the food vendors who fill the plaza in front. The plaza and area surrounding the church and convent were restored by INAH in 1993–94.

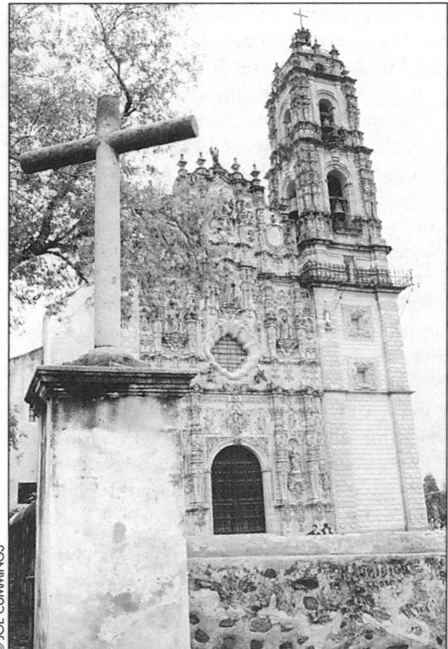
© JOE CUMMINGS
Templo de San Francisco Javier

Museo Nacional de Virreinato

This large and very impressive museum occupies a magnificent ex-convent that once served as a Jesuit college of Indian languages. The convent chapels, cloisters, library, refectory, kitchen, and other spaces were constructed between 1606 and 1767, and the overall three-story stone structure is considered an excellent model of the evolution of Spanish colonial architecture in Mexico. Even if you're not especially interested in the art contained in the museum, the convent architecture alone—with its thick walls, complex passageways, arched cloisters, and heavy wood-paneled doors and windows—is worth seeing. On the third floor is a terrace overlooking the town.

Several areas of the building conserve the convent's original art, which was extensive in and of itself, and in 1964, when INAH converted the ex-convent into a national museum, the collection was further enriched with religious art pieces from the Catedral Metropolitana in Mexico City. A few rooms are devoted to the history of Mexico's conquest, with displays of Spanish armor and weaponry. Other rooms contain an extensive collection of colonial textiles, including a display of religious garments worn by monks, nuns, and priests. There's no shortage of gold and silver, and you'll see vestments woven with these precious metals, plus candlesticks, chalices, and crucifixes of silver and gold inlaid with precious stones. Also worth noting are the collections of religious calligraphy, furniture, porcelains, and ceramics.

The selection of religious paintings rivals that of the Museo Nacional de Arte in Mexico City, added to which is a very ample supply of religious sculpture. A *capilla domestica* (domestic chapel, i.e., once meant for the use of convent residents only) on the ground floor contains exquisite *retablos* and religious paintings.

The museum is open Tues. 10 A.M.–5 P.M., Wed.–Sun. 11 A.M.–6 P.M. Admission costs $2.50, free on Sunday and festival days. For further information, call 5876-0245.

Food

On the upper floor of the old convent attached to the church, **La Ostería del Convento de Tepotzotlán Restaurant Bar** offers "pre-Hispanic" delicacies such as *guisanos de maguey* and *escamoles,* as well as such familiar central Mexican dishes as *chiles en nogada, crepas de huitlacoche, queso fundido, caldo tepotzotlán,* and *fajitas de pollo,* plus a long list of tequila brands. The average platter costs around US$5.50.

At the opposite end of the plaza in front of the church is a row of restaurants, including a *taquería* called **El Mexicanito** and **El Rancho Restaurante Bar.**

Food vendors on Plaza Hidalgo, in front of the Templo de San Francisco Javier and the Museo Nacional del Virreinato, sell *huaraches* and other *antojitos* as well as *pulque curado.*

Shopping

If you're setting up house in Mexico City, Tepotzotlán is a good place to look for rustic wooden furniture, custom wrought iron, and terra-cotta pottery.

Opposite the plaza in front of the church are a few *artesanía* shops.

TULA ARCHAEOLOGICAL SITE

Tollan, today known as Tula, was founded in the 10th century, after the decline of Teotihuacán and well before the arrival of the Aztecs. Evidence suggests that refugees from Teotihuacán caused a rapid increase in Tula's population. It is possible that the city was the capital of the Toltec-Chichimeca Empire. And though this was a powerful nation, it never grew as large as Teotihuacán, although it was a sizeable city. At its peak, archaeologists believe, Tollan covered an area of 13 square km and held a population of 60,000.

Scholars believe Tollan was engulfed in a great fire that destroyed much of the city, and by A.D. 1125, the empire began to decline. Sacked and looted by outsiders, Tollan was abandoned before A.D. 1200. The Aztecs, who arrived in the Valle de México shortly thereafter, considered the Toltecs their ancestors.

Little is left of the once-great city, which is not as frequently visited as nearby Teotihuacán. Despite the dusty desolation of the place, locals (and a few foreign New Age disciples) claim the site emits spiritual forces. The main attraction of Tula is the **Pyramid of the Morning Star** or Templo de Tlahuizcalpantecuhtli. The top of the pyramid is the resting place for four massive stone warriors known as the **Atlanteans,** for which Tula is famed. Each warrior is 4.6 meters (15 feet) tall, wears a butterfly-shaped breastplate and feathered headdress, and holds an *atlatl* (spear thrower) in one hand. Around the sides of the pyramid are reliefs of eagles eating human hearts, as well as coyotes, jaguars, and imaginary creatures.

Other structures at the site feature carvings of snakes, skeletons, and richly dressed nobles. If you look closely, you can see remnants of the paint that once covered the carvings. A ball court here is identical in size to one at the archaeological site of Xochicalco in Morelos. Some speculate that this is the original Mesoamerican ball court, where the "game" or "tournament" was conceived.

The site is open daily 9:30 A.M.–4:30 P.M. Admission is US$3, which includes parking and entrance to a small museum. Vendors sell soft drinks and souvenirs.

Accommodations

Most visitors to Tula are day-trippers from Mexico City, but if you have a keen interest in exploring the archaeological site, or if you're just looking to stay in a place where tourists rarely spend the night, Tula is well provided for.

Budget: Near the center of town, **Hotel Cuellar,** 5 De Mayo 23, tel. 773/732-2920, offers basic, small but clean rooms that open onto a brick-laid parking area and garden. Rates: US$17 s, US$19 d.

Hotel Catedral, Zaragoza 106, tel. 773/732-0813, offers similar quality rooms with cable TV and an open, street-front lobby. Rates: US$15 s, US$5 per added person.

Inexpensive: The most modern rooms in town are to be found at **Hotel Sharon,** Callejon de la Cruz 1, tel. 773/732-0976. A large facility with banquet areas and restaurant, the hotel has 120 rooms and a helpful staff. Rates: US$40 s/d, US$45 d/t.

Food

If you're planning a day trip to Tula and looking for a quick bite on the walk to the ruins, try **Pizzas In/Out,** Melchor Ocampo 20. The restaurant serves good Mexican food as well as hand-tossed pizzas and a dozen different types of burgers. There's another location on Hidalgo between Moctezuma and Zaragoza. Prices range US$2–5.

Taquerilla Parrillada Country, across the street from Pizzas In/Out, serves tacos, burgers, and good Mexican entrées in a down-home setting with checkered tablecloths and friendly service. Expect to pay US$2–6 for a meal. The restaurant's second location faces the town plaza between Leandro Valle and Hidalgo.

Across the street from Hotel Catedral is **Chicas Tortas,** a lively sandwich shop with loud music; open into the evening.

On Zaragoza across from the *iglesia* is **Cafetería-Nevería Campanario,** an excellent choice for well-made coffee drinks or a light meal.

For a more local experience, head to the **Plaza del Taco,** a cavernous "taco mall" on the corner of Colegio Militar and 5 de Mayo. Vendors operate individual stalls selling various specialty tacos—but don't expect anything fancy; this is strictly wooden benches and meat-laden tortillas.

Helados Danesa, on Melchor Ocampo between Hotel Sharon and In/Out, is an ice-cream shop that also sells snacks, soft drinks, and good coffee.

Getting There

Autotransportes Valle del Mezquital buses depart Mexico City's Terminal Central de Autobuses del Norte for Tula about every 15 minutes, 5 A.M.–11 P.M.; fare is about US$3. The bus will drop you off in town; you can either walk the three km to the site (about 15–20 minutes), flag a cab, or take the minibus marked "Tlahuelilpan." You might want to make arrangements with your cab or the minibus to be picked up for the return to town. The last bus to Mexico City leaves Tula at 7 P.M.

If you're coming by car, take México 57 from Mexico City toward Querétaro. At Tepotzotlán it becomes a toll road, México 57D. Continue till you see signs on the right directing you to Tula; this road is México 126, which takes you right through town. Look for signs directing you to Las Ruinas; from town the sign says Parque Nacional Tula.

PACHUCA

The state capital of Hidalgo lies in the Sierra Madre Oriental, an important part of Mexico's silver belt. Mining has driven the local economy since before the Spanish arrival in 1534, and it continues to be the most important industry. The hills above the city have been worked off and on for centuries and are riddled with mine shafts and ancient slag heaps. The region still produces more than a million ounces of silver a year.

Most visitors find themselves in Pachuca either to visit Fototeca, Mexico's national photography archive, or because they're on their way to Parque Nacional El Chico.

Around the Centro

Pachuca is a town of narrow, twisting streets climbing steep hillsides. Though not brimming with architectural treasures, it's certainly worth spending a couple of hours admiring buildings in the *centro.*

The center of town is the broad **Plaza de la Independencia,** punctuated by the 40-meter-high **Torre del Reloj** (Clock Tower), decorated with four carved statues and a carillon imported from Austria. The **Casa Colorado,** built in the 18th century, is now the city's law court, while the 17th-century **Las Casas** formerly served as a hall for storing the *quinta real,* or royal fifth, the percentage of the area's mined wealth automatically owed to the Spanish crown.

At the modern **Palacio de Gobierno,** in the civic center a few blocks from the Plaza de la Independencia, you'll find a statue of Benito Juárez by Juan Leonardo Cordero and murals by Pachucan painter Jesús Becerril.

South of the plaza and west of the civic center, **Parque Hidalgo** is a favorite Sunday haunt for Pachucans out for a stroll, vendors, and mariachis. On Avenida Guerrero near Salazar is the large enclosed **Mercado de Barreteros.**

Centro Cultural de Hidalgo/Fototeca

A 10-minute walk southeast of the Plaza de la Independencia leads to the former monastery of San Francisco, which has seen many different residents during its 400-year existence, including monks, horses, and criminals. The Conde de Regla, who made a fabulous fortune in local silver mines, is buried in the adjoining church. Today the Instituto Nacional de Antropología e Historia (INAH) runs a fine group of museums in the old ex-convent.

The **Museo Regional de Historia** displays archaeological and ethnological artifacts representing the Huastec, Aztec, Toltec, Otomi, and "Chichimec" (a derisive, all-inclusive Náhuatl term for the Amerindians of the north) cultures. You'll see displays of folk art, crafts, everyday utensils, and traditional dress. Open Tues.–Sun. 10 A.M.–6 P.M.; free admission.

On the second floor of the ex-convent is the **Museo Nacional de Fotografía,** a small but interesting collection of historical Mexican photography, from early daguerreotypes to Antonio Casasola's famed Revolution-era pictures to the work of modern photographers such as Gabriela Etrubide and Nacho López. Same hours as the Museo Regional; free admission.

In the same building as the photography museum but with a separate entrance is **Fototeca,** tel. 771/714-3653, fax 771/713-1977, email: sinafo@prodigy.net.mx, where INAH has cataloged 1.2 million photographs on computer and can search for them by photographer, date, location, or subject. The Fototeca will make prints of any of its photographs for US$2–18, depending on the size of the print, plus reprint permission fees if required. It's best to call ahead and arrange an appointment so a staff member can help you run a search. If you have the information needed, photos can be ordered by phone and delivered to you by courier for an additional charge. Hours are Mon.–Fri. 9 A.M.–2 P.M.

Accommodations

Budget: Two blocks below the plaza, **Hotel Noriega,** Calle Matamoros 305, tel. 771/715-1555, offers large, clean rooms in an old colonial building, popular with the occasional young traveler who comes to Pachuca. Rates: US$18 s, US$25 d.

Though not as nice as the Noriega and a bit more expensive, **Hotel de los Baños,** just off the plaza at Matamoros 207, tel. 771/713-0700, has decent low-priced rooms. Rates: US$20 s, US$26 d.

Inexpensive: Hotel Emily, on Calle Hidalgo, Plaza de la Independencia, tel. 771/715-0849, is one of the better places in the town center (though still nothing special), with a restaurant and parking. Rates: US$32 s, US$40 d.

Also on the square is **Gran Hotel Independencia,** Independencia 116, tel. 771/715-0515, formerly a bit of a dive but remodeled in 2001. Each of the simple, brightly painted rooms around the spacious open patio has a phone and TV. The rooms in the front of the building have a small balcony. Rates: US$33 s or d, US$42 d with two beds.

Expensive: Out on the highway exit to Mexico City is **Hotel Fiesta Inn,** Carr. México-Pachuca Km 85.5, tel. 771/711-3011, fax 771/711-4396, a modern hotel with an adjoining nine-hole golf course. The hotel has a restaurant and bar, and guests have access to a gym, tennis courts, and a pool at a nearby health club. Rates: US$90 s, US$105 d, US$155 junior suite.

Food

Pachuca's regional food specialties include *mixiotes,* tamale-type ingredients baked in maguey leaves; *barbacoa,* lamb wrapped in maguey leaves and baked underground; and *escamoles,* fried ant eggs. The large numbers of British miners who lived in Pachuca at the end of the 19th century introduced football (soccer) to Mexico and also brought with them the tradition of pasties. Here called *pastes,* these little pies stuffed with minced meat and vegetables are found all over Pachuca and surrounding towns. They make a great inexpensive midday snack.

A number of small cafés surround the town center. Right on the Plaza de la Independencia is **Restaurante La Blanca,** a cafeteria-style restaurant with inexpensive meals and snacks. Open daily 8 A.M.–11 P.M.

Excellent homemade tacos, with nine fillings to choose from, can be found at the cozy **Mesón de Los Ángeles Gómez** at Guerrero 723, just up from the Plaza Juárez. During the day you can buy breakfasts, *comida corridas,* and snacks, and it starts serving tacos in the evening. Open Mon.–Sat. 9 A.M.–11 P.M. **Hotel Noriega** also has a decent dining room.

Helados Santa Clara on Plaza Independencia serves good ice cream, sweets, and even a decent espresso.

Tourist Office

The tourist office, on the ground floor of the Monumento Reloj, tel. 771/715-1411, is open 10 A.M.–7 P.M.. It offers a selection of decent printed information, but mostly in Spanish. The state tourist office, Av. Revolución 1300, tel. 771/711-4150 and 718-4454, is a fair way out of the center of town and not convenient for pedestrians.

Services

The post office is at Juárez and Iglesias. Telephone service is available at Avenida Valle 106.

Several banks in the *centro* will change money.

The hospital can be found on the highway toward Tulancingo, while Farmacia del Pueblo is at Matamoros 205.

There's a *lavandería* at Centro Comercial Constitución L-14.

Transportation

From Mexico City, México 85D (toll road) is a good way to get out of Mexico City quickly, and the toll to Pachuca costs only US$2.

To get to Pachuca's **central bus station,** hop the bus that leaves from in front of the tourist office on Allende. Several lines run buses all day to Mexico City's Terminal del Norte (US$5). **Ovni** offers frequent buses 7 A.M.–7 P.M. to Tula (US$4). **ADO,** tel. 771/713-2910, runs three buses daily to Poza Rica (US$9.50) and one daily to Tampico (US$20). **Estrella Blanca,** tel. 771/713-2747, departs every hour for Querétero (US$11). The same company also runs the direct bus to the Mexico City airport 15 times daily for US$8. **Primera Plus,** tel. 771/713-3303, offers frequent buses to Puebla (US$7), as well as two daily to Jalapa (US$12) and Veracruz (US$18).

PARQUE NACIONAL EL CHICO

In the hills above Pachuca is Parque Nacional El Chico, a lovely pine-forested park covering 2,700 hectares, with campsites, hiking and mountain-biking trails, and fishing holes. El Chico has a reputation for being exceptionally safe and *tranquilo,* making it an attractive place to enjoy the outdoors close to Mexico City.

Rock-climbing

El Chico is best-known among Mexicans as one of the country's premier rock-climbing playgrounds, with several dozen bolted and mapped routes up the many rock formations in the park. Most routes rate 5.7–5.9. The two hardest routes are 5.12. **La Ventana,** the 150-meter tower reaching the highest point in the park, has three routes up it ranging between 5.8 and 5.10.

A fine place to start looking around for climbing routes and to talk to other climbers is the parking lot around the **Albergue Alpino Miguel Hidalgo,** a hostel of sorts where you can crash with a sleeping bag on weekends, on the south side of the main road running through the park. Right behind the building is a rock formation aptly named **La Botella** (the bottle), a 40-meter, free-standing rock with a couple of 5.7–5.8 routes. Behind La Botella are cliffs with dozens of bolted routes of varying difficulty.

Camping, Hiking, Biking

Apart from rock-climbing, the park is a wonderful place to wander about in the forest, breathe the crisp clean air, and enjoy the views. Several small valleys make great campsites, and locals charge only US$2 for permission to pitch a tent. You can also leave your car at the Albergue parking lot for US$1.50 and hike up to pitch a tent on the ridge above, with a lovely view overlooking the park and surrounding countryside. The Albergue itself has simple cots in a dormitory room to sleep in on weekends only for US$3.50 per person. Just across the road is a small restaurant and store, also open weekends only.

Mountain bikers will also find a couple of decent trails descending different sides of the hill from the area around the Albergue. One great trail descends from the south side of the main road, shortly before reaching the Albergue coming from Pachuca, and comes out after a hair-raising ride to a small reservoir by the village of **Estanzuela.** From here you can ride the paved road a couple of steep kilometers back up to the Albergue.

Other trails head downhill from the north side of the road near the Albergue through the woods to Mineral El Chico, and then return uphill on the paved road to the Albergue.

Getting There

To get to El Chico by car, take the highway leaving Pachuca toward Tampico. About 15 minutes from the city you'll see a paved road angling off to the left, clearly marked El Chico. Turn here and continue driving several kilometers into the park. This road continues all the way through the middle of the park to the town of **Mineral El Chico,** an attractive mining village that has become a favorite weekend spot for Pachucans.

Regular minibuses run between Mercado Benito Juárez in Pachuca and Mineral El Chico; the fare is about US$1 for the whole ride, or less to get dropped off at the Albergue. The last minibus descends to Pachuca at 7 P.M. In Pachuca, catch the buses at the north end of town, where the Viaducto turns into the highway leading to Tampico. Buses leave the central bus station in Pachuca for Mineral El Chico three times a day.

Cuernavaca

Nicknamed the "City of Eternal Spring" for its balmy climate, Cuernavaca was originally a Tlahuica city named Cuauhnáhuac (Place at the Edge of the Forest). It fell quickly to Spanish swords in 1521 and was granted to Cortés by the Spanish crown as one of his *encomiendas.*

Cortés was the first of many Mexico City residents to keep a vacation home in Cuernavaca, his built out of the ruins of the city pyramid. Many of Mexico's most powerful politicians and businesspeople, not to mention a few well-known drug traffickers, have built luxury villas here, giving a whole new meaning to the term "weekend getaway."

While you won't see much of Cuernavaca's wealthy residents, who are safely ensconced behind their mansion walls, the city center area is a very popular day trip for Mexico City residents, and it is mobbed on weekends. The city also hosts about 20 Spanish-language schools and a correspond ingly large contingent of foreign-language students.

If you read Malcolm Lowry's *Under the Volcano* and hope to find the village of Quauhnahuac in which the fictional consul passes a singular day, you will be disappointed. With a population of more than one million, Cuernavaca has grown dramatically in the past few decades, adding miles of nondescript concrete neighborhoods surrounding the colonial city center.

ORIENTATION

Although Cuernavaca covers a lot of territory these days, most places of interest to visitors are within easy walking distance of the two adjacent central squares, the Plaza de Armas and Jardín Juárez.

If possible, try to avoid visiting Cuernavaca on weekends, when the city center is invariably crowded with Mexico City tourists.

SIGHTS

Plaza de Armas and Jardín Juárez

Plaza de Armas is the larger of the two plazas in the center of town. The tree-lined plaza is con-

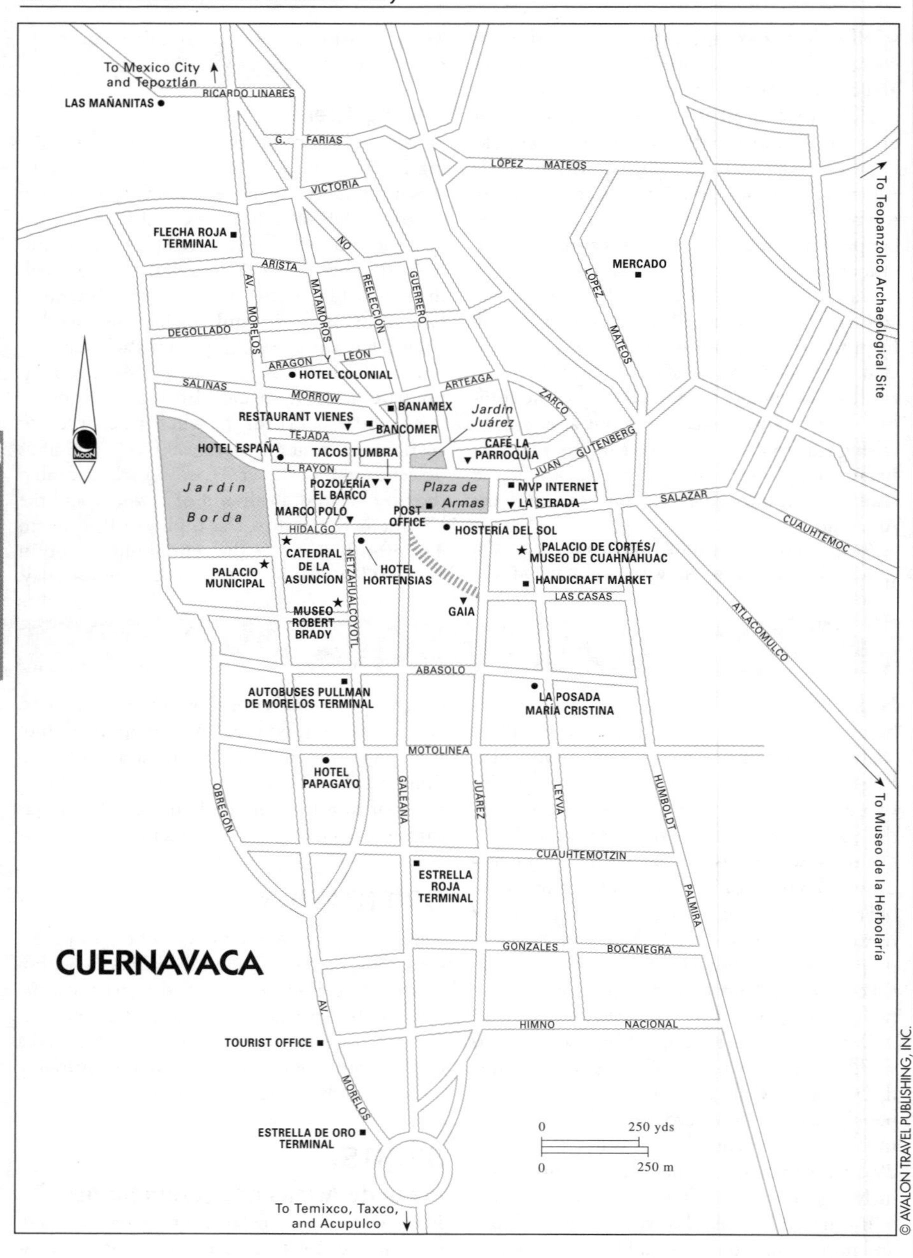

CUERNAVACA
To Mexico City and Tepoztlán
LAS MAÑANITAS
RICARDO LINARES
G. FARIAS
LÓPEZ MATEOS
VICTORIA
NO REELECCIÓN
FLECHA ROJA TERMINAL
ARISTA
AV. MORELOS
MATAMOROS
GUERRERO
MERCADO
LÓPEZ MATEOS
DEGOLLADO
ARAGON Y LEÓN
HOTEL COLONIAL
SALINAS
MORROW
ARTEAGA
ZARCO
BANAMEX
RESTAURANT VIENES
BANCOMER
Jardín Juárez
TEJADA
HOTEL ESPAÑA
TACOS TUMBRA
CAFÉ LA PARROQUÍA
GUTENBERG
JUAN
L. RAYON
Jardín Borda
POZOLERÍA EL BARCO
Plaza de Armas
MVP INTERNET
LA STRADA
SALAZAR
MARCO POLO
POST OFFICE
HIDALGO
HOSTERÍA DEL SOL
CUAUHTEMOC
CATEDRAL DE LA ASUNCÍON
PALACIO DE CORTÉS/ MUSEO DE CUAHNÁHUAC
PALACIO MUNICIPAL
NETZAHUALCOYOTL
HOTEL HORTENSIAS
HANDICRAFT MARKET
LAS CASAS
MUSEO ROBERT BRADY
GAIA
ATLACOMULCO
ABASOLO
AUTOBUSES PULLMAN DE MORELOS TERMINAL
LA POSADA MARÍA CRISTINA
MOTOLINEA
HOTEL PAPAGAYO
OBREGÓN
GALEANA
JUÁREZ
LEYVA
HUMBOLDT
CUAUHTEMOTZIN
ESTRELLA ROJA TERMINAL
PALMIRA
GONZALES
BOCANEGRA
HIMNO NACIONAL
AV. MORELOS
TOURIST OFFICE
ESTRELLA DE ORO TERMINAL
To Temixco, Taxco, and Acupulco
To Teopanzolco Archaeological Site
To Museo de la Herbolaría
0 250 yds
0 250 m
MOON

EXCURSIONS

tinually bustling with locals and visitors sitting on the many benches, reading papers, chatting with friends, or just watching the world go by.

Next to the plaza, smaller Jardín Juárez features a late-19th-century kiosk designed by French architect Alexandre Gustave Eiffel, who also designed Paris's famous Eiffel Tower.

Palacio de Cortés/ Museo de Cuauhnáhuac

Begun by Cortés in 1522, this austere, intimidating structure has more the look of a fortress than a luxury palace, a reminder that the Spaniards lived in fear of Indian uprisings. Cortés lived between here and his palaces in Mexico City until 1540, when he returned to Spain. Since then, the building has served variously as a prison and the state legislature and now contains a museum of colonial and pre-Hispanic artifacts.

After viewing the museum collection, head upstairs to see the Diego Rivera mural on the second floor, tracing the history of Cuernavaca from the Spanish invasion to the present. The mural was paid for by U.S. Ambassador Dwight Morrow, who kept a house in Cuernavaca during his three years in Mexico. On the ground floor are the barely visible remains of the ancient pyramid destroyed by Cortés to build the palace.

The palace stands at the southeast end of the Plaza de Armas. It's open Tues.–Sun. 9 A.M.–5 P.M.; admission is US$3.50, free on Sunday. A government-run shop on the premises offers an excellent selection of books on art, history, and travel in Mexico; open 11 A.M.–8 P.M.

Catedral de la Asunción

Opposite the Jardín Borda at the corner of Hidalgo and Morelos, Catedral de la Asunción was built by Spanish architect Francisco Becerra, under Cortés' orders, beginning in 1529. Becerra, who also designed the Palacio Cortés, gave the church a similarly intimidating, unadorned facade. Keep an eye out for the ominous-looking skull and crossbones over the main entrance, as well as a dramatic, Japanese-style painting inside depicting the martyring in Japan of Mexico's first saint, missionary San Felipe de Jesús. The painting (artist unknown) was discovered during remodeling work in the 1950s. The church is open daily 8 A.M.–8 P.M. For a taste of Catholicism with a singularly Mexican flavor, attend the mariachi Mass Sunday at 11 A.M.

On the other side of the cathedral courtyard is the smaller **Templo del Tercer Orden,** a newer baroque-style church with an ornate gilded altarpiece.

Museo Casa Robert Brady

Originally part of the cathedral cloister, the Museo Casa Robert Brady, Calle Netzahualcóyotl 4, is an unusual private art museum containing the collection of an American who lived in Cuernavaca for 24 years but who had an eye for works of art from around the globe. The house, known as Casa de la Torre, contains an eclectic collection of more than 1,000 works of native art from the world over, as well as colonial antiques and a number of paintings by well-known artists such as Frida Kahlo, Rufino Tamayo, and Miguel Covarrubias. The guided tour is required, but the guides are very knowledgeable and interesting. Spanish-speaking guides are available all day, but call in advance for either English- or French-speaking guides. The museum also houses a high-quality craft shop. Open Tues.–Sun. 10 A.M.–6 P.M.; admission is US$4.50.

Jardín Borda

Silver-mining empresario José de la Borda built this mansion and surrounding garden, which also served briefly as a holiday home for Emperor Maximilian and his wife, Carlota. Several of the rooms the ill-fated couple used have been restored and now house a small museum and occasional art exhibits.

The artificial lake is perhaps less lovely than in its former glory days, but the gardens are a lush haven in which to relax in the middle of the city. The entrance is on Morelos at Hidalgo, across from the cathedral. Open Tues.–Sun. 10 A.M.–5:30 P.M.; admission is US$1 or free on Sunday.

Next door stands the 18th-century **Iglesia de Nuestra Señora de Guadalupe,** burial place of José de la Borda.

Palacio Municipal

Adjacent to Jardín Borda at Morelos 265, the 19th-century town hall contains a museum displaying 20 paintings by Salvador Tarasona, each depicting a different facet of Morelos history (with a heavy emphasis on pre-Hispanic life). The museum is open Mon.–Fri. 9 A.M.–6 P.M.; admission is free.

La Casa del Olvido/ Museo de la Herbolaría

This small house and garden at Matamoros 200, about 1.5 km (one mile) southeast of the town center, received its nickname, "The House of Forgetting," because of a brief stay by Emperor Maximilian in the summer of 1866. For a few short weeks here, Maximilian consorted with Margarita Lefuisamo Sedano, the gardener's wife, avoiding his own fiercely ambitious, slightly unhinged wife, Carlota, and the unpleasant realities of his precarious situation as leader of Mexico. Maximilian hadn't really wanted to come to Mexico in the first place (Carlota convinced him to do so), and once here, he managed to alienate everyone with his well-intentioned but half-baked liberal ideas. He was deposed and executed the following year. Who can blame him for coming to this little spot and wishing it would all go away, if only for a short while?

Today the house holds a modest museum devoted to Indian folk medicine. Open daily 10 A.M.–5 P.M.; free admission.

Teopanzolco Archaeological Site

In what is now the neighborhood of Colonia Vista Hermosa northeast of the city center, you can see the remains of a Tlahuica pyramid, with an Aztec pyramid built around it. The first pyramid was built around 1200 A.D., while the second was still in progress when Cortés appeared on the scene. To get there, hop a Ruta 4 *combi* from Avenida Morelos in the city center. Open daily 10 A.M.–5 P.M.; admission US$3.50, free on Sunday.

ACCOMMODATIONS

As a long-time holiday city, Cuernavaca has a wide range of hotel options, from modest-but-decent rooms near the plaza to luxury spreads on the outskirts of town.

Budget

Hotel Hortensias, Hidalgo 13, tel. 777/318-5265, is a small family-run hotel around an interior courtyard, with cable TV. Rates: US$20 s, US$25 d.

Hotel Colonial, Aragón y León 104 (three blocks from the *jardín*), tel. 777/318-6414, is nice for the price. However, rooms vary widely in quality so look first. Some rooms have a TV. Rates: US$22 s or d, US$27 d with two beds.

A large, friendly place, with a restaurant inside, is **Hotel Espana,** Morelos 190 at the corner of Rayon, tel. 777/318-6744. The 30 tile-floored rooms are spacious and airy, with fans and TV. Rates: US$24 s, US$17 s (no TV), US$27 d.

Inexpensive

Hotel Papagayo, Motolinea 13, a short walk from the plaza, tel. 777/314-1711, email: hotelpapagayo@prodigy.net.nx, has 73 tidy rooms with linoleum floors in a brick building. The hotel has a swimming pool, playground, and parking lot in the central area. Rates: US$38 s/d.

Hostería del Sol, Privada Hidalgo 3, just off the plaza, tel. 777/312-4152, has only a couple of rooms (some with views) in a lovely old house, often taken by language students. It offers discounts for stays of a week or more. Rates: US$42 s, US$88 d, US$27 s by the week.

Moderate

On a quiet street up against Jardín Borda, **Hotel Ilebal,** Chula Vista 7, tel. 777/318-2725, has 35 rooms with TVs, safe-deposit boxes, and terraces. The hotel has a friendly, helpful staff and a steam room, hot tub, and pool for guests. Rates: US$68.

Named in honor of the Malcom Lowry novel set in a fictionalized Cuernavaca, **Bajo El Volcán,** on Humboldt Palmira 119, tel. 777/312-4873, www.tourbymexico.com/bajoelvolcan, has 27 tiled rooms; some have terraces. The patio features a medium-size pool. Rooms in the newer section of the hotel boast a view of the river and fields. Breakfast is included with the room. Rates: US$71 s, US$74 d.

Expensive

Just east of the Mexico City highway, **Hacienda de Cortés,** Plaza Kennedy 90, Atlacomulco, tel. 777/316-0867, fax 777/315-0035, www.haciendadecortes.com, is just what it purports to be: an old hacienda built by the legendary conquistador, on the outskirts of Cuernavaca just off the highway to Tepoztlán. Occupied briefly during the Revolution by the equally legendary Emiliano Zapata, and later destroyed, the hacienda lay in ruins until the 1970s, when it was restored. The 22 rooms are quite a good value if you don't mind staying outside of Cuernavaca. The gardens and outdoor pool are a great spot to relax. Rates: US$108 s/d, US$135 junior suite, US$165 suite.

Premium

The cozy, 14-room **Posada María Cristina,** Blvd. Juárez 300 (one block from the Palacio de Cortés), tel. 777/318-5767, www.maria-cristina.com, offers colonial atmosphere with amenities including a swimming pool, lovely gardens, and an excellent restaurant. Suites with king-sized beds and hot tubs are available. Rates: US$130–180.

Near the entrance to the Mexico City-Acapulco freeway, about a five-minute drive from the city center, **Calinda Racquet Club,** Francisco Villa 100, tel. 777/311-2400, fax 777/317-5483, www.hotelescalinda.com.mx, is for folks who really want to play tennis. The colonial-style building is surrounded by beautiful gardens and has all the amenities you expect at a luxury hotel. Rooms offer a variety of layouts including separate sitting areas. Rates: US$170–240.

Camino Real Sumiya, in Colonia José Parras near the highway exit to Tepoztlán and Cuautla, tel. 777/320-9199, fax 777/320-9142, U.S./Canada reservations 800/7-CAMINO, www.caminoreal.com, offers a taste of the Orient here in central Mexico. The main part of the hotel was carried across the ocean in pieces from Japan under the direction of heiress Barbara Hutton, whose fine art collection graces the hotel's walls. The hotel has 163 rooms looking onto acres of Japanese-style gardens and walking paths. The restaurant features an international menu highlighted by excellent Japanese cuisine. Rates: US$210 s/d, or up to US$420 for a top suite.

Las Mañanitas, Ricardo Linares 107, tel. 777/314-1466, fax 777/317-5483, www.lasmananitas.com.mx, a 15-minute walk from the city center, is considered one of the best hotels in Mexico. The verdant grounds, in addition to the resident peacocks, feature an elegant swimming pool and plenty of intimate nooks to sit and enjoy the refined ambience. The relaxing hotel bar is a great place to unwind even if you're not staying at the hotel. The hotel has only 22 rooms, and service is superb. Only American Express credit cards are accepted. Rates: US$151 s/d, US$345 suite.

FOOD

While not known for any particular regional cuisine, Cuernavaca has a large selection of quality Mexican and international restaurants catering to visitors and part-time residents.

Cafés

For breakfast and light meals, or just a cup of strong coffee, check out **Café La Parroquía** on the east side of Jardín Juárez, with tables out on the sidewalk.

Mexican

About a block from the *zócalo,* **Pozolería El Barco,** Calle I. Rayon 5-F, specializes in *pozole,* a flavorful hominy stew with your choice of beef, pork, or chicken (vegetarian upon request).

Right next door is **Tacos Tumbras,** a clean, unpretentious eatery serving low-priced tacos, *alambres, comida corridas,* and breakfasts daily 8:30 A.M.–9 P.M.

La Madriguera del Conejo, Av. Domingo Diez 1880, tel. 777/313-2604, is a very popular restaurant for its excellent, hearty food. As the name connotes, the house specialty is rabbit *(conejo),* but other types of meat and fowl are also on the menu. Open daily 1–8 P.M.

Las Mañanitas, Ricardo Linares 107, tel. 777/314-1466, serves delicious (though pricey) food and cocktails on a terrace overlooking the

© RAUL ORTEGA

stirring *cazuelas*

hotel gardens. It always has a fresh seafood meal of the day—a treat for the palate—as well as other specials. Open daily noon–5 P.M. and 7–11 P.M.

La Guelaguetza, Domingo Diez 64, tel. 777/313-7665, features Oaxacan specialties such as *enmoladas* (enchiladas in *mole* instead of chile sauce; US$5), or (for the adventurous) fried grasshoppers. Open daily 2–8 P.M.

Just off the *zócalo* is **Gaia,** Benito Juárez 102, tel. 777/312-3656, serving contemporary Mexican cuisine with a Mediterranean touch at midrange prices. Open Mon.–Sat. for lunch and dinner, Sun. lunch only. Vegetarian dishes available.

International

A couple of blocks from the *zócalo,* **Wah-Yen,** at Blvd. Benito Juárez 20, tel. 777/318-9648, serves a good plateful of Cantonese-style Chinese food at moderate prices. Open daily 2–9 P.M.

La Strada, Salazar 38, tel. 777/318-6085, in a 300-year-old building at the rear of the Palacio de Cortés in the city center (go to the left of the building and then almost to the bottom of the stairs), serves very respectable Neapolitan-style Italian food at moderate prices. Specialties include calamari in white wine and *medaglioni La Strada,* beef in red wine with purple onion. Open Mon.–Thurs. 1:30–11 P.M., Fri.–Sat. 1:30 P.M.–midnight, Sun. 2–10 P.M.

Another popular Italian restaurant is **Marco Polo,** Hidalgo 30 right in front of the cathedral, tel. 777/312-3484. The upstairs dining room is always packed, often with foreign visitors, enjoying the relaxed ambience and decent food. It serves a great cappuccino. Don't go in a rush as service is less than stellar. Open Mon.–Thurs. 1:30–10:30 P.M., Fri.–Sat. 1:30 P.M.–midnight, Sun. 1:30–10 P.M.

For a taste of German and Austrian cooking (or a close approximation, at least), try **Restaurant Vienes,** Lerdo de Tejada 11-B (a block from Jardín Juárez), tel. 777/318-4044. This is also a good spot to come for a cup of coffee and cake. Open daily 8 A.M.–10 P.M.

La Fontana Pizza has two locations in Cuernavaca: Juárez 19, Col. Centro, tel. 777/314-3040, and Calzada de los Reyes 14, tel. 777/317-9310. You can go in and enjoy a pizza, pasta, or *troncos* (baked sandwiches), or have it delivered. Open noon–midnight.

RECREATION AND ENTERTAINMENT

Golf

The city's several golf courses are all private, although some of the higher-end hotels can arrange access for you. Expect to pay US$50 weekdays and up to US$150 on weekends for greens fees. Local courses include **Club de Golf de Cuernavaca,** Vivero 1, Col. Club de Golf, tel. 777/312-0600; **Club de Golf Tabachin,** Fracc. Tabachin, tel. 777/312-3845; and **Club de Golf Santa Fe,** on the highway to Acapulco, about 20 minutes south of Cuernavaca.

Tennis

Many of the more expensive hotels in Cuernavaca have courts, and two public courts can be found on Domingo Diez. You can also rent courts by the hour at: **Tennis Palace,** Paseo del Conquistador 903, tel. 777/313-6500; **Villa International de Tenis,** Chalma 702, tel. 777/380-3845; and **Calinda Racquet Club,** Francisco Villa 100, tel. 777/311-2400.

Water Sports

Just eight km (five miles) down the free highway toward Taxco, **Temixco** is a *balneario* (Mexican bathing resort) with pools everywhere you look. It has 22 pools, filled with slides and other water games, as well as a wave pool. The resort occupies a former hacienda that started as a sugar plantation owned by Martin Cortés, son of Hernán, and then served as a fort during the Mexican Revolution. Vestiges of the old hacienda are still seen around the complex. The Ruta Temixco *combi* from Calle Galeana in Cuernavaca will take you there. If you're driving, follow the toll highway toward Acapulco and turn off on the Las Brisas exit. Open daily 9 A.M.–6 P.M.; US$10 entrance fee adults, or US$5 kids up to 1.25 meters tall. For more information call 777/325-0355.

Nightlife

The pedestrian street Fray Bartolomé de las Casas has several outdoor bars very popular with young folks both local and foreign to gather, shoot the breeze, and have a drink. A few of the places, such as Rincón Bohemio, El Garage, and Eclipse, have live music of varying quality.

Long-time nightlife stalwart **Barba Azúl** at Pradera 10 is known as a gay club but frequented by one and all for the thumping techno music. It charges a cover of US$8; drinks are US$2–3 each. Latin music lovers should drop in at **Zúmbale,** Bajada de Chapultepec 13, tel. 777/320-7430, where a live band keeps the salsa dancers swinging Thursday–Saturday. **Rumba,** at Paseo del Conquistador 178 in Col. Lomas de Cortés, also has live Latin music Thursday–Saturday.

Live performances of music and theater are often staged at the **Teatro de la Ciudad** at Morelos and Rayon, the **Teatro Ocampo** on the *zócalo,* and **Jardín Borda.** Ask at the tourist office for upcoming shows.

INFORMATION AND SERVICES

Tourist Information

The Morelos state tourist office, Av. Morelos Sur 187, tel. 777/314-3872 or 777/314-3920, stocks lots of literature in English, including information on the city's language schools and archaeological sites. It's open Mon.–Fri. 8 A.M.–5 P.M., Sat.–Sun. 10 A.M.–3 P.M.

The city runs small tourist booths in the bus stations, open daily 10 A.M.–5 P.M., but with limited information.

Services

The main post office is found at the south side of the plaza, next to the government palace; open Mon.–Fri. 8 A.M.–7 P.M., Sat. 8 A.M.–1 P.M.

For Internet access, head to MVP Internet, Gutenberg 2 just off the plaza, tel. 777/314-4567. It charges US$.5 a minute. Open Mon.–Sat. 9 A.M.–9 P.M., Sun. 10 A.M.–9 P.M.

Bancomer, on the Jardín Juárez, and Banamex, on Matamoros at Arteaga, just north of the Jardín Juárez, exchange dollars or traveler's checks at good rates.

Hospital General, Domingo Diez at Guadalajara, tel. 777/311-2209, has some English-speaking doctors. Farmacia Cuernavaca, Dr. Goméz Azcarte 200 (right next to the Hospital General), tel. 777/311-4111, is open 24 hours.

Language Schools

Cuernavaca has dozens of language schools. For a complete list of schools and prices, contact the local tourist office. Prices start around US$250 per week for one-on-one classes or US$135 for classes with five people.

Four of the better-known schools are: **Center for Bilingual Multicultural Studies,** Apdo. Postal 1520, Cuernavaca, Morelos 62000, tel. 777/313-0402, fax 777/317-0533, U.S. tel. 800/932-2068, email: admission@bilingual-center.com; **Cuauhnáhuac Escuela Cuernavaca,** Apdo. Postal 5–26, Cuernavaca, Morelos 62051, tel. 777/312-3673, fax 777/318-2693, U.S. tel. 713/292-1614, www.cuauhnahuac.edu.mx; **Cemanahuac,** San Juan 4, Col. Las Palmas, tel. 777/318-6407, www.cemanahuac.com; and **Spanish Language Institute,** run by Language Link of Peoria, Illinois, tel. 800/552-2051, fax 309/692-2926, www.langlink.com.

GETTING THERE

Driving

If you're coming from Mexico City, you'll leave from the southern part of that city either by México 95 *libre* (free) or 95D *cuota* (toll). For the most part the two run parallel to each other, but the narrow, truck-filled free road takes considerably longer. The toll road, which costs US$6, is a fine open highway. Whichever road you take, consider making a snack stop at **Tres Marías,** a roadside village high in the mountains; it's famed for excellent *sopa de hongo* (mushroom soup), quesadillas, and other Mexican treats. At Tres Marías is a turnoff east to a mountain lake park called **Laguna de Zempoala,** a popular picnic spot for weekenders from the city.

By Bus

Four different bus companies serve Cuernavaca, each from a separate terminal.

Autobuses Pullman de Morelos runs buses to Mexico City's Terminal Tasqueña every 15 minutes 5 A.M.–9:30 P.M. for US$5.50, as well as to Tequisquitengo throughout the day for US$2.25. A direct bus to the Mexico City airport (20 daily) costs US$10. It has two terminals, one in the center of town at the corner of Abasolo and Netzahualcóyotl, tel. 777/314-3650, and the other in Col. La Selva, northeast of the *centro,* at Plan de Ayala 102, tel. 777/318-4638.

Estrella de Oro also has frequent buses to Mexico City for the same price, leaving from its terminal 1.5 km from the center of town at Morelos Sur 900, tel. 777/312-3055. If you don't want to flag a taxi, take a local bus going up the hill on Morelos; you can get off at the city center.

Flecha Roja/Estrella Blanca, Morelos 503 (at Arista), tel. 777/312-8190, has buses to Taxco (US$4.25; 12 buses daily), Mexico City (US$5.50; 20 buses daily), and Acapulco (US$22; six buses daily)

From its terminal about eight blocks from the city center, **Estrella Roja,** at Galeana 401 and Cuauhtemotzín, tel. 777/318-5934, runs buses 6 A.M.–7 P.M. to Cuautla and Puebla, for US$3 and US$8.50 respectively.

To get to Tepoztlán, hop one of the frequent-but-slow buses leaving from the market on Avenida López Mateos, just northeast of the city center.

GETTING AROUND

It's easy to get around Cuernavaca on foot; most of the main tourist attractions are within walking distance of the center of town. Local buses to different parts of the city cost about US$.30. Street taxis are inexpensive and usually quite safe, but after dark, you might want to call a *sitio* taxi. One reliable service is **Radio Taxis,** tel. 777/317-3766 or 777/317-3776. Taxi prices increase after sunset.

Car Rental

Car rental agencies in town include: **Hertz,** Av. Emiliano Zapata 611, Col. Tlatenango, tel. 777/313-1607; **Solar Auto,** Av. Benito Juárez 45, Col. Las Palmas, tel. 777/312-2588; and **Deguer Rent-A-Car,** Av. Morelos Sur, on the corner with Galeana, Col. Las Palmas, tel. 777/318-5466.

NEAR CUERNAVACA

Xochicalco Archaeological Site

About 42 km (26 miles) southwest of Cuernavaca, this hilltop ruin was once a city populated by at least 10,000 people. Archaeologists place the apogee date at A.D. 700, a time when the lights were going out in so many other cultures of Mexico. Scientists continue to find hints of Olmecs, Toltecs, and Maya among the ruins.

The most outstanding structure here is the **Pyramid of the Plumed Serpent,** marked by intricate geometric patterns and stone reliefs of sinuous serpents and men with plumed headpieces. On the back side of the main acropolis is a tunnel leading to a cave used by the priests of Xochicalco as a kind of subterranean observatory; a long vertical shaft dug by hand let full sunlight into the cave only on two days a year, when the angle of the sun was perfectly aligned with the shaft. The priests used these fixed dates as a reference point to check the accuracy of their calendar. Guides waiting at the entrance to the tunnel will give you an informative tour. They don't charge a fee, but tips are appreciated.

Be sure to bring water and a sun hat, especially if you go in the dry season, as the ruins can get scorching hot. During the rainy season, views from the hilltop across the surrounding lush mountains are lovely. Admission is US$4—free on Sunday—and includes entrance to a small museum (at the parking lot) that provides background on the site; you'll appreciate the ruins more if you visit the museum first. If you want to bring a video camera in, you'll pay an extra US$3.50. The site is open daily 9 A.M.–5 P.M.

To reach Xochicalco from Cuernavaca by car, drive south on México 95 or 95D to the turnoff past the town of Alpuyeca. Continue past the town of El Cabrito and turn north on the paved road (signed Xochicalco). To get to Xochicalco via public transport, catch a **Pullman de Morelos Laser** bus from Cuernavaca to Coatlan, and from here take a US$2–3 taxi up to the ruins. Alternatively, hop a second-class bus from the Cuernavaca market directly to the ruins for a mere US$1. The last bus returns to Cuernavaca from the ruins at 6 P.M.

Lago Tequesquitengo

About 40 minutes south of Cuernavaca off the highway to Acapulco, this lake is a favorite among locals for camping, swimming, and water-skiing. Pullman de Morelos runs regular buses to the lake from its city center terminal for US$2.

Parque Acuático Las Estacas

A great spot for cooling off on a hot afternoon, especially during the week when it's not so crowded, is this water park five km from the small town of Tlaltizapán. Built around a small, crystalline river draped in jungly flora, with grassy meadows to relax on, Las Estacas has been the scene of several Mexican and U.S. movies, including one of the Tarzan series (1967) and more recently *Beat* with Keifer Sutherland and Courtney Love. The entrance fee is US$11. To get there, take a Pullman de Morelos bus from Cuernavaca (US$2) or from Terminal Tasqueña in D.F. (US$7 direct) to the town of Jojutla, and from there take either a minibus or taxi to Las Estacas. If you're driving, take the highway to Cuautla from Cuernavaca, and at the town of Yautepec turn south to Jojutla-Tlaltizapán. For more information, call locally 734/345-0077 or 734/345-0159, or in Cuernavaca 777/312-4412. In nearby Tlaltizapán was the general headquarters of Emiliano Zapata during the Mexican Revolution. The building now holds the **Museo de la Revolución del Sur** (Museum of the Southern Revolution). Nearby is an impressive 17th-century sugar hacienda, **Ex-Hacienda de San Francisco Temilpa,** worth a visit if you're coming this way.

Tepoztlán

Tucked into a lush valley up against a wall of cliffs about 30 km (18.5 miles) northeast of Cuernavaca, Tepoztlán enjoys a ruggedly beautiful setting. Mythical birthplace of the Mesoamerican god Quetzalcóatl, the town is steeped in Indian tradition. Older residents still speak Náhuatl, and the town's biggest festival of the year (September 8) honors Tepoztecatl, the god of *pulque,* drunkenness, and fertility.

For centuries a sleepy little village, Tepoztlán has in recent years developed into both a favorite weekend getaway for Mexico City residents and a budding artist community with a vaguely hippie/New Age feel. Although the people of Tepoztlán seem content enough with all the cafés, art shops, and weekend visitors, they keep tourism on their own terms. When wealthy developers tried to build a golf course outside of town in 1995, residents decided that was too much. They deposed the town government that had backed the project, organized a committee to run the town, and eventually saw the project canceled.

The town center of Tepoztlán turns into one big market on weekends. The many shops sell all variety of jewelry, art, and clothing from around the world, while locals sell Mexican handicrafts in outdoor stalls on the streets and in front of the church.

ORIENTATION

A small town nestled into one end of a narrow valley, Tepoztlán itself is quite easy to negotiate on foot. The main road leading into Tepoztlán from Cuernavaca and Mexico City is called Avenida 5 de Mayo until after it passes the town square, where it becomes Avenida del Tepozteco, dead-ending at the beginning of the trail up to a small pyramid in the hills. The pyramid, perched on a shoulder of one of the mountains directly behind town, can be seen from the town center.

Branching off 5 de Mayo to the right (east) next to the plaza, Avenida Revolución descends past the church and out of town on the free road toward Oaxtepec.

SIGHTS

Apart from the church and pyramid described below, among the town's main tourist activities are shopping in the weekend handicrafts market or simply enjoying a walk around town. (For information on hikes in the nearby hills, see Near Tepoztlán later in this section.)

Capilla de Nuestra Señora de la Asunción

Tepoztlán's imposing church and adjacent Dominican monastery seems more like a castle than a religious complex and reflects the tenuous situation of the Spanish missionaries when the church was built in the mid-16th century. Although it is simply decorated inside, the church's facade is adorned with interesting sculptures of both Spanish and Amerindian designs. The Christmas midnight Mass, held in the candlelit courtyard, is a lovely experience even for non-Catholics.

A Dominican monastery, **Ex-Convento de la Natividad,** has been restored and now serves as a regional museum. Open Tues.–Sun. 10 A.M.–5 P.M.; free admission.

Museo Arqueológico Colleción Carlos Pellier

This small museum at the rear of the church houses a tasteful though poorly displayed collection of pre-Hispanic pottery from Totonac, Aztec, and Olmec cultures. Open Tues.–Sun. 10 A.M.–6 P.M.; admission US$.50.

Pirámide de Tepozteco

Perched on a ledge in the hills 400 meters (1,300 feet) above Tepoztlán is a 10-meter-high pyramid dedicated to Tepoztecatl, the Aztec god of plenty and the legendary creator of *pulque.* The pyramid itself is not much to see, but the chance to hike up into the hills and catch views of the Tepoztlán valley below make it well worth the trip.

From town it's a hike of about two km to the pyramid. Although plenty of nonathletes make their way up the narrow and at times steep 1.2-km trail, be prepared for a good hour's workout. Wear sturdy shoes and avoid weekends or you'll feel as though you're hiking up with the entire population of Mexico City. Open Tues.–Sun. 9:30 A.M.–5 P.M.; admission US$2.

ACCOMMODATIONS

If you don't have a reservation on the weekend, it's unlikely you'll find a room in Tepoztlán. During the week it's usually no problem to show up without reservations, at least at the less expensive hotels.

Shoestring

At the bottom end of the price scale is the conveniently located **Hospedaje Mely,** Av. 5 de Mayo 5, tel. 739/395-1196. The friendly family rents out eight spartan but relatively clean rooms, each with two beds. It often has space even on weekends. Rates: US$13 for 1–4 people.

Budget

A major step up is **Mesón Amanda,** at Cuauhtemotzín 2, tel. 739/395-1537. A block off 5 de Mayo, it's a very quiet little family-run hotel with only four rooms (two more under construction at last report), each creatively decorated, well kept, and set around a small courtyard. Rates: US$27 s/d.

Moderate

Hotel Tepoztlán, Calle de las Industrias 6, tel. 739/395-0523, fax 739/395-0503, offers a full health spa with massage, sauna, and *temazcal* (an Aztec sauna). Rooms in the large concrete (not overly attractive) building are modern and clean, and prices include a buffet breakfast. Rates: US$72 s, US$82 d.

Expensive

By far the best hotel in town is **La Posada del Tepozteco,** Paraíso 5 (a block above the square), tel. 739/395-0010, fax 739/395-0323. Many rooms offer great views overlooking town and valley. The garden patio is a supremely pleasant place to sip a drink and contemplate the beautiful scenery. This is a fine place to come and enjoy a meal with a view, even if you don't stay in the hotel. Rates: US$137 s/d with breakfast.

Camping

About three km (1.8 miles) west of town, against the foot of the mountains, you can pitch a tent at **Mextitla** for US$4 per person. Showers and food are available. The hills behind the camp are a popular spot for hiking and rock-climbing.

FOOD

Budget travelers should check out the *mercado* (market), where several *loncherías* and *comedores* offer healthy and inexpensive *comidas corridas.* One of the stalls even offers a vegetarian *comida.* Or for a light snack, choose from the piles of magnificent produce grown in this lush region. The avocados are particularly sublime.

Downhill from the plaza, **Lilah's,** Av. Revolución 60, tel. 739/395-0387, serves remarkably well-prepared and healthy food in a small courtyard patio. Run by three sisters, the restaurant offers pita and submarine sandwiches, pasta, salads, and vegetarian dishes as well as a few treats such as grilled tuna or Cornish hen. Open Thurs. 1–6 P.M., Fri.–Sun. 1–9 P.M.

At the end of Avenida del Tepozteco, right at the foot of the hills in a house set amidst a jungle of trees and plants, is **Restaurant Axitla,** tel. 739/395-0519. It's well worth the 10-minute walk from the square for the extensive menu of tasty, reasonably priced meals, both Mexican and international. Most of the entrées come with rice or potatoes and a large salad. Open Wed.–Sun. 10 A.M.–7 P.M.; special arrangements can be made ahead of time for groups to eat later.

For classic, well-prepared Mexican specialties, go to **Colorines,** on Av. al Tepozteco three blocks north of the plaza. The ambience is colorful and cheerful, and the food is authentic, hearty, and moderately priced (US$4–6 a plate). Open Mon.–Fri. 9:30 A.M.–7:30 P.M., weekends 8:30 A.M.–8 P.M.

The classiest restaurant in town is **El Ciruelo,** Zaragoza 17 (behind the market), tel. 739/395-1203 or 739/395-1037, which features an outdoor patio with views of the mountains, an elegant atmosphere, and creative cuisine. Dishes include *enchiladas de pato* (duck enchiladas), chicken breast in mole and plum sauce, beef fajitas with nopal, and chiles rellenos stuffed with seafood and bathed in a goat-cheese sauce. Meals run US$6–10, or more with drinks and dessert. Open Wed.–Thurs. 1:30–6 P.M., Fri.–Sat. 1–11:30 P.M., Sun. 1–7:30 P.M.

TRANSPORTATION

Bus

Autobuses Pullman de Morelos, Av. 5 de Mayo, tel. 739/395-0520, run 16 buses a day to Terminal Tasqueña in Mexico City, between 8 A.M. and 7:30 P.M., for US$5. Travelers must take a minibus (free) up to the gas station outside of town from the terminal because the big buses are no longer allowed in town. It's also possible to go up to the toll booth above town and hop any passing first-class bus to Mexico from Cuautla for the same price.

A few blocks farther up the road toward Cuernavaca is the second-class bus terminal, where you can catch one of the frequent buses to Cuernavaca.

Car

The two-lane free road between Cuernavaca and Tepoztlán, which passes through farmland and several villages, takes about a half hour to drive. Most auto-equipped tourists coming to Tepoztlán from Mexico City take the Cuernavaca toll highway (US$6), turning off before Cuernavaca onto a branch toll road west to Tepoztlán (US$1.90). It's also possible to drive to or from Mexico City via a lesser known but lovely highway, which cuts across the mountains east of Tepoztlán and arrives in Xochimilco. The drive takes longer than on the toll road, but if you're not in a hurry the forests and mountain views are worth it.

NEAR TEPOZTLÁN

Forming the dramatic backdrop to Tepotzlán is the Sierra del Tepozteco, a jagged formation covered in dense vegetation. Above and behind the Sierra del Tepozteco rise the volcanic mountains forming the southern part of the Valle de México, which in this region is protected as the **Parque Nacional Corredor Chichinautzin.** Both ranges offer plenty of hiking opportunities for the adventurous.

San Juan

Perched on a high plateau in the Tepozteco mountains, San Juan is a Náhua town of farmers surrounded by pine forest, about 10 km (six miles) by road from Tepoztlán. San Juan is a good place to take a walk in the woods, either farther up into the national park or down to Tepoztlán; ask around in town for good places to go hiking. Following an old set of railroad tracks between Mexico City and Cuernavaca, passing through San Juan, is one recommended way.

To Tepoztlán, one can either follow the old railbed down from San Juan, then turn off on a path down to the Tepozteco pyramid, or go farther east from San Juan to the next valley, where a trail descends to the Mextitla campground just outside of Tepoztlán. Either hike would take a couple of hours—ask for directions in San Juan to find the trail entrances.

Those interested in trying a traditional Náhua sauna *(temazcal)* should consider trying the one in San Juan. Run by several Náhua women in a local community center, the *temazcal* is open on Saturday only, from early morning until early afternoon. The ladies are very friendly and helpful—if you speak some Spanish they'll tell you a great deal about the tradition of the *temazcal.* Clothing is optional, and visitors may get in or out of the large, mud-baked chamber as often as they like. Bathers are wrapped in blankets afterward and even served a bowl of delicious vegetable soup. The experience is perhaps not for everyone, but it's definitely interesting and physically rewarding. The cost is US$14 per person.

Buses run between Tepotzlán and San Juan every hour or so and cost about US$.50, while a taxi runs around US$3.

Amatlán

Another town that serves as a good place to start hiking into the mountains is Amatlán, at the far eastern edge of the Tepoztlán valley. Amatlán has in recent years become a favorite spot for artists and alternative lifestyle types from Mexico City and elsewhere to build houses. It's possible to hike from Amatlán up several different trails to different points in the Sierra Tepozteco, with great views of the valley and of Volcán Popocatépetl to the east.

Regular *combis* leave Tepotzlán for Amatlán (US$.50), or you can take a taxi for US$3–5, depending on how rich you look.

Toluca and Vicinity

The capital of the State of Mexico, Toluca lies 67 km (41 miles) west of Mexico City. Perched in the mountains at an elevation of 2,680 meters (8,816 feet), it's the country's highest state capital. Toluca is a large and growing industrial city not frequented by tourists, but the city center still has a few buildings and parks from its colonial past.

SIGHTS

Most of Toluca's sights of note are clustered around the broad, open Plaza de los Mártires or the adjacent Plaza Garibay and can easily be visited on foot. A block south of the Plaza de los Mártires, right behind the cathedral, are the *portales* (arched colonnades) where Tolucans come to eat, shop, and pass the time of day. The principal *portal* with 44 arches is **Portal Madero,** which runs in front of Avenida Hidalgo. **Portal Constitución** on the east side has 37 arches, and **Portal Reforma,** the smallest of the three with 35 arches, is on the west side. Between the *portales* and the cathedral is a small, hidden square, with a round, simple chapel in the middle.

© MAURICIO RAMOS

neoclassical house facade, Toluca

Plaza de los Mártires

Several colonial buildings, most built of the local dark volcanic stone, face the central plaza, including the **Catedral de la Diocesis de Toluca,** begun in 1573 and finished in 1797. The church is one of the largest in the country and sports a rather severe neoclassical facade, with two rows of columns. Facing the principal altar on the right side is a *portada* (entranceway) leading into a separate but adjacent church. For years the entrance was blocked off, but it was recently reopened. Other buildings in the plaza include the adjacent neoclassical **Palacio Municipal,** and, on the far side, the 18th-century **Templo de la Santa Veracruz.** Half a block west is the visually interesting modern **Teatro Morelos,** a brick cube ringed by copper arches.

Cosmo Vitral Jardín Botánico

This botanical garden, at the eastern end of Plaza Garibay, lies within the walls of a 19th-century market building sporting 54 stained-glass panels. The panels—created by Leopoldo Flores over a period of three years—portray the story of humanity. The blazingly colorful glass art makes a fine backdrop for the garden's 400 different species of plants and flowers from Mexico, Central and South America, Africa, and Asia. Open Tues.–Sun. 9 A.M.–5 P.M.; admission US$1.25.

Museums

Eight km (five miles) west of the city center, the **Centro Cultural Mexiquense** (Mexican Cultural Center) is an impressive complex holding three museums—**Museo de Antropología, Museo de Culturas Populares,** and **Museo de Arte Moderno**—that contain some of the state's finest exhibits. The creatively designed buildings (the art museum looks like a space ship sunken

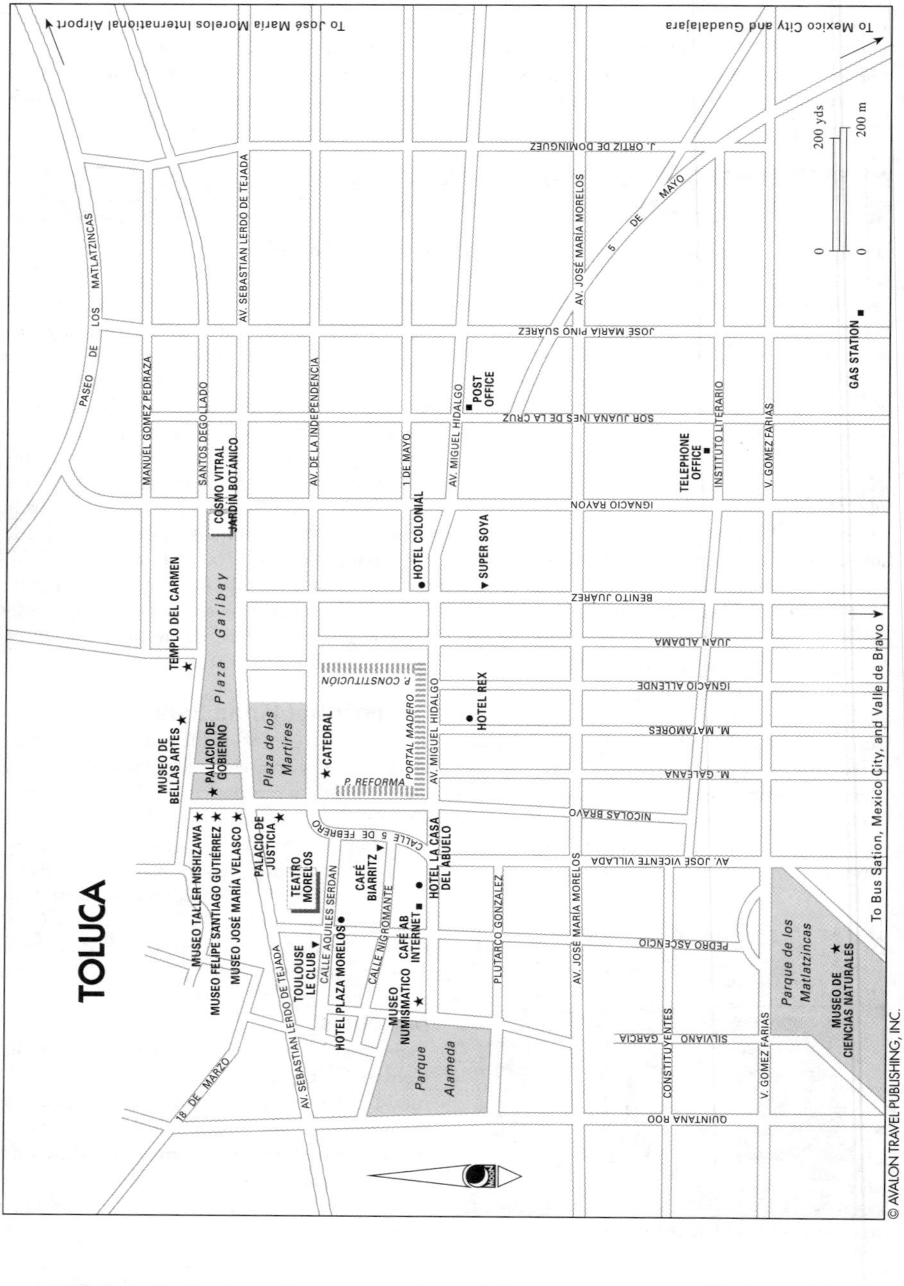

EXCURSIONS

TOLUCA

To José María Morelos International Airport
To Mexico City and Guadalajara
To Bus Sation, Mexico City, and Valle de Bravo

PASEO DE LOS MATLATZINCAS
MANUEL GOMEZ PEDRAZA
SANTOS DEGOLLADO
AV. SEBASTIAN LERDO DE TEJADA
AV. DE LA INDEPENDENCIA
1 DE MAYO
AV. MIGUEL HIDALGO
AV. JOSÉ MARÍA MORELOS
INSTITUTO LITERARIO
V. GOMEZ FARIAS
J. ORTIZ DE DOMINGUEZ
5 DE MAYO
JOSE MARÍA PINO SUAREZ
SOR JUANA INES DE LA CRUZ
IGNACIO RAYON
BENITO JUAREZ
JUAN ALDAMA
IGNACIO ALLENDE
M. MATAMORES
M. GALEANA
NICOLAS BRAVO
AV. JOSÉ VICENTE VILLADA
PEDRO ASCENCIO
SILVIANO GARCIA
QUINTANA ROO
CONSTITUYENTES
PLUTARCO GONZALEZ
18 DE MARZO
CALLE 5 DE FEBRERO
CALLE AQUILES SERDAN
CALLE NIGROMANTE
P. CONSTITUCIÓN
PORTAL MADERO
P. REFORMA

Plaza Garibay
Plaza de los Martires
Parque Alameda
Parque de los Matlatzincas

TEMPLO DEL CARMEN
MUSEO DE BELLAS ARTES
PALACIO DE GOBIERNO
COSMO VITRAL JARDÍN BOTÁNICO
CATEDRAL
MUSEO TALLER NISHIZAWA
MUSEO FELIPE SANTIAGO GUTIÉRREZ
MUSEO JOSÉ MARÍA VELASCO
PALACIO DE JUSTICIA
TEATRO MORELOS
CAFÉ BIARRITZ
HOTEL LA CASA DEL ABUELO
CAFÉ AB INTERNET
TOULOUSE LE CLUB
HOTEL PLAZA MORELOS
MUSEO NUMISMATICO
HOTEL COLONIAL
SUPER SOYA
HOTEL REX
POST OFFICE
TELEPHONE OFFICE
GAS STATION
MUSEO DE CIENCIAS NATURALES

0 200 yds
0 200 m

into the earth) comprise one of the finest cultural institutions in the country. Among the highlights are a huge, colorful "tree of life" from Metepec and artwork by famed Mexican painters such as Siqueiros, Rivera, and Orozco. Open Tues.–Sun. 9 A.M.–5 P.M.; admission is US$.60 per museum, or US$1.20 for all three. English-speaking guides are available. Get there via bus (Línea 2 de Marzo) or taxi. Opposite the complex is the imposing Tec de Monterrey University Toluca campus.

On Calle Santos Degollado find the 16th-century **Templo del Carmen** and, just to its west, the **Museo de Bellas Artes,** which houses paintings and sculptures from the 16th to the 19th centuries. Open Tues.–Sun. 10 A.M.–6 P.M.; admission US$.50. Around the corner on Nicolás Bravo are three small art museums: **Museo Felipe Santiago Gutiérrez, Museo José María Velasco** and **Museo Taller Nishizawa,** each free and open Tues.–Sun 10 A.M.–6 P.M.

Other museums (of limited interest to casual tourists) include the **Museo de Numismática** (money museum), Hidaglo Pte. 506, tel. 722/213-1927, and **Museo de Ciencias Naturales** (natural history museum), in Parque de los Matlatzincas, no telephone.

PRACTICALITIES

Accommodations

Hotel Rex, Matamoros 101, tel. 722/215-9300, offers 45 basic, unremarkable rooms. Rates: US$18 s, US$20 d.

La Casa del Abuelo, Hidalgo Pte. 404, tel. 722/213-3642, is a good deal in spite of the bizarre pink, Gaudiesque building that houses it, and it is often full as a result. Apart from basic, clean rooms, the hotel has a bar, restaurant, and private parking. Rates: US$22 s or US$27 d.

Hotel Colonial, Hidalgo 103 Ote., tel. 722/215-9700, two blocks east of the *portales* (arched colonnades), is about the best low-priced option. The large lobby is flanked by a restaurant on one side and a bar on the other—all around an interior patio. The hotel's 40 spacious rooms, each with TV and telephone, have high ceilings and wooden floors. Beware of rooms facing the street as they can be noisy. Parking is available. Rates: US$27 s, US$32 d.

At a higher price and comfort level, though in an unattractive modern building, **Hotel Plaza Morelos,** Aquiles Serdán 115, tel. 722/215-9201, is near the Teatro Morelos in the town center. The rooms, though a bit small, are clean and carpeted. Each has a TV and telephone. A parking lot and restaurant are downstairs. Rates: US$42 s, US$51 d.

High-end rooms can be found at **Hotel Fiesta Inn,** Paseo Tollocan Ote. 1132, tel. 722/276-1000, www.posadas.com.mx, with 140 rooms and four suites with all the amenities, as well as an indoor pool, gym, restaurant, and meeting rooms. Rates: US$125 s/d, US$135 junior suite.

Food

For snacks, head to the *portales* in the city center, where you'll find a couple of bakeries and plenty of vendors selling tamales and *atole* (a sweet, warm corn drink).

If you're looking for fresh juice, a *torta,* or a *comida corrida,* the health-food restaurant chain **Super Soya** has a branch at Juárez 111, half a block off Hidalgo. Open Mon.–Sat. 8 A.M.–9 P.M., Sun. 10 A.M.–7 P.M.

Coffee Station, in the *portales,* is an American-style café with espresso drinks, salads, croissants, yogurt, and baguette sandwiches at midrange prices.

Café Biarritz, at Nigromante 200 facing the side of the *catedral,* tel. 722/214-5757, is a good and inexpensive diner-type café with a large menu of standard Mexican meals. Open Mon.–Fri. 8 A.M.–11 P.M., Sat.–Sun. 8 A.M.–8 P.M. Similar is **Restaurant L'ambiant,** at Hidalgo 231 opposite Portal Madero, with an odd, bluish lighting (the "ambiant," perhaps?). Open daily 9 A.M.–9:30 P.M.

Toluca is known for its excellent cuts of meat and sausage, and one good place to give them a taste is **Las Costillas de Venustiano,** several blocks south of the town center at V. Carranza 201 at Aldama, tel. 722/270-4036. An unpretentious place with tables in front of a big grill and TVs invariably showing a soccer match (especially if the beloved Diablos of Toluca are playing), it serves an excellent *arrachera* plate with beans, guacamole, and tortillas for US$8. Also on offer is a variety of tacos and *alambres,* as well as the *chorizo mero toluca campeón,* a sausage named in honor of the soccer team's recent championship victories. Open daily noon–1 A.M.

For a cold beer and a game of pool, chess, or backgammon, check out **Toulouse Le Club,** at the corner of Aquiles Serdán and Pedro Ascencio, two blocks west of the cathedral. This relaxed spot is welcoming for old and young alike, and women will also feel quite comfortable here. Open Mon.–Sat. until midnight, Sun. until 10 P.M.

Information

The state tourism office, Paseo Tollocan and Calle Urawa, tel. 722/212-5836 and 722/212-6048, is east of the city center, past the bus terminal near the new IMSS clinic toward the exit to Mexico City; open Mon.–Fri. 9 A.M.–6 P.M. Unfortunately, they are quite unprepared to deal with the general public and not worth the effort it takes to get there.

Services

The main post office can be found at the corner of Hidalgo and Sor Juana Inés de la Cruz. Open Mon.–Fri. 9 A.M.–5 P.M., Sat. 10 A.M.–2 P.M.

Computel, 5 de Febrero 119 just west of the cathedral, offers long distance telephone and fax service and is open daily 7 A.M.–9 P.M.

Check your email or surf the Internet at Café AB, upstairs at Hidalgo 406, tel. 722/213-6557, charging US$1 for 30 minutes or US$1.50 an hour. The connections can be slow. Open Mon.–Sat. 9 A.M.–8 P.M.

Transportation

Flecha Roja, tel. 722/217-0285, and **Caminante,** tel. 722/217-0152, both offer buses between Toluca and the Terminal Observatorio in Mexico City every 10 minutes between 5 A.M. and 9:30 P.M. (US$3.50). Caminante also has direct buses to and from the Mexico City airport 17 times daily for US$8. **Primera Plus,** tel. 722/217-3485, runs buses to Morelia, six times daily, second class (US$14); Guadalajara, six times daily, first class (US$34); and Querétaro, every hour, first class (US$12). **Transportes Frontera,** tel. 722/217-1174, sells tickets for Taxco (US$8) and Acapulco (US$25) on Primera Clase; to Monterrey (US$55) and Nuevo Laredo (US$88) on Turistar Ejecutivo; and to Monterrey (US$55) and Nuevo Laredo (US$69) on regular first class Futura buses. **ETN,** tel. 722/217-7308, runs luxury buses to Guadalajara (US$45), San Luis Potosí (US$31), and Querétaro (US$16); all twice daily. It also has 20 buses a day to Mexico City (US$4.25).

Mexico-Toluca-Zinacantepec y Ramales, tel. 722/217-1596, has frequent buses throughout the day to Valle de Bravo (US$4). **TMT** runs frequent buses to El Oro (US$5). **Tres Estrellas del Centro** has frequent buses to Teotenango (US$.80), Ixtapan de la Sal (US$3.30), and Malinalco (US$3).

Once in Toluca, look for buses marked "Centro" if you're heading into the city center. To get back to the bus terminal, catch one of the buses on Morelos (near Juárez, two blocks from the *portales*) marked "Terminal." The terminal is about two km (1.2 miles) southeast of the town center. A taxi to/from the center costs US$2.

To leave the center of town by car, take Avenida Benito Juárez until it dead-ends into Paseo Tollocan, which exits toward Mexico City to the left (east) or to Valle de Bravo to the right (west).

NEAR TOLUCA

Teotenango Archaeological Site

The ominous-looking hilltop complex of Teotenango, 25 km (15.5 miles) south of Toluca, was established first by the local Teotenanca tribe, who were conquered by the Matlatzinca people in 1200 A.D. The Matlatzincas (whose name means "net-users" in Náhuatl, a reference to the people's frequent use of fishing nets) were in turn defeated by the Aztecs in 1477. One of the more fascinating artifacts found was a stone jaguar eating the sun, thought by some archaeologists to depict a solar eclipse. Other structures include a large ball court and several large squat temples. At the bottom of the hill where you pay your

US$1.25 admission, you'll pass a small museum holding some of the artifacts found during restoration. Open Tues.–Sun. 9 A.M.–5 P.M.

The site is just under a kilometer (half a mile) from the town of Tenango de Arista (also known as Tenango del Valle), which is serviced by frequent buses from Toluca (US$.80 with Tres Estrellas del Centro) and easily reached by bus and taxi combination. From Tenango tourists may either walk or take a US$1–2 taxi to get to the ruins. The town itself is a pleasant place to wander around for an hour or so to get a taste of rural life in the region. It's also known for its excellent *barbacoa,* which can be found in several restaurants or the local market.

Nevado de Toluca

The 4,691-meter (15,431-foot) Nevado de Toluca, sometimes called by its Náhuatl name, Xinantecatl (zee-nan-te-KAHT-el), is an inactive volcano with two small lakes in its crater and the fourth-highest mountain in Mexico. Tourists can drive up into the crater on a dirt road offering spectacular views, as long as it's not snowing (hence the name, *nevado,* which roughly translates to "snowy one"). From the crater it's another 500 meters or so of scrambling up to the actual crater rim. The 2–4-hour hike around the crater rim can be fun, but it is exposed and entails scrambling up lots of boulders and scree, so don't undertake it lightly.

In the late 1990s a Mexican development company had grandiose plans of building a ski resort on the mountain, but such ideas were put on hold by the local *campesinos,* who have part controlling rights of the forest. Apparently they feared that the necessary artificial snow-making would destroy their crops, or perhaps they just didn't like the idea of chopping up their mountain. At any rate, repeated protests put the project on indefinite hold.

To reach Nevado de Toluca by car, take México 134 heading west from Toluca. At Km 19, in the midst of pine forest, take México 3 south toward Texcaltitlán. Continue 7.3 km (4.5 miles), with great views of the volcano, to the dirt road turning off up the mountain, just past the village of **Raices.** From this turn, it's another 19 km (11.5 miles) of dirt road east to the crater, first through pine forest, and then above the tree line. Buses to Texcaltitlán and Sultepec can drop you at the turnoff, where you can hitch up on weekends. During the week there's very little traffic.

Part of the way up the road you'll pass a large *albergue* (hostel) with 200 bunk beds, hot water, and a kitchen. It's noisy on weekends but certainly cheap at US$3 per night. Camping is allowed anywhere on the mountain except in the crater.

El Oro

Right on the border with the State of Michoacán, 94 km northwest of Toluca via Atlacomulco, is this old mining town nestled into a hillside. Missionaries from the nearby Rancho de Guadalupe found chunks of gold around 1700, but it wasn't until the late 19th century that large-scale mining began, much of it undertaken by foreign miners. Although not a major destination for tourists, it's worth a day trip if you're interested in an offbeat place. There are no hotels to stay in in town, so plan on returning to Toluca or Mexico City by the end of the day.

The very friendly folks at the local tourist office, in the white and red **Palacio Municipal,** will happily take you on a tour of the town themselves if they aren't too busy, as they are eager to promote El Oro as a tourist destination. It's open Mon.–Fri. 9 A.M.–5 P.M., weekends 10 A.M.–4 P.M. Main sites include the Palacio itself, built in 1910, with an elegant old meeting hall on the top floor. Around the corner is the ornate **Teatro Juárez,** with four columns in front of its stone facade, open to the public to walk around daily 9 A.M.–5 P.M. Workers will turn the lights on for you to admire the interior if you ask. Several other buildings dating from the town's heyday are worth a look, including the old **Oro Club,** now housing a Bancomer bank. In the old railway station, a block uphill from the theater, is a collection of artisans selling their wares, including ceramics and woodwork.

A 10-minute walk above town is the free **Museo de la Minería del Estado de Mexico,** with lots of weird old mining gear, photos of the town during the mining boom, and rusted sculptures of two heroic looking miners and a woman sitting outside. During the week there's often no one around at all. Views over the town are good from the museum, making it a good excuse for a walk even if the exhibits don't do much for you. Open Tues.–Sat. 10 A.M.–6 P.M., Sun. 10 A.M.–3 P.M.

Several unpretentious eateries in town offer good food. One of the better ones is **Los Girasoles,** one block up from the theater on the second floor of a building formed by a fork in the road, run by a friendly matron who takes good care of her clients with very tasty *comida corridas* for US$4.50. Downstairs is a bakery. Open Tues.–Sun. 8 A.M.–8 P.M.

TMT buses run several times a day between El Oro and Toluca (US$5) and Terminal Observatorio in Mexico City (US$8).

IXTAPAN DE LA SAL

Thermal springs are the attraction at Ixtapan, a low-key spa/resort of about 25,000 people, 117 km from Mexico City. The mineral baths scattered around town have made Ixtapan a favored weekend getaway for people from Mexico City, Toluca, and Cuernavaca. All the locals will cheerfully tell you that the water is radioactive and can cure whatever ails you. More scientifically, the water comes out of the spring at 40.8°C, with a salt and mineral content of almost 10,000 parts per million. If your hotel doesn't have private baths, you can take a dip at the **Ixtapan Spa,** right at the entrance to town coming in from Toluca, Mexico City tel. 5254-0500, with pools ranging between 32 and 38°C, as well as regular swimming pools, for US$12 adults or US$6 for kids under 10. The **Balneario Municipal,** at the corner of Allende and 20 de Noviembre in the center of town, charges a mere US$2.50 for a hot bath or US$8 for a massage.

Between Ixtapan and Toluca, the highway passes very lovely stretches of countryside, with many hillside towns specializing in growing flowers. Two towns worth a visit if you're coming through in your own car are Santa Ana and Tenancingo.

Accommodations

Hotels in town tend to be of the all-inclusive variety, offering package rates that include room, meals, and spa services. One of the less expensive places in town is **Hotel Mari's,** right across from the municipal spa at Allende 7, tel. 721/143-0195, a family-run place with its own restaurant. Double or triple occupancy only unless there are not many visitors in town and you can negotiate. Rates: US$18 per person with breakfast.

Hotel Don Isidro, on Av. Juárez Norte just down from the Ixtapan Spa, tel. 721/143-0315, is also a decent low-priced option. Rates: US$27 s, US$33 d. **Hotel Casa Blanca,** Juárez 615, tel. 721/143-0036, has a hot pool and a restaurant that stays open all day. Rooms are spread around the one-level complex, with tropical plants everywhere. Rates: US$80 d with three meals.

A new upscale hotel outside of town, **Rancho San Diego,** Mexico City tel. 5254-7491 or Ixtapan tel. 721/143-4000, www.ranchosandiego.com.mx, offers all-inclusive stays with plenty of activities to keep you entertained, such as tennis, rappel, waterslides, mountain biking, or just relaxing on the many patios and enjoying the atmosphere. The complex is interestingly designed, with modern-style buildings painted in earth tones with wood beams. Rates: US$215 d with private mineral bath, US$193 d without.

Food

Check out the string of restaurants on Avenida Juárez Norte between the Ixtapan Spa and town. One good one is **Restaurante Los Arcos,** with a filling set meal for US$6, or US$4–8 entrées from the menu.

Transportation and Services

Tres Estrellas del Centro runs buses between Terminal Observatorio in Mexico City and Ixtapan de la Sal every hour 7 A.M.–7 P.M. (US$7); and to Toluca (US$3.30).

Tourist information can be found at the bus station, 1.5 km from town on the road toward Taxco.

Las Grutas de la Estrella

Past Ixtapan, about 17 km down the road toward Taxco, is the turnoff to Las Grutas de la Estrella, or Star Caves, carved out of a limestone mountain by millennia of rushing water. Pay a mere US$2 for a wander in an impressive series of caverns and side chambers, replete with bizarre rock formations. Through parts of the cave rushes the Río Zapote, which in the height of the rain season can flood the caverns. The caves were first explored thoroughly in 1956, revealing an altar to Tlaloc and other pre-Hispanic artifacts. Open Tues.–Sun. 10 A.M.–6 P.M. To get there by bus, take a Tres Estrellas bus from Ixtapan toward Taxco, and get off at the turnoff for the caves (US$2).

MALINALCO

This beautiful town is set amidst dramatic scenery in a remote corner of the mountains between Toluca and Cuernavaca. It's well worth the trip just to have a chance to see this not oft-visited region as well as to check out the 16th-century convent in the center of town and the impressive archaeological site on a hill just outside of Malinalco. Because of its natural beauty and bucolic ambience, Malinalco has become a popular spot for Mexico City residents to have a weekend home.

Malinalco was a strategic spot dominating a mountain pass and was not conquered by the Aztecs until shortly before the arrival of the Spaniards. The Aztec ruins are thought to have been a means of impressing the local population with the empire's dominance. After the Spanish conquest, a mission of seven Augustinian monks made their way to Malinalco in 1540 to begin evangelization of what was considered an important region. Malinalco also served as a strategic site during the Mexican Revolution, when it was used as a base by Zapata's troops.

Ex-Convento de la Transfiguración

Dominating the center of town is this impressive Augustinian monastery dating from the 1540s. Similar in style to the convent in Tepotzlán, the church itself (dedicated to San Salvador) is unadorned and fortresslike, while the cloister to the side is in two levels around an open garden. Decorating the walls of the cloister are very beautiful murals of flowers and animals. Visitors are free to wander around both the church and the cloister at no charge. Note an obviously pre-Hispanic carved rock sitting on a stump in front of the church.

Malinalco Archaeological Site

This famous temple complex sits on a bluff about one km west of the town of Malinalco, all uphill on a dirt road. The small but impressive site was built by the Aztecs starting in 1501, although archaeologists believe they built on a preexisting temple. The six monuments are carved directly out of the mountain rock, which was the only time the Aztecs used this technique. The principal structure is the **Temple of the Eagle,** thought to

© CHRIS HUMPHREY

trimming flowers for holiday decorations in the Ex-Convento de la Transfiguración

have been where Eagle and Tiger Aztec warriors were initiated into their cult. Two carved ocelots flank the steep stairway up to the circular temple, which has a carved eagle in the center and jaguars around it. Views from the ruins across the town and surrounding countryside are magnificent. The long stairway up to the ruins is a bit of slog, but it's broken up with interesting write-ups (in three languages: English, Spanish, and Náhuatl) on the site itself and local history, culture, and environment. Open Tues.–Sun. 9 A.M.–5:30 P.M., admission is US$3 (free on Sunday), and US$3 more for a video camera.

Visible from the stairway up is **Rincón de San Miguel,** a small chapel with pre-Hispanic ruins to one side. This is the where the town holds its annual festival on September 29. According to the guards at the main ruins, the hillsides around Malinalco are littered with unexcavated ruins. If you'd like to take a walk in the hills, one place to go is up the cobblestoned road past the turnoff to the ruins, which soon becomes a footpath across the mountains to the town of Tenancingo, about 15 km away.

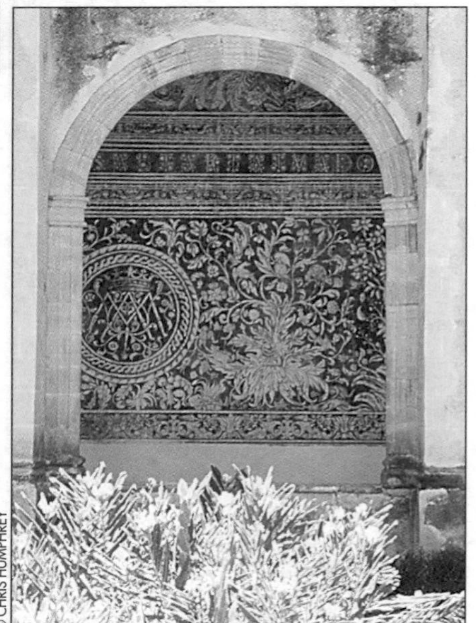
© CHRIS HUMPHREY

16th-century murals in the Ex-Convento de la Transfiguración

Accommodations

One low-priced spot right in the center of town is **Hotel Santa Monica,** at Hidalgo 109, tel. 714/147-0031, with simple rooms around a garden courtyard. Rates: US$10 s, US$20 d.

Not as good a deal, but acceptable in a pinch, is **Posada Familiar,** just down from the convent on Av. Juárez, tel. 714/147-0345, with clean rooms but somewhat lumpy beds. It has an inexpensive *comedor* also. Rates: US$17 s or d.

Food

For cheap eats, the restaurant at **Posada Familiar** is not bad, and it is open all week, unlike many of the more expensive restaurants which open only on weekends. US$3 will get you a full breakfast with coffee, juice, bread, and eggs.

Calle Guerrero leaving from the small square in front of the church up toward the archaeological site has several good restaurants on it. One of the best is **Las Palomas** Guerrero 104, tel. 714/147-0122, with tables around a small garden. Specialties include trout cooked with *epazote* and *hoja santa* spices and chicken breast with cheese and plum sauce. Prices are reasonable and quality is very good. Open Mon.–Thurs. until 6 P.M., Fri.–Sat. until 11 P.M., and Sun. until 8 P.M.

Two km south of town is a large trout farm, where you can fish yourself if you like or buy a tasty cooked trout from one of the several small restaurants nearby.

Transportation and Services

Tres Estrellas del Centro, Mexico City tel. 5264-3739, runs buses between Malinalco and Toluca (US$3) and Terminal Observatorio in Mexico City (US$6) regularly throughout the day.

The quickest route to drive to Malinalco from Mexico City is to take the Toluca highway and turn south at La Marquesa, following signs to Chalma. You'll also see signs to the Club de Golf Malinalco. The drive takes 1.5–2 hours. It's also possible to drive from Malinalco to Cuernavaca through beautiful, wild mountain country, but the road is in poor condition so expect to go slowly.

Tourist information can be found in the small office right on the higher of the two downtown squares, open daily 9 A.M.–4 P.M.

Chalma

About 11 km (7 miles) east of Malinalco, set amid forests and gorges, is the church of **Nuestro Señor de Chalma.** The 16th-century sanctuary was built at the site of an ancient sacrificial center, after the "miraculous" appearance of a crucifix on the site in 1533. The church is one of the most venerated pilgrimage sites in Mexico.

Valle de Bravo

Beautiful Valle de Bravo—usually shortened to "Valle"—lies 147 km (91 miles) west of Mexico City and 84 km (52 miles) west of Toluca and serves as a playground for wealthy city dwellers who flock here on weekends. Perched on a hillside above Lago Avándaro (Lake Avándaro), the ex-colonial town is crisscrossed by serpentine cobblestone streets lined with whitewashed stucco houses topped with red-tile roofs and draped with brilliant flowers and bougainvillea.

Actually a dammed reservoir created in the 1940s across a former river valley, Lago Avándaro measures three km (1.8 miles) across by seven km (4.5 miles) wide and is invariably dotted with dozens of small yachts and motor boats skimming the cool waters, particularly on weekends.

The gorgeous surrounding pine-forested mountains make a great outdoor venue for hikers, mountain bikers, and nature lovers in general. And as it happens, thermal conditions over the lake and nearby countryside make the area one of the premier locations in Mexico for hang gliding and paragliding. Right above town is a butterfly reserve, one of the best places in Mexico for visitors to see the legendary migrating monarch butterflies during the winter.

ORIENTATION

Valle is divided into two distinct sections, the main center of town up on the hilltop around Plaza Independencia and a second neighborhood down on the lakeshore and toward the road exit to Avándaro and Toluca. Most of the less expensive hotels, bike shops, government offices, the market, the bus station, and many restaurants are in the center of town. Down at the docks are a few of the better and more expensive restaurants, a couple of sport shops, and of course the lake. Visitors without wheels may find themselves trudging up and down the steep but short hill between the two with regularity, or you can flag down a passing cab for about US$.50. From the dock, a small road follows the lake shore north, bypassing the town center.

The road leading downhill to the dock from the plaza will eventually take you to the main exit toward Toluca. Just outside of town, a road branches off to the right leading to **Avándaro,** where many wealthy families maintain holiday homes. Leaving town in the other direction, to the north, a secondary highway passes the Avándaro dam and takes a longer and windier route back to Toluca.

While Valle doesn't have much in the way of tourist sights in town, the **Centro Joaquín Arcadio Pagaza,** at Pagaza 201, tel. 726/262-4016, frequently hosts small exhibitions by Mexican and international artists. A couple of blocks below the plaza, the Centro was once the home of Joaquín Arcadio Pagaza (1834–1918), a famed Mexican poet and translator born in Valle de Bravo. Open Tues.–Sat. 10 A.M.–6 P.M., Sun. 11 A.M.–7 P.M.; free admission.

RECREATION

With its large reservoir and encircling mountains, Valle is an outdoor recreation haven. While most Valle visitors live in Mexico and have their own gear, some rental equipment is available.

Water Sports

The going rate to rent motorboats on the lake is about US$28 for an hour's touring, or US$45 to go water-skiing (skis included). Fishing trips (perch and bass are plentiful) can also be arranged. To find a pilot, continue past the municipal dock south on the main street and look for a turnoff to the right leading down to a small marina. Be prepared to negotiate.

With a regular stiff breeze and just enough room to get up to full speed, Lago Avándaro is popular for small racing yachts and holds frequent regattas. While boat rentals are not easy to come by, it is possible to take racing classes if you're going to be in the area for a few weeks. The **Club Vela Santa María,** Marina Nacional 201, tel. 726/262-1012 or in Mexico City tel. 5606-4778, offers classes in a single-mast, twin-sail Ventura 21-footers for US$70 per class, four classes minimum.

Mountain Biking and Hiking

The pine forests and hills spreading in all directions from around Lago Avándaro are idyllic for taking long hikes or mountain bike rides along old dirt roads or narrow trails.

If you're just after a short stroll and a view of town, walk up Calle Depósito, off Bocanegra behind the church, which leads up to a fine lookout spot in the trees.

A great spot for a longer hike or bike ride is the ridgeline directly behind town. The easiest way to get up into the forest is to follow Calle Bocanegra from behind the church straight out of town without making any turns. After the road leaves town, it heads uphill and eventually turns to dirt. Look for a well-beaten trail on the right side just before reaching a crest in the road, about one km (0.6 mile)

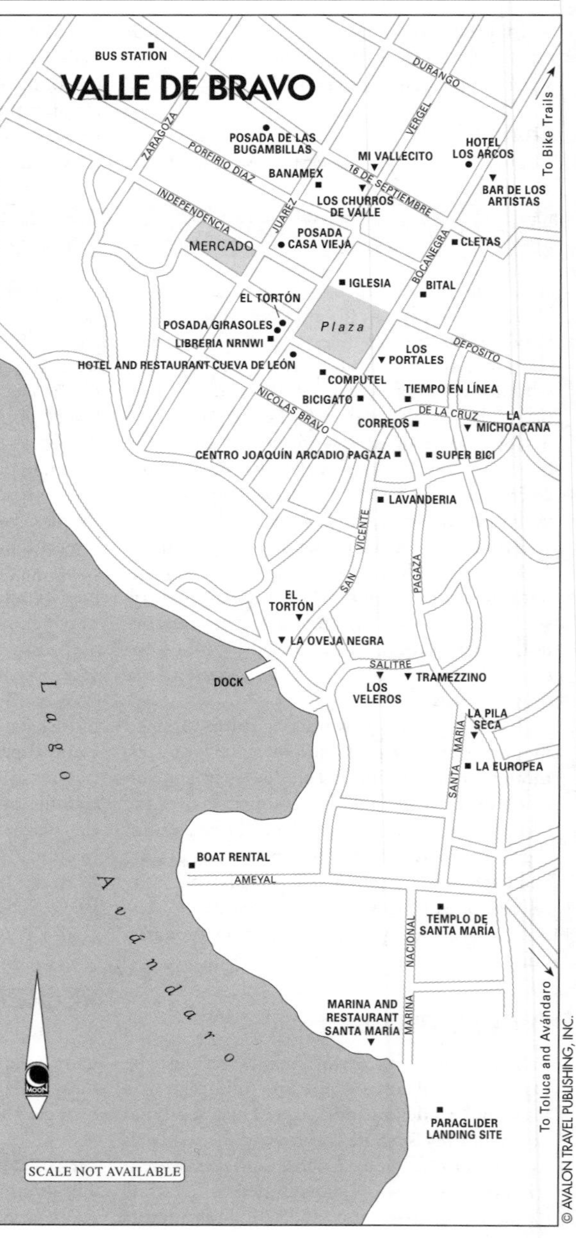

from where the pavement stops. This trail follows the ridge several kilometers south, with the town and lake to your right, and eventually arrives at **La Torre,** a peak used as a takeoff point for hang gliders and paragliders. Before the trail reaches La Torre, several other trails descend to the right back into town. From La Torre a dirt road winds about 14 bumpy km (8.5 miles) through forest and farmland back to the main highway coming into Valle from Toluca, about five km (three miles) above town. To find the turnoff coming from Valle, look for a dirt road on the left about 200 meters below the Pemex station, signposted S.M. Acatitlán.

Another fine area for getting into the woods is past the **Velo de Novia** (Bride's Veil) waterfall in Avándaro. To get there, take the road to Avándaro, pass through the small town center, and follow signs for Avándaro Spa. After passing the *glorieta* (traffic circle), look for a street to the right called Vega de Valle. Follow this a few hundred meters until you see a dirt lot on the right with a few food stands. If you have a car, park here and follow trails walking down to the waterfall or continuing around the lake.

Many longer trips are available in the surrounding mountains. One great multihour bike ride is to get a car ride up to the high point in the road heading back from Valle de Bravo toward Toluca; take a left-hand turn at a dirt road heading into a broad open meadow, called **Corral de Piedra.** From here trails and dirt roads wind way down the mountains through forest and remote farmland all the way back to Valle de Bravo.

Should you prefer to go on an organized trip rather than plunge off into the wilds on your own, or if you need to rent a bike, two shops operate in Valle. **Cletas,** 16 de Septiembre 200, tel. 726/262-0291, rents bikes for US$4.50 per hour or US$22 a full day or takes people on 2–4-hour rides for US$25 per person. The friendly owner will give bikers tips on where to go, and he'll give your bike a quick tune-up for US$4. Open during the week 10 A.M.–6 P.M., weekends 10 A.M.–8 P.M.

A block down from the plaza, **Pablo's Bikes,** Pagaza 104, tel. 726/262-3730, rents bikes at the same price and also organizes rides. Open Mon.–Wed. 10 A.M.–3 P.M. and 4–8 P.M., Fri.–Sun. 10 A.M.–9 P.M.

Monarch Butterfly Watching

Valle de Bravo was receiving seasonal vacationers for quite some time before Mexico City residents started showing up. Flocks of millions of monarch butterflies *(mariposas monarcas)* fly annually down from Canada to spend the winter in the western part of the State of Mexico and nearby Michoacán. Walking through forests covered with a brilliant blanket of brightly colored, constantly moving butterflies is a magical experience, not to be missed if you're in the area during the Dec.–Feb. season. At last count the monarchs wintered at 57 separate sites on the slopes of 11 volcanoes in central Mexico. Check the Monarch Watch website (www.monarchwatch.org) for blow-by-blow descriptions and best dates for viewing.

As the forests that provide winter homes for the monarchs are increasingly threatened by logging, the Mexican government has created a series of protected areas. One reserve is about 20 km (12 miles) from Valle de Bravo, near Los Saucos, a small roadside village. Keep an eye out for **Restaurant Las Tres Vírgenes**—that's Los Saucos. Just beyond the village toward Toluca, on weekends during the butterfly season, you'll see men with horses on the side of the road; they are offering inexpensive visits to the reserve. A 1.5-hour trip will set you back US$17 for a guide and US$11 for a horse (if you want one)—considerably less expensive than the better-known sanctuaries in Michoacán. Longer trips in the forests can be arranged without difficulty. If you don't see anyone on the road, ask in Los Saucos for a guide. The best month to visit is January, when the southward migration is mostly complete; it's best to visit during the week when there are fewer people around. In years when there are more butterflies than normal (as in 2001–2002), you'll see clouds of monarchs all the way down along the highway itself, along with local policemen waving cars to slow down as they pass through the area. And up in the forest, at "butterfly central," the sight is really staggering: about an acre of forested mountainside literally blanketed in butterflies,

© ELENA PAPPAS

One of Mexico's regular winter visitors: the monarch butterflies. Visit their sanctuary in the winter in the forests above Valle de Bravo.

to the point where it's hard to actually see the trees they are covering. If you sit still long enough, they'll start covering you, too!

Flying

While the thought of leaping into space and expecting to fly gives some of us visions of Icarus's ill-fated jaunt, hundreds of apparently sane people do just that each year from **El Torre,** the rocky peak behind Valle de Bravo. The equipment is of course much improved from the days of swan feathers and wax: modern wings of choice are either stiff-wing hang gliders or the newer paraglider, a type of soaring parachute. The debate continues to rage over which one is safer, but there's no doubt that paragliding is easier to learn and the equipment is more compact and convenient to transport, and thus more popular with beginners.

A visitor with no previous experience can take a tandem paraglide trip (that is, attached to a trained flier) for about US$110 to get a feel for what paragliding is like. Courses (usually a total of eight days spread over several weeks, though intensive courses are available) cost US$650–850.

Near the lake, **Alas del Hombre,** Fray G. Jiménez de la Cuenca 115, tel. 726/262-0934, www.alas.com.mx, has well-trained instructors who offer tandem rides and courses. The basic introductory paragliding course includes eight days of training over four weekends and costs US$1,100–1,500 per person, depending on how many people sign up for the course. It can also be reached in Mexico City at 5575-7760 or 5559-3629.

One U.S./Mexican company that runs hang gliding and paragliding trips to Mexico is **Fly Mexico,** tel. 512/467-2529 or 800/861-7198, in Valle de Bravo 726/262-2449, www.flymex.com, for US$695 (paragliding) or US$895 (hang gliding), for one week all included except airfare. Student trips cost more if you're not a certified flier already.

ACCOMMODATIONS

While Valle doesn't have a huge selection of hotels, there are a couple of good inexpensive options and a couple of lovely high-priced spreads. Rates are sometimes lower during the week. If you plan to visit on a weekend, be sure to make reservations.

Budget

The least expensive place in town to stay is **Posada Girasoles,** right on the main square at Plaza Independencia 1, tel. 726/262-2976. The hotel is small, but the brick and plaster rooms are quite spacious and spotless, with nice powerful showers to boot. A good deal. Rates: US$22 s, US$33 d, US$3 extra for a TV.

Inexpensive

An excellent midrange option, with not much in the way of amenities but lots of character, is **Posada Casa Vieja,** Juárez 101, tel. 726/262-0338. In a converted hacienda built more than 200 years ago and run by descendants of the original owners, the whitewashed rooms with wooden floors (no TVs or phones) spread around a tree-filled courtyard and are surprisingly affordable. If you come during the week it's less expensive, and you might even have the place to yourself. Parking is available. Rates: Mon.–Thurs. US$25 s, US$30 d; Fri.–Sun. US$35 s, US$40 d.

Posada de las Bugambilias, Av. 16 de Septiembre 406, tel. 726/262-1966, offers clean but very small rooms in a motel-like complex with parking. Rooms each have two double beds and cost the same for 1–4 people. Rates: US$40.

Right on the plaza, **Cueva de León,** Plaza Independencia 2, tel. 726/262-4062, fax 726/262-1361, features 14 rooms around a small interior courtyard filled with lots of hanging plants. The brightly painted rooms, with lots of pink trim, all have air-conditioning and color TVs. The attached dining room has mediocre food but a nice small patio overlooking the square. Rates: US$47 d, US$55 t.

Expensive

The most upscale place in the center of town is **Hotel Los Arcos,** Bocanegra 310, tel. 726/262-0042 or 726/262-0531, offering 24 wood-beamed rooms and suites, each equipped with TV and working fireplace, around an interior garden area with a small pool. Rates: US$100 s/d, US$115 junior suite.

Premium

An activity-oriented "therapy center" is the plush **Avándaro Golf and Spa Resort,** Vega del Río s/n, tel. 726/266-0200 or 726/266-0370; Mexico City tel. 5282-1212, fax 5280-0092; www.hotelavandaro.com. Composed of a hotel, health complex, and 18-hole golf course, the resort is secluded amid the pine forests in the town of Avándaro, southwest of Valle de Bravo. Rooms are spacious and bright, and the facilities include a palatial pool, seven tennis courts, a full spa, and the golf course. Guests must still pay an additional US$16 to use the spa or US$110 for the golf course, while the pool is included in room price. Nonguests may pay US$16 to use the spa but are not allowed in the pool or on the golf course. Rates: US$142 s/d, up to US$405 for Suite Monarca.

FOOD AND ENTERTAINMENT

If you visit Valle during the week, note that many restaurants are open only Thursday through Sunday, which means your options will be a bit limited on other days. Generally the less expensive eateries are clustered around Plaza Independencia, while the more pricey restaurants are found down toward the docks.

Mexican

La Michoacana, Calle de la Cruz 10, just off Pagaza, tel. 726/262-1625, serves great traditional Mexican dishes such as *sopa de tortilla* (tortilla soup), *cecina* (a type of dried beef), trout, and for the adventurous, *gusanos de maguey* (cactus worms). Meals are moderately priced, and the dining room's windows offer fine views overlooking the town and lake. Open daily 8:30 A.M.–11 P.M.

A very good, inexpensive local eatery is **Los Churros de Valle,** at the corner of 16 de Septiembre and Vergel two blocks from the plaza, with a small but tasty menu, much of it made with ingredients from the owner's farm. Specialties include a great artichoke dip, hearty soups, and of course the namesake *churros,* a sugary pastry served with hot chocolate.

Right across the street is another good place for inexpensive meals, **Mi Vallecito,** serving quesadillas, trout, beef dishes, and buffet meals. Open daily 9 A.M.–10 P.M.

Offering the best inexpensive food down by the lake is **La Oveja Negra,** in front of the town dock, tel. 726/262-0572. Breakfasts, including some creative egg dishes, run US$2–4, while a variety of entrées—pasta, meats, shrimp, and salads—cost US$3–6. Open Tues.–Sun. 9 A.M.–7 P.M.

Tacos, *Tortas, Comida Corrida*

Several small stands in the market, one block from the plaza, sell inexpensive breakfasts and *comida corrida* daily until 5 P.M.

For some of the finest *tacos de barbacoa* you're likely to find, go to the first stall on the right as you enter the market, where you'll see a crowd gobbling down this local specialty either *sencillo* or *con copia* (literally, "with copy," i.e., with two tortillas) daily while supplies last.

El Tortón, on Plaza Independencia next to Posada Girasoles, whips up decent jam, chicken, or sausage *tortas* for US$1.50. It also has a stand down by the dock next to La Oveja Negra.

Trout and Seafood

Just about every restaurant in town serves the locally famous *trucha* or trout. One popular low-budget place is **La Cascada,** a small restaurant on the road between Valle de Bravo and Avándaro, on the roadside next to a waterfall.

A much more upscale spot is **Los Veleros,** Salitre 104, tel. 726/262-0370, an exceptionally fine restaurant specializing in seafood (but also serving salads and meat dishes) in a beautiful old house. Diners may sit either in one of the interior rooms, decorated with pictures and drawings of sailboats, or on one of the outdoor balconies overlooking the lawn and garden. Open Fri.–Sun. 1 P.M.–midnight.

Restaurant Santa María del Lago, Marina Nacional 201, tel. 726/262-1012, is set in a large stone building right on the edge of the lake. The second-floor dining room and terrace have fine views of the lake and of the many paragliders who land right nearby on weekend afternoons. Apart from *huachinango* (red snapper), giant shrimp, trout, and other seafood, the restaurant also offers a tasty chicken or vegetable kebab. Entrées are US$7–13. Open Fri.–Sat. 8 A.M.–11 P.M., Sun. 8 A.M.–6 P.M.

Italian

Tramezzino, Salitre 104 C, tel. 726/262-4082, serves very tasty pizzas and pastas in a spacious dining room and courtyard that fills up regularly on weekends with out-of-town visitors. Pizzas run US$11 for a medium or US$14 for a large. Open Friday 4 P.M.–midnight, Saturday noon–midnight, and Sunday noon–8 P.M. It delivers.

Coffee and Snacks

The **Italian Coffee Company,** a chain coffee shop that started in Puebla, has a new place at Coliseo 104 a block above the plaza, with very good coffee, sweets, and a decent ham and cheese croissant for a light breakfast. Open daily 10 A.M.–10 P.M.

Shopping for Food

If you're renting a place in Valle and are looking for supplies, the first place to start is of course the **market,** one block from the plaza at the corner of Juárez and Porfirio Díaz. For more luxury goods, including a great selection of wines, cheeses, and other expensive treats, head to **La Europea** down near the lake at Santa María 114.

Entertainment

La Pila Seca, at the corner of Pagaza and Santa María, near the entrance to town, is a very chilled-out bar with good music and comfortable places to sit, popular with the alternative crowd living in or visiting Valle. Another, similar spot is **Bar de los Artistas,** a couple of blocks off the plaza at Bocanegra 303, slightly more upscale but still relaxed, sometimes with live music.

SERVICES

For information, tourist maps, and pamphlets stop in at the very helpful and friendly Oficina de Turismo, at the corner of Porfirio Díaz and Zaragoza, three blocks northwest of the plaza, tel. 726/262-1678. Open Mon.–Fri. 9 A.M.–7 P.M., Sat. 9 A.M.–2 P.M.

The Valle post office is on the corner of Pagaza and Calle de la Cruz, a block down from the plaza toward the dock. Open Mon.–Fri. 9 A.M.–4 P.M.

Computel, on the plaza opposite the side of the church, offers long-distance phone and fax service; open daily 7 A.M.–8:30 P.M.

Internet service is available at Tiempo en Línea, a block below the plaza at Calle de la Cruz 100, charging US$1.60 an hour. Open Mon.–Sat. 10 A.M.–9 P.M., Sun. noon–7 P.M.

Banamex, Bital, and Bancomer, all within two blocks of the plaza, change dollars and traveler's checks, and each has an ATM. On Saturday the banks are open 10 A.M.–2 P.M. only.

On San Vicente, a couple of blocks down from Pagaza toward the lake, is an inexpensive, no-name laundry service. Open Mon.–Sat. 9 A.M.–2 P.M. and 5–8 P.M.

Librería NRNWI, Coliseo 101, tel. 726/262-2557, sells magazines and newspapers, some in English. Open daily 9:30 A.M.–3 P.M. and 5–9 P.M.

Medical

Clínica de Especialidades, Nicolás Bravo 203, tel. 726/262-0018, a block south and west of the plaza, offers 24-hour medical attention.

The Cruz Roja ambulance service can be reached at tel. 726/262-0391, and the police at tel. 726/262-1126

Farmacia Santa Juanita, at Nicolás Bravo 103, at the corner of San Vicente, tel. 726/262-1065, is open 24 hours a day.

TRANSPORTATION

Bus

Zinacantepec, on 16 de Septiembre just past Zaragoza, tel. 726/262-0213, runs buses once an hour from Valle de Bravo to Toluca and Terminal Observatorio in Mexico City between 6 A.M. and 6 P.M., charging US$3 to Toluca (one hour, 45 minutes) and US$6.50 to Mexico City (two hours, 45 minutes). it also runs two direct buses to Mexico City per day, US$9, leaving in the afternoon.

Car

Two roads leave Valle de Bravo to Toluca, the windier and slower México 48 and the faster and more scenic México 134, which passes near Nevado de Toluca.

Around the Lake

Collective taxis running between Valle and Avándaro leave regularly from Pagaza, right next to the plaza, for US$1, while other taxis go to Colorines across the dam from Avenida 16 de Septiembre, just off Juárez, also for US$1.

Taxco

Soon after Cortés founded Taxco in 1529, the Spaniards discovered silver here and began mining in earnest. One of the city's hills, Cerro Barmeja, holds what was known as the King's Shaft, supposedly the oldest Spanish mine on the continent. The Taxco mines yielded vast quantities of silver—st of the country's supply came from here. But the veins were worked over so completely and efficiently that the city soon became a silver ghost town. It remained so for centuries, until American William Spratling opened a workshop in 1929 and began creating attractive original silver art designs. Since then the city has served as the locus of the most skilled silversmiths in Mexico, which accounts for its nickname as the "silver city."

SIGHTS

The city itself is built on and between seven hills covered by a maze of cobblestone streets. The steep, narrow streets climb up, down, and about, twisting in and out of the hilly landscape and occasionally opening up to reveal intimate plazas and cooling fountains. You need to watch your step when exploring this city on foot, as there's barely room for both cars and pedestrians on the steep, windy streets. Visitors with physical disabilities may have a rough go of it.

Although the maze of streets can be confusing at first, most of the main sites, as well as shops, hotels, and restaurants are all close to the center of town. The main drag, a section of the Mexico-Acapulco highway, is Avenida Presidente John

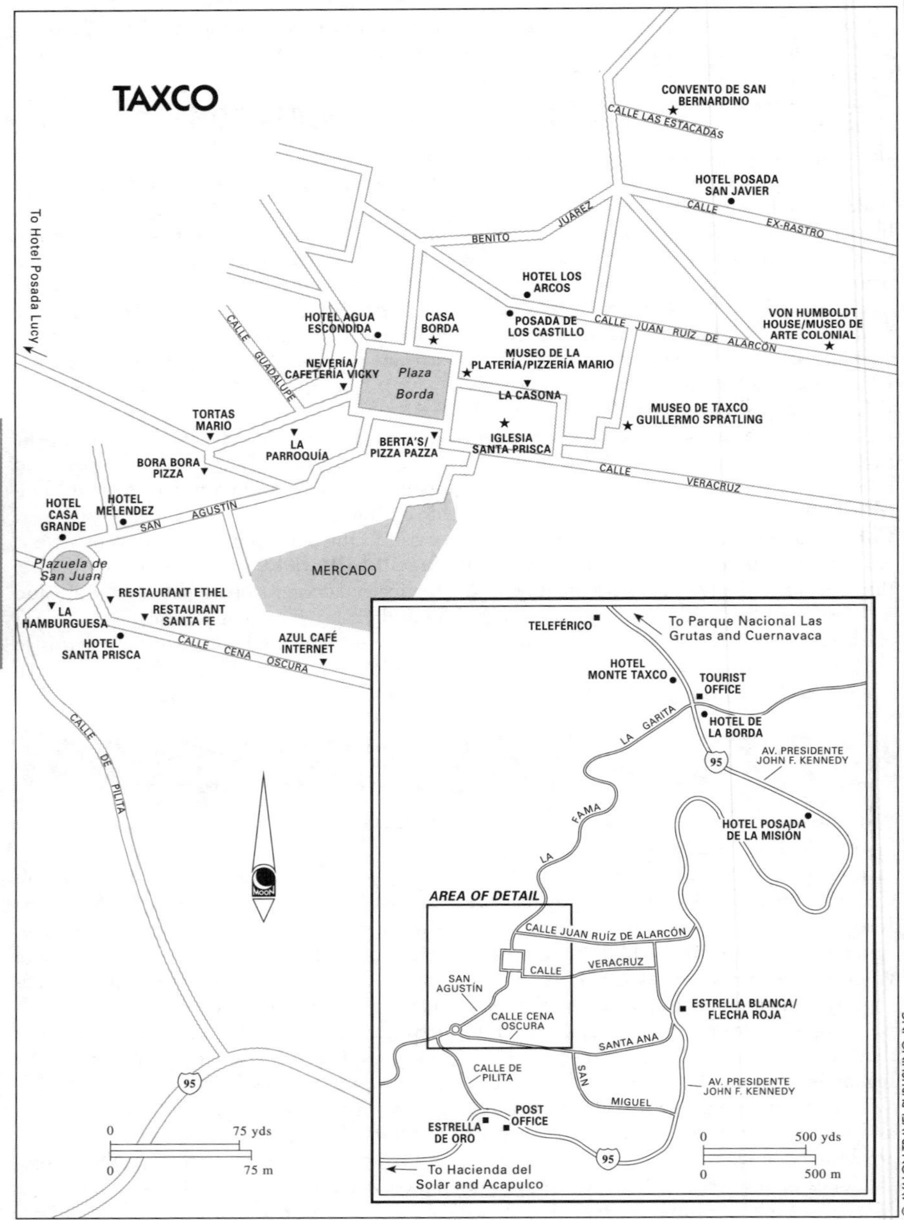
TAXCO
CONVENTO DE SAN BERNARDINO
CALLE LAS ESTACADAS
HOTEL POSADA SAN JAVIER
CALLE EX-RASTRO
BENITO JUAREZ
To Hotel Posada Lucy
HOTEL LOS ARCOS
HOTEL AGUA ESCONDIDA
CASA BORDA
POSADA DE LOS CASTILLO
CALLE JUAN RUIZ DE ALARCÓN
VON HUMBOLDT HOUSE/MUSEO DE ARTE COLONIAL
CALLE GUADALUPE
NEVERÍA/ CAFETERÍA VICKY
Plaza Borda
MUSEO DE LA PLATERÍA/PIZZERÍA MARIO
LA CASONA
MUSEO DE TAXCO GUILLERMO SPRATLING
TORTAS MARIO
LA PARROQUÍA
BERTA'S/ PIZZA PAZZA
IGLESIA SANTA PRISCA
CALLE VERACRUZ
BORA BORA PIZZA
HOTEL CASA GRANDE
HOTEL MELENDEZ
SAN AGUSTÍN
MERCADO
Plazuela de San Juan
RESTAURANT ETHEL
LA HAMBURGUESA
RESTAURANT SANTA FE
HOTEL SANTA PRISCA
AZUL CAFÉ INTERNET
CALLE CENA OSCURA
CALLE DE PILITA
95
0 75 yds
0 75 m
TELEFÉRICO
To Parque Nacional Las Grutas and Cuernavaca
HOTEL MONTE TAXCO
TOURIST OFFICE
LA GARITA
HOTEL DE LA BORDA
AV. PRESIDENTE JOHN F. KENNEDY
HOTEL POSADA DE LA MISIÓN
LA FAMA
AREA OF DETAIL
CALLE JUAN RUÍZ DE ALARCÓN
CALLE VERACRUZ
SAN AGUSTÍN
CALLE CENA OSCURA
ESTRELLA BLANCA/ FLECHA ROJA
SANTA ANA
CALLE DE PILITA
SAN MIGUEL
AV. PRESIDENTE JOHN F. KENNEDY
POST OFFICE
ESTRELLA DE ORO
To Hacienda del Solar and Acapulco
0 500 yds
0 500 m
© AVALON TRAVEL PUBLISHING, INC.

F. Kennedy, frequently known by locals as Avenida de los Plateros. The main part of town is basically uphill from Avenida Kennedy, so if you get lost, just go downhill to reorient yourself.

Iglesia Santa Prisca

A fine example of both Churrigueresque architecture and art, the church is a study in 18th-century detail, with an ornate pink facade punctuated by two steeples and a tiled dome. On the inside, you'll see magnificent paintings by Miguel Cabrera—a famed Zapotec Indian colonial artist—amid a bewildering assortment of gold leaf, sculptures, and nooks. One small painting is said to be unique in the world for its depiction of a pregnant Virgin Mary.

The church took more than eight years to complete and was paid for by rich miner José de la Borda. Open daily.

Plaza Borda

A shady spot under ancient laurel trees, Plaza Borda is a rare flat spot in the center of town.

© MAURICIO RAMOS

the detailed facade of Iglesia Santa Prisca

Bordering the square are Iglesia Santa Prisca and some lovely old buildings containing a variety of gift shops—look for pottery, Guerrero masks, local paintings, and of course silver. The plaza also holds court to an array of restaurants—most of which vie for the city's best view.

Museo de Taxco Guillermo Spratling

The two top floors of this museum house a fine collection of pre-Hispanic art, from Guerrero and central Mexico, gathered by William Spratling during his years in Mexico. Downstairs is an exhibit hall for temporary art displays. On Plazuela Juan Ruíz de Alarcón at Calle Delgado 1 behind Iglesia Santa Prisca, tel. 762/622-1660. Open Tues.–Sat. 10 A.M.–5 P.M., Sun. 9 A.M.–4 P.M.; admission US$2, free on Sunday.

Museo de la Platería

Aficionados of Taxco silver should definitely pay a visit to this small museum next to the Iglesia Santa Prisca, which traces the history of silver mining and craftsmanship in Taxco, and in Mexico as well. Several of William Spratling's most famed designs are on display here. The museum, which is run by a Taxco silversmith, has labels in Spanish only. On Plaza Borda, tel. 762/622-0658. Open Mon.–Sat. 10 A.M.–6 P.M., Wed. 10 A.M.–3 P.M.; admission US$2.

Von Humboldt House/ Museo de Arte Colonial

Originally built in the late 18th century as a private home, this building served as a guesthouse in later years and reputedly was where Baron Alexander Von Humboldt stayed when he came through Taxco in the 19th century. Now it's a small but interesting colonial religious art museum. At Calle Juan Ruíz de Alarcón 6, just a block and a half from the plaza, tel. 762/622 5501. Open Tues.–Sat. 10 A.M.–6 P.M.; admission US$1.50.

Casa Borda

Right next to the Iglesia Santa Prisca on the plaza is this mansion built for the Borda family in the mid-18th century. Now it's the town Casa de la Cultura, often with art shows by local artists. It houses a small café on the first floor that serves breakfast and lunch at reasonable prices. Open daily 10 A.M.–7 P.M.

Mercado

Beside the Iglesia Santa Prisca, this market is chock-a-block with stalls hawking all manner of food, herbal remedies, clothes, and some handicraft work also. On weekends the *mercado* is thronged with Indians who descend on Taxco from their villages in the hills above, whose fetching beadwork, brightly painted pottery, and textiles are sold for a fraction of their going price in Mexico City.

The *Teleférico* (Cable Car)

At the north end of town, a Swiss-built cable car takes passengers up 240 vertical meters to the top of a bluff overlooking the city. The cable car runs daily 8 A.M.–7 P.M.; fare is US$3 roundtrip, children are half-price. Views are predictably spectacular. At the top you'll find the pricey Hotel Monte Taxco, with a restaurant, disco, bar, shops, gym, spa, pool, horseback riding, and a golf course.

Rancho Spratling

The former workshop of William Spratling and current studio of some of Taxco's finest craftsmen is well worth the half-hour trip south of town. Directly off México 95 at Km 177.5, the ranch includes the accessible workshop where fine silver is crafted by artisans, a museum depicting Spratling's life, and a showroom of work. Open Mon.–Sat. 8 A.M.–1 P.M.; admission is free.

Parque Nacional Las Grutas de Cacahuamilpa

These extremely impressive caves comprise 15 interconnected chambers spanning 12 km (nine miles). About two km are accessible to casual tourists, with concrete footpaths and dim overhead lighting—a flashlight wouldn't hurt, though, to help see places the lighting doesn't reach, and also because power cuts are not unknown! Several of these "rooms" are quite massive—fully 70 meters tall and equally wide, filled with stalactites, stalagmites, and other stone formations. Guided tours leave every hour 10 A.M.–5 P.M., US$3, or US$2 for kids up to 12 years old. You must go with a guide, but not all guides speak English. Often it's very crowded, especially on weekends, although the caves are vast enough and the path easy enough to follow that escaping from the group is safe and easy. For a side trip, take the path branching to the right before arriving at the mouth of the caves, which leads to a place where the river flows into a 60-meter cave entrance. Minibuses (known in Mexico as *combis*) marked "Las Grutas" leave from in front of the Taxco terminal to the caves roughly every hour throughout the day and cost US$1.50 for the approximately 50-minute trip. If you're driving, take the highway east out of town toward Toluca and Cuernavaca, turn north on México 55 (toward Ixtapan de la Sal and Toluca), then watch for the marked turnoff, about 30 km from town.

ACCOMMODATIONS

Parking can be a hassle in Taxco, so if you're driving, look for a hotel with a parking lot.

Budget

Hotel Casa Grande, Plazuela de San Juan 7, tel. 762/6222-0969, fax 762/622-1108, offers 12 clean rooms with more on the way as soon as the addition is completed. Ask for a quiet room on one of the higher floors. The hotel's restaurant and bar, **La Concha Nostra,** that overlooks the plaza makes up for the softish beds and slightly funky bathrooms. Tacos, pizzas, and quesadillas are all good. Rates: US$17 s, US$26 d, US$32 t, US$27 q with private bath; US$13 s, US$21 d, US$23 t, with shared bath.

Posada de los Castillo, Juan Ruíz de Alarcón 7, tel. 762/622-1396, fax 762/622-1762, is a finely restored mansion from the colonial era with 15 rooms, a great place to stay in the center of town. There are plants, flowers, and hand-painted murals every place you look. A statue of La Virgen de Guadalupe guards the stairwell. Rates: US$21 s, US$30 d, US$37 t.

Inexpensive

Hotel Los Arcos, Juan Ruíz de Alarcón 12 (a block down the hill from Plaza Borda, opposite Posada de los Castillo), tel. 762/622-1826, fax 762/622-7982, was originally built as a monastery in the 16th century. The hotel is decorated with plenty of tile and has a great rooftop terrace. The 21 rooms, each with private bath, are simply furnished and have comfortable beds facing a verdant interior courtyard. Rates: US$32 s, US$37 d, US$43 t.

Hotel Posada Lucy, Carlos J. Nibbi 8, tel. 762/622-1780, a few streets north of the Plazuela de San Juan, offers 30 rooms with adjoining baths between them. Pleasant gardens surround the shotgun-style rooms. Rates: US$21 s, US$42 d, US$64 t, US$80 q.

Hotel Santa Prisca, Cena Oscura 1 (on Plazuela de San Juan, a couple of blocks west of Plaza Borda), tel. 762/622-0080, fax 762/622-2938, has 30 small but comfortable rooms around a patio and fountain. Grab one of the many English-language books from the library and enjoy a drink at the hotel's hole-in-the-wall bar. A section of the hotel is newer, with larger rooms and rambling junior suites. The dining room serves decent food. Rates: US$29 s, US$43 d, US$50 t.

Hotel Melendez, Cuauhtémoc 6, tel. 762/622-0006, fax 762/622-0613, is home to 33 newly decorated rooms surrounding an interior courtyard. Kitschy, brightly painted butterflies hover beside iron balconies in some of the rooms; other rooms open onto seating areas. Rates: US$30 s, US$40 d, US$50 t.

A beautiful garden surrounds **Hotel Posada San Javier,** Ex-Rastro 6, tel. 762/622-3177, fax 762/622-2351, with a swimming pool as centerpiece. This villa-style hotel features three terraces and quaint rooms, as well as spacious suites at reasonable prices. Rates: US$34 s, US$38 d, US$49 t.

Moderate

Hotel Agua Escondida, Plaza Borda 4, tel. 762/622-0726, fax 762/622-1306, enjoys a great location right on the Plaza Borda. The 50 rooms are freshly painted with decorative garden motifs and at least half now offer cable TV. Each has a private bath. Amenities include a rooftop terrace and snack bar, adjacent restaurant, video arcade, and a pool. Expect a crowd on weekends. Rates: US$ 40 s, US$50 d, US$60 t without TV; US$50 s, US$64 d, US$76 t with TV.

Expensive

Hotel de la Borda, Cerro del Pedregal 2 (opposite the junction of Av. Kennedy and Calle La Garita), tel. 762/622-0025, fax 762/622-0617, is larger and a little more modern than most Taxco hotels. It offers 120 large clean rooms and suites with charming balconies, a pool, and free parking. The attached **La Rotunda Restaurant & Bar** serves good food. Rates: US$85 s, US$85 d, US$100 t.

Hacienda del Solar, off México 95 south of town (opposite the tourist information office), tel. 762/622-0323, is an intimate hotel surrounded by beautiful views of the surrounding mountains. Balcony rooms and suites are available. Amenities include a pool, tennis court, gourmet restaurant **La Ventana de Taxco,** and strolling musicians. No children under 12. Rates: US$100 s/d.

Premium

Hotel Posada de la Misión, Cerro de la Misión 32 (just off Av. Kennedy), tel. 762/622-0063 or 762/622-5519, fax 762/622-2198, has 150 colonial-style rooms with private baths, and suites with fireplaces are available. On the premises you'll find a disco, piano bar, coffee shop, dining room, gardens, swimming pool, tennis court, and golfing. Parking is available. Weekday rates including breakfast and dinner: US$150 s, US$170 d, US$230 t, US$270 q.

The 156-room **Hotel Monte Taxco,** tel. 762/622-1300, fax 762/622-1428, has a choice location, perched on the top of a bluff on the north end of town near México 95. The hotel offers guests (and nonguests) a nine-hole golf course, tennis courts, horseback riding, steam baths and massage, a fitness center, three restaurants, bars, and a club. Rates: US$130 s, US$130 d, US$145 t.

FOOD AND ENTERTAINMENT

Budget/Midrange

La Hamburguesa, Plazuela de San Juan 5, tel. 762/622-0941, serves cheap burgers and tacos *al pastor* (pork cooked on a vertical spit). The piano bar gets lively in the evenings. Entrées run a little higher—around US$7–11. This cozy spot is open Thurs.–Tues. 8 A.M.–midnight.

For more than 40 years, the **Restaurant Santa Fé,** Hidalgo 2 (down from Plazuela de San Juan), tel. 762/622-1170, has been serving good, inexpensive food. Check out the *comida corrida* for US$6. Open daily 7:30 A.M.–11 P.M.

Restaurant Ethel, Plazuela de San Juan 14, tel. 762/622-0788, charges similar prices for *comida corrida* and specializes in good *antojitos.* Main courses are US$5–7; open daily 9 A.M.–9 P.M.

Restaurant Cielito Lindo, Plaza Borda 14, tel. 762/622-0603, serves sandwiches, good breakfasts, and Mexican and American cuisine for about US$3–12. Open 9 A.M.–midnight.

Nevería/Cafetería Vicky has a balcony that faces Plaza Borda. It's a great place to go for an excellent coffee drink or ice cream. The restaurant also serves affordable tacos, *sinchronizadas,* burgers, and beer. Open 8 A.M.–10 P.M.

Restaurant El Adobe on Plazuela de San Juan, tel. 762/622-1416, is a more refined place, with specialties such as *queso adobo* (melted cheese with herbs and veggies) or the *enchiladas oaxaqueños.* Meals run US$6–12. Open daily 8 A.M.–midnight.

For great views and low prices check out **Borda's Cafe,** next door to Restaurant Paco. The funky hole-in-the-wall grills cheap burgers, hot dogs, and serves excellent ice cream as well as mixed drinks and beer. Prices are US$3–6.

For fresh, local *tortas* go to **Tortas Mario** on Callejón de las Delicias, where the cook/owner will help you practice your Spanish. Prices are US$1–2.

More Expensive

El Corcel Negro, Cuahtemoc 8, tel. 762/622-7827, is a somewhat upscale restaurant and bar with a large deck and bright interior. The restaurant is open noon–8 P.M.; on weekends it turns into an evening bar scene with guitar music. Local favorites such as *molcajete* (a meat platter for do-it-yourself tacos) line the tables. Expect to spend about US$7–15 for a meal.

A small dining room and seemingly endless patio corners confront the visitor at **La Casona,** Celso Munoz 4, tel. 762/622-1071. Located beside the Iglesia Santa Prisca, the restaurant offers a panoramic view of Taxco. Mexican dishes run around US$8–12. Open 8 A.M.–8 P.M.

With a direct view of the Santa Prisca church through floor-to-ceiling windows, **Restaurant/Bar Paco** on the Plaza Borda is a pleasant place to spend the afternoon, with live music varying from Spanish guitar to synthesizer classics. The bar opens at noon and food is served 1–10:30 P.M. Expect to spend US$7–13 for a meal.

Del Ángel Inn, Celso Muñoz 4, tel. 762/622-5525, formerly a 10-room guesthouse, is now an elegant culinary haven. Steaks and meat-oriented dishes stand out in this patio-geared restaurant, though vegetarian Mexican meals are also available. Entrées are US$7–16.

White tablecloths will greet you at **La Parroquia,** Plazuela de Los Gallos 1, tel. 762/622-3096, as well as a menu replete with international favorites and Mexican specialties; dishes run US$10–15.

La Pagaduría del Rey, Colegio Militar 8, tel. 762/622-0075, is a hacienda-style restaurant just north of the city center. A serene setting both indoors and out, the high-end restaurant serves everything from fettuccine to filets. Expect to fork over US$8–20 for a meal without wine. Open daily 1:30–9:30 P.M.

La Ventana de Taxco, at the Hacienda del Solar (about seven minutes south of town on the highway to Acapulco), tel. 762/622-0587, gets high marks from *Bon Appétit.* With a chef from Como, Italy, good service, and Italian specialties, it's not to be missed—nor is the homemade chicken ravioli. The view is one of the best in town. Reservations recommended, especially on weekends; hours are 8 A.M.–11 P.M. Prices run from US$6 for appetizers to US$7–13 for entrées.

Pizza

The best pizza in town is **Pizza Pazza,** tel. 762/622-5500, next to the church on the plaza.

Apart from the excellent and reasonably priced pizzas, the menu includes pastas and other Italian dishes. Expect to pay about US$3–10 for a pie, and do your best to get a window seat for a good view of the plaza. Open daily 10 A.M.–midnight.

Bora Bora Pizza, Callejón de las Delicias 4, tel. 762/622-1721, also has very good pizza and other Italian dishes. If you're lucky you might get a table on one of the small balconies overlooking town, but if not, you'll still enjoy the tasty melted cheese and crispy crust amid the purple and pink decor. Internet services and a laundry send-out are also available at the expanding restaurant. Open daily 2 P.M.–midnight.

You'll find **Pizzería Marios** in an indoor square at Plaza Borda 1. The menu includes cheese fondue, good-sized pies, and spaghetti dishes. A nice terrace faces the plaza.

Nightlife

Taxco's most alternative bar is **Cafe Sasha,** opposite Hotel Los Arcos in Calle Juan Ruiz de Alarcón. A decent restaurant by day, at night Cafe Sasha becomes a hip place to sink tequilas and listen to reggae, drum 'n' bass, and world music. Open 8.30 A.M. to around 1 A.M.

Berta's Bar, next to the Santa Prisca church and adjacent to Pizza Pazza, tel. 762/622-0172, is something of a local institution and a great place to meet locals and travelers alike. It was opened in the 1930s by Berta, a Taxco resident, for whom a specialty house drink is named. The bar also claims to be the birthplace of the legendary margarita, which William Spratling supposedly invented. Hours are 11 A.M.–10 P.M.

If you get the urge to play pool while in Taxco, the closest place around is **La Estación.** The bar and burger joint is one floor below El Corcel Negro at Cuauhtémoc 8 between Plaza Borda and Plazuela de San Juan.

Fusion, Av. de los Plateros 190, tel. 762/622-0244, like most of Taxco's discos, is open only on weekends. The dance floor pulsates with the sounds of salsa, cumbia, and merengue. Taxco's trendiest disco is **Passagge,** Av. de los Plateros 34, where the DJs spin an eclectic mix of pop, techno, and salsa. Open Thurs.–Sat. from 11 P.M. Entrance is US$6–8 depending on the night.

EVENTS

Semana Santa

The Holy Week festival begins on the week before Easter. On Palm Sunday, the first procession begins in the nearby village of Tehuilotepec, when an image of Jesus is placed on the back of a donkey and carried to Taxco. Candlelight processions take place in town every following night, with *penitentes* making their peregrination (some on their knees) to the Iglesia Santa Prisca. On Holy Thursday, in front of Santa Prisca, the Last Supper is performed by the locals, and on Saturday, the Resurrection is staged about 9 A.M. The last procession takes place on Easter Sunday.

Fiesta Alarconia

The last three weekends are devoted to a festival honoring Taxqueño Juan Ruíz de Alarcón, a writer during the colonial era. Art exhibits, band concerts, Alarcón plays, and other cultural presentations take place all over town.

Feria Nacional de la Plata

The first week in December each year is dedicated to Taxco's most famous product, crafted silver. Hundreds of artists enter a contest overseen by a panel of judges, who choose what they consider to be the year's best silverwork. This is a great opportunity to see some of the country's most creative silver craftsmanship.

SHOPPING

Taxco offers some of the finest silver creations in Mexico and has more than 300 silver shops, but don't expect bargain basement prices. Besides silver you can purchase items with unusual mixtures of silver and ceramics, or silver, brass, copper, and ceramics. The bulk of the town's shops are in the city center; the ones closer to the plaza tend to be more expensive. When buying a piece, always look for the .925 stamp on the back, which ensures authenticity, and be sure to spend some time comparing prices before buying.

One of the best shops is owned and operated by the Castillo family, who sells its top-quality designs all over Mexico. Los Castillo is open daily

9 A.M.–7 P.M. Walk downhill from Plaza Borda until you see the sign. You can watch the silversmiths at work here and you can also get directions to the larger workshop outside of town.

Alejandro Viveros is another high-end silversmith-owned shop. Expect unique designs at this Patio de las Artesanías location. Other good shops are **Emma's,** a short distance down the street on the left of Santa Prisca and with slightly better prices than most, and **Elena Los Ballesteros,** next door, with high-end merchandise.

INFORMATION AND SERVICES

Tourist Office

The state tourist offices are both on Avenida de los Plateros (Avenida John F. Kennedy) at numbers 1 and 28, tel. 762/622-2274 and 762/622-0798 respectively; the former is open daily 9 A.M.–3 P.M. and the latter 9 A.M.–7 P.M.

Medical Emergencies

For medical attention, call the Red Cross, tel. 762/622-3232; Hospital Adolfo Prieto, tel. 762/622-0121/5552; or Clinic Santa Cruz, tel. 762/622-3012.

Post Office

The post office is below the *ayuntamiento* or town hall in Benito Juárez; open Mon.–Fri. 8 A.M.–7 P.M., Sat. 9 A.M.–1 P.M.

Language Courses

The **Centro de Enseñanza Para Extranjeros,** tel. 762/622-0124, www.cepe.unam.mx, a branch of Universidad Nacional Autónoma de México (UNAM), offers six-week intensive Spanish courses for US$375. Food and accommodations are extra, but the school can often set up rooms with local families. Call for starting dates.

Banks and Money Changing Services

Banco Santander, and Bital have 24-hour ATMs and cash travelers checks during normal banking hours. Banco Santander is on Calle San Augustin between Plaza Borda and Plazuela de San Juan, while Bital is in Plaza Borda next to the Iglesia Santa Prisca.

Laundry

Dirty duds can be left at Bora Bora Pizza at Delicias 1 between 1 P.M. and midnight and collected the following evening.

Internet

There are several Internet cafés within a stone's throw of Plaza Borda. Try La Estación on Cuauhtémoc, just 50 meters from the square, open daily 10 A.M.–midnight, or Moloko Plus, directly opposite.

GETTING THERE

Bus

Taxco has two bus stations, both on Avenida de los Plateros (Avenida John F. Kennedy). The **Estrella Blanca/Flecha Roja** station, near the intersection of Calle Santa Ana about halfway through town, tel. 762/622-0131, runs first-class buses to Terminal Tasqueña in Mexico City more than 10 times daily, US$9; to Acapulco once daily, US$15; and to Cuernavaca frequently, US$4. Frequent and less expensive second-class buses go to the same destinations as well as Toluca and Chilpancingo. **Estrella de Oro,** near the exit to Acapulco, tel. 762/622-0648, offers 6–10 first- and second-class buses to the same destinations for about the same prices.

Popocatépetl and Ixtaccíhuatl

The second- and third-highest mountains in Mexico, Popocatépetl (5,465 meters/17,925 feet) and Ixtaccíhuatl (5,230 meters/17,150 feet) form the southeastern lip of the Valle de México. On one of those rare clear days in Mexico City, the two snowcapped peaks can be seen in the distance from any tall building in the city center.

Until fairly recently, climbing Popo was probably the most popular mountaineering adventure in Mexico. In December 1994, however, the formerly dormant volcano began intermittently belching clouds of smoke and ash. As a result, the peak is now off-limits to climbers and is likely to remain so for years to come. For updated information on the volcano's activity, look on the Internet at www.prueba.cenapred.unam.mx/mvolcan.html.

The **Paso de Cortés** between the two volcanoes, a destination in itself for the brisk air and amazing views as well as the take-off point for an Ixtaccíhuatl climb, is reached by driving or busing 48 km (30 miles) from Mexico City to Amecameca, a large town at the base of the mountain.

CLIMBING IXTACCÍHUATL

Ixtaccíhuatl is still open for climbing and presents as much if not more of a challenge than Popo. While the single cone of Popo required a steep hike of 4–7 hours to reach the peak, the most common route up the broken, jagged Ixta, replete with false summits along the way to test your resolve, takes a solid 7–10 hours.

Below is only a general overview of what the route is like, and it does not pretend to serve as a blow-by-blow guide. To avoid difficulties, the safest bet is to hire a guide or go on a weekend and tag along with another hiking group. As the climb is entirely above the treeline, as long as you go during the day and don't get caught in a storm (rare in the December.–April dry season), there's not much danger of getting lost.

For more detailed route-finding information on Ixtaccíhuatl or other Mexican volcanoes, buy a copy of R.G. Secor's guide, *Mexico's Volcanoes,* 3rd ed. (Seattle: The Mountaineers, 2001).

La Joya Route

By far the most frequented route up Ixta begins at La Joya (4,000 meters/13,120 feet), a dirt parking lot perched on the southern flank of the mountain, reached by a seven km-long (4.5-mile) dirt road from the Paso de Cortés. The road is passable by passenger car most of the year but can get treacherous in the rainy season. No buses go to either the Paso de Cortés or La Joya, so if you don't have wheels, you'll have to hire a taxi in Amecameca (US$24 per carload).

In profile Ixta looks something like a sleeping woman, and climbers have labeled parts of the mountain accordingly. The La Joya climb starts at "Los Pies" (the feet) and continues up "Las Piernas" (the legs) to the brutally steep "Rodillas" (knees). From there it crosses the snowfields of "La Barriga"

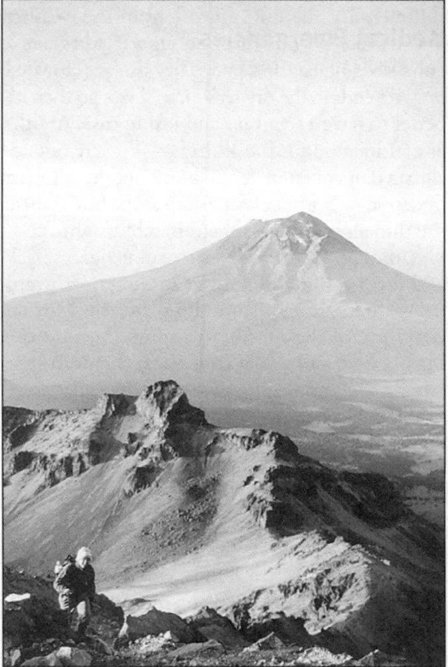

© CHRIS HUMPHREY

climbing Ixtaccíhuatl, with Popocatépetl in the background

(the belly) at a more gentle grade to reach the mountain's summit atop "El Pecho" (the breast). From El Pecho the views down onto the rock formation of "La Cabeza" (the head) are spectacular.

One popular schedule for climbing is to arrive at the parking lot at La Joya in the afternoon or evening, sleep until around 2 A.M. in your car or a tent, then climb most of the way up in the darkness, arriving at the peak sometime between 8 and 11 A.M. and returning to the parking lot in the early afternoon. Leaving at this ungodly hour provides spectacular sunrise views and ensures that the ice on the peak is hard, making it easier and safer to cross. The drawback is the possibility of losing your way if you're unsure of the trail.

If no one in your group has been on the mountain before, or if you just think getting up so early is for the birds, leave La Joya in late morning or early afternoon and spend the night about halfway up the mountain (at 4,750 meters) in a pair of climbing huts just below the "Knees." Although rudimentary, the huts are safe from the weather and will keep you warm enough if you have a good sleeping bag and pad. They can get crowded on weekends in the dry season, so if you go then it's better to have a tent on hand just in case. Another consideration is the altitude—if you're not acclimated, it's often better to knock out the climb in one shot, rather than try to sleep at the huts, where the thin air can make for a miserable night.

Although the trail is well worn, it zigzags back and forth across a long ridge leading northward up to the summit, sometimes on the Mexico City side of the mountain, sometimes on the Puebla side, and can at times be difficult to spot among the jumble of rocks and gravel. Go slowly and avoid energy-consuming detours.

Should you have no particular burning desire to go to the summit, a hike halfway up to the huts (either spending the night or returning the same day) crosses over only dirt and rock, not ice, and requires no special climbing equipment. The hike is still very arduous, especially with the altitude, and takes 5–8 hours round-trip.

Equipment and Safety Precautions

If you hike Ixta in the dry season (December–April), you can generally get away with just bringing an ice ax for emergencies, as the only stretches of ice you'll have to cross are mostly flat. The rest of the year you'll also need crampons. A rope is generally not needed. Check with a climbing shop in Mexico City (see the Sports and Recreation chapter) for current snow conditions. As with any mountain climb, keep a close eye on the weather and come prepared with waterproof, warm clothes, in case things take a turn for the worse.

Visiting climbers may be disheartened to see Mexicans young and old tromping gleefully past them on the trail, while they rest, wheezing, against a convenient rock. But don't forget, most of these locals live in Mexico City (elev. 2,240 meters) and are well acclimated. Don't just fly in from sea level or thereabouts and expect to hike up to the peak without a care. Even those who have spent some time in Mexico City may get struck by a splitting headache, fierce vomiting, and possibly worse. Should these symptoms befall you, the quickest remedy is a fast descent. Drinking plenty of water while climbing can help keep altitude sickness at bay.

Though not a technically challenging climb, this is a very large mountain and should not be taken lightly—don't go unless you have some experience climbing or you're with an experienced group leader. **Socorro Alpino** has a rescue crew at La Joya on weekends in case of problems, and someone is always around who can call for help at the ranger station at the Paso de Cortés. The closest medical help is the hospital at Amecameca.

Guides

Colorado Mountain School, P.O. Box 2062, Estes Park, CO 80517, tel. 970/586-5758, fax 970/586-5798, www.cmschool.com, offers a package trip from the U.S. to climb Ixta and Pico de Orizaba. A 10-day two-peak trip costs US$1,700 per person.

Two local guide groups that offer less expensive trips up Ixta are **Eco Grupos,** tel. 5522-5821 or 5522-5803 (the number of Hostel Moneda, owned by Eco Grupo partner Juan Pablo Rico), and **Río y Montaña,** Prado Norte 450, Col. Lomas de Chapultepec, tel. 5520-2041 or 5520-5018, email: rioymontana@compuserve.com.mx.

© CHRIS HUMPHREY

camping shelters on Ixtaccíhuatl

Transportation

Get on the Puebla highway leaving Mexico City, then take the turnoff marked Cuautla-Amecameca. After going through a US$1.50 toll, a secondary highway continues 22.5 km (14 miles) to Amecameca. One km beyond Amecameca, a road turns left (east) and snakes its way 30 km (18.5 miles) up the mountain to the Paso de Cortés, accessible by either car or taxi from Amecameca. By bus, ride from Terminal Tapo in Mexico City to Amecameca and take a taxi (see below for details).

Elsewhere on Ixta

The pine-forested flanks of Ixta are crisscrossed with dirt roads, giving access to the mountain from several different directions besides the Paso de Cortés.

On the Mexico City-Puebla highway, at the road's highest point above the valley of Mexico, 21 km (13 miles) from the toll gate leaving Mexico City, is the roadside village of **Llano Grande,** where you'll see a couple of dozen food stands and stores. Look for an archway on the north side of the highway—a dirt road turns in here and continues 10 km (six miles) up the northern side of Ixta, where it runs into a large meadow at 3,350 meters, with a forestry research station managed by the Universidad de Chapingo. From here secondary dirt tracks continue up the side of the mountain to a second, higher meadow with fantastic views of the peak, as well as down toward Cholula on the east side and toward San Rafael and Amecameca to the west. The climbing routes up Ixta from here all go by the "Head" of the mountain and are more technical, so don't attempt them without a guide.

While the forests on this side of Ixta are lovely for hiking and mountain biking, don't park your car near the village of Llano Grande, as robberies and assaults have been reported. Instead drive all the way up the dirt road as far as the research station, and leave the car there, where it's quite safe.

North of Amecameca, on the eastern side of Ixta, is the village of **San Rafael,** the takeoff point for another approach to the summit. Robberies have been reported recently around San Rafael, so at the moment it's not advisable to venture over this way.

PASO DE CORTÉS

Visitors who don't want to hike up to the high peaks might like to wander the many trails around the Paso de Cortés between the two peaks. The pass is so called because Cortés came through here from Cholula on his way to conquer the Aztec capital of Tenochtitlán.

Several food stands offer quesadillas and other snacks at the parking lot in the pass, and a visitor center can provide some information on the volcanoes. The **Albergue Alzomoni,** by the radio towers just off the dirt road leading to La Joya, rents beds for US$2 a night, with very minimal facilities. The lodge, atop a hill with great views of both peaks and the valleys below, can be crowded on weekends.

Transportation

Although no buses drive the 30-km (18.5-mile) potholed road to the Paso de Cortés from Amecameca, taxis in Amecameca are accustomed to taking up weekenders for a negotiable fee, usually around US$15 per car. If you did bring a car and don't mind a few bumps, consider continuing down the dirt road on the far side—it leads down through the forest to Cholula (46 km) and on to Puebla (10 km farther), where you can take the highway back to Mexico City. Driving up through Amecameca, enjoying the views at the pass, and returning to Mexico City via Cholula makes a great day trip.

AMECAMECA

On the way to the Paso de Cortés from Mexico City is Amecameca (elev. 2,475 meters/8,118 feet), a mountain town with clean brisk air. The market and picturesque town square, with the bright red **Iglesia de la Asunción** on the east side, are fun to explore for an hour or two. It's also a good place to grab a meal or pick up supplies before heading up the mountain.

Just west of town is a hilltop park known as **El Sacramonte** (Sacred Mountain), with two chapels on top. Each year on Ash Wednesday, the townsfolk carry a decorated image of Christ—supposedly made in 1521—in a candlelight procession from one of the churches to the nearby burial cave of Fray Martín de Valencia, who is said to have been the leader of the first group of missionaries to the area.

Transportation

Transportes Volcanes runs buses every 15 minutes or so, 5 A.M.–10 P.M., between Terminal Tapo in eastern Mexico City and Amecameca; the fare is US$1.75. Taxis from Amecameca's plaza to Paso de Cortés cost around US$15 per carload, or US$24 to La Joya, although prices vary.

Puebla and Vicinity

The Spanish founded the city of Puebla in 1531 as an intermediate supply depot and resting point between the port of Veracruz and the Mexican capital. Puebla became an important trading center in the colonial era, and the route from Mexico City to the coast via Puebla is still one of the country's main commercial arteries.

The capital city was laid out in the neat grid pattern typically employed by the Spanish. The historic city center is full of ornate colonial buildings replete with magnificent stonework, gold leaf, and Puebla's distinct signature, **Talavera tile,** which decorates rooftops, church domes, walls, and much else besides. Those with an eye for architecture will enjoy the city's plentiful baroque churches and Churrigueresque facades.

The **Cinco de Mayo** holiday, one of Mexico's greatest celebrations, originated in Puebla, when on May 5, 1862 a ragtag Mexican army beat back the invading French led by Maximilian. The French were eventually victorious, but Mexicans still celebrate Cinco de Mayo as a day of national pride and independence.

Today Puebla is the fourth-largest city of Mexico, with a population of about 1.5 million people. The city's colonial architecture provides a backdrop for bustling commerce, thick traffic, cafés, bars, shops, shoppers, museums, students, and scores of tourists. Agriculture, tourism, and the production of ceramics are major industries, and Puebla is also home to Mexico's Volkswagen factory, which produces the *bochitos* (Beetles) seen all over Mexican roads, as well as the sleek "new Beetle" so popular in the U.S.

© GREG BULL

banner of the virgin

SIGHTS

Orientation

Puebla was the first Mexican town built from a master plan rather than around an existing Indian city. With a few exceptions, streets running north-south are called *calles,* and those running east-west are called *avenidas.*

The intersection at the northwest corner of the *zócalo* forms the center of town for purposes of street labeling. Here Avenida Reforma/Palofax (east-west) meets Avenida 16 de Septiembre/5 de Mayo (north-south, one of the exceptions mentioned above). Coming from the west, Avenida Reforma becomes Avenida Palofax east of this intersection. Coming from the south, Avenida 16 de Septiembre becomes Avenida 5 de Mayo north of this intersection.

Even-numbered *avenidas* lie north of Avenida Reforma/Palofax; odd-numbered *avenidas* lie to the south. On the west side of Avenida 16 de Septiembre/5 de Mayo, all *avenidas* are labeled with the suffix "Poniente" (west); on the east side they're all labeled "Oriente" (east).

Even-numbered *calles* lie east of Avenida 16 de Septiembre/5 de Mayo; odd-numbered *calles* lie

EXCURSIONS

DOWNTOWN PUEBLA

TEMPLO DEL TERCER ORDEN AND EX-CONVENTO DE SAN FRANCISCO

BLVD. HÉROES DEL 5 DE MAYO

BARRIO DEL ARTISTAS

EL PARIAN

TEATRO PRINCIPAL

MUSEO DE ESTADA

MUSEO VIRREINAL

POST OFFICE

EL CONVENTO DE LAS CAROLINAS

MESÓN SACRISTÍA

CALLE DEL SAPO

CALLEJÓN DE LOS SAPOS

HOTEL COLONIAL

CAFE INTERNET

RESTAURANTE CHESA VEGLIA

MUSEO DE LA REVOLUCIÓN

HOTEL IMPERIAL

CASA DE LOS MUÑECOS

VITTORIO'S PIZZERIA

BARRA VEGETARIANA LA ZANAHORIA

MUSEO AMPARO

CASA DE LA CULTURA

IGLESIA DE SAN JOSÉ

MUNICIPAL TOURIST OFFICE

HOTEL PALACE

HOTEL ROYALTY

Plaza de Armas ZÓCALO

CATEDRAL

TOURIST OFFICE

MUSEO DE SANTA MONICA

IGLESIA DE SANTO DOMINGO DE GUZMÁN

CAFE AGUIRRE

RESTAURANTE CAFE EL VASCO

LA PRINCESA

TACOS TONY

MUSEO DE ARTES POPULARES

HOTEL ALAMEDA

HOTEL VICTORIA

HOTEL TERESITA

HOTEL AVENIDA

EL VEGETARIANO

GRAN HOTEL SAN AGUSTÍN

HOTEL CATEDRAL

HOTEL SAN MIGUEL

FONDA DE SANTA CLARA

HOTEL VIRREYES

MUSEO DEL FERROCARRIL

Parque Paseo de Bravo

AV. 5 DE MAYO

AV. 16 DE SEPTIEMBRE

AV. REFORMA

AV. PALOFAX Y MENDOZA

250 yds

250 m

to the west. On the south side of Avenida Reforma/Palofax, all *calles* are labeled with the suffix "Sur" (south), while on the north side they're all labeled "Norte" (north).

The historic section of town is bounded by Boulevard Héroes del 5 de Mayo on the east, Calle 11 on the west, Avenida 18 on the north, and Avenida 11 on the south.

Plaza

The city center (call it the *zócalo,* the plaza, the Plaza de la Constitución, or the Plaza de Armas) faces the cathedral and is bordered on three sides by the original broad stone *portales* (arches). The buildings exhibit a variety of architectural styles from across the centuries: baroque, Churrigueresque, neoclassic, Herreresque, and Renaissance. The 16th-century arches lining the plaza house sidewalk cafés, restaurants, shops, and newspaper stands. The broad *zócalo*—once a bustling 19th-century marketplace—is an island of tranquility with shady trees, benches, and a bandstand.

Catedral de la Inmaculada Concepción

On the south side of the *zócalo* you can't miss the cathedral, widely considered one of the most beautiful churches in Mexico (no small compliment). The twin-towered and tile-domed cathedral, begun in 1575 by Francisco Becerra and completed in 1664, shows medieval, Renaissance, and baroque styles on the facade, and even a few neoclassical hints on the inside, for example Manuel Tolsá's marble and onyx altar. Inside, past the lovely carved wooden doors, visitors will find 14 gilded chapels filled with religious paintings, relics, and sculptures, as well as a 12-meter-high pipe organ.

One tale about the church says the enormous 8.5-ton bell was placed in the bell tower by angels. How else would it have gotten up to the top of the 73-meter tower? The second tower has no bell because it was feared that the weight would cause the structure to sink into the ground. A tower tour is offered every day at 11 A.M.; English-speaking guides are usually available.

Casa de la Cultura

Formerly the archbishop's palace, the Casa de la Cultura is at Avenida 5 Oriente 5, across from the cathedral and next door to the tourism office. Built in 1597, the palace housed the colleges of San Pablo, San Pedro, and San Juan in the 17th and 18th centuries. In 1891 it became the Governor's Palace, and in 1973 it was reconstructed. Inside you'll find a movie room, exhibition space, workshops, a cafeteria, a coffee shop, and restrooms.

Up a flight of marble stairs to the second floor is the **Biblioteca Palafoxiana.** Believed to be the oldest library in the Americas, it was closed and awaiting restoration when we last visited. In 1646, Bishop Juan Palafox y Mendoza donated the first 5,000 volumes, including works of philosophy, theology, and history. The books cover a wide variety of scholars; many are in Greek and Latin, others in Hebrew and Sanskrit, and some were printed as early as the 15th century.

In 1773 Bishop Francisco Fabian y Fuero constructed the library, a parallelogram 43 meters long and 12 meters wide, covered by five domes on six Doric arches. Shelves of white cedar, divided into 2,472 sections, hold 50,000 volumes. Note the water flasks hung on the shelves in the event of fire.

Iglesia de Santo Domingo de Guzmán

Three blocks north of the plaza on 5 de Mayo lies what remains of a fine baroque Dominican monastery consecrated in 1690. Inside the exceptional **Capilla del Rosario,** the walls are covered with gilded ornate carvings, tiles, and cherubs.

Iglesia de San Cristóbal

Another baroque beauty, this one is on Calle 4 Norte at Avenida 6 Oriente. The interior is similar to that of the Capilla del Rosario. The elaborate relief figures are very well done but not gilded.

Other Churches

Puebla has around 60 churches, many dating from the colonial era. Church buffs might want to take a look at **Iglesia de San José,** nine blocks north of the plaza at Av. 18 Oriente and Calle 2 Norte, and the adjoining tile-domed **Capilla de**

Jesús. The church's interior is inaccessible but worth a look from the outside.

The Churrigueresque **Templo del Tercer Orden y Ex-Convento de San Francisco,** Av. 14 Oriente 1009 (at Blvd. Héroes del 5 de Mayo), was begun in 1535 and completed in 1667. The principal dome is an eight-sided star. *La Conquistadora,* the statue of the Virgin that according to legend accompanied Cortés on his battles of conquest, is also here—an ominous sight for those who can imagine the scenes the small statue witnessed.

Other churches worth a visit are: **Iglesia de Espíritu Santo,** Av. Palofax at Calle 4 Sur; **Iglesia del Carmen,** Av. 16 de Septiembre at Av. 17 Oriente; and **Iglesia de la Santa Cruz,** in an old neighborhood at Av. 14 Oriente and Calle 14 Sur (the site of Puebla's first Mass, in 1530).

Museo de Santa Monica

This religious museum at Avenida 18 Poniente 103 was founded as a convent in 1610. With the laws of the Reforma, promulgated by President Benito Juárez in 1867, the Catholic nuns of this convent literally went underground and remained hidden there until they were discovered in 1935. The building then was converted into a museum. Visitors can walk through narrow halls, winding stairways, hidden passages, and look through a secret window where the nuns watched Mass in the adjacent church. The museum entrance is through a private home, as it was when the convent was in operation. Open daily Tues.–Sun. 10 A.M.–4:30 P.M.; admission US$2, free on Sunday.

Museo Amparo

Three blocks from the *zócalo* at Calle 2 Sur 708, tel. 222/246-4646, this restored colonial mansion showcases an extensive collection of pre-Hispanic and colonial art. The displays are labeled in Spanish and English, with push-button recordings (headsets cost US$2). Open Wed.–Mon. 10 A.M.–5 P.M.; admission US$2.50, free on Monday. The museum restaurant is very good.

Museo Virreinal

Puebla's newest museum is dedicated to colonial religious art. Housed in the former Hospital de San Pedro, the museum has a permanent exhibit of art from the many churches around the city, displayed in a two-story gray stone building around a courtyard. Note several fine carved sculptures of saints, including the imposing San Cristóbal holding the baby Jesús. One of the rooms traces the construction of the building itself (begun in 1556) and its operation as a hospital. The museum is at Calle 4 Norte 203; tel. 222/246-6618; open Tues.–Sun. 10 A.M.–5 P.M.; admission US$2.

© CHRIS HUMPHREY

Shhh! A whispering 18th-century Santo Domingo at Puebla's Museo Virreinal

Museo Bello y González

José Luis Bello, a businessman who amassed a fortune, spent his riches on this seemingly endless collection of elegant furnishings from throughout Mexico, Europe, and Asia. The museum, Av. 3 Poniente 302, tel. 222/232-9475, displays all manner of art and collectibles, including porcelain, glass, Talavera ceramics, wrought iron, religious vestments, clothing, locks, and even original sheet music by Beethoven. The museum was closed awaiting restoration when we last visited. When last open, guided tours were available in Spanish (English guides by appointment), and museum hours were Tues.–Sun. 10 A.M.–4:30 P.M.; admission was US$1.50, free on Tuesday.

Museo de Artes Populares

This museum, at Calle 5 Norte 1201 (in the exconvent of Santa Rosa), tel. 222/246-2471, houses the Talavera-tiled kitchen with huge cauldrons and other earthenware utensils where legend has it that Dominican nun Sor Andrea de la Asunción created the first *mole poblano.* One of Mexico's most famed dishes, this mole has more than 25 ingredients, including a variety of spices and chiles, chocolate, and turkey. Mexican art is displayed on two floors, and a gift shop offers a selection of local handicrafts. Open Tues.–Sun. 10 A.M.–4:30 P.M.; admission US$1.50.

Museo del Estado Casa de Alfeñiqué

The intricate baroque facade of this building, at Av. 4 Oriente 416, tel. 222/232-0458, is a classic example of *alfeñique* architectural style, named for a white sugar candy made in Puebla. Built in 1790, it now houses the state museum, with old manuscripts related to Puebla history, ethnography on different indigenous groups in the state, and colonial clothing (including the original *china poblana* dress). Parts of the museum were closed for renovation when we visited. Open Tues.–Sun. 10 A.M.–4:30 P.M.; admission US$2.

Casa de los Muñecos (House of Dolls)

The top floor of this house, at Calle 2 Norte at Av. Palofax, is decorated with caricatures of the town fathers who refused to let the owner add the third floor. After going to Mexico City and getting the necessary permission, the owner exacted his vengeance on his opponents by making fun of them in stone. The building suffered extensive interior and exterior damage during a recent quake, though restoration is under way. When it reopens, look inside for a display of more than 200 colonial-era paintings.

Barrio del Artistas

Across the alley from the Teatro Principal, check out the Barrio del Artistas, an exhibition hall that in former years housed the fabric spinners of the local clothing industry. Nowadays it's used by local artists as a workshop and selling space. Open daily.

Centro Cívico Cinco de Mayo

Three km northeast of the *zócalo* at Blvd. Héroes del 5 de Mayo is a complex of parks and buildings on the site of the Battle of Puebla, which gave birth to the Cinco de Mayo fiesta. The **Fuerte de Loreto,** built in 1821, was the center of the battle; 2,000 Mexicans led by Gen. Ignacio Zaragoza tried to defend the fort against an attack by 6,000 French troops. The fort is now a museum containing dioramas of the battle, photos, drawings, and paintings. Open Tues.–Sun. 10 A.M.–4:30 P.M.; admission US$2. Cinco de Mayo is celebrated here each year with a reenactment of the battle and a major fiesta.

Also at the complex are a modern planetarium, the Museo de Historia Natural, and the Museo de Antropología—all open Tues.–Sun. 10 A.M.–4:30 P.M.

Museo del Ferrocarril

Choo-choo buffs should not fail to come to the railroad museum, Calle 11 Norte at Av. 12 Poniente, to study the collection of spiffed-up trains that have been put out to pasture. The antique steam engines and rail cars are open for visitors to examine and explore. In some of the cars visitors find pictures and displays illustrating the history of Mexican trains since 1837. Open Tues.–Sun. 10 A.M.–5 P.M.; free admission.

Africam

At this zoo about eight km from town, you can take a safari ride through 6,075 hectares inhabited by wild animals. Open daily 10 A.M.–5 P.M.; admission is US$8 adults, US$5 children 12 and under. Buses for Africam leave the Central Camionera (CAPU, north of the city at Calle

11 Norte and Blvd. Atlixco) three times daily. A taxi to the park costs about US$5.

ACCOMMODATIONS

Shoestring

At **Hotel Avenida,** Av. 5 Poniente 336, tel. 222/232-2104, the paint is peeling off the walls and the rooms are old and basic, but they're also very cheap and kept clean. Some rooms don't have private bath, so be sure to ask in advance if that's a concern. Hot water is available 7:30–11 A.M. only. Rates: US$8 shared bath or US$11 private bath.

Hotel Victoria, Av. 3 Poniente 306, tel. 222/232-8992, offers basic, rundown rooms with or without TV. Rates: US$12 s/d without TV; US$15 s/d with TV.

Hotel Catedral has two branches—one at Av. 3 Poniente 310, tel. 222/232-2368 and the other a few blocks west. Both offer private and shared rooms and baths at cheap prices. Some of the rooms are apartment-style with two stories and grubby makeshift kitchens. Rates: US$10 s, US$13 d.

Budget

A better value is **Hotel Teresita,** Av. 3 Poniente 309, tel. 222/232-7072. Rooms have recently undergone a facelift and the newly tiled bathrooms are nice. Rates: US$18 s, US$22 d.

Gran Hotel San Agustín, Av. 3 Poniente 531, tel. 222/232-5089, fax 222/232-5089, ext. 600, is a friendly place with clean rooms. Rates: US$21 s/d with breakfast.

A beautiful garden juxtaposed with garish, whorehouse decor mixes the sublime with the ridiculous at **Hotel Virrey de Mendoza,** Reforma 538, tel. 222/242-3903. Rates: US$22 s, US$27 d.

Hotel Alameda, Reforma 141, tel. 222/242-0882, is on the main drag closer to the plaza and has very tidy rooms at great prices. The building dates to the 17th century and has lovely hand-painted tiles and decorous hallways. Rates: US$21 s, US$28 d.

Hotel San Miguel, Av. 3 Poniente 721, tel. 222/242-4860, has a modern facade and a bright clean lobby. The rooms are a little dank and on the monastic side but good value for the increased cleanliness and security. Rates: US$22 s, US$28 d.

Inexpensive

A dramatic step up in quality is **Hotel Imperial,** Av. 4 Oriente 212, tel. 222/242-4981. This spacious hotel has 65 large rooms each with TV, telephone, and private bath. Amenities include a restaurant, pool table, parking lot, hot water all day, and bicycles for rent at US$3 a day. Anyone carrying a copy of this guide (not a photocopy) gets a 30 percent discount, making it that much better a value. Breakfast is included. Rates: US$30 s, US$37 d.

Hotel Colonial, a block from the plaza (and across from its own picturesque little square) at Calle 4 Sur 105, tel. 222/246-4612, is convenient for exploring downtown. The rooms are fairly large, and some have balconies, wood floors, and tile baths. The good restaurant has a gorgeous stained glass ceiling. Parking available. Rates: US$36 s, US$44 d.

You'll find nice rooms at the **Hotel Palace,** Av. 2 Oriente 13, tel. 222/232-2430. The restaurant El Sardinero is adjacent and offers room service. King rooms for just a few dollars more have better light and a street view. Rates: US$36 s, US$48 d.

At **Hotel Santiago,** Av. 3 Poniente 106, tel. 222/242-2860, fax 222/242-2779, the staff may go a bit overboard in their use of cleaning products, but the sparkling rooms and sterilized bathrooms of this modern hotel are nothing to scoff at. Rates: US$34 s/d.

Moderate

Hotel Royalty, Portal Hidalgo 8, tel. 222/242-0204, offers 44 rooms and an outdoor café under the *portales.* The hotel and café face the *zócalo* and make for a lively atmosphere. The hotel's interior is lovely, although rooms are somewhat small. Rates: US$45 s, US$56 d.

Expensive

Hotel Lastra, Calzada de los Fuertes 2633 (on the Cerro de Guadalupe), tel. 222/235-9755, www.hotellastra.com.mx, has 52 pleasing, large rooms with spic-and-span bathrooms. Rates: US$93 s/d.

Just one block north of the *zócalo* is **Hotel Posada San Pedro,** Av. 2 Oriente 202, tel. 222/246-5077, fax 222/246-5376. Housed in a 16th-century building, the hotel is a good mix of interesting architecture and modern amenities such as the interior courtyard pool, gym, and hot tubs. Rates: US$88 s/d.

The **Holiday Inn,** Av. 2 Oriente 211, tel. 222/223-6600, www.holidayinnpuebla.com.mx, has 75 recently remodeled rooms in an elegant old French-colonial building one block from the plaza. A white-linen restaurant (Aranjues), bar, rooftop pool, and parking lot are on the premises. Rooms have hand-painted bed frames and the lobby is decorated with antiques and Oriental rugs. Rates: US$105 s/d; US$15 per extra person.

Premium

One of the more interesting high-end hotel options is **Mesón Sacristía,** Av. 9 Oriente 16, tel. 222/246-6084, www.mexicoboutiquehotels.com/mesonsacristia, in the vicinity of Los Sapos. Each of the hotel's nine rooms is individually appointed with fabulous antiques and collectibles such as a '40s-era typewriter turned into a bedside lamp. An antique store, the lovely Restaurante Sacristía, and Bar El Confesionario are all within the 18th-century building that houses the hotel. Rates: US$165 s/d, US$190 suite.

Hotel El Mesón del Ángel, Hermanos Serdán 807, tel. 222/223-8300, www.mesondelangel.com.mx, is one of the better hotels outside of the city center. The 190-room modern hotel has a good restaurant, bar, and car service. Rates: US$148 s/d.

The **Best Western Hotel Real de Puebla,** and its modern yellow tower, is on the west side of the city at Av. 5 Poniente 2522, tel. 222/230-0122, toll free in Mexico 800/227-2700. Amenities include a pool, spa, workout room (you can schedule time with a personal trainer), dining room, cocktail lounge, coffee shop, and a popular disco. The tan-colored rooms feature minibars, satellite TV, twin double beds, plush carpets, and beautifully appointed tile bathrooms. Suites are available. Ask for a west-facing view to see Popocatépetl and Ixtaccíhuatl, or an east view to see Orizaba and Malinche. You have to be an early riser to catch a glimpse of these peaks though, because the smog covers them quickly. Rates: US$115 s/d.

The **Camino Real Puebla,** in the downtown area at Av. 7 Poniente 105, tel. 222/229-0909, toll free in Mexico 800/901-2300, is not what you might expect if you've seen other hotels in the chain. No swimming pool or tennis courts here, just top-quality rooms in the late-16th-century Ex-Convento de la Concepción. Amenities include two restaurants and a bar; for alfresco eating and drinking, tables are placed outside on the central patio—a very pleasant place on a sunny day. Rates: US$180 and up.

FOOD

Puebla is noted for its exceptional cuisine. In addition to mole, which was first made at the Santa Rosa convent, several other local specialties are worth a try. *Mixiotes* are made by wrapping barbecued meat (beef, pork, lamb, or goat) and spices in a maguey leaf (not edible) and steaming. *Tinga* is a meat and vegetable melange, sort of half salad, half stew, and delicious. *Chiles en nogada* consists of meat-stuffed green *poblano* chile peppers in a white sauce of crushed walnuts, cream cheese, and pomegranate seeds. The patriotic colors of the dish (red, green, and white) make it popular around Independence Day, September 16. *Taco árabe* is a Middle Eastern version of the taco—a pita bread wrapped around meat cooked on a spit. **Tacos Tony,** Av. 3 Poniente 149, tel. 222/232-0675, is a good place to try one.

For an outdoor seat and a good strong cup of coffee, the **Cafe Aguirre,** Av. 5 de Mayo 4, is a good choice any time of day. For a solid meal, try **La Princesa,** Portal Juárez 101, tel. 222/232-1195, where the breakfasts, appetizers, and *comida corrida* are all reasonably priced and hearty. This side of the plaza has several restaurants including **Restaurante Cafe El Vasco,** specializing in Spanish dishes including good Valencian paella.

The sidewalk café at **Hotel Royalty,** Portal Hidalgo 8, tel. 222/242-0202, is a relaxing spot for cocktails or a nice meal, though prices are slightly high.

Restaurant Bar Casa Real, Av. 4 Oriente 208, tel. 222/246-5876, two blocks from the *zócalo,* is open for breakfast, lunch, and dinner, and serves local specialties such as mole, *chalupas, chiles en nogada,* and a large selection of meats. Prices are moderate. On weekends (and some weeknights) live music is presented; shows start at 9 P.M.

Restaurante Chesa Veglia, Av. 2 Oriente 208, tel. 222/232-1641, serves good Swiss food including cheese, meat, and chocolate fondues. Dishes cost US$5–12. Open 1–11 P.M.

At **Vittorio's Pizzería,** Portal Morelos 106, tel. 222/232-7900, you can enjoy a cappuccino or espresso outside, or stay indoors if it's cold. If you haven't had a Mexican-style pizza yet, here's your chance. And if you haven't had your share of mole already, the restaurant offers a pizza version. Pizzas range US$4–12, and the restaurant delivers. The menu also includes pasta, salad, and *típico* fare. Hours are 7 A.M.–midnight.

Two vegetarian restaurants run by the same group are close to the city center. **Barra Vegetariana La Zanahoria,** Av. 5 Oriente 206, tel. 222/232-4813, and **El Vegetariano** both sell veggie versions of fast food and Mexican specialties as well as wheat germ and bulk health food products.

Legendary **Fonda de Santa Clara,** with locations at Av. 3 Poniente 307, tel. 222/242-2659, and Av. 3 Poniente 920, tel. 222/246-1952, is a popular and often noisy restaurant serving traditional regional food. Try the *mixiotes, ingas,* or *mole poblano.* The adventurous can even order *gusanos de maguey en salsa borracha* (maguey worms in tequila sauce). The menu is available in English. Prices are US$3–15.

Restaurante Típico La China Poblana's, one block south of El Parian at Calle 6 Norte 1, offers a small storefront room with three tables next to the kitchen and a larger dining room in the rear. It's decorated with local plates, masks, clothing, and a life-sized China Poblana. The food is good, but there's no written menu, so be sure to ask carefully. Double-check your order and the price if your Spanish is weak.

Plazuela de los Sapos, on the southeast side of the city's center, is another good arena for restaurants and mariachis. The small plaza and its surrounding streets are home to several upscale restaurants, good, cheap eateries, as well as interesting home furnishing shops to browse in. **El Resguardo de los Ángeles,** Calle 6 Sur 504, tel. 222/246-4106; **La Guadalupana Restaurante,** Av. 5 Oriente 605, 222/242-4886; and **La Bella Elena,** Calle 6 Sur 310, tel. 222/242-0702, are a few of the nicer spots for drinks or dinner, all offering local and international dishes for US$5–12.

The west side of town, Calle Juárez in particular, offers the city's largest array of high-end Mexican, European, and Asian restaurants. Cruise this strip in a taxi and you'll be sure to find what you're looking for if you've had enough of the historical district. **La Cava Restaurant and Bar,** Av. Juárez 2302, serves good-quality international food in a mellow, refined ambience with good service. Pasta dishes and salads range US$4–8, steaks and seafood run US$8–18.

Charlie's China Poblana, Calle Juárez 1918, has a tile facade, adjoining garden, and merry-go-round horses to greet you as you enter. The food varies from Poblano fare to international dishes such as salads, pasta, and steak. Charlie's is a fun alternative and lively nightspot in this chic neighborhood.

ENTERTAINMENT AND EVENTS

Theaters

Teatro Principal, Calle 6 Norte at Av. 8 Oriente, tel. 222/232-6085, and **Teatro U.A.P.,** Calle 4 Sur 104, both offer performing-arts events—mostly concerts. For a schedule, check at the tourist office.

Nightlife

For a taste of the bohemian life in Puebla, visit **El Convento de las Carolinas,** Av. 3 Oriente 403. This gallery, live music venue, bar, and *antojería* spot is popular with the local literati as well as young people.

La Leyenda Restaurant and Bar is more bar than restaurant and conveniently located next to Vittorio's. This hole-in-the-wall caters to a young crowd and the music is invariably techno. There are lots of small rooms to hide in and drinks are reasonable at US$1–4.

Librería Cafetería, Reforma at Calle 7 Norte, is a bookstore and coffeehouse that transforms itself into a hip nightspot come dark. Don't forget your black turtleneck. Open 7 A.M.–1 A.M.

Both the Juárez area and the road from Puebla to Cholula (eight km) are home to several of the area's discos. Most don't get started until about 11 P.M. It's best to ask around to find out which discos are the current favorites.

Sports

Soccer packs in the locals during the season (September–December and January–May) at Estadio Cuauhtémoc, Calz. Ignacio Zaragoza 666, tel. 222/226-2166. For **bullfights,** go to Plaza de Toros El Relicario, roughly five km (three miles) from downtown on the old highway to Tehuacán, tel. 222/236-1868. A *lienzo charro* (charro ring) holding 4,000 people hosts ***charreadas*** at Carretera Tehuacán Poniente 1032, tel. 222/283-6308. *Charrería* is big in Puebla, and *charreadas* are held most weekends and holidays.

SHOPPING

Puebla is an outstanding shopping city, filled with stores selling fine Talavera tile, pottery, onyx, handicrafts from surrounding regions, wool and cotton clothing, *amate* fiber paper, and a myriad of other artwork and handicrafts. On Sunday—market day in Puebla—Amerindian artisans from surrounding villages bring their folk crafts here to sell.

Market Days

Market days at a few of the surrounding cities can be an expedition of discovery: **San Martín Texmelucan**—Tuesday and Friday; **Huejotzingo**—Saturday; **Cholula**—Wednesday and Sunday; **Tepeaca**—Friday; **Tehuacán**—Saturday; **Puebla**—Sunday.

El Parian

A former 18th-century clothing warehouse, El Parian, on Calle 8 Norte between Av. 2 and Av. 6 Oriente, today houses rows of shops selling all manner of handicrafts. If you're looking for good quality Talavera, and don't mind the price, check out **Centro de Talavera La Colonial,** Av. 6 Oriente 11, tel. 222/242-2340.

Callejón de los Sapos

A quiet antique district during the week, this alley converts into a bustling flea market on Sunday. At Av. 7 Oriente and Calle 4 Sur, three blocks south and one block east of the *zócalo.*

Mercado Municipal

This sprawling indoor market at Calle 11 Norte between Av. 2 and Av. 6 Poniente is chockablock with all manner of foods from the region.

Amozoc

If you've always had the cowboy fantasy and want to indulge in all the accoutrements, take a short bus ride out to this small town 17 km due east of Puebla on the free highway to Tehuacán. Here you'll find superb craftsmen in dozens of shops fashioning what is reputed to be the finest ornamental silver and ironware for Mexican *charro* outfits. Particularly famous are the spurs, but they also make dagger handles, buckles, and *mancuernos,* chained brooches worn on clothing. Prices are not cheap but quality is excellent.

INFORMATION AND SERVICES

Tourist Office

The state tourism office, Av. 5 Oriente 3, tel. 222/246-2044, has a very friendly and helpful staff—many have a good command of English, and their love of the beauty and culture around them is evident. Maps and directions are cheerfully provided. Open Mon.–Sat. 9:30 A.M.–8:30 P.M., Sun. 9 A.M.–2 P.M.

An information kiosk at the CAPU bus terminal offers the usual printed literature and also sponsors tours of the city—a good way to get your first bearings. The tours begin at 10 A.M. and are conducted in English and Spanish; cost is about US$17, which includes entrance fees to museums. At 3 P.M. the microbus travels to Cholula, if enough people sign up. Check tour schedules as they tend to change.

The municipal tourist office, in the Palacio Municipal on the plaza, at the corner of Av. Palofax and Calle 2 Norte, tel. 222/246-1580, can also be helpful with city information. Open Mon.–Fri. 9 A.M.–8 P.M., Sat. 9 A.M.–5 P.M., Sun. 9 A.M.–3 P.M.

One tour company operating in Puebla and the surrounding area is **Servicios Turisticos Culturales de Puebla,** tel. 222/232-4055 or 242-1511, offering 2.5-hour tours to Cholula (US$16), as well as to Huejotzingo, Cacaxtla, and around Puebla city.

Communication

The post office is in the Archbishop's Palace at the corner of Av. 5 Oriente and 16 de Septiembre; it isn't well marked. Open Mon.–Fri. 8 A.M.–8 P.M., Sat. 9 A.M.–1 P.M. One Internet place in town is Café Internet, at Calle 4 Norte 7.

Money

Several banks scattered about the center of town exchange both dollars and traveler's checks. Try Bancomer, Av. 3 Poniente 116, and Banamex, Av. Reforma 135. Casa de Cambio Azteca, Calle 2 Sur 104, is another good place if you don't feel like waiting in bank lines.

Medical

Hospital UPAEP is at Av. 5 Poniente 715, tel. 222/246-6099 or 246-6464. Farmacia El Fenix del Centro has two locations: at Av. 4 Poniente 111, tel. 222/242-1974, and 5 de Mayo 803, tel. 222/242-2361.

GETTING THERE

Driving

The modern toll road (México 150D) goes from Mexico City clear to Veracruz and avoids larger cities. To Puebla it is 130 km, 90 minutes, and US$5.50 in tolls. The free road crosses the same mountain pass but can be difficult to follow leaving Mexico City. Coming into Puebla, the free road can be slow as it passes through several towns, but it also gives an excuse to stop at the impressive monastery at Huejotzingo.

Bus

CAPU, the large Puebla bus station, is north of the city at Calle 11 Norte and Blvd. Atlixco. From the station, you can get to the city center on a *combi* marked "Centro" (US$.30 cents) or a *sitio* taxi (US$3). First- and second-class buses depart here for Mexico City's Terminal Tapo almost constantly, all day and night; US$7 first class or US$5 second class. **Estrella Roja,** tel. 222/249-7099, runs the express bus direct to the Mexico City airport 15 times daily for US$13. **ADO,** tel. 222/225-9001, offers first-class buses to Jalapa (US$9.50), Veracruz (US$17), Mérida (US$73), Cancún (US$86), and elsewhere in the southeast of the country. **Cristóbal Colón,** tel. 222/249-7327, runs first-class buses to destinations in Oaxaca and Chiapas. **Autobuses Unidos,** tel. 222/225-9004, offers first- and second-class buses to Veracruz (US$17), Oaxaca (US$20), and elsewhere. **Estrella de Oro** has frequent buses throughout the day to Cholula and Huejotzingo.

GETTING AROUND

Most of the sights in Puebla are close to the *zócalo* and an easy walk from one another. For anything farther afield, **taxis** and ***colectivos*** are cheap and go everywhere. If you hail an unmetered taxi, don't board till you know the cost. One taxi company you can call for a car is **Radio Taxi,** tel. 222/243-7055 or 243-7212. Rent a car from **Budget,** Av. Juárez 1914, tel. 222/232-9108; **Renta de Autos Rams,** 16 Oriente 5029, tel. 222/235-9322 or 222-4205; and **Easy Rent A Car,** 7 Sur at the corner of 41 Poniente, tel. 222/243-9100 or 211-1413.

CHOLULA

The major population center in the region when Cortés arrived, the Cholulans planned a secret revolt against the conquistadors, which was discovered by Cortés's Tlaxcalan allies. The Cholulans paid with their lives, one of the more sordid episodes of the Spanish conquest. The tranquil scene today belies the dramatic bloodbath of the Amerindians that took place in Cholula, when 6,000 warriors were slaughtered in one day.

Cortés was so incensed by the Cholulans' almost successful ploy that he vowed to build a Catholic church in Cholula for each day in the year. He didn't quite make it, but there are at least 39.

Cholula had, and still has, the largest ancient structure in the Americas, the Great Pyramid of Tepanampa. It covers 18 hectares, is 60 meters (195 feet) high, and has a volume of three million cubic meters. Cholula lies 10 km west of Puebla.

Around the Plaza

On the east side of the *zócalo* is the fortresslike **Ex-Convento y Iglesia de San Gabriel** (San Gabriel Monastery) with its Moorish look and 49 domes. The Franciscan ex-convent is one of the original 12 built after the conquest. Construction began in 1549 and was completed in 1571. Check out the entrance door with 122 Roman nails, each a different design. On the north side of the *zócalo,* you'll find **Parroquia de San Pedro,** which dates to 1641.

The *portales* on this plaza are reputedly the longest in Latin America.

Gran Pirámide de Tepanampa

If it weren't for the church sitting on top, you might never realize this large hill is actually the largest pyramid in the continent, with a base measuring 450 meters on each side. Older than Teotihuacán, the Great Pyramid of Tepanampa of Cholula was in use before the birth of Christ.

As was the custom in ancient Mesoamerican civilizations, seven structures were superimposed over the original pyramid. The whole process, from original pyramid to seventh structure, spanned 600 years.

Guides are available at the pyramid and it's a good idea to hire one; you'll see and appreciate more than if you go it alone in this lighted, subterranean maze. The guides charge US$6. Excavations in the pyramid began in 1931 and continue today. About eight km of tunnels have been dug, but only a section is open to the public. The pyramid is open daily 10 A.M.–5 P.M.

On the south side of the pyramid is the **Gran Plaza,** also called Patio de los Altares. A large building west of the plaza, not generally open to the public, houses a 50-meter-long mural depicting a drunken bash of *pulque*-drinking from the 3rd century.

Follow the signs to a small museum containing pieces of pre-Hispanic art, obsidian, and ceramics.

Admission to the pyramid alone is US$2. Admission to the entire complex, including the museum, costs US$5; flash/video camera use costs US$3 more.

To get to the beautifully gilded **Capilla de la Virgen de los Remedios,** first built in 1594 and rebuilt after an earthquake in the mid-19th century, turn back the way you came and follow the steep, winding path to the top of the hill. On a clear day the views of Popocatépetl and Ixtaccíhuatl from the chapel are spectacular.

Accommodations

Budget: The basic **Hotel y Bar Reforma,** Calle 4 Sur 101, tel. 222/247-0149, has reasonably maintained rooms with private baths a block from the *zócalo.* Rates: US$20 s or d, US$26 d with two beds.

Moderate: Hotel Posada Señorial, Cinco de Mayo 1400, tel. 222/247-0049, is a clean, pleasant spot just outside of town on the road back toward Puebla. Rates: US$33 s, US$55 s/d, US$66 t.

Expensive: Villa Arqeológica, Av. 2 Poniente 601, tel. 222/247-1966, fax 222/247-1508, U.S. tel. 800/258-2633, is one of the resorts in the Club Med–owned chain of hotels built near various archaeological zones in Mexico. It's about 15 minutes from the Great Pyramid and offers air-conditioning, tennis courts, swimming, a well-stocked library, and a reasonably good French restaurant. Rates: US$84 s, US$95 d.

Food

One block off the main street, **La Casona,** Av. 3 Oriente 9, tel. 222/247-2776, is an attractive restaurant filled with trees and flowers. Take a seat on the outdoor patio (or inside if the patio is full, as it often is on weekends) and enjoy a good-quality traditional Mexican meal for US$4–8. Open daily 1–10 P.M.

La Pirámide, Morelos 416, is another popular spot with locals, offering moderately priced, traditional regional food. Open daily 1–11 P.M.

Cafe Enamorada and its adjacent shop frame the southwest corner of the *zócalo;* it's a good spot for outdoor dining. Open daily 9 A.M.–11 P.M. This side of the plaza is full of busy cafés, ice-cream parlors, and coffee shops. For a longer, more leisurely meal try **Los Cesones.** Dine inside the brightly painted restaurant or at one of the sidewalk tables that offer a good view of the square. A lunch buffet is available daily for US$3.

The Italian Coffee Company has managed to find its way into this ancient city just a few doors down from Los Cesones and next door to **Hawaiian Paradise Natural Fruit Juice.** There is also **Les Tolepanes,** whose mushroom *antojitos* are not to be missed, and nearby **Restaurant Concordi** with a four-course *comida corrida* including coffee or tea for US$4.

Restaurant-Bar Los Jarrones, Portal Guerrero 7, tel. 222/247-1098, is a charming spot with Mexican food ranging US$3–7.

Tacos Tony, at Morelos 212, serves inexpensive *tacos árabes,* a regional style of taco in pita bread.

Information and Services

The post office is at Miguel Alemán 314, two blocks from the plaza. You can change money at the Bancomer or Banamex on the plaza, or nearby at Casa de Cambio Azteca.

Getting There

Buses from CAPU bus station to Cholula, Huejotzingo, and San Martín depart every 15 minutes (Estrella de Oro) or every half hour (Estrellas Rojas) between 5 A.M. and 9 P.M. Minibuses also leave Puebla from Avenida 2 Poniente at Calle 13 Sur, across from the Railroad Museum.

If you are driving from Puebla, take Avenida Juárez west, go halfway around the traffic circle (México 190 to Cholula), and continue for about 10 kilometers.

Near Cholula

Just south of Cholula are two towns worth visiting: **Santa María Tonantzintla,** famed for its pottery as well as a 16th-century church; and **Acatepec,** with a lovely baroque church boasting a spectacular wood and tile facade.

West of Cholula, a dirt road heads to the town of **San Nicolás de los Ranchos** and continues up into the forest to reach the **Paso de Cortés** between the volcanoes of Popocatépetl and Ixtaccíhuatl, about 30 km from Cholula. From here a paved road continues down to Amecameca and from there on to Mexico City or Cuautla. This road is passable in any decent passenger car—if you don't mind a little dust—and the scenery is fantastic.

Fourteen kilometers northwest of Cholula, on the free highway back to Mexico City, is the dusty town of **Huejotzingo,** site of a 16th-century monastery, one of the first built in Mexico. The mix of indigenous and Christian motifs in the carvings on the church and adjacent cloister are fascinating. Note the ominous carved skulls on the courtyard towers. Inside is an interesting museum on the missionaries in Mexico, open daily 10 A.M.–4:30 P.M.

Tlaxcala and Vicinity

Tlaxcala, capital of the state of the same name, is a beautiful colonial city built on the site of the pre-Hispanic capital of the Tlaxcalteca people. This was the first major Amerindian city seen by Cortés and his band of conquerers as they marched toward the Aztec capital of Tenochtitlán in 1519. After fighting and losing to the Spaniards, the Tlaxcaltecas opted to join the conquerers in fighting the Aztecs, their hated enemies. Cortés and a group of Franciscan monks founded the colonial city in 1520. The first bishopric of the country was established here in 1527, and the chapels of the San Francisco convent were built in 1537. About 120 km east of Mexico City, Tlaxcala still has a population of only around 50,000. Though not atop anyone's list of must-see cities in central Mexico, the small city is a relaxed place to enjoy a day of touring or just to escape from the hectic capital.

SIGHTS

Plaza de la Constitución

In the center of the city, Plaza de la Constitución holds a 19th-century bandstand surrounded by flowers. The nearby octagonal fountain, topped by a carved stone cross, was given to the city in 1646 by Spain's King Philip IV.

Palacio de Gobierno

The 16th-century Palacio de Gobierno, on the north side of the plaza, has suffered a turbulent history. It was burned during an Indian uprising in 1692 and rocked by an earthquake 20 years later; only the lower part of the facade and interior arches remain of the original structure.

On the first floor are a series of murals by Tlaxcalan artist Desiderio Hernández Xochitiotzin depicting the history of Tlaxcala since pre-Hispanic times. The work, begun in 1957, is still in progress; it was interrupted for years due to disagreements between Hernández and local politicos on the content of the mural.

Tours are available; flashless photography only. The lobby is open weekdays 9 A.M.–9 P.M.

Tlaxcala cityscape

Parroquia de San José

Across the street from the Plaza de la Constitución, Parroquía de San José dates from early in the 17th century. The Bishop of Puebla dictated the original design, including the mortar images, tiled facade, and lone tower. The dome was damaged in an 1864 earthquake, and the resulting cracks were covered over with the tiles. Open Mon.–Sat. 6 A.M.–8 P.M., Sun. 7 A.M.–8 P.M.; no flash photography allowed. Masses go on much of Sunday morning.

Catedral de Nuestra Señora de la Asunción

The cathedral is part of the complex of the Ex-Convento de San Francisco, which began construction in 1520. Among the interesting details in the church are heavy cedar crossbeams decorated with stars and the wrought-iron gate of the Virgin's Chapel. In the Capilla de la Tercer Orden is the stone baptismal font first used in 1520 to baptize the four rulers of Tlaxcala. Open Mon.–Fri. 6 A.M.–2 P.M. and 4–8 P.M., Sat. 6 A.M.–7:30 P.M., Sun. 6 A.M.–8:30 P.M. No flash photography allowed.

Museo Regional de Tlaxcala

Next to the cathedral in the old cloisters of the Ex-Convento de San Francisco, this museum, tel. 246/462-0262, contains exhibits from pre-Hispanic to the independence era, as well as a

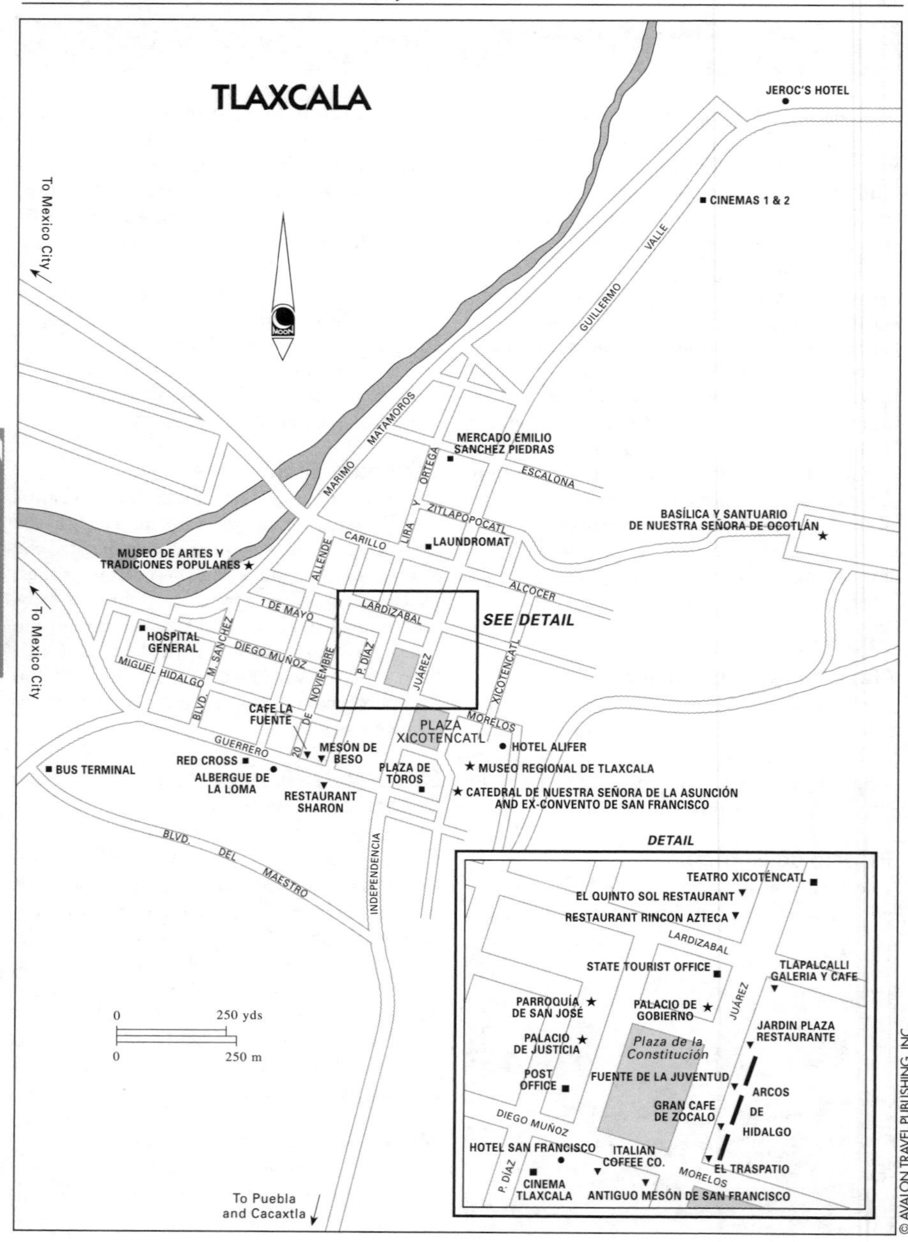
TLAXCALA
JEROC'S HOTEL
CINEMAS 1 & 2
GUILLERMO VALLE
To Mexico City
MARIMO MATAMOROS
MERCADO EMILIO SANCHEZ PIEDRAS
ESCALONA
LIRA Y ORTEGA
ZITLAPOPOCATL
BASÍLICA Y SANTUARIO DE NUESTRA SEÑORA DE OCOTLÁN
CARILLO
ALLENDE
LAUNDROMAT
MUSEO DE ARTES Y TRADICIONES POPULARES
ALCOCER
1 DE MAYO
LARDIZABAL
SEE DETAIL
HOSPITAL GENERAL
DIEGO MUÑOZ
MIGUEL HIDALGO
M. SANCHEZ
20 DE NOVIEMBRE
P. DÍAZ
JUAREZ
XICOTENCATL
BLVD.
CAFE LA FUENTE
MORELOS
PLAZA XICOTENCATL
GUERRERO
MESÓN DE BESO
HOTEL ALIFER
BUS TERMINAL
RED CROSS
ALBERGUE DE LA LOMA
PLAZA DE TOROS
MUSEO REGIONAL DE TLAXCALA
RESTAURANT SHARON
CATEDRAL DE NUESTRA SEÑORA DE LA ASUNCIÓN AND EX-CONVENTO DE SAN FRANCISCO
BLVD. DEL MAESTRO
INDEPENDENCIA
0 250 yds
0 250 m
To Puebla and Cacaxtla
DETAIL
TEATRO XICOTÉNCATL
EL QUINTO SOL RESTAURANT
RESTAURANT RINCON AZTECA
LARDIZABAL
STATE TOURIST OFFICE
TLAPALCALLI GALERIA Y CAFE
PARROQUÍA DE SAN JOSÉ
PALACIO DE GOBIERNO
JUÁREZ
JARDIN PLAZA RESTAURANTE
PALACIO DE JUSTICIA
Plaza de la Constitución
POST OFFICE
FUENTE DE LA JUVENTUD
ARCOS DE HIDALGO
GRAN CAFE DE ZOCALO
DIEGO MUÑOZ
HOTEL SAN FRANCISCO
ITALIAN COFFEE CO.
EL TRASPATIO
MORELOS
P. DÍAZ
CINEMA TLAXCALA
ANTIGUO MESÓN DE SAN FRANCISCO

EXCURSIONS

bookstore and library. Exhibits include a *chac mool* (sculpture of the ancient Maya god) and the original state constitution. Open Tues.–Sun. 10 A.M.–5 P.M.; admission US$2. Tours are available.

Basílica y Santuario de Nuestra Señora de Ocotlán

On a hill above the city is this high baroque church, with ornate sculptures of the 12 apostles, seven archangels, and other religious figures, framed by plaster columns. Note the star-shaped stained-glass window above the choir depicting the Immaculate Conception. Open daily 7 A.M.–7 P.M.; get permission before taking pictures.

Plaza de Toros

Dating from the early 19th century, the town bullring, just off Independencia on Calle Capilla Abierta, is Mexico's oldest existing *plaza de toros.* Open for touring daily 10 A.M.–10 P.M.

Museo de Artes y Tradiciones Populares

In this living museum on Marimo Matamoros, tel. 246/462-2337, the artists are on display along with the folk art produced. Exhibits highlight the traditional lifestyle of the region's Amerindian people and include an Otomí kitchen complete with three stone *tlecuil* (stoves) and large cooking vessels, a *típico* bedroom, designs for *huipiles* (blouses) and *titixtle* (woolen dresses), a *cuexcomate* (for storing corn), and a working *temazcal* (sauna).

Upstairs Otomí women spin wool into yarn using traditional methods and use different types of looms to make sweaters, blankets, jackets, and rugs. Another display shows the making of *pulque,* a regional drink of fermented cactus juice. Throughout the museum are exhibits of local costumes and masks.

In the bookstore downstairs you'll find lots of information about Tlaxcala, including some in English. A food stand offers visitors a taste of traditional Tlaxcalteca cuisine. Open Tues.–Sun. 11 A.M.–6 P.M.; admission US$2.

Santa Ana Chiautempan

This small town, six km east of Tlaxcala, is famous for its woolen textiles and makes a good afternoon outing. After a round of shopping, stop for a look at Santa Ana's two colonial churches, the **Iglesia de Nuestra Señora Santa Ana Chiautempan,** built in 1588, and the **Parroquia de Santa Ana,** finished at the end of the 17th century.

ACCOMMODATIONS

Budget

Albergue de la Loma, Av. Guerrero 58, tel. 246/462-0424, is small and pleasantly hidden at the top of a long and winding staircase facing the street. The 18 rooms—some with a view overlooking the city—are comfortable and well lit. The restaurant/bar serves inexpensive regional food, with a view over town to contemplate as you eat. Parking is available. Rates: US$20 s, US$24 d.

Hotel Alifer, Av. Morelos 11 (off Independencia), tel. 246/462-5678, has rooms of varying sizes, each with double beds, a writing desk, marble-tiled bath, and TV. Other amenities include a restaurant/bar and parking. Rates: US$28 s/d.

Moderate

Jeroc's, Blvd. Revolución 4-Bis. outside of downtown, tel. 246/462-1577, offers modern clean rooms with double beds, TVs, and stereo music; the common areas include a pool, tennis courts, conference room, restaurant, and disco. Rates: US$48 s, US$59 d.

Expensive

Hotel Posada San Francisco, Plaza de la Constitución 17, tel. 246/462-6022, fax 246/462-6818, faces the *zócalo* and is a large, roomy building with interior courtyards and all the amenities including a good restaurant, **Piedras Negras,** a billiards room, tennis courts, a boutique, a library, and the **Bar Rancho.** Rates: US$77 s, US$92 d.

Premium

Misión Tlaxcala, 10 km out of town on the highway to Apizaco, tel. 246/461-0000, fax 246/461-0178, has a drafty old section with iron-railed balconies and high ceilings, and a more standard modern new section. Amenities include tennis courts, a pool, and room service. The restaurant serves an excellent Sunday brunch for US$11 per person, open to nonguests. Rates: US$113 s/d and up.

FOOD

Restaurant Café del Teatro, at the 19th century–era Teatro Xicoténcatl at Av. Juárez 21, serves a decent breakfast, soups, sandwiches, and *antojitos* for US$3–4, and dinner entrées for US$4–7. The restaurant at **Hotel Albergue de La Loma** is a good spot to try delicious regional cuisine. For an interesting taste sensation, try *chamorro al pulque,* a pork dish prepared with *pulque.* Meals cost US$3–5.

Facing the plaza and shaded beneath the Arcos de Hidalgo are several lovely restaurants with outdoor dining as well as cozy, indoor tables. **El Traspatio,** Plaza de Constitución 8, tel. 246/462-5419, specializes in a *filete de res con huitlacoche* (beef steak smothered in a cream sauce made with delicious corn fungus) for US$6. Next door is **Gran Cafe del Zócalo** where the prices and setup are less fancy, but the cuisine is similar.

Fuente de la Juventud is a burger, salad, and juice joint with a *comida corrida* for US$3.

For regional versions of familiar dishes try the *quesadillas cacaxtla* or the *spaghetti tlaxcalteca* at **Jardín Plaza Restaurante** in the center of the Arcos.

The **Tlapalcalli Galeria y Cafe** on the *zócalo's* northern corner is the place to go for a dose of the bohemian life in Tlaxcala. Open 10 A.M.–11 P.M., the restaurant serves *comida corrida* for US$3 as well good coffee and crêpes. The gallery houses a higher caliber of art than is usually seen in the coffeehouse atmosphere and serves as a bookstore and venue for live music and performance art.

The southern end of the *zócalo*—home to the Hotel Posada San Francisco—offers the **Antiguo Mesón de San Francisco.** The restaurant is a few doors down and an affordable white tablecloth experience with prices around US$2–7. **The Italian Coffee Company** has a branch next door with gourmet coffees to sip or take away.

Restaurant Rincón Azteca, on Av. Juárez just off the plaza, offers regional and national foods. Regional specialties include *pechuga tlaxcalteca,* chicken breast stuffed with *huitlacoche* (corn fungus). Full meals cost US$4–7, while soups and snacks are US$2–4. Open Mon.–Sat. 7:30 A.M.–8 P.M., Sun. 9 A.M.–6 P.M.

El Quinto Sol, Juárez 12, is a good vegetarian option just a few doors north of Rincón Azteca. *Comida corrida* costs US$2. Hours are Mon.–Sat. 8 A.M.–7 P.M.

For a good cup of coffee and a snack break head to **Cafe La Fuente,** Guerrero on the corner of 20 de Noviembre. The small café is upstairs from the gift shop **El Regalito. Restaurant Sharon,** also on Guerrero between Porfirio Diaz and Juárez, has an excellent *comida corrida* for US$4, as well as *queso fundido* and *pozole* for US$2.

Across the street is **Mesón de Beso,** a lively hole-in-the-wall with cheap burritos, *sincronizadas,* and daily specials for US$2–3.

RECREATION

Balnearios

Dotting the countryside around Tlaxcala are many small *balnearios* or swimming spas, which make good places to cool off. They're usually crowded with Mexican families on weekends, so try to go during the week.

A few near Tlaxcala are **Zacatelco,** 18 km out of Tlaxcala by way of México 150 and 119; **Palo Huérfano,** 16 km from Tlaxcala via 150 and 119; **El Montecito,** 19 km from Tlaxcala via 150 and 119; **San Benito,** two km from Apizaco via México 119; **Los Pinos,** six km from Tlaxcala via 150 and 119; and **Santa Lucía,** 16 km from Tlaxcala via 150 and 119. For more information about these *balnearios,* ask at the tourist office.

ENTERTAINMENT AND EVENTS

Shopping

Bazar del Claustro, Plaza Xicoténcatl 8, tel. 246/462-2258, is a great place to browse for art, jewelry, and other collectibles, although prices can be high. **Museo de Artes y Tradiciones**

Populares sells the high-quality textile work of its artisans, but you might find the same quality at a lower price in the town of Santa Ana Chiautempan first. **Mercado Emilio Sanchez Piedras,** a standard town market for food and other necessities, is on the corner of Lira y Ortega and Escalona, four blocks north of the *zócalo.*

For high-end browsing, **La Tlaxcalteca Tendajón Cultural,** tel. 246/462-0014, ext. 24, can be found amid the row of restaurants beneath the Arcos de Hidalgo. Regional music, books, lithographs, textiles, carved wooden sculpture, and reproduction silver pieces are sold here. Hours are Tues.–Sun. 10 A.M.–8 P.M.

Regional Fiestas

Fiestas de la Virgen de Ocotlán take place on the first and third Mondays in May. On August 15 look for **Fiesta de la Virgen de la Asunción,** one of the biggest events in the state. The **Feria de Tlaxcala** comes to town the last week of October through the first week of November.

INFORMATION AND SERVICES

Tourist Information

The state tourist office is just off the *zócalo* at the corner of Juárez and Lardizabal, tel. 246/462-0027. A friendly and helpful staff will give you information and maps.

Money

Banamex is at Plaza Xicoténcatl 8, and Bancomer is at Av. Juárez 54.

Communication

The post office is on the Plaza de la Constitución. The telegraph is at Porfirio Díaz 6. Long-distance phones are available at Av. Juárez 56-C (8:30 A.M.–8 P.M.) and under the *portales* at the plaza.

Other Services

A laundromat is at Alcocer 30, about two blocks north of the Plaza de la Constitución; open Mon.–Fri. 8 A.M.–4 P.M. and 5–7 P.M., Sat. 8 A.M.–3 P.M. The Red Cross, on Allende between Guerrero and Hidalgo, tel. 246/462-0920, offers 24-hour ambulance service. Farmacia Iris is at Juárez 47, tel. 246/462-1151. The Hospital General is on Av. de La Corregidora, tel. 246/462-0357.

GETTING THERE

By Bus

The **central bus station** is a kilometer from the Plaza de la Constitución. Buses to Mexico City (Terminal Tapo), Puebla, and Jalapa-Veracruz leave often throughout the day with ADO and AU. Buses to Apizaco and Huamantla can be found on Allende, between Guerrero and Hidalgo, tel. 246/462-0217.

Driving

From Mexico City take the highway to Puebla and turn off before Puebla toward Tlaxcala. Driving time is roughly 90 minutes, depending on traffic leaving Mexico City. An alternative scenic route, probably an hour longer, is to follow México 136 east out of Texcoco.

CACAXTLA ARCHAEOLOGICAL SITE

A small hilltop ruins, for years Cacaxtla was not considered an important site. But in 1975, locals found an immense mural showing a man painted black and dressed as a bird in a polychrome panorama filled with details. The mural caught the attention of representatives of the Instituto Nacional de Antropología e Historia. Using clues from murals and ruins, archaeologists have been busily piecing together what life was like in the 1,100-year-old culture.

The People of Cacaxtla

The archaeological site lies 130 km east of Mexico City, a strategic junction point between traders from the Mayan coastal regions and the central highlands, dominated until A.D. 750 by the city of Teotihuacán. The inhabitants of the region are thought to have been originally Chontal Maya from the Gulf coast, near the border of present-day Veracruz and Tabasco, who migrated into the highlands shortly before the time of

Christ. After they populated several of the valleys around what is today Puebla and Tlaxcala, Cacaxtla rose some time around A.D. 300 as the capital of the region.

Cacaxtla is believed to have ruled over about 200 rural towns and villages, each controlled by a local strongman, or *cacique.* Perhaps because of competition among these many different local leaders, Cacaxtla society was extremely warlike, with the warrior as the most exalted figure in society. These traits are readily apparent when examining the spectacular battle mural. Some believe it may have been an invasion from Cacaxtla that finally toppled the rulers of Teotihuacán and put that city to the torch around A.D. 750. Cacaxtla slid into decline around A.D. 1100.

During its heyday, the white-stuccoed hilltop acropolis looming over the surrounding countryside must have been a striking sight. The ceremonial center measures roughly 1.7 km long by just under a kilometer wide and contains various platforms, pyramids, palaces, and other buildings. While the structures are impressive to modern visitors—particularly the **Gran Basamento (Great Base)** (now covered with a metal roof), **Templo Rojo (Red Temple),** and **Building A,** the real attraction is unquestionably the amazing mural paintings decorating the walls.

Scholars believe that murals once covered most of Cacaxtla's exterior, and that they were painted somewhere between A.D. 750 and 850. Motifs common to both Mayan lowland painting and also to those used in nearby Teotihuacán point to Cacaxtla's position as an intermediary of sorts between these two stronger cultures. The brilliant colors of the murals, depicting all sorts of people and creatures, remains shockingly bright considering the intervening centuries.

The largest and most impressive of Cacaxtla's murals, the ***Battle Mural*** (on the north wall of the North Plaza) displays 48 warriors, divided into two groups. Those dressed like jaguars appear to be the victors of a battle over those dressed as birds, who are shown wounded or already dead, in gory detail. It's uncertain whether the mural depicts the fighters of Cacaxtla defending against invaders, invading a foreign place themselves, or some other as-yet-unknown event.

Practicalities

The site is open seven days a week 10 A.M.–5 P.M.; admission US$4.50, free on Sunday and holidays. A snack shop, restrooms, and museum are at the entrance to the site.

Cacaxtla is 19 km southwest of Tlaxcala near the town of San Miguel de Milagro. From there take the "Nativitas" bus from the central bus station. You will find taxis and *colectivos* that will take you to the site. Be prepared for a lot of walking around when you get there.

If you're driving from Tlaxcala city, head toward Puebla on the free highway, which leaves town from near the bus terminal, and follow signs to Nativitas. Once you pass Nativitas look for a sign about two km out of town; the road will go to the right and is quite bumpy. Though the distance isn't great, many *topes* (speed bumps) slow you down.

LA MALINCHE

One of the best hiking areas in central Mexico is Volcán La Malinche (4,462 meters), Mexico's fifth-highest mountain. This extinct volcano is blanketed by thick forest protected by law as **Parque Nacional La Malintzin.** Climbing the peak is a perfect acclimatization hike for those looking to tackle the higher mountains of Pico de Orizaba, Popocatéptl, or Ixtaccíhuatl, and also makes an excellent hike for those who want to experience the high mountains of central Mexico without dealing with ropes, crampons, and glaciers.

The trail begins easily, heading up through lovely forest before coming out onto grassy fields below the peak. The last stretch up the sandy, exposed flanks of the mountain is tougher going. Allow 3–4 hours one-way. The views from the peak are stupendous, as the mountain lies between Popo and Ixta to the west and Pico de Orizaba to the east.

Getting There

Travel east from Apizaco (which is northeast of Tlaxcala) on México 136 about 13 km to a signed junction directing you to Campamento IMSS La Malintzin. The paved road leads to a camp on the side of the mountain at about 3,000 meters, then continues 4.7 km to its end at the trailhead, by the ruins of a building. You may want to leave your vehicle at the camp and walk up the last stretch of road as some cars have been broken into at the trailhead.

To get to La Malinche without a car, catch a bus to either Apizaco or Huamantla, and from there hire a taxi. The price should cost US$8 one-way, and usually it's no problem to arrange to be picked up. On weekends a bus winds its way around the volcano on bumpy dirt roads and down to the bus terminal in Puebla. Times vary, but the last one usually heads down around 5 P.M.

Camping

Camping is allowed in the forest above the camp for free, or in the camp itself for US$3.50 per person. Cabins at the camp, run by the Mexican Social Security Institute (IMSS), cost US$50 for a basic cabin sleeping six, or US$80 for a cabin sleeping nine. Prices are slightly cheaper during the week. Reservations (necessary for the cabins, but not for camping) can be made by phone, in Spanish, at 246/461-0700 or 461-0701 in Tlaxcala.

Basics

Getting There

AIR

Aeropuerto Internacional Benito Juárez

Mexico's airport, in the eastern part of the city near the exit toward Puebla, has two terminals, domestic and international. As you enter from the Circuito Interior, the domestic terminal comes first. Inside the domestic terminal, a wall between gates B and C features a mural (thoroughly ignored by the thousands of travelers swarming below it every day) by Juan O'Gorman illustrating the history of flight, from an Aztec nobleman eyeing the wings of a bat with curiosity to the Wright brothers and Charles Lindbergh.

Both terminals have several fast-food joints and restaurants of mediocre quality where you can get a bite to eat, as well as a few newsstands and plenty of money-exchange booths. One of the latter, Tamibe, in the arrival hall for international flights, is open 24 hours. **American Express** on the second floor of the international terminal is open daily 7 A.M.–10 P.M. Also in the international terminal is a 24-hour Servitel telephone office for long-distance calls. For general airport information, call 5571-3600. In the international terminal is an **Internet Café,** open daily 9 A.M.–9 P.M. Both Conaculta (the government culture institute) and Inegi (the government map and information service) have stores in the national terminal.

Although recently expanded, the airport is way past its capacity already, and the government is planning on building a new one not far northeast of the current location, near an old lakebed near Texcoco. However, the matter seems to have become a major political issue, so it may be some time before anything materializes.

the ancient steps of the Templo Mayor, in the heart of Mexico City

Arriving

When flying into Mexico City, your first airport stop is immigration, where you will fill out a tourist card if you don't already have a Mexican visa. While tourists are eligible to stay for six months, immigration agents will arbitrarily stamp the card with as many days as they feel like (often 60 days), meaning you'll have to go to an immigration office to renew it if you plan to stay longer. However, if before they've had a chance to stamp your card, you say authoritatively *"Ciento ochenta días, por favor"* (One hundred and eighty days, please) they'll usually give it to you. Once they start writing, don't bother as they apparently never rewrite a card once they've already started.

After immigration, you'll proceed downstairs to collect your luggage from baggage claim and pass through the customs station, where you may be randomly chosen for inspection.

If you are waiting to meet someone arriving on an international flight, be prepared to wait an hour or so (occasionally less, often more) along with a hundred or so others outside the glass doors past the customs checkpoint. While the bar at the Freedom restaurant looks like a great vantage point to wait for someone, the staff will only let you sit there if you order a meal.

Departing

Almost all departing international flights leave, logically enough, from the international terminal, but a few leave from the domestic terminal if the plane has a stopover in another city (such as Guadalajara or Cancún) while flying out to another country. Check with your airline by phone beforehand to be sure. When you depart Mexico, be sure to bring your tourist card as you will be asked for it before leaving the country.

Should you find yourself with a several-hour wait at the airport, because of a delayed flight for example, consider walking across the pedestrian bridge to the Hotel Marriott, where you can relax at a bar table in the lush courtyard or even take a swim or sauna at the hotel health club for US$12.

The duty-free shops in the international terminal have a large selection of tequila, cigars, and other consumer goods at good prices.

To and From the Airport

Metro: If you're arriving in Mexico City between 6 A.M. and midnight and don't have a lot of baggage, you could take the Metro into town from the Terminal station, a short walk up the sidewalk from outside the domestic terminal.

Taxi: No city buses service the airport, making taxis the only option besides the Metro to get into town. Because of the very high incidence of robberies by street cabs at the airport, tourists should use only the authorized airport taxi service. It's a bit expensive, but worth it. Buy a ticket from the taxi service window, in the international terminal right where passengers are let out after the customs checkpoint.

Fares are based on how far your destination is from the airport—a map next to the window tells you which zone you're going to (assuming you know the city well enough to find it). It costs US$8 to the Centro; US$9 to the Alameda area, Roma, and part of Paseo de la Reforma; US$13 to Condesa or the Zona Rosa; US$15 to Polanco or Coyoacán; and US$16 to San Ángel or farther west along Paseo de la Reforma.

Chauffeured cars (seating four) and vans (seating eight) are also available to nearby cities such as Pachuca (US$50 car, US$55 van), Toluca (US$57 car, US$66 van), and Puebla or Cuernavaca (US$60 car, US$70 van).

Bus: Bus companies have recently begun offering direct routes from the airport to several nearby cities. As there are no bus offices at the airport, you simply exit the domestic terminal near Sala D and buy a ticket on the bus when it arrives. Pullman de Morelos drives to Cuernavaca 21 times a day 6:30 A.M.–11 P.M. for US$10. Estrella Roja drives to Puebla 40 times a day 6 A.M.–midnight, US$13. Primera Plus goes to Querétaro 15 times daily 7 A.M.–10 P.M., US$20. Caminante goes to Toluca 17 times daily 7 A.M.–11 P.M., US$8.

Driving: The airport is just off the eastern side of the Circuito Interior ring highway, which is easily accessible from most major neighborhoods in the center, west, and south of the city. The airport exit is clearly marked. The entrance road first passes between the domestic terminal (on the right) and the domestic parking terminal

AIRLINE TELEPHONE NUMBERS AND WEBSITES

Domestic Airlines

Aero California: 5207-1392 or 5207-0068

Aerocaribe: 5448-3000

Aeromar: 5133-1111 or 800/704-2000

AeroMexico: 5133-4000 or 800/021-4000, website: www.aeromexico.com

Allegro: 5574-2200 or 800/715-7640

Aviacsa: tel. 5716-9004, website: www.aviacsa.com.mx

Mexicana: 5448-0990 or 800/501-9900, website: www.mexicana.com.mx

International Airlines

Aerolineas Argentinas: 5523-7154

Air Canada: 5208-1883

Air France: 5627-6060, website: www.airfrance.mx

Air New Zealand: 5208-1708

Alaska Airlines: 5533-1745

Alitalia: 5533-5590

America West Airlines: 5511-9788 or 800/235-9292

American Airlines: 5209-1400, website: www.aa.com

Aviateca: 5553-3366 or 5211-5940, website: www.grupotaca.com

British Airways: 5387-0300 or 5785-8714, website: www.britishairways.com

Canadian Airlines: 5208-1837 or 5208-1691

Continental Airlines: 5283-5500 or 800/900-5000, website: www.continental.com

Delta Airlines: 5279-0909 or 5202-1608, website: www.delta-air.com

El Al Israel Airlines: 5545-3317 or 5545-33190

Iberia: 5130-3030 or 5130-3000, website: www.iberia.com

Japan Air Lines: 5242-0149 or 5242-0154

KLM: 5726-0149 or 5563-1254

Lan Chile: 5566-5211 or 800/700-7600, website: www.lanchile.com

Lloyd Air Boliviano: 5591-1134 or 5535-3734

Lufthansa: 5230-0000, website: www.lufthansa-mexico.com

Northwest Airlines: 2122-1300 or 2122-1305

Qantas: 5628-0547 or 5628-0548

Swissair: 5511-5074

Taca: 5553-3366 or 5211-6640, website: www.grupotaca.com

TWA: 800/238-1997, website: www.twa.com

United Airlines: 5627-0222 or 800/003-0777, website: www.ual.com

Varig: 5280-9192 or 800/907-8800, website: www.varig.com.mx

(on the left). Another 500 meters beyond on the right side is the international terminal, with its parking lot just beyond, also on the right side. Returning to the city, just loop back around to the left at the cross-over past the international terminal and either bear to the right to get on the Circuito heading north or stay in the middle and cross over the Circuito to the southbound side.

BUS

Mexico's top-notch bus system has dozens of competing companies offering first- and second-class buses throughout the country at very reasonable prices. First class has more-comfortable seats, fewer stops, and, whether you like it or not, videos. The screens are usually spaced every four or five seats, so request a seat as far as possible from one if you don't want to watch. Second-class buses are 20–40 percent cheaper, but they're not as comfortable and always take longer, as they stop at seemingly every town on the route.

For trips to nearby major cities (such as Puebla, Toluca, Cuernavaca, or Guadalajara), there's usually a departure every 15 minutes or so throughout the day, so travelers can safely show up at the bus station and not have to wait very long. If you are going to destinations with less frequent service, want a particular seat, or are traveling during the holidays, it's best to go to the station and buy a ticket the day before your intended departure. Sometimes, if you're lucky or persistent, you can get information by telephone from individual companies, but it's not easy. A better option is to call a new service, **Ticket Bus,** which acts as a central reservation service for basically all of the main bus lines in Mexico. Its main phone numbers are 5133-2424 or from outside Mexico City 800/702-8000, www.ticketbus.com.mx. It has nearly 40 offices around the city where you can go to buy tickets. Some convenient ones are: Isabel la Católica 83 in the Centro, tel. 5709-9985; Paseo de la Reforma 412 (near the Diana monument), tel. 5207-9437; and Puebla 46 in the Roma, tel. 5511-2916.

First-class bus companies include: Omnibus de Mexico, tel. 5587-1927 or 5567-6756, www.omnibusdemexico.com.mx (north and central Mexico); Estrella Blanca/Turistar, tel. 5729-0707 (north, central, and western Mexico); Primera Plus/Flecha Amarilla, tel. 5567-7887 or 5567-7176, www.flecha-amarilla.com (western and central Mexico); Estrella de Oro, tel. 5549-8520 or 5549-8521, www.estrelladeoro.com.mx (Cuernavaca, Acapulco, Taxco); Uno, tel. 5522-1111, www.uno.com.mx (southern and eastern Mexico); ADO, tel. 5133-2444 or 5785-9659 (southeastern Mexico); Cristóbal Colón, tel. 5700-1089 or 5133-2400, www.cristobalcolon.com.mx (Oaxaca and Chiapas). Luxury bus line ETN, tel. 5273-7155 or 5277-6529, www.etn.com.mx, offers very comfortable reclining seats and nonstop rides at a premium cost, but it's worth it for a long haul. ETN serves north-central Mexico only, however.

Connections for U.S. Greyhound buses are available in Mexico City at Amores 707-102, Col. Del Valle, tel. 5669-1287 or 5669-0986, www.greyhound.com.mx.

Terminals

Mexico City has four intercity bus terminals, at the four main highway exits out of the city, corresponding more or less to the cardinal points of the compass. Each is accessible by Metro.

Terminal Central del Norte (North Terminal), Av. de los Cien Metros 1907, tel. 5587-5973. Take Metro Línea 5 to Terminal Norte station. From this station, there's bus service to Querétaro, San Miguel de Allende, Guanajuato, Zacatecas, Chihuahua, Monterrey, and Tijuana.

Terminal Central del Sur (South Terminal), also known as Terminal Tasqueña, Av. Tasqueña 1320, tel. 5689-9795. Take Metro Línea 2 to Tasqueña station. This terminal offers buses to Cuernavaca, Acapulco, Taxco, and Ixtapa/Zihuatanejo.

Terminal Poniente (Western Terminal), Av. Sur 122, tel. 5271-4519. The Metro stop is Observatorio. From this station there are departures to Toluca, Valle de Bravo, Morelia, Guadalajara, and Puerto Vallarta.

Terminal Oriente (Eastern Terminal, also known as Terminal TAPO), Calz. Ignacio

Zaragoza 200, tel. 5762-5977. Metro Línea 4 at the Morelos station or Línea 1 at San Lázaro station. Buses depart to Puebla, Veracruz, Mérida, Cancún, Palenque, San Cristóbal de las Casas, and Tapachula.

CAR

From the United States, Mexico City can be reached in 12–48 hours of reasonably sane driving, depending on which route you take. The shortest route is to cross the border at Laredo, Texas, taking México 85 to Monterrey, then México 57 on to Saltillo, San Luis Potosí, and Querétaro, all on good highway and almost entirely free of tolls. Other, longer routes extend from Ciudad Júarez on México 45 through Chihuahua, then México 49 on to Gómez Palacio, Zacatecas, and San Luis Potosí; the northwest highway from California and Arizona (México 15) passes through Hermosillo, Mazatlán, Tepic, and Guadalajara. In many places along Mexican highways drivers can choose between the free *(libre)* or the toll *(cuota)* road. The toll highways can be pricey, but the pavement is excellent and traffic is much lighter than on the congested free roads.

The highways connecting Mexico City to Guatemala (via Tapachula, 16 hours driving) and Belize (via Chetumal, 20 hours driving) are in worse condition than the northern roads and should be driven only during the day.

Try to avoid arriving in Mexico City on Sunday afternoon and evening, as the highways are invariably jammed with weekenders heading home. Conversely, Friday afternoon is about the worst time to try to leave the city.

Insurance

It's very important to carry a Mexican liability insurance policy on your vehicle when driving in Mexico. No matter what your own insurance company may tell you, Mexican authorities don't recognize foreign insurance policies for private vehicles in Mexico.

Vehicle insurance isn't required by law in Mexico, but it's a good idea to carry a Mexican liability policy anyway. Without it, a minor traffic accident can turn into a nightmare. Short-term—as little as one day's worth—insurance can be arranged at any of several agencies found in nearly every border town between the Pacific Ocean and the Gulf of Mexico.

One of the most popular, and reliable, Mexico insurers is **Sanborn's Mexico Insurance,** P.O. Box 310, McAllen, TX 78505, tel. 956/682-6677 or 800/222-0158, fax 956/686-0732, www.sanbornsinsurance.com, which has offices in or close to virtually every town along the U.S.-Mexico border except Tijuana and some of the smaller border crossings. Sample coverage for a vehicle insured at a value of US$20,000–25,000, plus US$50,000 property damage, US$80,000 liability, and medical payments of US$2,000 per person (up to US$10,000 per occurrence) costs around US$12 per day or around US$800 per year to drive anywhere in Mexico.

Another good source of Mexican insurance is **Lewis & Lewis,** 8929 Wilshire Blvd., Ste. 220, Beverly Hills, CA 90211, tel. 310/657-1112 or 800/966-6830, fax 310/652-5849, email: mexauto@gte.net. Lewis & Lewis premiums for a multiple-entry, one-year, comprehensive policy for Baja/Northwest Mexico start at around US$130 for under US$5,000 in coverage and rise to US$516 for US$100,000 worth of coverage; liability costs only US$74 per year.

For long-term visits, better deals can sometimes be negotiated from other sources, especially for drivers who will be making more than one trip into Mexico each year. Some agencies in Mexico offer annual policies in which you're only charged for those days you're actually in Mexico. Of course, this requires a trip south of the border to obtain such a policy in the first place, so you'll need a day or two's worth of border insurance for the trip.

Whichever policy you choose, always make photocopies of the policy and keep originals and copies in separate, safe places. It's also a good idea to carry a photocopy of the first page (the "declaration" or "renewal of declaration" sheet) of your home country policy, as Mexican customs law has in the past required that you cross the border with at least six months' worth of home country insurance. At the moment that law has been rescinded, but there's no guarantee all the Mexican customs officers will be aware of the repeal when you roll across the border.

To/From Querétaro

Take Paseo de la Reforma westward out past Chapultepec to the Periférico, turn north and look for the Querétaro signs past Satelite and Tlanepantla. It's also possible to follow the Eje Central north from downtown, but this is sometimes more complicated and with more traffic. Returning to the city, stay on the Periférico around the northwest side of the city and either get off at Paseo de la Reforma (for Polanco, the Zona Rosa, and the Centro) or continue farther south on the Periférico for San Ángel and Coyoacán.

To/From Toluca

Paseo de la Reforma and Avenida Constituyentes (a major avenue parallel to Reforma but farther south) both lead to free and toll highways to Toluca. The toll road costs US$7 for the 10-mile stretch to La Marquesa, where it meets back up with the free road. If you're not in a rush, take the free road and save your pesos. Coming in from Toluca, keep an eye out for signs directing you to Reforma (for Polanco, Paseo de la Reforma, or the Centro Histórico) or "Constituyentes" (for Condesa, Roma, or anywhere in the south of the city).

To/From Cuernavaca

Both Avenida Insurgentes and Calzado Tlalpan (the southern extension of Pino Suárez, the road on the east side of the Zócalo) lead directly to both the free and toll highways to Cuernavaca. Tlalpan is usually faster. The Periférico ring road also connects with the highway exit in the south part of the city. The US$6.50 toll highway to Cuernavaca bypasses the windy, scenic, and slow free road. Arriving in the city, watch for the major junction at the end of the highway, the right-hand fork leading to Tlalpan and downtown, and the left-hand one to Insurgentes, San Ángel, Coyoacán, Roma, and Condesa.

To/From Puebla

Navigating your way from the Centro through to the market neighborhoods to the eastern exit of the city is no simple task. It's often easier to head south along Pino Suárez and Tlalpan, turn off on the Viaducto Miguel Alemán heading east, and follow the signs to Puebla. It's also possible to follow Avenida Chapultepec east (farther on called Avenida Fray Servando) to Calzado Izazaga and the highway to Puebla, but a couple of turns are confusing, and traffic is usually bad. From the west and south of the city, take Viaducto Miguel Alemán.

Coming into the city, paradoxically, it's a bit of a trick to find the entrance to the Viaducto, whereas following Izazaga and then Fray Servando into the city center is fairly straightforward. Once you learn the Viaducto entrance, however, it's the quickest way to get into most of the center, south, and west parts of the city.

The toll road to Puebla costs US$5 and allows you to avoid all the curves and slow trucks on the free highway.

To/From Teotihuacán

Getting out on the highway to the ruins northeast of Mexico City, as well as to Pachuca, couldn't be simpler: just follow Avenida Insurgentes north and keep going straight. At the first toll booth, Pachuca drivers stay to the left, while those going to Teotihuacán stay to the right. Coming back is just as easy.

TRAIN

At last report, there was no passenger train service operating out of Mexico City. The last routes, to Apizaco in Tlaxcala and to Veracruz, have reportedly been discontinued. At last check the only passenger service in all of central Mexico is the **Tequila Express,** which runs day tours on Saturday and Sunday from Guadalajara to the town of Tequila and back—reputed to be lots of fun and very liquid. For more info look it up on the Web at www.ferromex.com.mx. **Expreso de la Independencia,** tel. 444/812-9720 or 812-5411, www.expresoindependencia.com, runs 13 restored rail cars on multiday tours of Guanajuato, Querétaro, San Miguel de Allende, and Zacatecas.

If for some reason you need to get to the train station anyhow, it is on Av. Insurgentes

Norte in Col. Buenavista, tel. 5547-1097, Metro station Buenavista.

A new suburban passenger train may be inaugurated in the next couple of years, servicing the hundreds of thousands of commuters living north of Mexico City.

Getting Around

Getting around Mexico City is cheap, efficient, and—with a little caution—safe. Within each neighborhood, walking is the best way to see everything; attractions are usually concentrated in each of the city's most popular areas.

To cover more ground, the options available include bus, taxi, and Metro. Those who have their own wheels will find negotiating the city not as daunting as might be expected, unless they're unlucky enough to be caught in one of the political demonstrations that frequently snarl the city center.

BUS

The most common of Mexico City's several bus types is the *pesero,* a medium-sized, box-shaped bus painted white and green. Fares (US$.20–50) depend on how far along the route you are going—ask and pay when you get in. To signal a stop, push the button above the rear door, and if that doesn't work, call out *baja, por favor* in a loud voice. *Peseros* tend to stop anywhere, not just designated stops. These buses can be extremely crowded during peak hours, and pickpockets are common, so watch out if you're standing.

The larger buses, some of them double-long, cost a bit more (US$.40) but are more comfortable and stop less often, and only at official stops. Some of the express buses running down Insurgentes stop only every kilometer or so. In some areas, particularly farther out from the city center, *combis* or *colectivos* (shared VW buses) are common.

To find the right bus for your destination, start by looking at the placards posted in the front window. These invariably only state the end of the line, so you most likely will have to ask drivers if they are going your way, and if not, which bus you should take.

At the end of each Metro line huge corrals of buses depart for destinations around the edge of the city.

TAXI

Taxis in Mexico City come in several varieties: two different kinds of roving taxis, hailed from the street, and various *sitio* taxi companies, based at a certain station and reached by telephone.

Street Taxis

The most common are the yellow or green Volkswagen Beetles, equipped with taxi meters *(taxímetros)* and powered by unleaded gas (hence their sometime nickname, "ecotaxi"). Yellow cabs, which use leaded gasoline, are a bit less expensive, but both are very cheap. Yellow cabs are being phased out and are now uncommon.

Metered taxis hailed from street corners in Mexico City have developed a bad reputation of late, not without reason. Armed muggings have become common, and foreigners are unquestionably a high-risk group. The U.S. embassy first issued a warning in 1997 advising all visitors never to hail cabs from the street, after the killing of an American citizen, and has since renewed the warning.

Obviously one way to cut the risk is never to hail a taxi. On the other hand, many people find taxi transportation worth the risk and take measures to lessen their risks (see the special topic Taxi Security) or just hope for the best. Many foreigners refuse to flag taxis from the street entirely and opt for calling a *sitio* taxi from a dispatcher (see below). For the record, the authors of this book often flag street taxis in Mexico City and have yet to encounter a single problem. Nevertheless it is definitely recommended that visitors, especially those who don't know the city well and/or don't speak Spanish, take only *sitio* cabs.

© JOHN NEUBAUER

Should you decide to take a street taxi, apart from safety precautions, be sure the driver turns on the meter as soon as you start driving. If possible try to have small bills when taking rides around town, as taxi drivers often don't have change. Tipping is not expected.

After 10 P.M. taxis are legally allowed to charge 20 percent above the meter reading. Some have special meters with a night setting, while with others you simply have to calculate the extra amount—ask when you get in. If it's late and you look desperate, taxi drivers may refuse to turn on their meter and will instead want to negotiate a price. Although this is technically illegal, it's common practice. Also, all rides going outside the city limits into the State of México cost extra. Note the amount the meter reads when leaving the Distrito Federal—all charges incurred after entering the State of México are doubled, then added to the amount accumulated on the meter while still in D.F.

Sitio, Radio, and Hotel Taxis

If you need to take a taxi in the city after dark, or you need one during the day and don't want to risk a street cab, a safer alternative is a *sitio* (pronounced SEE-tee-oh) taxi. These are taxis attached to a permanent taxi stand, or *sitio.* You'll find taxi *sitios* in various parts of the city, and you can recognize them by a short line of taxis, all painted the same color, with the name of the *sitio* emblazoned on the side. Often a curbside kiosk stands nearby where dispatchers log the taxis in and out. Such *sitio* taxis are highly unlikely to be occupied by rogue drivers trolling for robbery victims, but all the usual precautions should apply: check the *tarjetón* and make sure the doors lock.

Sitios with telephones and taxi radios will accept phone bookings, and with the increase in taxi robberies, the number of radio/phone *sitios* has been multiplying quickly. These taxis are considered to be the safest of all, and they're the second most expensive after hotel taxis. If you have any problem contacting the services listed below, the staff at your hotel will almost certainly be able to find one for you.

Servicios Ejecutivos Sitio 144, tel. 5654-3083 or 5649-0657, will get a taxi to just about wherever you are in the city in about 20 minutes, charging only the cost of the *taxímetro* plus US$.75 between 6 A.M. and 10 P.M., and US$1.75 other times.

Taxi Mex, tel. 5538-0912 or 5519-7690, is

TAXI SECURITY

The number of taxi robberies in Mexico City increased dramatically after the 1994–95 peso devaluation and ensuing economic crisis. Many foreign visitors choose never to take taxis off the street, since *sitio* cabs, operating from a radio base, are totally safe and easy to arrange. But should you either be forced to take one or think the convenience outweighs the risk, a few measures can improve your chances of a trouble-free ride.

First of all, keep in mind that it's safer to ride taxis in during the day. If you do plan on hailing a cab on the street, it's best not to board carrying a great deal of money or valuables.

Street cabs always have a green stripe painted across their license plate, and the plate number should match the number painted on the side of the cab. Before entering the car, ask to see the driver's *tarjetón,* a sort of oversized license bearing a photo that should match the driver's face. A good number of drivers don't have *tarjetones*—this doesn't mean they're thieves (many people don't have the money or don't want to pay the cost), but it's safer not to enter such a taxi anyway.

But the unfortunate truth is, license plates and *tarjetones* can be faked easily. One key mechanical factor cannot, however: make sure to check first that the passenger door lock works. Before getting in, with the door open, push down the lock on the inside, and check to see that the outer door handle does not open. If the door opens anyway, which is to say the lock doesn't work, don't get in. If the lock works, when you get in, lock the door immediately and roll up the window. Robberies almost always involve thieves, often accomplices of the driver, entering the cab through that door, so if you can prevent them from getting in your chances of getting away unscathed are much improved. Taxis are supposed to have their door handles on the passenger's side disabled entirely, so that only the driver can open the door from the inside, but many are not disabled.

Once inside the taxi, make sure the driver knows where you are going, and if possible tell him by what route. Even if it's a bit out of the way, sometimes it's best to go by a route you know, rather than trust the driver to find a shortcut. And if you don't know the way, make sure the driver clearly explains which way he intends to go. If you are in any way suspicious of the driver's words or actions, don't hesitate to get out immediately.

By far the most common modus operandi used for taxi robberies is for the driver to slow down, often pretending he is lost or confused. Suddenly the door pops open, and one or two other men get in, brandishing a knife or gun. Passenger(s) are pushed against the seat, told to shut up and close their eyes, and driven around the city for a good length of time as their pockets and bags are gone through. If bank cards are found, access codes are demanded.

Resistance is of course a temptation for some. The best time to prevent a robbery is just as it begins. If the driver starts to slow down or pull over for no apparent reason, quickly make sure the door is closed and locked, and start yelling at the driver *¡Maneja!* (Drive!). Should the accomplices actually get the door open and show a weapon, quiet down and try to remain calm. The robbery victims who have been physically abused or killed are invariably those who put up a fight. But by far the majority are simply let out in some outlying part of the city, broke, thoroughly frightened, but unharmed.

another good service charging the *taxímetro* plus US$1.25 during the day; add another 20 percent after 10 P.M.

Servitaxi, tel. 5516-6020 or 5516-6025, has taxis charging prices based on city zones (check with the radio operator first). Neighborhood bases include: Centro, tel. 5526-2300; Reforma, tel. 5566-1060; Polanco, tel. 5282-1428; Condesa, tel. 5553-5059; Insurgentes Sur/Del Valle, tel. 5687-8819; Coyoacán and Mixcoac, tel. 5534-3861; and Roma, tel. 5574-7356.

Radio Taxi, tel. 5674-6120 or 5674-6620, is

reliable and safe, but you're at the mercy of the drivers to name their price, as the operators will not discuss costs over the phone. Most often you can expect to pay about double the normal metered rate.

A very good unmarked taxi service, with reasonable prices, is **Radio Elite,** tel. 5660-1122 or 5593-3440.

Servicio Ejecutivo de Radio Taxi D'Lux, tel. 5756-6886 or 5756-3514, charges by zone in Mexico City and also can arrange day car-and-driver hires for trips outside the city. For example, a day trip to Puebla and Cholula costs US$100, plus toll highway costs (the company pays for gas).

Most high-end hotels have a cab service; these are the most expensive cabs, but they're quite safe and fares are usually posted. The cars are usually unmarked four-door Fords, and the drivers often speak some English (some are licensed guides as well). There may also be a taxi *sitio* near your hotel; ask the doorman to point one out.

Two companies offering chauffeur service around the city and elsewhere, with bilingual drivers, are: **Transportación Turística y Ejecutiva Chapultepec,** tel. 5277-2304 or 5516-0770, email: limorent@mpsnet.com.mx; and **Arguba,** tel. 5523-9958 or 5687-0617.

CAR

Driving in Mexico City can certainly be hazardous to both your physical and mental health and is not to be attempted by the faint of heart. Nevertheless, those who have driven in other large, chaotic cities will find Mexico City negotiable, as long as proper caution is taken and a few basic principals kept in mind.

One essential factor to peaceful driving in the city is to choose your hours carefully. Mornings (8–10 A.M.) can be congested, while midday traffic is usually fairly reasonable until around 3 P.M. During the week, mid-afternoon and early evenings are the worst, particularly on the main commuter routes in and out of the city and in the Centro. Traffic begins to dissipate around 10 P.M., or earlier in the city center. The worst traffic of all is Friday afternoon, and even worse still if it's a *viernes quincena,* a Friday that coincides with the twice-monthly payday. Unpredictable demonstrations along Paseo de la Reforma, Paseo Bucareli, and in the city center also regularly tie up traffic.

Navigation

As might be expected, learning your way around an urban area of several million inhabitants can be a bit confusing, but being familiar with a couple of major avenues can help you stay oriented. Avenida Insurgentes is the longest boulevard in the city and a major north/south route crossing Mexico City. To the northeast, Insurgentes takes you to the exit for Pachuca and Teotihuacán, while to the south it continues past San Ángel to UNAM and the exit to Cuernavaca and Acapulco.

Paseo de la Reforma is a broad avenue punctuated by large traffic circles (called *glorietas*) running northeast-southwest. Originally Reforma ran between the Alameda and Chapultepec, but now it extends west to the exit to Toluca and northeast to the Basílica de Guadalupe.

The city is circled by two ring highways, the inner Circuito Interior and the outer Periférico. The Circuito makes a complete loop, although it changes names (Río Churubusco, Patriotismo, Revolución, and Circuito Interior) along the way. The Periférico, however, extends only three-quarters of the way, with the northeast section (between the highway exits to Querétaro and Puebla) unfinished.

Cutting across these two loops is a grid of *ejes,* axis roads running in one direction with traffic lights (somewhat) timed, either east-west or north-south. Other important roads that are not technically *ejes* are the east-west Viaducto Miguel Alemán and the south-to-center Avenida Tlalpan, both of which are major, two-way arteries with few stoplights.

Finding specific addresses in the city can be tricky. The best tool is the *Guía Roji,* a bright red book of maps and indexes of the city. It can be found in Sanborns and is sold on many street corners for US$8. When driving, don't expect to see street signs placed in logical places, and be ready to ask for directions frequently. And always try to know the name of the *colonia* where your destination is located.

Hoy No Circula

In an effort to reduce the number of cars driving in the city, hence reducing air pollution, the city enforces a ban on each vehicle during the week based on the final digit of its license plate, a program known as *"Hoy No Circula"* (literally "Today No Drive" but often translated "Day without a Car"). Foreign-registered cars are not exempt from the program. Failure to comply can result in fines of up to US$80, or less if you are inclined to negotiate with the police officer who catches you. The ban is enforced 6 A.M.–10 P.M., five days a week. The schedule is as follows. Monday: No driving if final digit is five or six; Tuesday: No driving if final digit is seven or eight; Wednesday: No driving if final digit is three or four; Thursday: No driving if final digit is one or two; Friday: No driving if final digit is nine or zero; Saturday and Sunday: All vehicles may drive.

Perhaps worst of all are the armored cars—high-speed tanks, really—piloted by sunglass-wearing toughs who think that because they are driving money and guns, they are free to chug through red lights, make illegal U-turns, and perform all sorts of other lovely stunts.

In the last couple of years the city has enforced a new double ban when the pollution hits certain levels (250 points on the Imeca scale) as an emergency measure, but enforcement has been erratic.

Local cars are required to have a decal bearing either a "0," "1," or "2." A "0" means the car is exempt from any days off, regardless of the license number, because it has passed emissions tests. A "1" requires the car to not circulate on one day regardless of the conditions, and a "2" means the car cannot circulate on two days of the week during a pollution alert. Foreign-registered cars are not required to have these decals or to pass emissions inspections.

Drive to Survive

The best advice we can offer for how to survive the roads of Mexico City is to remain watchful and alert at all times. Expect anything to happen. Don't assume other drivers, even police cars, will follow the rules of the road. As most Mexico City drivers simply buy their licenses without taking any tests, they can hardly be blamed for not knowing the rules in the first place.

Drivers will pull out at inopportune moments, cut across in front of you to make a turn, drive the wrong way down a one-way street, all the while fully assuming you will get out of their way. Many intersections on side streets don't have stop signs in either direction, and the decision of who goes first seems to be the one who appears more determined. In the many *glorietas,* the standard rule of the person in the circle having right-of-way does not pertain. Expect drivers to come barreling into the circle without even looking to their left to check traffic.

Chilango drivers are aggressive in general, but some are worse than others and bear watching out for. The *pesero* bus drivers, in particular, are legendary for swinging their green-and-white machines around the streets with great abandon, expecting everyone to get out of their way. Be prepared for taxis to slow down unexpectedly and veer across several lanes to pick up a potential passenger. Perhaps worst of all are the armored cars—high-speed tanks, really—piloted by sunglass-wearing toughs who think that because they are driving money and guns, they are free to chug through red lights, make illegal U-turns, and perform all sorts of other lovely stunts.

Officials

If your car has foreign plates, you may attract an inordinate amount of attention from Mexico City's various police forces, particularly the brown-uniformed *tránsito* police, either on foot, in patrol cars, or on venerable, stylish (and sometimes barely functioning) Harley-Davidson motorcycles. If your car is in Mexico legally, the papers are in order, and you haven't broken the law, all will be well. Insist that you have done nothing wrong, and likely as not you will be allowed to go on your way.

If you did break the law in some way, you may find yourself being threatened with going to the *delegación,* the precinct house, if you don't pay a "fine" there and then. How you react to this will depend on your own moral compass, as well as how much of a hurry you are in. Fed up with the perennial corruption of the police, some Mexicans have taken to refusing to pay bribes (known as *la mordida*). Foreign visitors may well wish to take this road also—it's certainly the scrupulous thing to do. And because you are a foreigner, and also because the policeman will not want to bother taking you down to the *delegación,* you may well be let off with just a warning.

If you'd prefer to just pay a quick bribe and get out of there, the amount you pay will depend on your negotiating talents. They will invariably ask for several hundred pesos, but you can usually get off with US$5–10, or less if you really chisel. Just keep in mind that the policeman will almost never take you down to the station—it's far too much hassle. He's after a few easy pesos, nothing more.

The administrations of Cuauhtémoc Cárdenas and Andrés Manuel López Obrador have made some efforts to clean up corruption in the street police, but with little noticeable effect as yet. Perhaps their successors will have better luck, but don't expect anything dramatic for a few years at least. Old habits die hard.

A bit more serious than the *tránsitos* are the Policía Fiscal Federal, the Finance Secretariat police, who drive new-model blue pickup trucks and sometimes pull over foreign cars to check that their papers are in order. If they are not, the car will be impounded and you will go through a lengthy, nightmarish ordeal to get it out again. These policemen are not receptive to *la mordida.* The blue-uniformed *Seguridad Pública* police have no authority to stop you for traffic infractions, although of course they can stop you for other reasons.

A welcome change from all the spooky policemen are the men and women in bright yellow uniforms driving motor scooters around the city, forming part of the new Apoyo Vial road assistance program. Begun in 1996 under former Mayor Oscar Espinosa, Apoyo Vial takes care of all sorts of traffic and vehicle problems, basically doing most of what traffic police are supposed to do. Don't be surprised to run across a busy intersection, on Paseo de la Reforma for example, and see Apoyo Vial workers energetically and efficiently directing traffic, while a group of *tránsitos* lounge around their patrol car, smoking cigarettes and eyeing the traffic for someone to pull over and shake down.

Parking

Parking is an entire industry in Mexico City, employing many thousands of men (and occasionally women or children) who watch over certain stretches of sidewalk. As you pull up to park, they will hustle over and wave you into the spot. When you leave, they will again wave you out and expect a small tip in return. This can vary from US$.50 for a short stay in a normal area, up to US$2 for spots near crowded parts of the city or during events. While they have no particular right over that part of the sidewalk and probably wouldn't do anything if you didn't pay on leaving, the general custom is to pay them.

The next rung up the parking ladder is the *estacionamiento,* a type of parking lot found all over the city. Pull in, give the attendant your keys in return for a ticket with the time punched on it, and pay by the hour (usually US$.75– 1.50 an hour). Don't leave valuables in the car. The attendant will expect a small tip of a couple of pesos when he drives the car up when you leave.

Outside crowded clubs, bars, and restaurants, clients frequently leave their cars with a valet, for US$2–4.

Parking meters, called *parquímetros,* are installed only in a few areas of the city, particularly around the Zona Rosa and Paseo de la Reforma. Should the meter expire, the parking cops will eagerly slap a "boot" onto your wheel, which is costly and time-consuming to have removed.

Car Rentals

You'll find many car rental offices throughout the city and in the airport. Also, many agencies have rental desks in the bigger hotels. The major agencies are generally very expensive compared to U.S. prices. A small car with unlimited mileage will run an easy US$80 a day. Major U.S. companies operating in Mexico include:

Avis, with branches at the airport as well as at Leibniz 83 (near Hotel Camino Real) and Paseo de la Reforma 308 (near the U.S. Embassy), tel. 5588-8888 or 800/707-7700, www.avis.com.mx.

Budget, at the airport, tel. 5784-3011 or 5784-3118, and at Hamburgo 68 in the Zona Rosa, tel. 5533-0451, www.budget.com.mx.

Dollar, at the airport, tel. 5208-4313 or 5513-0128, fax 5525-7438, or in the Col. Roma at Av. Baja California 111, tel. 5564-6479 or 5564-6489, www.dollar.com.mx.

Remember that some of your best car rental bargains are obtained before you leave home. Avis leads the pack in bargain deals made in the U.S., and also offers some of the cheapest rates arranged in Mexico. It's always worth checking for discounts linked to airline mileage clubs and Costco/Price Club cards.

A myriad of local rental agencies offer cars at lower prices than the U.S. agencies. One very good agency we've used several times is **Casanova Renta de Automoviles,** with offices at Chapultepec 442 right near Metro Sevilla, tel. 5514-0449 or 5207-6007, and at Patriotismo 735 in Col. Mixcoac, tel. 5563-7606 or 5598-4814. It offers a no-frills (not even a cigarette lighter!) Nissan Tsuru (a simple four-door sedan) for around US$40 a day with 200 km mileage, or US$45 with unlimited mileage. The agency used to dealing with foreign renters and someone is always on hand who speaks English. Another good local agency is **Fresno Rent A Car,** at the airport, tel. 5784-4030 or 5785-3951; in the Centro at Dr. Andrade 246, tel. 5588-3809; or in the Roma at Monterrey 324, tel. 5584-2443.

METRO

Many visitors, expecting the worst, find themselves pleasantly surprised by Mexico's clean and efficient Metro system. At a cost of US$.20 per ride, the 11 lines *(líneas)* of the Metro move an average of five million people around the city each day. Just about all of the city's major sites, hotels, bus stations, and the airport are easily accessible from the system.

The Metro stations are well lit and generally safe. Directions are indicated by the last stops at each end, so you must know where you want to go in between these stops. Metro maps are posted on the walls of all stations. Signs marked Correspondencia indicate the walking route to take to transfer train lines—look for the name of the station at the end of the line in the direction you are going. For example, if you go into the Zócalo station and want to ride to Metro Revolución, go in the direction of "Cuatro Caminos" and get off at the Revolución station. There is no charge to transfer lines as often as you like, as long as you don't leave the Metro system. Try to buy several tickets in advance if you're going to use the Metro, as ticket booth lines can sometimes be very long. Operating hours vary slightly according to day of the week and the line, but they're roughly 6 A.M.–midnight, or until 1 A.M. Saturday nights.

For destinations beyond the reach of the Metro system, get off at the station farthest out in the direction you're going, then go outside where fleets of microbuses are parked and ask which one to take.

A *tren ligero* (light rail train) extends Metro service into the southern part of the city, from the Tasqueña Metro station as far south as Xochimilco.

A new elevated train line, heading from downtown northwest from Garibaldi past Tacuba to Naucalpan, Satelite, and beyond, was at last report the next Metro line planned.

For more information about the Metro, see its website www.metro.df.gob.mx.

Customs and Safety

Metro users are not known for their politeness, with people getting in at stations often shoving past others trying to get off. British travelers will no doubt find infuriating the local habit of standing on the left side of the escalators, thus blocking those who are trying to walk. Mexicans who find their path blocked, however, stop walking and wait for the end of the ride with the resigned aplomb for which Mexico City is legendary and don't even consider asking the person in front to move.

Foreign women, particularly those unaccompanied by a man, can expect plenty of looks at the least and very possibly some groping as well if the train is crowded—many female travelers avoid using the Metro if they're alone because of all the tiresome unwanted attention. Pickpockets are also rife on the Metro—after taxi robberies, probably the most common form of crime foreigners will run across is losing their wallet in the Metro.

These annoyances aside, the Metro is generally safe and easy to use, particularly if you don't try to use it during the morning and afternoon rush hours (7–9 A.M. and 6–9 P.M.). At peak hours in some stations the front couple of cars may be designated for women and children only—look for special roped-off lines, marked with signs.

Visas and Officialdom

TOURIST PERMITS AND VISAS

Tourist Permits

Citizens of the U.S. or Canada (or of 38 other designated countries in Europe and Latin America, plus Singapore) visiting Mexico solely for tourism are not required to obtain a visa. Instead they must carry validated tourist cards (*forma migratoria turista* or FMT), which aren't actually cards but slips of paper. Although you can get FMTs at any Mexican consulate, it's not necessary to arrange them before going to Mexico—just show up at the airport or the border and it will be taken care of with minimal hassle. The tourist card is valid for stays of up to 180 days and must be used within 90 days of issue. Your card becomes invalid once you exit the country—you're supposed to surrender it at the border—even if your 180 days hasn't expired. If you'll be entering and leaving Mexico more than once during your trip, you should request a multiple-entry tourist card, available from Mexican consulates only.

To obtain the FMT you need proof of citizenship—a birth certificate (or certified copy), voter's registration card, certificate of naturalization, or passport. A driver's license doesn't qualify, but it is helpful to back up a birth certificate.

Once you cross the border (or land at the airport in Mexico City), your tourist card must be validated by a Mexican immigration officer. You can arrange this at any *migración* office in Mexico (many *municipio* seats have them), but it's accomplished most conveniently at the border crossing itself. At airports you pass through immigration, where an officer stamps your paperwork with the date of entry and the number of days you're permitted to stay in Mexico.

In mid-1999, the Mexican government began collecting a 150-peso fee (around US$16 at the most recent dollar-peso exchange rate) from all tourists entering the country. If you fly in, this fee is tacked on to your airfare. If you arrive by land, you can pay this fee at any bank in Mexico. The bank issues a receipt, which you must show when you leave the country.

Before 1991, Mexican regulations required children under the age of 18 crossing the border without one or both parents to carry a notarized letter granting permission from the absent parent or both parents if both were absent. This regulation is no longer in effect, but we've heard that some Mexican border officers, as well as airline check-in crews, are still asking for the letter, apparently unaware that the regulation has been rescinded. Hence, unaccompanied minors or minors traveling with only one parent should be prepared for all situations with notarized letters. In cases of divorce, separation, or death, the minor should carry notarized papers documenting the situation.

In reality, minors with tourist cards are rarely asked for these documents. Children under 15 may be included on their parents' tourist card but this means that neither the child nor the parents can legally exit Mexico without the other.

Tourist Visas

Tourists from countries other than the 40 countries for which no visa is necessary need to obtain tourist visas in advance of arrival in Mexico. If

EMBASSIES IN MEXICO CITY

Argentina
Blvd. M. Avila Camacho 1, 7th floor
Lomas de Chapultepec
tel. 5520-9430 or 5520-9431

Australia
Rubén Dario 55
Polanco
tel. 5531-5225

Austria
Sierra Tarahumara 420
Lomas de Chapultepec
tel. 5251-9799 or 5251-1606

Belgium
A Musset 41
Polanco
tel. 5280-1258 or 5280-1133

Belize
Bernardo de Gálvez 215
Lomas de Chapultepec
tel. 5520-1346 or 5520-1274

Bolivia
Insurgentes Sur 263, 6th floor
Roma
tel. 5564-5415 or 5264-6169

Brazil
Lope de Armendariz 130
Lomas de Virreyes
tel. 5202-7500

Canada
Schiller 529
Polanco
tel. 5724-7900

Chile
Andres Bello 10, 18th floor
Polanco
tel. 5280-9682 or 5280-9689

Colombia
Paseo de la Reforma 1620
Lomas de Chapultepec
tel. 5202-7299

Costa Rica
Río Po 113
Cuauhtémoc
tel. 5525-7764 or 5525-7765

Cuba
Av. Presidente Masaryk 554
Polanco
tel. 5280-8039

Denmark
Tres Picos 43
Lomas de Chapultepec
tel. 5255-4145

Ecuador
Tennyson 217
Polanco
tel. 5545-6013 or 5250-4999

El Salvador
Temistocles 88
Polanco
tel. 5281-5723

Finland
Montes Pelvoux 111
Polanco
tel. 5540-6063

France
Campos Eliseos 339
Polanco
tel. 5282-9700 or 5282-9840

Germany
Lord Byron 737
Polanco
tel. 5283-2200

Greece
Paseo de las Palmas 2060
Lomas de Chapultepec
tel. 5596-6038 or 5596-6936

Guatemala
Av. Explanada 1025
Lomas de Chapultepec
tel. 5520-9249 or 5540-7520

Haiti
Cordoba 23-A
Roma
tel. 5511-4505

Honduras
A. Reyes 220
Hipódromo Condesa
tel. 5211-5250 or 5515-6689

India
Musset 325
Polanco
tel. 5531-1002 or 5531-1085

Indonesia
Julio Verne 27
Polanco
tel. 5280-5748 or 5280-6863

Israel
Sierra Madre 215
Lomas de Chapultepec
tel. 5201-1500 or 5201-1555

Italy
Paseo de las Palmas 1994
Lomas de Chapultepec
tel. 5596-3655

Jamaica
Schiller 326, 8th floor
Polanco
tel. 5250-6804

Japan
Reforma 395
Cuauhtémoc
tel. 5514-5459

Lebanon
Julio Verne 8
Polanco
tel. 5280-6794

Netherlands
Vasco de Quiroga 3000
Santa Fe
tel. 5258-9921

New Zealand
Lagrange 103, 10th floor
Los Morales Polanco
tel. 5281-5486

Nicaragua
Prado Norte 470
Lomas de Chapultepec
tel. 5540-5625

Norway
Virreyes 1460
Lomas de Chapultepec
tel. 5540-3486 or 5540-3487

Pakistan
Hegel 512
Polanco
tel. 5203-3636

Panama
Horacio 1501
Polanco
tel. 5250-4229 or 5250-4259

Paraguay
Homero 415, 2nd floor
Polanco
tel. 5545-0405 or 5545-0403

Peru
Paseo de la Reforma 2601
Lomas de Reforma
tel. 5259-0239 or 5570-2443

Philippines
Paseo de las Palmas 1950
Polanco
tel. 5251-9760

Portugal
Alpes 1370
Lomas de Chapultepec
tel. 5520-1989

República Dominicana
Guatemala 84
Centro
tel. 5522-7409

Romania
Sófocles 311
Los Morales
tel. 5280-0197 or 5280-0447

Slovac Republic
Julio Verne 35
Polanco
tel. 5280-6544 or 5280-6451

Spain
Galileo 114
Polanco
tel. 5282-2974 or 5282-2982

Sweden
Paseo de las Palmas 1375
Lomas de Chapultepec
tel. 5540-6393

Switzerland
Paseo de las Palmas 405,
11th floor
Lomas de Chapultepec
tel. 5520-3003

Thailand
Sierra Vertiente 1030
Lomas de Chapultepec
tel. 5596-1290

Turkey
Schiller 326
Polanco
tel. 5203-8984

United Kingdom
Río Lerma 71
Cuauhtémoc
tel. 5207-2449

United Nations
Presidente Masaryk 29
Polanco
tel. 5250-1231

United States
Reforma 305
Cuauhtémoc
tel. 5209-9100

Uruguay
Hegel 149, 1st floor
Polanco
tel. 5254-1163 or 5531-0880

Venezuela
Schiller 326
Polanco
tel. 5203-4233 or 5203-4435

Vietnam
Sierra Ventana 255
Lomas de Chapultepec
tel. 5540-1632

Yugoslavia
Av. Montañas Rocallosas 515
Ote.
Lomas de Chapultepec
tel. 5259-1332 or 5520-2523

you apply in person at a Mexican consulate, you usually can obtain a tourist visa on the day of application, although for some countries it can take a couple of weeks. Requirements include a valid passport, a round-trip air ticket to Mexico, three photos, and a visa fee of US$29.

Foreign visitors who are legal permanent residents of the U.S. do not need visas to visit Mexico for tourism. A free tourist card can be obtained by presenting your passport and a U.S. residence card to any travel agency or at the airport or border crossing.

Business Travel

Citizens of Mexico's NAFTA (North American Free Trade Agreement) partners, the U.S. and Canada, are not required to obtain a visa to visit Mexico for business purposes. Instead you can receive a free NAFTA business permit (*forma migratoria nafta* or FMN) similar to a tourist card at the point of entry (border crossing or airport); it's valid for 30 days. At the port of entry (the Mexico City airport if you arrive by air) you must present proof of nationality (valid passport or original birth certificate plus a photo identification or voter registration card) and proof that you are traveling for "international business activities," usually interpreted to mean a letter from the company you represent, even if it's your own enterprise.

Those who arrive with the FMN and wish to stay over the authorized period of 30 days must replace their FMN with an FM-3 form at an immigration office in Mexico. The FM-3 is valid for a period of up to one year, for multiple entries, and may be extended. Note that the FMN is not valid for those who will be earning a salary during their stay in Mexico.

Citizens of other countries visiting for business purposes must obtain an FM-3 visa endorsed for business travel, which is valid for one year.

Visitors to Mexico coming as part of human rights delegations, aid workers, or international observers should check with a Mexican embassy about the current regulations.

Overstays

If you overstay your visa and are caught, the usual penalty is a fine of US$50 for overstays up to a month. After that the penalties become more severe. It's rare that a Mexican border official asks to see your FMT or visa when you're leaving the country. Your main risk comes if you get into trouble with the police somewhere in Mexico and they ask to see your immigration documents. Having expired papers will only further complicate your situation in such cases, so the best policy is to stay up to date in spite of the apparent laxity of enforcement.

Pets

Dogs and cats may be brought into Mexico if each is accompanied by a vaccination certificate that proves the animal has been vaccinated or treated for rabies, hepatitis, pip, and leptospirosis. You'll also need a health certificate issued no more than 72 hours before entry and signed by a registered veterinarian.

Since 1992 the requirement that the health certificate be stamped with a visa at a port of entry or at a Mexican consulate has been repealed. The certificate is still necessary; the visa isn't.

Visitante Rentista and *Inmigrante Rentista* Visas

FM-3 visas may be issued to foreigners who choose to live in Mexico on a "permanent income" basis. This most often applies to foreigners who decide to retire in Mexico, though it is also used by artists, writers, and other self-employed foreign residents. With this visa you're allowed to import one motor vehicle as well as your household belongings into Mexico tax-free.

The basic requirements for this visa are that applicants must forgo any kind of employment while living in Mexico and must show proof (bank statements) that they have a regular source of foreign-earned income amounting to at least US$1,000 per month (plus half that for each dependent over the age of 15, e.g., US$1,500 for a couple). A pile of paperwork, including a "letter of good conduct" from the applicant's local police department, must accompany the initial application, along with an immigration tax payment (US$60) and various applications fees totaling about US$75.

The visa must be renewed annually but the renewal can be accomplished at any immigration office in Mexico. After five years in Mexico, you have to start over again or move up to the FM-2 or *inmigrante rentista* visa, which has higher income requirements and signifies an intent to stay longer. After five years on an FM-2, an *inmigrante rentista* is eligible to apply for *inmigrado* status, which confers all the rights of citizenship (including employment in Mexico), save the rights to vote and hold public office.

Many foreigners who have retired in Mexico manage to do so on the regular 180-day tourist visa; every six months they dash across the border and return with a new tourist card (issued at the border) on the same day. This method bypasses all the red tape and income requirements of the retirement visa. If you own a home in Mexico, however, some local immigrations officials may interpret the law to mean that you must have an FM-2 or FM-3 visa—not an FMT or tourist visa—to be able to stay in that home for any period of time whatsoever. Although it's clear from a straight reading that Mexico's immigration laws do not require any special visas for home ownership, each immigration district behaves like an individual fiefdom at the mercy of the local immigration chief.

Monthly income requirements for both *rentista* visas are keyed to the Mexican daily minimum wage (400 times minimum wage for the FM-2, 250 times for the FM-3), hence figures may vary according to the current dollar-peso exchange rate.

CUSTOMS

Entering Mexico

Officially, tourists are supposed to bring only those items into Mexico that will be of use during their trip. This means you can bring in practically anything as long as it doesn't appear to be in large enough quantities to qualify for resale.

Technically speaking, you're not supposed to import more than one still camera, one movie camera, and one video camera, and no more than 12 rolls of film or blank videocassettes for each. Anything more is supposed to require permission from a Mexican consulate. In everyday practice, however, Mexican customs officials rarely blink at more film or an extra camera or two. Professional photographers and others who would like to bring more cameras and film into Mexico can apply for dispensation through a Mexican consulate abroad. Regarding audio equipment, you're limited to one CD disc player and one audio cassette player (or combo), two laserdiscs, and up to 20 CDs or recording cassettes. Other per-person limitations include one musical instrument, one tent and accompanying camping gear, one set of fishing gear, two tennis rackets, five "toys," and one sailboard.

Other limits are three liters of liquor or wine, two cartons (20 packs) of cigarettes, 25 cigars, or 200 grams of tobacco.

Other than the above, you're permitted to bring in no more than US$300 worth of other articles. You will be subject to duty on personal possessions worth more than US$300, to a max of US$1,000, except for new computer equipment, which is exempt up to US$4,000.

Auto Permits

Foreign-registered motor vehicles—cars, trucks, motorcycles, RVs—do not require permits for border town visits of less than 72 hours. For longer visits, you *must* obtain a temporary vehicle importation permit at the border if you're going anywhere besides Baja California Norte and Sur, Puerto Peñasco, or Golfo de Santa Clara. To receive a permit, you simply drive your vehicle to a Mexican customs office at an official border crossing and present a valid state registration or similar document certifying legal ownership, a driver's license, and a credit card issued outside Mexico.

If you're leasing or renting the vehicle, you'll also need a copy of a rental/leasing contract with the owner. If the vehicle belongs to someone else, such as a friend or relative, you must present a notarized letter from the owner giving you permission to take the vehicle into Mexico. Contrary to rumor, you aren't required to present the "pink slip" (ownership certificate) unless the state registration certificate is for some reason unavailable. It also helps to bring along a few photocopies of your registration and driver's license as these may be needed in the import permit process. This will save having to stand in a separate line for photocopies at the customs office, as is necessary at some border crossings.

Once the Mexican customs officials have approved your documents, you'll proceed to a Banjército (Banco del Ejército or Military Bank) office attached to the customs office where your credit card account will be charged US$11 for the permit fee. This fee must be paid by credit card; cash is unacceptable. If you don't possess a credit card, you'll be required to post a bond issued by an authorized Mexican bond company. For vehicles manufactured before 1989, the bond is US$125; for later models it's 1–2 percent of the car's blue book value, plus issuance fee and taxes. You will also have to pay a sizeable fee to the bond issuing company (US$100–150) which is not refunded. Hence, it's much better to use a credit card if possible.

Banjército is the bank used for all Mexican customs charges. The operating hours for each bank module are the same as for the border crossing at which it's located.

Once the fee is charged to your credit card or the appropriate bond paid, the permit is issued and a hologramic sticker affixed to your front windshield. Make sure the validity period equals that of your tourist card or visa. You may drive back and forth across the border, at any crossing, as many times as you wish until the permit expires. You're expected to surrender the permit at the border when your trip is at an end.

Always carry your vehicle import permit when driving in Mexico. The permit may be checked at interior immigration checkpoints and the police may ask to see it during routine checks or stops.

Tourists who wish to renew their vehicle permits in Mexico City (only possible if your tourist permit or tourist visa has been extended) should go to the Secretaría de Hacienda (Finance Secretariat) at Hidalgo 77, Modulo 3, ground floor. After dealing with the paperwork there, you will have to make a second trip to Banjército, Av. Industria Militar, Col. Lomas de Sotelo (near the Toreo Cuatro Caminos, northwest of Polanco), where you will receive your new sticker. For more information on the procedure (in Spanish only), call the central Aduana (Customs) office, at 5228-6834 or 5228-6835.

Insurance

Visitors planning to drive their own vehicles in Mexico should carry Mexican vehicle insurance. Foreign insurance policies aren't valid in Mexico; without insurance, if you're involved in an accident adjudged your fault, you can be jailed until you pay damages. See By Car under Getting There for details on how to obtain Mexican insurance.

Returning to the U.S.

Visitors returning to the U.S. from Mexico may have their luggage inspected by U.S. customs officials. The hassle can be minimized by giving brief, straight answers to their questions (e.g., "How long have you been in Mexico?" "Do you have anything to declare?") and by cooperating with their requests to open your luggage, vehicle storage compartments, and anything else they want opened. Sometimes the officers use dogs to sniff luggage and/or vehicles for contraband and illegal aliens.

Nearly 3,000 items—including all handicrafts—made in Mexico are exempt from any U.S. customs duties. Adults over 21 are allowed one liter (33.8 fluid ounces) of alcoholic beverages and 200 cigarettes (or 100 cigars) per person. Note that Cuban cigars may not be imported into the U.S. and customs will confiscate the cigars if discovered. An estimated nine out of 10 cigars sold as Cubans in Mexico are fake anyway, so it's not worth the hassle. All other purchases or gifts up to a total value of US$400 within any 31-day period can be brought into the U.S. duty-free.

The following fruits and vegetables cannot be brought into the U.S. from Mexico: oranges, grapefruits, mangoes, avocados (unless the pit is removed), and potatoes (including yams and sweet potatoes). All other fruits are permitted (including bananas, dates, pineapples, cactus fruits, grapes, and berries of all types).

Other prohibited plant materials are straw (including packing materials and items stuffed with straw), hay, unprocessed cotton, sugarcane, and any plants in soil (this includes houseplants).

Animals and animal products that cannot be imported include wild and domesticated birds (including poultry, unless cooked), pork or pork products (including sausage, ham, and other cured pork), and eggs. Beef, mutton, venison, and other meats are permitted at up to 50 pounds per person.

Returning to Canada

Duty-frees include 200 cigarettes (or 50 cigars or 250 grams of tobacco) and 1.14 liters of booze. Exemptions run from C$20 to C$500 depending on how long you've been outside Canada. To reach the maximum exemption of C$500 you must be gone at least one week. Because Canada is also signatory to NAFTA, customs legalities will change over the next decade.

Returning to the U.K.

Duty-frees include 200 cigarettes (or 50 cigars or 250 grams of tobacco) and one liter of beverage with an alcoholic content of over 22 percent or two liters under 22 percent, plus two liters of wine. The total exemption runs £136.

Returning to Australia

Duty-frees include 200 cigarettes (or 250 grams of tobacco, including cigars) and one liter of alcohol. The total exemption runs A$400.

Special Note on Customs Regulations

Customs regulations can change at any time, so if you want to verify the regulations on a purchase before risking duties or confiscation at the border, check with a consulate in Mexico before crossing.

As NAFTA proceeds with scheduled decreases in trade tariffs among the U.S., Canada, and Mexico, expect a steady loosening of customs regulations in all directions until 2009, when all import tariffs are supposed to be erased.

Money

CURRENCY

The unit of exchange in Mexico is the *peso,* which comes in paper denominations of $20, $50, $100, $200, and $500. Coins are available in denominations of 5 centavos, 10 centavos, 20 centavos, 50 centavos, $1, $2, $5, $10, and $20.

Prices

The N$ symbol (standing for "new pesos" to differentiate from pre-1993 "old pesos") is sometimes, though rarely these days, used for indicating peso prices. Much more common now is the $ symbol for pesos. While it's highly unlikely you'll ever confuse dollar and peso prices because of the differing values, you should ask when in doubt. In this book, we use "US$" to signify dollars, and "$" for pesos.

Because coins smaller than one peso are often scarce, payments often must be rounded off to the nearest peso or at least to the nearest 50 centavos. For a marked price of $8.55, for example, you actually have to pay only $8.50; for a $8.75 price you may have to pay $9. Any denomination over $50 is difficult to break, so change them at every opportunity to secure a good supply of smaller notes and coins.

Old Pesos vs. New Pesos

Mexico's "old pesos" were discontinued in favor of "new pesos" in 1993. Old pesos were legal tender until January 1, 1996, when they were called out of circulation. It's highly unlikely you'll come across any of the old currency, but if it's ever offered as change you shouldn't accept it as it's legally worthless. Old peso notes came in denominations of 1,000, 5,000, 10,000, etc.—each bill shows three more zeros than the corresponding "new" pesos bills. Of course the new peso is now simply known as the peso.

Dollars vs. Pesos

A few commercial establishments in Mexico City will take U.S. dollars as well as pesos. Paying with pesos, however, usually means a better deal when the price is fixed in pesos; if you pay in dollars for a purchase quoted in pesos, the vendor can determine the exchange rate. If a bottle of boutique tequila, for example, is marked at $180, and the bank rate is $9 per dollar, you'll pay

US$20 for the tequila with pesos changed at the bank. However, if you ask to pay in dollars, the vendor may charge US$25 since vendors have the right—by custom rather than law—to charge whatever exchange rate they wish. Then again, if you're bargaining for price, it really doesn't matter what currency you use.

Devaluation

The Mexican peso entered a deflationary spin in 1976, when the government decided to allow the national currency to "float" on the international money market. From 1976 to 1987 the exchange rate slid from eight pesos to the dollar to more than 2,000. In 1988 the Bank of Mexico instituted measures to slow the decline to less than a centavo per day by the end of 1992.

After the switch to the new peso in '93, the peso actually gained a bit in value against the U.S. dollar for a while, until the 1995 devaluation sliced it down again. This was bad news for peso-spending Mexicans but good news for dollar-holding bargain hunters.

Since 1998, however, the peso has been remarkably stable, even gaining value at times, despite floating freely in the international market. In 2000 it was one of the only currencies in the world to gain value against the U.S. dollar. However, the peso is considered by many to be overvalued and may be expected to slide somewhat in the future.

CHANGING MONEY

In general, though changing money is not at all difficult in Mexico City, the most hassle-free way to get pesos is to use an ATM card, which are widely accepted in Mexican banks and invariably offer the best exchange rate.

Banks

Banks offer a standard exchange rate set by the Bank of Mexico. This rate is usually posted behind the counter where foreign exchange is handled and is usually the highest commercially available rate. Banks that handle foreign exchange generally accept a wide range of foreign currencies, including the Euro, English pounds, Japanese yen, and Canadian dollars. Either cash or traveler's checks are accepted, though the latter usually guarantee a slightly better exchange rate. The main drawbacks with banks are the long lines and short hours—Mon.–Fri. 9 A.M.–3 P.M., but the foreign exchange service usually closes about noon–12:30 P.M. With privatization, some banks are extending their hours.

Moneychangers

The second best exchange rate, generally speaking, is found at the *casa de cambio* or private moneychanging office. The *casa de cambio* (also called *servicio de cambio*) either knocks a few centavos off the going bank rate or charges a percentage commission. It pays to shop around for the best *casa de cambio* rates as some places charge considerably more than others. The rates are usually posted; *compra,* always the lower figure, refers to the buying rate for US$ (how many pesos you'll receive per dollar) or other foreign currency, while *vende* is the selling rate (how many pesos you must pay to receive a dollar or other unit of foreign currency). As with banks, the difference between the buying and selling rates is the moneychanger's profit, unless it charges a commission on top of it.

Moneychangers are usually open much later than banks; some even work evening hours, which makes them immeasurably more convenient than banks. U.S. dollar currency is generally preferred though many *casas* will also accept Canadian dollars. However, Canadians should always keep a reserve supply of U.S. dollars for instances where Canadian currency isn't accepted. Moneychangers usually accept traveler's checks.

One of the better *casas de cambio* in the Centro is Casa de Cambio Plus, opposite the south side of the Alameda on Avenida Juárez. It's open Mon.–Fri. 9 A.M.–7 P.M., Sat. 9:30 A.M.–1:30 P.M.

Other conveniently located *casas de cambio* in the Centro Histórico include Casa de Cambio Tiber, Madero 27 (Mon.–Fri. 9 A.M.–5 P.M., Sat. 10 A.M.–2:30 P.M.) and Casa de Cambio Velasco, Gante 12-B (Mon.–Fri. 9 A.M.–5 P.M., Sat. 10 A.M.–2 P.M.).

In smaller towns outside Mexico City you'll have to resort to a bank or local merchant. Many storekeepers will be happy to buy dollars at a highly variable and sometimes negotiable rate. Few will take traveler's checks, however, unless you make a purchase.

The bank exchange booths at the Mexico City airport offer regular bank rates and are open long hours (some stay open 24 hours), so the airport is a good place to change some money on arrival. You'll also find ATMs in the airport.

Hotels

Hotels, motels, *pensiones,* and other lodging places generally offer the worst exchange rates. If you're trying to save money, avoid changing currency where you stay. Pay for your room in pesos if possible—or better yet with a credit card—because the same low rate often applies to room charges paid in dollars.

Credit Cards, Debit Cards, and ATM Cards

Plastic money (primarily Visa and MasterCard, and to a lesser extent, American Express) is widely accepted at large hotels, restaurants catering to tourists or businesspeople, car rentals (you can't rent a car without a credit card), and shops in tourist centers. Usually card displays at the cash register or on the door will announce that *tarjetas de crédito* (credit cards) are accepted. If in doubt, flash one and ask *"¿Se aceptan tarjetas de crédito?"* or simply *"¿Está bien?"* A reference to *efectivo* means cash.

Many shops and some hotels, however, add a 3–6-percent surcharge to bills paid with a card, which more than offsets the exchange rate differential.

Cash advances on credit card accounts—a very useful service for emergencies—are available at Mexican banks.

Many banks now accept MasterCard or Visa debit cards ("cash" or "check" cards) as well as ATM cards on the Plus or Cirrus systems. Using such cards to obtain pesos from ATMs in Mexico is a much more convenient way to carry travel funds than traveler's checks. Some banks that issue ATM cards charge transaction fees for use of another bank's ATMs; check with your bank to see if these are reasonable. Some banks allow up to 10 free ATM transactions a month before service fees are collected. Most Mexican banks now charge nominal fees for withdrawing cash from their ATMs with cards from another banks.

Traveler's Checks

If you decide to bring traveler's checks, **American Express** is the most recognized type you could carry. Should you lose your Amex checks, or should you need to buy more, go to the American Express office, Paseo de la Reforma 350 at Lancaster, tel. 5207-7204 or 5207-7049, near the Zona Rosa. The office is open Mon.–Fri. 9 A.M.–6 P.M., Sat. 9 A.M.–1 P.M. Amex maintains a 24-hour hotline, tel. 5326-3625, for reporting lost or stolen checks or credit cards.

MONEY MANAGEMENT

Estimating Costs

Inflation in Mexico is running under 10 percent per annum, and if you believe Mexican Central Bank Governor Guillermo Ortiz, will converge with U.S. inflation rates by 2003. Because of Mexico's long history of inflation, however, this may be rather optimistic. Regardless, we've used dollar prices in this book on the belief that this will fluctuate less. This doesn't mean, however, that there won't be any increase in prices by the time you arrive. A couple of phone calls to hotels for price quotes should give you an idea how much rates have increased, if at all; this difference can be applied as a percentage to all other prices for a rough estimate of costs.

Student Discounts

A Tarjeta Causa Joven (Youth Cause Card) entitles the holder to discounts on air and rail tickets, hotels, cultural activities, museums, books, and various other educational goods and services. The card is available to anyone under the age of 26 who can show proof of current enrollment in a college or university. Obtain the card from official youth hostels anywhere in Mexico. Upon receiving the card you'll be issued a 100-page booklet listing the various discounts available.

Tipping

A tip of 10–15 percent is customary at restaurants with table service unless a service charge is added to the bill. Luggage handling at hotels or airports warrants a tip of US$.50 –1, or the equivalent in pesos, per bag. A few hotels maintain a no-tipping policy; details will be posted in your room. The tipping of chambermaids is optional according to Mexican custom—some guests tip and some don't. Remember that these folks typically earn minimum wage; even a small tip may mean a lot to them.

Taxes

A *impuesta al valor agregado* (IVA) of 15 percent is tacked onto all goods and services, including hotel and restaurant bills as well as international phone calls. Although by American standards this may seem high, this tax hike brings Mexico more in line with other countries that employ such value-added taxes—such as France, where the VAT runs over 20 percent.

Hotels add a further 2 percent lodging tax. Some hotel rate quotes include taxes, but to make sure you might ask *"¿Se incluyen los impuestos?"*

Bank Accounts

For long-term stays in Mexico—six months or more—visitors might consider opening a Mexican bank account. Now that peso deflation has been virtually halted, a *small* peso account seems quite safe. While the 1994–95 devaluation devastated the banking system, no depositers ever lost their savings. And in recent years, essentially all the major Mexican banks have been bought out by foreign banks (Spanish and U.S., in particular), meaning the banks are even safer.

Health and Safety

By and large, Mexico City is a healthy place. Sanitation standards, particularly in the areas most tourists are likely to visit, are relatively high compared to many other parts of Latin America.

FOOD AND WATER

Visitors who use common sense will probably never come down with food- or water-related illnesses while traveling in and around Mexico City. The first rule is not to overdo it during the first few days of your trip—eat and drink with moderation. Shoveling down huge amounts of tasty but often heavy Mexican foods along with pitchers of margaritas or strong Mexican beer is liable to make anyone sick from pure overindulgence. If you're not used to the spices and different ways of cooking, it's best to ingest small amounts at first.

Second, take it easy with foods offered by street vendors, because this is where you're most likely to suffer from unsanitary conditions. Eat only foods that have been thoroughly cooked and are served either stove-hot or refrigerator-cold. Many visitors eat street food without any problems whatsoever but it pays to be cautious, especially if it's your first time in Mexico. One rule of thumb is to eat street food only where you see a lot of other clients, which is a good indication of quality and also means there's a lot of turnover so the food isn't sitting around a long time.

Hotels and restaurants serve only purified drinking water and ice, so there's no need to ask for mineral water or to refuse ice. Tap water, however, should not be consumed except in hotels where the water system is purified—if so, you'll be informed by a notice over the washbasin in your room. Most grocery stores sell bottled purified water *(agua purificada).* Water purification tablets, iodine crystals, water filters, and the like aren't necessary for Mexico travel unless you plan on extensive backpacking.

Turista

People who've never traveled to a foreign country may undergo a period of adjustment to the new gastrointestinal flora that comes with new territory. There's really no way to avoid the differences wrought by sheer distances. Unfortunately, the adjustment is sometimes unpleasant.

Mexican doctors call gastrointestinal upset of this sort *turista* because it affects tourists but not the local population. The usual symptoms of *turista*—also known by the gringo tags "Montezuma's Revenge" and "Aztec Two-Step"—are nausea and diarrhea, sometimes with stomach cramps and a low fever. Again, eating and drinking in moderation will help prevent the worst of the symptoms, which rarely persist more than a day or two. And if it's any consolation, Mexicans often get sick the first time they go abroad, too.

Many Mexico travelers swear by a preventive regimen of Pepto-Bismol begun the day before arrival in the country. Opinions vary as to how much of the pink stuff is necessary to ward off or tame the evil flora, but a person probably shouldn't exceed the recommended daily dose. Taper off over the second week until you stop using it altogether.

Another regimen that seems to be effective is a daily tablet of 100-milligram doxycycline (sold as Vibramycin in the U.S.), a low-grade antibiotic that requires a prescription in most countries. It works by killing all the bacteria in your intestinal tract—including the ones that reside there naturally and help protect your bowels. It's available without a prescription in Mexican *farmacias* but you should check with your doctor first to make sure you're not sensitive to it—some people have problems with sunlight while taking doxycycline. Consume with plenty of water and/or a meal. Some physicians believe that when you stop taking the drug you're particularly susceptible to intestinal upset because there's no protective bacteria left to fight off infections. Hence, once you start don't stop downing the stuff until you return home.

If you come down with a case of *turista,* the best thing to do is drink plenty of fluids. Adults should drink at least three quarts or liters a day, a child under 37 kg at least a liter a day. Lay off tea, coffee, milk, fruit juices, and booze. Eat only bland foods, nothing spicy, fatty, or fried, and take it easy. Pepto-Bismol or similar pectin-based remedies usually help. Some people like to mask the symptoms with a strong over-the-counter medication such as Imodium AD (loperamide is the active ingredient), but though this can be very effective, it isn't a cure. Only time will cure traveler's diarrhea.

If the symptoms are unusually severe (especially if there's blood in the stools) or persist more than one or two days, see a doctor. Most hotels can arrange a doctor's visit or you can contact a Mexican tourist office or your consulate for recommendations.

SUNBURN AND DEHYDRATION

Sunburn probably afflicts more Mexico visitors than all other illnesses and injuries combined. The sunlight can be quite strong, especially at the Valle de México's generally high elevation. For outdoor forays, sun protection is a must, whatever the activity. The longer you're in the sun, the more protection you'll need.

A hat, sunglasses, and plenty of sunscreen or sunblock make a good start. Bring along a sunscreen with a sun protection factor (SPF) of at least 25, even if you don't plan on using it all the time. Apply it to *all* exposed parts of your body—don't forget the hands, top of the feet, and neck. Men should remember to cover thinned-out or bald areas on the scalp. Sunscreen must be reapplied after swimming or periods of heavy perspiration.

It's also important to drink plenty of water and/or nonalcoholic, noncaffeinated fluids to avoid dehydration. Alcohol and caffeine—including the caffeine in iced tea and Coke—only increase your potential for dehydration. Symptoms of dehydration include darker-than-usual urine or inability to urinate, flushed face, profuse sweating or an unusual lack thereof, and sometimes a headache, dizziness, and general feeling of malaise. Extreme cases of dehydration can lead to heat exhaustion or even heatstroke, in which the victim may become delirious and/or convulse. If either condition is suspected, get the victim out of the sun immediately, cover with a wet sheet or towel, and administer a rehydration fluid that replaces lost water and salts. If you can get the victim to a doctor, all the better—heatstroke can be very serious.

ALTITUDE SICKNESS

Some visitors who fly into 2,240-meter Mexico City airport experience mild altitude sickness shortly after arrival. Symptoms include headache, shaky stomach, breathlessness, and general malaise. The body needs time to acclimate to the change in barometric pressure and lesser amounts of oxygen. Those afflicted need to take it easy for a while: no running, no climbing the pyramids, no alcohol. The city's polluted air may exacerbate symptoms. Those with medical problems relating to the heart or lungs should probably consult with a doctor before even considering a trip to Mexico's higher climes. We find it takes us 2–3 days to fully adjust to the elevation when flying in from places at or near sea level.

Altitude sickness strikes some people at elevations as low as 1,600 meters. Others don't feel a thing until they reach much higher elevations. Above 3,000 meters acute mountain sickness (AMS) can occur—headache, loss of appetite, lethargy, shortness of breath, and insomnia are all pronounced. You're not likely to experience AMS unless you climb the higher volcanoes outside Mexico City. If you think you've been stricken, descending at least 300–600 meters should result in immediate relief. You can usually avoid AMS with a slow, step-by-step ascent. The climber's adage is to sleep no more than 300 meters higher than the place you slept the night before.

MEDICAL ASSISTANCE

The quality of basic medical treatment, including dentistry, is relatively high in Mexico City; ask at a tourist office or at your embassy for recommendations. Large hotels usually have a doctor on staff or a list of recommended physicians in the neighborhood. Sectur's 24-hour hotline, tel. 5250-0123, may also be able to offer suggestions. Polanco is the best area for private medical clinics, where a consultation will run US$25–45. Another good option is to call the Hospital ABC (see below), which has a referal service for quality doctors of different specializations.

An ambulance may be summoned via Cruz Roja (Red Cross) at tel. 5555-7557.

Hospitals

Hospital American British Cowdray (ABC), Calle Sur 136, No. 116, tel. 5230-8000 or 5230-8161, at the corner of Avenida Observatorio, south of Bosque de Chapultepec in Colonia Las Américas, is considered the best hospital in the city.

Another well-regarded hospital is **Hospital Español,** Ejército Nacional 613 in Polanco, tel. 5203-3735.

Emergency Evacuation

Over the years, several American companies have offered emergency 24-hour airlift service (accompanied by licensed physicians and nurses) from anywhere in Mexico to U.S. hospitals. Few have lasted more than a year or two. Two of the longer-running operations are Air Evac Services, Inc., 2630 Sky Harbor Blvd., Phoenix, Arizona, 85034 USA, tel. 602/273-9360 or toll-free in the U.S. and Canada 800/280-EVAC; and Advanced Aeromedical Air Ambulance Service, P.O. Box 5726, Virginia Beach, Virginia, 23471 USA, tel. 757/481-1590 or toll-free in the U.S. and Canada 800/346-3556, email: aeromed@norfolk.infi.net.

For information on other air evacuation services, contact the Association of Air Medical Services, 110 North Royal St., Suite 307, Alexandria, Virginia 22314 USA, tel. 703/836-8732, fax 703/836-8920, email: information@aams.org.

SAFETY

Until relatively recently, Mexico City enjoyed a reputation for being one of the safest large cities in the Americas, if not the world. The image suffered a reversal after the economic crisis of 1994–95, when the peso plummeted, unemployment soared, and some urban residents began resorting to robbery as a way to make up income shortfalls—or to lash out at the crisis, if you take the psychological explanation. In both cases, before and after 1994–95, the image was exaggerated. Mexico City was never as free from crime as, for example, Tokyo or Zurich, and nowadays it's nowhere near as bad as Nairobi or Bogotá, not to mention most large metropolitan areas in the United States.

To put things into perspective, FBI statistics

indicate that Washington, D.C., by comparison has a crime rate 230 percent above Mexico City's, while Los Angeles crime indices are 94 percent higher, New York's 63 percent higher, and Detroit's 292 percent higher. In 1999, the Secretaría de Turismo (SECTUR) received 1,509 complaints, a figure representing just 0.02 percent of the 7.5 million foreign visitors in Mexico City that year. On the other hand, there is general agreement that crime has increased substantially (most experts estimate a 35 percent increase) since the "crisis," and this has not improved despite overhauls of the city police department by successive governments.

Precautions

In general, visitors to Mexico City should take the same precautions they would when traveling anywhere in their own countries or abroad. Keep money and valuables secured, either in a hotel safe or safe deposit box, or in a moneybelt or other hard-to-reach place on your person. Keep an eye on cameras, purses, and the like to make sure you don't leave them behind in restaurants, hotels, or campgrounds. At night, lock the doors to your hotel room and vehicle.

Take extra caution after dark, when certain districts that are safe during the daytime—such as the Centro Histórico—become a little riskier. We advise against walking alone in the less populated streets of the historic center after 9 P.M., and after midnight it's best to take a cab even if you only have a few blocks to go. Even more touchy are areas north, northwest, and east of the Centro Histórico. Polanco, the Zona Rosa, the Roma, and the Condesa all seem to fare better after dark, though even in these areas you should stay alert. Stick to well-lighted areas and keep a steady, determined-looking pace. San Ángel and Coyoacán appear to be relatively safe places to walk around both day and night.

It's a good idea to carry limited cash and credit cards—no more than you need for an outing—when moving about the city. Don't wear expensive-looking clothes or jewelry. If confronted by someone intent on robbing you, don't resist. The only instances of violence we've heard about occurred where the robbery victims tried to resist.

If you'll be using ATM machines as a source of cash, we suggest you use off-street machines, such as those found inside many department stores (including Sanborns).

When riding the Metro or public buses, watch out for pickpockets, particularly when these modes of transport are crowded.

You must also be cautious about flagging taxicabs. Stolen taxis driven by thieves occasionally pick up unwary passengers—both Mexican and foreign—and rob them of their money and valuables. Take only cabs from taxi queues at a hotel or established taxi stand *(sitio)* and you should be okay. (For more on taxi strategies, see the special topic Taxi Security.)

Police

Mexico City police have a reputation for stopping motorists to extract *la mordida* (literally "the bite"), or minor bribes. While in much of the rest of Mexico this practice is on the downswing, in the capital it appears to be as bad as ever, despite recent attempts at reform by the new city government. Even if you're not driving, you're not entirely safe from predatory police. A few of our many acquaintances—both Mexican and foreign—in the capital have been robbed by police (or people posing as police) late at night in the Centro Histórico. In every case they were walking alone, so the best way to avoid such incidents is not to walk alone at night.

Help

"061" is the city's emergency telephone number for reporting criminal acts. It is designed to facilitate the reporting of crimes committed against tourists and residents alike. When an individual calls this number, a representative of the Ministerios Públicos Moviles (Mobile Justice Department) reports to the scene of the crime or, when tourists are involved, to their hotel to register the complaint. There are 32 such mobile crime units stationed around the city.

Another avenue to try is the Procuraduría General de Justicia, Florencia 20, tel. 5242-8154 or 5242-6328, a branch of the attorney general's office. The officials here are accustomed to dealing with foreigners and usually have someone on duty who speaks English. While not all Mexico City police inspire confidence (to say the least), these police will actually try to help you out, if they can. Interpreters are available, and someone is in the office 24 hours a day.

Sectur maintains a 24-hour traveler's aid hotline for emergencies of all kinds: 5250-0123 or 5250-0151.

Legal Matters

All foreign visitors in Mexico are subject to Mexican legal codes, which are based on Roman and Napoleonic law updated with U.S. constitutional theory and civil law. The most distinctive features of the Mexican judiciary system, compared to Anglo-American systems, are that the system doesn't provide for trials by jury (the judge decides) nor writs of habeas corpus (though you must be charged within 72 hours of incarceration). Furthermore, bail is rarely granted to an arrested foreigner—for many offenses, not even Mexican nationals are allowed bail. Hence, once you're arrested and jailed for a serious offense, it can be very difficult to arrange release. The lesson here is: don't get involved in matters that might result in your arrest. This primarily means anything having to do with drugs or guns.

The oft-repeated saw that in Mexico an arrested person is considered guilty until proven innocent is no more true south of the border than north. As in Canada, the U.S., and most of Europe, an arrested person is considered a criminal *suspect* until the courts confirm or deny guilt. You have the right to notify your consulate if detained.

If you get into trouble with Mexican law, for whatever reason, you should try to contact your nearest consulate in Mexico. Sectur and state tourist offices can also help in some instances. These agencies routinely handle emergency legal matters involving visiting foreigners; you stand a much better chance of resolving legal difficulties with their assistance.

Services and Information

COMMUNICATIONS

Postal Service

The Mexican postal service, though mostly reliable, is relatively slow. Delivery time has been shortened by 75 percent since 1989, the year a full government subsidy for Sepomex (Servicio Postal Mexicana) was discontinued and the Ministry of Communications and Transport ordered the agency to become self-sufficient. Average delivery time between Mexico and the U.S. or Canada is about 10 days, while to Europe you must figure two weeks. Mail sent to Mexico from outside the country generally reaches its destination more quickly.

Most post offices *(correos)* in Mexico City accept general delivery mail. Have correspondents address mail in your name (last name capitalized), followed by a/c Lista de Correos, the *colonia* name, and the postal code, e.g., Joe CUMMINGS, a/c Lista de Correos, Col. Condesa, México 06140 D.F., México. Mail sent this way is usually held 10 days. If you want your mail held up to 30 days, substitute the words "Poste Restante, Correo Central" for Lista de Correos in the address, e.g. Joe CUMMINGS, a/c Poste Restante, Col. Condesa, México 06140 D.F., México. Because delivery time is highly variable, it's best to use *poste restante* just to be safe.

In small towns and villages, residents often don't use street addresses, simply writing the addressee's name followed by *domicilio conocido* (known residence) and the name of the town or village. Even in large towns and cities, addresses may bear the name of the street without a building number (*sin número,* abbreviated as s/n), or will mention the nearest cross streets (e.g., *ent. Abasolo y Revolución,* or between Abasolo and Revolución).

The usual post office hours are Mon.–Fri. 9 A.M.–5 P.M., Sat.–Sun. 9 A.M.–noon. Offices in large cities and state capitals may stay open to 7 P.M., and some small-town *correos* close for a 2–4 P.M. siesta.

The Mexican post office offers an express mail service (EMS) called Mexpost. International rates are relatively high; a Mexpost express letter to the U.S. or Canada, for example, costs US$16, to Europe US$20. Mexpost claims to deliver almost anywhere in Mexico within 48 hours, to major cities around the world within 72 hours. A Mexpost parcel cannot exceed 1.05 meters along any one dimension or weigh more than 20 kilos. The main Mexpost center at Netzahualcóyotl 109, tel. 5709-9606, in the Centro offers packing services.

Some individual post offices with convenient locations include:

- **Palacio Postal,** Eje Central Lázaro Cárdenas and Tacuba, opposite the Palacio de Bellas Artes, Mon.–Fri. 9 A.M.–6 P.M.
- **Zócalo,** Plaza de la Constitución 7 (west side of the Zócalo), Mon.–Fri. 9 A.M.–2:30 P.M.
- **Zona Rosa,** Londres 208 at Varsovia, Mon.–Fri. 9 A.M.–5 P.M., Sat. 9 A.M.–1 P.M. (adjacent MexPost EMS office open Mon.–Fri. 9 A.M.–2 P.M. and 2:30–4 P.M., Sat. 9 A.M.–1 P.M.).
- **Paseo de la Reforma,** Paseo de la Reforma 77, Mon.–Sat. 9 A.M.–5 P.M.
- **Colonia Cuauhtémoc,** Río Misisipi 58, Mon.–Fri. 9 A.M.–3 P.M., Sat. 9 A.M.–1 P.M.
- **Colonia Condesa,** Aguascalientes 161; Mon.–Fri. 9 A.M.–5 P.M., Sat. 9 A.M.–1 P.M.
- **Roma,** Álvaro Obregón 31; Mon.–Fri. 9 A.M.–7 P.M., Sat. 9 A.M.–1 P.M.
- **Polanco,** Galileo 245, Mon.–Fri. 9 A.M.–5 P.M., Sat. 9 A.M.–1 P.M.
- **San Ángel,** Dr. Gálvez 16, Mon.–Fri. 9 A.M.–5 P.M., Sat. 9 A.M.–1 P.M.
- **Coyoacán,** Higuera 23, Mon.–Fri. 9 A.M.–5 P.M., Sat. 9 A.M.–1 P.M.

Courier Services

Several courier services operate in Mexico City. In our experience, DHL and UPS seem to offer the lowest prices and best services. MexPost, the express delivery offered by the Mexican Postal Service, is less expensive and a bit slower. All of the couriers listed below offer packing service. Central offices are listed below; each has many branches and also offers home pickup. DHL Internacional de México, Paseo de la Reforma 76, tel. 5345-7000; Estafeta Mexicana, Hamburgo 213, Zona Rosa, tel. 5270-8300; Federal Express, Insurgentes Sur 899, Col. Nápoles, tel. 5228-9904; Mexpost, Palacio Postal, Eje Central, Col. Centro, tel. 5729-3500; UPS de México, Insurgentes Sur 667, tel. 5228-7900.

American Express

Amex cardholders can take mail at the American Express office, Paseo de la Reforma 350, México 06600 D.F., México, tel. 5207-7204, open Mon.–Fri. 9 A.M.–6 P.M., Sat. 9 A.M.–1 P.M.

Telephone Services

The national telephone company, **TelMex,** was privatized in 1990 and has improved its services considerably over the last several years. Local phone calls are relatively cheap—a local phone-booth call costs only one peso—as are long-distance calls *within* Mexico. If you can find a working phone—many public phones seem permanently "out of order"—connections are usually good, though you may have to wait a while to get through to the operator during busy periods such as Sunday and holidays.

If you don't want to use a phone booth or a hotel phone (hotels usually add their own surcharges to both local and long-distance calls), you can make a call during business hours from a TelMex office or from a private phone office or *caseta de teléfono,* often set up in the corner of a local shop. Like hotels, private telephone offices add surcharges to calls.

Probably the best option to make local calls and long-distance calls within Mexico is the public pay phone service called **Ladatel** (acronym for Larga Distancia Teléfono), with phone booths where you can pay for local and/or long-distance calls with a *tarjeta de teléfono* (phone card) issued by TelMex. You can buy these cards in denominations of $20, $30, and $50 at many pharmacies, convenience stores, supermarkets, bus terminals, and airports.

In 2001, the Mexican government overhauled local area codes in the entire country, a process that left many people extremely confused about what number to dial, especially from outside Mexico. The numbers in this book all include the new area codes, but in case you need to check

TELEPHONE CODES

Long-distance operator (national): 020
Time: 030
Directory Assistance (Mexico): 040
Police, Red Cross, Fire: 060
International operator: 090
Long-distance direct dialing from Mexico via TelMex:
- **station to station (in Mexico):** 01 + area code + number
- **person to person (in Mexico):** 02 + area code + number
- **station to station (U.S. and Canada):** 001 + area code + number
- **person to person (U.S. and Canada):** 09 + 1 + area code + number
- **station to station (other international):** 00 + country code + area code + number
- **person to person (other international):** 09 + country code + area code + number
- **noninternational U.S. 800 number:** 001 + 880 + number (be aware these are not free calls when dialed from Mexico)

Access numbers for other long distance companies:
- **MCI:** 01-800-021-8000 or 001-800-674-7000
- **AT&T:** 01-800-288-2872 or 001-800-462-4240
- **Sprint:** 01-800-234-0000 or 001-800-877-8000
- **Canada Direct:** 01-800-123-0200

To call Mexico direct from outside the country, dial your international access code + 52 + number. Example: to call the number 5155-0631 in Mexico City from the U.S., dial 011 (international access code) + 52 (Mexico country code) + 55 (Mexico City code) + 5155-0631 (the phone number in Mexico City). The Mexico City area code "55" is the only two-digit area code in the regions covered by this book; all others are three digits.

Help: SECTUR (the Ministry of Tourism) maintains a 24-hour traveler's aid hotline for emergencies of all kinds: 5250-0123 or 5250-0151. If you're dialing from outside Mexico City, call 01-800-903-9200.

a number, look on the Web at www.cft.gob.mx/frame_camp.html for a complete list of the new area codes. Unlike most of the rest of central Mexico, Mexico City has a two-digit area code, 55, followed by an eight-digit phone number. To dial a Mexico City number from elsewhere in Mexico, call 01-55-5234-5678. All other locations covered by this book have a three-digit area code followed by a seven-digit phone number. For example, to dial a number in Cuernavaca from Mexico City, call 01-777-318-1234.

If you have a calling card number for Sprint, AT&T, MCI, or Bell Canada, you can use them to make long-distance calls within Mexico or to another country. Each of these has its own access code for direct dialing. (See the special topic Telephone Codes for each.)

One of the better long-distance telephone offices, **Servitel,** has two branches in the Zona Rosa at Florencia 70 and Hamburgo 108, which are open Mon.–Sat. 8 A.M.–10 P.M.

To direct dial an international call via TelMex, dial 00 plus the area code and number for a station-to-station call or 09 plus area code and number for a person-to-person or other operator-assisted call. Long-distance international calls are heavily taxed and cost more than equivalent international calls from the U.S. or Canada.

The appropriate long-distance operator can place a collect call on your behalf or charge the call to your account if you have a calling card for that service. If you try these numbers from a hotel phone, be sure the hotel operator realizes the call is toll-free; some hotel operators use their own timers to assess phone charges.

TelMex international rates now run about the same as AT&T's, sometimes cheaper depending on time of day and call destination. Since the deregulation of Mexican telephone service, several private, U.S.-based long-distance phone companies have set up their own phone systems—not just the lines and service but actual pay phones—in Mexico to take advantage of undiscerning tourists. The English-language signs next to the phone usually read Call the U.S. or Canada Collect or With a Credit Card or Just Dial Zero to Reach the U.S. or Canada. Often a company operates under several different corporate names in the area, charging at least 50 percent more per international call than TelMex, AT&T, MCI, or Sprint—as much as US$10–20 for the first minute, plus US$4 each additional minute, even on weekends. A percentage of these charges usually goes to the hotel or private phone office offering the service. At most private phone offices it's much cheaper to use TelMex (or a well-known international company such as AT&T, MCI, or Sprint), even if you have to pay a service charge on top of the rates, than to use these fly-by-night U.S. companies. If you're concerned about economizing, always ask which company is being used before you arrange an international call through a hotel or private phone office.

For international service, calling collect often saves hassles. In Spanish the magic words are *por cobrar* (collect), prefaced by the name of the place you're calling (e.g., *"a los Estados Unidos, por favor—por cobrar"*). This will connect you to an English-speaking international operator. For best results, speak slowly and clearly. You can reach an international operator directly by dialing 090.

In 1999 the "5" was added to the regular seven-digit numbers in D.F., so that now you must dial an eight-digit number, always beginning with 5. Some listings for Mexico City businesses still use the old seven-digit numbers; if you see a listing in the city for 256-1720, then you'll have to dial 5256-1720.

Internet Resources

A number of online service providers offer information on different aspects of Mexico, and the number of World Wide Web sites with data on the country are multiplying daily. You can expect a general search under the single keyword "Mexico" to turn up at least 100,000 references, perhaps many more. Many of these are commercial sites established by tour operators or hotels. The ratio of commercial to noncommercial sites is liable to increase over time if current Internet trends continue.

You'll do better to narrow your search by starting with a few known URLs (universal resource locators) and working from there using links to other resources. (See Mexico City on the Web for a list of some we've found.) Remember that all URLs mentioned here are subject to change without notice; a couple of them even changed addresses while we were compiling this section. You can of course use your own browser to conduct searches. Yahoo! (www.yahoo.com), Webcrawler (http://query.webcrawler.com), and Alta Vista (www.altavista.com) work well for blind searches.

Avalon Travel Publishing's website (www.travelmatters.com) contains occasional excerpts from this book and other Moon Handbooks titles, ordering information, and links to various related sites.

Email and Internet Access

If you're bringing a computer and modem to Mexico with hopes of staying on the infobahn, online options are limited to a handful of local Internet service providers and a few international ones. Baud rates can be slow—we have trouble logging on at speeds of 28.8M or greater, bottlenecked by low bandwidth and line interruptions in the Mexican phone system. With fiber optic on the way in many parts of the country, this could change rapidly, though much depends on the kind of equipment installed at any given town linked with fiber optics.

America Online and AT&T are the only international providers so far that we've found offering local access phone numbers in Mexico. Mexico's own TelMex/Prodigy is the most widely used local service. Long-term visitors can try their luck with local ISP accounts (average cost US$10–20 a month), but most people we know

MEXICO CITY ON THE WEB

While a substantial number of English speakers live in Mexico City, the Web offers paltry resources in English about one of the world's largest megalopolises. Yet for those Mexicophiles who feel the need to stay on top of city politics and tourism, government offices offer content-rich websites for those with some command of Spanish. You'll also find English language participation in bulletin boards, specialty guides, and an online rating courtesy of Deja.com.

Keep in mind that websites come and go, and URLs (universal resource locators, or World Wide Web "addresses") change. More websites are included throughout the book on different topics.

Directorio de Comunicación Social
www.precisa.gob.mx
An excellent directory of the entire Mexican government: all branches, the federal and state level, and state-run companies. As well, the site maintains updated lists of foreign embassies, foreign journalists in Mexico, media (radio, television, and newspapers) from across Mexico, universities, and political parties. Superb resource.

Mexico City Government
www.df.gob.mx/
Mexico City's website is well designed and, best of all, there is a great deal of content. If you're interested in city politics and administration, track down the addresses, phone numbers, and emails of the city's precinct leaders or participate in the online chat forums (www.df.gob.mx/foros/index.html) on topics including public security, tourism, and environmental affairs. Mixing thoroughness and creativity, the Mexico City website exemplifies what a government website can be. The only thing missing would be an email mailing list that provided press releases and announcements from specific departments. This information is posted online (www.df.gob.mx/noticias/index.html), but you have to hunt for it.

Mexico City Government Tourism Office
www.mexicocity.gob.mx/
The city's new tourism office has a fairly fancy website with plenty of good links, although descriptions are very limited. Check the Centro Histórico page (www.mexicocity.gob.mx/eng/enjoy/chistorico/index.asp) and the links for museums, theaters, cinemas, and walking tours. You'll also find the addresses for tourism *modulos* around the city (www.mexicocity.gob.mx/eng/modules/index.asp). Kudos to officials for posting an archive of statistics (www.mexicocity.gob.mx/eng/stats/index.html), which is a good resource for journalists and anyone interested in current affairs.

Instituto Nacional de Estadística, Geografía e Informatica
www.inegi.gob.mx
Inegi is the government statistical institute, and its website (although difficult to navigate) has a wealth of detailed information about the country's population, economy, environment, and much else besides.

Mexico City Virtual Guide
www.mexicocity.com.mx/mexcity.html
While the site does not seem to be updated often, it provides a first-time visitor with a wide range of information from city hotels to parks.

Guide2Mexico
www.guide2mexico.com/content/mexlinks.htm
An impressive collection of travelers' resources, including lots of useful links.

Mexican Wave
www.mexicanwave.com
Another general site for travelers, this one geared toward a European audience, but in English with lots of good information.

Centro Histórico
www.centrohistorico.com.mx/
As the name implies, this site focuses on the historic center of the city and on ambitious plans to renovate the district.

Mexican Embassy in Washington, D.C.
www.embassyofmexico.org
This is the place to come for the latest Mexican visa information.

Art and History Museums
www.arts-history.mx/museos/muse.html
This excellent site contains descriptions and opening hours of every important art and history museum in the capital.

Mexico City Art
www.arte-mexico.com
Online map of the city's many galleries and art museums and listings of current exhibitions and openings.

Rock en Español
www.rockeros.com
A compendium of links and commentary on *rock en español, la nueva onda, guacarock,* and other new rock movements in 13 countries in Latin America, plus the U.S. and Spain. MP3 downloads available.

Intellicast Forecast
www.intellicast.com
Want to know what the weather will be like tomorrow?

Environmental Information in Mexico City
www.planeta.com/ecotravel/mexico/df/mexinfo.html
A one-stop information center for anyone interested in environmental issues. This page is frequently updated and is part of the Planeta.com website.

Moon Handbooks
www.moon.com
Moon's website contains occasional excerpts from this book and other Moon titles, ordering information, an online travel newsletter with articles on Mexico, and links to various related sites.
—by Ron Mader, Mexico City resident and host of the *Eco Travels in Latin America* website (www.planeta.com), and Chris Humphrey

INTERNET CAFÉS

Because so few Mexicans own their own computers and/or have an Internet connection, public places to surf the Web have been multiplying throughout Mexico City. Travelers should have no problem at all finding places to log on. If the ones listed below are not satisfactory, just ask at your hotel for other suggestions.

Downtown

Escuela Superior Lafoel, Donceles 80 at the corner of República de Brasil, tel. 5512-3584, US$2.20 an hour; open Mon.–Sat. 10 A.M.–8 P.M.

Zona Rosa

Coffee Mail, Amberes 61, US$2.20 an hour; open Mon.–Fri. 10 A.M.–10 P.M., Sat. 11 A.M.–9 P.M.

Java Chat, Génova 44-K, tel. 5525-6853, US$2.20 an hour; open Mon.–Fri. 9 A.M.–11:30 P.M., Sat. 10 A.M.–11:30 P.M.

Monumento a la Revolución

Intermedios, Puente de Alvarado 70, right near the corner of Arriaga, US$.50 for 15 minutes; open daily 10 A.M.–11 P.M.

Condesa

ADN, Campeche 280, tel. 5584-1894, US$2 an hour or US$1 for half-an-hour; open Mon.–Fri. 10 A.M.–7 P.M.

Roma

Javanet, Orizaba 171, tel. 5584-1316, US$1.50 an hour; open Mon.–Sat. 9 A.M.–8 P.M.

W@ll Internet, Orizaba 39, tel. 5511-1749, US$1.50 an hour; open Mon.–Fri. 10 A.M.–8 P.M., Sat. 10 A.M.–4 P.M.

Polanco

Café.com, Virgilio 25, tel. 5281-3516, US$4.50 an hour or US$1.25 for 15 minutes; open Mon.–Fri. 10 A.M.–7:30 P.M., Sat. 11:30 A.M.–4:30 P.M.

San Ángel

Escape, Av. La Paz 23, tel. 5550-7611, US$3.30 an hour; open Mon.–Sat. 9 A.M.–10 P.M., Sun. 11 A.M.–7 P.M.

prefer using AOL, AT&T or TelMex/Prodigy over anything else available in Mexico so far.

RJ11 phone jacks are the standard in newer hotels, but in older hotels, motels, and *casas de huéspedes* the phones may still be hard-wired. A pocketknife and pair of alligator clips are useful for stripping and attaching wires, or bring along an acoustic coupler. You can also take your laptop to a local phone office and ask to plug into its system. Most phone offices are cooperative if you're polite and explain what you're up to. We've encountered a few small-town officials who seemed to fear that our laptop would suck all the electric power in the town dry, or that we would call Mongolia and charge it as a call to Mexico City. Sometimes a good bit of explanation is necessary. If the office or hotel telephone is hard-wired, ask if the office has a fax machine, because all fax units use standard RJ11 jacks.

Cybercafés where you can log on using public

terminals to send and receive email or browse the Web are multiplying in Mexico City. No doubt more public Internet access points will appear over the next few years. All allow access to any Web-based emailing such as Yahoo! or MSN Hotmail, or you can go through TelNet to check your account back home if you prefer, and provided you know the ins and outs of TelNet. (See the special topic Internet Cafés for a few suggested locations.)

Library

The **Biblioteca Benjamín Franklin,** Londres 16, Col. Juárez, tel. 5080-2089, www.usembassy-mexico.gov/biblioteca.htm, is an excellent library run by the U.S. Embassy, but it's open to the general public over 16 years of age. To check out books, you're required to show proof of residence in Mexico City and wait several days to get a card, but anyone is allowed to browse the periodicals or books at in the library. Open Mon.–Fri. 11 A.M.–7 P.M.

MEDIA

Newspapers

Among the national Spanish-language dailies, *Reforma* is widely considered the most informative and objective, and the newer daily *Milenio* is pretty good too. *La Jornada* and *UNO más UNO* lean well toward the left, while *El Financiero* is oriented toward business and politics. The latter also appears in a weekly English-language edition available at various Mexican consulates and cultural centers in the U.S., Canada, and Mexico. You can buy these newspapers at any of the many street-corner newspaper kiosks around the city, with the exception of Reforma which (because of a dispute with the newspaper union) is sold by vendors on street corners or in convenience stores only. Even if your Spanish is minimal, city newspapers are worth a glance for current information on museum exhibits and local cinema.

The News, a conservative English-language newspaper published in Mexico City, is heavily oriented toward Mexico City residents and carries stories off American wire services. *USA Today* and the *International Herald Tribune* are sometimes sold in hotel lobbies or bookstores.

Downstairs from the Club de Periodistas de México Prensa Nacional y Internacional (International and National Press Club), **La Torre de Papel,** Filomeno Mata 6-A in the Centro Histórico, sells more than 300 daily newspapers from around Mexico, plus about 50 from other

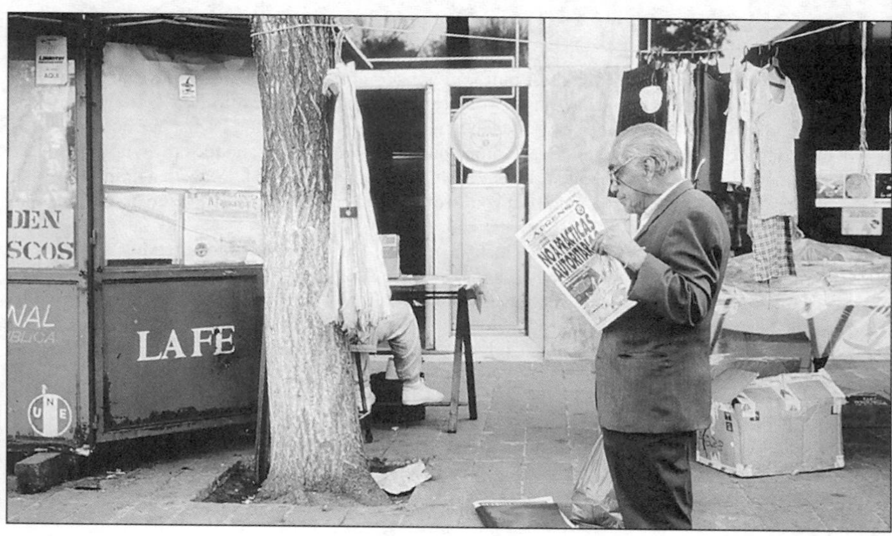

countries (mainly the U.S. and Europe). It's open Mon.–Fri. 9 A.M.–6 P.M., Sat. 9 A.M.–3 P.M. **La Casa de la Prensa,** a shop with a large magazine section and daily U.S. and European newspapers, has two branches in the Zona Rosa. The main store is at Florencia 57 and is open Mon.–Fri. 8 A.M.–10 P.M. and weekends 8 A.M.–4 P.M.; the other is at Hamburgo 141, open Mon.–Fri. 8 A.M.–10 P.M. and weekends 1 P.M.–9 P.M. In Polanco, **The Coffee Bar,** at the intersection of Temistocles and Presidente Mazaryk, has a similarly large selection.

Magazines

Formerly *MB* was a decent English-language read on Mexican business and politics, but in recent years its quality has slipped. *Latin Trade* is better, but it is heavily focused on business stories. The U.S. Chamber of Commerce puts out a magazine in Mexico City called *Business Mexico,* also heavily oriented toward business and finance, available in Sanborns around the city. In Spanish, *Proceso* is the leading muckracking magazine. Its stories on Mexican political machinations, though occasionally a bit over the top on the conspiracy theory, are often excellent. Two newer glossy weekly magazines are *Milenio,* which also has good international news stories, and *Cambio.*

La Torre de Papel and La Casa de la Prensa, both mentioned under Newspapers, stock many international magazines from the U.S. and Europe.

Television

Mexican TV offers a mix of American dramas and sitcoms dubbed in Spanish and Mexico's own versions of the same formulae. Mexico's famous *telenovelas*—soap opera series that run several months rather than several years—are exported all over Latin America.

Many hotels and motels maintain their own satellite dishes with as many as 50 channels from Mexico and the U.S. CNN International is widely available. The main movie channels in Mexico City are Cine Latino (Spanish), USA Network (English), Fox (English), Multicinema (mixed), De Película (Spanish), Multicinema (mixed), and Cinema Golden Choice (English).

Radio

Mexico City boasts hundreds of AM and FM stations. Most of the music stations play Mexican

WASHING YOUR DUDS

If you're tired of trying to wash those blue jeans in your sink (nightmare job) and want to have someone else clean the grime out of your clothes, you'll be pleased to hear getting your washing done in Mexico City is easy and inexpensive. Coin-operated laundromats are not common in Mexico—instead you normally drop your clothes off one day and pick them up either later that same day or the following day. Usually prices are charged in kilos, with a minimum of three kilos for wash, dry, and fold. If your clothes need special treatment be sure to tell the owners first.

Below are four places we've found which are reliable. There are many more in every *colonia* in the city, and many hotels will wash clothes for a fee also.

Lavandería Automática Esmafga, Mesones 42, Col. Centro, tel. 5709-0278; open Mon.–Sat. 10 A.M.–6 P.M.

Lava Jet, Danubio 119-B, Col. Cuauhtémoc (near Paseo de la Reforma), tel. 5207-3032, English spoken, US$6 for first three kilos; open Mon.–Fri. 8:30 A.M.–5:30 P.M., Sat. 8:30 A.M.–4 P.M.

Lavandería Automática Edison, Edison 91, near Monumento a la Revolución; open Mon.–Fri. 10 A.M.–7 P.M., Sat. 10 A.M.–5 P.M.

Lavandería Del Río, Jalapa 99, Col. Roma, tel. 5511-2538, , US$4 for three kilos; open Mon.–Sat. 8 A.M.–7 P.M., Sun. 8 A.M.–2 P.M.

top 40, but for visitors interested in authentic *música mexicana,* we can recommend several stations. Morena FM 89.7 FM broadcasts traditional *romanticismo,* romantic songs by such crooners as Luis Miguel, Alejandro Fernández, Tania Libertad, and Juan Gabriel.

Radioactiva 98.5 FM is an alternative rock/top 40 station presenting a mix of English and Spanish groups, with a greater emphasis on English. For *grupera,* La Zeta 107.3 FM is the one to listen to, and for *tropical* try Sabrosita 100.9 FM. Radio Uno 104.1 FM plays salsa daily 3–4 P.M. and 9–10 P.M.

One of the better radio news programs with news 24 hours a day is Formato 21, 790 AM.

MAPS

The government statistics institute, **Instituto Estadística, Geografía e Información (INEGI),** maintains three stores where the public can buy a variety of maps, as well as statistical yearbooks and other information resources. The main store is at Balderas 71, tel. 5512-8331, open Mon.–Fri. 9 A.M.–8 P.M. Other stores can be found at the INEGI Mexico City headquarters, Patriotismo 711, tel. 5278-1000, and at the airport's domestic terminal.

Mexico City Maps

The best overall street map of the city we've found for normal, everyday tourist use is Berndtson & Berndtson's *Mexico City City Streets* (1:11,000 scale, US$6.95) folding sheet map, which is very accurate and has very clear graphics. Another bonus is that it's laminated in heavy plastic, so it holds up well to frequent use. *Mexico City* (American Map Corp., US$9.95), another folding sheet map, also has good, clear graphics.

If you're planning to take up residence in the capital, you'll want to go a step further and get the thick *Cuidad de México Area Metropolitana* street atlas published by Guía Roji, which has a scale of 1:22,500 and costs around US$9 if you buy it in D.F., or around US$16–17 abroad. This one covers every corner of the Distrito Federal and includes two complete indexes, one by street name and one by *colonia* (neighborhood). Guía Roji also publishes a simple two-sided folding street map (US$4 in Mexico City, up to US$9 abroad), *Ciudad de México,* with a scale of 1:30,000, but it's really not a very good map. Another Mexican-made sheet map of similar quality is Pronto's *Ciudad de México,* which costs about the same as the Guía Roji sheet map.

Highway Maps

Among the many Mexico maps available to visitors who will be taking excursions outside Mexico City, two are particularly well suited to general-purpose Mexico road travel. One is published by the American Automobile Association (AAA) and is available from most AAA offices; maps are free to members, about US$4 to the general public. The excellent graphics on this map make it easy to read, and it's accurate and detailed enough for most Mexico auto trips. The map's coverage extends well into the U.S. border states. Distances are marked in kilometers for Mexico, miles for the United States.

Those planning to spend time on Mexico's back roads should buy a Mexican road atlas. The best available is the annual 127-page *Guía Roji por las Carreteras de México,* published in Mexico but available through Treaty Oak, P.O. Box 50295, Austin, TX 78763, tel. 512/326-4141, email: maps@treatyoak.com; Map Center, 2611 University Ave., San Diego, CA 92104, tel. 619/291-3830; and Map Link, 25 E. Mason, Santa Barbara, CA 93101, tel. 805/965-4402, fax 805/962-0884, as well as many travel bookstores abroad and in Mexican department stores. This atlas contains 38 double-page maps with a scale of 1:1,000,000 (one inch:25 km), along with color graphics to indicate forests and woodlands, deserts, and marshlands. Best of all, the atlas includes a fairly complete network of unpaved roads, villages, and *ejidos* that don't appear on the AAA or any other large-scale, single-page maps. Another plus is that the atlas includes 15 city maps.

Guía Roji also publishes state maps at 1:800,000 scale, simple to read and adequate for most purposes.

Topographical Maps

Because differences in elevation often determine backcountry route selection, hikers, kayakers, mountain bikers, and off-road drivers should consider using topographical maps. You can obtain these in advance from Treaty Oak or Map Link in the U.S., or in Mexico from INEGI.

TOURIST INFORMATION

Mexico City has its own tourist office, the **Secretaría de Turismo de la Ciudad de México,** at the 9th floor of Av. Nuevo León 56 in Col. Hipódromo Condesa, tel. 5286-9077, fax 5286-9022. For the most part this is an administrative office, so if it's information you need, you're better off visiting one of the several tourist suboffices *(módulos de información turística)* around the city and at the airport (see the special topic Tourist Modules for addresses). These small offices usually stock a variety of free brochures, maps, hotel and restaurant lists, and information on local activities, and are staffed by Mexicans who are trained to handle visitor queries. Some speak very good English, others not. The city tourist office has its own website at www.mexicocity.gob.mx.

The federal government also operates a national tourism secretariat, the **Secretaría de Turismo de México,** Av. Presidente Mazaryk 172, México, D.F. 11570, tel. 5250-0151 or 5250-0123, in the U.S. 800/482-9832, fax 5250-6610. SECTUR also maintains Internet information at www.mexico-travel.com.

TOURIST MODULES

Aeropuerto Internacional de la Cd. de México
Llegada Nacional Local 9
tel. 5762-6773
Daily 9 A.M.–8:30 P.M.

Alameda
Av. Juárez and Revillagigedo
Daily 9 A.M.–8 P.M.

Chapultepec
Corner of Paseo de la Reforma and Gandhi
Tues.–Sun. 9 A.M.–6 P.M.

Coyoacán
Jardín Hidalgo 1
tel. 5659-0056, ext. 181
Daily 8 A.M.–8 P.M.

San Ángel
Casa de la Cultura San Ángel
Av. Revolución and Madero
tel. 5616-1254 or 5616-2003
Daily 9 A.M.–8 P.M.

Xochimilco
Nuevo Embarcadero Nativitas
tel. 5653-5209
Daily 10 A.M.–6 P.M.

Zona Rosa
Londres and Amberes
tel. 5525-9380
Daily 9 A.M.–8:30 P.M.

100 Metros
Terminal de Autobuses del Norte
tel. 5587-1552
Mon.–Fri. 9 A.M.–4 P.M.

FILM AND PHOTOGRAPHY

Ordinary color print film is widely available in small photo shops, *farmacias,* and department stores throughout the city. If you're looking for something a little different, such as professional color transparency or black and white films, one of the best areas to shop for them is Calle Donceles in the Centro Histórico, particularly along Donceles between Calle Palma Norte and Calle República de Chile. Here you'll find shop after shop stocking most of the same films that are available in metropolitan areas of the U.S., Canada, and Europe. Film prices are about the same as or a little bit higher than in the United States. The same shops also sell camera equipment, although in this case Mexico is a rather expensive place to buy, because import tariffs on Japanese goods are high.

For film processing, the same applies. If all you need is to develop and print color snapshots, there are plenty of one-hour photo shops around the city. For quality slide processing or black-and-white proofing/printing, Calle Donceles is the most convenient place to go. On Donceles, we have found Photo Art Studio (Arce Bros.), Donceles 57, tel. 5510-8626, to be reliable for film sales and processing and for professional photographic equipment.

Profoto, Citlaltépetl 23 at Amsterdam in the Condesa, tel. 5286-5945, carries a full array of professional equipment and supplies. It's open Mon.–Fri. 9 A.M.–6 P.M., Sat. 10 A.M.–2:30 P.M.

Getting cameras repaired in Mexico City is no easy task. Considering the wait at professional shops, you might be better off holding off until you return home. Two places can offer quicker service than normal: **Servicio Bolaños,** Liverpool 9 near the Zona Rosa, tel. 5535-5564, open Mon.–Fri. 9 A.M.–5 P.M.; and a little hole-in-the-wall place called **Clásica Cameras Boutique,** Donceles 105, tel. 5694-5242, open Mon.–Sat. 10 A.M.–6 P.M. While the latter is really more of a street stand than a store, and it is littered with the carcasses of old cameras, we can state for the record that it fixed the light meter of a malfunctioning Nikon in one day for minimal money, and it's worked for three years without a hitch.

BUSINESS SERVICES

Computer Equipment Rental

The following businesses offer computer equipment for rent. Most will deliver to offices or hotels anywhere in the city: ABM Renta de Equipo, tel. 5741-6338 or 5741-0981; Consultores en Informática y Computación, tel. 5282-5777; Desarrollos Alem, tel. 5273-3746 or 5273-8296; Soluciones PC, tel. 5605-3436 or 5605-3572; Tecno-Rent, tel. 5661-9758; and XS Renta, tel. 5633-5464 or 5633-6955.

Translators and Interpreters

- **Amtrad Intertraducciones,** Holbein 18, Col. Mixcoac, tel. 5563-2745.
- **Berlitz de México,** Ejército Nacional 503, Col. Polanco, tel. 5545-0644 or 5545-0650, www.berlitz.com.mx.
- **Centro Integral de Traducción e Interpretación,** Av. Chapultepec 471-201, Col. Juárez, tel. 5286-8444, www.cititran.com.
- **Koiné,** Bajío 335-104, Col. Roma Sur, tel. 5264-6787 or 5564-5256, email: koine@infoabc.com.
- **Recursos Técnicos para Conferencias,** Eugenia 13-602, Col. Nápoles, tel. 5543-5011 or 5543-3517.
- **Traducciones Willy de Winter,** Horacio 528-404, Col. Polanco, tel. 5545-5764 or 5254-7446, email: willywinter@infosel.net.mx.

TIME, POWER, AND MEASURES

Time

Mexico City time coincides with central standard time in the U.S. and is six hours ahead of Greenwich Mean Time (GMT -6), from the last Sunday in October to the last Sunday in April each year. From April 25 to October 26 Mexico changes over to central daylight saving time (GMT -5).

Looking at the whole country, there are three time zones. The State of Baja California Norte runs on Pacific standard time (GMT -8 or GMT -7); the States of Baja California Sur, Sonora, and Sinaloa follow mountain standard time (GMT -7 or GMT -6); and the rest of the states are on central standard time (GMT -6 or GMT -5). This means you should set your timepieces an hour ahead when crossing the above zone boundaries going east or back an hour when crossing west.

Time in Mexico is commonly expressed according to the 24-hour clock, from 0001 to 2400 (one minute past midnight to midnight). A restaurant posting hours of 1100-2200, for example, is open 11 A.M.–10 P.M. according to the 12-hour clock popular in the United States. Signs in Mexico may be posted using either system.

Business Hours

The typical small business will be open Monday–Friday (plus Saturday for retail businesses) 9 A.M.–2 P.M., then closed until 4 or 5 P.M., and then reopened until 7 or 8 P.M. Official government offices typically maintain an 9 A.M.–7 P.M. schedule, with a 2–3 P.M. lunch hour.

Banks are open Monday–Friday 8:30 A.M.–3 P.M., but remember that the foreign exchange service usually closes about noon (probably to lock in the exchange rate before afternoon adjustments). A few competitive banks have extended their hours as late as 5 P.M.

Electricity

Mexico's electrical system is the same as those in the U.S. and Canada: 110 volts, 60 cycles, alternating current (AC). Electrical outlets are of the American type, designed to work with appliances that have standard double-bladed plugs. Small towns in some rural areas may experience brief interruptions of electrical service or periods of brownout (voltage decrease). In a few villages, gasoline-powered generators are the only sources of electricity and they may be turned off during the day.

Measurements

Mexico uses the metric system as the official system of weights and measures. This means the distance between Nogales and Mazatlán is measured in kilometers, cheese is weighed in grams or kilograms, a hot day in Monterrey is 32° C, gasoline is sold by the liter, and a big fish is two meters long. The U.S.-Metric Conversion chart at the back of this book will help Americans make the conversions from pounds, gallons, and miles to kilos, liters, and kilometers when necessary.

Working and Living in Mexico City

EMPLOYMENT

A great many foreigners find themselves looking for ways to get by in Mexico City for a couple of months or a couple of years. As one of the principal capitals of the Americas, and uniquely linked to the United States economy through the NAFTA free trade agreement, Mexico City is brimming with business activity. Apart from the ideas mentioned below, would-be residents could try contacting their embassy. The U.S. Chamber of Commerce, at Lucerna 78 near Paseo de la Reforma, tel. 5724-3800, maintains some information on jobs with U.S. companies in Mexico.

Teaching English

The most popular way of making cash for footloose visitors is teaching English at one of the hundreds of English schools in Mexico City. Hours are flexible, and pay is usually around US$7–10 an hour. The trick is to put together enough hours to make a decent living and to make sure the school pays you regularly (some are notoriously shifty in this regard). A livable, though hardly luxurious, wage is US$800–1,000 a month.

While some schools require a TEFL (Teaching English as a Foreign Language) certificate, most do not. Schools generally pay certified teachers better, and often they are able to arrange private classes on the side.

Angloamericano, with schools in Polanco, Coyoacán and Satélite, tel. 5658-6700 or 5659-2148, www.angloamericano.com.mx, has received decent reviews from foreign teachers. Apart from English, it sometimes needs teachers for French, German, and Italian.

Harmon Hall, tel. 5211-2020, www.harmonhall.com, has schools all over the city (in fact, all over the country) and is always looking for teachers, but its pay scale is among the lowest.

To find others, just open the yellow pages and start calling around. Beware that at some of the smaller schools, payment can sometimes be unreliable.

Modeling

For whatever combination of cultural and historical reasons, Mexican advertising is filled with tall, light-skinned, blue-eyed models. Perhaps the day will come when Mexicans will look at *mestizo* physiognomy with a little more pride, but for the moment much of the society idealizes European looks.

Because of such preferences, modeling agencies are constantly looking for European-looking models, and many foreigners with no acting experience find easy, well-paid roles in local commercials. Three agencies which have worked with foreigners in the past are: Glenda, tel. 5208-0045; Rebecca Bustos, tel. 5658-1261; and Contempo, tel. 5666-0438 or 5666-3022.

If you are found to have the right look, you will get calls for casting sessions, along with dozens of other hopefuls. If the directors like you, they'll call you back for the shoot. Pay can be between US$100–500 per day, although it's usually difficult to obtain more than a few jobs a month. While on rare opportunities you'll get paid in cash the day of the shoot, most often you have to wait a couple of months before seeing any money. Should the commercial run more than a certain number of times, you'll be entitled to extra royalties.

And who knows, maybe you'll become a star. One wild-eyed Austrian friend of ours recently become a minor legend in Mexico City after starring in a cereal commercial which ran for several months on a major station.

Journalism

As the number-one media center in Latin America, Mexico City can be an excellent place to get a start as a reporter. The favored place for inexperienced writers to get a foot in the door is *The News,* tel. 5510-9623, an English-language daily. Though hardly Pulitzer Prize material, *The News* is a good place to learn how to write (or edit) and get a crash course in Mexican news at the same time. Pay usually hovers around US$800–1,000 a month. As the newspaper is something of a revolving door, it's often looking for new hires.

Other English-language publications in Mexico City include: *El Financiero International* (a weekly English supplement to the Mexican daily), tel. 5227-7600, and *Business Mexico,* tel. 5724-3800, a publication of the U.S. Chamber of Commerce.

Mexican newspapers are often in the market for part-time translators. If your Spanish is good (and it better be if you want to translate!), pick up copies of all the major newspapers and start calling around.

APARTMENTS

Compared to large cities in Europe and America, housing in Mexico City is very reasonable in price. Wealthier residents tend to live in Polanco and farther west along Paseo de la Reforma, in the Bosques and Lomas neighborhoods. San Ángel and Coyoacán are also more upscale, though less so than the foregoing, while Roma and Condesa are favored by younger expatriates who can afford the steadily rising rents. Del Valle, south of Roma along Insurgentes, is also a quiet residential neighborhood with many apartment buildings. Colonia Cuauhtémoc, north of Paseo de la Reforma, has both inexpensive and higher-end apartments. Real penny-pinchers (or those fascinated with relentless urbanity) might consider checking out the many old, lovely buildings in the Centro.

Rents for a midrange, two-bedroom apartment in the Condesa/Roma/Cuauhtémoc areas run around US$500–1,000 a month, while Polanco apartments cost US$700–1,300. In the Centro, decent places can easily be found for as low as US$200–500.

Word of mouth is the best way to find a good apartment, but failing that, the ads in *Segunda Mano* (a weekly classifieds publication) will give you plenty of places to start. The daily ads in *El Universal* are also extensive. Another good technique is to choose a neighborhood you want to live in, and prowl the streets looking for Se Renta signs on buildings.

Red Tape

Most apartment contracts in Mexico City are fairly standard affairs, usually just a template bought at a local stationery store with the names, dates, and numbers filled in. Contracts usually extend by the year, although most landlords are amenable to shortening it if you notify them well in advance, and especially if you arrange for someone to take your place. If not, you may lose your deposit.

Landlords commonly request first and last month's rent, as well as an unusual requirement: a *fiador,* someone who owns property in Mexico City who is willing to sign a paper making themselves responsible for the rent if you do not pay.

Needless to say, many foreigners have a hard time finding a *fiador.* The options are twofold. The best plan is to try to convince the landlord that you are a responsible person, perhaps offering to pay a couple of months ahead of time.

Long used to Mexican tenants who go for months without paying (and who are very difficult to evict under Mexican law), landlords are often very well disposed toward potential non-Mexican tenants, as they have a reputation for paying on time. Thus they may sometimes waive the *fiador* requirement.

However, if the landlord is rigid, or if a real estate company (rather than an individual) is managing the apartment, the only option if you don't have a *fiador* is to buy a *fianza,* or a bond, from a local bank, which serves as your guarantee. The amount of the bond depends on the apartment rent but will run at least a few hundred dollars.

Utilities

Usually water is included in the rent, while tenants pay for electricity. This minimal fee can be paid at local banks if paid before the due date but only at the offices of Luz y Fuerza del Centro if you're late. It can take several days to reconnect after being cut off.

Water heaters and stoves invariably run on natural gas, which is either supplied from a tank attached to your building (in which case you will be charged each month) or sold in 30-kg tanks (US$14) to individual tenants from gas trucks that circulate a couple of days each week.

If a phone line is already installed, you will often have to buy it from the previous tenant or the landlord (usually US$100–200). If the apartment has no line, you'll have to go down to the local TelMex office, wait in line for an hour or two, and pay US$150 to get a new personal telephone line or US$300 for a commercial telephone line. Company workers will usually come to your apartment one or two weeks later to install the line. While TelMex has a monopoly on local service, clients may choose among several long-distance providers.

STUDY

Spanish Language and Mexican Culture

Mexico City is an excellent place to study Spanish. In the first place, the level of spoken Spanish in the city is among the highest in the country, and just as important it's a very friendly and open city where Mexicans generally don't hesitate to speak to strangers, whatever their nationality. This isn't necessarily the case in other state capitals in Mexico.

Since 1921, the Universidad Nacional Autónoma de México (UNAM) has operated the Centro de Enseñanza para Extranjeros (CEPE), a special division of the university dedicated to teaching Mexican history, culture, and language. The programs enjoy a very good reputation and are divided among five departments: Spanish, Art History, History, Social Sciences, Literature, and Chicano Studies. The popular Spanish courses generally run three hours per day. Sessions run year round, although the summer session, which combines language with cultural and historical studies, is the most intensive. A sampling of courses offered in the summer session include: Mexican Art, Popular Culture in Xochimilco, Traditional Medicine in Xochimilco, Traditional Mexican Dance, 20th-Century Mexican Theater, History of Modern and Contemporary Mexico, History of Science in Mexico, Myth and Rationality in Contemporary Mexico, Mexican Literature, Contemporary Mexican Women Writers, Images of Mexico through Literary Texts, Chicano-Latina Community in the United States.

UNAM also runs special training programs for teachers of Spanish as a Second Language (SSL). For all courses, tuition is reasonable, and CEPE can arrange housing either with local families or in dormitories. For further information contact CEPE-México, Apartado Postal 70–391, Ciudad Universitaria, 04510 México D.F, tel. 5622-2470, fax 5616-2672, www.cepe.unam.mx. UNAM/CEPE also has a branch in Taxco: CEPE-Taxco, Ex-Hacienda El Chorrillo, Apartado Postal 70, 40200 Taxco, Gro., México, tel./fax 7622-0124.

Universidad La Salle (ULSA), Benjamin Franklin 65, Col. Condesa, tel. 5728-0500, www.ulsa.edu.mx, offers good, inexpensive Spanish group classes and is closer to the center of the city than UNAM.

Resources

Chilango Slang

The Spanish spoken in Mexico is lined with a rich vein of colloquialisms, slang expressions, and turns of phrase. Most Mexican slang originates from working-class neighborhoods in the capital (particularly Tepito), but it's then frequently picked up by middle class and wealthier youth, from where it moves into general popular culture and is transmitted by the media to the rest of the country. In fact, because Mexican soap operas are by far the most popular in Latin America, people from other Spanish-speaking countries tend to understand a lot more Mexico City slang than would normally be expected.

A crucial aspect of understanding Mexican Spanish is getting into the world of the *albur,* a sort of pun made at the expense of another. When a group of Mexican men are standing around talking, you'll notice one after the other is constantly taking turns trying to twist someone's last phrase into something that will crack everyone else up. The trick is to make everyone laugh, but using clever phrasing, never just a straight insult or put-down.

As in Cockney English, another trick is to use words that sound similar to well-known swear words, thus making the meaning more acceptable, and more humorous, in polite company.

Rare is the foreigner who masters local slang enough to take part in this generally good-natured word competition, but it's entertaining to try. Keep in mind that everyone wants to laugh and will be looking at you expectantly when you open your mouth, so even if you're not sure what you're about to say, do it with the right expression and tone and you might be able to pull it off.

¿que hongo?—literally "what mushroom?," a play on ***¿que onda?***
¿que milanesa?—what's up?
¿que onda?—what's up?
¿que pasión?—twist on ***¿que pasó?*** or what's happening?
¿que pedo?—same as above
¿que pez mi acuaman?—same as above
¿que te picó?—literally, "what bit you?," meaning, "what's the matter?" or "what's your problem?"
a huevo—definitely, for sure
a toda madre—excellent
a todo mecate—similar to ***a toda madre,*** but softer, as ***"madre"*** has a slightly vulgar connotation when used in this sense
aguas—watch out!
ahí nos vidrios—a twist ("we'll windows") on ***"ahí nos vemos"*** ("we'll be seeing each other")
bailar lola—to screw something up, make a mess of it
bicla—bicycle
cámara—same as ***simón***
cantar oaxaca—to vomit
carnal—very good friend, a "brother"
chamba—work
chale—multipurpose exclamatory interjection ("really? wow! no way! right on!"). Often used as ***"chale, mano."***
chela—beer
chesco—soft drink
chilango—someone from Mexico City
chingar—to "screw" somebody, in both meanings of the word
chingón—really excellent
ciego—100 pesos
cualquier hijo de vecino—"some son of a neighbor," a softer way of saying ***"hijo de puta"*** (son of a bitch), an insult
cuero—handsome, good looking
de pelos—excellent
desvelar—to stay out late
diegos—10 pesos
douglas—two pesos
en un ratón—in a while, a twist on ***"en un rato."***
está del nabo, est· de la fruta—it sucks
está grueso—literally, "it's fat," but meaning, wow, heavy, that's serious

fajar—to make out, to kiss
faxear—variation of fajar
fresa—literally strawberry, meaning a prissy, an uptight person
gabacho—American
gu·cala—gross
guacarear—to vomit
guarra, guarura—bodyguard
güey—dude, guy. Common throughout Mexico, but used every other word by young ***chilangos,*** and even ***chilangas.***
hojaldra—same as ***ojete,*** but softened slightly
hueva—a drag, something boring or tedious
jefe, jefa—father, mother
jetón—asleep
jipiteca—Mexican hippie
la julia—the police van
la neta—the best, or also the truth, the real deal
la pura neta—even better
la puritita neta—better still
lana—"wool," i.e. money
mamón—stuck-up, arrogant person
mano—short for ***hermano*** (brother), and the Mexican equivalent of "Bro"
milanesa—1,000 pesos
melón—1,000,000 pesos
mochate—pass it along already, give me one, or give me some (often ***"mochate, güey"*** or ***"mochate, cabrón.")***
naco—someone with bad (i.e., lower-class) taste
nave—literally boat, but slang for car
ni madres—no way, not a chance
no mames—vulgar, meaning "no way, get out." Invariably said as ***"no mames, güey."***
no manches—means the same as ***no mames,*** but twisted at the end to make it sound less crude
ojete—a strong, vulgar insult, i.e., an asshole
órale—exclamation, "right on, wow"
pachanga—big party
pacheco—stoned (i.e., smoking marijuana)
pedo—literally "fart," but meaning either "drunk" ***("está·bien pedo")*** or a problem, i.e., ***¿que pedo?*** (what's the problem?) or ***no hay pedo*** (no problem)
pendejo—vulgar, insulting adjective, i.e., idiot.
pepino—a jerk
perro—as an adjective, something very difficult
perro—as a noun, a guy who sleeps around a lot
pinche—a vulgar adjective, i.e., ***"¡Abre la pinche puerta!"*** ("open the @#@!!%@ door!")
pitufos—literally "smurfs," meaning the blue-uniformed
reventón—big party
rola—a tune, a song
seguridad pública—police
que oso—literally "what a bear," but meaning "what a fool," i.e., "what a ridiculous spectacle they're making of themselves"
que poca madre—"can you believe that?" but with an indignant tone
quiúbule—also what's up? Usually, ***"quiúbule, cabrón"*** or ***"quiúbule güey."***
se puso hasta atrás—he/she got thoroughly drunk
se puso hasta las chanclas—he/she got thoroughly drunk
simón—a play on the word ***sí*** (yes), but more hip and current. A combination of "I agree" and "right on."
tamarindos—the ***tránsito*** police, with brown uniforms
tirar la onda—try to pick up on someone
tostón—50 pesos
tranzar—to deceive somebody
varos—***pesos*** (e.g., ***"cuesta diez varos."***— "it costs 10 pesos")
vientos—"winds," right on!
vientos huracanados—"hurricane winds," excellent
vientos huracanados aztecas—"Aztec hurricane winds," completely superb

Spanish Phrasebook

Pronunciation Guide

Spanish pronunciation is much more regular than that of English, but there are still occasional variations.

Consonants

c — as 'c' in "cat," before 'a', 'o', or 'u'; like 's' before 'e' or 'i'
d — as 'd' in "dog," except between vowels, then like 'th' in "that"
g — before 'e' or 'i,' like the 'ch' in Scottish "loch"; elsewhere like 'g' in "get"
h — always silent
j — like the English 'h' in "hotel," but stronger
ll — like the 'y' in "yellow"
ñ — like the 'ni' in "onion"
r — always pronounced as strong 'r'
rr — trilled 'r'
v — similar to the 'b' in "boy" (not as English 'v')
y — similar to English, but with a slight "j" sound. When standing, alone it's pronounced like the 'e' in "me".
z — like 's' in "same"
b, f, k, l, m, n, p, q, s, t, w, x — as in English

Vowels

a — as in "father," but shorter
e — as in "hen"
i — as in "machine"
o — as in "phone"
u — usually as in "rule"; when it follows a 'q' the 'u' is silent; when it follows an 'h' or 'g', it's pronounced like 'w,' except when it comes between 'g' and 'e' or 'i', when it's also silent (unless it has an umlaut, when it again pronounced as English 'w'

Stress

Native English speakers frequently make errors of pronunciation by ignoring stress; all Spanish vowels—a, e, i, o and u—may carry accents that determine which syllable of a word gets emphasis. Often, stress seems unnatural to nonnative speakers—the surname Chávez, for instance, is stressed on the first syllable—but failure to observe this rule may mean that native speakers may not understand you.

Numbers

0 — cero
1 — uno (masculine)
1 — una (feminine)
2 — dos
3 — tres
4 — cuatro
5 — cinco
6 — seis
7 — siete
8 — ocho
9 — nueve
10 — diez
11 — once
12 — doce
13 — trece
14 — catorce
15 — quince
16 — dieciseis
17 — diecisiete
18 — dieciocho
19 — diecinueve
20 — veinte
21 — veintiuno
30 — treinta
40 — cuarenta
50 — cincuenta
60 — sesenta
70 — setenta
80 — ochenta
90 — noventa
100 — cien
101 — ciento y uno
200 — doscientos
1,000 — mil
10,000 — diez mil
1,000,000 — un millón

Days of the Week

Sunday — domingo
Monday — lunes
Tuesday — martes
Wednesday — miércoles
Thursday — jueves
Friday — viernes
Saturday — sábado

Time

While Latin Americans mostly use the 12-hour clock, in some instances, usually associated with plane or bus schedules, they may use the 24-hour military clock. Under the 24-hour clock, for example, *las nueve de la noche* (9 P.M.) would be *las 21 horas* (2100 hours).

What time is it? — ¿Qué hora es?
It's one o'clock — Es la una.
It's two o'clock — Son las dos.
At two o'clock — A las dos.
It's ten to three — Son tres menos diez.
It's ten past three — Son tres y diez.
It's three fifteen — Son las tres y cuarto.
It's two forty five — Son tres menos cuarto.
It's two thirty — Son las dos y media.
It's six A.M. — Son las seis de la mañana.
It's six P.M. — Son las seis de la tarde.
It's ten P.M. — Son las diez de la noche.
Today — hoy
Tomorrow — mañana
Morning — la mañana
Tomorrow morning — mañana por la mañana
Yesterday — ayer
Week — la semana
Month — mes
Year — año
Last night — anoche
The next day — el día siguiente

Useful Words and Phrases

Mexicans and other Spanish-speaking people consider formalities important. Whenever approaching anyone for information or some other reason, do not forget the appropriate salutation—good morning, good evening, etc. Standing alone, the greeting *hola* (hello) can sound brusque.

Hello. — Hola.
Good morning. — Buenos días.
Good afternoon. — Buenas tardes.
Good evening. — Buenas noches.
How are you? — ¿Cómo está?
Fine. — Muy bien.
And you? — ¿Y usted?
So-so. — Más o menos.
Thank you. — Gracias.
Thank you very much. — Muchas gracias.
You're very kind. — Muy amable.
You're welcome — De nada (literally, "It's nothing.")
Yes — sí
No — no
I don't know. — No sé.
It's fine; okay — Está bien.
Good; okay — Bueno.
Please — por favor
Pleased to meet you. — Mucho gusto.
Excuse me (physical) — Perdóneme.
Excuse me (speech) — Discúlpeme.
I'm sorry. — Lo siento.
Goodbye — adiós
See you later — hasta luego (literally, "until later")
More — más
Less — menos
Better — mejor
Much, a lot — mucho
A little — un poco
Large — grande
Small — pequeño, chico
Quick, fast — rápido
Slowly — despacio
Bad — malo
Difficult — difícil
Easy — fácil
He/She/It is gone; as in "She left," "He's gone" — Ya se fue.
I don't speak Spanish well. — No hablo bien el español.

I don't understand. — No entiendo.
How do you say. . . in Spanish? — ¿Cómo se dice. . . en español?
Do you understand English? — ¿Entiende el inglés?
Is English spoken here? (Does anyone here speak English?) — ¿Se habla inglés aquí?

Terms of Address

When in doubt, use the formal *usted* (you) as a form of address. If you wish to dispense with formality and feel that the desire is mutual, you can say *Me puedes tutear* (you can call me "tu").

I — yo
You (formal) — usted
you (familiar) — tú
He/him — él
She/her — ella
We/us — nosotros
You (plural) — ustedes
They/them (all males or mixed gender) — ellos
They/them (all females) — ellas
Mr., sir — señor
Mrs., madam — señora
Miss, young lady — señorita
Wife — esposa
Husband — marido or esposo
Friend — amigo (male), amiga (female)
Sweetheart — novio (male), novia (female)
Son, daughter — hijo, hija
Brother, sister — hermano, hermana
Father, mother — padre, madre
Grandfather, grandmother — abuelo, abuela

Getting Around

Where is. . . ? — ¿Dónde está. . . ?
How far is it to. . . ? — ¿A cuanto está. . . ?
from. . . to. . . — de. . . a. . .
Highway — la carretera
Road — el camino
Street — la calle
Block — la cuadra
Kilometer — kilómetro
North — norte
South — sur
West — oeste; poniente
East — este; oriente
Straight ahead — al derecho; adelante
To the right — a la derecha
To the left — a la izquierda

Accommodations

¿Hay cuarto? — Is there a room?
May I (we) see it? — ¿Puedo (podemos) verlo?
What is the rate? — ¿Cuál es el precio?
Is that your best rate? ¿Es su mejor precio?
Is there something cheaper? ¿Hay algo más económico?
Single room — un sencillo
Double room — un doble
Room for a couple — matrimonial
Key — llave
With private bath — con baño
With shared bath — con baño general; con baño compartido
Hot water — agua caliente
Cold water — agua fría
Ducha — shower
Ducha eléctrica — electric shower
Towel — toalla
Soap — jabón
Toilet paper — papel higiénico
Air conditioning — aire acondicionado
Fan — abanico; ventilador
Blanket — frazada; manta
Sheets — sábanas

Public Transport

Bus stop — la parada
Bus terminal — terminal de buses
Airport — el aeropuerto
Launch — lancha; tiburonera
Dock — muelle
I want a ticket to. . . — Quiero un pasaje a. . .
I want to get off at. . . — Quiero bajar en. . .
Here, please. — Aquí, por favor.
Where is this bus going? — ¿Adónde va este autobús?
Roundtrip — ida y vuelta
What do I owe? — ¿Cuánto le debo?

Food

Menu — la carta, el menú
Glass — taza
Fork — tenedor
Knife — cuchillo
Spoon — cuchara
Napkin — servilleta
Soft drink — agua fresca
Coffee — café
Cream — crema
Tea — té
Sugar — azúcar
Drinking water — agua pura, agua potable
Bottled carbonated water — agua mineral con gas
Bottled uncarbonated water — agua sin gas
Beer — cerveza
Wine — vino
Milk — leche
Juice — jugo
Eggs — huevos
Bread — pan
Watermelon — sandía
Banana — banano
Plantain — plátano
Apple — manzana
Orange — naranja
Meat (without) — carne (sin)
Beef — carne de res
Chicken — pollo; gallina
Fish — pescado
Shellfish — mariscos
Shrimp — camarones
Fried — frito
Roasted — asado
Barbecued — a la parrilla
Breakfast — desayuno
Lunch — almuerzo
Dinner (often eaten in late afternoon) — comida
Dinner, or a late night snack — cena
The check, or bill — la cuenta

Making Purchases

I need. . . — Necesito. . .
I want. . . — Deseo. . . or Quiero. . .
I would like. . . (more polite) — Quisiera. . .
How much does it cost? — ¿Cuánto cuesta?
What's the exchange rate? — ¿Cuál es el tipo de cambio?
May I see. . . ? — ¿Puedo ver. . . ?
This one — ésta/ésto
Expensive — caro
Cheap — barato
Cheaper — más barato
Too much — demasiado

Health

Help me please. — Ayúdeme por favor.
I am ill. — Estoy enfermo.
Pain — dolor
Fever — fiebre
Stomach ache — dolor de estómago
Vomiting — vomitar
Diarrhea — diarrea
Drugstore — farmacia
Medicine — medicina
Pill, tablet — pastilla
Birth control pills — pastillas anticonceptivas
Condom — condón, preservativo

Suggested Reading

Description and Travel

Barros, José Luis. *Encuentros en la ciudad de México.* Miguel Ángel Porrúa, Grupo Editorial 1997. Collection of historic writings on the capital by such illustrative figures as Hernán Cortés, Thomas Gage, Guillermo Prieto, Miguel León Portilla, early Catholic friars, and others. Spanish only.

Gerrard, A. Bryson. *Cassell's Colloquial Spanish: A Handbook of Idiomatic Usage.* New York: Macmillan, 1980. Not as out of date as the publication year might suggest, Cassell's explains common *vulgarismos* (slang) used in Mexico, Central America, and South America; *pildora,* for example, is recognized as "the pill" in Mexico, but it refers to cocktail frankfurters in Argentina.

Legorreta, Jorge. *Guía del Pleno Disfrute de la Ciudad de México.* Mexico City: Jorge Legorreta/Metrópolis, 1994. This thin, spiral-bound guide to city nightlife, written by Mexico City politician Jorge Legorreta and oriented toward *capitalinos* rather than tourists, is a gem. Sadly out of print, the *Guide to the Full Enjoyment of Mexico City* contains critiques and descriptions of many classic Mexico City restaurants, cafés, cantinas, *pulquerías,* cabarets, burlesque shows, dance halls, and other nocturnal pursuits. Spanish only.

Martinez, Ruben. *The Other Side: Notes from the New L.A., Mexico City, and Beyond.* Vintage Books, 1993. A stimulating account of the growing pan-Latino culture extending from Los Angeles to El Salvador, with plenty of pop culture info on Mexico City.

O'Reilly, James and Larry Habegger, eds. *Travelers' Tales Mexico.* San Francisco: Travelers' Tales, 1994. If you only read one piece of travel literature on Mexico, make it this one. Forty-eight essays by travel writers, natural historians, journalists, and ecologists present a kaleidoscopic view of Mexico's mystery, beauty, tragedy, and internal contradictions.

Ryan, Allen, ed. *The Reader's Companion to Mexico.* New York: Harcourt Brace and Company, 1995. Contains 26 literary excerpts from works on Mexico—the oldest dates to 1888, the latest 1985—published by Katherine Ann Porter, Graham Greene, Paul Theroux, Langston Hughes, Paul Bowles, D. H. Lawrence, John Steinbeck, and a number of lesser-known authors. A full chapter is devoted to essays on Mexico City.

History and Culture

Arnold, Caroline. *City of the Gods: Mexico's Ancient City of Teotihuacán.* New York: Clarion Books, 1994. Illustrated with color photographs, Arnold's readable outing explores the ancient metropolis and extrapolates how the daily lives of the Teotihuacanos might have been.

Bierhorst, John. *The Mythology of Mexico and Central America.* New York: William Morrow, 1990. A good introduction to Mexican mythology, particularly with regard to Mesoamerican cultures.

Caistor, Nick. *Mexico City: A Cultural and Literary Companion.* New York: Interlink Books, 2000. An interesting and extremely atmospheric account of different aspects of Mexico City history and culture, written by someone who is clearly fascinated with the city.

Coe, Michael D. *Mexico: From the Olmecs to the Aztecs.* New York: Thames and Hudson, 1994. This textbook by curator/university professor

Coe provides a readable, well-illustrated summary of pre-Hispanic history in southern Mexico, wisely leaving the Maya for another volume.

Johns, Michael. *The City of Mexico in the Age of Díaz.* Austin: University of Texas Press, 1997. Well written, well researched, and ultimately fascinating chronicle of the capital during the rule of dictatorial president Porfirio Díaz.

Kandell, Jonathan. *La Capital: The Biography of Mexico City.* New York: Random House, 1988. A readable chronicle of Mexico's capital city that would have benefitted from a sharper focus on the city itself rather than the larger issues in Mexican history it tends to fall back upon.

Katz, Friedrich. *The Life and Times of Pancho Villa.* Stanford, CA: Stanford University Press, 1998. The larger-than-life bandit revolutionary Villa is portrayed here in all his complexity in exhaustive detail.

Krauze, Enrique. *Biography of Power: A History of Modern Mexico, 1810–1996.* New York: HarperCollins Publishers, 1997. One of Mexico's most respected historians traces the course of Mexican history, principally through the actions of its leaders. Because of his focus on personality, Krauze falls short on portraying the country's social dynamics.

Lewis, Oscar. *The Children of Sanchez: Autobiography of a Mexican Family.* New York: Random House, 1979. A gritty anthropological account of the city based on the lives of a family whose patriarch works as a waiter at Café Tacuba.

Oppenheimer, Andres. *Bordering on Chaos: Mexico's Roller Coaster Journey to Prosperity.* Boston: Little, Brown and Co., 1998. Miami Herald reporter Oppenheimer has some engrossing anecdotes on the turbulent times of the Salinas and Zedillo era, though at times he seems overly concerned about illustrating his own involvement with the power brokers, rather than focusing on the people and events themselves.

Oster, Patrick. *The Mexicans: A Personal Portrait of a People.* New York: Harper & Row, 1989. Reporter Patrick Foster presents 20 profiles of not-so-ordinary Mexicans, from a streetside fire-eater in Mexico City to a Sonoran *PANista.* Most of those profiled are Mexico City denizens. Despite a nearly overwhelming gloom-and-doom perspective, the essays provide hard information on Mexican politics and social schema.

Paz, Octavio. *The Labyrinth of Solitude: Life and Thought in Mexico.* New York: Grove Press, 1961. Paz has no peer when it comes to expositions of the Mexican psyche, and this is his best prose work.

Quiñones, Sam. *True Tales from Another Mexico: The Lynch Mob, the Popsicle Kings, Chalino, and the Bronx.* Albuquerque: University of New Mexico Press, 2001. An idiosyncratic and entertaining collection of stories from across Mexico, but particularly from the northern border regions.

Reed, John. *Insurgent Mexico.* New York: International Publishers, 1994. Famed American journalist Reed, of *Ten Days That Shook the World* fame, wrote this breathless, entertaining, and unabashedly biased firsthand account of time spent with Villa's troops in northern Mexico during the Mexican revolution.

Riding, Alan. *Distant Neighbors: A Portrait of the Mexicans.* New York: Vintage Books, 1986. Riding was the *New York Times* correspondent in Mexico City for six years, and when he finished he wrote this excellent exposition of Mexican culture and history through 1988.

Rodriguez, Jeanette. *Our Lady of Guadalupe: Faith and Empowerment among Mexican-American Women.* Austin: University of Texas Press, 1994. Explores the Guadalupe myth as the most powerful female icon in Mexican and Mexican-American culture and as a symbol of liberation for Mexican Catholic women.

Scarborough, Vernon and David Wilcox, eds. *The Mesoamerican Ballgame.* Tucson: University of Arizona Press, 1991. A well-researched history of the martial sport in all its gory details.

Simon, Joel. *Endangered Mexico: An Environment on the Edge.* San Francisco: Sierra Club Books, 1998. An superb collection of essays on Mexico's precarious environmental situation, and the many social factors propelling it, written by a journalist who has traveled far and wide to get his information.

Thomas, Hugh. *Conquest: Montezuma, Cortés, and the Fall of Old Mexico.* New York: Simon & Schuster, 1995. The definitive account of one of the greatest events in history: the meeting of the New and Old Worlds in Mexico in 1519. Detailed and extremely well written.

Womack, John. *Zapata and the Mexican Revolution.* New York: Knopf, 1970. This is considered the classic account of the legendary *caudillo del sur,* Zapata, and his role in the Mexican revolution. A must for anyone interested in understanding Zapata's mythic status in the Mexican pantheon of heroes.

Architecture

Opher, Philip with Xavier Sánchez Valladares. *Mexico City: A Guide to Recent Architecture.* Ellipse, 2000. This handy, pocket-sized guide is a good compendium of Mexico City's modern architecture.

Food

Adair, Marita. *The Hungry Traveler: Mexico.* Kansas City, MO: Andrews McNeel Publishing, 1997. A pocket-sized Mexican culinary lexicon, with plenty of references to Mexico City and nearby states.

DeWitt, Dave and Nancy Gerlach. *The Whole Chile Pepper Book.* Boston: Little, Brown and Co., 1990. Written by the editors of *Chile Pepper* magazine, this compendium of fact, lore, and recipes is the definitive culinary guide to chiles.

Quintana, Patricia. *The Taste of Mexico.* New York: Stewart, Tabori & Chang, 1993. Written by one of Mexico City's most famous chefs, this is perhaps the most authentic Mexican cookbook available in English. Also available in Spanish as *El Sabor de México.*

Walker, Ann and Larry Walker. *Tequila: The Book.* San Francisco: Chronicle Books, 1994. This small but beautifully bound and printed book contains the definitive history of agave distillate, along with tips on tequila etiquette and recipes for cocktails, *antojitos,* salads, soups, entrées, salsas, and desserts. Humorous anecdotes and place descriptions add to the reading fun.

Fiction and Poetry

Burroughs, William. *Queer.* New York: Penguin Books, 1987. Set mainly in Mexico City during the Beat era, this autobiographical novel fictionalizes Burroughs's flight to Mexico to avoid drug charges in the United States.

Kerouac, Jack. *Mexico City Blues: 242 Choruses.* New York: Grove Press, 1990. Beat novelist and poet Kerouac often tried to mimic the cadences of jazz in his writing. This work arguably comes closer to that goal than anything else he ever published, and it is evocative of 1950s Mexico City.

Lida, David. *Travel Advisory.* New York: Willam Morrow & Company, 2000. A collection of 10 gritty short stories set in Mexico (several in Mexico City) from an American writer who divides his time between New York and Mexico. Mexico has a bitter history with *americanos* and an even longer history with *malinchismo,* and some of these stories expose—rather than ignore—this essential cornerstone of modern Mexican culture. Lida has an especially good ear for dialogue, which he reproduces partly in Spanish.

Lowry, Malcolm. *Under the Volcano.* New York: Reynal & Hitchcock, 1990. Although when originally published in Canada in 1947 it only sold two copies in two years, Lowry's tale of the alcoholic demise of a British consul in Cuernavaca has become a modern cult classic.

Paco, Ignacio Taibo II. *Return to the Same City.* New York: Mysterious Press, 1996. Mexico City's favorite eccentric Marxist mystery writer resurrects his detective protagonist, Héctor Belascoarán Shayne. While chasing a Cuban arms-drugs dealer through D.F., Shayne gives us an insider's glimpse of the city and his existential way of coping with it. The novel's 1993 predecessor, *No Happy Ending,* is also set in *la capital.*

Traven, B. *The Rebellion of the Hanged.* New York: Hill and Wang, 1972. The mysterious B. Traven, author of the more well known *The Treasure of the Sierra Madre,* here chronicles Amerindian exploitation under Porfirio Díaz in another powerful work of fiction.

Internet Resources

While a substantial number of English speakers live in Mexico City, the Web offers paltry resources in English about one of the world's largest megalopolises. Yet for those Mexicophiles who feel the need to stay on top of city politics and tourism, government offices offer content-rich websites for those with some command of Spanish. You'll also find English language participation in bulletin boards, specialty guides, and an online rating courtesy of Deja.com.

Keep in mind that websites come and go, and URLs (universal resource locators, or World Wide Web "addresses") change. More websites are included throughout the book on different topics.

Directorio de Comunicación Social
www.precisa.gob.mx

An excellent directory of the entire Mexican government: all branches, the federal and state level, and state-run companies. As well, the site maintains updated lists of foreign embassies, foreign journalists in Mexico, media (radio, television, and newspapers) from across Mexico, universities, and political parties. Superb resource.

Mexico City Government
www.df.gob.mx/

Mexico City's website is well designed and, best of all, there is a great deal of content. If you're interested in city politics and administration, track down the addresses, phone numbers, and emails of the city's precinct leaders or participate in the online chat forums (www.df.gob.mx/foros/index.html) on topics including public security, tourism, and environmental affairs. Mixing thoroughness and creativity, the Mexico City website exemplifies what a government website can be. The only thing missing would be an email mailing list that provided press releases and announcements from specific departments. This information is posted online (www.df.gob.mx/noticias/index.html), but you have to hunt for it.

Mexico City Government Tourism Office
www.mexicocity.gob.mx/

The city's new tourism office has a fairly fancy website with plenty of good links, although descriptions are very limited. Check the Centro Histórico page (www.mexicocity.gob.mx/eng/enjoy/chistorico/index.asp) and the links for museums, theaters, cinemas, and walking tours. You'll also find the addresses for tourism modulos around the city (www.mexicocity.gob.mx/eng/modules/index.asp). Kudos to officials for posting an archive of statistics (www.mexicocity.gob.mx/eng/stats/index.html), which is a good resource for journalists and anyone interested in current affairs.

Instituto Nacional de Estadística, Geografía e Informatica
www.inegi.gob.mx

Inegi is the government statistical institute, and its website (although difficult to navigate) has a wealth of detailed information about the country's population, economy, environment, and much else besides.

Mexico City Virtual Guide
www.mexicocity.com.mx/mexcity.html

While the site does not seem to be updated often, it provides a first-time visitor with a wide range of information from city hotels to parks.

Guide2Mexico
www.guide2mexico.com/content/mexlinks.htm

An impressive collection of travelers' resources, including lots of useful links.

Mexican Wave
www.mexicanwave.com
Another general site for travelers, this one geared toward a European audience, but in English with lots of good information.

Centro Histórico
www.centrohistorico.com.mx/
As the name implies, this site focuses on the historic center of the city and on ambitious plans to renovate the district.

Mexican Embassy in Washington, D.C.
www.embassyofmexico.org
This is the place to come for the latest Mexican visa information.

Art and History Museums
www.arts-history.mx/museos/muse.html
This excellent site contains descriptions and opening hours of every important art and history museum in the capital.

Mexico City Art
www.arte-mexico.com
Online map of the city's many galleries and art museums and listings of current exhibitions and openings.

Rock en Español
www.rockeros.com
A compendium of links and commentary on rock en español, la nueva onda, guacarock, and other new rock movements in 13 countries in Latin America, plus the U.S. and Spain. MP3 downloads available.

Intellicast Forecast
www.intellicast.com
Want to know what the weather will be like tomorrow?

Environmental Information in Mexico City
www.planeta.com/ecotravel/mexico/df/mexinfo.html
A one-stop information center for anyone interested in environmental issues. This page is frequently updated and is part of the Planeta.com website.

Moon Handbooks
www.moon.com
Moon's website contains occasional excerpts from this book and other Moon titles, ordering information, an online travel newsletter with articles on Mexico, and links to various related sites.

—by Ron Mader, Mexico City resident and host of the Eco Travels in Latin America website (www.planeta.com), and Chris Humphrey

Index

Archaeological Sites

Aztecs

B

C

Churches/Church Buildings

Hernán Cortés

Cultural Museums

Handicrafts

History Museums

Frida Kahlo

L

M

Markets

Parks

Diego Rivera

UV

WXYZ

Acknowledgments

As usual, I've shamelessly pumped a myriad of folks for information on Mexico City and environs in putting together this book.

From Mexico City, there are the usual suspects: Eugenio "Secre" Aburto, Leendert de Bell and his ever-growing clan, Rodrigo, Margarida, and Marco Palacios, Cecilia Buck, Gideon Litchfield (how will I ever update that section without you?), Rob Randolph, Roger Magazine, Luis Briones, and the fount of all knowledge, Ron Mader. Thanks to David Lida for some great feedback on the first edition. Simeon Tegel helped me out in all sorts of ways, some legal and some not.

Many thanks to the Mexico-Washington, D.C., contingent (seems like I never left D.F. after all): Ana Morales, Manuel "El Chapulín" Felix, Fernando Flores, Guadalupe Paz, and Manuel Villegas. Thanks also to Bronwen Alsop, Alexei Monserrat, Kate Maloney, and Jackie Jones for sharing adventures in D.F. with me in the summer of 2001. And thanks to Elena Pappas for some great photos.

I would also like to recognize Chicki Mallan's contributions to the first edition of the guide: both Joe and I used portions of her work from *Moon Handbooks: Mexico* in the previous edition of this book.

Thanks also to travelers Joe Reid, Sophika Kostyniuk, and Kate Smith for their input. And last but not least, thanks to Joe Cummings.

—Chris Humphrey